HISTORY OF THE LATIN AND
TEUTONIC NATIONS

1494—1514

AMS PRESS

NEW YORK

HISTORY OF THE
LATIN AND TEUTONIC
NATIONS

(1494 TO 1514)

BY

LEOPOLD VON RANKE

A REVISED TRANSLATION BY

G. R. DENNIS, B.A. (LOND.)

WITH AN INTRODUCTION BY

EDWARD ARMSTRONG, M.A.

FELLOW OF QUEEN'S COLLEGE, OXFORD
AUTHOR OF "THE LIFE OF CHARLES V," ETC.

LONDON
GEORGE BELL & SONS
1909

Library of Congress Cataloging in Publication Data

Ranke, Leopold von, 1795-1886.
    History of the Latin and Teutonic nations (1494 to
1514).

    A rev. translation of the author's Geschichten der
lateinischen and germanischen Völker.
    Reprint of the 1909 ed. published by G. Bell, London.
    Includes index.
    1. Europe—History—1492-1517. I. Title.
D231.R313   1976   940.2'1   78-153636
ISBN 0-404-09258-6

Reprinted from an original copy in the collections
of the University of Chicago Library

From the edition of 1909, London
First AMS edition published in 1976
Manufactured in the United States of America

AMS PRESS INC.
NEW YORK, N. Y.

EDITOR'S NOTE

A TRANSLATION of Ranke's "Geschichten der lateinischen und germanischen Völker" by Mr. P. A. Ashworth was published in Bohn's Standard Library in 1887, but the volume has been out of print for several years. The demand for it, however, still continues, and it has therefore been decided to reissue the book in a revised form.

The translation has been subjected to thorough revision, every sentence having been compared with the original. Thus it is hoped that errors have been reduced to a minimum. A good many obvious slips and misprints in the German original have been corrected, and some more important historical inaccuracies have been pointed out in the Introduction. Considerable trouble has been taken in identifying the names of places, Ranke's spelling being often very misleading; as a rule, in the spelling of proper names, modern authorities, such as the Cambridge Modern History, have been followed. A new index and a full analytical table of contents have also now been added.

The thanks of the editor are due to Mr. R. H. Hobart Cust and Señor M. B. Cossio for help in solving various difficulties; to Mr. Cuthbert A. Williamson for similar help, and also for reading all the proofs; and especially to Mr. Edward Armstrong, who, in addition to contributing the Introduction, has given invaluable aid in clearing up doubtful and difficult points.

G. R. D.

January, 1909.

INTRODUCTION

MORE than eighty-four years have passed since Leopold
von Ranke published, in October, 1824, his earliest work,
"The Latin and Teutonic Nations." He was then not quite
twenty-nine; when he died, on May 23, 1886, he was in
his ninety-first year, but was still at work on his unfinished
"World History." Between the first book and the last
there is a close connection. It may, indeed, be said that
his "Latin and Teutonic Nations," his histories of the Popes,
of the Spanish and Ottoman Empires, of the Reformation,
of the Wars of Religion in France, of the Seventeenth
Century in England, and other works, were all exploratory
voyages for the discovery of the world, which was from early
years his goal. "You know," he wrote in 1826, "my old
aim, the discovery of the sea of World History".; and again
in 1828, "the discovery of the unknown World History
would be my greatest fortune." It is in this sense that
Lord Acton has called him the most prompt and fortunate
of European pathfinders. Thus, a quite peculiar interest
is inherent in the first essay of the great historian's ceaseless
historical activity, an essay which decided, or rather indi-
cated, the direction which his intellect was to take.

A revised translation of a juvenile work published not
far from a century ago is a lot, which has fallen to few
modern historians. As such has been Ranke's fortune, it
may be instructive to form some estimate of the causes.
These must be sought in the qualities of the writer, in the

choice of his subject, and in some degree in the changing fashions of historical reading. The two former causes will receive consideration here; publication can alone test the latter.

Ranke did not possess the high literary distinction of a Gibbon or a Froude. In point of style he can scarcely compare with Gregorovius, whose Teutonism was modified by Italian influence, as was that of Heine by French. Nevertheless there is a certain graceful simplicity which few German historians can claim, and a conscientious striving after clearness, not only of thought but of expression. Ranke, from the first, was not content to write for the learned few; he exacted no special knowledge, but appealed to the intelligent reading public. The existence of such a public in England explains the early appreciation which his works found here. He himself was not satisfied with his initial measure of success in respect of style and lucidity. He wrote to his brother that his "Latin and Teutonic Nations" was a hard book, but not, he hoped, obscure. Yet when Raumer praised its matter but criticized its language and form, he confessed that the criticism was just, and elsewhere he writes of the obscurities and unevennesses of his own work. In the full sunshine of his fame the prayer of Ranke was still for light—for clearness —for in clearness lies the truth.

Naturally enough, this deliberate simplicity, this absence of grandiose periods, dissatisfied some of the contemporaries of his earlier works. It was a pompous age, and the ambling paces of Ranke's narrative fell short of its ideal of a high-flying Pegasus. The very softness and sweetness of his style drew merriment from Heine, who compared it to well-cooked mutton with plenty of carrots. If Ranke's style was as transparent as water, it was said, it was also as tasteless. This characteristic undoubtedly increases the difficulty of translation, for the picturesque simplicity, natural in the German, if faithfully rendered into English, gives at times the impression of affectation.

Apart from his lucidity, the artistic element in Ranke, which is chiefly to be noticed, is his power of rapid portraiture. He rarely attempts an elaborate picture, and he is not always successful when he does. But the quick and true line-drawing enables the reader to seize the essential features of his characters without any interruption of the narrative. This art is less noticeable in " The Latin and Teutonic Nations " than, for instance, in "The History of the Popes," but an exception may be found in his portrait of the Emperor Maximilian, though this is, indeed, somewhat more detailed than is his wont. Ranke probably never aimed at being a colourist; his natural gift was that of an artist in black and white, or at most in tinted line. Nevertheless, when he takes up the palette, he shows a fine and delicate sense for atmosphere and texture, the result less of technical skill than of imaginative indwelling in his subject.

Literary merit alone could not have raised Ranke to his seat among the Immortals. The wings which bore him upward were an almost religious zeal for history, humanity, impartiality, and thought. His enemies called him a bookmaker and a fraud, but in truth history was for Ranke a religion; it was the manifestation of God's work upon mankind. In 1825 he told his brother, after his first success, that he meant to spend his whole life in the fear of God and in history, and his intention never faltered. Yet in this religion there was little that was abstract or doctrinal; it was eminently human. Personality was what Ranke loved to study; the personality of individuals, and then the personality of nations. Only through these could he attain to the personality of mankind at large. Abstract history had little charm for him; he would have nothing to do with types. "One must enjoy an individual," he wrote, "in all his aspects, just as one enjoys flowers without thought of the species to which they are to be referred." His very art of portraiture was probably unconscious, and is scarcely to be ascribed to style; it was the necessary outcome of his insight. History was for him a Muse who lived and breathed and moved; thus it is that his books are instinct with her life.

Impartiality must have been all the more difficult for an historian who felt so keenly as did Ranke. Yet when he describes such momentous conflicts as the French Wars of Religion or the English Great Rebellion, he is not a partisan. Even in his "History of the Reformation," where the cause of his own religion and nation is involved, he is scrupulously just. In quite modern times impartiality is regarded as being almost a matter of course in a true historian, but to a Prussian writer in the nineteenth century it was well-nigh an impossibility, especially if he were in State pay. Ranke, though born a Saxon, became a loyal subject of the Hohenzollern; he enjoyed the intimate confidence of his Emperor and of Bismarck, yet he cannot be fairly classed with the professional champions of Prussian policy; he preserved to the end the splendid isolation of his intellect. "He decided," wrote Lord Acton, "to repress the poet, the patriot, the religious or political partisan, to sustain no cause, to banish himself from his books, to write nothing that could gratify his own feelings, or disclose his own private convictions."

The range of knowledge and interest enjoyed by Ranke is now becoming rare. Modern research has the defects of its qualities; it is almost necessarily microscopic, and every new mass of materials that is unearthed must make it more so. The sphere of the more thorough modern historian is always narrowing, whereas that of Ranke was ever widening. He was by nature what he was still striving to be to the day of his death, a universal historian. He early had the impudence to criticize the antiquarianism of Niebuhr; he good-humouredly laughed at those who took the more trouble in proportion to the insignificance of their subject. As a teacher he may be said to have belonged to the Pre-Seminarist school. He had much belief in the educational power of lectures covering a long period of history, and though he had a weak and indistinct utterance he never yielded to the temptation of preferring the laboratory to the chair. Pupils were made to work out their subject for themselves. His method seems greatly to have resembled that of the Oxford or Cambridge tutor; pupils brought their youthful essays on somewhat general topics, and the Professor criticized as they read, or discussed the subject afterwards to the accompaniment of sausages and beer. Research for its own sake was actually discouraged; it must be the means, and not the end. Buildings, he would say, must always have sure foundations, but the highest aim of the student should not be the construction of cellar vaults. In Ranke's own practice archivial research was the last rather than the first stage. He thoroughly mastered his subject, and learned what to look for, he then resorted to archives for confirmation or illustration. Thus he appeared to know his way about collections before he had ever seen them. This was the despair of custodians who had to ply him with bundle on bundle of documents, and complained that he read with his hand, just as a recent Oxford professor was accused of judging books and examination papers by smell rather than by sight.

It was natural that Ranke's work should from time to time be depreciated by the growing school of archivist and researcher, or by those who worked on older methods. Leo Gervinus, Bergenroth, and Gindely all made him the butt of fierce attacks. Researchers complained that he neglected the most weighty stores of knowledge for the more showy, that he merely skimmed the documents which he professed to study, and peppered his pages with quotations, to give a show of erudition. One professor refused to place his books on the shelves of the University library ; another pronounced that nothing was to be learnt from his "Reformation." Doubtless in some of the strictures there was an element of truth. Ranke's researches were indeed considerable, but they were necessarily not so close and minute as those of workers who confined their studies to the history of a score of years. It is well to remember that so sound a researcher as Arneth declared before a Congress of historians that Ranke alone among writers of prose had furnished a masterpiece to every nation—to Germany, that is, and France, to England, Italy, and Spain, to the Ottoman Empire, even to Servia. Sufficient allowance was not made for his previous preparation, nor yet for the power of speed, which is a distinguishing mark of genius in archivial research as in all else. At any rate, Ranke had the good fortune to outlive most of his critics and their criticism. That he formed such pupils as Giesebrecht, Waitz, Sybel, Lorenz, and our own Lord Acton, is a proof of the educational value of his methods.

Lord Acton dwells upon this side of Ranke's work. He regards a prize essay on Henry I, set in 1834, and in which Waitz beat Giesebrecht, as the foundation of what has been for so long incomparably the first school of history in the world, not for ideas or eloquence, but for solid and methodical work. "Ranke has not only written," he elsewhere says, "a larger number of mostly good books than any other man that ever lived, but has taken pains from the first to explain how the thing is done." And again, "Ranke taught the modern historian to be critical, to be colourless, to be new. We meet him at every step. There are stronger books than any one of his, and some may have surpassed him in political, religious, philosophic insight, in vividness of the creative imagination, in originality, elevation, and depth of thought, but by the extent of important work well executed, by his influence on able men, and by the amount of knowledge which mankind received and employs with the stamp of his mind upon it, he stands unrivalled." Any one who has had any experience of a school of history will realize how well-nigh impossible it is to be at once a prolific writer and a fruitful teacher. Yet this was Ranke's feat.

The strength of Ranke consisted, perhaps, above all, in his power of thought. Whenever he wrote he thought. This is by no means a platitude. It is possible to write a very tolerable and useful history without any thought at all. History is frequently a mere matter of repetition— not of verbal iteration, but of idea and arrangement. Want of thought is, in fact, the danger to which the narrative, and especially the universal historian, is exposed. Ranke escaped this owing to his insight, his vitality, his power of co-ordination, his strategic mastery of his facts. A very appreciative critic, Dr. A. Guilland, has said that Ranke was intelligent rather than original. It is difficult now to judge equitably of the originality of an historian who wrote more than three-quarters of a century ago, because many of the thoughts and methods which were then original have become commonplace. The general lines of any given period have from much reading and much writing become fairly fixed, and the historian cannot stray far from them without becoming bizarre or paradoxical. But originality can always find its vent in the treatment of detail and illustration, and of this art Ranke gave convincing proof from his very earliest book.

This earliest book has a special interest for several reasons. It was accompanied by a subsidiary volume, which has not been translated, containing an elaborate critique of the authorities upon whom Ranke had mainly to rely. Their importance was at once recognized, and, what was better still, they provoked discussion as to the originality of his method. "A new art of employing authorities," wrote Lord Acton, "came in with Ranke in 1824." The result was the author's promotion from a school at Frankfurt on the Oder to the post of Extra-ordinary Professor in the University of Berlin. This was the making of Ranke's career; he could now both learn and teach in one of the world's chief intellectual capitals. The provincial schoolmaster was to become, in Döllinger's words, a *Praeceptor Germaniae*. Looking backwards from the close of this long career the reader will find that "The Latin and Teutonic Nations" contains the protoplasm from which Ranke's historical principles were gradually evolved, and in particular the blending of wide philosophical conceptions with illustrative detail. "What a wealth," writes Lorenz, "of ideas fermenting and in part obscure, set forth in a form which, while it makes reading difficult, nevertheless enchains the fancy." Ranke in after years had little parental affection for his firstborn, and wished first to exclude it from the edition of his collected works, and then to give it a new form. Lorenz himself saved it for posterity by insisting that he would spoil one of his most original and instructive contributions to history.

Ranke chose a magnificent subject, and this he himself admitted to the end. Until the close of the eighteenth century it would be hard to find two decades so rich in interest and importance as those whose history he tells. That this is now a commonplace is due mainly to the influence of this very book. It is true that the author owes something to accident, for his scheme comprised a larger period with 1535 as its concluding date. This would have led him into a fresh range of ideas, personalities, and aims. His final date, moreover, was singularly inconclusive ; no halt could have been possible until the year 1559. Even as it is, the date with which he closes is not, as will be seen, a scientific finale. The Preface sets forth that the author's intention is to confine himself in the main to the interaction of those nations of Latin and Teutonic origin, whose history is the kernel of all modern history. Internal or constitutional events he would only treat in so far as they were necessary to the understanding of external enterprises. For example, the growth of absolutism in Spain was a necessary condition of the success of the Spanish Crown in Italy ; the strength or weakness of Maximilian at his several Diets is reflected in the flux or reflux of his international influence. The common movements of a certain group of European nations is therefore the subject of this volume.

To prove how old the idea of this unity of European nations is, the Introduction opens with the dream of a Visigothic kingdom fusing the Germanic tribes with the old Roman world. At its close Ranke calls the three general movements of these nations—that is, the migrations, the crusades, and the colonization—the three deep breaths. It would almost seem as if he regarded the move of the Western powers upon Italy at the turn of the fifteenth and sixteenth centuries as a fourth deep breath. In a measure this does partake of the character of the other three. The southernly or easternly march of Germans, French, Spaniards, and particularly Swiss, was almost a migration. Then, again, to more than one mind Italy was the stepping-stone for a crusade against the infidel ; the threatened French advance from Naples upon Constantinople was to be the rival or the complement of the conquest of Granada. Charles VIII was too weak of purpose to abandon the pleasures of Naples for the sterner task of a crusade, but there is no reason to rate his high-flown expressions as mere bombast. And, finally, the colonizing enterprises of the European nations, especially those of the Portuguese, directly affected the fortunes of the Italian wars. Had the source of her commerce with the East not been tapped by Portugal, Venice might have made a better fight with Europe. The fourth great breath, in fact, began to be drawn in before the third was quite exhausted.

The offensive movement against Italy was begun by France, but Charles VIII's invasion in 1494 was rather the occasion than the cause for the enterprise of the other nations. These were prompted by no mere jealousy of France, or by a desire to preserve the balance of power. Maximilian had already begun his intrigues with Milan ; it was always certain that as soon as an Emperor was strong enough, he would revive his imperial pretensions. It was unlikely that the legitimate line of Aragon, which now wielded the forces of Castile, and which already possessed the ports of Sicily, would long acquiesce in its exclusion from Naples by the bastard branch. Julius II, as Cardinal, had long ago brought down the Swiss hordes, all too willing, upon the fat Lombard plains ; it was no mere raid that they now intended, but substantial occupation.

Upon Charles VIII's apparently futile expedition followed the partition wars, which form the bulk of the present volume. Louis XII doubted if he could realize the Orleanist claims on Milan without the co-operation of Venice, the most subtle antagonist of Charles VIII. Hence arose the Milanese partition war. The French king was then certain that the pretensions of his Crown to Naples were valueless unless he could offer a *quid pro quo* to Spain ; the outcome was the Neapolitan partition war.

The thieves quarrelled, to the disadvantage of the less clever but more enterprising thief, and Naples passed in its integrity to Spain. Alexander VI, after stealing oddments in the general confusion, was at the moment of his death balancing the prospects of a partition of Central Italy by an alliance with either France or Spain. Finally, Julius II, most fatal of all Italians to Italian freedom, engineered the most criminal of all partition wars. In the League of Cambray, France, Spain, and Germany were all to have their share of Venetian territory. It was of small advantage to Italy that the Pope himself, Mantua, Ferrara, and Savoy were to have such share of the spoils as fall to camp-followers. Julius recognized too late his own mistake, and bragged of the expulsion of all foreigners. The only result was a fresh partition, the temporary exclusion of France, the most humane and least persistent of partitioning powers, the permanent settlement of Spain, the introduction of the migrating Swiss, while, if he had had his will, the Austrian occupation of the Venetian mainland would have been anticipated by three centuries. Italy had become the Thieves' Kitchen of Europe, and Julius II had made himself responsible for the fixtures.

Such a theme as this gave full scope for Ranke's interest in personality, his range of knowledge, and his constructive power. Italy throughout occupies the centre of his canvas, but in the distance, and, it may be added, in the corners there are bits of landscape and seascape, which might well form separate pictures, but which, nevertheless, have their fitting place in the general composition. Beyond the Alps the fortunes of the Italian wars, and of Maximilian's shifting relations with France, are seen to affect not only the raids of the Duke of Guelders on the northernmost Netherlands, but the most technical details of constitutional reform in Germany. In a few lines something is learnt of the domestic peculiarities of Württemberg, a second-rate German state, which is in the process of conversion from a county into a duchy. At first sight this appears to be an otiose, if not inartistic, detail, but all of a sudden it is made to account for Maximilian's triumphant appearance before the Diet of Freiburg, and that leads to his enhanced reputation with the European powers. The quarrels of Swiss and Grisons with Swabians and Tyrolese contributed largely to Louis XII's occupation of Milan, their pacification led to Ludovico Moro's return, while an internal Swiss squabble determined the fate of Lombardy. Ranke touches but lightly and allusively on American exploration; but he levies heavy contributions on the shores of North Africa, on the Red Sea, and on the Indian Ocean, from Mombasa to Malacca. Here it is that he proves, in his most effective manner, the unity of the history of the Western nations. The Portuguese, after fighting the Moors on the shores of the Atlantic, found the same enemies at Mozambique, and strove with them for the spice trade of Calicut. The battles of Spaniards or Portuguese at Bugia, Tripoli, Diu have active connection with the clash of Latin and Teutonic nations in Italy. Until the French occupation of the hinterland of Algiers, there was, perhaps, only one statesman who comprehended the essential factors of the North African problem, and that was Ximenes.

Ranke perpetually brings the Western and Eastern incidents of his period into mutual relation. The Venetians, after Almeida's victories in 1507, sent metal and gun-founders and shipwrights to the Soldan, whose fleet was manned in part by Venetian and Dalmatian sailors. "His victory and his loss was their victory and their loss. Their maritime life and command of the seas were alike dependent upon the issue that was to be fought out in

India in the year 1508." Again, while February 3, 1509, crushed the trade of Venice, the battle of May 14 destroyed her mainland power; Italy, in the phrase of Ascanio Sforza, ceased to be the inner court of the world. Not only, indeed, were the profits of the Eastern trade withdrawn from Venice, but went to swell the resources of her enemies. The profit of one hundred and seventy-five per cent., which the house of Fugger derived from the despatch of three ships to Calicut, enabled them to finance Maximilian in his attack on Padua. And as with Portuguese so it is with Spaniards. In 1511 Ximenes had apparently persuaded Ferdinand to undertake in person the conquest of North Africa. Ferdinand, on his way to Malaga, was stopped by news from Romagna, and thus it was that the Spanish force, intended for the permanent occupation of North Africa, from Algiers to Tripoli, was shipped to Italy to be beaten at Ravenna.

It seems ungrateful to complain that one who has given so much should have denied a little more; and yet it must be confessed that the close of this volume leaves the subject incomplete. Ranke was, in this case, too much influenced by the chronology of reigns. He made the death of Louis XII his dividing line. This was natural, as the personality of his successor was so striking that it immediately calls up a fresh slide in the magic-lantern. Then, again, Francis I at once suggests the name of his rival, Charles V. Nevertheless, the scientific frontier line is not 1514, but 1516, for it was then that the Italian partition wars closed. Not until 1521 did the conflict between Charles V and Francis I for the domination of Italy begin; their relations were particularly friendly until at least the close of 1516. Ranke himself admits, in the Conclusion added in his second edition, that his work breaks off at the very moment of the crisis. The death of Louis XII left the situation in Italy indeterminate. It was as impossible that France should submit to defeat by the Swiss Cantons as it was that England should recognize Majuba or Magersfontein as a final verdict. It was not chivalry, nor mere love of fight, but political necessity that drove the French king and nation into the campaign of Marignano. The victory of Marignano connects itself with the defeat of Novara rather than with that of Pavìa. In 1514 Spanish troops were still prowling about Italy, seeking whom they should devour. While Spaniards occupied Brescia, Imperialists still held Verona, and these were the two chief cities of the Venetian mainland. The Swiss nominally in the service of the new Duke of Milan, Maximilian Sforza, were in reality absorbing Lombardy. The Holy League still stood in arms against France and Venice. Thus if Ranke must needs choose the end of a reign as his conclusion, it should have been that of Ferdinand, for the Spanish king had become of more weight in European politics than the French. Ferdinand's death occasioned the formation of the huge aggregate of Habsburg power, which was to be the dominating factor in the succeeding period. It was closely followed by four treaties, three of which have been of abiding validity. The treaty of Noyon, the most important for the moment, regulated the relations between France, Spain, and the Netherlands on the most amicable terms. The Eternal Peace of Freiburg bound the Swiss to French service down to the Revolution; it determined the curious, curly frontier which still twists in and out on the shores of Lakes Maggiore and Lugano. Their defeat at Marignano had decided that the Swiss should not be a substantial Italian power, a buffer state dividing the Habsburg and the Valois. Equally strange and equally permanent was the line drawn on the east between Venetian and Austrian territory by the treaty of December, 1516.

This line gave to Maximilian the uppermost slice of the
Lago di Garda, and the town of Roveredo on the Adige ;
instead of accepting the rapid Isonzo as the natural
boundary, racial and geographical, between Slav and Italian,
it created a highly artificial frontier, which to the present
day gives a breadth of the Friulian plain with its Italian
population to Austria, and leaves to Italy, heiress of Venice,
a *Slavonia irredenta* in the sub-Alpine hills. Finally, the
victory of Marignano determined the Concordat of Bologna,
which may be said to have guided the relations between
Church and State in France until almost yesterday.

It would be dishonest to pretend, that even within its
limits " The Latin and Teutonic Nations " is a perfect book.
Ranke well knew that it was not. He was still struggling
to attain his ideal of style—simple, smooth, and clear. The
volume has been criticized on the ground that it was based
solely on printed authorities ; but Ranke replies, in the
Preface to his second edition, that these authorities were
very numerous and very good, that only on reaching the
succeeding period he felt obliged to go behind the printing-
press. It may be regretted that this second edition was·
not more thoroughly revised in the light of later learning.
This appeared in October, 1874, to celebrate the jubilee
of Ranke's literary activity. He revised the pages on a
holiday in the country, away from books ; he confesses
that the work is essentially the same. Yet some of the
small mistakes might well have been corrected, and they
are probably responsible for errors in later text-books. In
1824· Ranke had not as yet visited Italy, and his geo-
graphy is occasionally at fault. He writes of Louis XII's
operations on the Adda as taking place among heights and
valleys, whereas the only excrescence on the plain was the
dyke of a canalized streamlet. It is elaborately argued
that the French attacked the Venetian vanguard, whereas

authorities printed by 1874 prove conclusively that it was the rear. The battle of Ravenna is a hotch-potch of bright anecdotes, without a feeling for tactics. Treviso is, by implication, placed in the Friuli, while Gian Galeazzo Visconti's widow is wrongly represented as giving Verona to Venice to obtain her alliance against Carrara. Caesar Borgia has enough crimes for which to answer, but it was not men, but bulls that he shot from horseback, as they charged across the *piazza* of St. Peters. A more serious mistake, often repeated by others, occurs in the very second paragraph of the book. Here René of Provence is made to disinherit his grandson, René of Lorraine, and leave Anjou to his nephew, the Count of Maine, who in turn bequeathed it to the Crown. But Anjou was an apanage which could not descend in either the female or the collateral line, and it lapsed to the Crown upon old René's death. But a Pharisee could doubtless have found motes in all the eyes of Argus. In spite of blemishes, " The Latin and Teutonic Nations " will remain an inspiring example of what can be done by a young writer who will both read and think. Most honest historians would be thankful if their last book were as good as Leopold von Ranke's first.

E. ARMSTRONG.

CONTENTS

PAGE

INTRODUCTION. By Edward Armstrong . . . ix

AUTHOR'S INTRODUCTION :

OUTLINES OF AN ESSAY ON THE UNITY OF THE
LATIN AND TEUTONIC NATIONS AND THEIR COMMON
DEVELOPMENT 1

1. The Migration of Nations 2
2. The Crusades 6
3. Colonization 17

BOOK I

1494–1501

CHAP. I. — THE SITUATION IN FRANCE AND IN ITALY.—EXPEDITION OF CHARLES VIII TO NAPLES

1. FRANCE AND CHARLES VIII

Retrospect 20
Success of Louis XI 21
Provence and Anjou united to the French Crown (1480) . 21
Revolt of the Duke of Orleans (1484) 22
Charles VIII begins to reign (1491) 22
His Marriage with Anne of Brittany 23
Peace of Senlis (1493) 23
Prosperity of France—The *Hommes d'Armes* . . . 24
Ambition of Charles 25
Ludovico il Moro urges him to an Expedition against Naples 26
Constitution of his Army 28
His Character and Appearance 29

2. THE SITUATION IN ITALY

The Houses of Sforza and Aragon 29
Ferdinand I (Ferrante) of Naples (1458–1494) . . . 30

2. THE SITUATION IN ITALY—*continued*

PAGE

Character of his Son Alfonso 31
Revolt of the Neapolitan Barons (1486) 32
Bona of Savoy, Duchess of Milan (1476) 34
Ludovico il Moro secures the Government of Milan (1480) 35
His Character and Policy 35
Lorenzo de' Medici in Alliance with Naples and Milan . 37
His Friendship with Innocent VIII 37
The Italian States 38
Rupture between Naples and Milan 39
Death of Lorenzo de' Medici and Innocent VIII (1492) . 41
Election of Alexander VI 42
His Alliance with Ludovico 43
Death of Ferdinand of Naples (1494) 44
Accession of Alfonso II 44
His Alliance with Alexander VI 44
Revolt of Giuliano della Rovere and the Colonna . . 45
Alfonso attacks Ludovico by Land and Sea . . . 46

3. CHARLES VIII IN ITALY

Charles sets out for Italy and is welcomed by Ludovico at
Milan (1494) 47
Death of Gian Galeazzo Sforza 48
Ludovico, Duke of Milan 48
The Situation in Florence 49
Piero de' Medici treats with Charles VIII . . . 50
The Medici expelled 52
Pisa freed from Florentine Rule 52
Charles enters Florence 53
Perplexity of the Pope 55
Charles in Rome 56
His Successful Advance upon Naples 57
Abdication of Alfonso in favour of Ferrantino (1495) . 58
Charles enters Naples 61

CHAP. II.—SPAIN AND THE LEAGUE AT WAR WITH
CHARLES VIII (1495-1496)

1. UNITED SPAIN

Castile and Aragon 62
Death of Henry IV of Castile and Accession of Isabella
(1474) 63

1. UNITED SPAIN—*continued*

War of Succession 63
Ferdinand and Isabella victorious at Toro (1476) . . 64
Establishment of the Inquisition (1480) 65
Consolidation of the Spanish Monarchy 66
War against the Moors (1481) 67
Conquest of Granada (1491) 67
Conquests in Africa 68
Discoveries of Columbus 69
Roussillon restored by France to Spain (1493) . . . 70

2. CONNECTION BETWEEN SPAIN AND ITALY

History of the Struggle for the two Sicilies . 71
Ferdinand protests against the Expedition of Charles VIII 72
Louis of Orleans threatens Milan 73
League against France (Treaty of Venice, March 31, 1495) 75

3. RETREAT OF CHARLES VIII

Negotiations between the Pope and the Sultan Bajazet . 75
Charles restores Order in Naples 76
He appoints Montpensier Viceroy and quits Naples . . 77
His Retreat 78
The Duke of Orleans in Lombardy 79
Battle of Fornovo (July 6, 1495) 81
Unsuccessful Attack by Giuliano della Rovere on Genoa . 84
Ferrantino re-enters Naples 84
Arrival of Swiss Reinforcements for the French . . 86
Treaty of Vercelli (October 9, 1495) 87
Charles returns to France 87

4. WAR IN NAPLES (1495–1496)

Gonzalvo in Calabria 89
Heroism of 700 Germans 90
Defeat of the French at Atella (July, 1496) . . . 92
Death of Ferrantino (October 6) and Accession of Federigo 93

CHAP. III

1. MAXIMILIAN OF AUSTRIA AND THE EMPIRE

Position and Objects of Maximilian 95
Philip of Ravenstein surrenders Sluys (1492) . . . 96
Character of Maximilian 97
The Diet of Worms (1495) 99

PAGE

1. MAXIMILIAN OF AUSTRIA AND THE EMPIRE—*continued*

Maximilian's Compact with Württemberg . . . 99
Betrothal of Philip and Margaret to Juana and Juan of
    Aragon 100
Use of German Auxiliaries in European Wars . . . 100
Constitution of the Empire 101
The Swabian League 102
Position of the Emperor 103
Struggle of Maximilian with the Estates 104
He accepts their Proposals 106
The Cameral Tribunal—The Common Penny . . . 107

2. MAXIMILIAN'S FIRST EXPEDITION TO ITALY.— THE
    FLORENTINES AND SAVONAROLA

Maximilian invited to Italy 108
Unsuccessful Attack by the Florentines on Pisa . . 108
Ludovico meets Maximilian at Münster (July, 1496) . . 109
Maximilian agrees to fight for the League against the
    French 110
His Schemes 111
His Arrival at Vigevano 111
He invests Leghorn 112
Description of the Florentines 112
Girolamo Savonarola, his Teaching and Influence . . 114
Reform of the Florentine Constitution 118
Failure of Maximilian at Leghorn 119
He Returns to Germany 120
Burning of the Vanities in Florence 121
Florence declares against the Pope 121
Savonarola urges the Reform of the Church . . . 122
The Pope reduces the Orsini 122
The *Bigi* and *Arrabbiati* in Florence 123
Piero de' Medici attempts to return (April, 1497) . . 123
Savonarola excommunicated 124
His *Triumphus Crucis* 125
Franciscan Challenge—The Ordeal by Fire (April, 1498) . 126
Death of Charles VIII (April 8) 127
Execution of Savonarola (May 23) 128

3. EXTENSION AND ASCENDENCY OF THE LEAGUE

Alliance between Ferdinand and Dom Manuel of Portugal
    (1497) 129
Henry VII joins the League (1496) 129

3. EXTENSION AND ASCENDENCY OF THE LEAGUE—*continued*

    Perkin Warbeck in Scotland 130
    Peace between England and Scotland (1497) . . . 131
    War in Roussillon (1496) 131
    Revolution in Württemberg 132
    Diet of Freiburg (1498) 133

CHAP. IV.—FALL OF THE HOUSE OF SFORZA-ARAGON

1. LOUIS XII AND VENICE AGAINST MILAN

    Failure of Maximilian's Attack upon France (1498) . . 134
    Character of Louis XII 135
    Cardinal d'Amboise 136
    Louis divorces Jeanne and marries Anne of Brittany (1499) 137
    Ferdinand makes a Treaty with Louis (1498) . . . 137
    Feud between Venice and Ludovico 138
    Ludovico aids the Florentines against Pisa . . . 138
    The Venetians assist Louis against Milan . . . 139
    Position of Ludovico 140

2. SWISS AND SWABIANS IMPLICATED IN THE WAR

    Maximilian supports Ludovico 141
    Outbreak of War between the Swiss Confederation and the
        Swabian League (1498) 143
    Alliance between Louis and the Swiss (1499) . . . 145
    Battle of Schwaderloch 146
    Battle of Frastenz 147
    Maximilian arrives on the scene 149
    His Troops refuse to follow him 150
    Battle of Dorneck 151
    Desperate Position of Ludovico 151
    His Castles surrender to Trivulzio 152
    Treachery of Francesco Sanseverino 153
    Fall of Alessandria 153
    Ludovico abandons Milan (September 1) . . . 154
    Louis in Milan 156
    Peace of Basel (September 22) 158
    Ludovico and the people of Uri 159
    Galeazzo Visconti collects Troops in Switzerland . . 159
    Guelphs and Ghibellines in Milan 160
    Ludovico returns to Milan (February 5, 1500) . . 162
    Negotiations with the Swiss 163

PAGE

2. SWISS AND SWABIANS IMPLICATED IN THE WAR—*continued*

Ludovico at Novara opposed by the French . . . 164
Capture of Ludovico (April 10) 166
Maximilian at the Diet of Augsburg 168
Establishment of the Council of Regency . . . 168

3. POPE ALEXANDER VI AND HIS SON AGAINST THE VASSALS
OF THE CHURCH

Situation of the Pope 169
Murder of the Duke of Gandia 170
Character of Caesar Borgia 171
He visits the Court of Louis XII (October, 1498) . . 172
French Marriage and Alliance (1499) 172
Caesar attacks Caterina Sforza 173
Fall of Imola (December, 1499) 173
Caterina surrenders Forlì (January, 1500) . . . 174
Caesar's further Conquests in the Romagna . . . 174
Assassination of the Duke of Biseglia (August, 1500) . 176
Treaty between France and Spain for the Partition of
Naples (September, 1500) 178
The Partition sanctioned by the Pope (April, 1501) . 178
Fall of the House of Aragon in Naples 179
War between the Turks and Venice (1499) . . . 181
Revolt of the Moors in Spain 183

BOOK II

1502–1514

INTRODUCTION

Summary of the Position of the Latin and Teutonic Nations . 185

CHAP. I.

1. THE WAR IN NAPLES AND THE ROMAGNA

Disputes between Spaniards and French in Naples . . 191
Outbreak of War (June, 1502) 192
French Successes 192
Description of the French and Spanish Leaders . . 193
Incidents of the War 196
Gonzalvo at Barletta 196

1. THE WAR IN NAPLES AND THE ROMAGNA—*continued*

Caesar in the Romagna 196
He takes Urbino and Camerino 197
Conspiracy of the *Condottieri* 198
They make a Treaty with Caesar (December, 1502) . . 199
He seizes the Leaders and puts them to death . . . 200
Suppression of the Orsini 201

2. THE DECISION IN NAPLES

Situation of Gonzalvo (February, 1503) 202
Defeat of Aubigny at Terranova (April 20) . . . 203
Battle of Cerignola (April 27) 204
Gonzalvo enters Naples (May 13) 205
Battle of the Garigliano (December 29) . . . 207

3. CHANGE IN THE PAPACY

Estrangement between the French and the Pope . . 208
Murder of Trocces (June, 1503) 209
Death of Alexander VI (August 18) 209
Illness of Caesar Borgia 210
Election and Death of Pius III (Sept. 22–Oct. 18) . . 212
Election of Julius II (November 1) 213
The Venetians invade the Romagna 213
Vacillation of Caesar 214
He surrenders his Castles to the Pope (April, 1504) . . 216
Fate of Caesar 217

CHAP. II.—SPAIN AND AUSTRIA AT VARIANCE

Philip concludes an Alliance with Louis (August, 1503) . 218
They are joined by Maximilian 219

1. MAXIMILIAN, THROUGH THE INFLUENCE OF THE FRENCH
     ALLIANCE, VICTORIOUS IN GERMANY

Assembly of Electors at Gelnhausen (July, 1502) . . 219
Opposition of Electors ceases after Conclusion of the French
    Alliance 221
Death of Duke Georg of Bavaria-Landshut . . . 221
War of the Landshut Succession (1504) . . . 222
Success of Maximilian 225
Diet of Cologne (May, 1505) 225

CONTENTS

PAGE

2. MAXIMILIAN'S COMPREHENSIVE SCHEMES.— PHILIP OF
CASTILE

Treaty of Blois (September, 1504) 226
Death of Isabella of Castile (November, 1504) . . . 227
Ferdinand summons the Cortes 229
He marries Germaine de Foix (October, 1505) . . . 230
Philip in England 231
He arrives in Castile 232
Meeting between Ferdinand and Philip 233
Ferdinand renounces the Regency 233
Maximilian in Hungary 234
Birth of an Heir to Wladislav II 235
Betrothal of Charles and Claude revoked . . . 236
Death of Philip (September 16, 1506) 237

3. FERDINAND, MASTER OF NAPLES AND CASTILE

Ferdinand sails for Naples (September, 1506) . . . 238
Settlement of Affairs there 239
Gonzalvo returns to Spain 240
Madness of Queen Juana 241
Account of Ximenes 245
Ferdinand enters Castile (August, 1507) . . . 248
Meeting of Ferdinand and Juana 248

4. FERDINAND'S EXTERNAL ENTERPRISES

Capture of Mers-el-Kebir 249
Colonization of America 250
Conquest of Oran (1509) 250
Conquests of Navarra in Africa (1510) . . . 251
Defeat of the Spaniards in Gelves 251

CHAP. III.—VENICE AND JULIUS II

1. VENETIAN COMMERCE, CONQUESTS, AND CONSTITUTION ;
ATTACK UPON THE ROMAGNA

Venetian Commerce 253
Venetian Conquests 255
The Venetian Constitution 258
Venetian Successes in the Romagna 260

2. FIRST EXPLOITS AND DOUBLE INTENTIONS OF JULIUS II

Julius enters the League of Blois (September, 1504) . . 261
Position of Giovanni Bentivoglio at Bologna . . . 262

2. FIRST EXPLOITS OF JULIUS II—*continued*

 Julius takes the Field against Bologna (1506) . . . 263
 Success of the Pope 264
 Revolution in Genoa 265
 Quelled by Louis (1507) 266

3. DISCOVERIES OF THE PORTUGUESE—DECAY OF VENETIAN
  COMMERCE

 Extent of Moorish Trade 268
 Portuguese Discoveries in Africa 269
 Expedition of Vasco da Gama to India (1497-8) . . 270
 Hostility of the Zamorin of Calicut 272
 Defeat of the Zamorin by Pereira (1503) . . . 273
 Expedition of Almeida (1505) 274
 Effect of Portuguese Voyages on Venetian Commerce . 277
 War between Portuguese and Moors of India and Egypt . 278

4. MAXIMILIAN'S ATTACK—THE LEAGUE OF CAMBRAY

 Diet of Constance (1507) 279
 Maximilian resolves to attack Venice . . . 280
 He adopts title of Roman Emperor Elect (Feb. 1508) . 280
 He advances into Italy and takes Cadore . . 281
 His sudden Retreat 281
 Successes of the Venetians under Alviano . . 283
 Campaign of Charles of Gelderland on the Lower Rhine . 285
 Venetians agree to a Truce with Maximilian . . 286
 The League of Cambray (December 10, 1508) . . 286

5. FALL OF THE POWER AND TRADE OF THE VENETIANS
  IN 1509

 Venice in Danger 287
 France declares War on Venice 289
 Beginning of the War (April, 1509) . . . 291
 Battle of Agnadello (May 14) 292
 Venice surrenders her Subject-Towns . . . 295
 Portuguese Victories in India destroy Venetian Trade . 296

6. WAR OF THE VENETIANS TO SAVE THEIR CITY AND
  PART OF THEIR TERRITORY

 Maximilian and Louis determine to destroy Venice . . 298
 The Venetians recover Padua 299
 Maximilian besieges Padua 300

PAGE

6. WAR OF THE VENETIANS—*continued*

He raises the Siege and retreats from Italy . . . 301
Further Venetian Successes 301
Rudolf of Anhalt lays waste the Country (1510) . . 302

7. ENTERPRISES OF THE POPE TO EFFECT THE LIBERATION OF ITALY

Venice released from the Ban (February, 1510) . . 303
Alfonso of Ferrara defies the Pope 304
He is excommunicated 305
Louis abandons his Alliance with the Swiss . . 305
The Pope concludes an Alliance with them . . 307
The Papal Army occupies Modena and threatens Ferrara . 307
Swiss Troops desert the Pope 309
Failure of the Pope's Attack on Genoa . . . 310
Louis decides on War against Julius . . . 310
The Pope in Danger at Bologna . . . 311
He is rescued by Spanish and Venetian Troops . 312
He succeeds in reducing Mirandola . . . 313
The Papal Attack on Ferrara fails . . . 314
Matthäus Lang endeavours to make Peace . . 315
The Bentivogli reinstated at Bologna (May, 1511) . 316
Cardinal Alidosi murdered by the Duke of Urbino . 317
Grief of the Pope 317
Desperate Condition of Venice . . . 318
Moral Reflection 319

CHAP. IV.—RISE OF THE AUSTRO-SPANISH HOUSE TO ALMOST THE HIGHEST POWER IN EUROPE

1. JULIUS II IN LEAGUE WITH SPAIN . . . 322

Schismatic Cardinals summon a Council at Pisa . 322
Julius summons a Council in the Lateran . . 322
The Holy League (October, 1511) . . . 324
Factions among the Swiss 325
Swiss Courier drowned in the Lake of Lugano . 325
The Swiss declare War against France . . 326
They cross the St. Gotthard into Italy . . 327
They are repulsed and retire . . . 328
The Venetians capture Brescia, and other Cities (February, 1512) 329

CONTENTS

PAGE

1. JULIUS II IN LEAGUE WITH SPAIN—*continued*

Gaston de Foix relieves Bologna 329
Capture and Sack of Brescia 330
Council of Pisa removed to Milan 331
Battle of Ravenna (April 11, 1512) 332
Receipt of the News in Rome 337

2. FORMATION OF A NEW LEAGUE—COALITION OF ENGLAND

The Situation in England 338
Death of Henry VII and Accession of Henry VIII (1509) . 339
Foreign Policy of Henry VIII 340
Alliance between Ferdinand and Maximilian . . . 341
Henry joins the League against France 342
Illness of the Pope (August, 1511) 342
Maximilian joins the League 343

3. THE CONQUEST OF MILAN

The Swiss again invade Italy (May, 1512) . . . 344
Julius opens the Lateran Council 345
Swiss Troops abandon French Army 347
Retreat of the French 347
Milan in the Hands of the Swiss 348
Bologna, Parma, and Piacenza submit to the Pope . . 348
Alfonso of Ferrara comes to Rome 348

4. THE CONQUEST OF NAVARRE

The Marquis of Dorset in Guipuscoa 349
The Sovereigns of Navarre allied with France (July, 1512) 350
The Duke of Alva advances on Pamplona . . . 351
Flight of Jean d'Albret 351
Surrender of Pamplona 352
Discontent of the English 352
Ferdinand gains Navarre 352

5. REVOLUTION IN FLORENCE.—OTHER SUCCESSES IN ITALY

Conquest of Pisa by Florence (June, 1509) . . . 354
Account of Cardinal de' Medici 355
Campaign of Cardona in Tuscany 357
Return of the Medici to Florence (September 14, 1512) . 357
Alfonso of Ferrara escapes from Rome 360
The Pope makes an Alliance with Maximilian . . 360
Death of Julius II (February, 1513) 361
Election of Leo X 361

CONTENTS

PAGE

6. STRUGGLE OF THE FRENCH AND SWISS FOR MILAN

    Conquests of the Swiss 362
    Massimiliano Sforza installed as Duke of Milan
      (December 30, 1512) 363
    Alliance between Louis XII and Venice (March 13, 1513) . 364
    The French invade the Milanese 365
    Battle of Novara (June 6, 1513) 366

7. GENERAL WAR MOVEMENT

    Strength of the Combination against France . . . 369
    Henry VIII at the Siege of Térouanne 370
    He is joined by Maximilian 371
    Battle of the Spurs (August 17, 1513) 372
    The Swiss invade Burgundy 373
    Queen Anne of France asks Help of James IV of Scotland. 374
    James crosses the Tweed 375
    Battle of Flodden (September 9, 1513) . . . 376
    La Trémouille arranges Terms of Peace with the Swiss . 377
    Henry VIII at Tournay 378
    Cardona drives back the Venetians 379
    Defeat of Alviano at Creazzo (October 7, 1513) . . 379
    Triumph of the League 380

8. FURTHER SCHEMES FOR THE ADVANCEMENT OF THE
    AUSTRO-SPANISH HOUSE

    Alliance between Louis and Ferdinand 381
    General Truce 382
    Treaties of Marriage 383
    Swiss Hostility to France 383
    Position of Maximilian in the Empire 384
    Subjection of Friesland 385
    Conclusion 386

INDEX 389

HISTORY OF THE

LATIN AND TEUTONIC NATIONS

INTRODUCTION

OUTLINES OF AN ESSAY ON THE UNITY OF THE LATIN AND TEUTONIC NATIONS, AND THEIR COMMON DEVELOPMENT

AT the beginning of his success, not long after the migration of nations had commenced, Athaulf, King of the Visigoths, conceived the idea of gothicising the Roman world, and making himself the Caesar of all; he would maintain the Roman laws.[1] If we understand him aright, he first intended to combine the Romans of the West (who, though sprung of many and diverse tribes, had, after a union that had lasted for centuries, at length become one realm and one people) in a new unity with the Teutonic races. He afterwards despaired of being able to effect this; but the collective Teutonic nations at last brought it about, and in a still wider sense than he had dreamed of. It was not long before Lugdunensian Gaul became not, it is true, a Gothland, but a Lugdunensian Germania.[2] Eventually the purple of a Caesar passed to the Teutonic races in the person of Charlemagne. At length these likewise adopted the Roman law. In this combination six great nations were formed—three in which the Latin element predominated,

---

[1] Orosius, vii. 34. Cf. Mascow, Geschichte der Deutschen bis zur fränkischen Monarchie, p. 369.

[2] Sidonius Apollinaris in Mascow, 480.

viz. the French, the Spanish, and the Italian; and three in which the Teutonic element was conspicuous, viz. the German, the English, and the Scandinavian.

Each of these six nationalities was again broken up into separate parts; they never formed one nation, and they were almost always at war among themselves. Wherein, then, is their unity displayed? Wherein is it to be perceived? They are all sprung from the same or a closely allied stock; are alike in manners, and similar in many of their institutions: their internal histories precisely coincide, and certain great enterprises are common to all. The following work, which is based upon this conception, would be unintelligible, were not the latter explained by a short survey of those external enterprises which, arising as they do from the same spirit, form a progressive development of the Latin and Teutonic life from the first beginning until now.

These are the migration of nations, the Crusades, and the colonization of foreign countries.

I

The migration of nations founded the unity of which we speak. The actual event, the movement itself, proceeded from the Germans; but the Latin countries were not merely passive. In exchange for the arms and the new public life which they received, they communicated to the victors their religion and their language. Reccared had, indeed, to become a Catholic before mutual intermarriage between the Visigoths and the Latin peoples could be legally permitted in Spain.[1] But, after this, the races and their languages became completely blended. In Italy the communities of Lombard and Roman extraction, in spite of their original separation, became so closely intertwined that it is almost impossible to distinguish the component elements of each. It is clear what great influence the bishops exercised upon the founding of France; and yet they were at first purely of

[1] Lex Flavii Reccaredi Regis, ut tam Romano, etc., in Leges Visigothorum, iii. 1, 1. Hispan. Illustr. iii. 88. Also in Mascow and Montesquieu, de l'Esprit des Lois, xxviii. 27.

Latin origin. It is not until the year 556 A.D. that we meet with a Frankish bishop in Paris.[1]

Now, although in these nations we find that both elements in a short time became welded and blended together, the case was very different with the Anglo-Saxons, the implacable foes of the Britons, from whom they adopted neither religion nor language, as well as with the other Teutons in their German and Scandinavian homes. Yet even these were not finally able to resist Latin Christianity and a great part of Latin culture. Between both divisions of this conglomeration of peoples there was formed a close community of kindred blood, kindred religion, institutions, manners, and modes of thought. They successfully resisted the influence of foreign races. Among those nations which besides them had taken part in the migration of peoples, it was chiefly the Arabs, Hungarians, and Slavs who threatened to disturb, if not to destroy them. But the Arabs were averted by the complete incompatibility of their religion; the Hungarians were beaten back within their own borders; and the neighbouring Slavs were at last annihilated or subjected.

What can knit together individuals or nations into closer relationship than a participation in the same destiny, and a common history? Among the internal and external occurrences of these earlier times, the unity of one particular event can almost be perceived. The Germanic nations, possessors from time immemorial of a great country, take the field, conquer the Roman empire of the West, and, more than this, keep what they have got. About the year 530 we find them in possession of all the countries extending from the cataracts of the Danube to the mouth of the Rhine and across to the Tweed, and all the land from Hallin Halogaland to that Baetica,[2] from which the Vandals take their name, and across the sea to where the Atlas range sinks down into the desert. As long as they were united, no one was able to wrest these territories from them; but their isolation, and the opposition between Arian and Catholic doctrines, led first to the destruction of the

---

[1] Plank, Gesellschaftsverfassung der christlichen Kirche, ii. 96.

[2] [Vandalitia (Andalusia).—Trs.]

Vandals. The loss that was caused by the fall of the Ostrogothic empire was to a certain extent retrieved by the Lombards when they occupied Italy—not entirely, for never at any time were they complete masters of Italy, to say nothing of Sicily or Illyria,[1] as the Goths were ;—but it was owing to these Lombards, who first destroyed the Heruli and Gepidæ, but thereupon left their hereditary and their conquered settlements to a Sarmatian people,[2] that the Danube was lost almost up to its sources. A fresh loss was the destruction of the Thuringian kingdom. The irruption of the Slavs far into the country lying to the west of the Elbe is probably not unconnected with this. But the greatest danger was threatened by the Arabs. They took Spain at a dash ; invaded France and Italy ; and, had they won a single battle more, the Latin portion at least of our nations might have been doomed. What could be expected when Franks and Lombards, Franks and Saxons, Angles and Danes lived in deadly enmity ? Let us not forget that the founding of the Papacy and the Empire warded off this danger.

If I may be allowed to state my own convictions, the real power of the Papacy—that which has really endured— was not established before the seventh century. It was not until then that the Anglo-Saxons recognized in the Pope, from whom their conversion immediately proceeded, their true patriarch, took to them a primate of his appointment, and paid him tribute.[3] It was from England, that Boniface, the apostle of the Germans, went forth. Not only on being made Archbishop of Mainz, did he swear allegiance, sincere devotion, and assistance to St. Peter and his successors, but the other bishops also swore to remain until death subject to the Roman Church, and to keep the ordinances of Peter's successors. He did yet more. For a hundred years before his day not a single letter can be found from the Pope of Rome, addressed to the Frankish clergy, so independent were the latter. Boniface, on Pipin's incentive, brought them also into subjection ; and the metropolitan bishops whom

---

[1] Manso, Geschichte der Ostgothen in Italien, App. v. 321.

[2] Paulus Diaconus, de rebus gestis Longobardorum, ii. c. 7.

[3] Schröckh, Kirchengeschichte, xix. 135.

he instituted received the pallium from Rome.[1] These were the three nations of which, with the Lombards, Christendom consisted in the West after the Spanish disaster. Charlemagne also freed the Pope from the enmity of the Lombards ; he made him the Frankish Patrician, so that he ceased dating his bulls by the years of the reigns of the Greek emperors, and drew him completely into the sphere of the newly founded world. Thus did the Pope become the ecclesiastical head of the Latin and Teutonic nations. He became so at the very time when the Arabs became powerful and gained ground ; his new dignity assuaged the enmity of the hostile races, and effected a material reconciliation between them. But they were only able to cope with the enemy, when relying on the power of the Pipins and the empire of Charlemagne.

Merit is due to Charlemagne for having united all the Latino-Germanic nations of the Continent, in so far as they were Christians, or were becoming so.—Egbert, moreover, who made the heptarchy of the Angles a monarchy, was his disciple—for having given them a constitution suited alike for war and peace, and for having taught them to advance again against their enemies along the Danube, to the east of the Saale and Elbe, and across the Pyrenees. But all had not yet been done. There appeared on one side, on every frontier, the Hungarians, in irresistible numbers, on horseback, and armed with bows and arrows ; and simultaneously on the other, on every coast, the Normans, both Vikings and Askemans, alike daring by sea and land. But at this very time the empire of Charlemagne perished through the mistakes made by his successors, whose nicknames almost invariably record their follies, so that the danger was renewed. It may be said that the migration of nations did not cease before these movements had been repressed. The Hungarians were driven back, and became Christians ; and at the same time the contiguous Slavonic nations became Christian also. All of them long vacillated between the Roman and the Greek form of worship before—and this was doubtless due to the influence of the Teutonic emperors—they decided

[1] Plank, vol. ii. 680 *seq.*

for the former. It cannot be said that these peoples belong also to the unity of our nations; their manners and their constitution have ever severed them from it. At that time they never exercised any independent influence, they only appear either subservient or antagonistic; they receive, so to speak, only the ebb or the tide of the general movements. But the Normans, of Germanic origin, were drawn into the circle of the other nations, and established themselves in France and England. They retaliated by carrying Germanic life in the eleventh century to Naples and Sicily. Their kindred at home had also meantime become Christians, and, except for an insignificant remnant, completely entered into the circle to which they naturally belonged.

Here, then, in the middle of the eleventh century, the movements of the migration of nations ended. The future development of the European languages, an intellectual fruit of these stormy centuries, had now been started in all its unity and diversity. If we glance at the French form of oath prescribed at Strassburg, we seem to find therein traces of the Italian, French, and Spanish dialects all at once. As this points to the unity of the Latin dialects, so does the fact that they have been recently combined in a single grammar bear still greater testimony to the unity of the Germanic dialects. The foundations of all modern kingdoms and their constitutions had been laid. Empire and Papacy were held in universal regard; the former represented the Teutonic, the latter the Latin principle of the great union of nations; the one supported the other.

2

After this, the original migratory impulse took a different turn, owing to the fact that it coincided with a complete devotion to Christianity. The Crusades may almost be regarded as a continuation of the migration of nations. The same people who had concluded the latter, viz. the Normans, took, in the same century, the most vigorous part in the first Crusade. Not only were they led by three eminent princes, namely, Robert of Normandy, whom the old chroniclers place above the supreme commander in point of nobility, wealth, and even intellectual excellence,[1] Bohemond of Tarentum, whose participation contemporaries rightly connected with his operations against the Greeks, and Tancred; but so many individual Normans took part in them,[2] that a war which was then in progress had to be brought to a close, owing to the dearth of warriors. It may perhaps have been a Norwegian, St. Olaf, who was the first to adopt the cross in war, both for himself and his army.[3]

The great armed pilgrimages to Jerusalem in the eleventh century appear to have originated with the Normans; the successful issue of them is at all events ascribed to them before all others by Roger de Hoveden.[4] All the Latin and Teutonic nations shared in this new enthusiasm. In the first expedition we find Spaniards, the counts of Cerdan and Canet.[5] Lope de Vega has left us a grand poem, immortalizing the meritorious services of the Castilians in the Holy Land. As early as the year 1121, Sigurd of Norway earned the name of Jörsalafar (pilgrim to Jerusalem); of the other nations it is known that they also took part in it. Never did a foreign nation, and only on one occasion did a foreign prince, Andrew of Hungary, participate therein, and he only did so as the leader of an Upper German expedition, and he was, moreover, the son of a French mother. The Crusades were in the main the unaided undertakings of the whole body of the Latin and Teutonic nations.

Now let us observe how the Crusades caused these nations to extend on all sides and in all directions. Their goal was, it is true, the Holy Land, yet they went to the coast of the Mediterranean besides, and not to that land alone. The Latin Empire at Constantinople would, had it longer existed, have turned the whole Greek Empire into

---

[1] Passage from Radulfus Cadomensis in Wilken, Kreuzzüge, i. 80.

[2] Gaufredus Monachus de acquisitione Siciliae, iv. 24.

[3] Gebhardi, Geschichte von Norwegen und Dänemark, i. 380.

[4] In Hugo Grotius, Prolegomena ad Histor. Gothorum, p. 60.

[5] Mariana, Hist. Hisp. x. c. 3. Capmany, Antigua marina de Cataluna, i. 124.

a Latino-German one. Had it not been for St. Louis' ill-luck, Egypt would have become a colony of France; and there appeared at this time a sensible, and certainly most instructive book upon the relations between the East and the West, written with the express intention of inciting to renewed operations against Egypt.[1] In the year 1150 King Roger of Sicily—known as Jarl Roger the Rich among his old countrymen—had possession of the coast of Africa from Tunis to Tripoli, and occupied Mahadia.[2]

But the most important and permanent achievements in the southern world were, without doubt, due to the Spaniards. Their Campeador, the Cid, lived to see the Crusades. In the same period they first succeeded in holding Toledo and the valley of the Tagus, which Alfonso the Emperor had just conquered, against the violent attack of the Almoravides, and then advanced under Alonso Ramon and took the valley of the Guadiana; (Alonso died under an oak-tree on Mount Muradal, at the extreme limit of his actual conquests, for all the rest were again lost). In the same period also they gained under Alonso the Noble the great battle of Navas de Tolosa, and set foot on the Guadalquivir.[3] And finally, at that very time, shortly before the first Crusade of St. Louis, St. Ferdinand subdued Jaen, Cordova, and Seville, and as Granada paid him tribute, the whole of Andalusia also, whilst, shortly before the second Crusade, Alonso the Sage subjected Murcia. In these days Portugal was founded and established as a kingdom. The union of Aragon and Catalonia, the conquest of Valencia, and the exploits of the Conquistador Jayme fall also into this period.

All this is closely connected with the expeditions to the Holy Land. The Archbishop Richard of Toledo, who came to Rome with a host of Crusaders, was sent back again by the Pope, because he and they were more needed at home; and instead of leading them against Jerusalem he now led them against Alcalá.[4] We know that it was

---

[1] Marini Sanuti liber Secretorum fidelium Crucis, in Bongars.
[2] Raumer, Geschichte der Hohenstaufen, i. 557.
[3] All taken from Rodericus Toletanus, de rebus Hispaniae.
[4] Rodericus, vi. 26.

chiefly Low Germans, English, and Flemish, who, proceeding on a Crusade, conquered his capital for the prince, who first called himself King of Portugal ;[1] and that seventy years later Alfonso II's most brilliant conquest was only effected by the same assistance.[2] In short, the conquest of the peninsula was only achieved by the co-operation of kindred races. Out of the plunder of Almeria, Alonso Ramon gave a splendid jewel to the Genoese as a thank-offering for their services. In the battle of Navas de Tolosa many thousands from beyond the Pyrenees[3] fought in the army of Alonso the Noble.

Concurrently with these operations and progressive advances of our nations on the coasts of the Mediterranean and in the South generally, there were others being carried on in the North which were prompted by the same spirit. Sigurd Jörsalafar, whom we have referred to, made it his first business, after his return, to land at Calmar and to coerce the Smalandic heathen, man by man, to embrace Christianity. With the same object in view St. Eric led the Swedes against the Finns. He shed tears on seeing the battle, but did not stay his hand until he had baptized the Finns in the spring of Lupisala. On the occasion of the second Crusade, on the receipt of a bull from Pope Eugenius III, the Danes, Saxons, and Westphalians leagued together to make a common expedition against the neighbouring Slavs, resolved either to convert them to Christianity, or else to exterminate them.[4] Not long after this, Bishop Meinhard came with traders and artisans from Wisby to Esthonia to preach there. These three undertakings led, if not immediately, at all events by degrees, to a brilliant success. On the west of the Oder the Slavs were, by the times of the Crusades, practically exterminated. German nobility, German citizens and peasants were the real stock of the new inhabitants of Mecklenburg, Pomerania, Brandenburg and Silesia. Since that time the

---

[1] Dodechini Appendix ad Marianum Scotum. Pistor. i. 676.

[2] Gotefridi Monachi Annales, 284.

[3] Epistola Alfonsi VIII ad Pontificem de bello, etc. in Continuat. belli sancti, Basel, 1549, p. 246.

[4] Anselmi Gemblacensis Abbatis Chronicon. Pistor. i. 965.

Eastern Pomeranians have always called the Western by the name of Saxons.[1]

In the year 1248, after long struggles, Finland at length became entirely Christian and Swedish.[2] Since that date Swedes have dwelt along the whole coast, and in the strongholds there. Proceeding from the unpretentious colony of Yxkull (Oesel), German rule extended over all Esthonia, Livonia, and Courland; nay, when the Knights of the Sword, who had been established there, despaired of being able to defend a certain fortress against the Prussians,[3] in spite of a great display of bravery, they were instrumental in bringing to their assistance the Teutonic Knights, who then made the land of the Letts a German country. A short time longer, and the joint possessions of both orders extended from Danzig to Narva. Here they met the Pomeranians, who were now either entirely germanized or partially so, owing to their subjection to the Emperor and Empire. Here, on the Gulf of Finland, they became neighbours of the Swedes. The German name embraced the whole of the Baltic.

To the same circle of events belong the operations of Henry Plantagenet in Ireland. He brought it to pass that thenceforth two nations have lived together in Ireland—the native Irish, the subjected, and the Anglo-Germanic, the dominant. The English, if not first brought over, were certainly established there by him.[4] At that time Venice taught the Dalmatians to speak Italian. This event must also be comprehended in our survey, for it is a new extension of our nations; and the Pope likewise instigated the attack upon Ireland, because that land would never obey him. Yet, in order not to depart from the principle we have laid down, those two undertakings, in the North and the South, must principally be kept in view, which sprang from the same tendency, and were carried out by the same arms, under the same symbols, and often with the assistance of the same men. They

---

[1] Kanzow, Pomerania, i. 216.
[2] Schöning in Schlözer's Allgem. Nord. Geschichte, 474.
[3] Dusburg in Script. rer. Pruss. i. 35 (note to Second Edition).
[4] Hume's Hist. of England, i. c. ix. p. 281.

show the unity of our nations in idea, in action, and in development.

But this principle is most clearly visible in the Crusades of the South and the North. This stirring energy, the result of an intellectual impulse, expanding in all directions, found a fitting expression in noble institutions and creations which belong to it, and belong to it exclusively. We will dwell on two alone. War may arouse every brutal passion in our nature, but it is the province of chivalry to save the true man, to soften force by manners and the elevating influence of women, and to refine strength by pointing it to what is divine. Its origin, in this sense, is coeval with the formation of the first two ecclesiastical orders of knighthood, and the zenith of its bloom coincides beyond doubt with the foundation of the third. After the Crusades it did not die out, but took another development which was different in different lands. It never spread to other nations; even the Hospitallers and Templars never owned a province in any other country, or more than a few possessions. The Teutonic Knights stood in constant contrast to the Letts and the Slavs. One noble blossom of chivalry is the poetry of these times. If it is true, as seems to be the case, that the story of Bechadas, by Godfrey of Bouillon, was the first novel,[1] and if the cycle of tales of Charlemagne and Arthur are, as appears very probable, immediately connected therewith, it is evident what a great share the Crusades have had in the foundation of modern poetry. This poetry, at any rate, binds all our nations exclusively together. The prefaces to the Wilkina-saga, and the Niflungasaga, confess that they were composed in Iceland after German models.[2] No other people had any share in it.

But war was not waged by knights alone; the freedom of the towns was also founded in war, and, in the case of all our nations, dates from this time. The first consuls of the Italian communities, chosen by themselves, and upon the

---

[1] Passage from Godefroy de Bigeois in Eichhorn, Gesch. der Cultur und Literatur d. neuern Europa, i. 82.

[2] Prooemium, quoted in Eichhorn, Geschichte der Cultur, Erläuterungen, p. 125.

selection of whom their whole freedom rests, appear contemporaneously with the first Crusade, in the year 1100. We certainly meet with them first in Genoa on the occasion of an expedition to the Holy Land. In the course of our period they procured for themselves the full powers of the old royal counts.[1] As early as the year 1112, we meet with the same institutions in France, free communes under magistrates and elders of their own election. As the king marches under the oriflamme, the standard of St. Denis—a device which appears to be the true origin of this imperial banner—so all the communes take the field with him, each under the standard of its local saint.[2] The cities in Castile, because of their martial ardour, were, in the year 1169, given a seat in the Cortes; and at the battle of Navas their assistance appears to have been not inconsiderable. The German cities, in the course of the same period, by freeing themselves from the "Vogt," developed to independent unions.[3] During the reign of Henry III the English towns were represented in Parliament.[4] It was in Gothland, upon Swedish soil, that Wisby flourished. Thus, hand in hand with chivalry and the crusades, the cities developed both in freedom and importance throughout the Latin and Teutonic nations from north to south. In the same way as the peculiarities of our poetry are due to chivalry, so our characteristic architecture appears to be due to the cities. In this same period it developed from the flat roof and the semi-circle to those beautiful Gothic proportions we admire in the façade of the cathedral at Strassburg, in the choir at Cologne, in the spire of Freiburg, and in the whole edifice at Marburg—of the year 1235—as well as in the cathedrals of Siena, Rouen, and Burgos.

Neither in chivalry nor yet in the development of the cities have other nations had a share. As late as the year

---

[1] Savigny, Geschichte des Römischen Rechts im Mittelalter, iii. 100, 121. Sismondi, Histoire des républ. ital. i. 373, from Caffaro.

[2] Ordericus Vitalis in Du Cange, s. v. Commune. Velli, Hist. de France, iii. 93.

[3] Document of the year 1255 in Vogt's Rheinische Geschichte, i. 426.

[4] Woltmann, Englische Geschichte, ii. 121.

1501, the Russians of Moscow begged that a knight,—an iron man, as they expressed it,—should be sent them, and marvelled at him as a wonder. The gates of the cathedral at Novgorod are the work of Magdeburg craftsmen.

Let us dwell yet upon another phenomenon. As the migration of nations was accompanied by the establishment of the Empire and the Papacy, so did the struggle between these two forces arise out of the Crusades. It is not merely a struggle between the Emperor and the Pope; it evidently affects all those confessing the Roman faith. The quarrel between Henry II of England and Thomas à Becket is quite analogous to it, both in respect of the interests the combatants had at stake, as well as in the kind of weapons they employed; the two princes and the two ecclesiastics were allied. This quarrel concerns moreover all our nations. Frederick I had Swedes in the army with which he invaded Italy in 1158; [1] it was mainly English gold which supported the popes in their struggles at Naples. The internal affairs of Castile act and react upon the history of Conradin.[2] Charles of Anjou, who brought these wars to a close, was the brother of the French king. Foreign quarrels could not fail to be influenced by internal dissensions. It was natural that in the midst of his Italian wars Frederick should sigh for Asia, where the strength and energy he lavished upon them would have guaranteed him more genuine glory and more perfect happiness.[3] But the internal forces also destroyed themselves. The Papacy was wrong in believing that it had gained in strength by the fall of the Hohenstaufen. Before Conradin had been dead forty years, it fell into the captivity of the French kings. Since that time it has never again been the old Papacy. Which of our nations could say that it has been unaffected by this?

We may distinguish two periods, in respect of these external enterprises; the first, that of their beginning, when they govern the thoughts and hearts of all; the

---

[1] Dalin, Schwedische Geschichte, ii. 88.

[2] Raumer, Hohenstaufen, iv. 586.

[3] Raumer from Ricobald. ii. 411.

second, that of their continuation, their effects and results. If this strikes the historian at the first glance in the migration of nations, it is almost even more striking in the case of the Crusades.

After the decay and fall of the two great powers, and when the universal interest in external operations had, in the fourteenth and fifteenth centuries, gradually cooled down, there arose in the heart of our nations, so to speak, a universal war of all against all. It was those who belonged most closely together that quarrelled most violently. The Provençals and Catalans are of one stock; but, owing to the claims of their princes,—the houses of Anjou and Barcelona,—to Naples, they at that time fell into an enmity that lasted for centuries. It was in this struggle that Naples and Sicily became sundered. Portugal was originally a fief of the crown of Castile. After this feudal bond had become severed, the pride of both nations caused a deadly hatred to take root in them. Moreover, the factions of the Nuñez and Gamboa pervaded the whole of Spain. Civil wars were only now and again interrupted by a campaign against the Moors, at other times it was the reverse. In Italy Guelphs and Ghibellines, whose names scarcely existed before the commencement of the thirteenth century,[1] nursed and fostered a feud that divided the whole land, town from town, and almost house from house. Owing to the strife between their royal houses, not, as was formerly the case, for a few fiefs, but for the crown itself, France and England became locked in deadly wars. At first it was France that was convulsed by English arms and a great English party; and then England itself was torn by the wars of the white and the red rose. In Germany, races and families fought together no less; Swabians and Swiss are both Alemanni, but they now fell into deadly feud. Austrians and Bavarians are the same race; the battle of Mühldorf shows how little they regarded it. Franconia became split up into the opposing factors of knightly and ecclesiastical domains. Wars of succession, wars of children against their fathers, and wars between brothers, laid waste Thuringia and Meissen. Brandenburg and

[1] Muratori de Guelfis et Gibellinis, Antiquitat. Ital. iv. 607, 608.

Pomerania were both peopled by Saxon colonists; but the claims of the Brandenburg princes to the country of the Pomeranians became a great offence between them, and in Pomeranian chronicles the people of the Mark are always mentioned with dislike. Besides this, we have the rising of princes against the sovereign power, and of freeholders against the princes; and, in cases where they were immediate subjects of the Empire, a rising of the knights against the cities; whilst in the cities the guilds rose against the families. Frequently, also, the crown was the object of contention. And it is not alone nations and races, states and cabinets, that regulate public affairs, but families, corporations, and individuals, every one in each matter for himself as best as he may.

In this state of things it might be thought scarcely possible that the unity of an empire, let alone that of the collective body of our nations, could have been preserved. Party feeling divides, but it also unites. It is mainly the Anglo-French wars that act and re-act upon the rest of the European complications, and bind them all together. What could appear to be wider apart than the rebellion of oppressed Scots against the English, and the struggle of Albert and Adolf for the crown of Germany? The battle of Cambuskenneth, in which the English were defeated, and that of Hasenbühel, in which Adolf fell, both in the year 1298, are all the same intimately con· nected. Albert was allied with the French, and through them with the Scots, Adolf with the English. The English party in Europe was defeated in both battles. The quarrel between Louis of Bavaria and Charles of Luxembourg for the same crown of Germany was decided not so much in Germany, as by the battle of Crecy. Shortly before, Charles had been raised with all pomp to the throne by four Electors; immediately after the battle—his party, the French, had lost—we see him hurrying back to Bohemia reft of dignity and power; but Louis sends and solemnly receives English embassies.[1]

In the interest of these two parties, and mainly with their assistance, Peter the Cruel and Henry of Trastamara

[1] Albertus Argentinensis apud Urstisium, ii. 139.

waged their war for the crown of Castile. Since Peter's avarice drove the Black Prince, who had assisted him, to the hearth-tax, and this tax goaded the latter's vassals to discontent,[1] which resulted in the decay of the English power in France, while Henry, on the other hand, conquered with the French in Spain, it may be said that the wane of English power in Spain was the result. Other threads connect these events with affairs in Holland and Gelderland, in Aragon and Sardinia, and in Venice and Genoa ; hence, not much credence can be placed in the assertion, so often made, that the nations in the Middle Ages were isolated from each other.

Even great intellectual movements pass through them all, and testify to their internal unity. About the year 1350 we find, almost as at the present time, a general tendency to make new constitutions. It was then (1347) that Cola di Rienzi, the Italian zealot, actually restored the good old state of things, as he called it—that is, a kind of republican form of government at Rome ; further, at that time (1356) plebeians and doge of Venice leagued together against the nobles, in order, in one murderous night, to restore their old rights ; and in France (1355), a first assembly of estates of the realm promised both to live and to die with the king, but curtailed his rights not a little ; a second demanded reforms and presented a list of twenty-two high personages who were to be deposed from office ; whilst a third finally ushered in a complete revolution, and forced the dauphin to don its red and green cap.[2] These movements were lawless and transitory. Others, at the self-same time, confined themselves within narrower limits and had more durable results. In Aragon, in 1348, in the place of the violent power of the union, the lawful influence of a Justicia was established. For the first time in their history (under Edward III) the Commons of England insisted upon the responsibility of the King's council ; and, perhaps in Germany also, it was similar intellectual movements which, in 1356, caused Charles IV to grant the "Golden Bull,"

---

[1] Le premier volume de Messire Jehan Froissart. f. 136.

[2] Villaret, Histoire de France, vol. ix. from page 147 on.

[3] Hieronymi Blancae rerum Aragon. Commentarii, p. 810.

that fundamental law of the Empire for centuries to come. At all events, the first union of the provinces into estates of the realm in Brunswick, in Saxony (1350) and elsewhere, took place at the same time.[1] Is it possible that this coincidence was accidental? The common development of our nations, it would seem, necessarily produced the same ideas in all.

In the midst of these movements, whenever, from time to time, the old feud between Emperor and Pope made itself felt, the minds of men turned invariably towards the East and a common expedition against the Infidels. The Pope frequently encouraged the enterprise. In novels, tales, and popular books, the general tendency was at once ventilated and nourished. In the fourteenth century the pastoureaux in France and in England believed that the conquest of the Holy Land was to be the work of the shepherds and peasants, and set out with this end in view. As late as the end of the fifteenth century, in the year 1480, many of the citizens of Parma fastened a red cross upon their shoulder, and pledged themselves to fight against the Infidels.[2] It was chiefly in Spain and Portugal, where the Moorish war was continued at intervals, and finally led to an attack upon Africa, that the crusading spirit was kept alive.

3

It was this crusading spirit that gave birth to colonization. The following book will show us how the first discoveries and colonies are in a twofold manner connected with the Moorish war; first, through expeditions against Africa, whence proceeded the scheme for the conquest of India, and secondly, through the idea of defending and extending Christendom. The intentions of the Portuguese were concerned directly with the centre of the Arabian faith. They desired to avenge Jerusalem upon Mecca. Their victories were once again fought and won in the enthusiasm

[1] Eichhorn, Deutsche Staats- und Rechtsgeschichte, iii. § 424, note.
[2] Diarium Parmense in Muratori, Scrip. Rerum Ital. xxii. 349.

of Crusaders.[1] The Spanish operations, on the other hand,
being directed, as they were, against heathen, and not
against Mohammedans, renewed rather the idea of the
Northern Crusades. A grant from the Pope, a proclamation
that "the enemy must be converted to Christianity or
utterly destroyed," was all the justification that was
necessary.[2] The peasants too, whom Bartolomeo de Las
Casas intended to lead upon a more peaceful expedition to
Cumana, wore each a red cross.[3]

As a fact, in both Spain and Portugal, migration of
peoples, crusades, and colonization form only one single
and connected event. The colonies, which moved from
the Asturian hills to the coasts of Andalusia and Africa,
and which were established as early as 1507 in Almeria,
and in 1512 in Oran, now begin on the other shore of
the Atlantic Ocean.[4] The Spaniards pride themselves on
nothing so much as that they planted there, instead of
barbarian peoples, as they say, the sons and descendants of
illustrious Castilian families.[5] The five million white men,
who are to be found there, are real Spaniards. A million
Portuguese dwell in Brazil. An almost equal number,
although degenerated, may be distinguished on the coasts
of Africa, and in the East Indies. Settlements on such a
great scale may be regarded as migrations. Another idea
that animates colonizations, and which they have in common
with the Crusades, is the propagation of Christianity. A
third that is peculiar to and characteristic of them, is
the idea of the discovery of the world,—of itself one of the
greatest conceptions, embracing the human race and the
whole earth. It was promoted and fostered by greed for
the spices of India, for the gold of America, and for the
pearls of the unknown seas, as well as by the interests of
trade.[6]

It is not necessary to describe the general participation

[1] Chronicon Monspeliense in Du Cange, s. v. Pastorelli.

[2] Hoieda's proclamation in Robertson's Hist. of America, i. 516.

[3] Oviedo, dell' historie dell' Indie, lib. xix.

[4] Oviedo, Historia de la conquista y poblacion de Venezuela. Cf.
Schäffer, Brasilien, p. 32.

[5] Sandoval, Historia del Emperador Carlos I, 189.

[6] *Ibid.*

of our peoples in these events (the Italians at any rate shared in the discoveries) ; and it is unnecessary to prove at length that they are exclusively peculiar to them. Other nations now and again took part in these movements, but in reality pursued other aims. The unity of a people cannot be better seen than in a common undertaking ; and wherein could the unity and the cohesion of several nations, like ours, be better demonstrated? The undertakings to which we have here referred, although continued through many centuries, are common to them all. They connect both the times and the peoples. They are, if I may so say, like three great respirations of this unique confederation.

BOOK I

CHAPTER I

THE SITUATION IN FRANCE AND IN ITALY —EXPEDITION OF CHARLES VIII TO NAPLES

---

1. FRANCE AND CHARLES VIII

TWICE during the Middle Ages did the Capets conquer France. They went forth from their dukedom, France, encountered the Eudons of Blois and the Plantagenets of Anjou, and were once cut off on all sides from the sea-coast. But Philip Augustus possessed himself of the provinces of North France, and St. Louis of Provence, whilst Philip the Fair subjected the Pope to his crown. This is the first conquest: by the direct line of Hugo Capet. After his line had become extinct, the kingdom was the bone of contention between his male descendants, the Valois, and the female line, the kings of England. King Edward III of England once held half France; on another occasion, one of his successors, Henry V, was in possession of Paris, and even of the crown. It may be described as a second conquest, when Charles VII of Valois again got the upper hand of the English. It was the Maid of Orleans who opened him the gate to victory. She restored to him Champagne; but he owed the recovery of his capital, as well as Normandy and Guienne, and the complete mastery over the country, to the Dukes of Burgundy and Brittany.

Yet the assistance rendered by the great vassals entailed

the consequence that the king was after all not completely sovereign.   Louis XI, who was made to feel this—he had one day to come and implore peace of the armed barons, —determined to put himself into full possession of the sovereign power.   He was very suspicious, very shrewd, and discerning enough besides.   Yet these qualities would not have enabled him to attain his object, had not the Dukes of Berry, Burgundy, Anjou, and Brittany, as though by a providential intervention, all died without leaving sons.   The first-named, his brother, he succeeded without any opposition.   In the case of the heiress of the second, her husband, Maximilian of Austria, failed to uphold her claim to Burgundy and the cities on the Somme ; in order to have peace, he was besides obliged to consent to the marriage of his daughter, Margaret, with the Dauphin, and to assign to the French Artois and Franche-Comté as her dowry.   The third, however, René of Anjou, who styled himself king of three kingdoms, duke of three duchies, and count of three counties,[1] might have made over the countries that he actually possessed, and his rights to the rest, to his grandson, René of Lorraine ; but he himself was not in favour of such a course.   He had once hoped to join Lorraine to Anjou ; and only because he had been taken prisoner had he acquiesced in the marriage of his daughter, of which his grandson was the issue.   Should he, then, now go so far as to allow his hereditary lands to pass to Lorraine ? The young prince would not even agree to exchange his arms of Lorraine for those of Anjou.[2]   Ill-pleased at this, René appointed his nephew Charles, bearing the name and the arms of Anjou, as his heir.[3]   But the latter, who was also not blessed with issue, seven years later, as the document says, for the sake of God and the love which he bears King Louis, the son of his father's sister, assigned to him the inheritance of all his kingdoms, possessions, and rights :[4] thus the territories of Provence and Anjou came directly to the Crown.

[1] Pasquier, Recherches de la France, vi. 557.
[2] Garnier, Histoire de France, xviii. 462, from Le Grand MS.
[3] Will in the Preuves in Comines, ii. 118.
[4] Extraits du Testament, in the same, 182.

Historically, the important point is that the great feudatory lands in the South and East, in contrast to the neighbouring princes who belonged to the Empire, were united with the French Crown. Brittany alone remained; but Louis had already purchased for his family the rights of the Penthièvre in the country, rights that had already once partly caused a great English war.[1]

But, in order to defend this last bulwark of the vassal-power, Louis of Orleans, the nearest relative of King Charles, who was still a minor, leagued himself with the Bretons and all the King's domestic and external foes. At St. Aubin, however, he lost the day, and was now in captivity at Bourges. Things were now in this position : the rebellion was checked, but not suppressed ; Brittany was, it is true, conquered, but ready to appeal again to arms, and was besides allied with the three most powerful neighbours of the French, England, the Netherlands, and Spain ; when Charles attained the age of nineteen years (1491), and began to take heart, and to be desirous of becoming his own master. He signalized his assumption of the reins of government by a noble and unexpected action. One evening he rode off from Plessis to the Tower of Bourges. He went to release the imprisoned duke, regardless of the fact that the latter had borne arms against him. He took him away with him.[2] They conversed and laughed together at table, and slept the night in the same bed.[3] He had well considered this : " Thus he would be called a good prince, and thus he would have faithful servants." And by this act he put an end to the old feud between the barons and the Crown. Immediately thereafter, Orleans, the Constable, and many notables combined together, no longer, as was formerly the case, for the public good, that is, the well-being of the vassals, but to obey and serve the King.

This opened the way for Charles to effect the conquest of Brittany. Dunois and other friends of the released

---

[1] Garnier, from Le Grand MS., xviii. 452.
[2] Extrait d'une histoire de France up to 1510, in Th. Godefroy, Charles VIII, p. 165.
[3] Extrait d'une histoire de Louys, in Godefroy, p. 375.

Louis went to Orleans, and addressed themselves to Anne,
the heiress of Brittany, who was betrothed to Maximilian,
and already called herself Queen of the Romans.[1]   They
represented to her that " Since Maximilian's first marriage
with Mary of Burgundy her country had not enjoyed a
single day's peace ; that its wealth had become the prey of
the Germans ; and that a still greater disaster was in store
for Brittany, because of the distance at which it lay."
They brought it about, that Anne came to Charles's court
at Langeais, and signed the document by which, for the
preservation of an eternal alliance and peace between
Crown and Duchy, she assigned to him all her rights in the
latter, and he all his to her.

By her marriage with the King she became Queen of
France.[2]   The day on which this took place, and before
it was known abroad, it is told how Margaret, hitherto
Charles's affianced bride, was seen walking sadly in the
garden at Amboise.   She told her attendant maidens she
had dreamt she had lost a very brilliant and large jewel ;[3]
and it was certainly a great misfortune for her, when it
turned out that the jewel signified the crown of France.
But what cared the Council of France for this, when it
found that it was upon Charles's marriage, not with her,
but with Anne, that the domestic peace of the realm
depended ?   Personal obligations retired when the consolidation of the French realm and its unity was at stake.
Nor did the injured neighbours offer any opposition to the
marriage.[4]   The renewed idea of the unity of France was
even in a certain way favourable to them.   Maximilian
concluded peace at Senlis, recovering Artois and Franche-
Comté, together with his daughter.   Henry VII, appeased
by a sum of money, returned to England.   When, too,
King Ferdinand of Spain had received back Roussillon
out of pledge—for Charles, mindful, probably, of St. Louis,

---

[1] MS. of Brienne in Daniel, H. d. F. iv. 478.

[2] Contrat du mariage in the Preuves in Comines, ii. 278.

[3] Pasquier, Recherches, p. 586.

[4] The political relations, as they obtained in the summer of 1492,
have been sketched in the oldest Venetian report of Zaccaria Contarini.
Cf. Ranke's Sämtliche Werke, xii. 34 (note to 2nd edition).

would not be burdened with foreign possessions—and had thereupon promised neither to ally his house with Henry, nor with Maximilian, nor yet with Naples,[1] and in nowise, reserving the rights of the Church, to lend the latter his support; when the old alliance between Castile and France had been renewed, king with king, country with country, and man with man;[2]—then, and then only did the French again enjoy perfect peace. It may be said that only now had the second conquest of the whole land by the Valois been accomplished.

Then did Charles journey in joy through the villages, which rose out of desolated places, to the towns, which now once more dared to extend beyond their walls. During the next thirty years after Louis XI, almost a third of the houses in the realm were rebuilt, arrangements being made at the same time for internal traffic.[3] The poor peasant, who in the midst of such great fertility could not obtain high prices for his produce, could scarcely, it is true, when the tax-gatherer came, find the money at which he was assessed;[4] yet he needed no longer, as formerly, in fear either of the English or of armed Frenchmen, to hurry his goods and chattels into the church, and to leave his village. The King vouchsafed to him law and right. He himself lived with the nobles in his service, the heads of the great houses, who had been brought up at court.[5] With them frequently were associated the second sons of the lower nobility, such as had neither inherited property nor had wished to enter the Church,[6] and who had learnt in a more illustrious house than their own,—perhaps with a trusty knight whom they had themselves chosen, or with a captain, to whom they had been assigned by the King—not the sciences, which they did not esteem, but how to run, wrestle, throw, ride, and shoot with the bow,—in one word, the use of

---

[1] Zurita, Historia del Rey Don Hernando, f. 6, 13, 18.

[2] Comines, Mémoires ann. 1482, i. 581. Corio, Hist. of Milan, p. 899.

[3] Claude Seyssel, Louanges du bon Roy Louys XII, p. 128.

[4] Continuation of Monstrelet, iii. 249. Machiavelli, Ritratti della Francia, p. 161.

[5] Trémouille's instance in the Memoirs, p. 121.

[6] Bayard's instance in the Loyal Serviteur, ch. 2.

arms.[1] In them this free chivalry became developed into a regular, quasi-military service. We find them mainly in the frontier towns, in corps of thirty, fifty, and a hundred men, under a prince or lord who could afford the expense, and who, although he received some pay, devoted as a rule his whole fortune to the service. Each had two archers, a young lad, who was trained up under him, and a servant. They all went together on the campaign.[2] They were called *Hommes d'Armes*. In times of peace one of them, in honour of his lady, would often institute a prize and invite all his neighbours to a tournament. Here they preferred to engage in masses rather than singly. Umpires were chosen, and after dancing in the evening, and mass the next morning, the prize was awarded. Others wandered through Spain and Portugal, through England and Scotland, to try the prowess of their neighbours. They imagined themselves Lancelots or Tristrams—with whom they were well acquainted; their king was to them an Arthur, or the Charlemagne of legend.[3] This intellectual and vigorous movement gave new life to the French nobility. With them their King rode from tournament to tournament. To humour them he called his son Roland; and since they all had inclination for fresh enterprises and he with them, an expedition to Naples began to be talked of.[4]

Now Charles had from his youth up both heard and believed that Naples, which through the adoption of both Joannas had become an hereditary portion of the House of Anjou, had devolved legally upon him with Provence. At the time of which we speak, all doubt upon this point was removed by the will of the younger Joanna, which a Genoese of the name of Calvo, a servant of the Queen, brought to his court, having found it, as he alleged, among the papers of his deceased father.[5] Several members of the

---

[1] Chartier l'Espérance, p. 316. Notes to Trém. Mémoires, p. 265, and Castiglione, Cortegiano, ed. Venet. 1587, i. 81.

[2] Principal passages in Marineus Siculus, lib. xiii. 428, and in Monstrelet, iii. 32.

[3] Instances in Bayard and Expilly's Supplément à l'histoire du Chevalier, p. 443.

[4] Histoire de Charles VIII, in Godefroy, 172.

[5] Senarega, Annales Genuenses in Muratori, xxiv. 537.

Parlement and several doctors of laws appeared before a full assembly of the princes of the blood royal and notables of the realm, and confirmed its validity.[1]   The bastard of the conqueror of Aragon, who occupied the throne of Naples, was declared an usurper.   Prince Antonello of Salerno, a fugitive from Naples, had for a long time been the mouth-piece of many other fugitives at the court of France; were he now to tell the truth, how cruel and detested the Aragonese was, that would surely move the young King to pity and rouse his hopes.   For some time past, Cardinal Giuliano della Rovere, who had fled from the Pope and the Aragonese, and who had still fortresses and adherents in the States of the Church, had also resided at the court.   He likewise urged the young King to undertake an expedition against Naples.   The messengers and letters of Ludovico il Moro, ruler of Milan, decided the matter.   " How long wilt thou," he wrote,[2] " leave the inheritance of thy crown a booty in a foreign land, and the name of France in con-tempt?   Thy people at Naples are oppressed and appeal to thee; I will assist thee with money and arms, with man and horse.   Half Italy is with thee, and God himself. Gird thyself, delay is ever hurtful.   And thinkest thou never, Charles, on thy great forefather, who advised that a war against the Turks should be begun from this kingdom? Sail from Brindisi to Avlona; and thou wilt crush the Turks, who are at present engaging in battle against the Hungarians, before they are aware of thy coming.   Thou wilt conquer the holy lands, where thy forefathers were once triumphant, and restore Jerusalem itself to Christendom and thy realm. Thou wilt fill the earth and the sea, yea, and heaven also with thy name."

What Charles of Anjou had, in the thirteenth century, undertaken with no small prospects of success, appeared capable of being carried out by his successor, who had at his disposal the martial forces of France, and was animated by the like chivalrous spirit.   The crown of Naples, to which the title and right of Jerusalem belonged, once

[1] Carlo Balbiano to Ludovico in Rosmini, Vita di Gian Giacomo Trivulzio, 1815, vol. ii.   Monumenti inediti, p. 194.
[2] Literae Ludovici in Corio, 891.

taken, Charles VIII would by the course of these events and the stirring of men's minds, as well as by right and power, become the chosen champion of Christianity against the common foe. André de la Vigne wrote a poem; in it Christianity came flying across Mont Cenis into the garden of honour, where she found Charles and his nobles, complained to him of her sufferings, and renewed the prophecy of a young Charles, who had been crowned in his thirteenth year, and who would crown her again with everlasting praise.[1] To the same effect were the visions of the monk Spagnuoli and the physician Jean Michel.[2] Master Guilloche, of Bordeaux, went still further: in his twenty-fourth year, Charles would have subjected Naples, and, in his thirty-third, the whole of Italy; he would then cross the sea, be called King of Greece, and at last enter Jerusalem, and ascend the Mount of Olives.[3] The old dreams of Christianity, of an Eastern and a Western potentate, who should make all the world believers, had not yet been forgotten—those dreams which the Germans interpreted as applying to the last King of the Romans: after his victory over the enemies of the faith, he would lay down his crown on Golgotha before the crucifix there appearing to him, and would die; whereupon, with the advent of the Antichrist and Enoch and Elijah, the end of all things would be accomplished.[4] The Italians referred the prophecy to the King of France; in Jerusalem he would lay down his crown, and dying, ascend up to Heaven.[5]

[1] André de la Vigne in the Vergier d'honneur; after Foncemagne's extract.

[2] Foncemagne in Histoire de l'Académie des inscriptions, xvi. p. 246, and Mémoires, xvii. 548. This prophecy is also given, though in an incomplete form, by Pilorgerie, Campagne et bulletins de la grande armée d'Italie, commandée par Charles huit, p. 431: "la vision divine révélée à Jehan Michiel très-humble prophète de la prosperité du très-crestien roy de France, Charles VIII, de la nouvelle réformation du siècle et la récupération de Hierusaleme à lui destinée, et qu'il sera de tous les roys de terre le souverain et dominateur sur tous les dominants et unique monarchie du monde" (note to 2nd edition).

[3] Foncemagne in the Mémoires de l'Académie, xvii. 845.

[4] Sebastianus Brandt, Revelatio Methodii, Basel, 1516. Preface of 1497.

[5] Alexandro Benedetto, Diarium Expeditionis in Eckardus, Script. Medii Aevi, ii. 1579.

Charles was susceptible by nature to such ideas. In quite early years, when he was received in Troyes with the mystery of Goliath and David, he saw therein typified his war against the Turks; he adopted the title of King of Naples and Jerusalem—"the latter especially appeared to him the fairest omen;"[1] and as though he meant to establish the Latin kingdom in the East, he had all the rights of the Paleologi to Constantinople and Trebizond ceded to him.[2] Tidings of the approaching expedition, for which all France was preparing, reached the Italian courts and cities. The army which Charles VIII equipped did not consist of his French troops and the Italian refugees alone, but many comrades from other countries also joined the expedition. Robert d'Aubigny, the brother of Matthew Stuart, who had shortly before taken part in the war against James IV of Scotland,[3] arrived with some Scotch archers. The Hoeks from the Netherlands, Philip of Ravenstein, who had just lost Sluys, and Engilbert of Cleves, who had lost Utrecht to Maximilian,[4] brought Flemish gunners[5] and German infantry.[6] The Bailiff of Dijon brought Rudolph Schwend of Zurich[7] and several thousand Swiss with him. At the foot of the Pyrenees the Gascons collected in their numbers, whilst horses came from the coasts of Brittany and from Portugal.[8] Ships were turned out of the dockyards of Marseilles and Genoa, and mounted guns, which, as was said of the Charlotte, "sung harmonies out of hell."[9] The King meantime amused himself in Lyons. Good and generous towards every one; pious to the extent that only in trivial matters[10] would he take an oath upon himself, he lived entirely in youthful dreams of great exploits, and of eternal fame won in the battlefield. Whenever he busied

---

[1] Balbiano to Ludovico in Rosmini, ii. 194.
[2] Treaty in Foncemagne, Mémoires de l'Académie, xvii. 572–578.
[3] Buchananus, Rerum Scoticarum hist. lib. xiii. 457, ed. of 1624.
[4] Wagenaar, allgem. Geschichte der Niederlande, ii. 265.
[5] Villeneufve, Mémoires, vol. xvi.
[6] Ferronus, Rerum Gallicarum, lib. i. 20.
[7] Stumpf, Schweizer Chronik, iii. 256.
[8] Corio, p. 899.
[9] Vergier d'honneur in Foncemagne, p. 588. Georgius Florus.
[10] Bayard, p. 14. Symphorian Champier in Godefroy, p. 314.

himself with these plans, his forehead appeared high, his eye large and fiery, and his brows prominent.[1]   But since he showed himself ignorant of the complications of the world, many attributed what he resolved and achieved to his servants.[2]   In personal appearance he was thin and mal-formed,[3] but was at the same time very keen for all sorts of knightly games and military duties.   Sometimes he hunted with his sparrow-hawk ;[4] and then it might happen that he saw a youth exercising himself in a meadow, who was there-upon brought into his service.   He made presents to the knights, who then again were generous on their side, and took part in the martial games which were held in the streets ; whilst at the corners the women sat upon benches and stages, exactly like what is told in the knightly tales of King Arthur at Caerleon.[5]

In Italy, meanwhile, many made vows and said prayers for his coming ;[6] they loved to call him the most Christian King, and said, " Blessed be he that cometh in the name of the Lord ! "

2. THE SITUATION IN ITALY

For about the last fifty years, two houses, which, owing to intermarriage, were almost one, had ruled over the greater part of Italy—to wit, that of Sforza at Milan and that of Aragon at Naples.   Alfonso of Aragon and Francesco Sforza had both simultaneously risen to fame in Italy.   The first-named had not been long in possession of Naples when the latter seized Milan.   Since that event their families had become allied, and spread in manifold affinities throughout Italy.   The Este at Ferrara, the Gonzaga at Mantua,[7] the brothers Bentivoglio, the princes of Urbino, Pesaro, Forlì,

---

[1] Prophétie du Roi Charles in Foncemagne, Hist. xvi. 245.   Bran-tôme after the testimony of a lady, Eloge, p. 22.

[2] Comines, Guicciardini, André.

[3] Passero, Giornale, p. 72.

[4] Zurita, Historia del Rey Hernando, f. 90.

[5] St. Gelais, Louis XII, p. 79.   Histoire de Charles in Godefroy, p. 172.

[6] Benedictus in Eckardus, ii. 1579.

[7] Diario Ferrarese in Muratori, xxiv. 253, 279.

almost all the heads of the States of the Church, and even some Neapolitan barons,[1] were among their connections. The power of the House of Aragon, which had been founded by Alfonso I, was shrewdly and rigorously maintained by his natural son, Ferrante. Once, when the great barons called in John of Anjou, and delivered to him the whole country, save the capital, the House of Aragon seemed to be lost. At that time the Queen once found herself compelled to sit with her little children at the convent of San Piero at Naples with an alms-box before her, and to beg the labourers to do voluntary work for her, and implore of other citizens a loan.[2] The dynasty and throne were only saved by the great barons again returning to their allegiance. The most distinguished of them was Ferrante's brother-in-law, Count Marsico of Sanseverino, whom the King in his compact styled the illustrious, the most powerful, who had saved him from the deepest misery; he made over to him Salerno, with all the rights of the exchequer and coinage.[3] Sanseverino's example was followed by the others, but they did not succeed in gaining the King's favour. Of some of his confidantes, who were instrumental in beginning the rebellion, as, for instance, his brother-in-law, Balzo of Taranto, he ridded himself by force.[4]

King Ferrante, once more firmly on his throne, thought to secure it mainly by foreign alliances. His son Alfonso he married to the daughter of Francesco Sforza; Popes Pius and Sixtus he gained over to him by investing the nephew of the one with Amalfi, and of the other with Sora.[5] Two men, who were invaluable to him, were entrusted with the conduct of home affairs, viz. Antonello Petrucci, and Francesco Coppola. The former was his most intimate counsellor, to whom he was wont to refer every one. This man was often obliged to come out to him when on the chase, and then return in dust and dirt to the council in the city; sometimes he had hardly crossed

---

[1] Porzio, Congiura dei Baroni di Napoli, p. 29.

[2] Pontanus, de bello Neapolitano, Haganoae, 1530, N. 4, S. 2.

[3] Pontanus, *ibid.* Dd. 4, Gg. 2.

[4] According to a document in Angelo di Costanzo, Istoria di Napoli, xix. 440, 467.   [5] Costanzo, 466.

his threshold, when fresh messengers would summon him back, although it was night. In return for his services, two of his sons were made counts and another an archbishop. Petrucci himself, though originally quite poor, was finally able to build churches and castles.

With the other, Francesco Coppola, a merchant, the King entered into partnership. By allowing no one to buy, unless Francesco had already done so, and by permitting no trading ship to come into port, unless it had previously sold its cargo, as well as by treating the oil and wine market almost as a monopoly, he increased his gains to an extraordinary extent. Francesco in a short time was made a count, and had a private dockyard for his ships.[1] By their advice and his own perseverance, the King became completely master of the country. The barons were obliged to maintain his stables. To his falconer he gave an abbey, and to the son of a Jew, in return for a sum of money, a bishopric.[2] The land was quite subject to him. He waged the wars of Italy. His power was steadily on the increase.

Brought up in the atmosphere of Ferrante's shrewd cunning, his son Alfonso developed into a totally different character, and one quite peculiar to the Italian princes of those times. They considered cruelty and licentiousness lawful things. To appear always in pomp—to hunt with hawks and falcons, which bore their arms in velvet and gold aloft into the air; at home to be seen in gorgeous apartments, surrounded by savants, musicians, and artists of all kinds; in public among the people to wear an imperious mien, and to be decorated with jewels; to be witty and eloquent; to command a goodly troop of soldiery, to foresee danger and to avert it: this appeared to them to be glorious and worth living for. There was no trace in them of the good qualities of human nature. They were unrighteous, and of true princely dignity they knew nothing; justice they considered bondage.[3]

This ideal, which instead of the strength and power

[1] Caracciolus, de varietate fortunae in Muratori, Scriptores R. I. xxiv. 69.

[2] Comines, vii. ch. xiii.   Porzio, Congiura, p. 116.

[3] Corio, p. 839.   Castiglione, Cortegiano, p. 388, and elsewhere.

that it intends, seizes only their shadow and their semblance,
Alfonso followed; and whilst the others wished to be
thought generous, he was nothing less than niggardly.[1]
He showed that he considered the wealth of Petrucci and
Coppola to belong to the royal house. Petrucci only
shrugged his shoulders when he heard of it, and tried to
pacify the King by making him New Year's gifts.[2] But
Coppola was differently minded.[3] He leagued himself
with the most powerful of the barons, Sanseverino of
Salerno, who also felt himself in danger. Alfonso had
been heard to say that Sanseverino looked almost like
Balzo of Taranto. They met together by night in solitary
places, devised plans for their protection, and gained over
others also.[4] For all the barons began to fear Alfonso, as
he threatened all who had not been zealous enough in
assisting him in his military expeditions.

They therefore allied themselves with Pope Innocent
VIII, who would rather have been possessor of Naples
than its feudal lord, and again arrayed themselves in open
war against the House of Aragon. Two princes and a
count of the house of Sanseverino, and two counts and a
prince of that of Balzo, were the leaders.[5] Many others,
among them Caracciolo of Melfi, gradually joined them.
They promised one another, with solemn vows, the Sacrament in their hands, to hold out together. But they were
weak and undecided. After the first unfavourable issue
they showed themselves inclined to come to terms;[6] when
fortune favoured them, they again took up arms.[7] Their
achievements were insignificant. When Alfonso had defeated the Pope and had laid siege to the city of Aquila,
which adhered to the baronial party and was their chief
hope, and was at the same time advancing in the kingdom,
they forgot their vows, promised one after the other what
was demanded of them, and surrendered.[8]

---

[1] Laurentii Medicei Epistola apud Fabronium, ii. 269.
[2] Caracciolus, p. 28.   [3] Porzio, Congiura, p. 28.
[4] Porzio, Congiura, pp. 39–49.
[5] Ludovico de Raimi, Annales Neapolitani, in Muratori, xxiii. 231.
[6] Machiavelli, Istorie Fiorentine, viii. 343. Pontanus, Bellum
Neapol. Hh.
[7] Porzio, pp. 80, 90.   [8] Porzio, p. 186.

The Aragonese had now asserted their superiority in a still more decisive manner than heretofore, and with their own forces. They next, father and son, resolved to wreak vengeance on their enemies.

Coppola and Petrucci had only taken a very doubtful, and at the most a very insignificant, part in the war; but they were the first victims of the peace. Ferrante promised to marry one of his nieces to one of Coppola's sons, and to celebrate the marriage in the new castle. Coppola and Petrucci rode up thither, each on a perfumed mule, and in all gala pomp; but as soon as they arrived both they and their sons were seized. They were all put to death.[1] The rest of the barons would have had time to escape on two barks,[2] and the Princess of Bisignano advised this course; but one was hindered in this way and another in that, and so remaining they were all taken on a single day,[3]—the six leaders above mentioned and Caracciolo. The people saw their food taken to them every day into the prison; but when the executioner was seen with the chain of the Prince of Bisignano, it was believed to have been all deception. In the church of S. Leonardo, the patron saint of captives, the Duke persuaded his father to commit the murder, and the executioner, or a slave, a Moor, did the deed.[4] Ferrante would scarcely listen to the expostulations of the Papal Nuncio on this matter. " Did not Pope Sixtus do with his rebels what he pleased? I shall also do the same with mine." This was the whole of his answer. Having delivered himself of it, he ordered the horns to be sounded, and rode to the chase.[5] But what he had devised for his security threatened to become his ruin. Many had fled to Rome, and now sent messages to Spain and to France to implore help. In France, Prince Antonello of Salerno, who had escaped from his clutches, aroused his real enemy. Those who still remained in the country only waited for the day when they could again

[1] Caracciolus, l.l. Raimi, 239.
[2] Literae Lutotii de Nasis in Fabronii Vita Laur. Med. ii. 352.
[3] Passero, Giornale Napolitano, p. 50.
[4] Angelo di Costanzo, 479.
[5] Infessura, Diarium Romanum, p. 1980.

D

take up arms against him. His first care was to provide
that they never should find an opportunity of doing so.
Such was the position of the House of Aragon in Naples.
Ludovico il Moro, at Milan, also owed to them his present
position.

After the eldest son of Francesco Sforza, Galeazzo
Maria, Duke of Milan and Lord of Genoa, had been
murdered, his widow, the Duchess Bona, took quiet
possession of his lands and cities in the name of her son,
Gian Galeazzo, who was still a minor. This was very
displeasing to Ludovico, Galeazzo's brother, who, when
sitting in the Corte dell' Arengha with the Municipal
Council, had to take his orders from the Castle and the
Council of State, and none the less so to the third brother,
Ascanio.[1]   But as soon as they agitated against it they
were driven out. It was only the war which Ferrante
began at that time with Florence, with which city Bona
was allied, that enabled the fugitives, with Ferrante's
assistance, to show themselves on the frontier, and to
stir up valley after valley in revolt, until they came to
Tortona;[2] whereupon, in a single day, forty-seven castles
belonging to the discontents went over to them. The
Borromei, Pusterli, Marliani, and all the Ghibellines, rose
in their favour. The disaffection spread even to Bona's
court. Whilst this confusion was at its height, Ludovico
returned,[3] and took upon himself the conduct of affairs.
But the attitude which he now adopted was quite unexpected. Although supported by the Ghibellines and in
good understanding with the Guelphs, he would neither
be dependent upon the one nor the other, nor consent
to see the heads of these families, his rivals, in power.
The Ghibellines, owing to whom the power of the Visconti
had been established in all the cities which Corio without
hesitation styles " ducal," he deprived of their weapons and
of their head, his brother Ascanio ;[4] he did not even spare

[1] Corio, Istoria di Milano, p. 840.

[2] Diarium Parmense in Muratori, xxii. 319.

[3] Diarium Parmense, p. 351.   Corio, p. 850.   Machiavelli, Istor.
Fiorent. viii.

[4] Corio, p. 848.   Diarium Parmense, p. 354.

those who had supported him in his flight; nay, he surrounded himself with Biragi, Terzagi, and Trivulzi, who
had retained their Guelph proclivities through centuries,
and to their party he granted his favour and his castles.[1]
Yet this was not done exclusively enough to gain to his
side the whole party: its most distinguished leader, Gian
Giacomo Trivulzio, was forced to seek safety in flight.
With the House of Aragon he entered into the closest
dynastic alliance.   Of this house came the wife of his
nephew, in whose name he governed.   Moreover, he
attached Pope Sixtus to his house by giving to his nephew,
Girolamo, Caterina Sforza to wife.   He procured the peace
of Bagnolo for the republic of Venice, when all Italy was
against her, by which event he increased her power and
made her well disposed towards him.   Upon this alliance
he relied: for his power had originated outside the State.
Under this protection he seized step by step the supreme
power within.   At first, Bona's favourite merely came into
the Council of State in order to carry some point or other,
and would say, "Her Serene Highness the Duchess so
and so."[2]   On Ludovico's initiative the twelve-year-old
Duke went one day into the castle, had the drawbridge
pulled up, and the favourite made a prisoner.   "I will
rule myself," he said, "and my mother may cultivate her
widowhood."[3]

After this, Ludovico shared the sovereign power for a
time with Eustachio, the commander of the castle.   After
the Venetian war, the young Duke helped his uncle,
into whose power he had entirely given himself, to get
rid of him also.[4]   Having thus acquired sole authority,
Ludovico showed himself kind and affable towards everyone, and perhaps the use he made of his power caused
the way in which it had been obtained to be forgotten.
He provided for the building of hospitals, the digging of
canals, the foundation of churches and monasteries, and
the protection of the country from brigandage and famine.

[1] Corio, 869.
[2] Diarium Parmense in Muratori, p. 351.
[3] Ibid.
[4] Senarega, Annales Genuenses, p. 523. Comines, Corio.

In accordance with the taste of the time, he fostered art and science. He summoned Leonardo da Vinci to Milan to be the instructor of the young nobles,[1] and gave him a salary. He was the first to have music publicly taught.[2] Jasone de Maino, in Alciati's opinion one of the five first jurists of the Middle Ages, lectured in Pavìa upon law to 3,000 students. Ludovico also honoured the grammarians. Demetrius Chalkondylas, who saw his auditorium in Pisa grow empty owing to Politian's more brilliant lectures, repaired with his Florentine wife and his favourite pupil, Johann Reuchlin, the teacher of the teacher of Germany, to his court.[3] It cannot be said that the Prince laid out badly the 650,000 ducats which the country gave him. Bellincioni's pastoral plays and farces, in which the people fancied they perceived the hand of the Prince himself, enlivened his court, as did also Gaspare Visconti, who was considered equal to Petrarch.[4] His farm at Vigevene was a masterpiece of rural economy. Here once had grown not even provender enough for the cattle, and no plant would flourish; only wild animals made their lairs in the low brushwood. Ludovico, who was first carried thither in the chase, cut dykes, and thus made meadows for the cattle, and then, by putting manure upon it, produced tillage land that vied with any other.[5] This done, he planted mulberry trees in long avenues, and lastly built spacious and clean stables with columns to hold 1,800 head of cattle and 14,000 sheep, and others for the stallions and mares.[6] In this castle a son was born to him; here woods were preserved for the chase and hawking.[7] The bounteousness of peace rested on the land. Every day saw new fashions and amusements, jousts and balls.[8] It was of the utmost

[1] Vasari, Vita di Leonardo da Vinci, iii. 21.

[2] Jagemann, Geschichte der Künste und Wissenschaften in Italien, iii. 650.

[3] Jovius, Vitae Virorum DD., p. 37. Reuchlini Praefat. ad Gr. Hebr.

[4] Bouterwek, Italien. Literatur, i. 339. Roscoe, Life of Leo X, i. 113.

[5] Carpesanus, Commentarii suorum temporum, ix. 1363.

[6] Desrey in Monstrelet, 239.

[7] Comines, Mémoires, p. 507.   [8] Corio, last book, beginning.

importance for him, so long as his rule was tolerated, to maintain the peace and the *status quo* in Italy, seeing that, were it disturbed, his ruin might easily ensue.

But the present conditions depended, before all else, upon Lorenzo de' Medici, the ruler of Florence, living on friendly terms with the King of Naples and the Duke of Milan.

Francesco Sforza, principally owing to the assistance of Cosimo de' Medici, had become lord of Milan, and, to the vexation of Venice, the Medici and Sforza had since then been the best of friends. When, after Galeazzo's death, the above-mentioned difference in the Sforza family arose, Lorenzo made cause with Bona; but the Sforza brothers and Ferrante attacked him, and succeeded so well that he made his resolve, went forth, came to Naples, and entered into friendship with them.[1] Since then, the King was his nearest ally, and Ludovico his second; in conjunction with both he sustained a very dangerous conflict with Ferrara, and eventually aided the King in the second Neapolitan war, which we have noticed. After it was over, Ferrante said, " I saved him, and he has now done the same for me." [2]

Pope Innocent VIII, who had espoused the cause of the barons and had been defeated, was at first highly dissatisfied with this arrangement. He even protested in his private garden at the palace, saying, " he did not recognize Ferrante as king, even though he called him such." [3]   He exclaimed, " I will put him under ban. If the Italians will not then assist me, I will cross the mountains, like the Popes did in the days of old, and appeal to those dwelling on the other side, and I know I shall stop their feuds and that they will help me." [4]   Lorenzo undertook to pacify him, and was able to effect this by giving his daughter to the Pope's son, Franceschetto Cibò, to wife.[5]   Hereupon a thorough change supervened. His old friends, Giuliano della Rovere and the Colonna, fell into disfavour with

[1] Machiavelli, viii.   Diarium Parmense, p. 335.
[2] Fabronii Vita Laurentii Medicis, ii. 369.
[3] Literae Petri Victorii, ap. Fabronium, ii. 344.
[4] Literae Philippi Pandolphini, *ibid.*, p. 353.
[5] *Ibid.*, p. 313.   Letters and documents.

Innocent, who inclined to the Orsini, Lorenzo's relations and his old enemies. At last the Neapolitan complications were settled, and the King confessed that in everything he perceived Lorenzo's faithfulness and goodness.[1] We see how it is that Lorenzo, owing to his position, became the mediator of Italy; upon this was founded the subsequent greatness of his house, for, owing to the co-operation of the three, his son Giovanni was made abbot of Miramondo in the province of Milan, of Monte Casino in the kingdom of Naples, and a cardinal of the church.[2]

And thus they all lived in peace together; all of them, except the Pope, in usurped dominions, each menaced by his subjects, and only careful that the latter did not anywhere find assistance in any neighbour : but each supporting the other. They were neither nations nor races ; neither cities nor kingdoms ; they were the first States in the world, and their origin was as follows.

The appellation of "State" was originally given to the friends most nearly devoted to a single family ; and we find Foligno de' Medici complaining that their "State" had decreased, only numbering fifty men instead of a hundred, and these ill provided with children.[3] The most illustrious members of the State, who came to Lorenzo with the deputies of the city, in order, as he says, to entrust to his care the public duties, were not from the country — for this is called "Dominio" and has not the slightest influence—but they were the friends, the old State, without which Lorenzo declared it difficult to live in Florence.[4] Now, as the party united with these "nearest friends," and the party was master of the city, and the city of the land, the name of the original unit became applied to the whole. Nowhere did real liberty exist. Whence, then, sprang the lively attraction towards the beautiful, through which this people at this time became the stimulus and the model for

[1] Literae Philippi Pandolphini, ap. Fabronium, ii. 351.

[2] *Ibid.*, p. 374, and in Roscoe, Leo X, the letters in Appendix, from p. 486 on.

[3] Foligno de' Medici, Notizia in Fabroni, ii. 7.

[4] Lorenzo de' Medici, Ricordi *ibid.*, p. 42. A further proof is contained in Varchi, storia Fiorentina, ii. 8 : "andavano cercando che lo stato si ristringesse e a minore numero si riducesse " (note to 2nd ed.).

all later peoples;—whence came the semblance, yes, the effect of liberty? It grew mainly from the antagonism of parties, ever covertly or openly existing, from the vigilance of all human forces engaged in conflict, from the universal enthusiasm which was devoted to art, active work, science, and antiquity, and from the reverence in which the savants were therefore held.

Since the era of the migration of nations, Italy now for the first time stood independent, and formed an ideal unity, combined with the greatest variety. These States, though based upon violence and faction, entertained notwithstanding the most universal relations. Venice was dependent upon commerce, Florence upon artistic industry and manufactures, the kingdom of Naples upon the great European balance of power, which had now found a moment of rest, the duchy of Milan upon the trade of war as it was followed by the Condottieri, and the State of the Church upon the idea of the supreme hierarchy. The nation was at the zenith of its culture. Would it not have been possible for it to have progressed and developed further in the same way, and so in later times have itself exercised influence, instead of being subjected to that of other nations?

But this retired and singular world was convulsed by a great and violent movement. The sea is calm, and reflects the sky; then comes a storm: when it is past and gone, the sea is the same as before. If a movement and a storm comes into the hearts of men, there will also return a day of calm: but meanwhile the world has altered.

In the year 1480 Ferrante had two grand-daughters at his court, who, it might be, often quarrelled when playing at his feet: Isabella, ten years of age, the child of his son Alfonso, and Beatrice, aged seven years, his daughter Leonora's child by her marriage with Ercole d'Este.[1] At the beginning of his rule Ludovico betrothed the elder of these two to his nephew, Gian Galeazzo, who would one day be duke, and himself to the younger. After some time Isabella was taken to Milan: and while there she was forced to see how the uncle ruled her husband like

[1] Diarium Parmense, p. 311. Diarium Ferrarense, p. 254.

a boy, and neither allowed him nor herself the least power;
she endured this, nevertheless. But the time came for
Beatrice also to go as a bride to Milan,[1] and as Ludovico
was actually prince, Beatrice and not Isabella was honoured
as princess. Here, then, we see the younger girl in the joy
of her youth, with every wish gratified, full of hopes, sometimes sitting as mistress at the games and tournaments in
Milan, and anon at Genoa—whither she has come secretly
to enjoy herself—so soon as discovered, the recipient of
princely honours amid the gorgeous pomp of the merchants;[2]
anon driving to her father at Ferrara with her attendant
ladies, with many coaches and mules, the streets covered
with carpets and green boughs, whilst the populace shouts
her husband's name.[3] The elder, meanwhile, the lawful
duchess, has the pain of being bound to a man who is
a mere nobody, and who even repeats to his uncle what
she confides to him; moreover, she has little prospect
either for her own future or that of her children. For
Ludovico now declared, that the sovereignty belonged to
him, who was born whilst his father was reigning duke,
rather than to the son of one who was born before,[4] and
entered into negotiations to procure his investiture. A
heart perceiving danger threatening its whole house and
enduring in silence, were nothing less than divine. Isabella
acted like a mortal in not tolerating this treatment; at
first she complained in Milan, then threatened,[5] and finally
appealed for assistance to her father in Naples.[6] She
wrote, "Whilst his newly-born infant is designed to be
Count of Pavìa, we and ours are ever held in contempt,
and are even in peril of our lives; and I am like a widow,
a helpless woman. We have courage and understanding,
and the people are favourable and pitying. If thou hast
the heart of a father, and love and generosity, and art
touched by tears, then save us."

[1] Diarium Ferrarense, p. 279.
[2] Folieta, Historia Genuensis, lib. xi.
[3] Diarium Ferrarense, p. 283.
[4] Comines and Georgius Florus, p. 3.
[5] Marcus de la Cruce to Trivulzio in Rosmini, ii. 192.
[6] Literae Isabellae, *verbatim* in Corio, p. 884.

"We ought to help them," said Alfonso, "even if they were strangers to us." He consulted with his old father, and with his grown-up son. He then called upon Ludovico to crown his noble actions by the most noble of all, and to retire from the government in favour of his nephew. He received no answer. But in this silence lay the breach of friendship and peace between them ; nay, of the peace of Italy itself.[1] Alfonso's friends said Ludovico must be content to be podestà in Milan ; they wagered that he would not exist one month longer.[2] But he, on his side, thought that he possessed the means of securing his rule, and at the same time of endangering the existence of his enemy.

Now, Lorenzo de' Medici and Innocent VIII at this time died in quick succession, and Alfonso as well as Ludovico had to cast about to gain the favour of their successors. Lorenzo's son, Piero, was heart and soul devoted to the House of Aragon, from whom, in the great hall at a splendid festival, he had received his wife, Alfonsina Orsini.[3] But the successor of Pope Innocent was of entirely opposite feelings.

Amidst the universal corruption, it was a universal misfortune, and redounded little to the credit of the human race in general, that, in the retired cells of the Conclave assembled to elect a Pope, amid high and holy ceremonies, and among men who had no further wants and no one to provide for, it was not the weal of Christendom, so sorely in need, that determined the election, nor that of a nation —no, nor even genuine affections and emotions. The highest dignity in the Church was regarded as the inheritance of all cardinals; given, because alas! it was indivisible, to the one who promised the others most. Brother Albus of Venice, ninety-five years of age, who could scarcely talk any longer, and always nodded his head, still took 5,000 ducats.[4] He received them from Rodrigo Borgia (Borja) of Xativa in Valencia, and the others took similar presents. The revenues he received from

[1] All in Corio.   [2] Cruce to Trivulzio, 191.
[3] Oricellarius in Fabroni, ii. 316.
[4] Infessura, Diarium, p. 2007.

three cathedrals and several monasteries, whose head he was; the income derived from the vice-chancellorship that he held, as well as numerous connections with foreign princes, furnished him with the means of making these bribes.[1] Ascanio Sforza and Giuliano della Rovere still resisted him; but the former gave up his opposition when Borgia sent to his house four mules laden with silver, and promised him the vice-chancellorship. The latter would not receive anything, and kept complaining that the Italians were excluded, but at last he too gave way.[2] Calamity was expected to result from the election. Sinibaldo de' Sinibaldi died of grief occasioned by it. It is said that a tear was seen in the eye of the old Ferrante, whose rule, established by so many misdeeds, was threatened with utter ruin by this election.[3] The great Popes of early days provided, after their lights, for the Church; the later ones had nephews to provide for; and in these days even sons—Borgia, who called himself Alexander VI, had three, Juan, and Gioffredo of temporal, and Caesar of spiritual rank, as well as one married daughter, Lucrezia.[4] Men said, "This man, who when Cardinal, made his son Duke of Gandia, what will he do now he is Pope?" The Sforza gained him over to them

[1] Jacob Volaterranus, Rom. Diarium, p. 130.

[2] Infessura, p. 3008, and Corio.

[3] Infessura, 3009. Zurita, i. 15. In the Codice Aragonese of Trinchera this tradition is traced back to Guicciardini, and denied, no mention being made of the true authors of it. The account which follows, however, records the hostile relations between the new Pope and the King of Naples, which immediately showed themselves. "Sappiate," we read in a letter of the King, of 7 June, 1493, addressed to Antonio d'Alessandro (Cod. ii. 2, 43), "che 'l pontifice succedendo in pontificato, con la majore pace in tutta Italia: et con lo majore reposo che mai altro pontifice: stando tutti li potentati in summa amicitia: ipso pontifice non guardando al ben publico, ma sequendo el suo naturale." (Cf. Gregorovius, Geschichte der Stadt Rom., vol. vii. p. 329.) The accounts given in the Codice are of great moment for the epoch 1493-1494; yet they go so deeply into the details of the intricate and vacillating policy of those times, that it is impossible to incorporate their contents in this place; the general view here given will not be affected by this (note to 2nd edition).

[4] Vannozza de' Cattanei was the mother of Caesar, Juan, Gioffredo, and Lucrezia. Her monument stands in Santa Maria del popolo. Pedro Luis, Duke of Gandia, was born of another alliance. Cf. Reumont, Gesch. von Rom, iii. 2, p. 838 (note to 2nd edition).

by giving Giovanni Sforza, lord of Pesaro, to his daughter for a husband; he dissolved the marriage with her former husband, whom he satisfied with money. In the presence of one hundred and fifty Roman ladies, whom these clerics in frivolous play pelted with sweetmeats served up in more than a hundred silver dishes, the new betrothal was celebrated.[1] Hereupon the Pope nominated three Cardinals in the interest of the Sforza.[2] After that, he endeavoured to divorce King Wladislav of Hungary from Ferrante's daughter, in order that he might wed a Sforza; and, as Ludovico was allied with all his relations at Ferrara, Mantua, Forlì, Pesaro, and Bologna, and had even gained over Venice[3] and despatched his envoys and his letter to Charles VIII, Alexander now entered into a league with him also. Their plan was to put an army into the field under a joint commander. The Pope approved Ludovico's proposals that he should invest Charles,[4] and thereupon invited him to come.[5]

That the adherents of the Aragon dynasty did not despair in the face of such dangers, was owing to their reliance upon the tried shrewdness of their old king, Ferrante. But he now appeared to have lost all pleasure in life. He cared neither for the chase nor for amusements, and would even scarcely take food. No one could please him in rendering the small services of everyday life.[6] He was bowed down by the weight of years and the dread of this third war, by far the most dangerous of all, as the King of France was taking part in it; and he was moreover harassed by his barons. It was said that an ancient book had been found in Taranto, addressed to the King alone and his most intimate adherents. The people believed that therein was prophesied the destruction of Ferrante's race and dynasty.[7] Yet he did not abandon the cause as lost. He thought of paying tribute to Charles as his vassal, but his envoys

[1] Infessura, 2010, 2011.
[2] Senarega, Annales Genuens. in Muratori, xxiv. 534.
[3] Alegretto Alegretti, Diari sanesi, p. 827.
[4] Zurita, i. 26.   [5] Infessura, Diarium, p. 1016.
[6] Caracciolus, de varietate fortunae, p. 72.
[7] Giacomo, Cronica di Napoli, p. 173.

returned with the presents he had sent. He next thought of securing Alfonso by a Spanish marriage, but King Ferdinand evaded it. His sole safety he now saw in going to Milan, and taking Isabella back home with him. But grief and fear, as well as the recollection of what he had done, broke his heart. In crowded assemblies he was heard to give vent to frequent and deep sighs; in the midst of a conversation he would utter meaningless words, which, however, had reference to his danger.[1] In this state he died, two days after his return to the city, on the 25th January, 1494.

When Alfonso mounted at once his black steed, and, riding through the streets with a bold air, received the ovations of the people, there were still some who hoped. But the tradition goes that many were obliged to join in the acclamations under the point of drawn swords; and meanwhile the old Queen sat with her sixteen-year-old daughter Joanna in a dark room. They lamented: "Wisdom is dead, and light is extinguished. In what plight has he left us behind, and to whom? All power is gone: the realm is helpless and lost!" Alfonso came to them, and said: "I shall uphold the kingdom as well as did my father." But they were afraid of his cruelty, and only implored him to spare the people.[2]

Alfonso's first care was to gain over Pope Alexander, in which endeavour he was so far supported by the King of Spain, that he married Maria Enriquez, his uncle's daughter, to Juan Borgia.[3] Alfonso promised the latter an estate of 12,000, the younger son Gioffredo one of 10,000 ducats, in addition to his daughter Sancia; so that the Borgia were thus received into relationship with the genuine as well as with the spurious House of Aragon. For the sake of these great advantages, Alexander forgot his former engagements, paid no heed to the protestations of the Consistory, and allied himself with Alfonso.[4] This connection first caused

---

[1] Senarega, Annales Genuenses, p. 538, and Caracciolus, de varietate fortunae.

[2] Zurita and Passero, Giornale, p. 57.

[3] Zurita, i. 29, 34.

[4] Diarium Burcardi in Eccardus, 2036, 2040.

alarm to Cardinal Giuliano. On a former occasion he had once invited the Pope to Magliano. The Pope came ; but on hearing a chance shot fired, he feared it was a signal meant for him, and returned without tasting food.[1] Since then Giuliano had banded himself with the discontents in Ostia. Now, when the Orsini also were reconciled with the Pope, he sailed with two caravels through the pirate ships of Villamarino across to France, came into his legation at Avignon, and leagued himself with Charles.[2] Whereupon the Colonna, under their own standards, as well as those of Rovere and France, occupied Ostia, closed the Tiber, cared not that their houses were destroyed, and awaited the coming of the King.[3]

Alfonso was crowned on the 8th May. His coronation apparel was valued at more than a million and a half ducats ; yet, amidst all the pomp and splendour, he looked sad and brooding.[4] On this very day he heard certain tidings of the approaching French expedition. His silver shield could not gladden his heart, for he needed an iron one. Yet he did not think of awaiting the attack, as his father had advised. " Shall I hide," he said, " like a stag in the wood ? " He received the coronation presents and exacted payment of a whole year's income from landowners and his tithes ; the foals from his studs were trained for military service, and his ships equipped with newly-invented bombards; he then had an interview with Alexander at Vicovaro. In accord with the latter, he resolved to attack Ludovico on two sides[5]—with his fleet in Genoa, and by land in the territory belonging to Milan. In view of the operations against Genoa, two exiles, Cardinal Fregoso and Obietto Fiesco, offered their services. They had been expelled in order that the city might obey Ludovico, and they now placed their hopes in the King of Naples.[6] He

[1] Infessura, 2010.

[2] Senarega, Annales, p. 539.   Zurita, 34.   Infessura, 2016.

[3] Burcardus, p. 2048.

[4] Passero, 61.   Caracciolus, de varietate fortunae, 43.   Diurnale di Giacomo Gallo, 7.

[5] Benedicti Diarium.   Corio, 919.   Oricellarius, de bello Italico, p. 10.

[6] Senarega, Annales, 520.   Folieta, 263.

hoped to effect an entrance into Milan through the instrumentality of the Papal vassals, who were pledged to obey
their suzerain; the upper hand he hoped to gain through
the Guelphs, whose head, Trivulzio, marched with him ;
whilst the complete victory should be his through the
devotion of the people to their own prince, Gian Galeazzo.
In August, 1494, thirty-eight squadrons of horse started
from the Abruzzi ; they were to take their way through the
Romagna, in order to set free the young Duke of Milan.[1]
Infantry they had none; but they had officers with them
to recruit them.   The land army was led by Ferrantino, the
son of Alfonso ; whilst the fleet, which put to sea at the
same time, was commanded by Federigo, Alfonso's brother.
Thus did the war in Italy break out.

Ludovico awaited the coming of his enemies, already
not without French help; he was to be aided against the
landing of troops, which the Neapolitan fleet had on board,
by Duke Louis of Orleans, who had come to Genoa with
a few companies of Swiss.

At last the beacon-fires flashed from cape to cape ; the
enemy was approaching.   The Aragonese then effected a
landing on the Riviera, and occupied Rapallo[2] with their
troops.   But what availed these troops, which were neither
picked nor disciplined—to-day recruited, and to-morrow
dismissed—troops whose highest aim it was to run about
and shout the name of the leader[3] who had hired them ;
what availed they against the Swiss battle array?   They
could not hold their position ; Aubigny and one of the
brothers Sanseverino from the borders of Ferrara offered
resistance to the troops advancing by land.   Ferrantino, at
all events, was driven back.

3.   CHARLES VIII IN ITALY

Whilst the Italian League, as now constituted, was
attacking Milan and Genoa by land and sea, King Charles
was ordering processions to be held, and prayers offered

[1] Emilia Pia to Gibert Pio, in Rosmini, 202.
[2] Georgius Florus, de bello Italico, 7.   St. Gelais, Louis XII, p. 82.
[3] Nardi, Vita di Tebalducci.

up in all churches, for the success of his crusade against the Saracens.[1] After the old custom of French kings, he had the bodies of St. Denis and his companions brought up into the church from the vaults.[2] On the 29th of August, 1494, he attended mass at Grenoble, took leave of the Queen, and started for Italy. He had arranged who, in his absence, should govern the kingdom, and who rule each duchy. He had borrowed 100,000 ducats from the house of Sauli in Genoa;[3] the chamberlains had arranged his journey, and so, with high expectations, he proceeded from Briançon over Mont Genèvre, down the valley of Cesanne, and through the valleys of the Waldenses to Turin; mules brought up the baggage in the rear. At the gates of Turin they were received by Blanche, the lady of Savoy, seated on her palfrey, and by the young Duke, who, though still a child, had been taught to express himself in graceful language;[4] for close relationships and frequent appeals for their decision in disputes touching wardships, had procured for the French kings the dignity of real suzerains in Piedmont. To the music of clarions and trumpets, the cavalcade passed through the streets, where Charlemagne's wondrous exploits were represented in devices.[5] The Princess gave her ornaments in pledge for a small loan. Philippe de Bresse, the uncle of the Duke, joined the expedition; with a light heart they marched upon Asti, on the borders of Milan.[6]

Here Ludovico met the King. "In Italy," said he, "we have three great powers. One, Milan, you have on your side; another, Venice, sits quiet. How should Naples single-handed oppose him, whose forefathers have conquered us all together? Only follow me, and I will make you greater than Charlemagne was. We will drive these Turks out of Constantinople ere we finish."[7]

[1] Baudequin MS. in Foncemagne, Mémoires de l'Acad. xvii. 572.
[2] Desrey in Monstrelet, p. 228.
[3] Desrey, 214, 215.
[4] Georgius Florus, 6.
[5] Philiberti Pignoni Chronicon Augustae Taurinorum, p. 41.
[6] Comines and Desrey, 216. On the 1st September Charles arrived at Briançon, on the 5th at Turin, and on the 9th at Asti.
[7] Comines, p. 444.

But before they had come up with the enemy, Ludovico took complete possession of Milan. Gian Galeazzo was sick unto death; but Ludovico had received the investiture of the dukedom from the Emperor,[1] who had a few months previously wedded his niece. Now if Galeazzo were to die whilst the French army was in the country, who should then stand in his way? At Pavìa Charles saw the sick man, whose mother had been his own mother's sister, and who apologized even then for not having come to meet him, for he was too ill; but he offered him homage on behalf of himself and his children.[2] A Pavian physician, who accompanied the King, assured Rucellai that it was evident he had been poisoned.[3] However, Charles bade him be of good heart, and taking his chain from his neck, hung it on him. He had scarcely reached Piacenza, when he heard of the young man's death.[4] Sympathy with the innocent victim was universal, as was the horror felt of him who was considered to be the murderer. The King invited the citizens to the funeral and gave presents to the poor, while Ludovico hurried to Milan, assembled the Council of State, and proposed the son of the deceased as his successor.[5] "We need a man, not a child," the Treasurer Marliano replied. All the members were of one opinion, that Ludovico must be their duke; they handed him the sceptre, a garment of cloth of gold was brought and put on him; he then rode, accompanied by the notables of the city, to Sant' Ambrogio, and was there proclaimed duke by popular acclamation.[6] If Isabella had felt that her letter had caused her father a most perilous war, and her husband his death, what must her feelings have been now, when she

[1] Documents in Corio, 900, 912, 935.

[2] Georgius Florus, de expeditione Caroli, p. 9. Marino Sanuto, La Spedizione di Carolo ottavo in Italia, pubblicata per cura di Rinaldo Fulin, p. 671 (note to 3rd edition). Charles started from Asti on the 7th of October, and arrived at Pavìa on the 14th.

[3] Oricellarius, de bello Italico, p. 33.

[4] Desrey, 218. On October 18 Charles arrived at Piacenza; and on the 21st Gian Galeazzo died.

[5] Florus Navagero in Muratori, xxiii. 201.

[6] Corio, p. 936; Ludovico to Aubigny in Rosmini, Trivulzio, ii. 206.

heard that Ludovico was duke, and her children were without hope and robbed! The first she had endured, but this crushed her to the earth.[1]

The King stood on the borders of the Florentine and Papal territory. At Piacenza two of the Medici had come to him, Piero's cousins of the younger branch, who, though more generous, more affable, more endeared to the people, and not less rich than he, were exiles, because, when at play with Piero, they had quarrelled with him and evinced French sentiments.[2] They told the King he need only advance into Tuscany, for he had friends in Florence. Among the old adherents of the Medici, there were many who were discontented with Piero. His father had once written to him, " Though thou art my son, thou art all the same no more than a citizen of Florence, like myself." [3] But the son of an Orsini, whose brother was Cardinal, whose father had been the mediator of Italy, and who felt himself even superior to the latter in point of physical strength, good looks, and graceful deportment, and, it might be, his superior in classical education—for he expounded Virgil to his brother, and could improvise cleverly[4]—might easily forget this warning. Like many others, he forgot, over external show, what was really deserving of praise. He had no liking for agriculture and commerce, as his fathers had, but only taste for hunting, hawking, and Tuscan games with hand and foot, brilliant cavalcades by day, and nightly carouses.[5] He had himself painted in his armour.[6] In civic business, on the other hand, he approved what his counsellor, Bibbiena, proposed. It was not until Charles had crossed the high mountains and had arrived at Pontremoli, that Piero perceived how little the Florentines were inclined to support him against the King. " I never dreamt I should come into these straits," he wrote; "never have I mistrusted such great

[1] Petrus Martyr, Epistol. xi. 193.
[2] Corio and Comines.
[3] Literae Laurentii in Fabroni, Vita, p. 264.
[4] Literae Petri in Fabr., Vita Laur. p. 298.
[5] Nardi, Istorie Fiorentine, p. 9.
[6] Jovii Elogia virorum illustrium, p. 187.

E

friends of this city, but I am forsaken by all, and have neither money, credit, nor authority, so as to be able to sustain the war."[1] This he wrote when already on the road to Pisa to meet Charles, to deliver himself unconditionally into his hands.[2] Only with the King's help was it possible for him to maintain himself in the city.[3] The course he pursued was not so ill-advised as has been asserted,[4] namely, to grant the King all he wished, the

[1] His letter to Bibbiena in Fabroni, Leo X, p. 262.

[2] Second letter in same work. On 23rd October Charles left Piacenza, and arrived on the 29th at Pontremoli. On the 26th Piero started from Florence.

[3] Georgius Florus, p. 9. Nerli, Commentari, p. 61.

[4] Even in the most recent writings there has been attributed to Piero, una stoltezza veramente incredibile (Villari, storia di Girolamo Savonarola). We should scarcely anticipate such a quality in a Florentine, a Medici. All was antagonism of parties, more or less false calculation, and agitation of the moment. Extremely remarkable are the letters of the time of the crisis given in the collection of Desjardins, Négociations diplomatiques de la France avec la Toscane. We can perceive that Piero was at variance with his State in Florence, in consequence of his alliance with Alfonso, and his general attitude. For the Florentines were at heart well inclined towards France ; they perceived the danger which threatened them from France with all the greater ill-humour, as it was not the policy of the Commonwealth, but merely a personal one of the head of their republic, that implicated them in it. Florence itself could not be defended against the superior forces of the French which threatened it from the sea side. Coerced by his opponents within, and menaced from without, Piero resolved to seek in person the favour of the King of France. He did this not without anxiety on his own account, and before setting out implored his fellow-citizens to provide for his family, in case any disaster befell him. But as he went to the French camp in the double capacity of head of the Republic, and its envoy, his opponents in the city bestirred themselves ; they appointed an embassy, which should, either in conjunction with Piero or without him, enter into negotiations with Charles VIII. They also were ready to meet the French demands. Meanwhile, it had not caused Piero much difficulty to open negotiations with the French. He was really of opinion that he was doing his old ally, Alfonso, the best service, by throwing himself entirely into the arms of France. He did not hesitate to deliver into their hands the fortresses which the French coveted, until their business with Naples was settled. He at once issued orders to Pisa and Florence to receive the King of France in a manner worthy of his dignity and the old connection with him. The new envoys had not received any orders that were directly contradictory ; they only laid stress upon the authority of the Republic as such. Every minute the opposition to Piero in the city itself waxed stronger. He

fortresses of Sarzana, Sarzanella, Pietrasanta, Pisa, and Leghorn, which command the mountain-road and the coast from the Magra to the mouth of the Arno.[1] He meant by this means to estrange him from his friends, and to gain him for himself. But he was far from being sure of this when he learnt that his action was condemned at home. He hurried back to Florence. In order to maintain his authority, he massed his troops under Paolo Orsini, and proceeded—it was on the 9th of November, 1494, a Sunday evening—with an armed retinue to the palace. The assembled Signori were not in accord. One of them, of the name of Lorini, ushered in Piero, and refused to give up the key to the bell, with which the others proposed to call the people together. But the latter had the upper hand. A Nerli and a Gualterotti, both sprung of families formerly Medicean to the core, stepped towards Piero, as he entered, exclaiming, "Alone and unarmed, otherwise he does not enter here." Others opened the bell-tower.[2] With Piero had returned Francesco Valori, who had hitherto been envoy to King Charles, and was convinced that he would not support Piero de' Medici.[3] This man mounted his horse, summoned the people to liberty, and increased their confidence.

Girolamo Savonarola had for the last four years preached to the same people : " A king will come over the mountains,

considered it wiser to return to Florence, in order to remain master of the city. But he was not quite assured of the protection of France ; in the French camp it was, on the other hand, perfectly well known that he and not the Signoria was the real enemy of France. One of the civic envoys, Valori, came back from the King, convinced that he would leave the internal affairs of the Republic to its own management. Thus it came about that Piero, whilst thinking to gain possession of the palace, met with opposition, and the population rose up against him. The moment is of the greatest importance ; it was really decisive for the later times of Tuscany (note to 2nd edition).

[1] Comines, 449.

[2] Nerli.   Nardi, p. 13.

[3] The alleged bulletins of Charles VIII's army (Pilorgerie, Campagne et bulletins de la grande armée d'Italie commandée par Charles VIII), are worthy of note, in so far as they explain the political negotiations that accompanied the expedition of the King, and his intentions : they are of little value for the internal Italian movements (note to 2nd ed.).

a great king, sent by God to punish evil-doers, and to regenerate the Church."[1] This king seemed now to have come. As Piero went across the square, he saw stones flying about him, and the people at the sound of the bell running together towards the palace and disarming his myrmidons. He saw these weapons of slavery, the few that had escaped his control, brandished for emancipation from his own yoke.[2] Giovanni, his brother, shouted in the street, " Palle !" (Their watchword was " Bullets.") They endeavoured to rouse their partisans in the suburb of San Gallo; but no one stirred, and Paolo's troops were afraid. Thus the Medici, Lorenzo's sons, left Florence without saving anything; their treasures, their jewels, the cups of sardonyx, the most precious antiquities, the 3,000 medallions, the manuscripts and books, which it was their pride to show strangers,[3] the gardens, in which Torrigiano and Michael Angelo were brought up, all were left to the people to pillage. They yielded up the power which their fathers had possessed for sixty years, and fled; they durst not turn their steps to Charles, but crossed the Apennines to Bologna.

The advent of him, in whom the prophets foretold a Saviour, and whom people loved to address as " Holy Crown," set Pisa free also on the same Sunday. How that came about is not without uncertainty. One historian has much to say of Simone Orlando, who exercised great influence upon both people and prince.[4] On the way back from mass, or on the way thither, the people of Pisa, young and old, prostrated themselves before the King, complained to him of the great oppression which they had suffered for the last eighty-seven years at the hands of the Florentines,[5] and said that they wished to be free and under his rule. Hereupon the monarch, who had a tender heart and hated all injustice, at once threw

[1] From Savonarola's sermons in Fabroni, Vita Leonis X.
[2] Nardi, Nerli, Guicciardini.
[3] Comines, pp. 451, 455. Vasari, Vita di Torrigiano, v. d. P. iii. p. 136.
[4] Jovius, Historiae sui temporis, fol. 19.
[5] Desrey, p. 219. Nardi, 12.

an inquiring glance at one of his councillors, who accompanied him, his master of petitions, Jean Rabot, and when the latter had judged that they were right, and when all his knights showed their sympathy, he nodded to them and promised to maintain them in good freedom. Hereupon the people, shouting "Franza !" "Libertà !" and "Gioia !" threw the Florentine lion into the Arno, and expelled the Florentine commander.[1]   The chroniclers add that two strangers had a share in this ; a Milanese, on account of certain claims of the Sforza, called Galeazzo Sanseverino, and a Sienese, for the sake of Tuscan liberty, named Bartolomeo Sozzini, a teacher of law at Pisa, who had once for a long time been a prisoner in Florence.[2]

So much for the story told by the Florentines and French.   Since the day of its enslavement there have been no Pisan annals.[3]   Charles intended to wrest this city from Piero ; but as yet he could not know how the latter stood with the Florentines.

These, against whom he now advanced, were partly his enemies, for their ruler had waged war against him, and partly his friends, in that they had expelled this their ruler. Upon the hills before Signa, with the unprotected plain of the city before him, negotiations were opened.   Since Lucca, which was in nowise under an obligation to him,[4] had received him with offerings in its best palace, he now demanded the same of Florence, viz., perfect confidence and unconditional surrender to his good-will.[5]   The Florentines appeared ready to accede to his terms, and brought him (on the 17th of November) the keys of the gates. Youths in French garments bore a baldachin over his head and conducted him, fully armed, just as he was, past the mystery of the Annunciation to their cathedral, and to the palaces of the Medici.[6]   But the subsequent negotiations did not proceed so smoothly.   Can it be true, as is said,

[1] Comines, 452. Ferronus, p. 10.
[2] Alegretto Alegretti, p. 836.
[3] Sismondi, note to p. 1406.
[4] Chronicon Venetum in Muratori, xxiv. 8.
[5] Negotiations in Oricellarius, de bello Italico.
[6] Desrey, p. 219. Nardi, 15.

that Piero Capponi seriously challenged the French inside
the city to fight a battle which his party had not dared to
accept outside?[1] Certain it is, at any rate, that the citizens
and the French did not agree well together,[2] that the King
feared treachery, and the town pillage.[3] At last an understanding was arrived at. The principal point of dispute
concerned the House of Medici, whom the King wished to
have restored. However, he only so far attained his point,
that the most rigorous edicts that had been launched against
the Medici, their lives and their house, were withdrawn.
All else was left for the future. Pisa, Leghorn, and the
fortresses ceded by Piero were to remain in French hands
until the conclusion of the expedition against Naples. The
French reserved to themselves great influence, in respect
both of policy and arms.[4] After this had been ratified, the
bells were rung, and " feux de joie " were kindled in the
streets and squares. The king caused messages of peace,
favourable to the renewal of liberty, to be affixed to the
walls; he then prepared to continue his expedition to
Rome and Naples.[5] Savonarola came and warned him
to lose no time; God had sent him, of this he was assured,
but he conjured him not to allow the insolence of his
soldiery to bring to nought the accomplishment of his
object.[6] Charles VIII, in a kind of manifesto, announced
that he had left his wife, his Dauphin and only son,
and his realm; that he was not come to injure anyone,

---

[1] Machiavelli, Decennale. Oricellarius.

[2] Machiavelli, Clizia Commedia. Atto i. Sc. i.

[3] A very vivid picture of the mistrust existing between the French
and the Florentines may be found in the Diario Fiorentino dal 1450 al
1516, by Luca Landucci, edited in the year 1883 by Jodoco del Badia.
Therein we read, under date of the 24th October (p. 85) : " Che ognuno
attese a riempiere le case di pane e d'arme e di sassi e afforzarsi in casa
quanto era possibile, con propositi e animi ognuno volere morire co
l'arme in mano e ammazzare ognuno, se bisognassi, al modo del vespro
Siciliano " (note to 3rd edition).

[4] Petrus Parentius, Diary in Fabroni, Leo, 263. Désjardins,
Négociations, i. 601. The text of the treaty has been published by
Gino Capponi in the Archivio Storico Italiano, Sér. i. vol. i. pp.
362-375 (note to 2nd edition).

[5] Petri Criniti Carmen, cum Carolus ad urbem tenderet, in Roscoe,
Life of Leo, i. Appendix, 510.   [6] Nardi.

but to take possession of Naples, which had been assured
both to his forefathers and to himself by twenty-four in-
vestitures of Roman Popes and holy councils, and whose
harbours and seaboard afforded him the best base of
operations for attacking the Infidels. He demanded a
free passage, otherwise he would proceed by force.

Florence having been metamorphosed by his advent, he
next advanced against his second foe.[1] Pope Alexander
was thrown into perplexity rather than into fear. He said
to Rudolf of Anhalt, who was at that time in Rome:
"This King will demand the name of emperor, as he does
the sovereign power. But assure Maximilian that I would
rather have a sword at my throat than agree to it."[2]
Ferrantino was moving on the one side towards Rome;
he had been long since forsaken by the Florentines and
by the princes of Urbino and Pesaro,[3] and by Caterina
Sforza also, now that he had showed himself incapable of
resisting Aubigny. The people declared they did not
desire war with the French;[4] they even showed themselves
hostile to him and barred his way. Without divesting
himself of his armour,[5] he took the Roman road through
the Romagna. The Pope seriously believed that, with the
assistance of the Neapolitans, he would be able to withstand the King of France advancing from Tuscany.[6] He
did not listen to the assurances of the Sforza and their
adherents. Charles VIII entered Siena through garlanded
gates;[7] he there proclaimed his ban against those who
had been expelled, and left some soldiers behind him. At
Casciano he received the youth of Pisa, who brought him
an offering of roes, hares, and other fruits of the chase.[8]
Thus did Charles VIII arrive within the territory of the
Church.[9] Cardinal Perrault persuaded the inhabitants of
Montefiascone to receive the King peacefully; for such

---

[1] Charles left Florence on the 28th November.
[2] Burcardus, Diarium, p. 2050.   [3] Baldi, Guidobaldo, p. 135.
[4] Passero, Giornale, p. 63.   [5] Zurita, f. 52.
[6] Burcardus, 2053, and Zurita, p. 50.
[7] Desrey, 218.   Sanuto, Spedizione di Carolo, viii. 144 (note to 3rd
edition).
[8] Alegretto Alegretti, pp. 835-837.
[9] Burcardus, Diarium, 2051.

had been the old and real promise of the Pope. As early
as the 10th December he was praying before the relics of
Santa Rosa at Viterbo;[1] and there even an Orsini, whose
family was closely allied with Piero and Alfonso, surrendered to him all his castles and supplies. On all sides,
even on the Tiber, the enemy appeared; Comines narrates,
as an undoubted fact, that a portion of the city wall had
fallen.[2] Ferrantino, on the other hand, had left Rome on
hearing of the King's superior force. Then the Pope sent
his master of the ceremonies, to escort the King into the
city.[3] On the 31st December, 1494, he made his entrance
by torchlight through illuminated streets, amid the ovations
of the people.[4] It could not be Charles's intention to bring
about a reformation of the Church by force, or to seize
the imperial power; purposing, as he did, to attack the
enemies of Christianity, he dared not stir up the whole
of Christendom against himself.[5] But if he had Caesar,
Alexander's son, as a hostage in his train, he was assured
of the Pope. If he occupied Terracina and Cività Vecchia,
the chief harbours from the French to the Neapolitan coast
would be in his hand.

There was at this time in Alexander's keeping a certain
Djem, the brother of Bajazet, who had fled from the latter
to the Christians, but yet had many adherents among the
Turks; a man of resolute principles, who would only
kiss the Pope's arm, and not his feet. Charles, by taking
this man with him, considered himself as good as assured
of success against the Turks.[6] Having obtained these

---

[1] Desrey, 220. On the 22nd December Charles left Viterbo.

[2] Comines, 462. That is also narrated by Sanuto, p. 163 (note to
3rd edition).

[3] Burcardus, on the 31st December.

[4] Trémouille's Memoirs, 147, 148.

[5] From a letter of the Archbishop of St. Malo to Queen Anne of
France, we definitely learn that the deposition of the Pope Alexander
and a thorough reform of the Church were talked of. "Si nostre roy
eust voulu obtempérer à la plupart des Messeigneurs les Cardinaulx ilz
eussent fait ung autre pappe en intention de refformer l'église ainsi
qu'ilz disaient. Le roy désire bien la réformaçion, mais ne veult point
entreprandre de sa depposicion." Pilorgerie, p. 135 (note to 2nd ed.).

[6] Infessura, 2060. Alexander to Maximilian in Datt, Wormser
Acten, p. 852.

advantages, which were moderate, though important, he said, standing on the steps of the papal throne, "Holy Father, I have come to make my obeisance, as my forefathers did."[1]   He was present at the ceremony of the universal Indulgence, received the blessing, and left Rome on the 28th of January, 1495.[2]

Now only Alfonso was left to deal with.   Whilst in Rome he had entered into negotiations with the King through the Pope.   He had offered him large sums of money; a million ducats down and 100,000 ducats annually as a kind of tribute.   The Venetian Republic and the King of Spain were to guarantee the payment.   But, certain of his hereditary right, and filled with his plans against the Turks, Charles VIII rejected all his overtures.[3]   Even then Alfonso did not abandon all hope.   Charles would not, he conceived, be able to advance upon Naples before the spring; meanwhile he would fortify his frontiers, and succour would arrive.[4]   He expected such aid from the King of Spain, who, on a proposal being made him for his youngest daughter for Ferrantino, had shown himself inclined to accede to the request.   He had offered, through Ram Escriva, 500 lances, and even a large army under a grandee, under certain conditions.   It was known of Bajazet, against whom the French expedition was so publicly proclaimed, that he was fitting out a great number of galleys for sea in Constantinople, and had others on the stocks, and further that the Anatolian army had received orders to cross the strait by the first of March, and the Greek army orders to get ready without delay.[5]   His envoy accompanied Alfonso from the army to the capital.[6]

But this winter was just like spring; no rain fell, and even in Lombardy there was no snow; the French expedition suffered no hardships, and met with no resistance anywhere.[7]   Aquila surrendered as soon as the French showed

[1] Desrey, 220.   [2] Burcardus, 2064.
[3] Letter of the Archbishop of St. Malo to Queen Anne in Pilorgerie, p. 138 (note to 2nd edition).
[4] Zurita, f. 49, f. 50.
[5] Chronicon Venetum, p. 11.
[6] Passero, p. 63.   [7] Diarium Ferrarense, p. 290.

themselves.   The Neapolitans began to inquire of one
another whence all this success came.   Many said, "It is a
secret of God;" others, "Their Latin and Greek made
them cowards." [1]

Alfonso himself was at length startled at the universal
despondency.   And when the people rose up in tumult
—no one knew why—and only Ferrantino's presence
calmed them,[2] Alfonso perceived that he could not stand
his ground, and remembered the prophecies which had
been made about him.   He hid himself for three whole
days; the consciousness of his wickedness paralyzed his
energies.   But when the people again rose with the cry,
"The King is dead, for who has seen him alive?" and he
saw that all was lost as regards himself; feeling that he was
loathed and hated with just cause, but that his son, innocent, uncontaminated, young, and brave, the darling of the
people, would assert himself, Alfonso renounced the realm.[3]
They all wept when Jovianus Pontanus drew up the document.[4]   Alfonso bade his son mount a horse and ride through
the city in company with his uncle Federigo.   Even then,
the horror did not leave him; the spectres of his innocent
victims visited him by night; upon his conscience lay the
warning of his father, after whose death people believed all
was going to destruction: "crime entices thee as with an
alluring face, before thou hast committed it; afterwards,
when it is done and a calamity has happened, it still retains
its features; but they are now a hideous picture; for hairs
it has snakes; it is a veritable Medusa's head."   "We will
away from here," said Alfonso to his stepmother, and when
she desired to wait a little longer, exclaimed, "I will throw
myself from the window.   Dost thou not hear how they all
shout the name of the French?"   He tarried no longer,
but fled to Mazzara into a monastery of the Olivetans.[5]

With the intention not to yield, Ferrantino meanwhile
joined his army at the pass of San Germano.   With the

---

[1] Romoncine, Tesoro politico, in Vecchione, p. 107.

[2] Passero, 64.

[3] Passero. Gallo, 8.   Cronica di Napoli di Notar Giacomo, 185.

[4] Bembus, 32, 33.

[5] Comines, 462-467.   Tranchedin to Ludovico in Rosmini, ii. 207.

same intent, Alfonso Davalos held in front of him Monte
San Giovanni, which was considered impregnable.[1]   If
they could only hold out for a while on the frontier, the
people might be gained over, they thought, and succour
arrive. But they could not hold their ground. One day,
after the midday meal, Charles arrived from Bauco before
San Giovanni and ordered it to be stormed. He did not
require to repeat his order, for one and all were determined
to gain honour in his eyes.[2]   On renewing their onslaught
for the third time—for they met with staunch opposition—
they gained the fortress, and spared no one ; they showed
great cruelty. But Charles was on the Garigliano.[3]   The
rapidity and fury of this conquest inspired terror into
Ferrantino's friends and roused the courage of his
enemies.

The citizens of San Germano would resist no more. At
Teano one night Messer Renaudo came to Ferrantino :
" Sire," he cried, " away hence, else you will be delivered over
to the enemy by your own camp."[4]   No hope remained,
save in the citizens of Capua and Naples. On the 16th of
February, Ferrantino felt himself sure of the Capuans ; he
thereupon hurried to the Neapolitans to gain these over
also ; he called a gathering of them in Santa Chiara. " Ye
Sirs, my fathers and brethren," he said, " do ye know me ?
Among you I grew up and was reared. Now that all
forsake me, and I have no one I can trust, will ye also
forsake me ? Not yet ! Only not for fourteen days. If
I have then received no help, do as ye list." He stood
before them in tears ; they were silent, for many loved him.
" Our lord," said a nobleman, " we have neither provisions
nor guns." Ferrantino replied, " There are the keys of the
Castel Nuovo, go and take what you need ; there are a
year's supplies for the whole of Naples there." He was still
speaking, when a messenger came with the tidings that the
enemy was attacking Capua ; in despair he rushed away
and took the road thither.[5]   On his arrival at Aversa, he

---

[1] Passero, 65.   [2] Villeneufve, Mémoires, p. 4.
[3] Chronicon Venetum, p. 13.   Desrey.
[4] Passero. Martinellus to Ascanio in Rosmini, 208.
[5] Passero, 66.   Giacomo, 185.

learnt that of his three chief captains, Trivulzio had gone
over to Charles with his whole army, which had been kept so
long in pay for him.   This he did on the very first day that
he had an opportunity of reciprocating this outlay with his
service.[1]   The other two had fled, and the citizens, on the
16th, and early on the 17th, had sent envoys to Charles,
who begged for mercy with folded hands.[2]   All the same,
it is said, he ventured up to the walls of Capua ; but here he
was met by the Germans, who had alone remained faithful
to him, Caspar's and Gottfried's companies ; they had made
a sortie against the enemy on the other side, but had been
deserted by the Italians.   They had hardly been permitted to withdraw through the town in parties of ten men
each.[3]   It was now evident that all was lost.   Perhaps
Ferrantino when he turned round to go back to Naples,
still hoped, for had not his grandfather here resisted all his
enemies ?   But he found that the nobles, instead of equip-
ping themselves for battle, were plundering the Jews, and
that the populace, when he went into the stables to give
horses to his servants, ran after him and stole them.   Now
all was over ; he felt that the hatred cherished towards his
father and grandfather was now turned against himself.
Full of despair, he drew his sword and turned about with
the words, " What have I done unto your children ? "   But
a faithful servant led him away to his castle out of the
throng, for he would otherwise have been murdered.[4]

Whilst, then, Alfonso Davalos held the castle with 400
Germans, whilst the houses round about, the arsenal and
some ships were burning,[5] and whilst the old Queen
lamented, " O fate, no lance has been broken, and thou
destroyest this kingdom ! " and all were on shipboard, she,
her daughter and the young King, intending to escape to
Ischia, Giacomo Caracciolo, without asking leave, opened
the gate to the French herald, and shouted " Franza ! "

---

[1] Florus, as against which Rebucco in Rosmini, Trivulzio, i. 227, is
improbable.
[2] Desrey.
[3] Jovius, Historiae sui temporis, fol. 30.
[4] Passero.   Johann. Juvenis, de fortuna Tarentinorum, p. 127.
[5] Chronicon Venetum, p. 13.   Navagero, p. 1202.

Hereupon, twenty deputies of the Neapolitans advanced to meet Charles, with the words, " Holy Crown, thou hast been awaited these hundred years in Naples. Now thou art come. Enter as our King and Lord ! "[1] But Charles, whose success had been so brilliant, and who now saw this kingdom, like the French duchies, united to his crown, entered as though into his rightful inheritance. Yet in Capua he had fancied himself wonderfully reminded of his expedition against the Turks ; Djem still lived. It was said that the prestige of the French had prevented the Bassa of Avlona from crossing, and had scared away the Turks from many islands ; even from Negropont they were flying to Constantinople. When Grimani with Venetians passed by Lepanto, they thought it was the French, and retired from the castle and the shore. The peninsula and the mainland gathered fresh hope.[2]

[1] Diarium Ferrarense, p. 294.
[2] Corio, 939. Bembus, 34 b. Benedictus, p. 1583. Chronicon Venetum, p. 8.

CHAPTER II

SPAIN AND THE LEAGUE AT WAR WITH CHARLES VIII

1495–1496

———◆◇◆———

1. UNITED SPAIN

AT this time Spain was first heard and spoken of; this country had a short time previously become consolidated into a united and powerful kingdom out of two disunited and feeble principalities, Castile and Aragon.   With regard to Castile, the manuscript of Alonso de Palenzia records that there existed a law of Henry of Trastamara to the effect that, "without permission of the King of France, no Englishman should go to Castile, nor a Castilian to England." Such a disgraceful compact was actually kept by these weak monarchs.[1]   John I relied in battle even more upon the French than upon his Castilians; John II appeared to many to be almost bewitched by his favourite Alvaro de Luna;[2] the Portuguese, Pacheco and Giron, after overthrowing Alvaro, obtained control over Henry IV.   Henry, though a huntsman, and an enemy of baths and wine, but deprived of noble indignation and manly strength by early profligacy,[3] had scarcely turned away from them—not to be his own master, but to take another favourite—when they revolted, and with them all the nobles.   They declared his daughter Juana to be illegitimate, and favoured his brother's

[1] Ferrera's Spanish History from this Manuscript, vii. B. p. 47.
[2] Rodericus Santius, Historia Hispanica, iv. c. 31.
[3] Hernando Pulgar, Claros Varones, p. 4.

succession, and, when the latter died, that of his sister Isabella; but she did not desire to be called queen, and was content that the succession should be assured to her issue.[1]

Near kinsmen of this family ruled in Aragon, yet with no better fortune, in spite of their having inherited from Ferdinand I. a crown adjudged him by the three counties of which Aragon consisted, great estates in Castile, and valid claims to Naples. These claims Alfonso took over from his son, and succeeded in establishing them; yet he afterwards gave Naples to his illegitimate son, and separated it from Aragon. The estates in Castile devolved upon Henry; but at Olmedo, where he fought against John II, and was defeated, they were lost to the house, and came into the hands of those Portuguese favourites. Even the crown was in danger, when John of Aragon, to whom it had passed, was attacked by his eldest son, and by all the Catalans.

Let us now picture to ourselves how the union and the consolidation of these kingdoms was brought about. The same men who had seized the Aragonese estates had procured for Isabella the succession in Castile. Now, when John's enemies were dead and he triumphant, and they began to feel alarmed, Isabella betrothed herself with the man whom they dreaded most, namely, Ferdinand, the youngest son of John, and his heir. Seated on a mule, in disguise, Ferdinand came to Valladolid to celebrate the nuptials;[2] then they did not hesitate to swear allegiance to Juana, and to offer her hand and realm to the King of Portugal.[3] This was the origin of the war, a war that was waged on all points between Fuenterrabia and Gibraltar at the same time: a war in which Juan Ulloa fought against Rodrigo Ulloa,[4] his brother, Pedro Zuñiga against his father,[5] and the Count of Salinas against his sister;[6] while the cities, which sided with Aragon, fought against their castles, which

[1] Antonius Nebrissensis, Rerum a Fernando et Elisabe gestarum Decades, p. 801.

[2] Ferdinand himself in Zurita.   [3] Antonius Nebriss. p. 802.
[4] Ibid. 821.   [5] Ibid. 835.
[6] Ibid. 895.

favoured Portugal. But at last Ferdinand and Isabella
were victorious at Toro, and succeeded in ridding the
country of the enemy.   They founded the convent of
St. Francis at Toledo, and proceeded in two directions to
pacify the country—the Queen to the Andalusian cities,
and the King to the castles on the Duero.   Against the
castles—for, as a fact, the country had been pillaged, and
all robbers had sheltered themselves in them—he was
assisted by the cities and their Hermandad, who, in order
to punish robberies and murders in the streets, squares,
and houses, maintained 2000 horsemen and a proportionate
strength of infantry.[1]   They lent their assistance, as though
their sole aim was the general peace, yet their object was
also a political one in the interest of Ferdinand.   He
wrested the castles from his enemies.   Isabella, meanwhile,
presided at tribunals of justice at Seville every Friday,
surrounded by bishops and lawyers, and with clerks before
her.   But here, where the Duke of Medina Sidonia and
Juan de Cordova were of her party, and the Marquis of
Cadiz and Alfonso de Aguilar against her, and where the
enmity of the old Christians, the new converts, the Jews,
and the neighbouring Moors, divided streets and families,[2]
her rigour was ineffectual.   She resolved to pardon all
offences, save and except heresy.   The latter, with which
the judgment hall of the Hermandad was as incompetent
to deal as the Dominican Inquisition, which had been long
since abolished, was reserved for another tribunal.

In September, 1478, she quitted Seville; on the 1st
of November, Sixtus IV, who at the same time revoked
the dispensation granted to the King of Portugal to marry
Juana,[3] gave the Kings (under which title Ferdinand and
Isabella were now known) the right to appoint inquisitors
against heretics, apostates, and their patrons.[4]   Unexcep-
tionable accounts testify[5] to the fact, that it was the
representations of Tomas de Torquemada, a prior of the
Holy Cross, who declared that "those who had been

[1] Antonius, 851.   [2] *Ibid.* 861.
[3] Ferrera's Hist. of Spain, vol. xi. § 235.
[4] Llorente, Histoire de l'Inquisition, vol. i. p. 145.
[5] Marineus Siculus, p. 481.

converted, went by night into the synagogue, kept the
sabbath and the Jewish Easter, and celebrated, barefooted,
the day of Remembrance," which primarily caused the insti-
tution of this tribunal; a lamentable fatality, if, as Pulgar
states,[1] the Torquemadas were also originally Jews, and it
was thus a quarrel between the converted and the unconverted Jews which brought the Inquisition upon the people
of Castile and Aragon. But if we remember that the
influence of the Jews over the grandees, due to their
farming their revenues, their affluence, and their relationship to them, conflicted secretly and at all points with
the Kings' interests,[2] that the first order of the Inquisitors
threatened the Marquis of Cadiz, an opponent of the
monarchs, in case he sheltered the fugitive Jews, and that
it was a Jewish book against the Government that brought
matters to a crisis,[3] the general connection of events becomes
clear. The Inquisition harmonized with the Hermandad
in form—for they each had originally two judges and a
fiscal—as also mainly in aim; viz. the termination of this
war and the consolidation of the royal power, under the
cover of a far wider plan; yet the ecclesiastical power of
the one was far more arbitrary than the civil power of the
other. After some hesitation, Isabella had the Quemadero
erected on the plain before Seville, between the four
prophets;[4] the convent of the Dominicans in the city
was soon too small to hold the accused,[5] and 5000 houses
in Andalusia were empty.[6] But the people began to obey.
As soon as Pacheco consented to resign a great part of his
estates, and the King of Portugal to renounce his claims,
and when everybody surrendered, the civil war came to a
close, and the royal power was at the same time re-established. For these institutions still continued under the
pretence of general policy, and others were added to them.
When the grand masters of two of the Spanish orders

[1] Claros Varones, p. 24.

[2] Caracciolus, Epistola de Inquisitione, in Muratori, Scrip. xxii.
97. Cf. as to the condition of the Jews, Bernaldez, Reyes Catolicos in
Prescott, Hist. of the Reign of Ferdinand and Isabella the Catholic,
i. 339 (note to 2nd edition).

[3] Llorente, pp. 148, 149.   [4] *Ibid.* p. 152 and fol.
[5] Ferrera, xi. § 320.   [6] Marineus Siculus, p. 483

of knighthood had died, and the third was inclined to
retire, Ferdinand undertook to manage all three. In truth
a goodly power; for the order of Santiago alone could put
1000 heavy cavalry into the field; and a schedule of the
fifteenth century ranks its grand masters among the princes
and independent heads of Europe.[1] Further, since the
Pope had given way in the matter of some disputes touching the sees of Saragossa, Cuenca, and Tarragona, the rule
was established that no one could be raised to the rank of
bishop upon whom the King had not previously declared
his willingness to confer this dignity.[2]

Let us now observe : the Hermandad. was modelled on
a former independent coalition of the citizens against the
nobles, and it now committed the civic power into the hands
of the King. The grandmasterships, through the Enco-
miendas, bound the knights who had received them, as
well as all noble families, out of gratefulness or expectation
of future favours, to the King. The latter, by his Inquisition and the election of bishops, became almost the head of
the clergy. We perceive that it was not so much that
Ferdinand and Isabella extended the royal power handed
down to them from their ancestors, as that they gave it
a new basis ; they placed themselves at the head of the
Estates who might have resisted them, and who resisted
their forefathers, and, concentrating their powers in their
own persons, became their real chiefs. In all this the
Church, by handing over to them the Inquisition and
Mayorazgos, and by conceding to them by degrees even
the Tercias of the ecclesiastical tithes in perpetuity, rendered
them the greatest service, and they had no more dangerous
foes than the enemies and apostates of the Church of Rome.
The traditional liberties still continued ; even in Castile
the noble might surrender his fief back into the King's
hand,[3] and retract his allegiance, whilst the citizen might
shut his house against the royal officer;[4] but obedience

---

[1] In Sanuto's Venetian history in Muratori, xxii. 963.

[2] Mariana, de rebus Hispaniae, xxiv. c. 16.

[3] Mariana, xiii. 599.

[4] Hallam from Marino, Ensayo critico, in The State of Europe
during the Middle Ages, i. 762.

to duty became established. The rigorous Isabella, who rode in person after the son of the Admiral Fadrique Enriquez who had broken her safe-conduct and fled; who had the alcalde, who had killed a royal servant, hanged on the very spot where he had committed the deed; and who ordered the hand of the grand alcalde Villenas, to be cut off merely for not preventing it,[1] soon brought it about that travellers from Spain spoke of it as one of the wonders of that land, that there no one dared do wrong, not even the authorities themselves, since it was immediately punished.[2] And thus Isabella sat amongst the images of the saints in her chapel, with her escutcheon quartered with a castle, a staff, a lion, and an eagle, behind her; Cardinals, Archbishops, Bishops, and Orators, on the one side, and the Constable, Admiral, Dukes, Marquises, and Counts, on the other, the priests in full canonicals before her, all awaiting her sign.[3] Her policy aimed at absolute power over an orthodox kingdom.

Now that the internal disorders had ceased, and the government had been reorganized, the Kings turned their eyes unceasingly towards the outer world, Christian as well as infidel, and first towards the latter. According to the example of their forefathers, Ferdinand the Great and the Saint, the four Alonsos, the Emperor, Ramon, the Noble, and the Eleventh, who ventured not to wage war with the Moors until they had first been victorious in a civil war, but who engaged in the former as soon as they had succeeded in the latter, thus did they, under the standard of the Cross, each division under a crucifix, as the song goes, invade the plain of Granada.[4] They swore not to leave it until they had taken the city; they centred the attention and the obedience of the whole nation upon this point, and at last conquered it. But as the different kingdoms had always been in the habit of dividing beforehand what they intended to conquer, and were hardly less jealous of what they coveted than of what

---

[1] Ferrera, viii. 92.
[2] Senarega, Annales Genuenses, in Muratori, xxiv. 534.
[3] Marineus Siculus, p. 506.
[4] Guerras Civiles de Granada, by Perez de Hita, tom. iii. p. 145.

they had already taken, so at the present time they claimed
the African kingdoms of Oran and Tlemcen for the crown
of Aragon, and for Sicily, Tunis and the eastern slope of
the Atlas. These claims were also confirmed by the Pope,
and they hoped to push on in an easterly direction to
Egypt, and to come as far as Jerusalem. In the West,
Castile claimed all that had formerly been Mauritania and
Tingitana. This led to a war with Portugal. At last they
agreed together, that, with the exception of Melita and
Caçaça, Portugal should be at liberty to conquer the whole
of Fez. But this was of minor importance. For, when
Pope Alexander promised the conquest of the whole of
Africa to the united crowns, those maritime expeditions
were endangered, in which the Portuguese, planting their
standard ever further and further afield, had learnt of an
Eastern and Christian monarch, the King of Abyssinia,[1] and
by which they hoped to find this potentate—for already a
Portuguese had been in Goa and had discovered the Cape
—and by his help, proceeding along the coast,[2] to reach
the real India and the land of spices. But, finally, the old
treaties remained valid ; the right of navigating to Guinea
and the coast downwards was assigned to the Portuguese,[3]
and they were entitled to prevent any one else from sailing
on this route. But Providence willed that something unexpected should result from these differences ; and what
actually happened far surpassed human calculations.

At Lisbon there lived two brothers from Genoa, Bartholomew Columbus, who drew maps for the use of sailors,[4] and
Christopher, the elder, who had navigated with varying
fortune the Mediterranean and the Atlantic from the
Canaries to Iceland.[5] These two often discussed together
what every one knew, and became convinced that the
safest plan to discover that land of precious stones, pearls,
and spices,[6] that Sypango of which Marco Polo had written,[7]

[1] Barros, Asia, iii. c. 2, 3, 4.
[2] Sommario Pietro Martir's in Ramusio, 3, 1.
[3] Mariana, xxiv. c. 10.
[4] Antonius Gallus, Commentariolus de navigatione Colombi, p. 300.
[5] Jagemann, Geschichte der ital. Literatur, iii. 111.
[6] Petrus Martyr, decas Oceanea, i. f. 1.
[7] Barros, Asia, iii. c. 9.

a land into which Christianity could be introduced, would
be, not by voyaging along the coast of Africa, but by
sailing ever westward, and thus circumnavigating the globe.
But no King, no Duke, and no Signoria, would believe the
brothers. At length the two Kings, in their joy over the
victory of Granada, being at Santa Fé three months later,
took the advice of the same Alonso Quintanilla who had
first projected the new Hermandad,[1] and hazarded this
venture. They put three caravels at the disposal of the
elder Columbus, and had them manned for the most part
by sailors from the vicinity of Palos.[2] Tradition goes, that
these coast-seamen, after spending week by week between
heaven and water, only gazing upon seaweed and seeing
no land, threatened to murder their captain. The captain
the while, working by day with the lead, and by night
keeping his eye intent upon the fixed stars, and even in his
dreams full of visions of success, remained firm of purpose
and managed to curb all opposition ; until at last looming
clouds inspired hopes, and in the night a sailor shouted,
" light and land ; " when day broke, hills, high trees, and
green land were discovered ; he shed tears, and falling on
his knees, said the " Te Deum Laudamus." They erected
on the coast an enormous cross, heard the notes of the first
nightingale, saw the timid good people,[3] and returned to
tell their king of the country they had taken posssession of
in his name.[4]

The immediate result of this divine favour and the
discovery of Columbus was to continue the quarrel between Portugal and Castile. The wind drove the returning
party to Lisbon. As soon as the King of Portugal saw
that the natives, who had been brought back, looked like

[1] Oviedo, Sommario, in Ramusio, iii. 80, compared with Antonius
Nebrissensis, p. 847.

[2] Oviedo, p. 81, and Dillon's Journey to Spain, ii. 102.

[3] All taken from the Sommarios of Pietro and Oviedo, p. 16,
p. 810, and from the Decas, i. 1. It is evident that in this short
mention of the great event neither its worldwide importance could be
enlarged upon, nor its course critically examined in detail ; it is treated
only in its local origin with reference to the undertakings which at that
time proceeded from the Iberian peninsula (note to 2nd edition).

[4] Christophori Columbi Epistola in Hisp. Illustr. ii. 1282.

the Indians, as they had been described to him, and heard from Columbus, that he had there been told of a land called Sybang,[1] he began to be afraid that he had been forestalled. He requested the Kings to send expeditions, not south-wards, but northwards, according to the old compact.[2] They also believed, as he did, that they had come to the point where east and west touched ; they little knew the size of the world; they bargained long together, and finally fixed a mark, 370 *leguas* from the Canary Islands, to the east of which Portugal should conduct discoveries, and to the west, Spain.[3] This was quite a different matter from their quarrel about Fez and Tingitana ; but they still went on in the old fashion.

Such were the operations of the united kingdoms against the Infidels, and, if the conquest of Granada was celebrated in all Christian lands with feasting and games, much more did the report of a new earth and a new race of men ring throughout Europe. These kingdoms now turned their eyes again towards the interior of Christendom. The grandees had delivered up those crown estates to which they could show no legal title, and which were, at the lowest estimate, computed to be worth nearly thirty million mara-vedi. Cadiz and the Isla were recovered from the family of Ponce de Leon, and Roussillon was restored by France. The time had come, in which the idea of a United Spain for the first time asserted itself. The Pope initiated the title "Serene Kings of the Spains," seeing that Northern and Central Spain, Baetica, and a portion of Lusitania had become united, in the sense in which the title "Catholic King" is said to have been originally framed.[4]

The renewed unity of the French kingdom impelled Charles VIII to look towards Naples, and in the same way the unity of Spain, asserting itself now for the first time, induced Ferdinand and Isabella to turn their attention thither also. The rights of the former clashed here with those of the latter.

[1] Barros, Asia, iii. 9.
[2] Zurita, Historia del Rey Hernando, i. 30, 31.
[3] Zurita, f. 36.
[4] Márineus Siculus, p. 164. Franciscus Tarapha, de Regibus Hispaniae. Hispan. Illustr. i. 567.

2. CONNECTION BETWEEN SPAIN AND ITALY

The two Sicilies had from time immemorial been the source of strife between the Spanish and French houses, a strife which began with the death of the last Hohenstaufen, and had not yet been fought out. It was on the point of being taken up on both sides by third houses. At first it had been carried on between the Angevins, who had been called in by the Pope, and the Barcelonese House of Aragon, the heirs of Conradin, that is, between the Provenças and the Catalans, who are in reality one race, of the same origin, and speaking the same language. The former took Naples, the latter Sicily, and ever since they had been in feud with each other.

Secondly, this long-standing dispute devolved upon Alfonso I, of the House of Aragon, and the younger branch of the Angevins. Alfonso with the Catalans was victorious, and gained possession of Naples. Although before the people he took his stand upon the new right conferred by his adoption, although this had been revoked, yet he confessed after the victory that his greatest joy was, that he had regained what had belonged to his ancestors.[1] Connected with this is the war of Ferrante with John of Anjou.

Thirdly when the rights of the Angevins had at length passed to the crown of France, the united kingdoms, in opposition to them, felt themselves pledged to protect the interests of the Cataans. Ferdinand had often been urged by the barons to make war on Ferrante, but had always answered, "He is my brother-in-law." [2] But now if Charles was victorious, he would lose one prospect, viz., the establishment of his rights, and saw even Sicily threatened. The Kings of Spain were bound by the treaty of Roussillon, but had never approved the enterprises of Charles VIII.

While Charles was making his preparations, they proposed to him an expedition against Africa with their rights to support him; when he was already in the Alps, they equipped a fleet in Biscay; when he turned against

---

[1] Marineus Siculus, de Vita Alfonsi V.
[2] Zurita, "casado con su hermana."

Tuscany, they endeavoured to rouse Ludovico's ambition by offering him an alliance with their house and the royal title. Charles arrived at Florence; they then despatched Lorenzo Figueroa to Venice, in order to arrange an alliance, perhaps without any formal proclamation.[1] But when the French King was in arms in Rome, and had already occupied the cities of the Church, they laid hold of a clause in their treaty, "*reserving the rights of the Church*," a clause which Charles agreed to, so long as Alexander was a friend to the Sforza and belonged to his party. Ferdinand was the first to make it important by helping to win over the Pope. If the Catholic Kings displayed any care for Christendom as a whole, it was agreeably to their own interests. Relying on this clause, their envoys,[2] one for Aragon and one for Castile, betook themselves to the States of the Church, met Charles near Rome, and, on his refusal to accede to their demand that he should restore the cities and uphold the treaty, tore up the document embodying it. This cannot be exactly called faithlessness, but a faithful observance of treaties it certainly was not. Ferdinand and Isabella then took under their protection Alexander, whose son had long since fled from the French King, and Ferrantino, who had betrothed himself with their niece Juana, and had fled with her from Naples, and promised them certain Neapolitan castles as security for their war expenses. They were now in a position to form a new league against Charles.

Now after Charles had left Ludovico il Moro, differences arose between them on account of some transactions in Tuscany, Rome, and Naples. Sarzana and Sarzanella, which had been objects of contention between the Genoese and Florentines until Charles's arrival, Ludovico had vainly hoped to obtain from the latter for his city. He found fault with the peace concluded with Alexander, because he himself was not sufficiently benefited by it.[3] He was vexed on seeing his rebels, the Milanese Trivulzio, and the Genoese Fregoso and Fiesco taken into Charles's

---

[1] Zurita, f. 38, 41, 46, 47.
[2] Argensola, Annales, p. 50. Florus, p. 15.
[3] Ludovico to Ascanio in Rosmini, ii. 208.

service at Naples, and in consequence refused to allow French ships to anchor at Genoa.[1] Meanwhile a danger threatened him nearer home. Duke Louis of Orleans, upon whom there had devolved, through a legitimate daughter of the House of Visconti, better claims to Milan[2] than were those which the Sforza deduced from an illegitimate offspring, was at Asti, as though only waiting for a favourable opportunity to assert these claims. His servants openly declared that he would soon be Duke of Milan; and as he was collecting troops, and had at least no resistance to fear from Charles, Ludovico began to tremble for his own power.[3] He addressed himself first of all to Maximilian, who had only a short time previously solemnly conferred upon him the investiture,[4] and who, among all princes, was almost his nearest relative. Maximilian, too, had received Alexander's message, and might well be anxious for the imperial dignity. His envoys throughout Italy also complained when they saw the lilies displayed instead of the eagle, for the suzerainty belonged to the Emperor.[5] Yet most of all was he moved by this, and was ever repeating it to the princes of the Empire: that Charles was threatening Genoa, and Louis Milan, so that urgent help against them was necessary. But the need of the Venetians was more urgent than Maximilian's, and quite as sore as Ludovico's. They feared for their own existence, now that Aubigny had penetrated as far as Forlì. They raised money when Charles was in Florence; directly he reached Rome, without meeting with resistance, they gathered a force of several thousand light Albanian cavalry, their Stradioti;[6] and now that he had Naples, and the castles had fallen into his hands, and they had heard of Louis' plans, they were seized with the utmost fear. One morning they were sitting together, as was their wont, sixty or seventy in number, in the Doge's chamber, when the French ambassador entered. They

[1] Ludovico to Charles in Rosmini, 213.
[2] Extrait d'un discours, touchant le droit sur le Duché de Milan, by Tillet. Comines, Preuves, ii. 321.
[3] Instructio Casati in Rosmini.
[4] Sanseverino to Ludovico in Rosmini.
[5] Allegretto Allegretti, Diari di Siena, p. 838.
[6] Chronicon Venetum in Muratori, xxiv. 8, 9, *seq.*

sat, with their eyes fixed on the ground, and their heads resting on their hands. No one broke silence, no one looked at him. The Doge then spoke : " Your master has the castles of Naples; will he remain our friend ? " The envoy assured them that such would be the case.[1] What troubled them was not the destruction of the unity of Italy only, but their own danger. For we must remember that the claims of Louis of Orleans to Milan might also be extended to a great part of the Venetian possessions, which had once been in the power of Gian Galeazzo Visconti, his ancestor, and which had afterwards been conquered by the Republic. If the one were taken, there was certainly reason to fear for the rest.

We see that Maximilian, Ludovico, and Venice were natural allies. It was to Ferdinand's advantage to join this league, not by himself, but with his allies Ferrantino and the Pope. But could Ludovico trust Alexander, who had only shortly before this broken faith with him ? Suarez insisted that it was not his power, but his name that was wanted.[2] And further, could they receive into the league Ferrantino, who no longer possessed anything or could afford any assistance ? Yet, all the same, his ambassadors went to Worms and appeared before the Emperor, praying to be included in the league.[3] At length, on the 29th March, 1495, after frequent negotiations had been carried in secret, even by night, an understanding was arrived at. Suarez exclaimed, " Charles made the wound, and we have found its cure."[4] The Venetians now invited the French ambassador again. " We have concluded an alliance," said the Doge, " against the Turks for the peace of Italy and the security of our possessions." A hundred nobili were there, holding their heads high, bold and joyous, for they knew that an army of more than 50,000 men would take the field against Charles.[5] The ambassador departed, it is said, surprised and perplexed. On the stairs Spinello, the

---

[1] Comines.   [2] Zurita, f. 61.

[3] Datt, de pace publica, p. 523.

[4] Peter Justinianus, Historia Veneta, from Hieron. Donatus, Apologia, p. 148.

[5] Comines, Mémoires, i. 490.

Neapolitan envoy, met him with a beaming face and in a
fine new dress. Coming down, he begged the secretary who
accompanied him to repeat to him what the Doge had said.[1]
It is Comines of whom this is related ; he himself will not
confess to it ; he asserts that he knew everything. In the
afternoon the envoys of the allies, to the number of fifty,
were conveyed in pleasure barks, decorated with the arms
and ensigns of their respective masters, to the strains of
music and song, through the Grand Canal, between the
marble halls on either side. They passed under the
windows of Comines, and the Milanese envoy, at all events,
pretended not to know him. In the evening, torches,
cannon and illuminations proclaimed the new League.[2]
Ten days later, Venice had 21,000 men in the field ; on
Palm Sunday the League was proclaimed in the countries of
the respective allies. Comines and Louis of Orleans wrote
six times within six days to France that fresh troops were
needed. King Charles was informed of the danger that was
approaching.

3. RETREAT OF CHARLES VIII

It is both the life and the fortune of the Germano-Latin
nations that they never become united. These negotiations
and these preparations, with which the real struggle of the
Spaniards and French began, were the beginning of a
far-reaching and long-lasting division, which completely
altered the face and form of Europe. In the first instance,
if Charles's expedition threatened danger to the Turks,
they were certainly advantageous to the latter.

Djem was now dead. An instruction of Alexander to his
Turkish ambassador and letters of Bajazet to the Pope are
extant, of perfectly horrible contents. The Pope is asked
to "raise Djem from the troubles of this world into another,
where he might enjoy greater repose ; in return for which
he, Sultan Bajazet Chan, would pay him 300,000 ducats."[3]
And it is well that we have reason to doubt the genuineness

---

[1] Bembus, Historiae Venetae, pp. 34–36.
[2] Comines. Carraciolus, Vita Spinelli, Cariati Comitis, p. 43.
[3] Burcardi Diarium, p. 2056.

of the documents. Djem, however, actually died suddenly;
and whilst the Christian writers speak of poison, the Turkish
annals[1] contain this passage: "Mustapha Bey killed Djem with
the help of the Pope." Little blame is due to Charles for not
having actually embarked on the expedition he had intended
to make, and on which he had already despatched the Archbishop of Durazzo and the Despots of the Morea.[2] He would
gladly have concluded a treaty with Ferrantino. Federigo,
too, before the League was formed, came once more, found
the King sitting under an olive tree near the new castle, and
begged a territory for Ferrantino, and the title of King; but
Charles cautiously answered, "Not here, but in France;"
and thereupon they separated.[3] He contented himself
with bringing nobles, citizens and people of Naples into
peace and harmony. All the barons came to pay allegiance to him, and received back their estates, which they
had lost through the Aragonese kings. With the exception
of a few, who still held out, all cities sent their syndics
with the keys, and received marks of favour:[4] Taranto,
for instance, permission to select its syndic from among
the middle class of citizens, the Onorati,[5] and the Neapolitans a like permission to choose an Eletto with a council of
twelve from their midst.[6] He remitted to the propertied

---

[1] Leonclavii Annales Turcici, p. 154. Daru, Histoire de Venise,
iii. 164, from Saadud-Din-Mehemed-Hassan.

[2] Oricellarius, p. 66.

[3] Desrey, 223. Passero, 70. Giacomo, 188. The negotiations
can be followed in a letter of the King, dated 28 March, 1495, to
Bourbon, which contains this passage: "Frédéric (Federigo) me
supplia et requist, que je voulusse bien laisser à son nepveu (Ferrantino)
le tiltre du royaume et quelque pension pour vivre telle qu'il me
plairoit adviser." The King replied, before his departure his right and
title to the kingdom had been investigated in France and solemnly
recognized, and then further, "Je n'estois point déliberé de riens
laisser ni quitter de mon héritage et dudit tiltre—que s'il s'en vouloit
venir en France, je luy donneroye pour son état xxx mille livres de
rente et xxx mille livres de pension chacun an, et des gensd'armes,
avecques ce que je le maryerois en quelque lieu de mon royaume de
manière qu'il auroit cause de se contenter" (Pilorgerie, Campagne et
Bulletins, p. 212) (note to 2nd edition).

[4] Passero, 7.

[5] Joh. Juvenis, de fortuna Tarentinorum, p. 127.

[6] Giacomo, 204. Gallo, 67. Cf. Reumont, die Caraffa von
Maddaloni, i. 124 (note to 2nd edition).

classes 200,000 ducats of their annual dues, and to those who had nothing he promised 12,000 ducats as an annual present. He fed the poorest on Maundy Thursday,[1] and when he visited the wonders of the land—the grotto of Posilippo, which he was told had been artificially made by Virgil, the wondrous springs, the chasms in the earth, full of hot wind[2]—and gazed on the fatness of the land in spring : when he sat at the tournament, and saw how French and Italians tilted in the ring together, and how the Princess of Melfi rode as straight as a knight on her horse, the red and white feathers waving from her hat, her hair floating in dainty tresses about her ruff and her knightly tunic of green brocade ;[3] amid such amusements and occupations he undoubtedly felt contented and happy.   With satisfaction he noted in his letters the restoration of good order and justice in the land hitherto so oppressed, and the homage paid him on all sides in consequence.   They evinced the feeling that he had happily accomplished a great undertaking.   In the midst of these pleasures, the news of the League and its preparations reached him.   The restoration of Roussillon and Artois had, after all, been in vain.   How could the powerful foes in his rear at Milan, Venice, and Rome have permitted a Turkish campaign ?   In order not to be cut off from France, he must of necessity return thither.   Once more he entered the city, with a crown on his head and an orb in his hand, to make and to receive the vow.[4]   The citizens lifted up their sons of five, ten, and twelve years of age to him, in order that he should dub them knights.[5]   He appointed Bourbon, Duke of Montpensier, viceroy, lord, and commander of the kingdom, took one half of his troops with him, and returned on the road by which he had come.[6]   He hurried, in order not to be overtaken by the heat.

The Pope fled before him from Rome to a fortress ;[7]

---

[1] Lettre à la Duchesse de Bourbon in Godefroy, 739.

[2] Desrey, 224.

[3] Lettre, *ibid.*   [4] Giacomo, 190.

[5] André de la Vigne, Histoire du voyage de Naples, in Godefroy, p. 200.

[6] *Ibid.*, and Desrey, p. 224 b.

[7] Navagero, Historia Veneta, p. 1204.

those who are well-informed assert that Charles would otherwise have taken further steps against him.[1] At Siena he
heard the complaints of the Riformatori against the Nove—
these were the factions of the city—and took the part of the
complainers, who called him their king and lord. He left a
garrison behind him there.[2] On the first day of his arrival
at Pisa, the children greeted him, all dressed in white silk,
embroidered with lilies ; and, on the next day, the men—
they desired to be his subjects ; on the third, the ladies and
citizens' wives, but these barefooted and in mourning, praying that he would see fit to take them under his protection.[3] These good people had scarcely a piece of fine
cloth left in their shops that they did not give to the commanders of the army.[4] Particularly they gained over the
Swiss, who appeared before the King at the play with their
axes over their shoulders, and begged him to guarantee the
freedom of the city. Charles so far agreed as to say that he
would act so that every one should be contented.[5] And
there he stood again at the foot of the Apennines, where the
Bardonian Alp from the Magra across to the Taro—a pass
which even the Longobards thought it worth while to fortify
with castles and strongholds [6]—separates Tuscany from
Lombardy. In Naples the League had been ridiculed in a
comedy; [7] and as yet Charles had seen no enemy, nor
feared any. But Savonarola had told him that the God who
had brought him in would surely lead him out ; nevertheless,
because he had not ameliorated the condition of his Church,
he would be scourged.

The League had actually already occupied Naples, which
he had only just quitted, as well as the territory of Milan
which lay before him. In Naples there appeared under
Gonzalvo de Aguilar, Ferdinand's Biscayans, Galicians, and
horsemen. Gaeta revolted, and Ferrantino pushed forward
into Calabria. This first attack was repulsed by the French,
who took Gaeta, not even sparing those who clutched the

---

[1] Oricellarius, de bello Italico, p. 68.   [2] Allegretto Allegretti.
[3] André de la Vigne, pp. 204, 205, 206.   [4] Nardi, p. 24.
[5] Comines, 501.
[6] Paulus Diaconus, v. 27, vi. 58.
[7] Burcardus, Diarium Roman. p. 2067.

crucifix for their protection,[1] and drove Ferrantino back.
Only one Neapolitan, Juan de Altavilla, comported himself bravely. Seeing the King fall with his horse, he dismounted, gave him up his own, and by a soldier's death
gained the eternal glory of fidelity.[2] All the rest fled. But
now Otranto, of its own accord, raised the Aragonese cry of
" Fierro : " [3] and in Naples, when two persons met in the
street, they asked, " Brother, when comes the Sponsor ? "
meaning Ferrantino. The decisive issue was expected in a
short time. On the 4th of July the beacons of Capri
announced that he was really coming.[4] Lombardy was in
great commotion on both sides. The Duke of Orleans,
immediately on the outbreak of hostilities, took the field
forthwith with his lances, Gascons, and Swiss, which were
sent to the King's assistance.[5] He was invited to go to
Milan and Pavìa, for the new taxes that Ludovico had
imposed for the purposes of the war had excited the
populace. Following the two Opizi, he had been received
in Novara and proclaimed Duke. Immediately on the
receipt of this news, Ludovico betook himself to the
Venetian envoy, to entreat his good services with the
Republic; he pressed a valuable emerald into his hand.[6]
He himself collected all his energies to rid himself of the
enemy. Venice bestirred herself in real earnest. In spite
of her strong army in the field, she issued orders throughout
the province that one man of every family should equip himself for active service.[7] The allies at once invested Novara,
and intercepted Charles's retreat. It was improbable that
he would advance by way of Bologna; yet there also they
prepared to meet him. He must either take the road from
Parma or from Genoa. Early in June, a strong force was

---

[1] Passero, 74.

[2] Jovii historia sui temporis, 48.

[3] Galateus, de situ Japygiae, p. 14.

[4] Passero, 72, 76.

[5] St. Gelais, Extraict d'une histoire, in Godefroy, p. 180. His
feelings are shown by a letter of 23rd April, given by Cherrier,
Histoire du Charles VIII, vol. ii. p. 491 : "Je pense faire ung tel
service au roi, que en long temps en sera parlé" (note to 2nd edition).

[6] Corio, 941, and Jovius, 38.

[7] Chronicon Venetum, p. 23.

in position in the Parmese mountains ; and Ludovico wrote
to Genoa, "We are ready ; get ready also." On receipt of
this message, Conradin Stanga made every preparation for
resistance.[1] If Charles took the road by the Riviera, Louis
of Orleans would be isolated ; but, on the other hand, did
he take his old road across the mountains, he would be
obliged to forego all hopes of conquering Genoa, his fief,
which Ludovico had now forfeited. He chose the more
difficult of the two; he chose to march across the
mountains,[2] whilst Fregoso, Giuliano, and Philippe de
Bresse made an attack upon Genoa. On his road he was
continually reminded that he had Swiss with him. These
troops had always caused him much trouble. At the very
outset, on the expedition to Naples, their sack of Rapallo
roused almost the whole of Genoa to arms against them.
At Siena their bad discipline again made itself felt. At
Rome it was within an ace that an open battle took place
between them and the Spaniards ; and in Naples, on one
occasion, the shops had to be closed in consequence of
their tumultuous behaviour.[3] And now, on the retreat,
they fell upon the city of Pontremoli with pillage and
murder, in spite of the assurances of the commanders to
the contrary, because they thought that they had something still to avenge from their previous march through.[4]
Their exuberance of health and physical strength incited
them to take disproportionate vengeance for every little
insult. The same exuberance of health and vigour, however, rendered them amenable to every good impression.
In the same way as they had formerly offered to forego the
pay for which they had undertaken to serve, on condition
that Charles would promise to guarantee the liberty of Pisa,
so now they soon regretted having destroyed supplies that
were urgently needed, and presented themselves before the
King saying, that if he would forgive them they would
harness themselves to the cannon[5] which he was at a loss

[1] Chronicon Venetum, p. 23.
[2] *Ibid.* p. 21. Comines.
[3] Florus, Allegretti, Burcardus, and Passero.
[4] Comines. Spazzarini, Framenti Storici, in Rosmini, ii. 217.
[5] Comines, 508.

how to transport across the mountains. A brave knight of the King's retinue, of the name of La Trémouille, undertook to lead them. He once, while still a boy, when Louis XI was fighting with the barons, had, in childish earnestness, taken the side of the King, and in his early youth he had ridden away from his parents to serve King Charles. He now threw off his upper garments ; and when the Swiss, in gangs of one hundred to two hundred men, attached themselves to a cannon, and, pulling all together, dragged it forward a distance, then to be relieved by a fresh relay, he would himself lend a hand, and address them with words of encouragement. He had trumpets and clarions sounded until they were over the summit and down at the bottom of the precipitous incline, where men and horses rested. He then appeared, black from the intense heat of the sun, before the King, who said, " You have done as Hannibal did; I will so reward you that others also shall gladly serve me." [1]

With difficulty they made their way from the source of the Magra, which flows to the one sea, to hard by the springs of the Taro, which flows to the other. At length the last summit was gained. There they saw before them Lombardy, covered with ripe waving corn and fruit and vines, dotted with smiling villages, and intersected with streams. But in the foreground, not far from the foot of the range, they descried countless tents and the standards of Venice and Milan—an army of nearly 40,000 men. Nevertheless, unmolested they pursued their way down, and on the 5th July the King took his repast at Fornovo.[2]

He was resolved not to make terms, but to accept battle. On both sides of the Taro the valley of Vergerra broadens out down towards the Po, surrounded by hills. On the right bank, the Lombards had taken up their position. What can have been the reason that they did not occupy both banks, and so directly face the enemy ? Their main desire was to protect the Milanese territory and Parma, which was always in a state of sedition, against attack ;

---

[1] Jean Bouchet, Histoire de Mons. de la Trémouille, in the Mémoires, xiv. 150.

[2] Desrey, 225.

Ludovico himself was strongly opposed to a battle.[1] They were drawn up in nine divisions and 140 squadrons; for their custom in battle, as in more serious tournaments, was as follows : the greater number remained in camp and looked on, whilst the divisions one after another successively attacked, fought, and relieved each other.[2] Although under arms, they allowed Charles's army to occupy the left bank of the shallow river.   Forthwith the 3,000 Swiss kissed the earth, placed themselves with Engilbert's Germans and the King's gigantic arquebusiers in the vanguard, and advanced against the enemy.   The rearguard and the " Bataille," with the great standard surrounding the King, consisted of the hommes d'armes.[3]   The latter made the sign of the cross on their foreheads and thirsted for the fray.   The King sat on his one-eyed black charger, Savoye, a magnificent animal ; the colours of France and Brittany waved in the plume of his helmet ; the crosses of Jerusalem adorned his coat of mail ; his forehead, his eyes, and his whole visage wore a martial aspect.   He spoke : " What say ye, sirs ?   Will ye live and die with me ?   Be not afraid, though they are ten times our numbers.   God has led us hither, and he will lead us home." [4]   Whilst he was creating new knights, some shots were fired, and three divisions of the enemy, in a storm of rain, dashed across the river ; the Milanese against the vanguard.   When the Milanese saw the lowered spears of the Germans and Swiss, they hesitated to attack.   The Venetians under Gonzaga, mounted upon great horses clad in mail, even better harnessed than the French, were in splendid array.   The Stradioti, who were appointed to fall upon the flank of the royal army,[5] shouted " Marco Victoria ! "[6]   An actual collision took place only between the regular cavalry of the Venetians and that of the French.   When the first advanced to the charge, the French sentinels cried, " Voilà

---

[1] Benedictus, Diarium, p. 1589.   Balt. Visconti to Ludovico in Rosmini, ii. 218.   Carpesanus, Commentarii, 1213.

[2] Excursus in Porzio, Congiura dei Baroni di Napoli, p. 138.

[3] Comines, 521.   Desrey, 226.

[4] André de la Vigne, p. 209.

[5] Comines, whence Guicciardini.   Oricellarius, p. 70.

[6] Navagero, Storia Venet. p. 1206.

l'ennemi!" and the King was urged to hasten into battle.
He drew the centre and the rearguard together, faced
about, came close to the enemy, and met his first onslaught.[1]
The attack was directed against his right wing, and was
dangerous so long as lances were being used, for those of
the Italians were longer. As soon as swords were resorted
to, the left wing of the King's army, the twenty shields
under the standard of Aymar de Prie, the noblemen of his
house, and some valiant Germans,[2] fell upon Gonzaga's
flank, which tapered off to a thin end, and afforded no
broad front, as was their habit. When at length the
Milanese, who had lost courage, were broken and hurried
down the banks with drawn swords, Gonzaga himself
retired towards the river.[3] A hand-to-hand scuffle took place,
in which even the French baggage boys surrounded the
cuirassiers, four or five round each, and with their mattocks
drove holes through their armour. But an Italian troop
charged once again, and penetrated as far as the King,[4]
who, however, escaped through his own gallantry, and by
the aid of his horse. The advantage undoubtedly remained
with the royal army; but it was not decisive. Pitigliano,
who escaped from French captivity, and rode back into the
Italian camp, kept shouting, "You have conquered," until
they halted; and, as the French saw many lances held
aloft, they did not venture to follow up their victory.[5] The
Taro flowed with blood. Trivulzio had a bottle of water
fetched from it for his little son, who was thirsty, as
though it were red wine.[6] The boy said, "How salt this

---

[1] Symphorian Champier, Trophaeum Gallicum in Godefroy, 306.
Graville to Bouchage in Rosmini, 218.

[2] Mémoires of de la Trémouille, p. 153.

[3] Benedictus, p. 1597.

[4] According to an account of Gilbert Pointet, the intention of the
allies was to take the King prisoner (Pilorgerie, Campagne et bulletins,
p. 356) :—"Nous rompre et prendre ledit seigneur aussi fièrement que
vindrent lesdits ennemis, aussi fièrement furent-ils recueilliz, tellement
que quasi tous furent tuéz." But he distinguishes from this the charge
upon the King, who had only three warriors about him :—"Il avait
son espée traicté combattant contre les ennemys " (note to 2nd edition).

[5] Bembus, p. 44. Jovius, 43. Corio, 949. Nicole Gilles,
Chroniques de France, f. 117.

[6] Rebucco in Rosmini, i. 268.

wine is ! "   " My son," answered his father, " there is no
other in this country."

The French had repulsed an attack that was never very
seriously meant. They had not gained any real victory, but
they were enabled to continue their march. The battle took
place on the 6th July ; on the 7th, before daybreak, when
mass had been said and while the watch-fires were still burning, the King arose, without sound of trumpet or war-cry,
and took a road, along which all the fortresses were occupied
and their gates shut against him, so that his knights often
came with a handful of hay—for they had not more
wherewith to feed their horses—and the army marched
from early morn until late at night, ofttimes so thirsty,
that wherever there was a pond or a pool they jumped
in up to their waists.[1] Along the whole line of march
they left fresh graves behind them. During the same days
two other decisive events took place.

On the 6th July, Giuliano advanced towards the French
into the plain of Santo Spirito, to attack Genoa. The
Spinola and Adorni made a sortie,[2] which was repulsed ;
but on the 7th the Genoese assaulted Rapallo, which was
in the occupation of the French, and made a simultaneous
attack upon their ships in the bay—both with good success,
so that Giuliano lost courage, drew off from Genoa, and
took the road [3] upon which the King had proceeded. The
most important event of all took place at Naples. On the
6th July, Ferrantino appeared with sixty-nine sail in the
Gulf of Naples ; though he showed himself neither resolute
nor quick. But, on the morning of the 7th, as he was
sailing past Naples from Torre, as if bound for Pozzuoli,
he suddenly heard from within tumultuous cries, stopped, and
approached. He saw the flag of Aragon flying upon the
bell-tower of Carmelo ; and then heard the loud pealing of
bells. Then a bark shot towards him, whence came shouts
of " Lord King, the city is yours." [4] A certain Merculiano,

---

[1] Comines, 537. Vimercatus to Ludovico in Rosmini, ii. 221.
Gilles.

[2] Senarega, 553.

[3] Folieta, p. 270. Senarega, 554.

[4] Passero, 75.

so Jovius narrates,[1] the previous day crept stealthily in from the fleet and assembled his friends. When they were about to lay hands on him, the tumult burst forth—some one having produced an Aragonese flag from under his coat; hereupon general shouting, waving of flags, and ringing of bells. Some ran to the Maddalena, where the King had alighted, fell at his feet, and brought him a horse. He rode to the gates between Alonso Pescara and his private secretary Chariteo,[2] who was making Provençal poems the while. The whole populace came out of their houses. They caught hold of his sword, and did not heed being wounded so long as they could kiss his hand or his coat; and ever and anon they shouted " Fierro " so loudly, that he turned to Chariteo and quoted from Juvenal, " It is iron, that they love." [3] So they came into the city, whence the French were fleeing and were being robbed or slain.[4] Gaetans were seen with a Frenchman's heart between their teeth. Jean Rabot, who lived in luxury and opulence, scarcely saved the most indispensable clothing of his household.[5] But the people kissed the King's feet, the ladies wiped the sweat from his brow, and maidens threw garlands in his way; all cried, " Long live our true sovereign." At the same time the Venetians fell upon Monopoli and took it, and Federigo captured the city, court, and castle of Trani, and threw its captain, who defended himself with only eight others, into the hold of his galley. In the whole kingdom the Aragonese party was astir and doing.[6] After these events, having at last arrived at Asti across the dyke of Tortona, Charles could no longer dream of conquering—he must confine himself to rescuing the Duke of Orleans, who had meantime been shut in Novara, and was in great distress.

By permission of Maximilian, Friedrich Cappeler von Pfirt and Georg von Wolkenstein had brought 10,000 Germans, probably Tyrolese and Swabians, across the

[1] Historia sui temporis, f. 49, 50.
[2] Edictum Friderici in Vecchioni, Passero, p. 106.
[3] Passero, 77. Juvenalis, vi. 112.
[4] Villeneufve, Mémoires, p. 13.
[5] Lettre in Godefroy, p. 717.
[6] Villeneufve, p. 873.

Alps ; [1] and these, after having been reviewed by Ludovico and his wife, lay with the Venetians in one camp, living in tents full of abundance (there being before the door of almost each one a spring of water), well paid and contented.[2] In order to procure suitable troops for the French, wherewith to oppose this force, the Bailiff of Dijon repaired to Switzerland. On the 24th of August he was seen with large ships, with music, drums, and joyous cries, sailing up the lake towards Lucerne from the Forest cantons, where he had been well received.[3] In Lucerne he feasted daily with his friends, was lavish with his money, and was regarded as a prince. The latest decrees prohibiting foreign expeditions were not heeded. Where the magistracy insisted on their observance, the young men climbed over the walls. Where it was permitted, flags were flown from the gates and the fountains. Even old men, who had seen Duke Charles at Nancy, joined the bands. And so they marched, troop by troop, from Martinach, across the mountains, and down to Ivrea. On the 7th of September, the first detachment, all grand, martial fellows, appeared before the King in Moncagliere.[4] And none too soon ; for Duke Louis in Novara, who, although suffering from intermittent fever, was yet obliged to visit the guard every day, and his brave companion-in-arms, ill from bread made of hand-ground coarse meal from unripe corn,[5] signalled their great distress by lowering and raising their torches three times every night on the highest towers. Even this flour was exhausted, and in the streets there were dead and dying to be seen.[6] Charles now despatched some Swiss to Provence, to cross thence to Naples ; but the greater part of them he kept in his camp at Vercelli. Their numbers increased daily, and made the enemy fear for the result of a battle, and therefore more inclined to make terms.[7] An arrangement between

[1] Acta of Worms in Datt, 873.

[2] Benedictus, Diarium.

[3] Ludwig von Diesbach's letter to Lucerne in Glutzblotzheim, Schweizergeschichte, p. 516.

[4] Tschudi, Supplementum MS., in Fuchs, Mayländische Feldzüge, i. 212. Stettler, Schweizer Chronik, 325.

[5] Benedictus, Diarium, 1603. Notizie di Novara in Rosmini, 222.

[6] Benedictus, 1619.   [7] André de la Vigne, 226.

Charles VIII and Ludovico had been already mooted.
The first opportunity for the opening of overtures was
made by the death of the Marchioness of Montferrat, when
Charles, on the occasion of settling her inheritance, sent a
message to Gonzaga, expressing his sympathy. This led
to the envoys of both parties incidentally talking of peace.
At first, heralds went over, and concluded a truce, by virtue
of which the Duke of Orleans was permitted to leave Novara,
and received food for his troops. Hereupon negotiations
were opened as to the peace itself. There sat in Ludovico's
chamber, himself, his wife, and the envoys of the League,
on one side of the table, and on the other the French; at
the end were two secretaries for the two parties and the two
languages, and the negotiations were carried on between
them. Frequently, when one, two, or three Frenchmen all
began talking at once, Ludovico interrupted them with
" Ho, ho ! one at a time ; " and thereupon himself carried on
the conversation. He brought it about, that at the expiration of fourteen days, on the 9th of October, all parties
were agreed.[1] He promised to support the French from
Genoa, as a fief of Charles, against Naples, as soon as
his country belonged entirely to him again. Upon these
conditions peace was concluded. Early on the morning of
the 10th, the Venetians burnt their camp, and marched
away.[2] How could it, as Bembo says was the case, have
been so disagreeable to them, when the danger that they
had dreaded was removed, and the expense that they so
unwillingly bore was at an end ? The treaty moreover was
concluded under their very eyes. The Duke of Orleans, a
part of the French nobility—the numbers of his adherents
are reckoned at about 800 lances—and the Swiss, who
had joined the expedition in order to enrich themselves,
submitted but unwillingly to the arrangement. But
Charles VIII kept saying, " I have sworn to it, and I
will keep it." His attention was to pacify Upper Italy, in
order to save Naples for himself.[3]

He now came to Lyons, and paid his vow in St. Denis ;

---

[1] Comines, 553–557.
[2] André de la Vigne, 227. Benedictus, 1622–1624.
[3] Comines, 553–557.

he found France just as he had left it ; but in Italy the effect
of the impulse he had given continued to be felt.[1]   Scarcely
ever has a military expedition been undertaken, which, after
such a brilliant beginning, resulted in fewer immediate consequences, and which was yet indirectly of the greatest
influence upon the world.   The expedition of Charles VIII
may be regarded as the last enterprise undertaken in the
chivalrous spirit of the Crusades.   This spirit now disappeared.   But from this expedition sprang that great
rivalry between the Spanish and French monarchies which
from this time forth filled the world, whilst Italy was at
the same time torn to pieces.

The ideal unity of the peninsula, which we have traced
above, has never been re-established.   Italy became the
battlefield of neighbouring nations, and the sovereignty over
it the prize for which they continuously strove.   Even among
the Germans the Imperial journeys to Rome, which appeared
to have been almost forgotten, were again discussed.

4. WAR IN NAPLES, 1495-1496

In Naples the war still continued.   Its object was the
possession of the city.   This was gained by the favour of
the populace, who drove the enemy into their castles, paid
500 men for their King, each placing as much as he could
give into a collection box, and even marched against
the Swiss at Sarno, and repulsed them.   It succeeded
further, because the enemy in their castles despaired of
all help.   After the peace of Novara, two Genoese ships
arrived, and the French hoped that Ludovico had sent them
to their assistance.[2]   But Ludovico had never intended any
such thing.   When the Venetians called out to the Genoese
sailors, "Chi vive?" the latter replied, "San Giorgio e
Fierro ! Fierro !"   Hereupon in the city, trumpets, flying
flags, and congratulations on the part of the officers of the
galleys; in the castles, sheer despair.[3]   The castles surrendered.   Capua, Nola, and the greater part of the west

<hr />

[1] Desrey, 227-228.   [2] Passero, 78-90.
[3] Villeneufve, 43-45.

coast, followed their example; and the Colonna going over, Aquila and a part of the Abruzzi did the same.

Gonzalvo had also advanced from Reggio. The whole southern tableland of Calabria, La Sila (which was conquered by the ambushes, stratagems, and surprises his soldiers had learnt in the similar country of the Alpujarras) in a northerly direction as far as the foot of the mountain range, where a steep road, in winter quite impracticable, hewn in the solid rock, leads from Rotigliano to the Cosentine villages—all this, together with the places lying on both sides, he had taken either by force or faction. Here he stopped.[1] It was now December. In spite of their sudden change of feeling, it is not quite correct to complain of the inconstancy of this people. Whenever a party which has inherited its allegiance, and which has seen itself the victim of sudden oppression, becomes roused at the first opportunity, this must be called obstinacy rather than inconstancy. We will suppose two almost equal parties, united not only by disposition, but also by property; for the one has often lost its goods to the other, or wrested them from it in return. In their case, a successful campaign and battle won, or favourable tidings, may help up the one, whilst a chance accident, and the crime of an individual, may oppress and dishearten the other; so that, in order not to subject itself, but to await another opportunity, it hastens to secure itself on this occasion as far as possible by making terms. No one will accuse the English of natural cowardice, but in those days they acted in the same manner, and for the same identical reasons. Where relationships are sundered by disunion, by an enmity which only aims at the recognition of a privilege, or a superiority of the one and not the complete destruction of the other, in proportion as hatred is weakened, martial ardour is diminished. Often, when they had already taken the field in order to fight, the Aragonese thought of the losses of their Angevin relatives, would not engage, and were considered cowardly.[2] Under such circumstances, the war could not be brought to a close in a moment.

[1] Zurita, f. 72, compared with Séjours d'un officier en Calabre, 1821, geographically better than Bartels.

[2] Zurita, f. 86, 95.

From the west he turned eastwards across the hills. Here there stretches away the plain of Apulia, arid in spite of a few rivers, on which, at all events in those days, not a single tree grew, and where fennel stalks served as fuel. Upon this plain there was no village, but at harvest time the respective owners of the soil came from their towns and castles with waggons and oxen, remained all night in the open, and only returned when they had finished their work. At times, there grazed upon the royal meads of Tavoliera, eighty miles in extent, a strange herd of cattle.[1]   For towards the winter there came down from the Abruzzian mountains, passing by Serra Capriola, several hundred thousand sheep, goats, and oxen, which remained there until the early spring, when they returned to the fresh herbage of their hills.   In those days they paid considerable duties to the revenue authorities in Foggia—the King's best source of revenue, as they once were of the Roman Republic, bringing in 100,000 ducats.   In order to collect this revenue both Ferrantino and Montpensier hurried across the plain in February, 1496—the former towards Foggia, the latter towards San Severo.   In the little guerilla warfare which they began there a marvellous deed is recorded. About 700 of Ferrantino's Germans, who had taken the road from Troja to Foggia, were suddenly surrounded and attacked by several thousand French.   At once forming a ring, they beat off the enemy with their muskets ; and then, for they wished to proceed on their way, they opened their ranks, and 200 of them dashed ahead to clear the road. But their captain, Hederlin, fell ; they bound his corpse on a horse, took it in their midst, and pushed forward.   They would then have remained unharmed, had they not had to cross a river.   In so doing they divided their forces, which made it easy for the enemy to attack them.   Over the whole plain of Massaria, and along the road, lay the bodies, just as life and blood had left them.   They all died.   Italians and Spaniards have sung their praises once or twice since then ; but never a German.[2]   This deed is remarkable not for its success, but for the prowess displayed.   Yet Ferrantino

[1] Leander Alberti, Descriptio Italiae.
[2] Jovius, 71.   Passero, p. 97.   Zurita, 73.

immediately after had the advantage again. He had pledged five places in Apulia, the best situated in the country, to the Signoria of Venice for their war expenses, and pledging was almost tantamount to selling. The Stradioti, who in return for this transaction joined him, even took the cattle away from the French, which were being driven for them to San Severo.[1] Here, there, and everywhere, always attacking and never awaiting the enemy's attack, they made the King master of the plain, so that both Ludovico in the west and Venice in the east aided Ferrantino to victory; yet the Republic afforded by far the greatest assistance. In the south, Gonzalvo, as early as February, had mounted up to the Cosentine villages on the hills, had subjected Cosenza, except its castle, and all the fortresses of the valley of the Crati, whether they would or no, as well as the whole mountain chain as far as the second passes, where it slopes down from Castrovillari to Campo Tenese, and had instituted everywhere Aragonese judges.[2]

The Colonna had possession of the Abruzzi in the north, the western and eastern slope of the hills were Aragonese[3]; and so the French were obliged to pass through their midst into the province of Molise, although they were disunited, without money, and ignorant of hill-warfare. Ferrantino immediately went in search of them there. At Morcone they both again faced each other; at Frangete only a ditch parted them. A collision appeared to be inevitable. At Naples, processions were held for two days, because the King would have to fight at Benevento. In Calabria, too, he was not quite safe. At Laino were gathered the barons who had fled before Gonzalvo, and who now cherished the plan of joining Aubigny, who was still at Tropea, in order with united forces to relieve Cosenza. Before they could make up their minds,[4] Gonzalvo sallied forth at night, seized the passes, occupied the bridge between the town and castle of Laino, possessed himself of both, and

    [1] Bembus, 57. Also Guicciardini, ii. 149.
    [2] Zurita, 84. 96.
    [3] Tarfia, Historiae Cupersanenses, in Graevius. Ital. Thes. ix. 48.
       [4] Passero, 100.

took fourteen barons and many knights prisoners.[1] Whilst he was coming up from the south, Ferrantino drove the enemy before him from the north, by way of Ariano and Gesualdo, from place to place, until he caught them up at Atella.[2] Here he occupied the hills, covered with woods and vineyards, which surround the valley on three sides. He only left the road from Venosa open. This road Gonzalvo blocked.[3] When now the French made an attempt to break through, Ferrantino was the first to break his lance upon them ; and when his knights said to him, " Sir, how dare you expose yourself so much ?" he replied, " It is my affair also." In this way he fired the zeal of his troops, and soon drove the enemy back.[4] The latter hoped against hope in their King, but he was too far away, and they were perishing from hunger. They accordingly begged for a thirty days' truce; if at the expiration of it they were then unable to take the field, they pledged themselves to leave the kingdom and surrender their strongholds. The days passed; succour did not arrive, and at length they were all—for Aubigny had also surrendered—conducted to the coast. Here, heat, hunger, and dire diseases left only 1,500 men out of 6,000, and these took ship in such an exhausted condition that they had almost to be lifted on shore, if they were ever to breathe the air of the land again.[5] Others came into captivity, sat behind wooden and iron gratings in dark cells, where they saw no living creature, except perhaps the Moor who brought them their food.[6] At last they were set free. These fugitives might be seen, with the iron chains of their captivity still about their necks, betaking themselves to holy places and to the court of the King. They were contented to see his face once more ; they took his presents, and wished him long life.[7]

After this great victory over the French, Ferrantino returned, on the 5th October, 1496, with his young wife to

---

[1] Jovius, Vita Consalvi Magni, p. 220.
[2] Baldi, Guidubaldo, p. 156.   [3] Zurita, 91–95.
[4] Passero, 101. Unrest, Oesterreichische Chronik, p. 798.
[5] Schödeler in Fuchs, 111, Anshelm.
[6] Villeneufve, Mém. p. 74.
[7] *Ibid.* p. 87.

Naples.[1] The people, whom he had allowed to choose a fuller as their Eletto, who was permitted to carry the Mappa[2] on Corpus Christi day, which had been a privilege of the nobles—and who, if he lived, might hope for many other favours at his hand—loved him from the bottom of their hearts. Many of them imitated him, how he raised and bowed his head,[3] and they believed they had a hero in him. And now he came back to them ; but he was sick to death. The people spent the whole night before the saints on their knees. Early in the morning, they carried a wonder-working image of Mary through the streets, and brought it to him ; in the evening there followed in grand procession, clerics and laymen, men and women, and even the nobles, behind the head and blood of St. Januarius, which their Archbishop carried before them through the streets, until they were come to the gate of the palace. Here the old Queen knelt down, and the people cried, " Misericordia." He spoke to them, and said, " Finish your prayers ; God will do as seemeth him best," and then died. " O our master," they said, " wherefore hast thou left us so soon? Thy prowess, thy prowess in battle, equalled by no hero of old, where is it now? By thy death it is gone." Another said, " How shall I now live, O my master, I that have borne so many hardships to earn thy favour ? " Some remembered that he had often been in danger of poison ; but he had escaped such a death, and now he had passed away gently at the goal of his victories.[4] Federigo, his uncle, succeeded to the throne in his stead.

And now it almost appeared as though Charles's expedition, which certainly never vanquished the Turks or took Jerusalem, was not even productive of any lasting effects upon Italy—Ludovico and Federigo were even reconciled. Yet it was not so in reality. The Florentine Popolari, the Orsini, who now opposed the Pope instead of the Colonna, as well as the unconquered cities in the kingdom of Naples, Taranto, Bitonto, Sora, Rocca Guglielma,

[1] Passero, 105, 107. Giacomo, 205.
[2] Passero, 101, 102. Giacomo, 209.
[3] Castiglione, Cortegiano, Book i.
[4] Passero, 107-110.

formed a strong party, and every day Charles, their suzerain, thought of returning to them again.   These were confronted by the League.   The Italian members of it would have been quite contented with a victory over their enemies in Italy. The foreign members desired more.   Ferdinand was thinking of his claims to Naples, and made inquiries of the Pope in respect thereof.[1]   Maximilian hoped, with the assistance of this League, to strike a blow at France itself.

[1] Zurita, i. 101-103, whence Mariana, 26, 14.

CHAPTER III

1. MAXIMILIAN OF AUSTRIA AND THE EMPIRE

THE real objects of Maximilian were to aid the League to conquer in Italy, and then to place himself at its head and attack France.

He was lord of Austria and the Netherlands. It might have been about 600 years previously that, in the valley of the Danube, between the Alps and the Bohemian mountains, the mark of Austria was first founded round and about the castles of Krems and Melk.[1] Since then it had grown, first in the valleys towards Bavaria and Hungary, and afterwards through the House of Hapsburg, across the whole of the northern slope of the Alps to the point of separation of the Slavonic, Italian, and German tongues, and down to Alsace; from a mark it had become an archduchy. On all sides the Archdukes had claims; on the German side to Switzerland, on the Italian to Venetian possessions, and on the Slavonic to Bohemia and Hungary.

To such a pitch of greatness had Maximilian by his marriage with Mary of Burgundy brought the heritage received from Charles the Bold. True to the Netherlander's greeting, in the inscription over their gates, "Thou art our Duke, fight our battle for us," war was from the first his handicraft. He adopted Charles the Bold's hostile attitude towards France; he saved the greatest part of his inheritance from the schemes of Louis XI. He thought day and night how he might conquer it entirely.

But after Mary of Burgundy's premature death, revolution followed revolution, and his father Frederick being too old to protect himself, it came about that in the year 1488

---

[1] Kurz, Beiträge zur Geschichte von Oesterreich, iii. 226. Cf. Büdinger, Oesterreich. Geschichte, i. 167 (note to 2nd edition).

he was ousted from Austria by the Hungarians, whilst his
son was kept a prisoner in Bruges by the citizens, and they
had even to fear the estrangement of the Tyrol.   Yet they
did not lose courage.   At this very time the father denoted
with the vowels A. E. I. O. U. (" Alles Erdreich ist
Oesterreich unterthan "—all the earth is subject to Austria),
the extent of his hopes.   In the same year, the son negotiated for a Spanish alliance.   Their real strength lay in the
imperial dignity of Frederick, and in the royal dignity of
Maximilian, which they had from the Empire of the
Germans.   As soon as it began to bestir itself, Maximilian
was set at liberty ; as soon as it supported him in the
persons of only a few princes of the Empire, he became
supreme in the Netherlands.   The standard of the Kennemer, with its device of bread and cheese, floated before
Leyden for the last time, and the last Hoek, Philip of
Ravenstein, surrendered Sluys to him.[1]   It was the same
help which secured him the Tyrol, and enabled him to
reconquer Austria.[2]

Since then, his plans were directed against Hungary and
Burgundy.   In Hungary he could gain nothing beyond
securing the succession to his house.[3]   But never, frequently
as he concluded peace, did he give up his intentions upon
Burgundy.   He might have hoped to compass them if
Anne of Brittany had become his wife.   On the day that
he learned that she was not to become so, he threw himself
in a fit of bitter disappointment into the saddle, and took
part again and again in the tournaments.[4]   On this occasion,
however, the Empire did not come to the assistance of his
anger.   But now that he had allied himself with a Sforza,
and had joined the League, now that his father was dead,
and the Empire was pledged to follow him across the
mountains, and now, too, that the Italian complications
were threatening Charles, he took fresh hope, and in this
hope he summoned a Diet at Worms.

[1] Pontus Heuterus, Rerum Austriac. Hermanni bellum Gelricum,
530.
[2] Speech of Berthold of Mainz of the year 1492 in Müller's Reichstagstheatrum.
[3] Document in Sambucus, Appendix ad Bonfinium.
[4] Ehrenspiegel, p. 1368.

Maximilian was a prince of whom, although many portraits have been drawn, yet there is scarcely one that resembles another, so easily and so entirely did he suit himself to circumstances, so little was he controlled by one occupation or one inclination,—a prince of whom his contemporaries have left behind them detailed descriptions of manners and habits, yet not a single satisfactory history. His soul is full of motion, of joy in things, and of plans. There is scarcely anything that he is not capable of doing. In his mines he is a good screener, in his armoury the best plater, capable of instructing others in new inventions. With musket in hand, he defeats his best marksman, Georg Purkhard; with heavy cannon, which he has shown how to cast, and has placed on wheels, he comes as a rule nearest the mark.[1] He commands seven captains in their seven several tongues ; he himself chooses and mixes his food and medicines.[2] In the open country, he feels himself happiest. He rides by copses listening for the nightingale,—it may be to the forests of Brabant, to hunt the boar,—to the Tyrol mountains, where he has forbidden the shooting of the chamois because firearms have left so few remaining.[3] Here he leaves his horse behind, and in pursuit of them climbs the steep rocks where, if he makes a false step, he may fall four hundred to five hundred feet, where sometimes, when the climbing iron has given way, a bush or projecting stone alone saves him from destruction, and where, on one occasion, in the Hallthal, he hears the avalanche thunder at his back.[4] The common people tell stories of how he was once let down by strong ropes from the heights into the valley beneath, and on another occasion, when this was impracticable, and a crucifix was already raised towards him from the valley as though to receive his dying prayer, an angel rescued him from the Martinswand.[5] On his return from such an expedition, his fowler brings him all

---

[1] Weiskunig, 83, 90, 99.
[2] Grünbeck, Historia Friedrichs und Maximilians, p. 84. Cuspinianus, Vita Maximiliani in Vitae Imperatorum, p. 613.
[3] Weiskunig, 91.
[4] Grünbeck, Ehrenspiegel, 1381.
[5] Pontus Heuterus, 343, and the legends.

H

manner of singing birds into his chamber, so that he can
hardly hear himself speak.   Or, again, he goes to the
wedding of one of his servants, or listens confidentially to
the prayers of his subjects, or it may be relates a story to
his councillors and secretaries.   Sometimes he dictates a
piece from his enigmatical and almost unfathomable works,[1]
a note for his diary, as, for instance, how priest Lasla is to
compile the Chronicles,[2] or one of his very exact instructions
as, for instance, how, at Beutelstein, with a makeshift musket
one might shoot obliquely into the kitchen,[3] or perhaps a
letter.   Such is his character.   But this has little to do
with history.   What really distinguishes his public life is
that presentiment of the future greatness of his dynasty
which he has inherited from his father, and the restless
striving to obtain all that passed to him from the House of
Burgundy.   All his policy and all his schemes were con-
centrated, not upon the Empire, for the real needs of which
he evinced little real care, and not directly upon the welfare
of his hereditary lands, but upon the realization of that
sole idea.   Of it all his letters and speeches are full.   Yet
each individual plan he keeps extremely secret.   There
are projects that he communicates to none of his councillors;[4] at such times he places the foreign embassies
in positions where they learn nothing, and from which
they cannot escape; then he sends his cook on ahead
only an hour before he himself sets out.[5]   Whenever
he fancies his plans are discerned, the veins in his neck
swell, and he becomes wrath.[6]   It will sometimes happen
that the matter upon which he is bent, after he has undertaken it, presents difficulties for which he is not prepared;[7] but, as he has always other schemes, which lead to
the same end, he soon forgets his failures.   Thus, in such
matters, he behaves like a huntsman, who is bent upon

---

[1] Grünbeck, 90.   Henric. Pantaleon, de Viris illustribus, p. 1.
Roo, Annales rerum ab Austriacis principibus gestarum, 316.

[2] A passage therefrom in Hormayr, Oesterr. Plutarch, v. 159.

[3] Instruction in Göbler, Chronika der Kriegshändel, f. 1.

[4] Machiavelli, Principe, c. 23, p. 60, out of the mouth of Pre Luca.

[5] Machiavelli, Legazione alla corte di Massimiliano, p. 193.

[6] Hubertus Thomas Leodius, Vita Friderici Palatini, lib. iii. No. 7.

[7] Histoire de Bayard, 179.

climbing a very steep hill, first by this path and then by that, and if he fails, attempts another and yet another way without losing patience; for it is still early in the day, and he gradually mounts higher and higher, his sole care being to hide himself from the wild animal he pursues.

In March, 1495, Maximilian came to the Diet at Worms. He showed to the full his knightly prowess, when he himself entered the lists with a Frenchman, who had come to challenge all the Germans, and conquered him. He appeared in the full glory of his regal dignity, when he sat in public between the archbishops and his chancellors. On such occasions, the Count Palatine sat on his right and held his orb, on his left stood the Duke of Saxony and held his sword; before him stood the envoy of Brandenburg with the sceptre, and behind him, instead of Bohemia, the hereditary cupbearer of Limburg, with the crown; and grouped round him were the rest of the forty princes, sixty-seven counts and lords, as many as had come, and the ambassadors of the cities, and others, all in their order.[1] Then a prince would come before him, lower his colours before the royal throne, and receive his investiture. There was then no perception of the fact that this mode of investiture denoted a certain compulsion upon the King, or that the insignia of royal power resided in the hands of the princes.

At this Diet the King made two important arrangements, which opened up to him great prospects of advantage. In Württemberg there had sprung of two lines two counts of quite opposite characters, both named Eberhard. The elder was kind-hearted, tender, always resolute, and dared " sleep in the lap of any one of his subjects;"[2] the younger, volatile, unsteady, violent, and always repentant of what he had done;[3] but the elder, by special favour of the Imperial court, also managed the land of the younger.

---

[1] Bernh. Herzog, Elsasser Chronik, ii. f. 150, in Datt, de pace publica, 613. Linturius, Appendix ad Rotewinkii Fascicul. tempor. in Pistorius, Scriptt. Germ. ii. 594.

[2] Pfister, Eberhard im Bart, p. 60.

[3] Ulrich's lamentations in Sattler, iv., and in Spittler's Geschichte von Württemberg, 46.

In return for this, he furnished 400 horse for the Hungarian war, and despatched aid against Flanders. With the elder, Maximilian now entered into a compact. Württemberg was to be raised to a dukedom—an elevation which excluded the female line from the succession—and, in the event of the stock failing, was to be a "widow's portion" of the realm for the benefit of the Imperial treasury.[1] Now, as the sole hopes of this family centred in a single weakly boy, this arrangement held out to Maximilian or his successors the prospect of acquiring a splendid country. Yet this was the smaller of his two successes. The greater was the espousal of his children, Philip and Margaret, to the two children of Ferdinand the Catholic, Juana and Juan, which was here settled.[2] This opened to his house still greater expectations,—it brought him at once into the most intimate alliance with the Kings of Spain.

These matters might possibly, however, have been arranged elsewhere. What Maximilian really wanted at the Diet of Worms was the assistance of the Empire against the French, with its soldiery who were already world-renowned and much sought after.

For at that time in all the wars of Europe, German auxiliaries were decisive. The troops upon which Wasil-jewitsch depended when he led his Muscovites against the Poles,[3] and those who subjected Sweden to the Union,[4] were German, as were also those which died in England for the cause of York on the very spot[5] where they had awaited the battle. Those who made the possession of Brittany by the crown of France uncertain, as well as those who conquered it, were also Germans;[6] the defenders as well as the conquerors of Naples; the subduers of Hungary, as long as it suited them, as also those who saved it by going home with their booty,[7] all were Germans. But these were the quarrelsome, wandering portion of the nation, those

1 Pfister, 271, 297.
2 Zurita, f. 79. Petrus Martyr, Epp. 96.
3 Letter in Raynaldus, Annal. Eccles. xx. 141.
4 Kranz, Vandalia, xiv. 27.
5 Polydorus Virgilius, Historia Anglica, 26, 729.
6 Müller, Schweizergeschichte, v. 318.
7 Maximilian's proclamation in Datt, 496.

hirelings whom the peace proclamations inveighed against. In Germany there still lived peasants, like the Ditmarschers, who awaited a victorious army, under a king of three realms, behind their walls, and defeated it, and who hung up the Danebrog in a village church. In the cities there dwelt behind their impregnable walls and their cannon, citizens versed in the use of arms, who practised their good arts and games until irritated by an enemy, when they met him, as the Strassburgers did Charles the Bold before Nancy.[1] Less secure perhaps were princes and lords, yet these had castles to protect them against the first attack, and feudal tenants and faithful subjects ever about them. If Maximilian had united the whole of this power in his hand, neither Europe nor Asia would have been able to withstand him. But God disposed that it should rather be employed in the cause of freedom than for oppression. What an Empire was that, which in spite of its vast strength allowed its Emperor to be expelled from his heritage, and did not for a long time take steps to bring him back again?

If we examine the constitution of the Empire, not as we should picture it to ourselves in Henry III's time, but as it had at length become—the imperial dignity devoid of any material possessions, the several estates legally independent, and with the power of election of a sovereign, who afterwards always maintained certain rights over the electors,—we are led to inquire not so much into the causes of its disintegration, for this concerns us little, as into the way in which it was held together.

What welded it together, and preserved it (leaving tradition and the Pope out of the question), would appear to have been chiefly the rights of individuals, the unions of neighbours, and the social gradations which universally obtained. Such were those rights and privileges which not only protected the citizen, his guild and his quarter of the town against his neighbours and more powerful men than himself, but which also endowed him with an inner independence ; those rights and privileges which secured his rightful possessions to the greatest, and his existence to the least ; a legacy left by each generation to the succeeding,

[1] Königshofer, Strassburger Chronik, 379.

unalterable either by emperor or empire who had confirmed them, but which were without them a mere nothing. Next, the unions of neighbours. These were not only leagues of cities and communities of peasants, expanded from ancient fraternities—for who can tell the origin of the Hansa, or the earliest treaty between Uri and Schwyz?—into large associations; or of knights, who strengthened a really insignificant power by confederations of neighbours; but also of the princes, who were bound together by joint inheritances, mutual expectancies and the ties of blood, which in some cases were very close. This ramification, dependent upon a supreme power and confirmed by it, bound neighbour to neighbour; and, whilst securing to each his privilege and his liberty, blended together all countries of Germany in legal bonds of union. But it is only in the social order that the unity is really manifest. Only so long as the Empire was an actual reality, could the supreme power of the Electors, each with his own special rights, be maintained; only so long could dukes and princes, bishops and abbots maintain their authority in the eyes of their neighbours, and through court offices or hereditary services, through fiefs and membership of the Diet give their vassals a distinctive position to the whole. Only so long could the immediate cities of the Empire, carefully divided into free and imperial cities, be not merely protected, but also assured of a general participation in the government. Under this sanctified and traditional system of suzerainty and vassalage all were happy and contented, and bore a love to it such as is cherished towards a native town or a father's house.

In this system, the House of Austria had for some time past enjoyed the foremost position. It also had a union, and, moreover, a great division on its side. The union was the Swabian League. Old Swabia was divided into three leagues—the league of the Forest Cantons (the origin of Switzerland); the league of the knights in the Black Forest, on the Kocher, the Neckar, and the Danube; and the league of the cities. The cantons were from the first hostile to Austria. The Emperor Frederick brought it to pass that the cities and knights, that had from time out of mind lived in feud, bound themselves together with several princes, and formed, under his protection, the league of the land of Swabia. But the division was scattered throughout the whole Empire.

Almost every German house was divided into an elder and a younger line; and, as through some fate, it happened that one, generally the younger, attached itself to the Emperor. Of the Bavarian House, it was at this time that of Munich; of the Palatinate, that of Veldenz; of the Württemberg House, the Urach line; of the Saxon, that of Dresden; of the Hessian, that of Marburg; and of the Guelph, that of Brunswick. The most friendly to the Imperial House were the Houses of Brandenburg and Baden, which was for a long time undivided; the most hostile, since Frederick the Victorious, was the Palatinate. Any one who steeps himself in these dry studies, and has access to all the historical documents, especially the electoral rolls of the ecclesiastical princes, will be able to discover, from Frederick II's time, a new history, unlike Häberlin's, founded upon persons and living actions.

But it is not this upon which the Emperor's hallowed position in the nation reposed. This was based before all else upon his dignity, the sublimest in Christendom, the keystone of the social order, and upon the custody of traditional rights—a custody, so to speak, of times past for times to come—which lay in his hand, and which was bound up with the distribution of new rights through the medium of privileges and fiefs. His position was based, moreover, upon the universal judicial office he filled, as well as upon the great influence he exercised upon public matters by his motions, proposals, and party in the Diet. "His name is great," says a papal deputy; "in a land of factions he can do much. Every one looks to him; and without him nothing can be done."[1] In this respect there were, however, great deficiencies. Privileges were often bestowed out of mere personal considerations, and to the prejudice of others; judicial business was frequently kept in arrear, if the parties did not come to court with sufficient money; domestic matters were often made affairs of general policy,

[1] Campanus ad Cardinalem Papiensem in Freherus, ii. 148.

and real needs neglected. The princes complained that the Emperor did not consult them, but his councillors. We can see that there was much arbitrariness and determination to take all that could be got, on the one side, and lack of complaisance and goodwill and the rendering of as little service as possible on the other.

Maximilian had first intended to remain a fortnight at Worms ; and then, before Charles had returned from Naples, with the help of the vassals of the realm, to undertake an expedition against him. Yet his proposal did not express this intention. It was as follows : " Whereas the Turk twice each year assailed Christendom ; and whereas the King of France threatened to transfer to himself the prerogatives of the Empire and the Church, a speedy and, more than this—for they had equipped themselves for a long campaign,—a continuous aid for ten to twelve years was needed." [1]

But here lay the chief difficulty, to induce a government only framed for peace, or at most fitted to carry on a short war, to undertake a protracted campaign at a distance. To this end either the dormant military power of the vassals, princes, knights, citizens, and peasants could be utilized, or else the landsknechts, who were always ready to serve for pay. But the feudal system had fallen into decay, owing no less to the Emperor, who left the individual unaided, than to the individuals who did not, on their part, support him. It still lived on only in respect of *meum* and *tuum*, and not with any view to war; it existed more in claims and in parchments than in actual fact. It was impossible to unite the vassals in military obedience for any length of time, so as to undertake a real campaign. Maximilian's intention, therefore, was to raise money through his claims upon them, and with this money to form an army of landsknechts. This was the tenor of his proposal.

This proposal was received by the Estates at Worms in full assembly at the Rathaus. Hereupon they withdrew— the Electors into one chamber, the princes into a second, and the representatives of the cities into a third, and began to examine article after article. The printed records do not

[1] Reichstagsacta von Worms, 13.

quite disclose the relations of the princes to the electors; but of the cities thus much we know, that their commission was, to agree in the main to what the electors and princes resolved, and otherwise only to protect the interests of each city. They would not, even when asked, make known their opinion until the princes had declared theirs. Often they learnt from the Elector of Mainz what had been proposed to them, and what they had determined upon. In case they had any scruples they sent, after lunch perhaps, to him direct. The King, when confronted by the full assembly, appeared at a great disadvantage. In a case when he desired a rapid decision, he was even obliged to go out whilst they were deliberating, and await the result outside.[1]

These Estates, then, that have in their hereditary independence as little in common with the representative estates of a military monarchy, as the Empire of those days with a political state, answered the King, that, before all else, order in the Empire must be secured. When, in 1486, Frederick pressed them for assistance against the Hungarians, they cast in his teeth complaints as to his administration of justice; and when, in 1492, he proposed a French campaign, they replied, led by Berthold of Mainz: " It was an evil innovation to ask for assistance in money. Many were excused the contribution; many paid only half; many, again, too late; those that paid it were ruined; and, finally, it was spent for different objects than it had been granted for." All the same, they did not declare themselves against pecuniary assistance, but they wished to counteract those two evils by the aid of the tribunals, and by assisting in the appropriation of the moneys voted.

At the present moment, both parties, they and the King, pursued their own ends. On three occasions, Maximilian was particularly pressing. The first occasion was in April, when the preparations of the Duke of Orleans threatened Milan, and Charles's retreat menaced the Pope and Genoa, and he could still hope to find him in the field, far away from his country. But the princes took upon themselves to propose to him a Council of Regency which should consist of a president appointed by the King, and sixteen members

[1] Reichstagsacta, § 15, § 65, § 19.

chosen by the Electors, the four archbishoprics, the four territories and the cities, and which should, in reality, exercise all internal power. In this first dispute Maximilian gained the day. Berthold of Mainz said: "They did not wish to mortgage the King's person for this assistance they voted him; they would acquiesce in his wishes and trust him." Acting upon this sentiment, they promised him that, although he rejected their Council of Regency, they would, within six weeks, raise 100,000 guilders from the Estates; 50,000 he should raise himself, and both sums should be covered by a general tax levied on the country; only he should not leave the land before peace, right, and a tolerable state of order was established. This was the first time.[1]

The peace was not established, the money was not paid, and the six weeks had long passed by.

On the second occasion, when Charles was in Florentine territory, and messengers announced that Milan was in danger, he declared as follows: "For two days, from eight o'clock in the morning until eight at night, he had busied himself with the peace project; in two days he hoped to have settled it; in the meanwhile they should be good enough to vote him the money." Many were opposed to this, especially the cities. But he prevailed upon some princes to grant him the money; and Berthold induced the representatives of the cities, at all events, to write home about it. He was successful on this occasion also. It was in July.[2]

After this, at the beginning of August, when Novara was being besieged, and a victory of the Swiss was apprehended, in case the landsknechts, who had been sent thither, were not regularly paid, he made fresh demands. But on this occasion he could prevail upon nobody. On the afternoon of the 4th of August he adopted the proposals provisionally, and on the 7th definitely, and received on the 9th a fresh vote of 150,000 guilders.[3]

[1] Acta, § 25. Müller's Reichstagsstaat, p. 11. Besserer's letter to Esslingen in Datt, de pace publica, 521.

[2] Acta, § 47, § 55, § 56.

[3] Acta, §§ 69–74, in Datt, de pace publica, pp. 873–883. Cf. Ullmann, Kaiser Maximilian I, p. 374.

What can it then have been that the King was unwilling to face? Certainly not the public peace, that had been so often proclaimed, but the Cameral Tribunal (*Kammergericht*), a Court constituted with the advice and consent of the Diet, and which, moreover, as was plainly evidenced by later references to the events of this day, was composed in the way in which it was intended to compose the Council of Regency, so that hereby a great part of his absolute judicial power was taken from him. Yet in the matter nearest his heart still greater difficulties presented themselves. It was resolved to raise the Common Penny, no small tax, as it would amount to the thousandth part of the property of the public, and in many districts taxes and assessments were at this time unknown.[1] The object was to bring every individual in all Germany immediately under the Imperial government, and always to keep a good sum in reserve for public matters.

This tax was for the King, but it was not proposed to leave it to his absolute control. Seven Imperial treasurers were to raise it, and an annual diet was to keep watch over its application. On the evening before the Feast of the Purification in each year, the King, the princes, and all the Estates should assemble, and remain a whole month together to deal with the public peace and justice. This assembly could not but diminish the King's independence and his whole prestige. What availed him the money, when another could determine how it should be employed? But on this occasion it could not be avoided. With but few knights, without any reception, Maximilian arrived at Frankfurt. On the Grossbraunfels there, he delivered the simple red judge's staff with its black handle to the first justiciary, Eitel Friedrich von Zollern, and then, in disgust that his chief object had been defeated, betook himself to the Tyrol. Charles was home again ; in Milan peace prevailed, and all his plans had been thwarted.[2]

---

[1] Kanzow, Pomerania, ii. xvi. 414.

[2] § 57, 7, Datt, de pace publica, 606, 717. Vogt, Rheinische Geschichten, iii. xiv. 365. MS. of Latom in Lersner's Chronik von Frankfurt a/M. 128.

2. MAXIMILIAN'S FIRST EXPEDITION TO ITALY—THE FLORENTINES AND SAVONAROLA

In the Tyrol, Maximilian was visited by the ambassadors of Italy ; they represented to him that "the King of France was every day threatening to return. The Popolari at Florence, his keenest partisans, had been bold enough to attack Pisa. Against the former, as also against these latter, they prayed him to come and wage war, and not, when they had so great need of him, to be again detained by a Diet." Maximilian turned his attention entirely to Italian affairs, and inclined to the hope that he would be able, even without material assistance from Germany, to carry out one of his plans.

The condition of things in Pisa and Florence was now as follows. When King Charles took Pisa under his protection, he forgot that it had ever been Ghibelline, against the House of Anjou and against his rights, and that its last action had been to hoist the Burgundian colours.[1] Later, he came to terms with Florence, and insisted only upon an amnesty for Pisa. Relying upon this, the Florentines commenced the war. The castles upon the heights of the Era and Elsa, originally belonging to Pisa, and not far from the coast, were soon taken. Leghorn was ceded to them, and Charles gave orders to his captain in the citadel of Pisa to surrender this also.[2] But the captain acted contrary to expectations. Whether or not it was compassion, bribe, or, as is said, a lady of Pisa, who pleased him too well, he disregarded his sovereign's commands. When the Florentines, upon his invitation, rushed through suburbs, fortifications, and across the Arno, in order to take the city and to receive the citadel from him, he fired point-blank amongst them and drove them back. He was the first to make the people of Pisa perfectly free, by surrendering to them their citadel.[3]

But what sort of liberty is that, which from the first outset

---

[1] Sismondi, Histoire des Répub. Ital. viii. 152.

[2] Nardi, Istorie della città, 26. Guicciardini, ii. 121. Jovius, Historiae sui temporis, 56.

[3] Comines, viii. 567.

hesitates to protect itself? It was enough for the people of Pisa not to be subjected to their old enemies. And he who protected them against their foes was also acceptable to them as their lord and master.

When, then, on the occasion of the renewed attacks made upon it by Florence, Ludovico and the Venetians took the part of Pisa, they may, perhaps, have intended to injure the French party; certain it is that Ludovico reflected, that the city formerly belonged to the Visconti, and that it was favourably situated for both Genoa and Milan; and certain it is that the Venetians considered what an excellent acquisition Pisa would be to add to the Apulian cities which were already theirs, and to Taranto, which had just raised the cry of "San Marco!" and how it would enable them to plant their flag on the Tyrrhenian sea. At first, as though no one knew the others' thoughts, they held together; but every day Ludovico became more jealous. He retired. His general on one occasion, on being invited to advance, answered that he must first take his breakfast. But matters did not progress much in this way,[1] and it was a clever idea of his to help to transfer this war to the Emperor, his nearest relative, who was an enemy of the Popolari, and no friend of Venice.

When, in May, 1496, Trivulzio came over the mountains, fortified Asti, and spread the report that close behind him were coming the Duke of Orleans, and after him the King, with 2,000 hommes d'armes, and 10,000 Gascons and Swiss, the Venetians were induced—for Charles threatened to avenge their attack at Fornovo—to agree to Ludovico's proposal.[2]

Accordingly, in July, 1496, Ludovico set out with his court and journeyed through the Valtelline, and by way of Bormio across the Umbrail to Münster, there to await Maximilian. The next morning, before daybreak, the Emperor arrived attired in a black hunting costume, with his golden bugle-horn at his side, and accompanied by 200 huntsmen with the long poles, with which they clamber from

---

[1] Chronicon Venetum, 36. Bembus, Historia Veneta, 66. Bursellis, Chronicon Bononiense, 914.

[2] Francesco Visconti to Ludovico in Rosmini, 238.

rock to rock, and by many nobles all decorated with the Burgundian Cross of St. Andrew. After the meeting was over, he might have been seen following the chase on the highest peaks of the Piz Umbrail—merely to gaze up at which made the spectator dizzy—his feet shod with climbing irons, where the cleft rocks ran sheer down into the abyss beneath.[1] Meanwhile, the Duchess sat in a small hut, and chamois were driven down from the ravines and round the jagged rocks, and the sport went on before her eyes. In this way they amused themselves. The most important event, however, was, that Maximilian entertained the proposals of the Italian envoys: "they should pay him 40,000 ducats every three months, and he would then come and wage their war for them." [2] But first he must return to Germany.

In his ill-humour he had abandoned all the decrees of the Diet. At all events, he ought, by his presence in the first assembly, to have inaugurated the new constitution ; but when the Feast of the Purification arrived, he said that in Worms he had been treated as no city treated its burgomaster, and remained away. A few plenipotentiaries came, but in a short time every one went home. In the meanwhile, the Common Penny had been raised; abbots and ecclesiastics paid it, and the cities also paid it into the hand of their priests. But as the assembly, which should determine how the contribution should be expended, had broken up, how was it likely that any should show great enthusiasm, especially as all were unaccustomed to these proceedings, and annoyed at their property being investigated? Maximilian, accordingly, at Whitsuntide, 1496, wrote : " Each one must appear at Lindau with his soldiers all ready equipped, and with the money that had been raised by tax to pay them." Immediately afterwards, just as if nothing had been pre-arranged and determined, he demanded that, " eight days after St. John's Day, the summer solstice, the strength of the nation should accompany him across the mountains, for King Charles was already on the

[1] Ebel, Anleitung, die Schweiz zu bereisen, iv. 510.

[2] Ghilinus, de adventu Maximiliani in Italiam, ap. Freherum, iii. 82. Navagero, Stor. Venet. 1207.

march;"[1] and in August he declared that he was full of great hopes for the success of his Roman campaign; the country should support him at once with loans and the Common Penny.[2]

But how was the war to be begun, without the decree of the Empire? That no such decree was issued in no way disheartened him. The princes of his party afforded him some assistance, namely, those princes who at that time were living at his court at Innsbruck. The deputies of a few Swiss cities accompanied him. Yet his real army was to be provided by Italy. At Linz he took counsel with his son Philip. Philip, who now ruled the Netherlands, had come gladly, sometimes taking part in the bird-shooting of respectable burghers, and sometimes joining in the patrician dances. At Augsburg, where they made a pile of maypoles and garlands forty-five feet high for the St. John's Day bonfire, the fairest damsel with a wax taper in her hand kindled it with him in the dance, whilst the trumpets, cornets, and kettledrums all brayed to the fire and the dance.[3] At Linz his father disclosed to him his bold plans. He hoped to keep the French back from Italy and Leghorn; Florence would then league itself with him; nay more, aid him to cross over in René's interest from Tuscany into Provence. This done, Philip should invade France from the Netherlands and Ferdinand from Roussillon. At Lyons, they might all three meet, and then Burgundy would be won.[4] With these hopes, in August, he took the 200 horse that he had equipped, and arranged that Albrecht of Saxony should follow him with some infantry; and in the hamlet of Meda, beyond the Valtelline and Morbegno, among houses and gardens, he met the envoy of the Pope and Ludovico. In Vigevano they took counsel together.[5] A

[1] Letter of the Esslingers in Datt, de pace publica, p. 550. Maximilian's proclamations, *ibid*. 544, 546. Trithemius, Chronicon Hirsaugiense ad annum 1496.

[2] Letter of Maximilian of the 29th August from Carimate (read instead of Calmia) in Datt, p. 552 *seq*.

[3] Pontus Heuterus, Rerum Aust. xv. 230. Gasser, Augsb. Chronik, 257. Cursius, Ann. Suevici, ad hoc ann. [4] Zurita, i. 98.

[5] Maximilian proceeded from Augsburg, where he had resided for two months, about the middle of June, 1496, to Innsbruck, by way of

few days later, the Venetian envoys arrived. The first danger, the arrival of the French, was past. In France, Louis of Orleans, when his baggage was already on the road and he was about to start between evening and morning, suddenly changed his mind, and Charles did not wish to compel him. It would have been all the easier to have attacked Asti, but the Venetians would not give it up to the man who had refused them Pisa. An immediate attack upon Florence was concerted. In a short time Maximilian, full of his schemes, stood before the towers of Leghorn, in order first to wrest this city from Florence.[1]

The Florentines at that time owned sway over 800 walled towns, consisting partly of such as were closed in the

Landsberg. Here he remained from the 27th of June to the 5th of July (Reports of the Venetian envoy, Francesco Foscari, in the Achivio storico Italiano, vii. 734, 749). Thence he journeyed by Imst (10th July), Pfunds (13th), and Nauders to Mals, where he arrived on July 17. On the 20th the meeting with Ludovico took place at Münster. Maximilian escorted Ludovico on the same day as far as Mals. From Mals, which he left on the 26th of July, he returned to Imst, where he arrived on the 2nd August (not on the 28th July, as Ullmann, Kaiser Maximilian I, p. 447, states ; for in Foscari's report in the Arch. stor. Ital. vii. 790, "jeri giunsi in questo loco dove si trova l'Arciduca Filippo e nel quale S. M. arrivò il di precedente ;" by "jeri," seeing that the letter was dated 4th August, the 3rd is meant, and accordingly is "il di precedente" the 2nd August—in the Itinerarium of Maximilian, by Stälin, Forschungen, i. 355, Imst does not occur), and had an interview with his son Philip. On the 4th August Maximilian again left Imst, and proceeded by Landeck, Prutz, Pfunds, and Nauders to Mals, which he reached on the 13th. Thence he set out on the 15th, and betook himself by Bormio, Tirano, Sondrio, and Carimate, to Meda, where he met on the 31st August the envoy and Ludovico. On the 1st September Maximilian went back to Vigevano, where he arrived on the 2nd, and Ludovico and the papal legate on the 3rd September (Sanuto in Arch. stor. vii. 946). (Note to 3rd edition.—It should be the 13th September ; see Foscari's Report in Arch. stor. Ital. vii. 865, Sanuto, Diarii, i. 304 ; and cf. Rawdon Brown, Ragguagli sulla vita e sulle opere di Marin Sanuto, pp. 35, 40.)

[1] Senarega, Annales Genuenses, 560. Burcardus, Diarium, 2075. Ghilinus, 88. Comines, 576. On the 23rd September Maximilian started from Vigevano, and proceeded by way of Tortaea (Foscari, p. 886) to Genoa, which he reached on the 27th. Here he embarked on the 8th October, and arrived on the 21st at Pisa. On the 27th October he came with the Venetian ships to Leghorn (Foscari, pp. 914, 922).

evening and opened in the morning—the half at least with a market—as well as over 12,000 open hamlets. One hundred and thirty towns brought them every St. John's Day a taper or a piece of cloth, and owned the city as their protectress.[1]   Such was the power they exercised over Pistoia and Volterra by party influence; by their commerce and money over Arezzo, which they had purchased from Coucy d'Enguerrand;[2] over Cortona, which had surrendered to King Ladislas and had been bartered by him to them; over Pisa, which had on one occasion been betrayed and sold to them by Gabriele Visconti, and on another by the head of the exiles, then the head of the city—for the city had resisted and had called back its exiles into it—and, finally, over Leghorn, which Tommaso Fregoso had made over to them for 100,000 ducats.[3]

Now we must remember that not all the 10,000 fathers of families at that time in Florence belonged to the ruling classes, for the most of them were citizens without the rights of citizens. The benefit of the city, as it was called, was shared in by only 576 houses of the greater, and by 220 of the lesser trades, and probably never by more than 2,000 citizens. They had also private property; and the 800 palaces and 32,000 estates in the vicinity of the city were for the most part in their hands. It was these 2,000 against whom Maximilian waged war.[4]

In spite of their great affluence and power, they had not as yet forsaken their original employment, trade, nor abated their innate severity of life. They had 270 woollen factories which imported wool from France, Catalonia, and the best from England, and exported cloth to South Italy, to Constantinople, and by way of Brusa to the whole of the East. They had eighty-three manufactories for silk fabrics, brocade, and damask, for which their own ships fetched the silk from the East, and which found their chief markets in Lyons, Barcelona, Seville, London, and

[1] Benedetto Dei in Varchi, Istorie Fiorentine, 262.
[2] Sismondi, Histoire des Républ. Ital., vi. 407, vii. 287.
[3] Belius, Historia Patriae in Graevius, v. 27, 42, 90.
[4] Varchi, Digressione intorno il governo di Firenze in the Istorie, ii. 65. Istorie, 208.

I

Antwerp.[1] The East sent them silk, and the Western world wool; they manufactured both, and exported their silk stuffs to the West and their woollens to the East, and thus ministered to the wants of the world. Hence it came that their first Signori were cloth and silk merchants, and the third a banker.[2] For their thirty-three banks, having agencies in all parts, did perhaps the best business of all; they founded the fortune of the Medici.[3]

The first business of such a Florentine was to go to early Mass. This done, in summer clothed in black Lucco, frilled round the neck, and a black silken cap with a long point, and in winter in black mantle and sober cowl,[4] he walked through the streets to his business in the market or in the palace. At midday, after dinner, he saw his children and related to them a new or an old story.[5] He then arranged his papers, or went to the Loggie which the patricians had at their houses. They always addressed each other as "thou;" and only a knight, a doctor, or an uncle was called "you" and "Messere." Almost every one bore the nickname that had been given him by his playfellows in his youth. The beautiful language that the whole of Italy learnt from them was formed in their society. At the hour of the Ave Maria they were all at home. In winter, they stood with wife and child for a while around the fire; and whilst the lower orders, and those that lived by the sweat of their brow, made good cheer in the inns, they themselves partook of a frugal meal at home at the third hour of the night. Many stayed up half the night at their looms and their spindles.[6]

Among these rich, influential, educated, and austere people, a Dominican friar of Ferrara, one Girolamo Savonarola, had succeeded in making himself universally esteemed. He was, it is true, strict with himself and others, a solitary walker, a friar by inclination, and a man who

---

[1] Benedetto Dei in Fabroni, Vita Laurentii Medici, ii. 337.
[2] Neumann, Introd. to Aretinus, Staatsverf. von Florenz, 39.
[3] Roscoe, Life of Lorenzo, from his Ricordi, 120. Benedetto Dei.
[4] Varchi, Storie, p. 265.
[5] Machiavelli's comedy, Clitia, act ii. sc. iv. p. 141.
[6] Varchi, 261, 267.

also knew how to control his rough voice. He admonished his brother friars to give up all their property. He spared no one, neither his fellow-citizens, the Brescians or the Florentines, nor his liege lords, the Pope and Lorenzo de' Medici, and all this helped to secure him a certain influence. But what made him really powerful were, before all else, his teaching and his prophetic gifts.

His teaching is indeed worth examining:—"Like a piece of iron between two magnets, so does the human soul waver between divine and earthly things, and between belief and feeling. Its purity consists solely in withdrawing itself from the love of things earthly, and in voluntary flight to God. Sacrament and prayer lead to Him; His nature it is that draws it heavenwards to participate in His goodness.[1] But the soul has a domestic enemy, an adversary in the form of a friend, the flesh, that rebels against it, and oppresses it to sin. With its help the devil lies in wait for it, like the vulture after the heart of its prey. Since the world began he has deceived and devoured it a thousand thousand times, yea, a number without end and count, and is not yet satiated, but still lurks and waits like a hungry wolf. The world accordingly is divided between two banners, of Christ and the devil, a black and a white one."

"Now the sinner is like a dead man, reft of life. His face is dark, he durst not open his eyes. God hates him. A man may pour bad wine from his golden vessel and keep the vessel; but God breaks both sin and the vessel of sin. And no one begs for mercy of God, as in Florence no one dares to entreat for an exile."[2]

"The faithful man, on the other hand, when he bows his knee, when he follows the commands of Love, when he disregards all things earthly, and only aims at being merged into God, feels God and is illuminated by him. In this way, a simple man and a maiden of low estate come further than Plato and Pythagoras came. But he

---

[1] Savonarola, de simplicitate christiana, 80, 18, 78. Edition of 1615. Triumphus crucis, i. c. 12.

[2] Seven consoling sermons by Savonarola in Latin. (Sieben schöner tröstlicher Predigten, von Hieronym. Savonarola in Latein, durch Michael Lindenern verdeutscht. Wittenberg, 1668.)

who is by nature inclined thereto, and who is quite free
of earthly care, by constant habit and watchful carefulness
attains in his old age the greatest bliss, he sees God.
Such a man communes with angels and saints; and the
devil has no power over him, but he over the devil." [1]

"When the wicked man's day is done, where is then
his pomp? His journeying and his riding? His hurrying
and scurrying, and his golden ornaments? Down, down,
where his body is food for worms. But the soul is free,
and begins to think of itself and to lament: 'O woe! who
hath soiled my vesture, which by baptism was made whiter
than snow, and made it now more filthy than pitch?'
Satan then comes to it and says: 'My playmate, stand up,
I have done it. For thou hast followed my advice and
worked faithfully with me. Come, follow me into my
kingdom. There is hunger without meat, thirst without
drink, there is an unquenchable, dull, violent, smoking fire,
and by the side of it, cold without measure and remedy.
Come with me. The devils are coming to meet thee with
their song of lamentation.'" [2]

"But on the other side, the joy of the elect cannot be
described in language. It will be splendid and clear, like
the sheen of the sun, quick like the ray of light that in one
moment gleams from east to west. Being with God he
will know all things, present, past, and future; he will
wish for nothing that he cannot obtain; there will be a
life and existence in constant admiration, in sweet delight,
in ecstatic love, in the ceaseless singing of praises, in bliss
and triumph, without ending for evermore." [3]

When Savonarola delivered this teaching, with an eloquence which is often nothing but rapture, a shout of joy
and triumph,[4] and especially when he corroborated it out
of the Holy Writ, the Florentines, as he himself has said,
stood and gazed at him like marble pillars, with their faces

---

[1] De simplicitate, **13, 41**, de divisione omnium scientarum, edition
of 1594, p. 793. Dialogus: solatium itineris mei, ed. of 1633, p. 165,
228. Expositio orationis dominicae, edition of 1615, p. 190.

[2] Sixth Sermon. Solatium itineris mei, lib. vi.; de vita futura,
p. 250.

[3] Seventh Sermon. Solatium, 254–263.

[4] For instance, Sermo in vigilia nativitatis Christi.

turned to his.[1] It was all the more impressive because it distinguished good and evil, as in their city Ghibellines and Guelphs, Bianchi and Neri, had often been contrasted. Besides, they considered him a prophet. He had foretold the advent and the victory of Charles, and had prophesied in unmistakable language the expulsion of the Medici.[2] The majority believed him entirely. He was master of their minds, and in the new order of things in Florence he attained the greatest influence.

It was Piero's nearest relatives and friends who had summoned his enemy to Tuscany, had expelled him from the Signoria, and overthrown him. It was not that they were minded to share their government with the populace —when would this ever occur to the ruling party in any city? — but, because Piero intended to be prince, they hated him. They hoped under Lorenzino and the junior line of this house to attain to greater influence. With this idea, immediately after Piero's flight, they summoned a parliament. They called it a parliament, when they collected the people together in the square by the sound of a bell, placed armed youths at all the entrances, who thrust back every one who was displeasing to them, and then, finally, allowed the collected throng to vote by acclamation. Such a parliament, on this occasion, with loud shouts of consent, entrusted to twenty men among them the business of a Balìa, that is, the supreme government.[3]

Savonarola, whose theory based the right of government purely upon agreement,[4] opposed them, and preached his principle that all true citizens ought to participate in the sovereign power. He even convinced some of the leading men. Antonio Soderini publicly professed his views ; others visited him at night. Owing to this, differences and general dissensions gradually arose, which were followed at last by a peaceable and complete dissolution of the Balìa.[5]

[1] Triumphus crucis, p. 100.

[2] Fabroni, Vita Laurentii Medici, ii. 291.

[3] Nerli, Istorie Fiorentine, 58, 63.   Cf. Sismondi, Histoire des Républiques Ital. xii. 233.

[4] Savonarola, del governo.

[5] Nardi, Le storie della città, 23.   Corio, Istor. di Mil. 966.

The new order of things was framed in accordance with Savonarola's principles. All those who enjoyed the benefit of the city, that is all whose fathers and grandfathers had, since the political government of the Medici, been drawn for the three dignities of Signori, Gonfalonieri, and Buonuomini, that is to say had been elected or at least declared eligible, entered into the government under the name of the Consiglio Grande. Such an arrangement is far from being a declaration of the rights of man ; for Savonarola conceived of social distinctions and grades to have been original and given by God :[1] to many it will appear to have been nothing more nor less than an enlarged aristocracy. Only inside the Council no privilege should be tolerated. It received a thoroughly democratic constitution. Just as in Venice there were Doge, Consiglieri, and Pregadi above the Grand Council, so here also the Gonfaloniere had the administration of justice, and the eight Priori and the Council of Eighty the essential attributes of government. In Venice the greater part of the dignities were conferred for life, but in Florence for two months and not by a regular election. Only after certain names in each quarter of the city had been proposed by chance, by lot, did voting take place upon them. The elections were rather committees and commissions, than official elections in our sense of the term. "A city is well governed," says Savonarola, "when the magistracy have short notice given them of the day when their stewardship shall be inquired into. What otherwise is the meaning of free election? for every one will only be obedient to the best."[2] For this assembly a hall was at once built. It was the largest in Italy, and yet was finished in a marvellously short time. It was approached by broad steps. The middle was occupied lengthways and crossways by benches for the citizens, on each side upon a raised dais three yards high and broad were seats for the Eighty. At the east end, the Gonfaloniere and Priori had their places, and here two doors led into the chambers set apart for secret deliberation, and for the registry of taxes;

[1] Savonarola, de simplicitate vitae christianae, 65, 70, 85, 90.
[2] Nerli, 44, 66. Varchi, Digressione intorno il governo, 67 ; Savonarola, del governo.

at the west end there stood a tribune and an altar with a picture by Fra Bartolommeo, at which mass was said. The hall had also an ecclesiastical appearance, and Savonarola said: "the angels have assisted in the work."[1]

This constitution was in full operation when Maximilian was investing Leghorn. It is true there was no demand now for brocade or cloth; the Stradioti laid waste the country estates; there was no importation either by sea or land, for Siena also was hostile; but that made little impression upon the citizens. They came in such numbers to hear Savonarola's sermons, that in the Cathedral of Sᵗᵃ Maria del Fiore, in spite of its great size, galleries had to be built at the entrance, opposite the pulpit, as in a theatre. The fasts were most strictly observed. The games that the friar condemned were abandoned; and, in view of the approaching war, they awaited the arrival of the fleet which Charles was fitting out in Marseilles. But soon they had to learn that this fleet had been wrecked in a storm. Weiskunig narrates that Maximilian saw the French fleet arriving; and hereupon, as soon as he had weighed anchor and spread his sails, there came first a cloud, and from it wind, and then more clouds, and thereout there arose such a storm, that the enemy's ships were driven with him into the harbour, and part in battle and part in storm were wrecked and lost. Where was now their hope and the promise of God's immediate help that the Dominican had made them? Yet they retained sufficient courage, even at this critical moment, to receive within their walls a host of fugitives, who had been beggared by the war. They could not do aught else but carry the image of the Virgin through the streets, followed by all men and women, clerics and children, with psalm‑singing, prayers and lamentations. They had just arrived with their tabernacle at the Porta Sᵗᵃ Maria, when they perceived a messenger on a mare careering across the Ponte Sᵗᵃ Trinità, and waving an olive-branch from afar. They stopped and listened; some ships fitted out by their merchants, which had long struggled with the same storm, had at last, owing to the wind having unexpectedly shifted, been driven right past Maximilian into the harbour,

[1] Vasari, Vita di Simone Cronaca, iii. 253.

and so to Leghorn. The news was true. They seized the horse's reins; every one wanted to hear it for himself from the mouth of the messenger. We may imagine, though the historians do not record it, how fervently they thanked God, the God who had heard their prayers, for these tidings.[1]

What saved them, thwarted Maximilian's plans. The Florentines would now no longer entertain the idea of being separated from Charles VIII, of whose return Savonarola had always reminded them. Leghorn was held for them by Swiss legions. Moreover, the south-west wind levelled their enemy's tents on land, and scattered his ships on the sea. Maximilian, meanwhile, saw the months, within which the money was promised him, draw to a close; the Venetian and Sforza parties were already at variance as to which should hold the harbour when they took it; and he heard of letters from Venice itself, written with the object of inciting the army against him. Overcome by the feeling of the impossibility of being able to achieve anything under such circumstances, he said, "No! against the will of God and men, he would not wage this war." He turned towards Pisa, arrived at Vico, appeared as if he still intended to do something, but did nothing, and, though invited to the chase, hurried away to Pavìa and home to Germany.[2]

After this the Florentines cherished no doubt of Savonarola's prophetic mission. At Christmas, 1496, 1,300 children under eighteen years—for only with their eighteenth year were they wont to adopt the long cloak, and to rank as young men—partook of the Sacrament with the priest. On the following Shrove Tuesday the children of every quarter went to the houses and begged for the " Anathema," that is " the accursed thing." Their distribution into companies,

[1] Nardi, 29–32. Weiskunig, 201, and in other passages. Ghilinus, 90.

[2] Jovius, Historiae sui temporis, 83. Navagero, Storia Venez., 1207. Zurita, 108, and Coccinius, de bellis Italicis, 277. Machiavelli, Legazione a Pisa. The French ships put into the harbour of Leghorn on the 29th Oct. (Foscari in the Arch. Stor. ital. vii. 938. Sanuto, Diarii, i. 373); about the middle of November Maximilian raised the siege. On the 16th Nov. he was at Vicopisano, on the 2nd Dec. at Pavìa, on the 26th at Mals; at the commencement of the year 1497 he returned thence to Innsbruck.

their processions, and songs at vespers under Correttori were familiar.[1] The men gave them cards, dice, and dice-boards, the women false hair, paint, and perfumed waters. Many produced their Morgante, Boccaccio, and indelicate pictures ; some sacrificed their harps, remembering perhaps for what purposes they had used them. Bartolommeo Baccio took the naked figures—for they should not be where young maidens congregated—from his workshop and offered them. In the market-place a stage was erected in the form of a pyramid with many steps mounting up to it, and upon this all these things were piled. On the day of the Carnival, the whole people came together, and the Signori took their seats. Then came the children from the mass, dressed in white, with olive-branches round their heads and red crosses in their hands, and sang Italian hymns of praise. Four advanced to the Signori, received from them burning torches and lighted the pyramid, which blazed up amid the blare of trumpets. Meanwhile alms were collected for the poor who were ashamed to beg.[2]

The severe religious tendency of this city forms a material link in the struggle between the League and the French party. By declaring against the Pope, who regarded himself as the head of the League, it gave the quarrel a new phase.

In Ferrara, Savonarola's native place, we remark a similar condition of things. Frequent fasting was observed, blasphemy was punished, and swearing was prohibited. Beadles were sent through the streets to report on everything. There is no doubt what was the object of all this. The inhabitants of Ferrara, who had but, little sympathy with the League, because it united both their natural enemies, Venice and the Pope—being, as they were, of French sympathies, even to wearing French dresses and shoes—endeavoured to counteract the Pope's influence by still deeper piety.[3] In spite of the great perils surrounding them, they made processions every third day. In the King of France, Charles VIII, we

[1] Varchi, 259, 265.
[2] Nardi. Vasari, Vita del Fra Bartolommeo, t. iii.
[3] Diarium Ferrarense, 320, 323, 386.

remark a kindred tendency. He asked his doctors whether or not the Pope was not bound to hold a Council every ten years; whether, in case he neglected to do so, the princes were not entitled to summon it; and further, in case all the others neglected this duty, whether the King of France alone could not summon a Council. He made known his intention of restoring the order of St. Benedict to its original form, and of permitting no bishop to absent himself from his diocese.[1] Savonarola was the head of all enemies of the League and the Pope. He condemned the wealth and the pomp of the clergy, for thereby the barrier was broken which separated Church and world. By this means the children of the world had entered into God's vineyard. But God's Word still endured, and they were in no way bound to trust a prelate as much as it. Nay, no one ought to teach God's Word except so long as his works were not prejudicial to the operation of the doctrine. Acting in accordance with these principles, he invited Charles orally, and the Emperor and the Spanish King in writing, to undertake the reformation of the Church. But it was inevitable that he should arouse hierarchical antipathy against himself. A man named Mariano de Genazzano, who had once preached at his side in Florence to the admiration of the classical scholars, hurried to Rome to the Pope, and there began one of his sermons with, " Cut this monster off from the Church, holy Father!"[2]

Whilst Pope Alexander was at that very time giving dispensation from oaths, in order that his enemies might die in prison,[3] he resolved at the same time to use his ecclesiastical weapons against Savonarola and his adherents, as being heretics. But before this, he had another battle to fight out with the partisans of the League in his own land, the Orsini.

The Orsini were no despicable foes. They killed his son, the Duke of Gandia, to whom he had committed the staff of the Church to war against them, and he was

---

[1] Questions in Garnier, xx. 519. Brantôme, 39. Comines, 592.
[2] Meditationes in Psalmos, Lugduni, 1633, p. 128. Del Governo. Letters in Mansi. Nardi.
[3] Zurita, i. 97.

obliged to call Gonzalvo to his aid. Gonzalvo had just taken Taranto, which had in vain flown the Venetian colours—for the League would not allow Venice to take its side [1]—and had subjected Sora to Federigo. He now vanquished a pirate, who had taken Ostia and threatened to starve out Rome, and compelled the Orsini to make peace. At this time the Neapolitan, Papal, and Spanish flags were all flying in conjunction on the ships of Villamarino, which were now victorious everywhere. Even Cardinal Giuliano was obliged to come to terms.[2]

After this, when the Pope had leisure to turn his attention to Savonarola, it happened that a factious rising in Florence aided him, and he it. The leading Florentines could not forget the power they had enjoyed under the Medici in former days, and their sons would not submit to the rigorous discipline of the friar. Probably under the impression that Piero would now have learnt to know them better, they allied themselves with his professed adherents, the Bigi (they themselves were called the Arrabbiati), in order to effect his recall. They were not successful. Benivieni, whom the Signoria in their alarm sent to Savonarola, often related how he found the friar reading in a book from which he looked up and said : " O ye of little faith, God is with you ! Mark ye, Piero will come as far as the gates and will then turn back." Nardi adds : "And so it really happened. One of those who had already been seized by the Medici, escaped and came before daybreak to the gate in order to close it, whereupon Piero found it closed and all quiet, and went back again." But how fierce and violent must this party feeling in the city have been, to bring such an excellent and pious man, as the friar was, from his path.[3] To him especially is due the law that where any one is accused of

---

[1] Johannes Juvenis, de fortuna Tarentinorum, vii. 3. Navagero, Stor. Ven. 1209.

[2] Jovius, Vita Gonsalvi, 220. Arnold von Harve, Reise, in the Conversationsblatt of 1823, No. 2. Burcardus, 2080.

[3] Nerli, 71. Nardi, 36. Jovius, Vita Leonis, 19. Cf. also contemporary records in Matthiae Döringii Continuatio Chronici Engethustani, in Mencken, Scriptores Rerum Saxonicarum, ii. 53.

a political crime, he shall not be judged by the Signoria, or a Commission as a court of last instance, but shall be allowed to appeal to the Council. This law mitigated the Italian usage, that every victor should, as of right and under certain legal formulas, be able to decide the question of life and death in the case of his adversaries. But in August, 1497, when it was believed to have been discovered who had taken Piero's part, Savonarola allowed his good law to be infringed, and the accused were denied the right of appeal. His opponents became, in consequence, only more violent and secret.[1]

The Pope now sided with them. The Tuscan Dominicans, whom Savonarola had separated from the Lombards, the Pope joined with them again, interdicted him from preaching, summoned him to Rome, and appointed the Lombard Vicar of the order as his judge. But Savonarola continued preaching, received more brothers into his convents daily, and refused to recognize his judge, saying " he could not come to Rome on account of his enemies." It availed him nothing that in Florence signatures were collected attesting the fact that his teaching was sound and productive of good fruit. In spite of all he was placed under ban.[2] After that his life depended upon the fact that his party never allowed its enemies to become strong, for, by the then existing law, he could be at once put to death. The Pope only required the secular arm.

In Florence, however, towards the close of the year 1497, open dissensions burst out. Some of the clergy condemned the processions of others, some the Mass that others celebrated, and some again, as in an heretical city, desired not to perform divine service any longer. The Franciscans, the old opponents of the Dominicans, joined the party of the Arrabbiati and the Pope. Sometimes the friar found his pulpit soiled. On one occasion some young men lifted a heavy money-box during his sermon, let it fall and fled. He was escorted to church by armed

<hr />

[1] Machiavelli, Discorsi sopra la prima deca di Livio, I. c. 44.

[2] Alexander Papa priori, etc. Responsio fratris Hieronymi in Burcardus, and in Gordon, Vie d'Alexandre, Appendix ii. 488. Epistolae Petri Martyris, xi. 191.

men, and whilst he was preaching one stood by him with
a halbert. But sometimes, when some of the Arrabbiati
joined the Signoria, and the others were timid, he remained
in his convent altogether.[1]

Yet he did not lose courage. The moral of his teaching was that a pious and learned man must not give way
to a wicked and ignorant Pope.[2] He comforted himself
in his convent with his successes. " Every day a greater
number, out of yearning for a more perfect life, forsake
parents, friends, and goods, and betake themselves where
each must do or not do as his superior wills ; where no
one has anything except what he absolutely needs, and
where he can for a time be deprived by his superior even
of that. But here every one becomes daily calmer, and
· confesses that Christ is his only joy. Only he who prays
without ceasing attains to a holiness, from whose rays his
face beams with rapture." [3]   He found himself in the midst
of the struggle between Popolari and Arrabbiati, the League
and its enemies, the true and the Roman Church, between
heaven and hell. He openly interpreted those two flags,
the black and the white, in this sense. He felt certain
of victory. At Christmas he published his treatise,
" Triumphus Crucis." Therein he represented Christ upon
a triumphal car, above his head the gleaming ball of the
Trinity, in his left hand the Cross, in his right the Old and
the New Testaments ; further below, the Virgin Mary ;
before the car, patriarchs, prophets, apostles, and preachers ;
on either side the martyrs and the doctors with opened
books ; behind him, all the converts ; at a further distance
the innumerable crowd of enemies, emperors, powerful
rulers, philosophers, and heretics, all vanquished, their
idols destroyed, and their books burnt.[4]

But the longer it lasted, the more furious waxed the
conflict. At Shrovetide, 1498, his children desired to
repeat the celebration of the previous year ; but the

---

[1] Nardi and Nerli.
[2] Del governo.
[3] Triumphus crucis, 121, 195, 114.
[4] Triumphus crucis, p. 11.   Machiavelli, Lettere, tom. vi. ed. 1783,
p. 6.

torches were torn out of their hands. At first, the children, and then even the men, stoned each other. A significant instance of the extent of the feud was afforded by the action of the painters, Baccio and Albertinelli. They had always worked together, and had had all things in common. They now left their workshop. The former went into a convent, the other became an innkeeper.[1] How was it possible that these differences could be settled but by force? When, at last, a Franciscan friar presumed to declare that he would prove in the fire that certain doctrines of the Dominicans were erroneous, it appeared also to the latter that they had found another and the true decision—the ordeal. The Franciscans argued thus: if Savonarola would allow their friar to perish in the fire, he was no saint; and upon this they built. The others, who were half mad, who indulged sometimes in the market places in round dances to the accompaniment of a spiritual song, and who had chosen for their war cry "Viva Cristo!" hoped to conquer by the truth of their faith. During the sermon, hundreds cried, "Look! look! I will go for thy doctrine, O Lord, into the fire." Accordingly two piles of oak logs and brushwood, well saturated with pitch and oil, were built up side by side, 40 feet in length, leaving a very narrow passage between them, and on the 7th of April the Signoria, on this occasion only Arrabbiati, sat awaiting the trial.[2]

The Franciscans came quietly, the Dominicans with burning torches, red crosses, and loud singing, led by Savonarola. The monks approached the pyre; the Dominican seized the Host. At this moment the crisis arrived. The Franciscans would not permit him to have the Host, as this would be a test of the whole Christian faith, but he would not be prevented. Hereupon ensued a quarrel, confusion, a shower of rain, and a general stampede. Some rushed into the convent, others resorted to arms. Scenes of violence followed, and the Arrabbiati would not allow the favour of the Signoria and the

---

[1] Vasari, Vita del Mariotto Albertinelli in the Vite, iii.

[2] Nardi and Nerli, Declaratio fratris Hieronymi, in Burcardus, 6. Eccardus, 2090.

propitious moment to pass by without taking advantage of it. They attacked the Popolari in the streets and in the convent; and, although they did not take the convent by storm, they remained masters of the situation. Savonarola took no part in these proceedings. At first he exhorted his followers from the pulpit, afterwards he prostrated himself in the choir of the church and prayed. When all was quiet, he went out, and delivered himself up to his enemies.[1]

There was now no doubt that the League was victorious in Italy: the Arrabbiati were as devoted to it as the Popolari were to the French. On the 7th of April the Arrabbiati asserted their supremacy in Florence; on the 8th, Charles died, and the League was victorious even in France. Charles was at the last occupied with the internal affairs of his realm. Of his Grand Council he formed an ordinary Court of Justice, consisting of seventeen members, something similar to the later Reichshofrath of the Germans; in all commanderies he had a general book of customs compiled; he intended to live on his demesnes, an' twice every week he sat to hear the complaints even of the poorest. Having made all these arrangements, and equipped with better alliances, he was again about to attempt to assert his right to Naples. Savonarola, too, had always referred to his return. But on the 8th of April, whilst passing through a gallery on his way to look at a game of tennis, he suddenly fell down, and, though a moment before in perfect health, died in a few minutes.[2]

Many are of opinion that this event first determined Savonarola's fate. Many accusations had been brought up against him; and as often as torture was applied, he confessed all that was wanted. But as soon as he came to himself again, he denied everything, saying that "on the rack he would certainly confess to it again."

---

[1] Nardi and Nerli. Burcardi Diarium, 2087, 2094. Excerpta ex Monacho Pirnensi, probably a pamphlet, mentioned by Trithemius in Mencken, ii. 1518.

[2] Garnier from the Lettres patentes, 515, and a letter of Charles there cited. Comines, 591. St. Gelais, 120. Bayard, 56. Brantôme, 44.

Meanwhile his soul communed with itself. His pride was broken; if he ever had thought himself holy, he thought so no longer. It often seemed to him as if Despair, with a strong army with lances and swords, the standard of Justice before it, and surrounded by instruments of torture, appeared in the town, called him from afar, and, coming nearer, whispered into his ear all his sins; and then again Hope, shining with the light of heaven, would comfort him. He spoke to himself thus: " Thou hast loved the Lord many years, and hast wrought out of love to Him; then didst thou exalt thy heart; then didst thou follow thine own thoughts, and live in the vanity of thy mind; then did the Lord take His hand from thee, and thou art like a sinner plunged into the depths of the sea." He had arrived at this holy self-enlightenment, when he was doomed to die; his body was consigned to the fire.[1]

With his death the essence of his teaching and his influence was not destroyed. Simone Cronaca, a good artist, honoured him whilst he was alive, and spoke of him when he was dead. Even after thirty years, the accomplishment of his most famous prophecies was expected to take place. But at that time, as we have said, the Arrabbiati attained the principal offices. They did not now consider the recall of Piero necessary for their safety. They were so devoted to the League, that all its members, except the Venetians, considered it better to restore Pisa to them.[2]

[1] Meditatio in Psalmum; " In te, Domine, speravi," I. quam morte praeceptus absolvere non potuit, 84, 97. The history of Savonarola has since then commanded the greatest attention in all civilized countries, and has been the subject of various treatises. The account that I gave here as the result of my former studies, I could not alter by the light of them, although on the occasion of a lengthened visit to Florence I have not neglected to make researches. I still hope to be able to publish in a later volume the results of my labours at that time, which have especial reference to the history of Florence in the first epoch of the Medici. [Note to the 2nd edition.]

[2] Vasari, Vita di Simone, detto il Cronaca. Zurita, i. 143.

3. EXTENSION AND ASCENDENCY OF THE LEAGUE

Thus the object of the League was attained, and Italy subjected to its views. But the extension and ascendency of the League is fraught with other consequences for the whole of Europe, and for later times. The alliance of the Houses of Hapsburg and Aragon is one result of the conditions which obtained during these years. Ferdinand knew how to draw the maritime princes into the sphere of his alliances, and among them first Dom Manuel of Portugal. He had protected him whilst he was still Duke, and had made military preparations in his favour when he inherited the throne after John's death.[1] But Dom Jorge, John's natural son, of whom all were afraid, was led by Jacobo Almeida before the King to kiss hands,[2] and war was averted. Ferdinand promised his daughter Isabella to this Manuel. Isabella, who considered a second marriage a bad thing, demanded that Manuel should at all events expel from Portugal the Jews and all those whom the Inquisition had condemned. She would not consent to be his wife until he had promised her this.[3] After that day, peace and union existed between Portugal and Spain for a century and a half.

At the same period, in August, 1497, and ever since the treaty with Brittany, Ferdinand was negotiating with Henry VII of England. If Spain and France quarrel, England must take part in it. In June, 1496, Henry joined the League;[4] he received hat and sword from the Pope, and received the envoys of all the allies.[5] His councillors, indeed, asserted that this was tantamount to bringing the war to England; but this monarch, who never cared about taking the field, except it might be against a rebel, well knew what he was about, and that he was working at the iron wall, with which, as he said, he intended to gird his

[1] Zurita, 78.

[2] Hieronymi Osorii de rebus Manuelis libri xii. lib. i. 3, a.

[3] Zurita, f. 124. Osorius, i. 14.

[4] Burcardus, 2067. Cf. Brewer, Calendar of State Papers, i. 247 (note to 2nd edition).

[5] Chronicon Venetum, p. 41.

realm.[1] But, at present, great dangers threatened him from
without: in Flanders, from Margaret of York, widow of
Charles the Bold, who, if she did not actually incite his
first rebel, Lambert Simnel, who declared himself to be
Edward of Warwick, at all events raised him to some importance by means of 2,000 Germans, whom she found
means to send to his assistance.[2] No one doubted that the
second rebel, Perkin Warbeck, who called himself Richard,
Duke of York, was also really her creature.[3] The latter
found his most reliable support in Scotland, where King
and nation united in their eagerness to cross the Tweed.
James IV allied Perkin with his house, brought him to
Scotland, ravaged the country, and was alternately in his
palace and on the border;[4] whilst the people, whenever a
truce was made, broke it on their own responsibility. In
both countries, Flanders and Scotland, the effect of the
marriage arranged between Katherine of Spain and Arthur,
Prince of Wales, was felt. Ferdinand was enabled by it to
render the King of England secure on either side. At first,
through the Austrian alliance, the treaty of general intercourse between England and Flanders was renewed; "rebels
were to be extradited, including Margaret's territory."[5]
The English merchants came in triumph to Antwerp, and
Maximilian, though hesitatingly, promised to ignore the
so-called York.[6] In Scotland, Pedro de Ayala was plying
his negotiations with sly circumspection, in order to draw
the King into the great political league. He understood
how to persuade Perkin—and this appears to have escaped
the notice of the English historians[7]—that the Kings of
England and Scotland had already come to an agreement,
and that there was therefore nothing left to him but to
flee; and when Perkin, on the ship of a Spaniard of San

[1] Bacon, Historia Henrici Septimi, p. 300.
[2] Polydorus Virgilius, Historia Anglica, lib. 26, p. 730.
[3] Bacon, p. 194.
[4] Buchanan, Rerum Scoticarum, lib. xiii. 460, 465.
[5] Bacon, p. 268. Treaty in Rymer. Wagenaar, Allgem. Gesch.
ii. 269.
[6] Zurita, pp. 88, 99.
[7] Hume and Rapin, besides Bacon and Polydore Virgil, the source
of all.

Sebastian, had joined the rebels of Cornwall, he persuaded King James not to undertake the invasion of England just at that moment,[1] whereupon Perkin fell into Henry's power. King James then married Margaret, daughter of Henry VII,[2] whence resulted a long peace between the Scots and the English, and finally the union of both kingdoms. The close relationship in which James stood to John of Denmark, who possessed Norway and claimed Sweden, cemented the peace which the Danes and English had, after a long war, recently concluded.

The chief members of the League were Ferdinand, Henry, and Maximilian, the old allies of Brittany, yet now united, not merely by their advantage, but by the blood of their children.

All that now remained was that, if not Henry, at all events Ferdinand and Maximilian should, as they had agreed, invade France. But this scheme was confronted by the consideration that Ferdinand had something to lose by it, whilst Maximilian would gain. Between Aragon and France there lay certain frontiers, where ravaging was so regular, that whenever any one went on a pilgrimage, or took to him a wife, he had to submit to pillage at the hands of both parties. Thus in this war also, Enrique Enriquez crossed the frontier, and pillaged for three days and three nights; then well-armed Gascons, Swiss, and French appeared on the other side, and the French succeeded in surprising the Castle of Salsas. Thereupon, out of apprehension for Roussillon, Ferdinand concluded a truce.[3] Maximilian was discontented with these doings. Not only the death of Charles, but a new phase of German politics aroused him to fresh hopes.

---

[1] Zurita, p. 134.

[2] Buchanan, 488. From the information given by Bergenroth, Calendar of State Papers, i. 97, it is plain that the chief impetus to this alliance was given by the Catholic sovereigns, who only regretted that they had not two daughters to dispose of, so as to be able to marry one to the King of England and the other to the King of Scotland, and therefore counselled that a marriage should be arranged between the latter and the daughter of the former. [Note to 2nd edition.]

[3] Hubert Thomas Leodius, Vita Frederici Palatini, ii. No. 45. Comines, 581. Zurita, 79, 114.

After his return from Italy, his prestige in the Empire was at first at a low ebb. The Elector Palatine was on good terms with Charles, sent knights into his service, entreated a good reception for his merchants, and delegates of both sides held meetings.[1]

The total setting aside of the decrees of Worms made the Elector of Mainz extremely disaffected. He openly complained of Maximilian: "From top to bottom there was little trace of earnestness; contrary to their resolutions Milan and Savoy had been regranted; he was ill pleased to find that ordinances were made and sealed, and yet not adhered to; in this way the Empire could not possibly maintain its position."[2] Maximilian also perceived that he could not undertake anything, until he had gained over both Electors and the Chancellor of Mainz, Doctor Stürzler. He never attended any meeting of the Diet. However, in consequence of the death of the elder Eberhard of Württemberg, he effected a change. For Eberhard had appointed for his cousin and heir a council of twelve men, four from each estate, without whom he could do nothing, but who without him could discharge the daily business of the State, and perform even the most important functions, if he did not accept their invitation to appear;[3] and had entrusted to this Government his principles, and his devotion to the Emperor. But was it likely that the younger Eberhard would follow his cousin after his death, seeing that he never cared to follow him in his lifetime? Immediately after his arrival, he dismissed the old councillors, took a prisoner, Doctor Holzinger, out of gaol, and made him Chancellor. Thereupon Hug von Werdenberg refused to be Chamberlain any longer; the Twelve complained that Eberhard intended to surrender the country to the Count Palatine; but the Estates were not minded to agree to that. They took his servant prisoner, and seized his cities. He

[1] Epistolae Galliae Regis Caroli et Philippi Archipalatini, in Ludewig: Reliquiae Manuscriptorum, vi. 96.

[2] Müller, Reichstagstheatrum, ii. 144. Also in Hegewisch: Leben Maximilians, i. 144, and in Menzel.

[3] Esslinger-Vertrag in Eisenbach; Geschichte Ulrichs von Württemberg.

escaped with silver and jewels to Ulm. The Estates, the new Chamberlain, the Councillors, the Chancery, the officials and the courtiers turned against him, and renounced their allegiance.[1] Maximilian, alarmed for the estrangement of the country, hurried thither, and heard both sides. But for what purpose? It seems that he had previously decided upon his verdict, "that the Estates and Councillors had done right ; the young Ulrich should be Duke under the guardianship of the Twelve, and later should receive Sabina, the King's niece, to wife ; but that the country should not, if his race died out, pass to the Empire, as was formerly determined, but to Austria."[2]

Eberhard renounced his duchy, repented of his action, fled to the Count Palatine, assigned to him his silver plate and all right and title to his land, repented of that also, and was imprisoned at Lindenfels until his death. But Württemberg was completely loyal to the King.[3]

In the new prestige which the compact with Württemberg had gained for him, Maximilian appeared in June, 1498,[4] at the Diet of Freiburg, which had opened eight months previously. On this occasion he received from the Estates 70,000 guilders, without reckoning what had been received by the Common Penny tax in his hereditary lands.[5] It appeared now possible for him to acquire Burgundy, if not Brittany. With this hope he ordered his army to advance to the borders of Burgundy. The bold landsknechts boasted that if they were victorious this time, France and Switzerland also would be in their power.[6]

---

[1] Ufkündigung der Pflicht, in Sattler, i. Suppl. No. 12. Document A. p. 157. Naucleri Chronographia, at end.

[2] Sattler's Geschichten, p. 32. Decree in Lünig, ii. 722.

[3] Sattler, 33. Eisenbach.

[4] Neidhart's letter to the Diet, in Datt, p. 594.

[5] Datt, p. 904.

[6] Hugi, Vogt zu Domeck, in Glutzblotzheim, p. 518.

CHAPTER IV

FALL OF THE HOUSE OF SFORZA-ARAGON

1. LOUIS XII AND VENICE AGAINST MILAN

THE situation was now as follows. The attacks of the French upon Naples and Milan had leagued the King of Spain and the Pope with Ferrantino, and Venice and Maximilian with Ludovico. Ferrantino had mainly been saved by Ferdinand, whilst Ludovico owed his safety principally to Venice. In the midst of the dissensions that Charles' advent had produced in Central Italy, a Spanish general from the one side and Maximilian himself from the other had taken the field against the French party. This party had been completely defeated. Round France itself there had become formed, in the interest of the League, an alliance of all the sovereigns.

Relying upon this, Maximilian, in the summer of 1498, undertook a three-fold attack upon France. He sent one corps against Langres,[1] a second against Châlons,[2] and a third, under the command of his Marshal of Franche-Comté, Guillaume de Vergy, against Dijon and Burgundy.[3] Three thousand Swiss were in his pay. He expected the help of the League, and considered himself assured of success. But the first corps was in July weakened and lamed in its movements by the heat, which suffocated the horsemen in armour, and also by a want of provisions, which was increased by the soldiers, who, impatient to see fire, preferred to burn down the rich villages to plundering them. The second was driven back by the rains. The third saw the enemy approach and retire, but concluded a

---

[1] Life of Götz von Berlichingen, p. 7.
[2] Zurita, f. 152.
[3] Fugger MS. in Kurzbeck's notes to Weiskunig.

treaty.[1] This campaign was crowned with so little success, that it has been overlooked by all later historians.

These failures were due to the fact that the League at this precise moment ceased to exist. Ferrantino was now dead, and his successor was hated by the King of Spain. Venice was in feud and almost in open war with Ludovico on account of Pisa. But the new King of France succeeded in winning over to himself the defenders of Milan, and the defender of Naples. He drew the Pope to his side, and repulsed the attacks of Maximilian. He made matters look at the moment as though there never had been a League. It is our acquaintance, the Duke of Orleans, now King Louis XII.

He was standing, the story goes, at his window, without knowing that Charles was dead or even ill, when the royal bodyguard drew up before him, and shouted " Vivat ! " to their new Lord and King.[2] On this he spoke, as well as he knew how, in terms of laudation of Charles VIII, sprinkled his body with holy water,[3] and received the fealty of the grandees.

Louis was a perfectly developed man, more in the apogee than in the perigee of life, and already a little afflicted with the gout.[4] That wildness of his early youth, when his chamberlains dared not chastise him unless disguised—for fear he should revenge himself—that impetuousness of later days, disclosed at revelries, tournaments, and in domestic wars, were passed and gone.[5] But he was still beyond all others a prince, and a true knight. The first thing he conceived he ought to guard was his honour. Whoever attacked him, or accused him of the smallest breach of faith, would be refuted by the sword. After that, his lands and his rights were nearest to his heart. " I will endure everything," said he, " save where my honour and my lands are concerned." [6] He had not such bold plans

[1] Weiskunig, 260.
[2] Corio, Storia di Milano, 967.
[3] Extrait d'une histoire in Godefroy, 198.
[4] Maximilian to Esslingen, in Datt, 564.
[5] Extrait de l'histoire de Louis, 337.
[6] Zurita. Machiavelli, Legazione, v. 355.

as had Charles, and had not Maximilian's love of conquest. Only his rights he was resolved to assert, and therefore did not select a " Plus Ultra," but a porcupine for a symbol. It was he who finely said, " The King does not avenge what has been done to the Duke." He preferred to sell his demesnes for the purpose of carrying on his wars, rather than to exhaust his poor subjects with taxes.[1] The same feeling made him forbearing and kind towards others. Moreover, increasing years made him more economical every day. His first action was to defray the expense of his predecessor's interment at Blois out of the savings of his own private exchequer.[2]

The internal government he committed from the first into the hands of the Archbishop of Rouen, Georges d'Amboise. When at the Court of Louis XI, Georges had taken the side of the present King, even in opposition to his own brother. For his sake he had suffered imprisonment, for endeavouring to advantage him at the expense of Charles VIII. They were only three years apart in respect of age, and were entirely devoted one to the other; and, especially after the death of Dunois, Georges had the full and undivided confidence of his master.[3]

The first duty of the King and his Archbishop was to provide that internal peace was perfectly assured. Charles's sister, Anne of Bourbon, demanded, at the least, a compensation for the increment her grandfather, her father, and brother, had acquired for the Crown. She was content when her daughter Suzanne was guaranteed an almost relinquished right of succession to all the possessions of her house.[4] The Prince of Orange regained his sovereignty. All who were afraid of Louis, because they had offended him whilst Duke,—perhaps in his feud with the Queen Regent,—were comforted, when he showed a mark of favour to the brave La Trémouille, who had formerly taken him prisoner, and marked the names of the others with the red cross of pardon.[5] Only he would not brook any

[1] Monstrelet, 249.   [2] Historie de Charles in Godefroy, 169.

[3] Le Gendre : Vie d'Amboise, 12, 27, 39.

[4] Zurita. Garnier, Hist. de France, tom. xxi.

[5] Vie et gestes de la Trémouille, 158.

limitation of the rights of the Crown. A new tribunal
decided against René's claims to Provence. The weightiest
question that he had to determine concerned Brittany, which
by Charles's marriage with Anne had become attached to
the Crown, but which, owing to his death, had now become
separated from it again. Louis XII did not scruple to
divorce his wife Jeanne,[1] in order to re-marry with his
predecessor's heiress, Anne.   Jeanne was certainly not
beautiful, nor had she borne him children. She now betook
herself to Bourges, where, with some sisters in connection
of the order of the Annunciation, she dispensed alms with
true benevolence, and was reverenced as a saint[2] by the
people, who always remained attached to her.

Anne made it a condition that Brittany should neither
pay taxes, nor have officials appointed in it, nor be called
upon to make war, without her consent. Louis united on
his coins the arms of Brittany and France.[3]

Upon other coins, as soon as he had entered Paris,
he styled himself King of Naples and Milan.[4] He was
certain of his rights to these countries; he had fought
for both; and now he wished to enforce them. It was a
great advantage to him that the League collapsed, and
that half of the allies even took his side. After Enrique
Enriquez had been killed in a riot at Perpignan, and
Roussillon was threatened by the French and was not
minded to defend itself, Ferdinand concluded a treaty with
Louis, securing his own interests and the possessions of the
House of Burgundy; yet it did not include Federigo.[5]
The Pope hoped to obtain from Louis so many advantages
for his house, that he was quite ready to pronounce the
divorce from Jeanne.   The Venetians sent him sixty falcons
from Candia and two hundred valuable furs, as a coronation
present.[6]

The successive enterprises of Louis with the Venetians,

[1] Decret in Nicole Gilles, Chroniques de France, 118.
[2] Hottingeri Historia Ecclesiastica.
[3] Coins in Daniel, Hist. de France, iv. 596.
[4] *Ibid*. 597.
[5] Zurita, 140.
[6] Petrus Justinianus, Historiae Venetae, 359.

with the Pope, and with Ferdinand, are distinguished more by unity of event than by unity of action. Never more than one of his allies was engaged at a time; they appear as so many distinct and different enterprises.

The first was the expedition against Milan. It was supported by the feud between Venice and Ludovico.

After the death of Savonarola, when the Florentines again attacked Pisa, Ludovico took the side of the assailants, "for it belongs to them;" Venice sided with the attacked, "for a promise must be kept." Hereupon, the Venetians won over Pitigliano, and Ludovico the Marquis of Mantua. The former threatened a French alliance, the latter replied that such would be to their own damage. In the Council of the Pregadi conflicting opinions were expressed; some old fathers could not conceal their apprehensions; others were for combating Ludovico unaided. Others again, those who hated him most cordially—"for if ever they had a secret plan did he not at once adopt public measures to thwart it? and a neighbour, served by their traitors, was the most intolerable of all:"—this third party proposed an alliance with France.[1] How could Ludovico believe that they, who had waged a great war against a man, because they would not have him for a neighbour when Duke, would call him in, after he had become King? He did not fear this. He continued his hostile operations against Pisa, without paying any attention to the Venetians, who supplied it with both money and men.

In this quarrel he really retained the upper hand. Through his influence Paolo Vitelli was entrusted with the command of the Florentines, and, with his assistance, he succeeded, between June and October, 1498, in taking castle after castle round about Pisa, as well as Vico and Librafatta, and in reducing the city to extremities. Against him the Venetians tried first of all their own resources. They knew that they were deceived by the lords in the Romagna, and nevertheless they took them into their service. Thus they were enabled to place a large body of cavalry in the field, though not without the heaviest expense; 16,600 horse in all. They then, now by Bologna

---

[1] Chronicon Venetum, 53-57.

and now by Perugia and now again by Siena, attempted to threaten Florence itself which lay on the other side of the Apennines. On one occasion Alviano succeeded in crossing over, and opposed Paolo Vitelli.[1] But though their men hurried by day and night to his succour through the Ferrarese territory, Ludovico's cavalry, under the brothers Sanseverino, with no less despatch, spurred their horses, and rode day and night to come to Vitelli's aid at Forlì, Imola, and Faenza. At last great detachments, as many as 300 men at once, deserted from the Venetian camp, which by these means had been surrounded in the hills, "for they had neither straw, nor money, nor bread." Others dashed after them to take from them the recruiting-money, until the whole army became disbanded; so that this undertaking resulted in failure for Venice.[2] In their indignation at this ill-fortune, "for which Ludovico was alone to blame," they resolved on a campaign against him himself. They left Ercole of Ferrara, who was not particularly friendly to them, to settle the Pisan affair. Meanwhile, they made a proposal to King Louis: they offered to assist him with 6,000 horse in an expedition against Milan, on condition that he would guarantee them a portion of the territory of Cremona and the Ghiara d'Adda. The King no sooner heard the conditions than he acceded. On the 10th of February the agreement was arrived at, and the man who had attacked Ludovico, and the city which had mainly defended him, were now both leagued together against him.[3]

Ludovico was not dismayed. He considered himself the cleverest man in Italy. On one occasion, when the papal master of the ceremonies wished to explain to him how he must address a cardinal, he answered, "Have you ever seen a Duke of Milan who has done what I have done? I shall know also how to act on this occasion."[4] In Milan there might often be seen a painting of a rose branch, with the motto, "With time," or a painter's brush

[1] Nardi, Istorie Fiorent. Nardi, Vita di Tebalducci, 57, 63. Bembus, Histor. Venet. 87.

[2] Diarium Ferrarense, 355, 357.

[3] Chronicon Venetum, 67–72. Bembus, 93.

[4] Burcardi Diarium, viii. 63.

with the motto, " With merit and time." [1] The mulberry
tree, " which does not shoot forth its leaves until spring
is at hand, and then quicker than all other trees," he may
perhaps have regarded as the emblem of his cleverness. [2]
He said, " In one hand he had peace, and in the other
war ; but even in war the pen could do more than the
sword." [3]

Time was the only thing his shrewdness took into
calculation ; in other respects it employed the boldest
schemes and the most dangerous means. Alfonso of
Calabria was made to assist him against Venice, and
Venice against Alfonso. His country was on one occasion
defended for him by the Duke of Orleans, notwithstanding
he desired it for himself, and on another by Maximilian,
to whom it belonged of right. His cavalry had emblazoned on their standard a Moor with his right hand
holding back an eagle's wing, and with the left strangling
a dragon. Ludovico was a gambler, who staked the
whole of his existence upon a throw of the dice ; for he
knew the dice obeyed him. He only accepted advice from
the stars. He never concluded a truce, even for three days,
without consulting his astrologer. [4]

I cannot say what his astrologer may have told him on
this occasion ; but, as things were, he needed not to be
much alarmed. His brother Ascanio—a man ever full of
schemes and secrets, and untiring [5]—was with him, and
kept the Ghibellines, as he himself kept the Guelphs, on
his side ; under these circumstances, he was justified in
feeling assured of his country. Should he then fear an
attack on the part of Venice? In the Turks he could
arouse an enemy to that city, who would keep it sufficiently
employed. Or should the lances of the French strike
terror into his breast ? He had other and stronger fortresses
to throw in their way. It would be more dangerous if
Louis enlisted Swiss ; for no Italian infantry could stand

---

[1] Leunclavius, Pandectae Historiae Turcicae, 193.
[2] Jovius, Elogia Virorum bellica virtute illustrium, 196.
[3] Chronicon Venetum, 53.
[4] Benedicti Diarium, 1611, 1623.
[5] Arluni, de bello Veneto, i. 22.

against them. But Ludovico also was firmly allied with Schwyz and Unterwalden, and with Bern and Lucerne ; [1] and in case these could not prevent an enlistment being made by the French, they could, at all events, easily provide him with an equal number of their men, whom he could lead against the King. In this way he was on an equal footing with his enemies. Through his alliance with Maximilian, and through the landsknechts who, in consequence, were at his disposal, he was even superior to them. Besides, it did not so much depend upon the collective strength of the States, as upon how much money each could employ. Ludovico was thus of good heart. Three years previously he had had coins struck, one of which bore a device of a snake, his emblem, guarding a lily, and another that of a snake bending down the cup of a lily, a sign of his power over France : [2] at this time he had a picture in his hall representing Italy full of cocks, hens, and chickens—intended for Gauls, Frenchmen—and in the midst of them a Moor sweeping them out with a broom.[3]

2. SWISS AND SWABIANS IMPLICATED IN THE WAR

Maximilian was as much interested in this struggle as Ludovico.

Valentina, Louis' grandmother, had a hundred years previously helped to kindle the deadly enmity between Burgundy and Orleans. An Orleans was now reigning in France, and even possessed Burgundy ; and the head of the House of Burgundy was King of the Germans, and demanded Burgundy back. The Sforza, whom the former attacked for his grandmother's sake, the latter was bound to defend for the sake of his wife. The Duke of Gelderland, who was related to Louis, Maximilian wished to destroy as a rebel to him ; so that they were enemies on three accounts.

---

[1] Tschudi MS. in Fuchs, Mailändische Feldzüge, i. 234.
[2] Reproduced in Rosmini, Trivulzio, i. 255.
[3] Nardi, Istorie, viii. 63.

Although Maximilian's son, Philip, had been obliged to promise never to attempt to take Burgundy by force of arms, and moreover to serve King Louis against every soul without any exception,[1] yet he was never inclined for peace: " peace was like corn that had been harvested while yet unripe; by peace he would never conquer his land." In vain René and Frederick the Wise endeavoured to mediate.[2] Forthwith in the country of the Duke of Gelderland, who had received French aid, the war was continued which had been already waged at Leghorn and on the Saône.

It is evident how closely Ludovico and Maximilian were allied. Ludovico desired no treaty with France, if the German King had none, for he would not sever himself from the fortunes of his ally.[3] Maximilian repeated : " the Duke would be able to defend himself without foreign aid ; but, in case he could not do so, he would in person come to his assistance with the whole strength of the Holy Empire, and protect Milan as well as the Tyrol." [4]

Since, then, Ludovico's superiority was due to this alliance it was important for the French King to try to occupy the German King in another way. He could cause him trouble in Germany, and there are letters extant, wherein he reminds the Count Palatine of the century-long alliance of their House, and promises one of his sons a pension at his Court, and to another high ecclesiastical dignities.[5] But how if he found ways and means of attaching the Swiss to himself, so as to be enabled to avail himself of their infantry ; to ally them so closely with himself that Ludovico would receive no assistance from them, and at the same time to involve them in war with Maximilian, so that he would have to fear for himself, and would not dare to come to the assistance of another ?

Without any action on his part, the desired opportunity arose. The accident that in the year 1498, Georg

[1] Jean Amis, Procès verbal, in Garnier, xxi. 108.
[2] Zurita, f. 121. Spalatin, Life of Frederick the Wise, 78.
[3] Ludovico to Brascha in Rosmini, ii. 256.
[4] Somentius to Ludovico in Rosmini, 258.
[5] Instruction of Mathieu Pelleyt in Ludewig, Reliquiae, vi. 117.

Gossenbrod of Augsburg, Royal Councillor in the Tyrol, journeyed with his wife to the watering-place of Pfäffers,[1] and there met an enemy, Count Jörg of Sargans,[2] and that the latter tried to take him prisoner, was ordained to determine the course of public affairs, and bring this great struggle to a head.

Count Jörg had once schemed to bring the Tyrol to the crown of Bavaria, and on that account had been outlawed by the King.[3] Unconcerned thereat, he lived with one cook in the castle of Ortenstein by selling his estates, and slept in the tower, where his bed may still be seen; for he was on terms of friendship with the monks of Chur, and made common cause with them. The Abbot o. Pfäffers, to whom Gossenbrod owed his preservation and who was also a friend of Maximilian—the latter confided to him his schemes and successes—was forced by Jörg to leave his monastery. Now between Chur and the Tyrol there had existed, since time out of mind, differences, which had lately been revived. These differences affected the Engadine as far as Pont'alto, where their frontiers touched, the administratorship of the Minster in the Münsterthal, to which both laid claim, as also the hereditary office of cup-bearer, which Maximilian declined to receive, as former Counts had done, as a fief from Chur.[4] Gossenbrod availed himself of this feud to take revenge. He mocked the people of the bishopric of Chur, and encouraged the Tyrolese, until the latter, who had been posted by him in strong detachments on the border,[5] invaded and occupied the Münsterthal; the others at once sallied out and recovered it. Upon this, both appealed to their allies; the people of Chur summoned to their aid the Upper League and the Ten Jurisdictions, with which they formed the Grisons Confederation, and the people of Uri, with six other Swiss cantons, with whom they had allied themselves in 1497, "until the end of all

[1] Stettler, Chronik des Uechtlandes, p. 329.
[2] Müller's Schweizergeschichte, v. 322.
[3] *Ibid.*, p. 190.
[4] Münster, Cosmographie, p. 763.
[5] Pirkheimer, de bello Helvetico, p. 13.

things " ;[1] and these called in the others who were members of the Confederation. The Tyrol called to its assistance the princes, lords, and cities of the Swabian League.[2] In a trice the whole frontier was in arms; on the one side the Swiss, and on the other the landsknechts; each waited to see what the other would do.

This was not a plot of the King of France, yet the event relieved him of perplexity. It was still doubtful whether there would be war or not; for Maximilian could not be anxious for it, and, moreover, on the 5th February, 1499, the recess[3] of Lucerne declared that terms had been arrived at, and that it was doubtful whether the cantons which favoured Milan would join the others. It came to pass quite spontaneously. In German countries it frequently happens that among neighbours, questions of cattle and landmarks, and especially boundaries of properties, aided by boasting, scoffing, and diverse claims, create hatred such as that which exists between two brothers who have quarrelled—the more intense as its origin becomes more and more obscure. The least stimulus arouses it. So here, when the Swiss, thinking peace was assured, retired from their frontier and passed through Gutenberg, the German landsknechts crept on all fours over the walls and lowed at one another like cows. Where the Rhine separated the two peoples, the Germans dressed up a cow, danced with it and cried that they had the bride, and the others should send them the bridegroom. In Bendre they christened a calf " Amman Reding ; "[4] and amused themselves at Constance, Diessenhofen, and elsewhere with variations of the same joke. Enraged thereat, some troops from Zürich and Zug crossed the Rhine on the 6th of February, routed the enemy, and ran across hedge and ditch away to the Lake of Constance, where they again attacked the landsknechts, whose leaders had become despondent and wished to return, with such onslaught, that they drove some of them into the ditches, where they were drowned, others into the

[1] Simleri Respublica Helvetiorum, p. 36.
[2] Gasser, Augsburger Chronik, p. 258.
[3] Recess in Glutzblotzheim, p. 77.
[4] Stettler, 331. Edlibach and Tschudi in Glutzblotzheim.

morasses, where they died of cold, while others fled before them to Ulm and Augsburg, where they told their tale of terror.[1]

This event made war a certainty and united the Swiss. Schwyz and Unterwalden, Lucerne and Bern had previously joined the League; and Glarus wanted to make a fifth.[2] They had joined in Maximilian's interest, who, owing to this, had Swiss envoys with him on his Leghorn expedition, and Swiss soldiers in his war with Burgundy. The same cantons were allies of Ludovico. But now it was a case of another alliance, directed, if not expressly against Ludovico, at any rate against Maximilian, by whose councillors the feud had been caused, and whose landsknechts had made it burst forth. The Confederation held better together than the League; all the cantons united for war. Louis saw it, and as he had come to terms with Venice and the Pope, and as in the interior of Germany the Houses of the Palatinate and Bavaria-Landshut, both opposed to the House of Austria, entered into a close alliance, he offered the Swiss his alliance.[3] Although Ludovico let it be known that he "had never supported the Swabians, and he desired to be mediator between them and the Swiss,"[4] for he too saw the danger, and although there were many among the Swiss who were opposed to a war with Austria, yet the contrary opinion was the prevailing one: "for what had the House of Austria ever done for them, save abuse in words and war in deed; but that was the way to bring its plans to nought." On the 21st March, 1499, they all concluded a treaty in these terms:[5] "The King promises to assist them in their wars with men and money, and to give in peace, besides, to every canton 2,000 Rhenish guilders annually, in return for which they concede to him free enlistment, and to no one else in opposition to him;"[6] and appended their ten seals to the document. They then

---

[1] Pirkheimer, de bello Helvetico, p. 14. Tschudi.
[2] Stettler, 325–328.
[3] Tschudi in Fuchs, p. 239.
[4] From Ludovico's letter, p. 240.
[5] Stettler, 337. Glbl. p. 93.
[6] Anshelm, Berner Chronik, ii. 360 (note to 2nd edition).

emblazoned the Crucifixion on their standards and guarded their frontiers.[1]

High among the mountains, where spring the sources of the Inn and the Adige, along the Rhine valley lying between Sennwald in Appenzell and the red wall of the Vorarlberg, on both shores of the Lake of Constance, down to where the Rhine finishes its upper course and leaps downwards to the plain, they stood ; men from the Grisons against the Tyrolese and troops from Appenzell and St. Gall against the King's landsknechts and countrymen, the nine districts in Thurgau against Constance and the cities of the Swabian League, Zürich and Solothurn, against the nobles of Sundgau and Hegau. Between them flowed the Rhine, both its banks adorned with the gorgeous mantle of spring. But among them many a Swabian might have been heard to boast, how he would fire and burn in the enemy's country, so that St. Peter would not for the very smoke be able to find the gate of heaven ; and, should he die, his comrades were conjured to crush his bones to make powder wherewith to exterminate the foe.[2] The Swiss, on their side, swore by the saints that they would take no prisoners, but slay all their enemies, as their fathers had done before them.[3] The former only wished to vent their hatred, the latter to protect their freedom that was threatened ; and thus they waged their war.

At the same time, the Confederates on one occasion crossed the Rhine to attack the men of Wallgau, whilst the Leaguers crossed the bridge of Constance and marched towards the Schwaderloch. Hereupon the landsturm was called out ; on the Swabian side by the firing of shots, and on the Swiss side by smoke, and the people ran to their places of rendezvous. The men of Thurgau, Bischofzell, and St. Gall assembled at the Schwaderloch to the assistance of the whole Confederation, and sallied forth to find the landsknechts. These were already on their way home, their waggons full

---

[1] Unrest, Oesterreichische Chronik in Hahn, collectio monumentorum, tom. i. p. 803.

[2] Stettler, p. 331, Anshelm, ii. 302.

[3] Recess of 11th March and a Military Ordinance in Glutz-blotzheim, p. 86.

of corn,[1] and their muskets and field-pieces hung with pans, kettles, and all manner of pillage. But their enemies, by taking shorter roads through the woods, caught them up and engaged them in bloody encounters; and when the leader of the infantry, Burkard von Randeck, who was considered the bitterest foe of the Swiss, had fallen, and the leader of the horse, Wolf von Fürstenberg, had taken flight after a chivalrous struggle, the landsknechts left both their muskets and booty behind, and fled towards the city-bridge, and to the ships in the lake.[2] This was the battle of Schwader-loch.

Meanwhile Swabians, with men from Algau and Etsch-land, collected at Frastenz. The miners came out of their pits, arrayed themselves in steel, vaunted themselves greatly, and came to the battle. They did not dare to follow up their enemy, but entrenched themselves behind ramparts, and so awaited their onslaught. Above, on the top of the Lanzengast were posted 300 arquebusiers, and at its foot the miners.[3] The Swiss advanced against them in two divisions; the main body against the rampart in the valley, whilst a detachment of 2,000 scaled the Lanzengast. At the first pause Heini Wolleb rode in front of the 2,000; he then dismounted, ordered them to kneel, and said the Lord's prayer: he cried, "in God's name follow me." He led them through the ravines, where each one had to draw up his fellow by his lance,[4] first into the fire of the arquebusiers, and then into close quarters with them, until they were routed; this done, they attacked the miners, and drove their first and second line behind their entrenchments; and here, already victorious, he met with the main body.[5] With united forces, they scaled the great barricade, and saw the enemy drawn up in three bodies, in act of preparing their guns for action. For one moment they threw themselves flat on the ground, until the shots had passed over their heads: they then wanted to rise up. "Not yet, confede-rates!" cried Heini, "wait for another shot, and then at them." They all knelt down except himself. He, a tall,

[1] Tschudi in Gltzbl., p. 103.   [2] Pirkheimer, p. 15.
[3] Stettler, p. 341.   [4] Tschudi in Gltzbl., p. 99.
[5] Hauptmann und Fähndrich an Luzern, Glutzblotzheim, p. 522.

powerful man, stood up in the midst of all to maintain discipline ; careful for all, but fearless for himself. The bullets flew again, but all missed save one, and this laid him low. " Lay me by and attack them," he cried.[1] Within two hours the Swabians had been driven from their camp. The corpses with their red crosses floated down to Feldkirch. The men of Wallgau came even upon the battlefield to the victors with the sacrament, priests, women, and children, and begged for mercy.[2] The Swabians took comfort and said, " Where is now your Wolleb ? " The Swiss replied, " He is playing dice with Randeck."

The Swiss were everywhere in advantage. From Thiengen the landsknechts retired before them in their shirts, a white staff and a piece of bread in their hands.[3] The lady of Blumeneck carried her husband away from the castle as the dearest treasure that she was allowed to take. On the Malserheide the three bands of the Tyrolese fled before the men of the Grisons when the horn of Uri echoed from afar.[4] The King's troops, on the other hand, climbed the topmost hills commanding the Engadine, and pursued the enemy down the side. But when they had reached the valley, they found the bridges, across which they had to go, on fire, villages, in which they intended to pass the night, in flames, and stores that they wanted to eat, all destroyed. They, the plunderers, had to pluck grass to satisfy the cravings of hunger, and were half mad from want ; the fresh waters of these mountains were their sole comfort.[5]

Such was the character of this war : there was no question on either side of conquest or attack. No ! it was merely defence and revenge. They entrench themselves, sally forth, pillage, plunder, burn, and return home again. The neighbouring cities might easily, at that time, have joined the league of the Confederates ; but these were as cruel as their enemies, and throughout the whole of Swabia,

---

[1] Stettler, 342.
[2] Münster, Cosmographie, p. 631.
[3] Stettler, 343. Tschudi and Anshelm in Gltzbl.
[4] Stettler, 345.
[5] Pirkheimer, 19-21.

on every Wednesday evening and every Saturday, after the sermon, they prayed for the League, the widows and orphans, and the general peace.[1] Conquest was not the intention of the Swiss either; their war served no one save the King of France.

For in this way it came about that Maximilian became involved in an arduous war. Ludovico had to forego all assistance from him, and found himself, as his ally, even deprived of Swiss aid. Danger threatened him, if the French succeeded at the same time in leading Swiss against Milan. To effect an arrangement with the Swiss, Ludovico sent Galeazzo Visconti with thirty horses across Valais to Bern. Schwyz, at all events, declared for him, but all to no purpose: he could not bring about any arrangement.[2] There was only one way of escape, viz. if Maximilian were to engage the Swiss in such a conflict, that they would forget to lend their aid to others.

In June, 1499, Maximilian came upon the scene. The daily invitations addressed to him by his people had at last induced him to leave those enemies in Gelderland whom he was for ever pursuing, and never catching. In an open letter to the Estates of the empire he enumerated the crimes the Confederates had committed against the Empire and Austria ; and he succeeded in raising a considerable number to assist him. In a short time, a strong army of the Empire and the League was assembled at Constance. The soldiers of Gelderland and Burgundy were at Dorneck under the command of Count Fürstenberg. He felt sure of success.[3] If the Swiss ever really offered him, as is related, that they would serve the Empire, and wage his wars against the Turks, it must have been on this occasion.[4]

He threw them into great alarm and trepidation, but did not succeed in preventing them from joining the French. Yet when Louis XII made them a proposal in these terms, " He was taking the field, in order to take his

[1] Crusii Annales Suevorum, i. 513.

[2] Fuchs, 242. Weiskunig, 271.

[3] Weiskunig, 261. A letter in the Swiss Museum and in Glutzblotzheim, 113.

[4] Unrest, Oesterreich, Chronik in Hahn, Collect. Monument, i. 803.

hereditary land of Milan; how if his allies showed themselves on the hills with only three thousand men?" the cantons refused him this request; but a few thousand individuals were induced by his pay—for their country had nothing to give them—to forget their country, and, in spite of all, to join the King's hommes d'armes, who were collecting at Asti.[1]

The decision on both sides now depended on arms and open war alone. If only Maximilian was victorious over the Swiss, Ludovico could join the Swabian League, and this might come to protect Milan.[2]

On the 13th July, 1499, with his artillery, and accompanied by his knights in coats of mail and waving plumes, Maximilian advanced over the bridge of Constance towards the Schwaderloch. Scarcely recognizable in his old green tunic and his great hat, he rode about and gave his commands. The Eagle of the Empire waved in the hand of the Cupbearer of Limburg. The astrologers prophesied success. He waited for the enemy to come down from the mountains; but they did not come. He therefore resolved to hunt them out in their native hills; and many of his followers expected, as he himself did, to strike a grand blow. But his nobles remembered Sempach and Charles the Bold. Should they risk their noble blood against peasants?[3] The captains of his Württembergers declared that, "they were tired out with marching, and must wait for the strength of the whole League to come up." They would not follow him. The King threw away his glove, and rode off; they returned hastily to the city.[4]

After this, Count Fürstenberg, at all events, resolved to make a raid from Dorneck. One day a provost of the Cathedral at Basel had a banquet prepared in the Cathedral tower, in order, with his friends, to look out upon Dorneck in flames. The same day, Nicholas Conrad, bailiff of Solothurn, sat at table at Liestal, when he learnt that the castle was threatened. He did not wait for other

---

[1] Tschudi MS. in Fuchs. Recess of 22nd June.
[2] Ludovico to Stanga in Rosmini, ii. 261.
[3] Life of Götz von Berlichingen, 19. Münster, Cosmographie, 632.
[4] Coccinius, de bellis Italicis, ap. Freherum, ii. 278. Tschudi.

confederates, but with his own followers mounted the
heights above the enemy's camp. The horsemen were
scattered about the villages ; the landsknechts were drink-
ing and dancing, or else shouting and quarrelling ; their
captains made themselves comfortable in undress. Upon
this camp Conrad fell, and the Bern and Zürich soldiers
followed him. At first it looked as if they must succeed.[1]
But when the experienced landsknechts had drawn themselves up in line, and were supported by their cavalry, it
was doubtful, and some Swiss fled into the woods near the
Scharfenflue. All at once horns and shouts and the sound
of feet. Both sides looked up to see who was coming, and
which party's lot was to be victory and life, and whose
defeat and death. There appeared a flag, folded like a
banner; it was the flag of Lucerne. The brave fellows,
from Lucerne and Zug, had been informed of the battle
that was raging and had seen the fugitives in the wood;
they forthwith hung up their knapsacks on a great pear
tree,[2] came, and fell upon the enemy. The confederates,
thereupon, took courage, and the landsknechts lost heart.
Count Heinrich fell, and four thousand men with him.
Maximilian's hopes were over. At first he shut himself up
in his castle at Lindau, and would not admit any of the
princes; but soon he composed himself. In the evening
he opened his door, and dined in public; he then gazed
from his window at the stars, and spoke of their nature.[3]
He was inclined for peace ; he accepted Galeazzo's mediation, and agreed to a conference at Schaffhausen.

But before any terms were arrived at—nay, even before
any regular meetings had taken place, even whilst fighting
was going on in the Hegau, and Laufenburg was being
threatened,—the French threw themselves upon Ludovico.

Ludovico saw his fate approaching. Against him was
arrayed, on the one side, the same Trivulzio of whom
only three years previously he had publicly announced
that "a halter awaited him as soon as caught;"

---

[1] Dornecker - Lied and Letter of the Bernese Captains in the
Appendix to Glutzblotzheim, 524, 526. Stettler, 352.

[2] Inscription by Gerber, *vide* Glutzblotzheim, p. 134.

[3] Pirkheimer, p. 24.

against whom he had roused warrior upon warrior to prove to him his treachery and cowardice; of whom, finally, he had had a picture exhibited in all his cities, representing him as hanging by the legs.[1] Now, however, Trivulzio had 1,500 lances and 15,000 men on foot under his command. On the other side, the Venetians were arming against him. He had hoped for assistance from the Swiss, but they were leagued with his enemies; from the Germans, but they were fighting against the Swiss; even a little from the Arrabbiati at Florence, but they were engaged on a campaign against Pisa. Finally, he had relied upon Bajazet; but how could Bajazet help him? for Venice was fitting out two armies, one against the Turks, and one against him.[2] At this critical moment, all his foreign alliances, which had made him what he was, failed. The pen availed him nothing; the sword could alone decide. He still relied upon his castles, and those favourites in them, whom he had from the first honoured more than his party; he still trusted to his two armies on his two frontiers, who were not to engage the enemy in open battle, but to come to the assistance of the menaced castles; he relied, finally, upon the fidelity of his Milanese, whose beneficent lord he had ever been.

But even this calculation proved false. For castle after castle surrendered as soon as Trivulzio showed himself. Those favourites of Ludovico were Guelphs, and their head, Trivulzio, was more to them than he was. The garrison of Valenza had just prepared itself to give the enemy battle outside the walls, and awaited their attack, when the commander, Donato, let them in through the castle, and they saw themselves taken in the rear. At one stroke, Tortona, Voghera, and the whole country across the Po was lost. It was said that Trivulzio had brought with him 300,000 escus for the commanders; that Donato received 5,000; and that there was no castellan, and no official in any castle in Milanese territory, who had not been bribed.[3]

---

[1] Documents in Rosmini, ii. 224, 244; i. 276, 299.

[2] Chronicon Venetum, 96.

[3] Corio, 969. Jusmondus to Ludovico in Rosmini, ii. 271. Antonius ex Marchionibus in Rosmini.

Everything now depended upon the preservation of Alessandria, and into it Galeazzo Sanseverino threw himself with one of the two armies. Ludovico meant to exert all his strength to keep it. He summoned Francesco Sanseverino, who was in command of the other army, to come to the aid of his brother.[1] Many warned him, and this commander's name was mentioned among fifteen others suspected of treason. "Whom shall I trust if not Francesco?" he exclaimed. He had loaded him with favours, and had treated him as a son. Yet, when Francesco had arrived at the Ticino he refused to cross and come to his brother's assistance. Ludovico, indeed, persuaded himself that he was unable to do so without risking a battle, and this must, under all circumstances, be avoided; but everybody else said that Francesco's treachery was patent.[2]

In this strait, Galeazzo thought also on self-preservation. He saw his walls crumbling under the enemy's fire and his foes making ready to storm the city. He would not surrender, and neither would he defend himself to the last push. He arranged with Constantin de Montferrat, one of the leaders of the enemy, for permission to march off privily: and, accordingly, on the 28th August, 1499, between the third and fourth hour of the night, Galeazzo and his hommes d'armes took to flight. They took different roads; some the direction of the Po, in order to gain the main road, others the road to Montferrat, to reach Milan by way of Genoa. They were four hours gone, when the reveille sounded in the French camp, and the pursuit of the fugitives began. Galeazzo, two of the Sforza, the Count of Melzo, and Luzio Malvezzi escaped across the Po.[3] But in Montferrat, Constantin could not keep his plighted word; the hommes d'armes were deprived of their horses and weapons.

The city had fallen; the country was defenceless; and Galeazzo's army was annihilated. "Haste," wrote Ludovico

---

[1] Nardi, iii. 62. Senarega, 568. St. Gelais, 147.

[2] Ludovico to Somentius. Corio, 971.

[3] Ludovico, Commissione ad Ambrogio et Martino, che narrassero, etc., in Corio, 979. Zorzo to Ludovico in Rosmini, 27. Corio.

to Visconti: "haste to his Imperial Majesty; announce to him this calamity. Kneel before him and implore him not to allow us to perish, but to come at once to our aid with as great an army as he can muster. In this citadel we will shut ourselves up and wait until his Majesty comes to deliver us."[1] That was Ludovico's first resolve, and he still relied upon the Milanese, whom he considered faithful to him, and whom he had already organized into companies. But their feelings towards him proved unreliable; they were willing to remain faithful to their lord, but it should, if possible, be to their advantage, and certainly not to their harm. To risk life for him, life that was to them the greatest of all goods, never entered into their calculations.[2] When the Venetians were come across the Oglio and would entertain no new proposals, Guelphs and French sympathizers showed themselves even in the capital. On the 30th August, the Treasurer, Landriano, was attacked on his way to the palace by an insolent fellow who had twelve horsemen in his pay, and was thrown wounded under his horse. This occurrence showed Ludovico plainly that he could not count upon the Milanese, and could not trust himself and his family to them.[3] On the following day he lifted up his sons, Massimiliano, aged nine, and Francesco, aged seven, kissed them, gave them into his brother's keeping, and sent them with his treasure to Germany. This done, on the 1st September he chose four men; these again co-opted eight others from the first families, all Ghibellines. He granted each of them an estate, and committed the government into their hands.[4] He too intended to cross the mountains. After having committed his castle and his jewels[5] to the keeping of Bernardino da Corte, whom he had brought up and raised from the dust, and had received the kiss of fealty from him, all was arranged, and he said to his companions, "God be with you." He then went forth alone to the Church of the Madonna delle Grazie. His wife, Beatrice,

---

[1] Ludovico's Letter in Rosmini, i. 322.
[2] Chronicon Venetum, p. 93.
[3] Corio, 972.   [4] Corio, 973.
[5] Burcardus, Diarium Rom. 2103. Commissione, 980.

the companion of his prosperity, with whom his good fortune
had died, lay here entombed. Here Leonardo da Vinci had
painted them both, him with the elder child on his lap,[1]
and her with the younger. The beams of the setting sun
slanted through the windows. He stood at the foot of her
grave. The monks of the convent escorted him out of
the church. He looked once more around. What a fabric,
closely woven of coloured threads, which can never be
altered, happiness and fortune, guilt and calamity, is this
mortal life ! He burst into a flood of tears. Thrice he
turned, and then stood long, lost in thought and motion-
less, with his head bowed to the earth.[2] In the castle yard,
meanwhile, the bustle of horses and men, who were to
escort him on his way, was heard. The next morning, at
break of day, they all took the road to Como. Of all
other cities the people of Como were the most Ghibelline
and ducal in their sympathies. Once again they welcomed their Prince, and gave him quarters in the episcopal
palace. The following morning they came together at his
command in the garden by the lake. He stood amongst
them on a rising knoll and addressed them.[3] " Citizens,
my most faithful subjects ! My fortune stood high, but
now it has changed. I have spared neither energy, nor
friends, nor strength. Yet all in vain ; no one can resist
treachery. I will now give way a little to fate, and will
not struggle against God, will not destroy so many peoples,
and still save my own. I go to my nephew, the august
King of the Romans, and I hope, with his assistance, in a
short time to return as conqueror. Follow, then, my advice.
When the French come, do not oppose them, but obey
them. But preserve your allegiance to me, so that when
I come I may not be received as an enemy, but as your
true and first lord and master. If I can do you any favour,
tell it me, for I am still among you." Codito, a citizen,
answered him in these words. " With thy departure, O
Prince, we pass from day to night. If thou wilt still do us

[1] Vasari, Vita di Leonardo da Vinci, in vol. iii.
[2] Histoire MS. de la conquête de Milan in Daru, Histoire de
Venise, iii. 221.
[3] Corio, 976. Paulus Jovius, Elogia.

a favour, relieve us of toll for ten years, so that we may each day praise thy generosity, and deliver the citadel into our keeping." He did not hesitate to grant the first request, but at the second he showed some hesitation. They shouted loud : " Go not away from us, Prince ! we will have no other lord but thee. But if thou wilt go, give into our hands the castle, wherein is our safety and our destruction." As he granted this petition, a cry was raised that the enemy were already in the Borgo. He instantly embarked, sailed down the lake and journeyed up the Valtelline. Having arrived at the baths of Bormio, at the foot of the Umbrail, on the frontier of his land, he rested once more, and then crossed over into Germany.[1]

Thus Venice had avenged and, at the same time, compensated itself for the loss of Pisa : for Cremona surrendered, and in the cathedral there an altar was raised to S. Marco.[2] And Louis XII had acquired the inheritance of Valentina. Bernardino da Corte in the castle quieted his scruples, on the King making him rich presents and a yearly allowance, and assigning to him the treasures and the artillery of the fugitives.[3] He kindled no torch and waved no flag, as he had promised his lord to do, to announce good or bad tidings. Unattacked by the enemy, he surrendered to them the impregnable fortress, the sole refuge of his benefactors. By this treachery he drew down upon himself the contempt of the one side and the curses of the other. But he could not endure it long ; he went forth and hanged himself.[4] The King now came into his new country. Attired in a white mantle and cap, he rode through the white draped streets of the city : and some were heard to call him the Great King, their deliverer.[5] In order to win the most influential classes over to him, he allowed the nobles to hunt big game, gave the professors greater incomes, and made the appointments of officials permanent. He then caused it to be publicly announced in the open squares

[1] Corio, 977. Senarega, 567.
[2] Chronicon Venetum, 102, 108, 122. Bembus, 98.
[3] Burcardus, 2103. Ferronus, p. 48.
[4] Tschudi in Glutzblotzheim, 188.
[5] Chronicon Venetum, 119, 120. Burcardus, 2107.

and streets of Milan, that tolls upon wine, wheat, maize,
millet and nuts, should from thenceforth be no more
levied in the town and suburbs, or within the ecclesiastical
district of Milan, whilst other burdens should be removed
in the whole dukedom. He lowered the taxes, moreover,
to 622,000 livres ;[1] he thought thus to satisfy everybody.
Genoa, too, recognized his suzerainty. After Corradin
Stanga had been recalled, and the Adorni showed themselves more and more violent, many became alienated from
Ludovico. Now that he had fled away, the Adorni were
also obliged to abandon their castles, and to flee. When
the King arrived, the city sent twenty-four men to him,
who arranged a capitulation, and thereupon received the
oath of the new governor, Philip of Ravenstein, to it. He
now ruled as far as Lesbos, where the Genoese had
formerly held sway.[2] The less powerful princes joined him.
The Marquis of Mantua entered into his service,[3] and
Ercole of Ferrara, whose falcons and leopards he had had
brought to him at Milan, put himself under his protection
and claimed his friendship.[4] The Popolari at Florence
approached him by sending an embassy. When it came
to war, the young Arrabbiati chose them a leader, whom
they called " Duke," and the Popolari another, whom they
called " King," and they both performed plays in the
market-place, displaying their respective tendencies.[5] The
party of the Popolari, owing to Ludovico's fall, gained the
upper hand, and came to renew their old relations with
France. Venice is Leonardo's lion, whose breast opens
and is full of lilies.[6] As the Pope also was dependent upon
the assistance which the French rendered him against the
Sforza of the Romagna, and as the Angevins in Naples longed
for the arrival of the King, he, hitherto only lord of Asti,
had suddenly become by far the most powerful potentate

[1] Ferronus, iii. 49. Forma Cridae in Rosmini, ii. 278. Gilles,
Chroniques de France, f. 120.
[2] Senarega, 563–570. Folieta, 272.
[3] Chronicon Venetum, 122.
[4] Diarium Ferrarense, p. 370.
[5] Filippo Nerli, Commentarii, p. 80.
[6] Vasari, Vita di Leonardo da Vinci, tom. iii. p. 25.

in Italy. Having happily accomplished all those things, he returned to France.

The quarrel at Milan had not, however, as yet been finally disposed of.

Ludovico, far from giving up his cause for lost, thought of Ferrantino; how he once had fled away and had returned to his own, chiefly owing to the people of Naples and the favour of the Milanese. As late as November, the King heard in Milan the cry of "Duke and Moor!" and, in December, a coin was seen bearing the device of a Moor and a Turk, with the motto: "In winter we will fiddle; in summer we will dance."[1] Here also public opinion was manifested in play; when the boys, representing the two parties of the King and the Duke respectively, played together, the Duke's adherents were always the conquerors, and brought the leader of the royalists, who played King, back to the city dishonoured, tied to the tail of an ass.[2] Ludovico considered himself sure of Milan. In Switzerland, Galeazzo Visconti negotiated, to his advantage,[3] a peace with the neighbouring Germans. Ludovico himself was obliged to pay the fine levied upon Wallgau and the Bregenzerwald, and to undertake to pay the 20,000 ducats, without which Constance would not cede the jurisdiction in the Thurgau to the Seven Cantons, which demanded it. It was only after this was arranged, that the other differences were on the 22nd of September submitted to arbitrators at Basel; where a thanksgiving service was held in the cathedral and the peace ratified.[4]

On the conclusion of peace, the Swiss Cantons again evinced their old tendencies and dissensions. Ludovico had here also a faction favourable to his cause, and, as he could again avail himself of the landsknechts, he determined to venture on a second struggle.

On either side of the St. Gotthard are the green Alpine valleys of Urseren and Leventina; the inhabitants of the latter formed eight Italian communes, originally connected

---

[1] Diarium Ferrarense, pp. 375, 377.
[2] Chronicon Venetum, p. 137.
[3] Pirkheimer, p. 27.
[4] Document in Fuchs, p. 269.

with the cathedral and the leading houses of Milan, while
those of the former were a German settlement, ruled by
the people of Uri. The valleys were frequently in feud,
usually about the pasturage, and each called its patron to
its aid. But, sometimes, when the people of Uri drove
their oxen through the Val Leventina to the market of
Varese, they themselves were insulted, and became thus the
more enraged. On such an occasion, in 1402, the Val
Leventina was forced to acknowledge the protection of
Uri. That was no sufficient advantage for the people of
Uri. The pass near Bellinzona is so narrow that the town,
with its three gates, could entirely close it. They acquired
Bellinzona also, partly by force and partly by purchase.
Since then they had had, on this account, many a quarrel
with Milan. There was a time when they had given up
both. Francesco Sforza had restored the Val Leventina to
them ("in gratitude for this they had to bring every August
four falcons and a new crossbow to Milan"), but not
Bellinzona.[1] They conceived that they had an established
right to this place also, and followed the Duke of Orleans
to Novara : they were always on his side, because he had
promised it them. But now that the Duke no longer
thought himself bound by his promise, which was made
under other circumstances, Ludovico, who had changed
sides with them, was inclined to promise them something.[2]
Like the oxen of Uri, the horses of the Valais had also their
market in Milan ; thence the inhabitants of the Grisons
procured a definite quantity of corn and wine. They could
not live without the Dukedom, and enjoyed old privileges
from the Sforza. Ludovico knew how to turn all these conditions to his account.

First of all, it appears, he availed himself of the state of
affairs in Uri. For at the self-same time, in October, 1499,
he promised Bellinzona and Val Bregna to the people of
Uri,[3] and Galeazzo collected some troops for an incursion
into the Valtelline.[4] But on this occasion—for the Bailiff

[1] Simler, Respublica Helvetica, p. 43. The rest Müller and Ebel.
[2] Ludovico's Capitulation in Müller, v.
[3] Fuchs, 274.
[4] Stettler, 361.

was also at this moment enlisting troops, the cantons were calling back their sons who had gone away, and the King was promising the people of Uri various possessions— the troops were disbanded as soon as collected.[1] But one advantage accrued to Ludovico therefrom. The Bailiff dismissed many in the midst of winter without pay, and some were frozen to death on the tops of the mountains. By these doings he made himself and the King enemies enough.

Galeazzo availed himself of these enemies, the universal dissatisfaction, and the relations existing between the Grisons and the Valais, to make a second attempt. The Valais declared that the King was an intolerable neighbour;[2] 2,000 men of the Grisons enrolled themselves at Chur under his standard. All whom the Bailiff had wronged or rejected he welcomed to it. In January, 1500, he was enabled to venture over the mountains between the Engadine and the Valtelline.[3] His advent was victory. At the first cry, Chiavenna opened its gates; the Ghibellines of Lugano and Locarno rose; the people of Bellinzona reconquered their castle for the Duke. The French fled from Como, in dread of Ascanio's arrival. Giovanni Orelli marched into Pavìa, and, as there was a lack of corn, provisioned it with chestnuts.[4] All depended upon whether the Duke's party in Milan would be able to hold that city.

In Milan, the Ghibelline families, the Landriani, Marliani, Visconti, Cribelli, and especially some ecclesiastics amongst them, would never obey Trivulzio. On one occasion, even, they made common cause with the French prefect against him.[5] Between the Ghibellines and Guelphs there existed an open feud. Sometimes no one dared to speak of terms; sometimes the leaders had a conference and concluded a formal peace. Trivulzio, who behaved

[1] Tschudi in Glutzblotzheim and the Recess of Lucerne, 7th January, 1501, in Glutzblotzheim, p. 532.

[2] Hans Krebs in Fuchs, 171.

[3] Benedictus Jovius, Historia Novocomensis, 58.

[4] Bened. Jovius, Historia Novocom. 60. Zurita, i. 176. Life of Aloysius Orelli, 40.

[5] Arluni, de bello Veneto, i. 7. Andrea da Prato, Cronaca, in Rosmini, i. 337.

himself as these party leaders were wont to do when they were victorious, ever kept alive the arrogance of the rest. When then, on the 1st February, 1500, the tidings arrived that the Sforza were there, both rushed at once to arms. Trivulzio, with his Guelphs, was the first to occupy the square between the cathedral and the palace. The Ghibellines showed courage, and surrounded him and his men. The two parties kept up a contest of words. As long as Trivulzio spoke them fair, saying that "he desired no better fortune than to share Milan's fate; he was willing to die for his country, but they must be faithful, and then they would obtain great liberties," his opponents only replied with mockery; "was he not the same person, who had always sought his own advantage in his country's calamities? Was he not the old fox that had ever deceived them? He was only now making them promises which he would never be able to keep." But when he began to command them to lay down their arms, threatening that the King would destroy the city, they also became violent. "If Guelphs could carry arms, Ghibellines could do the same; instead of giving orders, he would now have to receive them; but why was he still allowed to live? If his life was the ruin, his death would be the saving, of his country." One Ghibelline or other was for ever shouting these words; every hour, as the Sforza drew nearer, their courage waxed stronger. The next morning, Trivulzio retired to the park and the castle. In the city nothing was heard but "Duke and Moor, and death to the Guelphs!" All the shops were closed, and the streets barricaded; Trivulzio saw that the city was lost, provided for the castle and fled to the Ticino.[1]

These tidings, with the invitations from his party, reached Ludovico in Innsbruck. He was not yet ready, he had not landsknechts enough, and Maximilian did not approve of his starting at that moment;[2] but Ludovico could not be restrained. He took Claude de Vaudrei's Burgundian horse, and as many landsknechts as he had,

---

[1] Epistola Hieronymi Moroni ad Varadeum in Rosmini, ii. 280. Chronicon Venetum, 137.

[2] Maximilian's letter of complaint of the year 1507, in Fuchs, ii. 91.

and crossed the Alps.[1] They came from the villages and towns to meet him, saying, "All hail, Ludovico, our prince!" The people of Como brought him in triumph into the Duomo.[2] All the nobles in a body met him before the gates of Milan. As a sign of his mercy, he carried a green ensign, displaying a Moor, dressed in gold, touching the shoulders of four barons kneeling before him. Thus did he enter the city.[3] After this, the people of Cremona only waited for an occasion to revolt from Venice, and in Genoa the rulers did not dare to commit the watch to any Italian, for the city was full of the report that, "Giovanni Adorno had written and was on the march with succour from Naples."[4] In Ferrara itself three hundred boys followed the drum of a Servite monk; they thundered at the door of the Venetian Visdomino, and shouted "Moor!"[5] The whole country would at one stroke have come into Ludovico's hand, had not the traitors given their castles over to the enemy; these must be retaken, were he to assert his supremacy. He raised his army, in spite of their small pay, to 12,000 men and 2,500 horses; his brother Tommaso followed him with the guns that he had just had cast in Germany. He said to the people, "I will be your prince and your brother; but you must help me with money." And although many thought that they had made sacrifices enough for him, and others did not believe that they could rely upon his good fortune, most of them perceived that his need was their need, and assisted him. Hereupon Ascanio besieged the castle of Milan, and Ludovico the castle of Novara.

Trivulzio, in the face of this movement, had retired along roads which the peasants endeavoured to render impassable by trees and stones, in return for which he left their villages desolated in his track, and proceeded despondently—for his own party upbraided him—past Pavìa to Mortara and Vercelli. Thither the King despatched La Trémouille to take the supreme command; thither also came a few Swiss, who had been in the pay of Caesar

---

[1] Benedictus Jovius, 61.   [2] Chronicon Venetum, 137.
[3] Chron. Venet. and Ferronus, iii. 51.   [4] Senarega, 571.
[5] Diarium Ferrarense.

Borgia.[1] But to withstand an army as great as that which Ludovico had with him, fresh recruiting must be resorted to. For this the Florentines and Venetians gave money, and the Archbishop of Sens and the Bailiff started at once for Switzerland.

The Swiss of those days were bold in the face of steel, but weak in the presence of money. They were united as soon as they had an enemy before them; but before that disunited, as also in negotiations. As they had no great general interests to consult, they blindly followed each special and momentary advantage. If those who joined Ludovico's colours remained faithful to his cause, whilst others were allowed to give their oath of allegiance to the Bailiff representing the opposite side, the murder of relatives by relatives, and a domestic war, terminating with the break-up of the Confederation, might ensue. It was, perhaps, owing to these apprehensions that they did not agree to the first offer of the Bailiff on the 21st February: "The King," they said, "should first of all pay up all arrears and confirm the terms;" and so, grumbling to himself: "it will be a matter of crowns, and so I suppose I shall have to open the purse," he left the assembly, and went through all the cantons.[2] On the 11th March they again assembled. Maximilian represented to them that: "in their terms with the French King, the Empire was excepted from those countries against which they were to lend assistance; but Milan was now a crown land, and Ludovico a subject, a vassal, of the Empire." That was at that time no unfounded assertion, as Ludovico had completely allied himself to the German King of the Romans; but now that they had received their money, they would not listen to any counter reasons.[3] The Zürichers chose a captain and Venner for their companies; the Freiburgers sent their councillors with them. Although the enlistment was at once prohibited in Bern,[4] the people, in spite of the prohibition, followed the drum. They marched, some up the Soane and across

[1] Moronus ad Varadeum, 285. Chronic. Venet. 143. Ferron.
[2] Anshelm and Tschudi in Glutzblotzheim, p. 171.
[3] From Tschudi in Fuchs, p. 287.
[4] Bern to Maximilian, p. 299.

the St. Bernard, others over the St. Gotthard, and came to Vercelli. They did not know what they were doing. Many a one had a brother, a brother-in-law, or a father opposed to him in Novara.

Either the oath would have to be broken, or the Confederation was at an end.

Ludovico still considered his camp to be blessed by good fortune;[1] he still hoped to draw all those who had crossed over the hills to his standard, He thought to take advantage of the wishes of the people of Uri, and sent a message to the Swiss to this effect: " Bellinzona, Mendrisio, Lugano, Locarno, and Val Maggia he would cede to them, give them 40,000 ducats at once, and pay a yearly sum of 24,000, if they would only rid him of the King." [2] Thereupon, the common people of Bern, in town and country, having, as they probably had, relations on both sides, implored their councillor, their Bailiff, to see that peace was made. This councillor proposed[3] to the confederates to dissuade both princes and both lords from using the sword, else great damage and great strife was unavoidable ; and in this direction the German envoys likewise exerted their influence. As a matter of fact, a decision was arrived at on the 31st March, such as Ludovico desired : " On the 8th of April two deputies from each canton should meet in the inn at Uri, and thence haste, in God's name, to bring the two princes to an understanding." [4]

But before the decision was known, the French sallied out. Ludovico was bold enough to oppose himself outside the walls to an army three times as strong as his, and to draw up Swiss to face Swiss. But both stopped; they refused to fight each other.[5] He retired to Novara, his enemies after him. He awaited, it appears to me, the decree, from which he hoped everything, and the reinforcements, which on the 9th of April had arrived at Como.[6] At length the decree arrived ; but it was not so unequivocal that the

---

[1] Ludovico's signature in Fuchs, p. 304.
[2] Stettler, 364.   [3] Letter of Bern, 298 and 302.
[4] Recess in Fuchs, p. 292 ; in Glutzblotzheim, p. 174.
[5] Testimony of Meyer in Gl. 175.
[6] Benedictus Jovius, Hist. Novocom., p. 61.

French could not make use of it. People in Lucerne were
not quite at one in the matter; the ducal party had gained
something, but not everything, and the essence of the decree
was quite contradictory in terms : " The soldiers should be
warned by both sides to return home, or, at all events, to go
over to one side." [1] It is evident that this determined the
matter. The French could rely upon faithful men; Ludovico
had to deal with captains who defrauded him of 500 guilders
in a single levy.[2] These latter went over into the enemy's
camp, and let the enemy into theirs. The two became
almost one. It was soon resolved to interpret the decree
in favour of the French. The cry was raised, " It is all over
with the Duke." [3] The French then came so close to him
that they might almost have taken him prisoner in a room.[4]
When he complained of the conduct of his captains, they
asked : " When did they ever promise to fight against confederates ? " If he only wanted advice, they told him that
he should apply to his wise councillors ; but if he would
take their counsel, he would mount a good horse, and ride
off to Bellinzona or the Eschenthal.[5] In this state of embarrassment, he entered into negotiations with the leaders of
the French, and Ligny was for allowing him to escape ; but
the others opposed this, and Trivulzio said: " He is as
good as ours." [6]

The enemy without, treachery within ; for his Italians
also became slack and drew back. There was only one
way of escape, namely, that which Æmilius Paulus advised
to Perseus, and of which Cato gave an example to the great
Romans—the last expedient in the struggle with fate, before
one succumbs. But Ludovico was not the man to perceive
it or seize it.

On Friday morning, the 10th April, 1500, Ludovico
Maria Sforza, called the Moor, sat in his room at Novara,

---

[1] Recess in Glutzbl.

[2] *Ibid.* p. 532.

[3] Anshelm in Fuchs, 309.

[4] Testimony of Tapfervogt in Fuchs, 321.

[5] Testimony of Pfister and Zellweger in Fuchs, Glutzb., and in
Aloysius Orelli's life, p. 54.

[6] Morone to Varadeus, 290.

read, and appeared to pray. Galeazzo Sanseverino entered and said: "he had only looked for two hundred Swiss to give him an armed escort, but had not found a single one." Then came certain Swiss captains and said: "they were obliged to go. If he would venture to escape in their midst, he must disguise himself and come." He hardly heard them, but went on reading.[1] They came again to him. "All is ready," they said. They found him still hesitating. So throwing a Swiss blouse over his scarlet skirts,[2] they sat him, partly by force and partly with his will, upon a horse, put a halberd in his hand, concealed him in their thickest company, and rode out of the gate. The French stood on both sides with lowered spears, and with guns ready pointed, so as to find him and not allow him to escape.[3] Some of them fell upon the landsknechts, and upon the Burgundians, and took Jacob von Ems prisoner.[4] Others rode up to the Swiss: "they had him, and for dear life they should surrender him; they must point him out, or they would be destroyed."[5] The cavalcade stopped. The Duke, now as a Minorite, and now as a Swiss trooper with a halberd, once taken, but again let go, as he was not recognized, was here, there, and everywhere, and few knew him. At last the Bailiff rode up and offered 500 ducats to him who would point him out.[6] Thereupon a man of Uri, named Turmann, who was standing behind him—a man of whom nothing evil had ever been known before—was allured by the proffered reward, and lifting up his hand, said in a low tone, "There!"[7] No one resisted. The Bailiff seized and recognized the Duke, and struck him with the flat of his sword across the shoulders. Trivulzio stept up to him and said, "Sforza, you have your reward."[8]

---

[1] The same, testimony in Fuchs, 331.

[2] Anton, p. 110.

[3] Testimony of Zimmermann, 323.

[4] Bebelii-Epitome laudum Suevorum, p. 141.

[5] Testimony of Brüchli Scherer and Tapfervogt.

[6] Paulus Jovius, Epitome Historiarum, p. 87.

[7] Testimony of Scherer, 322.

[8] Anton, p. 110. Ferronus, 52. Monstrelet, 230. In the "Anzeiger für Schweizerische Geschichte," 1884, No. 80, p. 279, is published a letter of Geoffrey Carles (of the 15th April, 1500), who

At the first report, the Milanese rushed terrified from their houses to the palace. Ascanio went out to them and said, "The Moor is a prisoner." He said nothing more. He had forgotten his eloquence. He thought only of his own escape.[1] Francesco Sforza had had five sons, all excellently endowed by nature and well brought up by their wise mother; but the first was murdered by conspirators; the second fled away from his sister-in-law and was drowned; the third died in exile. The fourth was Ludovico, and Ascanio, too, the fifth, did not avoid his destiny. He fell into the hands of Venice. No city was able to defend itself. They came out everywhere to meet the victors with olive branches.[2] But the victors treated them as great criminals. The Vogheresi also waited for Ligny, their lord, but he rode by them, as though he did not see them. They began to entreat him, but he would not hear until Louis d'Ars interceded for them. They brought him silver plate, and he gave it at once to Bayard.[3] The latter said: "God forbid that the gifts of such wicked people should come into my hand," and distributed it among others. In this way they took possession of the country. In Milan the heads of the leading Ghibellines were fixed on the palace gates, the rest were spared.[4] But the two Sforza were sent to France. Bourges and Loches lie not far apart on the left bank of the Loire, Bourges with its high round tower, commanding

belonged to the French who, at the revolt of Milan in January, 1500, had retired into the citadel; in this it is also stated that Ludovico had endeavoured to escape among the Swiss, to whom he made great promises. The French let the Swiss file by man by man. They recognized Ludovico also by the fact that he could not speak German (cognitus pour ce qu'il ne sceut respondre Alemand). The treachery of Turmann is not mentioned here. Everything is attributed to the work of the French commander. So, also, in Trivulzio's letter to the Signoria (in Sanuto, Diarii iii. p. 226). But we must, after all, take our stand upon what the Swiss accounts tell us. (Note to 3rd edition.)

[1] Arluni, de bello Veneto, i. 2.

[2] Chronicon Venetum, 151.

[3] Bayard, p. 84.

[4] Chronicon Venetum, 162.   Seyssel, Louanges du bon Roi, p. 48. Appendix to Monstrelet.

the country for miles round;[1] thither came Ascanio; Loches with its towers and bastions built on a steep rock, and surrounded by such deep moats that the English declared it to be impregnable.[2] Here Ludovico was imprisoned. Here he often spoke with his servant from Pontremoli of his sins and his fate.[3] "That is the star of Francesco Sforza," said the astrologers in Italy; "it means fortune for one man, but disaster for his descendants."[4]

As Maximilian was engaged in this war, he was also affected by this disaster. On that same momentous 10th of April on which Ludovico was taken prisoner, he opened a Diet at Augsburg. His prestige in his Empire did not depend only upon internal development, it depended almost still more upon his war and peace, and upon his foreign successes. Now that, since the diet of Freiburg, the four military enterprises in which he had been engaged had failed, viz., in Burgundy, in Gelderland, in Switzerland, and Milan, he was forced to acquiesce in a Council of Regency, such as had already been proposed at Worms. It consisted of twenty members, one elector, one spiritual and one temporal prince, one count, one prelate, and fifteen deputies. These twenty had the right of summoning the princes in small numbers or collectively, of deciding upon war, of recruiting infantry and horse for the "Common Penny," which they were to administer, even of disposing of any conquered territory, and finally, of making peace again.[5] What then remained of the royal dignity? "They would have liked to depose us," said Maximilian, "but a certain person required time and leisure." On the 2nd of July, 1500, this Council of Regency was resolved upon. On the 21st, Louis XII went to meet an embassy sent by it; he had to expect more assistance from it than resistance to his plans. He had gained a complete victory over Maximilian.[6]

---

[1] André du Chesne, Antiquités, p. 482.   [2] *Ibid*. p. 520.
[3] Paul Jovius, Elogia, p. 200.   [4] Arluni, de bello Veneto, i. 24.
[5] Gasser, Augsburger Chronik, 258. Regimentsordnung in Müller's Reichstagsstaat, 25-48.
[6] Maximilian's kurzer Begriff seiner Reichsverwaltung, p. 120. Monstrelet.

3. POPE ALEXANDER VI AND HIS SON AGAINST THE VASSALS OF THE CHURCH

Had the star of Francesco Sforza really possessed the significance assigned to it, its pernicious effect would have extended to the whole House of Sforza-Aragon. To his ruin it was disclosed for what purpose the Pope had entered into a league with Louis XII. But, in order to understand how the Pope was situated, it is necessary to begin with a general sketch.

Laws and customs, representing the unity of society in each individual member, do not merely exist for the purpose of protecting others against you, or you against others, but also for the purpose of protecting you against yourself. Moderation and self-restraint, the neglect of which entails self-destruction, and which, nevertheless, natural inclination and pride will never tolerate, become by means of them a habit, and lead him, who submits to them, unharmed and peacefully through all the days of his life. Yet, as the human race ever needs new laws, some one must be raised up to originate and to guard them, and over such a one their restrictive force cannot have power.

A great danger this, and yet one which high and low ever vie with each other in arrogating to themselves, and which the German-Christian nations, while yet united, reposed in a single individual, an old man chosen by old men ; a man who, with the exception of his name, had given up all connection with the world, and whom they believed God's Spirit did not allow to go astray. But inclinations are exceedingly deep-rooted and obstinate, even in old men ; and who is there that could be dead to the world and yet rule it? It was fortunate that the Popes were not entirely without fear, either when they fought with the Emperors, or when the Ghibelline party was at its height, or when they were at Avignon in the power of the French kings. After this, they were held in check by the schism, the fear of a fresh schism, or by the proximity of the Turks.

It was only when they had become accustomed to this constant fear, and when, in the whole of the Western world, there was none who could withstand the coalition even of the few whom the Pope could always command, that he became quite fearless. Two things tended to make this a particular misfortune; corrupt election, and the prevailing infidelity. If a strong man, whose mind in the course of a long life had become impure by sensuality, greed, and all the vices of the world, attained this position, and suddenly found himself honoured as semi-divine, would he use his power to a good or an evil end? A fear of Him, of whose very existence he was uncertain, could not restrain him. Alexander every Maundy Thursday imitated the Author of the faith by washing the feet of twelve poor men; but the feet had first to stand in a golden basin full of perfumed herbs, and a Cardinal had first to pour water over them out of a golden vessel, and not until then did he touch them.[1] Diaries, the truth of which it is impossible to doubt, accuse him of a sensuality which found its gratification even in that of others, of a cruelty which employed murderers [2] by day and night, and of such premeditated villainy, that he would by means of promises induce a man, good in other respects, to confess to something that he had not committed, and then punish him as if he had been guilty of it.[3] A man who had once spoken ill of his son, he punished by cutting off his hand and the tip of the tongue, and causing the latter to be exhibited stuck on the tip of the little finger.[4]

Through his son Don Juan, to whom Federigo had promised a principality in return for his investiture, Alexander had become closely connected both with Federigo and with all the House of Sforza and Aragon. But, in consequence of Juan's sudden death—his body was found in the Tiber [5]—this connection began to be severed. Juan, as a German chronicle relates, was Alexander's joy, and his soul was wrapped up in him. He now sat from Thursday to Sunday shut up in his chamber, without food, without

---

[1] Anton Harve, Reise 3.

[2] Raphael Volaterranus, Vitae Paparum, p. 167. Burcardus. Valerianus, de infelicitate literatorum, p. 272.

[3] Burcardus, 2085.   [4] *Ibid.* 2137.

[5] *Ibid.* 2082. Zurita, f. 125. Mariana, xxxi. 169. Guicciardini, iii. 182.

sleep, and always in tears; he thought of abdicating, for his wickedness was the cause of his son's death.[1] On Sunday he came forth, went on foot to St. Peter's, ordered five cardinals to make new arrangements for his court, and bade his children leave it.[2] But his children controlled him. All his passions were in still greater intensity found in his son Caesar: sensuality, thirst for power, bloody revenge, also the power of concentrating all his mental forces upon a single object, his princely generosity and his apparent magnanimity.[3] Caesar was an active, well-grown man, skilled at throwing, riding, and at slaying the bull when running with a single blow; his dark-red face was full of pimples, which readily festered and gave to his eye keenness and brilliancy and a snake-like movement, which he only restrained a little in the presence of women.[4] After his brother's death, which was attributed to himself, his tastes were all for arms and princely honours. Instead of removing from the court, he proposed to his father to relieve him from the office and dignity of Cardinal, and to endow him with a principality.[5] The Church is built up upon the inextinguishable character of the priestly state, and it was quite without precedent that the highest rank in it should be given up. But the Pope cared little for this, and he, in fact, proposed to Federigo that he should give his eldest daughter and Don Juan's possessions to Caesar.[6] Now Gioffredo Borgia and Lucrezia Borgia, the latter of whom had been torn away from the side of Giovanni Sforza, lord of Pesaro, and married to Alfonso, Duke of Biseglia, were already allied to the house of Aragon by marriage. But Federigo knew Caesar. A quiet, moral, noble gentleman as he was, and a father who loved his daughter so tenderly, could not sanction this. The Sforza plied him with entreaties upon entreaties, representing to him that the Pope would otherwise take other steps for the destruction of Italy. But his reply was that: "nothing in

---

[1] Matthias Döring, Continuatio chron. Engelhusi, ap. Menken, iii.
[2] Nardi, ii. 42. Burcardus.
[3] Petrus Martyr, Epistolae xv. 143.
[4] Jovius, Elogia virorum bellica virtute clarorum, 201-203.
[5] Burcardus ; also in Gordon's Appendix, d. 57.
[6] Burcardus, 2098.

the world should induce him; rather would he die a poor nobleman, and endure all the ills of the world, than do this. Let them not speak of it any more." From that time Alexander began to enter into serious negotiations with France. After Louis XII had promised Valentinois to Caesar, the latter came into the Consistory of Cardinals: " in spite of always having been addicted to the world, he had yet always been raised to spiritual dignities and benefices. His propensities would not be curbed. He now gave back his benefices, and begged to be relieved of his office."[1] How could he be refused what had long since been determined? In short, in October, 1498, he made his public entrance as Prince into Chinon, where Louis was holding his court. Sixty-six laden mules preceded him; he himself rode in, covered with jewels from his hat, in which gleamed ten rubies, down to his boots. His horse was shod with silver shoes; and behind him there came twenty-four mules caparisoned in red velvet.[2] The Pope was soon heard to say that, " he would give a fourth part of his papacy if only Caesar would not return;" and again —for he believed himself offended—" If only Caesar were there, he would act differently;"[3] and hence we can perceive how completely he was in Caesar's power. In France, Caesar received Valentinois, the bishop of which styled himself Count, as a Dukedom, and in May, 1499, Charlotte, Alain d' Albret's daughter, to wife.[4] Through this marriage he became related to the Kings of Navarre and of France. He next schemed to attain a larger lordship. If Louis attacked the Sforza in Milan, he, on his part, would destroy the despots of the Romagna, and all the vassals of the Church.

In September, 1499, Ludovico fled for the first time; in November, the Pope declared his great-nephews to have forfeited Imola and Forlì.[5] Caesar did not recollect that their father, Girolamo Riario, after having risen to power, lived

---

[1] Burcardus, 2096.
[2] Brantôme, Capitains étrangers, from an original.
[3] Zurita, 159, 160.
[4] Fleuranges, p. 12. Ferronus, p. 48.
[5] Burcardus, 2107.

as he himself did, and what his end was.   With French and
Swiss assistance, Caesar made war upon Caterina, Ludovico's
niece and Girolamo's widow.   The lady had no support.
Florence and Milan had formerly been her allies: the
former, because her court was full of Florentines;[1] besides,
her third husband, Giovanni di Pier Francesco de' Medici,
had come from Florence, and her son had at times been in
the service of the city.[2]   Milan was so devoted to her that,
for a time, Giovanni da Casale, Ludovico's agent, had the
whole government in his hands, and was present at her
most secret audiences.[3]   Aided by both, she had in the
previous year resisted the Venetians, and in this year had
supported both, especially Ludovico, with troops.[4]   But
now Ludovico was an exile, and her enemy was master of
Milan.   Now, too, in Florence, instead of the notables, who
were her friends, and the friends of her late husband,
Giovanni de' Medici, and of her child, the Popolari were
supreme; and although she went thither saying that "her
feast was the eve of that of the Florentines," they still
considered it dangerous to resist the French and Caesar.
In consequence of this state of things, Imola, both city and
citadel, was soon lost, and the nobles welcomed the enemy
into the city of Forlì.[5]   The citadel of Forlì, which had
been so strongly fortified by Pino Ordelaffi as to appear
impregnable, still held out.   Caterina, who, since her
husband's death, had withstood all her enemies, herself
commanded it, went about on the walls, and was nothing
daunted.[6]   In order to compass her rescue, a musician took
a poisoned letter to Rome, and desired an audience of the
Pope.   His chamberlain was a native of Forlì, and with
this chamberlain's help he thought he would be able to
succeed.   Yet he betrayed him.   "Didst thou think to
escape, in the event of succeeding?"   "At all events," was
the answer, "I should have saved my Princess; she reared

---

[1] Machiavelli, Legazione alla Contessa Caterina Sforza, lett. iv. 16.
[2] Commissione a Machiavelli, p. 1.
[3] Machiavelli, Legazione, lett. ii. 7.
[4] *Ibid.* p. 17.
[5] Nardi, ii. 61.
[6] Chronicon Venetum, p. 128.

me up, and I would suffer a thousand deaths for her."[1]
Caesar had promised 10,000 ducats to the man who would
bring her to him alive; but amongst such faithful adherents
he could not hope to find a traitor. She took no notice of
the Pope's promise to grant her an annual allowance; she
met Caesar's attack with energy. At last the wall was
pierced by 400 shot, and was scaled. She defended herself
to the last; but at last she was taken, and brought before
Caesar. The French captain demanded the 10,000 ducats;
Caesar then spoke of 2,000. "Wilt thou break thy word?"
answered the former, and was on the point of killing her.[2]
After this she lived many years at Florence, and enjoyed
much honour.

The return of Ludovico delayed this undertaking,
for, on account of it, French and Swiss had to turn towards
Milan.

After a while a messenger brought the tidings of Ludovico's captivity. The Pope gave him 100 ducats. The
Romans shouted "Orso e Franzia" in the streets.[3] Caesar,
who had since received the mantle, hat, and staff of
Gonfaloniere of the Church, advanced against Giovanni
Sforza at Pesaro.[4] Giovanni relied upon his people, upon
Venice, and Urbino. In his hall, the nobles and citizens
at his request had promised him allegiance and assistance;
immediately afterwards he discovered a conspiracy. He
hurried to Venice, which had always protected him; but
on this occasion he was reminded of how he had received
Turkish ambassadors. The Duke of Urbino gave him
poor encouragement, saying he ought to keep himself for a
better opportunity.[5] When Caesar approached, he fled,
and abandoned to him both city and country. Pandolfo
Malatesta also would not await him at Rimini. Before
that year, Venice had sent a Proveditor to protect him, so
that Caesar had retired, whilst he hurried to the feet of
the Signoria,[6] to express his gratitude. But now Venice
had declared for the Pope, who had granted to her
ecclesiastical revenues wherewith to fight the Turks; his

[1] Burcardus, ii. 61.
[2] Chronicon Venetum, 135.
[3] *Ibid.* 2116.
[4] Burcardus, 2114.
[5] Baldi, Guidubaldo, 215.
[6] Chronicon Venetum, 241.

people hated him, and so he also fled.   Hereupon, since everything appeared to succeed, in November, 1500, Caesar advanced against Faenza.

The Faentines were distinguished among all the Romagnols for their unanimity and their industrial cleverness; their linen was the whitest; their potteries had acquired a special reputation; and they had, moreover, been renowned for their loyalty, ever since they had defended the Bolgherelli against Frederick II's superior force, and had saved them from harm.[1]   At the time of which we speak, there lived two youths, descendants of their old princes, the Manfredi, of whom the elder, Astorre, aged fifteen years, was an angel in cleverness and beauty.   Their sole ally was the winter; but they made such good use of it that Caesar retired on the tenth day.   In April, 1501, he came again.   They killed 1,000 of his men to sixty citizens on their side; 1,400 they blew up in a bastion;[2] and the Pope sometimes was so angry that he did not go to chapel.   But Caesar was not weakened by his losses, as the charitable offerings of piety were at his disposal, and the Faentines were ruined by their success.   At last, utterly exhausted by three successive attacks, they surrendered, after Caesar had guaranteed them safety, and liberty to their princes.[3]   After this Caesar was called Duke of the Romagna, and up to this point Louis acquiesced in his undertakings.   But when he threatened Bologna, Giovanni Bentivoglio, under French protection, resisted him, and escaped with a few fines.[4]   When after this he made an irruption into the Florentine territory, as though intending to restore the Medici, the King and the Pope warned him to depart; and he was obliged to content himself with money and a condotta.[5]   When he made a descent upon Appiano of Piombino, the King would not have been displeased, had Genoa previously acquired the fine fresh-water harbour by purchase.   But Caesar was too quick; and as soon as he had Elba and Pianosa, its Prince was obliged to relinquish to him

---

[1] Leander Alberti, Descriptio Italiae.
[2] Zurita, i. 209.   [3] Diarium Ferrarense, 393, 395.
[4] Nardi, 70.
[5] Nardi.   Nerli, v. 86.   Machiavelli, Discorsi, i. 38.

Piombino, and take refuge in the valley of the Scrivia, on the estate of a Spinola.[1] Even Alfonso of Ferrara was not strong enough to resist him, and was obliged to make terms, by marriage with this family.

Caesar is like a wolf in the fold, that has made friends with the shepherd. His soldiers wore a belt from the right shoulder to the left thigh, representing a scaly snake, picked out in gold and colours, darting downwards with its seven heads.[2] But what symbol could express the damnation of a man who, during these struggles, came once to Rome, caused the Via S. Pietro to be closed, and six human beings brought into it, and hunted with arrows, whilst he stood by and shot them until they died like hunted game;[3] who promised Astorre his liberty, and then outraged this innocent boy, this noble blood, in an unnatural manner; and, still fearing him, at last caused him to be thrown with his brother into the Tiber,[4] with a stone round his neck.

God's judgment was over Italy. Destruction was abroad, and stalked from one palace to the other. Only the true Aragonese, Federigo and his house, still survived ; but destruction was in their wake. At the first attack upon the Sforza, Alfonso di Biseglia, Alexander's Aragonese son-in-law, fled from Rome. If he had only never returned ! But now, when crossing the Piazza di S. Pietro in broad daylight,[5] he was attacked by murderous bands, and carried to his house wounded in three places : but, as he did not succumb at once to his wounds, Caesar employed his executioner, Michelotto, to despatch him in bed.[6] Beatrice, daughter of Ferrante the elder, and wife of King Wladislav, was far away in Hungary. After losing a better

---

[1] Senarega Annales. [2] Baldi, Guidubaldo, p. 216.
[3] Burcardus, 2121. [4] Nardi, iv. 71. Burcardus, 2138.
[5] Burcardus, 2123.
[6] Passero, 123. Cf. Römische Päpste, i. 33 ["History of the Popes," Eng. translation, i. 39], and the Report of Paolo Capello in Appendix 3 [iii. 6]. The accounts of the Neapolitans, from the reports sent to the court of King Federigo, are strange, *e.g.* that of Giacomo, who describes very exactly the wounds inflicted, p. 235 : " Una alabardata alla spalla, una ferita dereto la testa et una stocchata in li fianchi." (Note to 2nd edition.)

husband, she had brought the crown to this one. But
Wladislav was long since tired of her. Alexander, who
had always hitherto been prevented by some consideration
or other, now pronounced his divorce from her. Anne de
Candale, of the royal house of France, took her place.[1] In
Federigo himself, the life of this dynasty was threatened.
When Milan was first conquered, the French levies boasted,
"they were now in the midst of a hundred years' war
without a day's peace;[2] they had still to war against the
Turks, and to cross the Alps, but first of all to Naples."
Federigo had sometimes attempted to negotiate, but he
only found himself dallied with. In April, 1501, the
preparations were no longer a secret; and, in May, Louis
communicated his intention to the German Imperial
Council, which had concluded a truce with him until the 1st
of July, and had tied Maximilian's hands.[3] In June, the
army advanced into the Florentine territory; and in Rome
shelters were erected for the men, and stables for the
horses, whilst a residence was prepared for the King.[4]

Many thought then how closely Ferdinand was related
to Federigo, and how the former, even in breach of his
treaty, had come to the aid of Ferrantino, and saved him;
now Gonzalvo was in Messina ready for action. A long
war—possibly a reversal of the whole of the French
successes—might be expected. Federigo had asked
Gonzalvo if he could depend upon him, and he answered:
"my master is your friend."

Yet it was not so. Ferrantino would scarcely have been
so energetically supported had he not been married to
Juana, Ferdinand's niece. For the old kinship, from the
time of the first Alfonso, was hateful to Ferdinand, since it
had ousted his line from Naples, and it went for nothing
with him. Federigo, also, had looked for a new alliance
and had begged for Ferdinand's youngest daughter, or his
niece Juana, for his son;[5] but he refused the first proposal
and for the second demanded an exorbitant dowry. He

---

[1] Burcardus, 2116. Zurita, 180. Petrus Martyr, xi. 190.
[2] Burcardus.
[3] Altobosto's statement in Müller's Reichstagsstaat, p. 107.
[4] Burcardus. [5] Passero, p. 120. Zurita.

now began to think of his own claims. He had already negotiated with Charles VIII upon the matter of compensation for his claims to Naples, in case Charles should again invade it, to take the form either of Calabria, which should be detached from the kingdom, or of a partition of the whole of Italy between the French, the German, and himself the Spanish King.[1] Charles died, and therefore, at the beginning of Louis XII's reign, he concluded a treaty with him, without regard for Federigo.[2]

When then this King was making ready for his campaign, Mosen Gralla, Ferdinand's ambassador, visited Cardinal d'Amboise, and said to him, as though only expressing his own ideas : "How if you were to come to some arrangement with us respecting Naples, as you did with Venice regarding Milan?" Amboise had always feared the Spanish claims, and so replied, "We two shall have to keep up the friendship between our kingdoms."[3] But Gralla had long since received his instructions from his master. On the 22nd September, 1500, a real treaty was arrived at, in these terms : "The territory of Naples to be divided into two halves; one half, comprising the Abruzzi and Lavoro with the title of kingdom, to belong to Louis; the other, consisting of Apulia and Calabria, as a dukedom, to Ferdinand. A further arrangement especially respecting the Dogana to be made after the conquest."[4] This treaty was still unknown when the French entered the Florentine territory. But on St. Peter's day, 1501, both envoys submitted it to the Pope, who at once invested both princes.[5] These were the first tidings that Federigo received of what was proceeding against him. Thereupon Gonzalvo sent him a message to the effect that: "he renounced his fief in Naples, for he was obliged to renounce the oath[6] he had taken in respect of it." And the Pope rejoiced when he saw the French army, 2,000 horse and 12,000 infantry, with 42 guns, file past in the garden of the Castle of St. Angelo on its way to the Neapolitan frontier.[7]

[1] Zurita, 132–138. Comines, end. [2] Zurita, f. 140.
[3] *Ibid*. f. 168. [4] *Ibid*. f. 192.
[5] Guicciardini, iv. 266. [6] Zurita, f. 212.
[7] Burcardus, 2131.

When Federigo looked about him, he found nothing upon which he could rely. The east coast was in the hands of Venice, and the fortresses, by virtue of old treaties, in those of Spain. Should he trust in his barons, who would not even all be present at his coronation,[1] who outlawed in their respective territories all who adhered to him, and whom he could only possibly have subjected with Gonzalvo's assistance ?[2] The Colonna alone were faithful, but they alone were of no account, entrusting, as they did, their possessions in the States of the Church to the cardinals. Their stewards were compelled to swear allegiance to the Pope, and an assembly of Roman citizens resolved to destroy their city of Marino.[3] Federigo's sole hope lay in the cities, and he had their walls repaired and hand-mills provided, whilst the peasants were driven in and located in barns.[4]

There is no spectacle more depressing than a country which allows itself to be conquered without drawing the sword. Gonzalvo was master of fifteen towns, without transporting a single horse thither. After Capua had held out for a moment, thanks to German mercenaries, the Count of Polenta rode out, as though he wished to see how things stood with the enemy, and, whilst doing so, surrendered a gate.[5] The city fell. Now Federigo lost all hope of being able to resist. The two great kings were his enemies, and on the march against him ; the Pope was leagued with them, and his vassals were in revolt. He now only thought of how he could save himself and his family, and prevent his country being given up to the ravages of war. Before the gate of the arsenal in Naples, the King assembled his citizens and nobles and addressed them : " since fate was driving him away, he released them from their oath."[6] He himself came to the following arrangement with the French : " if within six months he could not appear at the head of an army, he would retire to France upon estates which should be assigned him, and thither would bring also his treasures, his acquaintances

[1] Zurita, f. 126.
[2] Zurita, 130, 132.
[3] Burcardus, 2129.
[4] Caracciolus, Vita Spinelli, p. 47.
[5] Arluni, i. 17. Zurita, 215.
[6] Passero, p. 125.

and friends." [1] Hereupon he betook himself to Ischia. Thither came also Beatrice of Hungary, and Isabella of Milan, his whole family and the few who remained faithful to him. He was never again able to show himself at the head of an army, and so passed the remainder of his life in France. How different were his expectations and all anticipations thirty years before, when, in the flower of youth and hoping for the hand of the daughter of Charles the Bold, he passed through Rome! [2] He was neither king nor heir to the throne, but the cardinals strove together as to which should be the first to welcome him. In him the Aragon dynasty was extinguished, as was the House of Sforza ; both of which a short time previously had flourished above all others in Italy. If we inquire what they achieved, the answer is that it was owing to them that, almost for the first time in their history, the Italians remained for a while free from the influence of foreign nations. If Francesco Sforza had not become lord of Lombardy, the French would have been : had Alfonso not given Naples to a spurious son, a Spanish viceroy would have been even at that time established there. It was due to this assertion of their independence, that the Italians, untrammelled by foreign influence, and in progressive movement and rivalry within, were enabled within a somewhat limited sphere to develop their intellectual energies to a degree that the Germanic-Latin nations have always regarded as the highest perfection of culture to which they ever attained. They acknowledge the fact that every new science and art traces its birth to this era. These two families had to separate, chiefly on account of two women ; the one called in the French, the other the Spaniards : after they had weakened each other, union availed them nothing. The two invoked forces joined hands, and destroyed both. They both sprang up together, flourished together, and perished together.

After this event, it was possible to journey under French safe-conduct from the Pyrenees to Naples. The Spaniards made further progress in the south of Italy. In order not to be completely ruined by this powerful enemy, Maximilian

[1] Zurita, 218.
[2] Jacob Volaterranus, Diarium Romanum, xxii. 95.

was obliged at Trent to promise the King of France the investiture of Milan.[1] Three independent and pre-eminently active members of Christendom were now annihilated, and only three large States still existed in Italy. That was the result of Charles VIII's movements. To us, however, it is a matter of regret; for we must always feel sad when a particular existence, one of God's own creations, perishes. But one consideration may tend to calm our feelings.

If we remember that Otranto was once in the hand of the Turks, and that a certain Boccalino, on another occasion, ceded to them Osimo, that at Naples sometimes the kings and at other times the barons summoned them to their aid; that at Pesaro in the States of the Church, their agents were well received, and that, on Ludovico Sforza's invitation, they made an incursion into Friuli; if we remember how unanimous and powerful they always were or soon became, and how disunited and weak the Italians showed themselves, we cannot deny that Rome might just as readily have fallen into their hands as Constantinople, and that the same fate which befell the Hungarians might easily have overwhelmed all Italy, and primarily Naples, to which the Turks already laid claim. But now more powerful neighbours occupied the frontiers, and offered them resistance.

The Turks themselves, and almost the whole of the Mohammedan world, were involved in this war.

Abuayazid, whom we know as Bajazet, induced by the messages of Ludovico the Moor, considered that Louis XII after conquering Italy would probably carry out the other plans of his ancestors; that Venice forced the Turkish ships to salute hers, which was an insult to him; and that he had remained five years quietly in Stamboul, and the day had at last arrived when he could take Inebecht, that is Lepanto.[2] Entertaining this idea, he gave Andrea Zancani, who entreated peace of him, only an Italian letter of compact, which he did not consider binding, and not a Turkish one.[3] Whilst Andrea went joyfully on his way

[1] Dumont, iv. 1, 16.
[2] Leunclavii Annales Turcorum, p. 35. Ejusdem Pandectae Historiae Turcicae, p. 192.
[3] Bembus, Histor. Venetum, 91a, 92a.

home, thinking that "the Othman of the Othmanis, the
Grand Turk, had assured him of all good will," the latter
equipped 270 ships for sea in the Hellespont, collected
250,000 horses in Adrianople, and despatched them in
June, 1499, to pillage Zara.[1] But in August they set out,
he by land, and his fleet by sea, both bound for Lepanto.
Antonio Grimani awaited the fleet near Sapienza. Antonio,
from being a prosperous merchant, in whose hands earth
appeared to turn into gold, had become supreme commander of the Venetian forces, and they believed they
had in him an Alexander or a Caesar.[2] He had kept back
in harbour a ship of pilgrims about to sail for Jerusalem
for this holiest deed, namely, to do battle against the
Infidel; he had already issued his orders to the effect that
"he would, with God's assistance, attack the enemy;" but
when the Turks sailed out from Portolungo, and ·the
Christians from Sapienza, both sides showed themselves
but little inclined for the combat, and, after manœuvring
about, turned back. At length both became more resolute.
The largest Turkish ship put out for action. Two other
Christian ships had just made ready to engage her,
when there came from Corfu that valiant hero Andrea
Loredano and joined the fleet. The crew shouted their
acclamations, and after having asked the general whither
he wished him to go, he embarked on one of the two ships.
They put out and grappled the Turk. All three caught
fire. Whilst the Turks hastened to rescue their men in
boats, the Christians stood thunderstruck. Loredano made
no attempt to escape; he said: "Under this flag I was
born, and under this flag will I die," and threw himself into the flames. The rest jumped into the water,
and were taken prisoners. Thus was this battle lost.[3]
Grimani retreated; the Turks attacked Lepanto both by
land and sea, and took it.[4] Two thousand others
pillaged in Friuli, so that in Treviso, and even in Mestre,
the inhabitants dared not to open their gates. Zancani

---

[1] Chronicon Venetum, 74.
[2] Chronicon Venetum, 125, 126. Jovius, Elogia, p. 300.
[3] Chronicon Venetum, 86, 96, 109. Petrus Justinianus, p. 354.
[4] Annales Turcici.

who was sent against them dared not venture out of Gradisca.[1]

Zancani was banished; Grimani was also banished. In the following year, Melchior Trevisano, Grimani's most bitter enemy, went against the Turks, but he was neither able to capture Cephalonia, nor to relieve Modon, but Abuayazid took Coron, Modon,[2] and Navarino.

It must be recorded that at the same time the Moors of Granada rose against the Kings of Spain. Ximenes, Archbishop of Toledo, had won over some Alfaquins by gifts of silk dresses and red hats, and one Zegri by imprisonment and presents, and then baptized them, as well as a large number of others from the Albaycin. But when he had burnt upon a pile nearly five thousand of their books, all beautifully wrought in gold and silver and artistically decorated, the people revolted, killed his servants, and scarcely spared him. The King came sorrowfully to the Queen: "their monk had undone all their conquest."[3] Three days later, the Moors living in the city recollected themselves;[4] in order to escape punishment they allowed pictures to be hung in their mosques and submitted to baptism. But the Moors of the mountains, who dwelt upon the impenetrable peaks of the Alpujarras of the red, white, and snow-bound Sierra, could not be pacified.

Two brothers, Aguilar by name, took the field against Moors and Turks; the elder, Alfonso, against the Moors, and he was slain. Since a great number would on no account become Christians, they were sent to Africa, and every day galleys went backwards and forwards to transport them thither.[5] Troops were left to hold the remainder in check. The younger brother, Gonzalvo, the Great Captain, went to the assistance of the Venetians, and his advent brought them good fortune. Abuayazid, who was lamed by gout, had returned to his palace to study Averroes, and Trevisano had just returned from his pursuit, full of pride that within sight of Europe and Asia he had succeeded in hanging some of his enemies on the gallows.[6] Gonzalvo

[1] Bembus, 105, 106.
[2] Petrus Martyr, xiii. 217
[3] Gomez, Vita Ximenis, 958-961.
[4] Zurita, 172.
[5] Zurita, 202, 203.
[6] Zurita, 195.

combined forces with him in order to capture the castle of Cephalonia ; he sent in word to the Turkish commander Gisdar : "that it was the conquerors of Granada who were attacking him." The Turk answered, " Has not each of us seven bows and seven thousand arrows ? Moreover, the day of our death is from the first written on our brow," [1] and in this conviction he defended himself with his accustomed weapons. The Biscayans withstood all his arrows, scaled his castle, and killed him. This done, Gonzalvo turned towards Sicily and Naples. But afterwards Portuguese ships and even papal troops came and took part in the Turkish war, and the French troops stormed Mitylene eighteen times. The Christians did not succeed further than to surprise Santa Maura, and even this they were obliged to restore as the price of the peace. What Venice lost remained lost; she gained but little advantage from Cremona ; and Ludovico comforted himself in his prison with the reflection that, at all events, one ally had not broken faith with him.

[1] Jovius, Vita Gonsalvi.

BOOK II

1502–1514

INTRODUCTION

THE position of the Latin and Teutonic nations at this time may be briefly summarized as follows :—

Italy had been visited by a great disaster ; it was not political unity, which the country had really never possessed, that was imperilled, but that internal accord and independence in dealing with foreign countries, which might have stood in its stead. These were lost and gone, and this result had been effected, not so much by the expedition of Charles VIII and its immediate consequences, as by the feuds between Venice and Milan, and between the Pope and Naples. The papal authority, which was paramount in Naples, was mainly instrumental to this end. Alexander VI cannot aptly be compared with the Popes of the thirteenth century, who, when hard pressed by the enmity of the Hohenstaufen, appealed to the French for aid to rid themselves of them ; in his case, the marriage of his infamous son, an alliance supported by the one and opposed by the other side, was the motive for delivering Naples at once into the hands of the French and Spaniards. The after-consequences of this step swayed the destinies of Italy in the ensuing centuries.

Of all princes of that time, Louis XII was the most powerful. Among the ordinances by which he guaranteed the French an appropriate constitution, and gained for himself in their esteem a place between St. Louis and Henry IV, the following is, perchance, the most characteristic : " A tribunal should never be venal : in the event of his commanding such a thing, the Chancellor should not seal it ; and, in the event of his having sealed it, neither Bailiff nor Seneschal should obey." Such was the ordinance which by the King's unbiassed judgment placed law above caprice.[1] In this way he kept his people well inclined towards him. From Italy not merely his own subjects flocked to his court, but the deputies of the independent States in almost still greater numbers. Every day there arrived mounted couriers bearing letters, instructions, and money ; every one was desirous of currying favour with a member of the King's Council. No prince or city in Italy felt themselves secure without being first assured of French protection. Florence was itself powerful, yet was not in a better position than the rest.[2] In addition to politics, the daily occupations of Louis were hunting and hawking. With the month of May, the huntsmen made their appearance at the court all in green, and each with his horn and his hound. In September, when the stag-hunting was over, the falconers appeared in their cocked hats, and took the place of the others.[3] Louis followed them both, through field and through wood.

His principal allies were Alexander VI, the kings of Denmark and Scotland, and certain German princes.

Alexander had assigned the legation at the court of France, the most important office the Pope had to bestow, to Cardinal Georges d'Amboise for life ; and this was considered such an extraordinary act of favour, that the University of Paris opposed it. The neighbours and vassals who enjoyed Louis' protection, were taken likewise by the Pope under his. The Duke of Urbino allowed exiles and refugees free asylum and social intercourse at his court ; Alexander had guaranteed him his nephew's succession. Giovanni Bentivoglio, relying upon his new treaty with Caesar, founded ironworks in the mountains near Bologna, and cut canals in the plain ; he believed he was acting for his children.

The Baglioni, Vitelli, and Orsini, were in Caesar's pay.

[1] Ordonnance of 1499. Article 40 in Röderer, Mémoir pour servir à l'histoire de Louis XII. Paris, 1822, p. 255.

[2] Machiavelli, Legazione alla corte di Francia, iii. 64, 66, 80.

[3] Fleuranges, Mémoires, 19.

Pandolfo Petrucci, the head of the Nove, and, through the three privy councillors, chief of the whole municipality of Siena, became also, in the persons of these his friends, allied with the Pope. Ercole of Ferrara proceeded to build palaces, to ride in processions, and to enjoy the pleasures of the theatre, without anxiety; his son was married in the Lent of 1502 to Lucrezia Borgia. Alexander remained the devoted friend of the King.[1]

James IV of Scotland, who, since his marriage with the daughter of Henry VII, had forgotten his English wars, was building in Falkirk, celebrating tournaments at Stirling, and receiving constant visits from French knights.[2] Both expeditions of the King of Denmark were unsuccessful; that against the Ditmarschers, whom he, in league with France, had attacked against Maximilian's wish, at the time of the Milanese War,[3] failed, by reason of the enemy's bravery; that against Sweden was completely foiled by Sten Sture, and in 1502 he was forced to rest. Several German princes maintained an open understanding with France; since the treaty of Trent, they paused in their opposition to Maximilian.

This combination was confronted by another, formed by the house of the Catholic Kings, and cemented not only by league, but by blood-relationship, a genuine family union. In the year 1497, all the children of Ferdinand the Catholic were together, with the exception of Juana. Juan, with his consort, Margaret, was destined for the Spanish throne; Isabella for the Portuguese; Katherine for the English; and Mary for some other throne, which was at present the object of negotiation. At the court all was still; all who desired to gain favour, went about with downcast eyes and modest pace; the royal pair had prescribed the strictest ceremonial, extending even to the interchange of kisses on hand and mouth, between the ladies of the court.[4] But here

---

[1] Castiglione, Cortegiano. Baldi, Vita di Guidubaldo, vi. 223. Bursellis, Chronicon Bononiense, 912. Allegretti, Ephemerides Senenses, in Muratori, xxiii, 763. Diarium Ferrarense, 325, 358, 276.

[2] Buchananus, Rerum Scoticarum, lib. xiii. p. 468, ed. Francf, 1624.

[3] Gebhardi, Hist. of Denmark and Norway, ii. 41. Note 2.

[4] Zurita, i. 118. Petrus Martyr, p. 99. Marineus Siculus, 567.

changes now took place, which were of great importance for the State, and had still greater influence over its future.

Just as every one was hoping to see the unity of Spain established for ever under a native sovereign, by a son of Juan, Juan himself died. He had been the hope of the realm. A native prince of good disposition is a great blessing. But now black flags floated over the walls of the city, and for forty days all business ceased. All the inhabitants were dressed in black. If a grandee rode out, it was only his horses' eyes that were undraped. The child, too, of which Margaret was delivered after Juan's decease, died as soon as born.[1]

Hereupon, Isabella who had since become Queen of Portugal, returned with her husband, and after receiving at Toledo the allegiance of the Castilians, as successor to the throne, she came to Saragossa, in order to obtain it likewise from the refractory Aragonese. The whole peninsula would in course of time have thus become united; but whilst at Saragossa Isabella also died, and her son Miguel shortly after her.[2]

Thus the succession devolved upon Juana, the consort of the Archduke Philip, and passed to the house of Hapsburg with all the greater certainty, since on St. Matthew's day, 1500, she gave birth at Ghent to a son, Charles. " The lot fell upon Matthew," said the old Queen of Castile, and rightly, for round the life of this child was centred the greatest combination our nations have for centuries known. In the year 1502, Philip and Juana were in Spain; now received by the Commanders of Orders, so gorgeously attired that even their stirrups were of gold, and anon welcomed by the Biscayan nobility, who begged for a bounty in order to be able to celebrate high festival. The succession was then assured them; in Toledo by the prelates, grandees, and procurators of the cities of Castile; in Saragossa, by the bishops, by the thirty-two Ricoshombres, and the deputies of the Caballeros and Infanzones; in Aragon by the Jurados of the cities.[3]

---

[1] Comines. Petrus Martyr, pp. 100, 106.
[2] Osorius, de rebus gestis Emanuelis, i. 19. Zurita, 139.
[3] Hubert Thomas Leodius, Vita Friderici Palatini, lib. ii. Zurita, 227.

Meanwhile, Katherine had gone to marry Arthur, Prince of Wales; Mary to marry Manuel of Portugal, and Margaret, Juan's widow, to marry the Duke of Savoy.[1] All these houses formed a natural union.

The French League and the family of the Spanish Kings, confronted each other. Philip, at once vassal of France and heir to the throne of Spain, made a compact with Louis to the effect that their children, Charles and Claude, who were both as yet in the cradle, should one day marry; and thus he became the mediator between both parties. This induced Maximilian to abandon completely the interests of the Sforza, and, in October, 1501, to promise the King of France the investiture of Milan. Philip journeyed through France on his way to Spain, sat among the peers in the hall of justice, came before the King, and readily comported himself as a vassal. Juana, on her part, gave Claude a large diamond, in testimony of the new alliance. Philip also prepared to return through France.[2]

At this time our nations ruled over hardly a single foreigner, and were subjected to none. We find even the Grandmaster of Prussia now refusing allegiance to the King of Poland, and this action of his gained the support of many German princes. Ivan Wasiljewitsch's attack upon Livonia in the year 1501 was repulsed by the general, Walter von Plettenberg, in two great battles; peace for fifty years being thus secured.

Certainly, at this juncture a general campaign against the Turks, who were now engaged in war with Venice, would have been a feasible undertaking. Immediately after the treaty with Maximilian, and when Christendom was enjoying universal peace, Louis proclaimed this crusade.[3] For this, both France and Italy, and Upper and Lower Germany, but especially the latter, had been prepared by a marvellous apparition of certain coloured crosses, which were said to have suddenly made their appearance everywhere, upon

[1] Treaty in Dumont, iv. 1, 15.
[2] Pontus Heuterus, Rerum Austriac. libri. From the MS. of Lalaing, a fellow-traveller of Philip, p. 259.
[3] Appendix to Monstrelet, 247.

linen and wool, and upon dresses and all manner of cloths. Maximilian, in anticipation of this war, founded a special order of knighthood.[1]   But, as yet, Italian affairs, as well as those of the usurping powers, were not so firmly established as not to give occasion for a fresh quarrel, a quarrel destined to spread even more widely than the former.

[1] Joh. Francisci Pici Mirandulani Staurostichon.   Carmen ad Maximilianum.   Apud Freherum Rer. Germ. tom. ii.

CHAPTER I

1. THE WAR IN NAPLES AND THE ROMAGNA

IN Naples a fresh war broke out between the Spaniards and the French. The immediate cause was the treaty of partition, which they had concluded together. In this partition Lavoro and the Abruzzi were guaranteed to the French, and Apulia and Calabria to the Spaniards, whilst four smaller provinces, the two Principati, Basilicata and Capitanata, had not been expressly divided. Now, seeing that, according to the fundamental institutions of the countries, institutions inaugurated by the Emperor Frederick II, the Principati shared their court of justice with Lavoro, whilst the other two had their court in common with Apulia,[1] a little good-will, after the Dogana question had been settled, would have sufficed to settle this dispute also, had not there been other motives for quarrelling, notably, the internal factions of the country. The Colonna, whose possessions lay in the French portion, placed themselves under the protection of Spain, whilst several towns in Apulia raised the French banner. The Angevins summoned the French to Calabria, whilst the Aragonese called Gonzalvo to the Abruzzi. The same factions were already engaged in fighting for Manfredonia and Altamura.[2] It turned out, that, live in whatever division they might, the one party would only obey the French and the other only the Spaniards, whilst these powers were always ready to help them to gain the ascendency. The attitude of their respective armies was decisive for the issue. When, on one occasion, the Spaniards had made an incursion as far as the

[1] Lebret, History of Italy, iii. 166. From Matthaeus Afflictus.
[2] Zurita, 231, 219. Jovius, Vita Gonsalvi, 230.

springs of Troia, and a skirmish was the result, Ives d'Allègre sent a message to Mendoza, inquiring : " Whether this meant an open breach, and was intended to rouse them from their tranquillity ; if so, he was ready to give satisfaction." Mendoza replied : " We came to Italy, I and my army, not for peace, but for war. We would gladly engage, even without orders." And this was the feeling of the majority. At this time the two commanders, Gonzalvo and Nemours, who had advanced close to each other, the first to Atella, and the latter to Melfi, often met at the high altar of a chapel dedicated to St. Antony, situated on the ridge of the Apennine chain which lay between them. But, in spite of all their orders to the contrary, the struggle broke out quite spontaneously.[1]

On the 12th June, 1502, when the Spaniards forcibly entered Tripalda—alleging it was a widow's portion, belonging to Juana, the sister of their King—and when Aubigny set forth from Naples to recover it—holding that it belonged to the French portion—open war could no longer be avoided.[2]

Gonzalvo, who had under his command but few of his 5000 men—for he had brought so many with him—was at once obliged to fall back. In Apulia lay one of the four castles, which were considered the strongest in the whole of Italy,[3] viz. Barletta, and thither he proceeded. The French pursued him. They forced Pedro Navarra to retire from Canosa, though with honours.[4] In August they took Quadrata and Biseglia ; and by September they had on their side all the Sanseverino of Bisignano, Bitonto, Melito, Capurso and Acquaviva di Conversano. Of the whole of Apulia they left the Spaniards nothing but Bari, Barletta, and some surrounding places. These districts also were attacked by the French, and first and foremost Barletta, "for the honour of their chivalry ; "[5] for Bari was being defended by a woman, Isabella, the widow of Gian Galeazzo.

[1] Zurita, 238, 240.
[2] Passero, Giornale Napolitano, 129.
[3] Leander Alberti, Descriptio Italiae, p. 369.
[4] Petrus Martyr, xv. 140.
[5] Jovius, Vita Gonsalvi, 235. Zurita.

" We are still six leagues away," wrote Nemours on the 19th November, " and keep the enemy shut in; the King shall see that we defend his rights staunchly, and that everything is going from good to better." [1]   In December, Aubigny advanced to Calabria.   He fell upon the Spaniards —for here also they were much too weak—at the very moment when they were in the act of retreating across the Aspromonte and through the passes to the Retromarina. They managed, however, to make good their escape; but the whole of Calabria, with the exception of a few castles on the sea-board, was lost to them.   They held their ground in Gerace and in the Mottas.

The rest of the Spanish possessions (like the plank of a ship fought for by drowning men) were the object of a chivalrous war, waged with good weapons.   Here were the heroes whom Ariosto had seen when he began to sing of his Rogeros and Rinaldos.   In Calabria we meet with that Imbercourt to whom, whenever there was a battle to fight, the heat of an Italian noontide seemed like the cool of morning, and with that Aubigny who, in order to ransom him, although he had been chosen before himself, sacrificed his silver plate. [2]   Before Barletta were the discreet La Palice, to whom the enemy first gave the title of " Marshal," and Montoison, who, though bowed down by weight of years, was still, when on horseback, the falcon of the fray ; there, too, was Fontrailles, called the " Fearless," as well as many others of those who, if there was a battle to fight and they happened to be on shipboard, contending with contrary winds, would land and march one hundred leagues in three days. [3]   Among them also was that Bayard who, from the very hour when his mother came down from the tower to give him her small purse at parting and to commend to him four virtues—the fear of God, truth, kindliness and generosity—had never neglected a single day to practise them.   He always prayed, before leaving his chamber, and no one ever heard

[1] Lettera del duca di Nemorsa a Ciamonte in Machiavelli, Legazione al duca Valentino, 222.

[2] Brantôme and Garnier, from Anton's MS., 362.

[3] Brantôme, 115, 116.   Anton, Histoire de Louys XII, p. 159.

him praise himself. Once when he had captured 15,000 ducats, and another, though he had no claim, demanded them of him, he first of all established his legal right; this done, as soon as the money had been paid down, and his adversary remarked, "I should be happy for all the rest of my life if I only had the half of it," he replied, "Then I will give you just half;" and thereupon gave him the one half and his followers the other. "O, my lord, my friend," cried the other, upon his knees, "no Alexander was ever so generous."[1] Bayard's life was as clear as crystal, his heart ready in every danger, and his soul mild and gentle. The Spaniards resemble the French; but the resemblance is that between the Moorish and Christian knights of Ariosto. Among them was the small, thin Pedro Navarra, who had raised himself from a common soldier to the dignity of Count; no rock was so hard that he could not mine it; his mouth tightly closed, his nose pointed and severe; a thick and pointed beard fell from his chin.[2] There, too, was Pedro de la Paz, who, when mounted, could scarcely be seen above the head of his horse; a squinting, withered and deformed dwarf, yet the boldest heart in the world. He, accompanied only by his Moor, each with a torch, he himself with a naked sword in hand, ventured into the ill-famed grottoes of the Gaurus, in order to dig out hidden treasure; for he feared ghosts as little as he did the enemy in battle.[3] Their leader was Gonzalvo Fernandez Aguilar de Cordova, whose plumed crest had, in his first battle, been seen thick in the midst of the fray, now a true captain. He never interfered when Spaniards, who made disgraceful conditions, were slain by their fellows for degenerate conduct; but that an enemy retiring under treaty should be robbed of a gold chain, this he would not tolerate, and himself pursued the robber into the sea. He said, "I would rather tame lions than these Asturians;" but yet he tamed them. His

[1] Histoire du bon chevalier Bayard, commencement, 407, 113. Brantôme. Pasquier, Recherches de la France, from the Histoire.
[2] Jovii Elogium Navarrae. Vita Alfonsi Estensis, 171. Fleuranges, Mémoires, 84.
[3] Histoire de Bayard, 114. Passero, Giornale, 151.

infantry consisted of those whom the Spanish soil would no longer tolerate, on account of their crimes ; but he made them all loyal to his King, eager for honour, untiring in besieging and defending, and dauntless in the battle.[1]   He was the first to combine in a single corps Spanish, Italian, and German soldiers, an organization which proved irresistible for a century and a half.   At the head of men like Leyva, Pescara, Alva, Farnese, and many other famous leaders, who for one hundred and fifty years hardly ever quitted the field with that army whose nucleus he had first formed, he may fairly be called the Great Captain.

These, now, and their comrades, fought, not merely for victory, but for the prize of strength, dexterity, and chivalrous bearing.   Sometimes individuals would engage in a single-handed combat ; they first knelt down and prayed to God, threw themselves flat upon the ground, and kissed it, and then appealed to the sword.[2]   It might happen that the French would announce that on the morrow they would prove that their hommes d'armes were superior to the Spanish ; whereupon the Spaniards would come in like numbers to the appointed place, in order, as they said, to fight for their King's, their country's, and their own honour.[3]   Or both sides, the one coming from Ruvo, and the other from Barletta, charged each other on horses with iron masks about their heads and plates on their breasts and shoulders, and struggled together until one side was exhausted and gave way.   Or they would have recourse to stratagem in order to gain the advantage ; the French, for instance, would fly, but only to the ambush which they had laid, whereupon the Spaniards on their part would retire also, but only behind their ambush, so that the French were again compelled to fall back, yet not unwillingly, for they had still a third ambush in reserve, and this was their last, enabling them to remain the victors.[4]   In this rivalry of the knights the Italians also

[1] Jovii Vita Gonsalvi, 206 ; further Castiglione, Cortegiano, iii. 287.
[2] Histoire de Bayard, 103.
[3] Zurita, 249.
[4] Ferronus, Rerum Gallicarum, lib. iii. p. 59.

joined. In Barletta, which Gonzalvo defended against
the besiegers with his Spaniards and Italians, a French
prisoner once observed to a Spaniard, that the Italians
were cowards by nature, and their allegiance but empty
air. " Were ye not there, we should extinguish them as
water extinguishes fire." [1] This roused the Italians to
challenge the French to a combat of thirteen against
thirteen on the plain lying between Andria and Barletta.
This encounter took place on the 13th February. The
Italian historians and poets have graphically described
it; how both sides confronted each other like two tall
forests, between which flowed a small brook, and how
the French attacked in vain—for Ferramosca restrained
the ardour of his Italians—and how the latter at length
made their onslaught, like a subterranean mine, that
seethes internally until at length it bursts its bonds and
sends rock and castle into the air,[2] and conquered, driving
twelve as prisoners before them (the thirteenth was slain);
whereupon they were received with the ringing of bells
and salvos of artillery, and with the cry of "Italia" and
"Hispania." [3]

Thus was the war protracted from June, 1502, until
February, 1503. The Spanish were at a disadvantage, but
they held their ground. During precisely the same months,
Alexander also warred in the Romagna in the same cause,
yet in how different a manner and in what a different
spirit! He well knew that the King required, if not his
help, at all events his sanction, and he knew how to extort
from him both sanction and help.

Caesar renewed his campaign in the Romagna with
insatiable greed, duplicity, and violence. In June, 1502,
he planned an expedition against the Varani of Camerino,
and borrowed for this purpose Guidobaldo of Urbino's
artillery. Guidobaldo had, besides, made him a present of
a few thousand men and a horse splendidly caparisoned.

---

[1] Passero, 133. Jovius, Vita Gonsalvi.

[2] Marci Hieronymi Vitae, 13. Pugilum Certamen, Milano, 1818,
vs. 316 and 390.

[3] Jovius. Guicciardini. Sabellicus. Carpesanus, 1250. Brantôme,
106, wrong.

Caesar, in return, saluted him as the best brother he had in
Italy; yet he did not long rejoice in this name, for this
expedition was primarily directed against him.   On the
20th of June he was sitting at supper in the shady vale of
Zoccolanti, when at sunset a messenger appeared and
announced that " Caesar's cavalry was advancing upon his
city Fossombrone." [1]   He struck the table and sprang up;
he felt he was deceived.   At that instant other messengers
arrived with the news that : " the enemy had been seen in
the vicinity of Marino and San Leo, and that Caesar himself
was advancing upon Cagli."   Guidobaldo saw that he was
defenceless, and caught in a net.   He assembled the
citizens of Urbino and addressed them.   " A year has 365
days, and a day twenty-four hours.   Of these days one,
and of these hours one will surely at some time be
auspicious for my return."   Thereupon he took flight.   On
the mountain roads on which he sped, hired peasants
shouted after him the murderers' war-cry of " Carne Ammazza!"   Soon he heard bells ringing, the firing of shots,
and the crackling of fire all around, intended to rouse the
whole country to find him.   On one occasion he was only
saved by a girl, who was coming from market and gave
him some information; but he succeeded in eluding the
enemy.[2]   His country, his city, and his library, in which
he frequently studied with his tutor Odasio, fell into the
hands of Caesar.

In July Caesar also took Camerino.   Old Giulio Varano,
who has been compared to Priam, because he only saved one
son in a foreign country, he allured to his side with all his
other sons by specious promises, and then caused them all
to be strangled.[3]   In August he allied himself afresh with
Louis XII ; which done, in order both to make Bologna
the capital of his duchy, and also to give his father the
glory of having in his day conquered a city which no former

[1] Baldi, Vita di Guidubaldo, duca d'Urbino, vi. 234. Nardi, Istorie
Fiorentine, iv. 78. Burcardus, 2138. Raphael Volaterranus, Vita
Alexandri, 166.

[2] Lettera del duca Guidubaldo, in Leoni, Vita di Francesco Maria,
pp. 15–21, in authentic form ; extracts in Baldi.

[3] Baldi, Vita, 253.

Pope had been able to conquer,[1] he turned against the Bentivogli.

For these ends he made use of the Baglioni of Perugia, the Vitelli in Città di Castello, of Oliverotto of Fermo, and of all the Orsini. All these were warriors by inclination and profession. Of the first named, it was said that they were born with the sword at their side; the second had been the first to introduce Swiss arms into Italy. They pursued each their own aims and ends, as, for instance, Oliverotto, who, by murdering seven leading citizens of Fermo, who were related to him and had brought him up, made himself master of the city. Thus acted the others also, who were desirous of restoring the Medici to Florence. Caesar indulged them in this.[2] But now that he had allied himself with the King, and had begun to oppose their enterprises and to attack the Bentivogli, whose case was almost like theirs, they were filled with apprehension that, " the ruin of all the lords in the States of the Church had been resolved on." They thereupon sent envoys and assembled. They entered into a close alliance with Petrucci and Bentivoglio, and at last at Magione decided to make war upon Caesar.[3]

They resolved on war; the people of Urbino began it. The signal for its outbreak was given on the 5th October by a carpenter, who let a beam, which he was instructed to convey to the castle of San Leo, fall upon the drawbridge there.[4] Thereupon, in an instant, armed men rushed across the bridge and took the castle. Thence the cry of " Feltre e Duca " spread through the whole duchy, and roused it in revolt. In the city the peasants, who had come to market, first seized the cannon, and then gained the castle. Guidobaldo returned, and even those who only saw him lying on his bed—for he was at that time suffering from his malady, the gout—went

[1] Machiavelli, Legazione al duca Valentino, 200.

[2] Leander Alberti, Descriptio, 125. Machiavelli, Principe, 8. Nardi, 81.

[3] Machiavelli, descrizione del modo tenuto dal duca Valentino nell' ammazzare Vitellozzo Vitelli, etc., 92. Nardi, 83.

[4] Caesar's own story in Machiavelli, Legazione, p. 130.

away satisfied. Camerino summoned the last of the Varani.[1]

But what could have been the reason that the allies of Magione, menaced as they were and warlike as they were by nature, did not attack Caesar, who was all defenceless at Imola? They did not wish to destroy him; they wanted only to show him how indispensable they were to him. Caesar knew that full well. "They wished to secure themselves, nothing more," said he. He sent and asked them why they had deserted him, urging that only the title belonged to him, and that the possession of all his past and future conquests belonged to them: "he sent them a blank sheet of paper with his signature, and only waited for their conditions." And now that Alexander had remarked to Cardinal Orsini that he would resign the papacy in his favour, they believed that they had attained what they wished. The Cardinal smiled and said: "The Pope needs me, we are always good friends." [2] On the 25th October, Paolo Orsini came to Caesar about the matter of the treaty. Caesar now said: "They are ogling me; I will abide my time." [3]

At Imola he received not only the assurances of King Louis, the proposals of the Florentine Popolari, and money from his father, but in June he gathered round him 230 French lances, 2,500 soldiers, half French and half German, 2,500 Italians, a Bolognese refugee with mounted arquebusiers, and some Albanians; all in his pay. Meanwhile, Paolo journeyed with the draft of the peace proposals from Imola to Perugia, and thence to Magione and the camps of his friends; no trouble deterred him, and he persuaded them one after another to sign it, and although Vitellozzo Vitelli remained a long time obdurate, he too at last followed suit.[4]

On the 2nd December the following treaty was agreed to: "Caesar to receive back Camerino and Urbino, but to give a pledge to the Bentivogli by arranging a matrimonial

---

[1] Baldi, Vita di Guidubaldo, vii. 7 f.
[2] Burcardi Diarium, 2142.
[3] Machiavelli, Legazione, 161.
[4] *Ibid.* 145, 156, 174, 183. Del modo tenuto, 94.

alliance between their house and that of Borgia, and to use
the old weapons again." [1] Hereupon Caesar ordered the
barons to take the field against the revolted districts and
against Sinigaglia ; he himself remained with his army at
Imola. He only gave audience to very few, from whom
he expected to hear important news ; he only admitted
three or four servants to his presence, and never left a
certain chamber before nightfall.[2] It was never possible
to learn from him what his purposes were ; but his confidantes said, " We have been wounded with daggers and
we are now to be healed with words : even children would
laugh at such terms." [3]

The treaty with the Orsini restored forthwith to Caesar
both Camerino and Urbino, the only condition being that
the people and Guidobaldo's private possessions should
be protected. Sinigaglia was next prevailed upon by four
heads of the Orsini, namely, Paolo, Vitellozzo, Oliverotto,
and the Duke of Gravina, to promise to surrender its castle,
but only to Caesar himself.

The time he had longed for had at length arrived. On
the 31st December, 1502, he advanced with his army upon
Sinigaglia. Vitellozzo did not wish to await his coming :
but as the others trusted Caesar, and Paolo coaxed him to
remain, he did not care to break the league. Unarmed,
and attired in his citizen's cap with its green lining, he
mounted his mule and rode forth to meet him. Their
troops were quartered in the outlying villages, with the
exception of Oliverotto's companies ; and these latter dispersed at Caesar's request, " for they might otherwise
quarrel with his troops about their quarters." The four
chiefs escorted him to the lodging prepared for his reception. He would not part from them, " as he had something to say to them." Full of apprehension—but they
could no longer refuse—they entered his apartments with
him. Now he had them in his power.[4] His principle

[1] Zurita, 261.

[2] Machiavelli, Legazione, 250 f.

[3] *Ibid.* lett. 23, p. 215.

[4] Machiavelli, del modo tenuto nell' ammazzar, 95, 36. Nardi, 85.
Guicciardini, Book v. 290.

was : " He who does not avenge himself, deserves to be always insulted." He said, it is right to deceive those who are experts in all treachery and treason.[1] Moreover he had always sought after territories, but never only after the land but against the head of its lord as well. When the door was closed behind them, Michelotto, the trusted executor of all Caesar's murders, stepped forward with a few armed men. Each of them was addressed with, " Sir, you are a prisoner," and forthwith they were thrown into prison. Their troops were surprised and slain. Caesar, talkative and vivacious once more, rode through the streets.

The work begun by the son was continued by the father. He invited Cardinal Orsini to him, as if to narrate to him the story of the fall of Sinigaglia ; but on the Cardinal looking down into the courtyard from the room into which he had been shown, he saw his mule being unsaddled and led off into the papal stables. He and all his friends with him were captives also.[2]

And now for murder and conquest, and the final accomplishment of these undertakings. Oliverotto and Vitellozzo, bound back to back, the former accusing the latter—it was the anniversary of the death of the Seven of Fermo,—and the latter praying for the spiritual blessing of the same Pope who had condemned him to die, were, on the first night of their captivity, strangled with one rope ; the other two suffered shortly after. The Cardinal's mistress, in male attire, brought the Pope a valuable pearl, his mother sent a sum of money, and the Cardinal promised a still more considerable sum. But all these endeavours could only attain a momentary alleviation of his lot. His life could not be saved. When he died, all the world was convinced that he had been poisoned by order of the Pope. The houses of the Orsini in Rome were pulled down ; and an old lady of the family, eighty years of age, was compelled to seek shelter under a public archway. Almost all their castles, the cities of Perugia and Città di Castello, as well as many villages, fell into the hands of the Pope. Caesar compelled

[1] Machiavelli, Legazione, 266, 268.
[2] Burcardus, 2148.

the Sienese to expel Petrucci.[1] Never in history had a Pope been so powerful in the States of the Church as Alexander. Both factions of barons had been expelled, if not annihilated; there was now not a lord in the land, save his son and his son's family—for the Bentivogli and the Este had been received into it—Siena was conquered, Florence friendly, all successfully accomplished.

It was primarily the name and assistance of France that achieved this result. When Caesar was in peril, Louis said: "Whoever helped Caesar he would love the more the quicker he did it; he would give the Pope and his son the whole of the States of the Church."[2] As the Orsini were in negotiation with the Spaniards,[3] their destruction was also to the advantage of Louis. It was expected that the troops of Caesar would come to the aid of the French in Naples.

2. THE DECISION IN NAPLES

In February, 1503, Gonzalvo, now shut up in Barletta, appeared to be in a sorry plight. Neither the German nor yet the Spanish troops, for which he had written, made their appearance. The transport of supplies was impossible so long as the French galleys under Préjean held the sea; and yet troops and supplies were both urgently needed.[4]

A change for the better began when, under the very eyes of the Venetians, some Spanish sloops and galleys succeeded in gaining possession of the coast so completely that Préjean hurriedly threw his guns overboard, set free his slaves, forsook his ships, and escaped by land. Six days later, Gonzalvo ventured once more to leave Barletta. Whilst Nemours had gone to subdue a revolted town, he himself succeeded in reducing Ruvo, after a siege of seven hours, and taking many brave men prisoners, among them La Palice. His spirits rose, but as yet he was much too

---

[1] Machiavelli, in both places. Burcardus, 2150. Carpesanus, Historiae, p. 1248.

[2] From Louis' letters in Machiavelli, Legaz. 156.

[3] Zurita, 261.

[4] Caracciolus, Vita Spinelli, in Muratori, xxii. 50.

weak to make an attack in full force. But lack of provisions impelled him to risk it, and he was preparing to try his luck in a sortie on the following day, when a Venetian ship laden with wheat, and immediately afterwards a Sicilian corn ship, put into harbour. Three others brought 7,000 tumbanos of corn with them.[1] He was thus enabled to wait for re-inforcements. On the 8th March, the Spaniards arrived at Reggio[2] with 3,000 Catalan, Galician, and Asturian infantry, and 300 heavy and 400 light cavalry. On the 10th April, the 2,500 Germans—the contingent Maximilian had promised,[3] and Juan Manuel had raised—at length arrived at Manfredonia, under the command of Hans von Ravenstein. The Spaniards were now equal, if not superior, to the French in numbers. They were in a position again to carry on the war in earnest. Serious encounters had already taken place in Calabria. Near Terranova, the Spaniards from Gerace and Reggio were collected under the joint command of Andrada Caravajal, Benavides, and Antonio Leyva. In the plain below, but across the river which intersects it, Aubigny showed himself, and sent his herald Ferracut up into the Spanish camp : "They should come down into the valley where he had once vanquished the most gallant king." The Spaniards gave the herald a silver dish and a golden goblet, replying : "They would come." They then came down, and the infantry, covered by the cavalry, crossed the stream in the plain. At this moment Aubigny attacked Benavides.[4] In Ubeda and Baeza the lion of the Benavides and the black standard of the Caravajals had often met in conflict.[5] But now Caravajal forgot the old feud, and with his Ginetes made an onslaught upon Aubigny's rear. The French were defeated. Aubigny, surrounded by his body guard of Scots, escaped to Gioia.

This took place on the 20th April. On the 27th of the

[1] Zurita, 266, 267. Jovius, 245.

[2] Zurita, 256.

[3] See also Viti Prioris Eberspergensis Chronica Bavarorum, in Oefele, ii. 739.

[4] Jovius, Vita Gonsalvi, 251. Zurita, 278.

[5] Molina, Nobleza del Andaluzia, Sevilla, 1518, fol. 217 and 222.

same month Gonzalvo marched out of Barletta with all his forces also to do battle.[1] The French, stationed at Canosa, saw him depart and likewise set out, but neither side very willingly. Gonzalvo had received provisions, but no money; he scarcely succeeded in quieting his Spaniards with promises of rich booty and with the small sum of six carlins[2] for nine months' pay. The French had received express orders from their king to finish the business forthwith, otherwise he would summon them home again to their wives, and send other hommes d'armes in their stead.

Here stretches away the treeless plain of Apulia, where the month of April is always very hot. Of Gonzalvo it is told how his Germans in early morning licked the dew-drops from the high fennel stalks, and fell down at noon exhausted from thirst; how he refreshed them with the last drain of Ofanto water the bottles contained; and how at last he let the most weary mount behind the horsemen. Nemours must have had to contend with scarcely less considerable difficulties on his march. Yet, after ten months of weary waiting, the satisfaction of at length finding themselves in the field enabled them to endure their hardships, and, on the 28th April towards evening, both arrived in extreme exhaustion before Cerignola. The Spaniards, who were the first to arrive, threw up light entrenchments in a vineyard.[3] But as soon as the French came up, and both armies saw each other, they forgot exhaustion and thirst— the soul conceals within it secret wells of ever new refreshment—and the armies prepared for battle. On either side, the infantry was in the centre, and the cavalry on the flanks. Nemours would not for a long time consent to attack; but he was compelled to undertake it by the pressure of Ives d'Allègre, and the other captains. In order to show, as he said, who he was, he dashed at the trench behind which the Germans were posted. He came up to it, wheeled about, came up to it again and cried, "We must get over this rampart." As he dashed at it, a German gun laid him low,[4]

[1] Petrus Martyr, 16, 147.

[2] Zurita, 1. 330.

[3] Jovius, Vita Gonsalvi, 254.

[4] Ferronus, Rerum Gallic. lib. iii. p. 66.

and his comrades, who met with an equally hot reception, began to retire. Further to the left, the Swiss attacked, though somewhat later; but as soon as they perceived their commander, recognizable by his white plume, and at the same moment many others also, laid low by the Galician bullets and javelins, they likewise turned and fled. Allègre, who led the left wing and was furthest in the rear, did not venture then to attempt anything more. The Spaniards were left victors on the field, and passed the night in the French bivouac. Nothing further was now needed to give the Spaniards the upper hand in this kingdom, rent and torn as it was by factions. The understandings which Gonzalvo had maintained from the Abruzzi as far as Castel a Mar awoke to life and energy. On a single day he took thirty castles, and on the 13th May with the cry of "Spagna, Spagna," the Count of Tramontano opened to him the gates of Naples. Inigo Davalos brought the keys of the castle of Ischia. Rocca Guglielma, which since Charles VIII's expedition had held for the French, fell in June. Meanwhile, Andrada took stronghold after stronghold in Calabria, and at length Aubigny himself surrendered to him. With the exception of Gaeta, whither the French army had fled, almost the whole kingdom was now in the hands of the Spaniards. At the end of July Navarra went to that stronghold, in order to try the same means as had opened to him the fortress of Naples.[1]

We shall consider immediately the great change which was brought about by the death of Alexander VI., which took place in August of this year. During the agitation for the election of his successor, French and Spaniards fought together. In Rome, even the troops were on one occasion arrayed against each other. This event, however, exercised no immediate influence upon the war in Naples. The decision there depended solely upon the superiority of arms.

In October, 1503, a fresh French army, under the Marquis Gonzaga, made its appearance on the Garigliano, in order to invade the lost territory. The Spaniards were resolved to prevent their crossing the river. Accordingly,

[1] Passero, Giornale, 138. Jovius, 258. Zurita, 291.

both armies marched backwards and forwards for a while, intently observing each other, until Gonzalvo threw a bridge across at Sessa, and, under cover of his guns, which mounted on barks swept the river, actually succeeded in gaining the opposite bank. As soon as he had crossed, a battle began, in which Gonzalvo fought on foot, and a Spanish ensign who had lost his right arm exclaimed: "Have I not still the left?" and again seized the standard. In this encounter the French held the bridge and the head of the bridge, but they never advanced a step further.[1]

But the opposing armies were not kept apart so much by the river, although it actually separated their camps, as by the swampy ground on either bank—for the season was very wet, and the country as far as Mondragone almost one great morass. Some of the Spaniards kept the outer lines of the trench they had dug; the rest were encamped under huts made from oak trees.[2] The French endeavoured to find shelter in the neighbouring villages, at all events for their horses; the Swiss companies lay alternately in the camp and in the same villages. Both armies were in need of provisions, money, and clothes.[3] This depressing state of things resulted in the very reverse of the merry war before Barletta. Words of abuse were heard more than the ring of arms. The Spaniards were abused for their stealing and hanging proclivities; the French were called drunkards; the Swiss were called cattle-vultures, and the Germans "Schmocher;" whilst the Italians were called "Bougres."[4]

The question was, which of the two would hold out the longer. Gonzaga, hearing himself called "Bougre" by the French, and all disaster attributed to him, would no longer tolerate this want of discipline, and so drew up an account of his operations, and after having it signed by his captains, left the army. Gonzalvo, on the other hand, who was beset by his bravest officers, stating that they could not and would not endure this state of affairs any longer,

---

[1] Jovii Gonsalvus, 263. Petrus Martyr, 261. Zurita, 313 f. Passero, 141.

[2] Machiavelli, Legaz. a. c. d. R. 316, 342, 382.

[3] Caracciolus, Vita Spinelli, 52.

[4] Zurita.

replied : " Rather a step forwards to death, than one backwards to victory," and so held out.[1]

At length the enemy crossed over and attacked. On
the 29th December, 1503, Gonzalvo made an onslaught
upon the French bridge, and a simultaneous attack upon
their camp with his main army, which, with Alviano's assistance, he had been enabled to bring across the river. This
battle decided the fate of the kingdom. Bayard fought like
a hero, but all in vain ; the French disorganization was too
great, and the onslaught of the Spaniards overwhelming.
Gonzalvo was victorious on both banks. In Gaeta, too,
whither French had at first fled, the Spanish standard was
flying by the 3rd January, 1504. The French were obliged
to retreat homewards ; many by sea—the ships set sail as
soon as they were filled, none waited for the other—the rest
by land ; the latter said to Gonzalvo : " Give us strong
horses to bring us back again." [2]

Yet this favour was not to be their's so readily. The
superiority of the Spaniards was due to their greater
proximity, owing to the possession of Sicily, between which
and Naples existed an old natural alliance, as well as to the
prudent and cautious treatment of the factions opposing one
another in the south of Italy; for this was Gonzalvo's
peculiar merit, that he controlled different factions and
nations by the deep respect in which he was held, as might
be seen in the manner in which he succeeded in uniting
Colonna and Orsini in one and the same camp. He did
not spare his enemy. The remainder of the Angevin army
in the Abruzzi and Otranto was vanquished by Morgan and
Pedro de la Paz ; the Marquisates of Bitonto and Salerno
were seized, and many barons dispossessed.[3] Gonzalvo
rewarded his captains, including those of the Orsini family,
with the estates of those thus expelled, and ruled the
kingdom entirely in the spirit of the Aragonese party.

At the same time, the French and Spanish forces were
opposing each other, not only on the Neapolitan frontier,

[1] Ferronus, Rerum Gallic. lib. iii. pp. 70, 71.

[2] Sabellicus, Euneades, 12, 2. Bayard, Guicciardini, 330. Jovii
Gonsalvus, 267. Zurita, 315-317.

[3] Treaty in Dumont, iv. 1, 52. Zurita, 321.

but also on the borders of Roussillon.[1] Here Ferdinand,
in person, protected those garrisons, which wrote to him
saying : " they were ready to die, but he ought to see that
he did not lose many brave men," as well as the frontiers of
his own empire. On showing himself on French soil with
20,000 infantry and 8,000 lances, he obtained in November
a truce for Roussillon.[2]

In the February following their reverse, this truce was
also extended to Naples, where the French still entertained
the greatest hopes.

3. CHANGE IN THE PAPACY

The former good understanding between the French and
the Pope did not long endure. The French complained
that he had appropriated the purchases of supplies made by
their commissioners in the States of the Church,[3] and consequently, that their troops had been compelled to fight at
an inconvenient season ; that he had despatched troops to
Aquila, but only for the purpose of seizing it for himself ;
and, finally, that he had taken good care that Caesar's army
should not support the French.[4] If we inquire what it was
that could have estranged him from the French alliance, to
which he owed all his successes, we find the reason in the
state of affairs in Tuscany. Caesar had twice threatened to
attack Florence, and on each occasion Louis XII had
dissuaded him. Louis had granted all that he was capable
of granting. His most faithful allies, the Popolari at
Florence, could not possibly be sacrificed to the Borgia.
But this very city of Florence, on the other hand, Ferdinand
the Catholic was ready to hand over to the Pope. He had
long since proposed to the German King to make Caesar
King of Tuscany.[5] Here we can perceive how great the
prestige of this Pope was. The King of France was
desirous of making his son lord of the Marches and of the

[1] Appendix to Monstrelet, 236.

[2] Petrus Martyr, Epistolae, 151, 2.

[3] Garnier, 399. From Anton's MS. compared with Monstrelet and
Gilles, Chroniques de France, 121.

[4] Carpesanus, 1254.   [5] Zurita.

Romagna, whilst the King of Spain even wished to make him King of Tuscany. In the struggle between the two princes it was of vital moment to which side the Pope would incline. Hitherto he had been regarded as a supporter of the French. But now, when a French envoy could be attacked and almost slain in the streets of Rome, when envoys from Pisa (the enemies of the Florentines), who had long since offered their city to Caesar, had the *entrée* of the court, and when the Pope most energetically opposed the union of Florence and Siena, which Louis XII exerted himself to compass by the restoration of Petrucci,[1] it was palpable that the Pope was abandoning the French cause, in order primarily to subdue Pisa, Siena, and Florence. When Francesco Trocces, the favourite of the Pope and his privy chamberlain, attempted flight, and was seized and put to death the same night, this act was ascribed to the suspicion that Trocces communicated to the French the plot that was being hatched against them.[2] We have it from the most unimpeachable source, that in or about March, 1503, Alexander proposed to the Catholic King to enter into a league with Venice in order to expel the French from Italy.[3]

Thus the whole success of the campaign in the Romagna would have been turned against Louis, and a league might easily have been formed against him, as against Charles VIII. In the same way as, when in league with the French, Alexander had conquered the States of the Church, he would now, deserting his former allies, have conquered Tuscany in league with the Spaniards. He would have become master of central Italy, and a powerful arbiter between the great powers.

Everything bearing on these undertakings had been well considered, except one thing, and this occurred. Alexander died, and Caesar at the same time fell dangerously ill.[4]

Alexander also had been ill for a few days previously to

[1] Cardinal Soderini in Machiavelli, Legazione alla corte di Roma iv. Titzio in Lebret a. h. a, 544.

[2] Carpesanus, 1255. Biagio Buonaccorsi, Diar. Fiorent. 78.

[3] Zurita, f. 270.

[4] Machiavelli, Principe, c. 7.

his death, but little more was known in the palace than that he was ill of a fever. But, after his death, which took place on the 18th August, the sight of his corpse, with the face black as coal, and the tongue so swollen that the mouth would not close, a sight more ghastly than had ever been observed in a dead body, gave rise to sinister reports.[1] It was said that the Pope one evening went to a banquet in the vineyard belonging to Cardinal Adrian of Corneto, at which he intended to poison several rich cardinals; being thirsty, he called for wine to drink and by mistake drank of the wine which Caesar had told his servant was the best, but which had really been poisoned for the purpose of murdering the guests. Caesar also partook of the wine, and both he and his father were carried off half dead. Caesar was sewn up in the still reeking hide of a mule, and escaped death, but Alexander died.[2] At any rate the Cardinal of Corneto told the historian, Giovio, that the poison, which carried off the Pope, was intended for him among others, and that he narrowly escaped.[3] Others added that Alexander had forgotten the sacred Host which he was in the habit of carrying about with him for protection; others, again, that the compact had expired which he had made with the devil, who had come in the form of a courier to fetch him away.[4]

At all events, in the midst of his greatest expectations, his career was cut short.

It has been said, that the Pope had sometimes been warned, as though by God, in the midst of his crimes: for instance, by a flash of lightning that once struck the ground before him, just as he had persuaded the Archbishop of Cosenza to accuse himself guiltlessly,[5]—by a popular tumult, from which he barely escaped with his life into a church, immediately after he had caused Alfonso di

---

[1] Burcardus in Brequigny, Extraits et Notices, 66, 67.

[2] Guicciardini, iv. 314. Petrus Martyr, 269. Mariana, 222.

[3] Jovii Vita Gonsalvi, 260. I have given in my History of the Popes the results of certain later investigations. In my opinion they place the matter beyond all dispute. [Cf. English Translation (1907 ed.), vol. i. p. 41, and vol. iii. Appendix, p. 9.]

[4] Tommaso Tommasi in Gordon, Vie d'Alexandre VI. 298.

[5] Burcardus in Eccard, ii. 2085.

Biseglia to be put to death [1]—and he likewise received the express warning of the astrologers that he would die for his son's sake. [2] There never was a Pope, who so completely subordinated all ecclesiastical considerations to secular interests, and still less was there ever one, who strove to compass his ends by such terrible means. No acquisition of land has ever been stained with so much blood and cruelty, as was the establishment of his direct sovereignty over the Papal States by stamping out all their small potentates. But this appropriation was not after all intended for the papacy ; a single despot was to unite it all in his hand, and this despot none other than the Pope's own son. What a check would not such a principality have exercised upon future popes !

After Alexander's decease, Rome and the Romagna became involved in the greatest confusion. In Rome Caesar was master of the Castle of St. Angelo ; he had a large body of men under his command and, moreover, his father's treasure stored in two large chests, which he had removed from the palace. [3] But since he lay sick, the cardinals were not prevented from enlisting troops ; the Orsini too now ventured again to make their appearance. It is related of Fabio Orsini that he slew one of Caesar's attendants and washed his mouth and hands in the blood. The citizens often closed the streets and shops because of the tumult of the fighting parties. [4]

In the Romagna, the authorities, Caesar's adherents, fled, and the lords of the land returned. When Guidobaldo came back to Urbino, even the patrician ladies under captains followed the drum through the streets in the evening, to show that they also were ready to fight for him. [5] In Città di Castello a golden calf was carried through the streets as a device of the Vitelli. Sinigaglia, headed by the Rovere, flew to arms at the bidding of Cardinal Giuliano. Giampaolo Baglione returned to Perugia

---

[1] Zurita, i. f. 186.   [2] *Ibid.*

[3] Burcardus in Brequigny, 67. 68. Victorellus ad Ciacconium, 1356.
[4] Sismondi, xii. 289, from Ulloa. Raphael Volaterranus, Vitae Paparum, 167.
[5] Baldi, Vita di Guidubaldo, ix. 115.

under French protection. The others likewise returned from their several asylums.[1]

But how matters would develope depended entirely upon the election of the new pope.

The cardinals hastened to meet. Ascanio Sforza was once more released from his tower at Bourges, in order that he might give his vote for the French candidate. Giovanni Colonna came from Sicily, where he had been living upon an annual allowance from the Catholic King. He was entirely Spanish in his leanings.[2] As soon as the French forces occupied Nepi, the Spanish advanced under Mendoza to Marino, both places being in close proximity to the city. Under the protection of the French party, both in the conclave and in the field, Georges d'Amboise publicly aspired to the highest dignity in Christendom. Gonzalvo was not less open in his counter-declaration : "If the Holy Ghost chose another than Caravajal, the Spanish party would not oppose the choice."[3] Neither Amboise nor Caravajal was elected. But in Piccolomini, of Siena, Pope Pius III, whose election was finally agreed to, the Spaniards believed they had gained a friend on the papal throne, while the French saw in him an enemy, as Pius II, also a Piccolomini, had been.[4] The Spaniards appeared as the victors. But Pius had scarcely taken possession of the Vatican, and had not even entered St. John Lateran, when he died, and the struggle between the rival parties began afresh. Baglione and Alviano once more entered Rome with their troops ; the former with his French on the right bank of the Tiber, and the latter with his Spanish on the left. When the cardinals entered into the Conclave, both sides retired.[5]

Now at this time, the man who enjoyed the greatest esteem of all the cardinals was Giuliano della Rovere, who had opposed three popes, and always with the utmost

---

[1] Baldi, viii. 108, ix. 116–122.

[2] Zurita, 299. Arluni, de bello Veneto, i. 21.

[3] Zurita, 329.

[4] Epistola Francisci Cardinalis Senensis in Ciacconius, 1356. Gilles, Chroniques de France, 121.

[5] Machiavelli, Legazione alla corte di Roma, 285.

courage,[1] a man whom even Alexander admitted was a man of his word, the same man, who had just directed the capture of the castle of Sinigaglia. He was a native of Savona, and might be considered a French subject. He had always favoured the party of the Colonna, and was not altogether unacceptable to the Spaniards. Now that Amboise despaired of becoming pope himself, and Ferdinand of placing a Spaniard on the throne, both parties decided in favour of Giuliano. He had always been well disposed towards the Venetians, and he now promised security for Caesar. And so it came to pass that, within an hour after the close of the Conclave, he was sitting at a separate table as pope, signing the capitulation of the cardinals, and placing on his finger the papal ring that had already been engraved with his monogram.[2] He styled himself, slightly changing his baptismal name, Julius II. In this choice the French believed they had gained a victory such as the Spaniards had vaunted in the case of Pius. At all events, Amboise, who, in addition to the French legation, received that of Avignon, and whose nephew was the first cardinal, lived harmoniously together with him in the palace and assisted at his most private councils.[3] The first difficulty to be encountered was the state of things in the Romagna, which became more and more complicated. On the part of Tuscany, the Aretins and Pisans, with Pandolfo Petrucci and Giuliano de' Medici, offered their services to Gonzalvo ; on the part of Genoa, both the French and the Adorni ; and on the part of Lombardy, 600 nobles and Ascanio Sforza with them.

For, precisely at the time that Julius became pope, the Venetians invaded the Romagna. They occupied the country round about Imola, purchased Rimini from the Malatesta, and threatened Faenza.[4] But as this country owned Caesar as its lord, and since Julius, though

---

[1] Infessura, 1977. Jacobi Volat. Diarium.

[2] Machiavelli, Legazione, 287-293. Zurita, 330. Burcardus in Eccard, 2159, in Brequigny and in Rainaldus, Annales Ecclesiastici, vol. xx. p. 2.

[3] Machiavelli, Legazione, 361, and in many passages.

[4] Bembus, Historiae Venetae, 145-147. Sansovino Orig. 79.

promising to let him remain so, had not undertaken to defend him, this invasion, consequently, resolved itself into a war between the Venetians and Caesar.

Therefore, when the Pope upbraided them for their conduct, asking, "whether he had done them so few services, that they had resolved to rob the Church during his pontificate," they replied: "it was a robber, and not the Church that they were attacking: and that they too were ready to pay their tribute." Whereupon the Pope replied: that "though he wanted lords over his cities, he only wished for such as he could control," and held frequent councils.[1] Although Caesar was not exactly an acceptable personage—for how could he possibly trust him?—the Venetians were even less desirable.

Since his father's death, Caesar appeared to have lost all confidence, boldness, and decision. He even vacillated in the papal election; to-day making a compact with Amboise and on the morrow with the Colonna; to-day promising to join one army, and then on the morrow betaking himself to the other. But, as soon as the first intelligence of the Venetian operations reached him, he completely lost his senses. Men said of him: "The strokes of adverse fortune have stunned him, and he no longer knows what he wants."[2] Where we see men displaying energy as soon as disaster befalls them, we shall always find them at the bottom to be good and noble natures; those, on the contrary, who are not such appear strong only so long as they are in good fortune and no longer.

In order to invalidate the excuse advanced by the Venetians, Caesar expressed his readiness to surrender for a time all his castles and towns to Pope Julius. But the latter, apprehensive lest it might be difficult for him to restore them again, refused the offer.[3] He considered it to be best for Caesar to proceed by sea to Spezzia, and thence to go by way of Ferrara, whilst the army advanced against Imola through the Tuscan and Perugian territories. Caesar was neither supported by Florence, nor yet by

---

[1] Machiavelli, Legazione, 300, 305, 320.
[2] Soderini, in Machiavelli, Legazione, 319.
[3] Machiavelli, Legazione, 337.

Baglione; but he made the venture. On the 19th November, 1503, he despatched his army through Tuscany, whilst he himself went to Ostia, to take ship. He still hoped that the star of his fortune would return; but all the world mocked at him: "Whither," said they, "will the wind waft him, where will he meet with his troops again?"[1] Everything depended upon his relations to the new Pope, and upon the latter's good-will towards him.[2]

[1] Machiavelli, Legazione, 332. Burcardus, 2139.

[2] The divergent opinions that have been expressed about this event cause me to reproduce here, more in detail than I have done in the text, the account given by Zurita, who utilized the information received by King Ferdinand. According to Zurita, the proposal to deliver over his castles to the Pope proceeded from Caesar himself. He wished to secure them from Venice, which would recoil in terror before the name of the Church. Soon after he repented of his offer, and was kept under restraint until he had performed his promise. He was taken to Ostia, with the express assurance that he should enjoy complete liberty as soon as the strongholds had been given up. He was under the care of the Cardinal of Santa Cruz. Two galleys were put at the latter's disposal, in order to release Caesar as soon as he had kept his word. The Cardinal was invested with full powers to this end not only by the Pope, but also by the College of Cardinals; and it actually came so far that of the three castles in question, two were surrendered, and a money security given in the case of the third, so that the Cardinal set him at liberty. At this moment the war between the French and Spaniards which had been interrupted by a truce threatened to burst out afresh. Caesar, who was still well furnished with money and accustomed to pay his soldiers well, and who was fawned on as their lord and master by those insolent characters to whom wild and cruel deeds are congenial, and being, as he was, thoroughly well acquainted with the internal relations of the various Italian factions, and accustomed to turn them to his own account, would have been welcome as an ally either to the French or Spaniards. Gonzalvo sent a message to the Cardinal of Santa Cruz to the effect that he would oblige the King of Spain if he would contrive that Caesar joined his side (seria gran beneficio de toda la Christiandad divitirle de otras empressas: y que no se diesse lugar que veniesse a Francia); which now came to pass. Caesar came with a strong escort to Naples, but it was not his intention to remain long quietly here. His first idea was to prevent the surrender of Forli to the Pope, which had not yet taken place, to revive the war in the Romagna, and to retake Urbino and the other cities, which had been lost to him. He was desirous, for this purpose, of employing the Spanish and Italian infantry, with which Gonzalvo had gained his victories. Gonzalvo quickly perceived that Caesar was influencing his troops, and being moreover informed that he was in communication with Forli, began to be apprehensive lest he was plotting, not merely to renew the war in Italy, but

He was but two days gone, when Julius received tidings that Faenza was in the greatest danger of being taken by the Venetians, and that it was open to doubt whether Caesar would arrive quickly enough, and with sufficient forces, to be able to take effective measures against them. These tidings deprived the Pope of sleep, and in the night of the 22nd November he resolved to take the risk and to accept Caesar's castles for the time being. In the morning he summoned Cardinal Soderini to him; but he still kept his own counsel, for he wished not to do wrong, and did not confide to him his resolve. Towards evening he again sent for him, told him, and sent him after Caesar. But now the latter refused. On the 29th, he was brought to Rome by the papal guards; when there, he was sometimes to be found in Magliana, and sometimes in the treasurer's apartments, or in Amboise's lodging. He there heard how Baglione had surprised and annihilated his army; and so, at length, he consented to surrender the signs of power, by which the governors of his castles were pledged to him.[1] But they delayed and made fresh difficulties. It was not until April, 1504, that the castles were delivered to the Pope, and Caesar again enjoyed full liberty at Ostia.

Thus it came to pass that Julius II interfered against Venice on behalf of Cesena, Imola, and Forlì, as their immediate lord, and defended these cities against attack. But, meanwhile, Faenza was lost. We shall see what important events resulted from its fall.

At Ostia, Caesar was again seized by his old vacillation. His father had first of all been French in his sympathies, and then Spanish, and then again French, and again Spanish. Lescun, and the Marquis of Finale, both set out at the same time to Caesar, the latter offering French aid, and the former a Spanish safe-conduct. What should he do? Louis was

to weaken him (Gonzalvo) so much that Naples would be forced to fall into French hands. Thereupon he resolved to make sure of this dangerous personage : the King approved his conduct. (Zurita, 324.) Mariana has borrowed his account from Zurita, and has not made it clearer, though he has lent it a classic colouring. (Note to 2nd edit.)

[1] Machiavelli, Legaz. 347, 355, 366, 373. Baldi, Guidubaldo, 147. Burcardus and Nardi.

his kinsman, and always kept his promise. Ferdinand had the reputation of being faithless, and the Aragonese safe-conducts were well known, as was also the fact that, a short time previously, Federigo's son had been allured to avail himself of them, and had been made prisoner, and carried off to Spain. But was he still capable at that time of making a choice? It might be said that his fate was upon him. Lescun was the first to come, and Caesar followed him. In the same way as Michelotto stepped up to his prisoners, so at last did Runno de Ocampo address Caesar with the words: "Sir, you are a prisoner." Caesar drew a deep sigh, surrendered himself, and was imprisoned in a castle in Spain. This firebrand, the Spaniards said, was safe in no other hands but in theirs.[1]

Later, Caesar escaped from the castle and reached Navarre once more, but was slain, shortly after his flight, in a skirmish.

[1] Zurita, 328. Jovii Gonsalvus, 274. Mariana, 233. Guicciardini, vi. 339.

CHAPTER II

SPAIN AND AUSTRIA AT VARIANCE

THESE Neapolitan affairs are intimately connected with a quarrel between Spain and Austria, which broke out even before their negotiations had been concluded.

When Philip, in the early part of the year 1503, set out on his return journey to the Netherlands through France, the Spanish cause at Naples was in a sorry plight, and Philip believed himself commissioned to conclude a treaty with Louis. He arrived at his court at Lyons,[1] and, on the 5th of April, had just agreed upon a peace with the King, a peace, of course, most advantageous to him and to this effect: "That Naples should be governed in the name of Charles and Claude, but with his co-operation, and should at a future day devolve upon them," when the prospects of the Spaniards at Naples improved. They now entertained hopes of victory, and Ferdinand ordered his commander-in-chief to disregard any orders he might receive from Philip.[2] In vain his heralds came and departed; instead of the peace, the battle of Cerignola took place. Philip had long been on bad terms with his father-in-law; the latter had refused him the revenues of a prince, had, in Roussillon, prohibited his attendants being provided with horses, and had given orders to have all the cannon at Salsas ready for action whenever he visited that fortress.[3] Both foresaw Isabella's death, and that they would then have to fight for the succession in Castile. This Neapolitan affair further fanned this bad

---

[1] Hubert Thomas Leodius, de vita Friderici Palatini, p. 41.
[2] Zurita, 259, 260.   [3] *Ibid.* 258.

feeling. The quarrel with Ferdinand's envoys, who denied that Philip had been commissioned to conclude a peace, at first deprived this young and noble prince—who was ill at the time—of consciousness.[1] But he soon recovered, and in his own name he now concluded an alliance with Louis, which was proclaimed at Lyons in August. It was aimed immediately at Ferdinand. Louis promised the Archduke 1000 lances for the conquest of Castile, as he knew that he would need them.[2] Philip then induced his father, who was always in accord with his son, to join this alliance and to reiterate his promise concerning the investiture of Milan, which had not yet been bestowed; and to this step Maximilian was also persuaded by the state of affairs in Germany.

1. MAXIMILIAN, THROUGH THE INFLUENCE OF THE FRENCH ALLIANCE, VICTORIOUS IN GERMANY.

It is worthy of remark how intimately German domestic affairs are connected with French war and peace.

The Council of Regency, which had been constituted after Louis' victory over the Sforza and Maximilian, passed, as early as September, 1501, independent resolutions of its own. But owing to Maximilian having, on the 3rd of October following, entered with Louis into the treaty of Trent, not one of its resolutions was put into force ; nay, from that hour it entirely fell to pieces.[3] For a whole six months neither Kammergericht nor Hofgericht was held throughout the Empire, the Estates lost prestige, there was no prospect of a Diet, and public peace was not to be dreamt of. In spite of this, the Neapolitan war of Ferdinand and, as we have seen, of Maximilian also, against Louis was allowed to break out in June, 1502, before any steps were taken. In July, the Electors assembled at Gelnhausen, and agreed to hold yearly meetings, to which they proposed to summon all the Estates, each bringing

---

[1] Pontus Heuterus, from Lalaing's MS. apparently.

[2] Zurita, i. 289; ii. 9.

[3] Müller, Reichstagsstaat, i. c. 21, § 3 ; c. 23.

his neighbours, in case the King himself did not summon a Diet.

The intention was the same as that with which certain meetings had been agreed upon at Worms, and a committee of the realm appointed at Augsburg; namely, to deliberate upon such subjects as war with the Turks, the public peace, the Cameral Tribunal, and all internal matters. Such meetings were actually held.[1] To these the Electors referred everything which Maximilian demanded of them individually; and when he summoned any of their number before his Court they flatly opposed him.[2] All the judicial power now left to the King was the right of reversing appeals, and the bestowal of expectancies.[3] During the months in which the French were victorious in Italy, the breach was most strongly marked. Maximilian loudly complained of Berthold of Mainz, stating that: "he was most vexed with him, because he had not followed his suggestions in the Diets; and had, moreover, always hindered him in his endeavours for the prosperity of the realm and of Christendom."[4] In February, 1503, he would gladly have made common cause with the Swiss, who crossed the St. Gotthard to defend Bellinzona, and would with them have entered Milan, in order to settle the Neapolitan question, had it not been that the situation at home tied his hands. To enable him to engage in the slightest enterprise, he needed a certain tranquillity on the part of the German princes, and, for this, peace with France.[5]

Thus it was that, in concluding this treaty, his son's advantage coincided well with his own.

It can scarcely have been by corruption that Louis contrived to keep the princes on his side; it was to their advantage also when the French gave the German King plenty of trouble; they need not then fear him

[1] Müller, Reichstagsstaat, book ii. pp. 248, 260, and cap. iii. § 8.
[2] Letter in Müller, ii. cap. 5.
[3] Häberlin, Reichshistorie, ix. 229, from the documents.
[4] Correspondence in Gudenus, Codex Diplomaticus Moguntinus, iv. 547, 551.
[5] Weiskunig, 278.

for themselves.   However that might be, after the reconciliation between Louis and the House of Austria, in
November, 1503, the Electors excused themselves apolo-
getically for their previous conduct, and resolved only to
meet once every two years.[1]   These meetings never took
place again.   This opposition was now virtually at an end.
But at that very time Maximilian found an opportunity of
destroying another older and more deeply rooted combination, which even foreigners class among the great factions
of Europe, viz., the opposition of the Palatinate.

Forty years previously, Friedrich, Arrogator of the
Palatinate, in league with Bavaria-Landshut, victoriously
resisted the grand attack of the Emperor and his whole
party.   We have seen the correspondence in which the
Elector Palatine engaged with Charles VIII and Louis XII.
In the days when Louis concluded the Swiss treaty against
Maximilian, the Elector married his son Ruprecht to the
only daughter of Georg of Landshut.   Those who forty
years before had fought together were now dead; but the
old hate and the old leanings still survived and lived on
in their children.

It happened that Duke Georg of Landshut, when about
to proceed in his carriage, accompanied by four physicians,
to Wildbad, at Michaelmas, 1503, was suddenly taken so ill
on the road that he could only reach his castle at Ingol-
stadt; so sick was he.[2]   Should he allow his country to pass
to Duke Albrecht of Munich, his old enemy and Maximilian's brother-in-law, who was, nevertheless, his rightful
heir according to the feudal law of descent?   In order to
pass it to Ruprecht, his sister's son and his son-in-law, he
committed to him his fortresses and his treasure, and
called together the Estates for the 10th December.   But he
died before they met; and this last scion of the house
of Bavaria-Landshut was borne to the grave by foreign
knights, save one only, whom he had summoned to protect
his son-in-law.[3]

The young Ruprecht was the first to appear before the

---

[1] Documents in Müller, Reichstagsstaat, ii. viii. pp. 276, 287.
[2] Zayneri de bello Bavarico liber memorialis in Oefele, Rerum
Boicarum, tom. ii. p. 350.   [3] Zayner, 363.

Estates, with his knights and yeomen. "How," he exclaimed, "could any one wish to defraud the grandchildren of Duke Georg, who were males, and of his own flesh and blood? The whole succession of the House of Burgundy had descended through a woman; Bavarian blood also coursed through his veins." Then appeared Albrecht's envoys: "The land was a male fief, and, further, Albrecht was in the fourth, whilst Ruprecht was only in the eighth degree from Georg."[1] The Estates did not seem able to arrive at a solution, and so declared their readiness to submit to Maximilian's arbitration; yet this was also a decision, for the King had long since taken a side.[2]

Maximilian considered his own advantage, and had three aims in view. The first was for Albrecht, his sister's husband, in whose company he entered Augsburg, on the 30th of January, 1504, to assist at the Diet. His second aim was for himself, to obtain certain districts of Landshut; and the third was the humiliation of the Palatinate, which, besides, he wished to deprive of the Landgraviate of Hagenau.[3] His proposal "that that part of Bavaria lying across the Danube should be assigned to Ruprecht, and all the rest should belong to Albrecht," as well as others of a like nature, was rejected now by one party and now by the other. At last, on Easter Day, after the Dukes of Munich had held two hours' private conversation with him, he announced the same evening to the Estates of Landshut, in a garden at Augsburg, that "the war must unfortunately take its course."[4] His final decision gave the whole country to the Munich line. On the 24th of April, Ruprecht's consort took possession of the city and of a large portion of the Landshut territory.[5] Forthwith all the old enemies of 1461 rose up in arms, Württemberg, Veldenz, and Hesse against the Palatinate; the Munich House,

---

[1] "Handlung zwischen Herzog Ruprecht und gemeine Landschaft," in Zayner, 370.

[2] Maximilian's Letter in Müller's Reichstagsstaat.

[3] "Der Echte Fugger" from the MS. in Oefele, ii. 471.

[4] "Handlung zu Augsburg von gemeine Landschaft wegen," in Zayner, 392, and especially p. 401.

[5] Proclamation when Landshut was taken, in Zayner, 438.

with the assistance of Brandenburg, Saxony, Swabia, and the city of Nuremberg against Landshut. The war began.

But how about the French alliance of the old Count Palatine? His followers wore white crosses like the French; he sent his son repeatedly to Louis.[1] But all to no purpose; the new alliance with Maximilian prevented the French King from listening to him. The Count Palatine resolved to keep only the fortresses garrisoned, and to maintain two armies in the field, one at Heidelberg, and another at Landshut, with the view either to prevent or to requite pillage and plunder. The enemy, he reflected, was not so rich as he was, and would be first exhausted.[2]

The Palatinate itself was assailed on three sides. On the east of the Rhine, Ulrich of Württemberg made the attack. He took Maulbronn, and 2000 balls discharged from the Niederberg forced the people of Besigheim, Walheim, and Weinsberg to accept him in their churches as their lord and master. Bretten alone was defended by the good pieces of ordnance that Georg Schwarzerd had cast, and by a company of Swiss from Thurgau.[3]

West of the Rhine, Alexander the Black of Veldenz drove off herds of oxen and swine, levied contributions, and allowed his soldiers to cut up silk altar-hangings to make jerkins, or to send them home to their wives. In Sonwald we find him lying in wait for the cattle to be driven out of a castle, so as to surprise the open gate. But now and again Johann Landschad would march against him from Kreuznach with better men, and deal with him likewise.[4]

Wilhelm of Hesse ravaged first the Bergstrasse lying to the right of the Rhine, and then the Alzheimer Gau, on the left; and it was only the peasantry of Ingelheim in their monastery, and the garrison of Kaub, that offered him any formidable resistance.[5]

[1] Zayner, Preface ; and Zurita.

[2] Vendii Ephemerides belli Palatino-Boici, ex Kölneri libris tribus concinnatae, in Oefele, ii. 480.

[3] Sattler, Eisenbach, Stettler. Crusii Annales Suevici, 525.

[4] Trithemius, Chronicon Hirsaugiense, 608–613.

[5] *Ibid.* 613–623. Münster, Kosmographie.

Whilst all this robbing, murdering, and pillaging was taking place—for we cannot call it regular warfare—the archives were ransacked for evidence of the King's claim to this territory, and this, with Hagenau and Ortenau, passed into his hand.[1] Overjoyed at his success, which had been achieved without heeding the solicitation of any of the Electors,[2] by merely confirming the enemies of the Palatinate in the possession of what they had conquered, he proceeded to Bavaria, where some of his councillors kept a vigilant watch over Kufstein, and others over Weissenhorn, to both of which he laid claim.

He arrived just in time. Here also the war was being waged more with fire than with sword. Now it was the country about Munich itself, and anon the neighbourhood of Landshut, that was ravaged. Municipal guards and patrols came into collision. One or the other fled. There was nothing done and no results.[3] Just as some Swabians and Brandenburgers on the Munich side had retired, and the Landshut troops appeared to have gained the upper hand by the aid of their 2500 Bohemians, Maximilian arrived on the scene. Three miles from the city of Regensburg, whence peals of bells, inviting to processions and prayers, accompanied him into the field, he fell upon the Bohemians who were entrenched behind a triple barricade of waggons, and behind long stockades made with iron spikes driven into the ground and bound together with chains ; surrounded by his knights he fought on, and although once unhorsed by a pike —his life was only saved by the devotion of Erich of Brunswick—at last succeeded in mastering them.[4] Thereupon he marched into Regensburg, with music playing and drums beating, the standards and the prisoners he had taken preceding him.[5] He had now gained the upper hand, and took for himself Weissenhorn, Mauerstätten, and Kufstein.

Now when the old Count Palatine looked about him,

[1] Note of Häberlin from a document in Lünig, ix. 278.

[2] Müller, Reichstagsstaat, 406.

[3] Life of Götz von Berlichingen, edited by Hagen, p. 41, f.

[4] Zayner, 448. Vendius, 484. Wimpheling, Epitome Rerum Germanicarum, p. 196. Bünting's Braunschweiger Chronik, ii. 63.

[5] Regensburger Chronik, vol. iv. part i., Regensburg, 1822, p. 84.

and saw both countries ravaged, and partly in the enemy s hand; when he found himself bereft of his son Ruprecht, as well as of his daughter-in-law, both of whom had died during the war; when he saw too the Union of Electors broken up, France leagued with Maximilian, his enemies unbroken, and no hope left, his courage sank, and he had recourse to entreaties. Maximilian, at length in possession of what he had coveted, able to boast that he had it in his power to crush the Palatinate utterly, and mindful that Munich also had not always favoured Austria, was prudent and forbearing enough not to desire its destruction, and so, in September, commanded a truce.[1]   He then, in accordance with his original proposal, founded the so-called " Junge Pfalz," on the other side the Danube, for the children of Ruprecht and the grand-children of Georg.

After this great victory, who was there in Germany whom he should still fear?   Berthold of Mainz, the life and soul of all the opposition he had hitherto met with, died in December, 1504, and the King had long since taken into his service his chancellor, Stürzler.[2]   In May, 1505, he again held a Diet at Cologne, where he had always wished it to meet, but the princes would never consent. We must especially lament that there was no one in those days who had either the opportunity to study, or the inclination and skill to chronicle, the active participation of the princes and their councillors in public business.   Such a one would tell us how the great ideas of a universal participation of the Estates in internal government, of the contribution of all Germans towards the common burdens, and of a real unity of the nation in opposition to the imperial power, were all born of the three attempts of the Estates to frame a constitution, namely, the yearly Assembly, the Council of Regency, and the Union of the Electors, and how, after attaining a certain development, they all perished at Cologne.

To live on in the memory of posterity is one half of

---

[1] Hubertus Thomas Leodius, Vita Friderici Palatini ii., No. 42. No. 47, and Zurita.

[2] Häberlin, ii. 283.   Trithemius.   Der echte Fugger, i. 1.

life; but these attempts have almost been forgotten.[1] At Cologne those ideas were relinquished, and the constitution began to return to its old groove. The Emperor was guaranteed for a year a force larger than ever before. This force was raised by the Estates according to their resources, which were no longer computed according to parishes and population, but by a matricula; it was fixed at 1000 horse and 3000 foot soldiers, the pay of the former being reckoned at ten, and that of the latter at four guilders a month, amounting to 264,000 guilders in all; this force was, moreover, to be equipped by the Estates.[2] No Council of Regency cared how it was to be employed. The Cameral Tribunal, the payment of which was transferred to him, passed in consequence into his hands. He was powerful enough to carry out his plans.

2. MAXIMILIAN'S COMPREHENSIVE SCHEMES. PHILIP OF CASTILE.

These successes were entirely due to the French alliance, and the same alliance was the basis of all new projects.

Negotiations were in progress in France during the whole of the Bavarian war; Ferdinand at first appeared willing to consent to assign Naples to the joint names of Charles and Claude, but had ended in August by flatly refusing;[3] at last on the 22nd September, ten days after the battle of Regensburg, Maximilian, Philip, and Louis united in a most intimate alliance: " they would be one soul in three bodies, each be the friend of the other's friends, and the enemy of their enemies, and would intermarry their children. Louis would pledge his governors in Milan, Genoa, Asti, Brittany, Blois, and Burgundy, all of which provinces had been detached from the Crown, to deliver them all over into the hand of Charles and Claude, in the event of his dying

---

[1] This remark is responsible for my later investigations, which I have published in the first volume of my "Deutsche Geschichte." (Note to new ed.)

[2] Müller, Reichstagsstaat, ii. 441. Imperial recess in Müller, 509.

[3] Lettres du Roi Louis XII, vol. i. 1–7.

without male heirs of his body."[1]   We do not find any having references to Naples; but Ferdinand complained that it had been dealt with at Blois, as if it had been the Tyrol.[2]

Hereupon, in April, 1505, in Hagenau, which had just been taken, Amboise received not only for Louis but for Charles and Claude as well, the investiture of Milan, Pavìa, and Anghiera, whilst Philip received Gelderland for himself and his son.[3] In July, 1505, the Duke of Gelderland, stripped of all French assistance, and forsaken by his barons, Wisch, Bronkhorst, and Batenburg, actually threw himself at Philip's feet at Rosendaal, gave up the greatest part of his country, and entered into his suite.[4]

After this, greater enterprises were undertaken.   In November, 1504, Isabella, Queen of Castile, and Philip's mother-in-law, died.[5]   Philip, without delay, took the royal sword and the royal title instead of the ducal hat, and was bent upon becoming her heir.[6]   But old Ferdinand was no less determined to remain the real King of the Castilian kingdoms, under the title of a Gobernador. Hence the schism in the Austro-Spanish house, and Philip made preparations to drive his father-in-law out of Castile.

Maximilian turned his eyes towards Hungary, with a view of securing the succession, which was disputed; and for this purpose the Empire had voted him supplies.

If both these objects were attained, attention could be turned to Italy.   The treaty of Blois pointed to a general war upon Venice.   Naples was demanded because it belonged to Castile.   If we survey the whole state of things, and reflect that, after Ferdinand's death, all the Aragonese possessions, and, after Louis' death, all the rest of Italy together with a third of France would fall to the same heir, these plans must be regarded as jeopardizing European

[1] In Dumont, iv. 1, 55.

[2] Zurita, 343.

[3] Acte de foi, in Dumont, 60. Pontus Heuterus, 226.

[4] Barlandus, Duces Brabantiae, 137. Teschenmacherus, Annales Geldriae in Annal. Cliviae, etc., p. 527. Heuterus, 274.

[5] Luc. Marineus Siculus, 512. Petrus Martyr, Epist. 270.

[6] Heuterus, 270. Wagenaar, History of the Netherlands, ii. 281.

liberty. But Maximilian dreamed of an universal monarchy over all the Latin and Teutonic nations. In the year 1505 he proposed to the King of France to repeal the Salic law, in order that Charles and Claude might succeed him on the throne of France.[1] In the year 1506, he placed Schwente Nielsen, Erik Johannsen, and other leaders in Sweden, who would not recognize the union nor the King of Denmark, under the ban of the Empire with the words : " their possessions belong to the first comer." [2] He declared that through his mother he had as good a claim to the kingdom of Portugal as King Manuel. He had the pretensions of a fugitive member of the House of York to the crown of England transferred to himself.[3]

But God willed it that this should not happen. The development of the Latin and Teutonic nations that had just begun, would have been interrupted and hindered thereby. When Louis XII, in the spring of 1505, fell dangerously sick, all patriots who desired to see the kingdom in a state of union, as well as all friends of the royal power, which had been established with so much bloodshed, began to dread that in a short time the realm would become divided, and the old civil war revive.[4] It was primarily the partisans of Louise of Savoy, the mother of the heir presumptive to the throne, Francis of Angoulême, who opposed it. The King himself repented his alliance of Blois. Did he not swear at his coronation at Rheims never to suffer the realm to be diminished? It was Queen Anne who specially favoured the betrothal of Claude and Charles, seeing, as she did, that the latter was destined to attain the highest dignity in our nations. On one occasion she had not spared a considerable sum of money, in order to degrade and dismiss from court Marshal Gié, who, during a former weakness of the King, had dared to counteract her schemes.[5] She was heart and soul in favour

---

[1] Zurita, ii. f. 152.

[2] Extract from the Document in Dalin, Swedish History, ii. 665.

[3] Zurita and Wagenaar, from the Chartr. van Brabant Layc. Engleterre, ii. 269. Cf. Hormayr, Oesterreich. Plutarch, v. 178.

[4] Garnier, Histoire de France, xxi. 3–9. Saint Gelais, 225 *sq.*

[5] Garnier, from the Trial of Gié, xxi. 463, 476.

of the alliance. But the King being so sorely sick, the wife was fain to concede to the husband, what as Queen she refused to the King, and Anne at length gave way, forgot her difference with Louise,[1] and consented that Claude should be betrothed to Francis of Angoulême, instead of to Charles. Amboise and the high dignitaries at court swore to further this scheme. It was as yet kept a secret. But the treaty of Blois had been broken, and the plans of the Austrian house thwarted in the chief point upon which they were based. Louis gradually recovered from his illness.

Not long afterwards, the Inquisitor of Catalonia, Brother Juan de Enguera, repaired to the French court, in order to investigate the ground.[2] He was despatched thither by Ferdinand the Catholic, who was primarily threatened by Maximilian's plans, and wished for an alliance with France.

Should he cease to be King of Castile and the head of the European political world, and return to the insignificant position enjoyed by his ancestors? Isabella, by her last will, left him a few estates and rights in Castile. The succession she devised to her daughter Juana, decreeing at the same time that, " previous to her arrival, all Cortes should be prohibited, and afterwards, only if it should be proved that she was either incapable or unwilling to conduct the government, should a peaceful administration be provided." [3] But Ferdinand was not content with this, but assumed the title of a Gobernador, and summoned the Cortes without delay. The grandees, whose independence he had broken, were against him ; notably Pacheco of Villena, who, at the beginning of Ferdinand's reign had lost his estates, his share of the Aragon plunder; and Manrique of Najara, who saw his nephew prejudiced by Aguilar ; their complaint was that, "he tempted the notables in the cities, and the alcaydes in the castles, with presents, and was even bent upon reviving the long-forgotten affair of Juana, Henry IV's daughter; thinking to marry her, only

[1] Fleuranges, Mémoires, 154.
[2] Also Nardi, Istorie Fiorent. p. 110.
[3] Zurita, i. 349. Gomez, Vita Ximenis, 981. Petrus Martyr, 279. Mariana, 278.

Manuel of Portugal would not give her to him; he was illegally striving to become lord of Castile." They did not appear in the Cortes.[1] The procurators of the seventeen cities, on the other hand—for Ferdinand had once, aided by the Hermandad of the cities, overcome the nobles, and the cities favoured him—appeared, declared themselves the representatives of the united kingdoms of Castile, recognized him as administrator in the room of his daughter, and received from him the oath.[2]

In spite of all this, Ferdinand could not possibly hold his ground, were Philip, strengthened by the alliance of Blois, to arrive in Castile, and the grandees there to declare for him. Nothing but a reconciliation with Louis promised him security.

Now that Isabella was dead, Ferdinand also could adopt Louis's maxim, a maxim which he used against every proposal advocating terms respecting Naples, and from which proceeded the intention to marry Charles and Claude together, namely, that, " it was incompatible with his honour and conscience alike to sell his good rights to strangers." In October, 1505, Louis assigned his Neapolitan rights to his niece, Germaine de Foix. Ferdinand promised to marry her, to pay a million gold ducats within ten years, and to restore all the Angevins to their estates.[3] In addition to this, the two Kings promised each other mutual help against all enemies. Almazan, Ferdinand's other self, confided to some, that nothing would come of the marriage between Charles and Claude.[4]

The schemes of Maximilian and Philip, who after meeting in Brabant, in December, 1505, separated, the father to look after his Hungarian, and the son after his Castilian affairs, were thwarted by the alliance Louis had contracted, not with them, as he had promised, but with their enemies. But they gained another in its place. When Aragon and Castile were at variance, it had frequently happened that England had allied itself with the

[1] Zurita, ii. 12. Carta in Zurita, ii. 22, 23.
[2] *Ibid.* ii. f. 6.
[3] Documents in Dumont, iv. i. 72. Extract in Guicciardini, iv. 357.
[4] Bacon, Historia Henrici VII, p. 369.

one and France with the other. This natural state of things combined with chance to procure an English alliance for the Austrian house.

In January, 1506, Philip had provided the expenses of his voyage by the sale of his crown-lands, and the enforced impost of the sixteenth pfennig. Four hundred nobles, with several thousand landsknechts, Flemings and Swiss,[1] embarked on board his fleet of about fifty sail, and Philip himself on the ship of two brothers Huybert. The squadron steered through the Bay of Biscay, making for a Spanish port, not far from Cordova, when the wind suddenly changed, and a storm arose. In the stress of weather, the Huyberts, though Philip vainly bade them "Watch,"[2] could devise no other means of safety than running for the English coast. At length, escaping through the race off Portland's chalk cliffs, they landed on the quay of Weymouth.[3] Here Philip was received as a most welcome guest, not like a shipwrecked man, and was escorted with all pomp and ceremony to Windsor, a castle of King Henry VII. Yet not for nought. Here in his most private chamber, Henry placed his hand upon his guest's shoulder, and said, "You have been saved on my coasts, and should I then suffer shipwreck on yours? I mean Suffolk, give him up to me." Philip had still a Yorkist, Edmund de la Pole, Earl of Suffolk, in his keeping, and much as he resisted: "for he would appear to be acting under compulsion," he was obliged at last to surrender him.[4] This done, Henry swore upon a portion of the true Cross, to come to the aid of his guest, in defence of his kingdoms, either such as he now possessed or should possess, against every one who should attack him in them.[5] And thus strengthened, almost against his will, with a new ally, in April, 1506, Philip embarked for Corunna.

[1] Wagenaar, ii. 281. Ehrenspiegel, 1165. Nardi, Istorie Fiorent. iv. 111.

[2] Bayle, Dictionnaire, s.v. Huybert, from a "mémoire communiqué au libraire."

[3] Petrus Martyr, Epist. 296. Polydorus Virgilius, Historia Anglica, 777.

[4] Bacon, Historia Henrici VII, pp. 336, 370.

[5] In Dumont, iv. 1, 77.

He arrived. " Now that he was come, the Galician and Castilian nobles should prove their promised allegiance." The Duke of Najara was already equipped : should he not receive the new prince in the same manner as the old ? Not only Villena, but Benavente, who through the House of Aragon had lost his market of Medina del Campo, Giron, of the oppressed house of Portugal, Garcilasso de la Vega, who hoped to be able to revive with Philip the influence he had enjoyed with Isabella, the Duke of Bejar, the Marquises of Astorga and Priego, and many others accompanied him.[1] They complained that " old Ferdinand wished to merge Castile into Aragon; the Jurado of Saragossa in his scarlet dress, and with his mace, had already entered into Valladolid and was now preparing for resistance; Philip should not trust in his assurances ;[2] every noble who placed himself on his side was denaturalized, and forfeited the protection of his rightful suzerain."

On the other side, Ferdinand urged upon his party to ally itself with him, giving as his reason that its lady and true Queen was kept prisoner by her husband, so that none could serve her, and none address her. Philip was treating her as no yeoman ever treated his wife; they should, therefore, aid in liberating the Queen. In this endeavour he would risk his person and his whole power.[3] He retained on his side the cities, a few grandees and prelates, and the governors, who owed their positions to him, and whom, as he said, Philip wished to displace. But, in a short time, all the grandees and prelates, and even his relatives, including the Condestable and the Almirante, had forsaken him,[4] and only a single man, the Duke of Alva, who never wavered, remained faithful to him. In the cities the relatives of those imprisoned by the Inquisition looked towards the young King, and these were all the more numerous since Luzero had recently, by the use of false witnesses incarcerated knights and dames, and monastic

---

[1] Zurita, ii. 47-55.
[2] Petrus Martyr, 305.
[3] Carta, con que el Catholico se justifica, in Zurita, ii. 57, 58.
[4] Ferdinand's words, in Zurita, fol. 71.

and secular clergy.[1]   After this, a recourse to force was impossible ; only in an interview could Ferdinand hope to assert his personal ascendency over his son-in-law.   Fray Francisco Ximenes de Cisneros arranged this meeting for him.

Upon a hill, in the midst of the mountain range of Gamoneda between Puebla de Sanabria and Rionegro, hard by the farm of Remessal, and close to a grove of oak trees, stands a chapel.   Hither, on the 20th June, 1506, came Ferdinand from the one side with 200 light-armed troops seated on mules, all in cloaks and red caps, with a sword hanging loosely from their belts, whilst from the other there approached 1000 Germans with muskets and spears, the finest and most stalwart men who could be found, and behind them, surrounded by his grandees, all wearing armour under their tunics, came Philip.[2]   The old monarch, distinguished by his bald head and severe nose, rich in exploits ; the youth, of red and white complexion and full of hope ; the latter on this occasion more serious than his wont ; the former more cheerful.   In the chapel, while Ximenes waited on the grassy slope before the door, they conferred with each other.   Ximenes had already had nego-tiations with Philip, endeavouring to induce him to agree to a joint administration—urging that the shrewdness of age and the vigour of youth would then combine—and trying to persuade him, at all events, to leave Granada, which needed a practised eye, to the more experienced monarch.[3]   And this is, probably, what Ferdinand also attempted on this occasion.   In any case he pointed out to him the intentions and the character of his grandees.   But all to no purpose.   They departed as they came ; yet, whilst journeying up the Duero, several miles apart, they con-tinued their negotiations.   Finally, Ferdinand was obliged to content himself with half the Indian revenue, and a limited control of the grandmasterships.   He renounced all

---

[1] Llorente, Histoire de l'Inquisition de l'Espagne, i. 346.   Zurita, 99, 116.   Letter of Gonzalo Ayora in Llorente.
[2] Jovii Gonsalvus, 278.   Gomez, Vita Ximenis, 990.   Mariana, 28, 252.
[3] Literae Ximenis, in Gomez, 987.

other share in the government.[1] But here his dissimulation manifested itself. Whilst conceding this, after much resistance, he declared to the people, that "he had had no other intention from the first but this; if he had formerly taken the government upon himself, yet he had only done this in order that his goodwill towards his children might be made the more clear."[2]

He went yet further. On the 28th June, after declaring with Philip, that, "it was to be known that the gracious Queen must in no case interfere with the Government in any respect; otherwise, the complete ruin of these realms would be the result," he protested secretly to Almazan, that "he made this confession only out of fear; in reality he was resolved to liberate his daughter."[3] On his way home he found the gates of several cities closed against him by the grandees; yet he comforted himself with the reflection that he had once been still more powerless, and yet had ruled them many long years. Full of fresh cares and anxieties, he hurried back into Aragon.

After this all the cities opened their gates to the young King, and swore allegiance to him. If there was any governor of a castle, who at first was not inclined to yield, he did so, as soon as a few companies of troops showed themselves. The grandees and prelates were besides in Philip's retinue.[4] The House of Austria had succeeded in taking possession of Castile.

During this time Maximilian was in Hungary; fifteen years previously, the prelates, barons, and cities of this country had been obliged to swear to him that: "should Wladislav die without male heirs, Maximilian, or, in case he was not alive, one of his sons should succeed; failing these, one of the heirs male of their body, begotten in direct descent, should succeed as lawful heir to the crown."[5] Now Wladislav, a monarch who never said

---

[1] Zurita, ii. 63.   [2] Relacion del Catholico, in Zurita, 70.

[3] Concordia entre el Catholico, etc., and Protestacion del Catholico, in Zurita, 67, 68.

[4] All in Zurita.

[5] Bonfinius, Rerum Ungaricarum Decas, v. 2, 509, and the document in Sambucus, Rerum Ungaricarum Appendix, 546.

anything but "Dober" to the Bohemians, and "Bene" to the Hungarians, was old and weak, and had only one daughter. Some said he would marry her to a grandson of Maximilian; others, that he was willing to give up his kingdom to the latter.[1] The Hungarians, however, and the Saxons, who dwelt amongst them, did not desire a German sovereign. The magnates assembled, and resolved that whoever advocated the election of a foreign king should die; and Count John, of the house of Zapolya, aspired to the crown for himself. Maximilian reminded them of their oath, and that "their welfare, as well as successful resistance against the Turks, depended upon an alliance with Austria." But they gave a defiant answer; as he himself expressed it, "they summoned their power by the bloody sword." [2] He determined to attack this power, and, without ravaging the country—for otherwise it might become hostile to him — only to proceed against the magnates. On the right bank of the Danube he first compelled Oedenburg and the Count of Bozin, whose dominions extended a whole day's journey wide on these borders, to accept his terms. Next, during an eight days' truce, he passed over to the left bank and reduced Pressburg. Having taken the island of Schütt, he thought he had conquered: for "it was the heart of Hungary." But a message from Wladislav to the effect that "he must go to his wife, who was expecting her confinement," was followed shortly by another that, "on the 1st July she had been delivered of a child, who though very weakly, was yet a boy." [3] The magnates then gave his people 3000 pieces of cloth, and 2000 head of oxen, and recognized his rights.[4] How was it likely that a boy, who had had to be placed in the warm skins of freshly slain beasts, in order to be kept alive, would eventually survive? [5] Maximilian left the country, but his prospects were saved.

Now that Castile had been taken, and the succession in

---

[1] Linturius, Appendix ad Rolewinkium, in Scriptt. Struvii, 600.
[2] Maximilian's proclamation in Datt, 568, and in Müller, 528.
[3] Müller, 531.
[4] Anton, Chronicques Annales, ii. p. 11.
[5] Michael Brutus' testimony in Struve, Corpus Historiae Germanicae.

Hungary assured, he turned his eyes towards Italy, in order to receive the Imperial Crown in Rome.

It was just about this time that he first heard for certain, that the betrothal between Charles and Claude had been revoked by Louis XII. This was not publicly announced until May, 1506. The deputies of the cities, who, in the official account of this affair were, almost like the Cortes of Toro, simply styled Estates, appeared at Tours before the King, sitting with his prelates on his right and his grandees on his left, and entreated him to agree to the betrothal of Claude to Francis of Angoulême. This was ratified in their presence. Under their hands and seals, each and all, the councillors of Brittany with them, vowed to see that a marriage resulted therefrom.[1]

Maximilian then learned that the road through his fief of Milan had been closed to him, whilst Philip received the tidings that Charles of Gelderland, who had escaped from his escort, had, by means of French and Aragonese money, renewed the war in the Netherlands. Both were extremely indignant. Maximilian complained that " Louis had never really cared about the treaty ; it was only the fiefs that he had coveted. He revoked the fiefs he had already granted in favour of his grandson Charles."[2] Philip was determined upon a general war. " My heart is not so cowardly, nor my relatives, and my worldly goods so insignificant," he wrote, " as that I could allow myself to be prejudiced in my good right. I would rather appeal to my whole party throughout Christendom, for, as I believe, it is stronger than that of my opponents."[3]

And first, Maximilian was resolved to invade Italy as best he could. His envoys, who with their attendants were fully armed, went first to Venice, in order to entreat a peaceful passage.[4] But the Venetians would not allow a passage to the man who had so often and so publicly laid

---

[1] Récit de ce qui s'est passé, in Röderer's Mémoire pour servir, etc., in the Appendix, p. 425, and this Mémoire altogether. St. Gelais, 181. Mémoires de Fleuranges.

[2] Proclamation, 533.

[3] Writing in the Lettres de Louis XII, i. 51.

[4] Lascari's letter in Machiavelli, Legazioni, Opere, v. 127.

claim to their territory. Whilst his landsknechts were wandering about, they had time to occupy all their passes with infantry and cavalry.[1] Maximilian therefore hurried to the Carniolan ports, whither Gonzalvo had promised to send him ships; but the latter was dissuaded by the grand promises made by Ferdinand. Resolved upon daring the utmost, he went to the Karst in the Windish Mark, whence in four days the coast of the Romagna could be reached, in confidence that the Pope would receive him with joy and would crown him.[2]

But the most unexpected calamity befell him here. On the 16th September, his son Philip died at Burgos, of the Mazucco, an infectious fever.[3] He had never felt eager for this journey, nor looked forward to his Crown. He came not to live as king, but to die.

This death, which threw the affairs of Castile and the Netherlands into the greatest confusion, put an end to all Maximilian's further schemes and projects.

3. FERDINAND, MASTER OF NAPLES AND CASTILE.

When Ferdinand saw that Castile was lost to him, he had been seized with anxious apprehensions regarding Naples.

Here, where the kings had always ruled only for short periods by their armies and their factions, and where a paternal, ecclesiastical, and hereditary monarchy was unknown, Gonzalvo, who had installed the captains of his army in rich possessions, and levied taxes as he thought right, enjoyed as much popularity as ever a king did.[4] He was dissatisfied with Ferdinand, who had refused to ratify his grants, and who in Spain had appointed a Neapolitan council, which forced him to dismiss his Germans.[5] Now the Castilians maintained that Naples belonged to them, for

[1] Proclamation, and Bembus, Historia Veneta, 157a.
[2] The same proclamation, Müller, 540. Zurita, i. 389.
[3] Machiavelli, Legazioni, v. 162, from the letter of Soderini, and Dr. Tozzetti.
[4] Zurita, i. 320, 321, 330.
[5] Caracciolus, Vita Spinelli, in Muratori, xxiv. 52, 53.

it had been conquered by their money and their blood. Ferdinand rejoined that his were the rightful claims, and that the land was his. As a matter of fact, all depended upon whom the General would make lord of the country. Gonzalvo inclined to the side of Philip and the Castilians; he refused to retain Philip's envoy to Julius, who was believed to be animated with the like feelings towards Austria. Maximilian sent a message to him to the effect that, " he should behave like a good knight of Castile, and then he should be assured of protection in Naples; he could then receive for himself Pisa and Piombino, which he was at that time supporting." At this time Gonzalvo, as we are aware, sent his ships to the Carniolan ports.[1]

These circumstances filled Ferdinand the Catholic with apprehension. At first he was for taking Gonzalvo prisoner; but reflected how disastrous such a step would be, were it to fail.[2] The day following his interview with Philip, on the 21st June, 1506, he took a different view of the state of things, and drew up a document stating that, " he swore by his royal word, by God, the Cross, and the Gospels, to transfer to Gonzalvo the Grandmastership of Santiago as soon as he should return to Spain."[3] Ferdinand's ambassador needed no more than ten days. On the 2nd July Gonzalvo sent his reply to the King. " No one," he wrote, " was more anxious to live and die in his service than he was. For the rest of his life he desired to recognize no other King and master but him alone. This he swore by God, being a Christian, guaranteed it as a knight, confirmed it with his name, and set his seal thereunder."[4] He had now pledged himself, and Ferdinand took courage, and, on the 4th September, set sail for Naples. But Maximilian arrived in vain at the Carniolan ports.

On his way, Ferdinand received the tidings of Philip's death, yet this event did not induce him to abandon the enterprise upon which he had embarked. On the 1st November, in company with his consort Germaine, he rode through

[1] Zurita, ii. 30, 33, 46.
[2] Argensola, Annales de Aragon, from Almazan's papers, p. 75.
[3] Cedula del Maestrazgo, in Zurita, 65.
[4] Carta satisfactoria, in Zurita, 67.

the five Saggi of Naples. The nobles and ladies came out of their houses to kiss his hand, Gonzalvo giving him their names.[1] He who gave the names was none other than the man whom he had come to take away with him, whilst those who kissed his hand, were in great measure those whose old enemies, the Angevin barons, he was about to recall. Bent upon accomplishing his purpose, his time was so busily occupied, that he did not even allow himself to pay one visit to the castle garden.

When, in the previous year, the first news of his treaty had been brought hither, every one lamented that such a shrewd King was intent upon restoring those who had always proved so disloyal. Could his object perhaps be to make almost independent lords of the Sanseverino from Salerno to Reggio, of the Caracciolo in Apulia, of Bitonto in the Abruzzi, and of Traetto on the Garigliano? His own party would thus become powerless, and the royal power sink into insignificance.[2] But all the same he adhered to his intention. All that had belonged to Don Caesar in Aragon, to the Borgias of Gandia, Squillace and Don Juan, and the portion of the dowager queens, all this he acquired, either by purchase or as feudal lord, and divided it among the injured parties. The knights who had conquered the country had now to retire from their new possessions and content themselves with compensation in money.[3] Dignities and incomes were not even spared. Difficult though the task was, he succeeded in carrying it through, thus satisfying among others also the plenipotentiary of France, who took part in the transaction. He restored all the exiles, princes, counts, and barons to their own, and reinstated among them Sannazzaro, Federigo's most faithful follower, in his country seat of Margolina, whose beauties, hill and slope, brook and dale, he had so often sung.

This settlement assured him the possession of Naples more securely than many victories would have done. The real object of contention between the rival parties was property, from which each was ever being ousted by the other:

[1] Passero, Giornale, p. 147. Jovii Gonsalvus, 279.
[2] Zurita, ii. 34. [3] *Ibid.* f. 112, 114.

of this he made an end. He contrived to keep the Colonna in obedience and to win over the Orsini to his side again. It was, perchance, owing to the marriages which, as we have seen, were constantly taking place between Angevin and Spanish families, Sanseverino and Villahermosa, Bisignano and Richesenza,[1] that from this year forth the nobles of Naples remained loyal to a distant King. Henceforward the chronicles of Naples teem with accounts of the wonders done by a picture, to which pilgrimages were made barefooted and which was often presented with golden chains, with stories of murders and marriages, or it may be of an insurrection which broke out against a royal official, a new law, or a despotic landlord.[2]

With respect to Gonzalvo, Ferdinand issued a letter addressed to all princes and barons, and all men now and hereafter : "Through glorious deeds of bravery and generosity, Gonzalvo had regained for his crown the kingdom this side of the Faro ; he had governed it with unwavering loyalty, and he, the King, was his great debtor."[3] He then demanded of the Pope his sanction of the transfer of the Grandmastership, but, "it must," he urged, "be kept secret, so that the thirteen electors do not oppose it."[4] To please him, he took from the faithful and reliable Spinello, who was an enemy of Gonzalvo, the office of accountant of the realm.[5] He gladly allowed Gonzalvo's retinue to outshine his own following. But, as soon as he had attained his object, when on the 4th June, 1507, he saw him take leave of all the nobles and ladies, who had accompanied him to the shore, and embark on one of his ships, he then felt himself recompensed for all his duplicity and sacrifice, and he gradually laid aside the mask. Spinello received a letter with the superscription : "To the Count of Cariati," and with it a fuller share of administrative power that he had ever enjoyed. The Grandmastership was never mentioned again.[6] Whenever Gonzalvo's friends said, "The great ship is running aground," he

[1] Passero, 163, 176.
[2] *Ibid.* 150, 155, 167 f.
[3] Escritura, in Zurita, 139.
[4] Zurita, 128.
[5] Caracciolus, Vita Spinelli, 56.
[6] Jovii Gonsalvus, 282.   Passero, 149.

would reply, "The tide will raise it again."[1] On one occasion afterwards he had hope for it, but it never came to pass. The life of man is a long growth, a short bloom, a long decay; the first is full of hope, the last full of regrets. Gonzalvo had to content himself in Loja with thinking of his daughter's marriage, and in keeping up communication with the world by letter. Then he often thought how he had once conducted Federigo's son and Caesar to Spain, and how he at last had returned home in the same manner. Both these actions he regretted, and a third that he did not mention.[2]

At length King of Naples in reality, with Gonzalvo safe on his ships, Ferdinand hurried to Castile, which Philip's death had plunged into great confusion.

Before this occurrence, the old hereditary factions of the Nuñez and Gamboa, whose heads were Najara and the Condestable, had already again showed themselves among the grandees.[3] What took place after Philip's death, was closely connected with the Queen's state of health. The malady from which she was suffering first declared itself on Philip's journey to Lyons, that is in the year 1503. At that time, after taking leave of him with many tears, she never more raised her eyes, or said a word, save that she wished to follow him.[4] When she learnt that he had obtained a safe conduct for her also, she would not wait for her mother any longer, but ordered her carriages to proceed to Bayonne; then—for horses were refused her— she attempted to set out herself on foot; and, when the gate was closed, she remained, in spite of the entreaties of her attendant ladies and her father confessor, in her light attire sitting upon the barrier until late into the November night; it was only her mother who at length contrived to persuade her to seek her chamber.[5] At last she found her husband. She found him devoted to a beautiful girl with fair hair. In an outburst of jealous passion, she had the

---

[1] J. Oronius, in Jovius, 286.
[2] Jovii Gonsalvus, 290, 291, 274.
[3] Petrus Martyr, Epp, 317, 331.
[4] Petrus Martyr, xv. 144. Gomez, 972.
[5] Zurita, i. 271.

girl's hair cut off. Philip did not conceal his vexation.[1]
Here—who can fathom the unexplored depths of the
soul, see where it unconsciously works, and where it unconsciously suffers, who can discover where the root of its
health or sickness lies?—her mind became overshadowed.
In Spain her love for Philip, and in the Netherlands her
reverence for her father were her guiding passions: these
two feelings possessed her whole being, alternately influenced her, and excluded the rest of the world. Since
then, she still knew the affairs of ordinary life, and could
portray vividly and accurately to her mind distant things;
but she knew not how to suit herself to the varying
circumstances of life.[2]

Whilst still in the Netherlands, she expressed the wish
that her father should retain the government in his hands.
On her return to Spain, she entered her capital in a black
velvet tunic and with veiled face; she would frequently sit
in a dark room, her cap drawn half over her face, wishing
to be able only to speak for once with her father.[3] But it
was not until after her husband's death that her disease
became fully developed.[4] She caused his corpse to be

[1] Petrus Martyr, Ep. 272.   [2] Gomez, 999. Zurita, ii. 28.
[3] Zurita, ii. 47, 73.

[4] In the year 1868 no little sensation was caused by an opinion
put forward by G. Bergenroth, who was employed by the English
Calendar Commission to make researches among the records of
Simancas, which opinion was diametrically opposed to the views here
given by me and generally accepted. In his work, "Supplement to
vol. i. and vol. ii. of letters, despatches, and state papers relating to
the negotiations between England and Spain" (cf. Sybel's Hist. Zeit-
schrift, xx. 231), he attempts to prove that Juana's madness was a
mere myth, invented in order to exclude her from the succession in
Castile, either in favour of her father or her husband. Queen Isabella,
he urges, had already intended this, induced by deficiencies in the
Catholic faith, of which Juana had given proof. All this he attempted
to prove from correspondence, which had been hitherto carefully concealed, but which had come at last into his hands in Simancas. In the
first place he refers to the correspondence of the Sub-prior of Santa
Cruz, Tomas de Matienzo, who was despatched to the Netherlands in
1498, in order to inform himself as to the state of the Archduchess.
A clerical question is here really involved. The Archduchess made
her confession to certain brothers of a monastic order, who did not
follow the strict observance, but, being bound to no monastery, proceeded to the Netherlands, and thence back to Paris, whence they had

brought into a hall, attired in half Flemish, half Spanish dress, and the obsequies celebrated over it. She never, the while, gave vent to a sob. She did not shed tears, but only sat and laid her hand to her chin. The plague drove

come. The Archduchess had made them what was, under the circumstances, a considerable present. Now, her old teacher and father confessor in Spain, who had remained there, reminded her that in this way she was not caring for the welfare of her soul. She should treat no one as her father confessor who possessed or accepted property worth even a pin's point ; she ought only to make presents to the monastic houses, who in return therefor would care for the welfare of her soul. Now, that Sub-prior, as being a monk of the strictest observance, was destined for her confessor. In spite of a very cool reception, he succeeded nevertheless in ingratiating himself with the Archduchess. Following on his first reports, in which he expresses himself as a man who is offended, came others, in which he declares himself as perfectly satisfied. He could find no fault with the religious bearing of the princess ; her court even, he declared, reminded him of monastic discipline. What she was accused of was chiefly a want of strict surveillance over her household, under which the Spaniards had specially to suffer. At first he was struck by the fact that the Archduchess never mentioned her relations. Later she said she did not care to mention her mother, Isabella, for she longed so greatly for her that she could not avoid giving way to tears whenever she thought of her. We are very grateful to Bergenroth for the communication of this correspondence, which contains much welcome and reliable information. Only he ought not to have regarded the Sub-prior as an Inquisitor of faith ; for there is nothing in the whole story but petty jealousies between monks. There is not a trace to be found therein of facts which could cause the Queen to feel any scruples respecting the succession of her daughter in Spain. If Isabella later entertained any such scruples, they were due to Juana's extraordinary behaviour in Spain which I have already alluded to, and which certainly awoke doubts as to her healthy condition. Yet her insanity was of a melancholic character, a sort of monomania as regarded her husband, a state of health which modern psychiatric investigations have proved never develops into madness. It was a matter of doubt whether she was insane at all or not. She is sometimes declared to have been so ; whilst other observers never noticed anything of it. When the proposal was made in Castile to exclude her from the government and to pass it instead to her husband, one of the grandees of the realm, the Almirante of Castile, was opposed to the plan. He had an audience of the Queen, in which she gave, though short, yet sensible replies, so that he contrived to defeat this proposal in the Cortes. She was always a subject of variance between the parties in Castile after the death of her husband, but still more so after that of her father. From the correspondence which passed between the Marquis of Denia and the Emperor Charles V touching her state, as well as from sundry other documents, it has been attempted to prove that the poor

her away from Burgos, but not away from her loved corpse.
A monk had once told her that he knew of a king who
awoke to life after being fourteen years dead. She took
the corpse about with her. Four Frisian stallions drew the
coffin, which was conveyed at night, surrounded by torches.
Sometimes it halted, and the singers sang mournful songs.
Having thus come to Furnillos, a small place of fourteen
or fifteen houses, she perceived there a pretty house with
a fine view, and remained there : " for it was not fitting for
a widow to live in a populous city." There she retained
the members of the Government which had been established,
the grandees of her court dwelling with her. Round the
coffin she gave her audiences.[1]

After Philip's decease there existed as good as no
sovereign power in Castile. At first the grandees of both
factions entered into an agreement under Ximenes, at all
events for three months.[2] But as the Condestable and his

princess was subjected to the cruellest ill-treatment. Denia is said to
have asserted that she had even been put to the rack by her mother.
It is likewise said that her father, whenever she refused to take food
because her will had not been performed, had her put to the rack. " She
was to be put to the rack to preserve her life." But as a matter of fact the
Spanish words of the text, p. 143, " dar cuerda por conservarle la vida,"
have an opposite meaning. The King had given orders that in such
cases she was to be humoured, in order to preserve her life. The phrase
" dar cuerda " can still less bear the meaning attributed to it, as it has
no pronoun attached to it. Just as little have the words " hazer pre-
mie," in the passage, the meaning attributed to them (cf. Bergenroth,
405 note) ; they signify a coercion, which may certainly have been
employed upon her under certain circumstances, but in the manner
previously recommended by Denia. In order to remove her from
Tordesillas, which favoured the Communeros, she was to be placed
in a carriage at night and conveyed to Arevalo, which city was loyal to
the Crown. For her state was such that the party of the Communeros
endeavoured to oppose the mother to the son, who was now Emperor,
and this involved danger for the latter. We may reject Bergenroth's
conclusions with all possible certainty, prompted as they are by a previously formed opinion and a not unjustifiable hate of the Inquisition.
This latter does not come here into question at all, but only that condition of the Queen, which, in spite of long intervals, when she evinced
interest in matters and shewed good sense, yet really rendered her
incapable of governing. This opinion has come and gone like a
meteor. (Note to the second edition.)

[1] Petrus Martyr, 316, 8 ; 320, 4, 8 ; 332, 5.
[2] Escritura in Zurita, ii. f. 81.

party were desirous of inviting the King of Aragon, whilst Najara and his partisans were for appealing to the Emperor to undertake the administration of the kingdom in the name of the young Charles, and seeing that the Cortes could not be constitutionally convened for deliberative purposes without the royal sanction, the result was that the whole country resolved itself into factions. One party actually did invite Ferdinand, and the other Maximilian. The first boasted that "the Catholic King would come and punish all his enemies;" the others, that "the father would be received like the son, and given a contingent of 2000 lances." Pimentel said : "I have two suits of armour, but I will use up both before I will tolerate the King of Aragon in Castile." Thereupon, throughout the whole country, the old feuds burst out afresh between the Ayalas and Silvas at Toledo, the Arias and Lassos at Madrid, and the Benavides and Caravajals at Ubeda. Some seized strongholds, and exclaimed, "Castile, Castile for Queen Juana." These were Ferdinand's partisans. Galicia and the Asturias both adhered to their prince, and hoped for Maximilian's coming. At court the heads of both these parties, the Condestable and Najara, were armed ; their troops were constantly arrayed against each other.[1]

In this crisis the nation might well congratulate itself that it still possessed one powerful man, belonging to no party, Archbishop Ximenes of Toledo. His position he had won for himself; and he, accordingly, deserves a short notice.

Ximenes, the son of an advocate, well versed in both theological and juristic knowledge, and somewhile resident at Rome, had already received appointments from two of Isabella's adherents—Mendoza, who made him vicar of his diocese, and Cifuentes, who entrusted him with the management of his estates—when he bade adieu to his brilliant career, and retired into a Franciscan convent not far from Toledo. Here he went about barefooted, dressed in sackcloth, slept on a scanty layer of straw, and scourged himself frequently. In his happier hours he might

[1] Zurita, f. 88, 99, 107, 134. Llorente, Histoire de l'Inquisition, i. 348. Petrus Martyr, 343.

be seen lying under some broad-spreading chestnut trees, in order to shield himself from the rays of the sun, which in those climes blazed so fiercely. He often reclined in the grass, the Bible in hand, or else knelt and prayed. Here he experienced all the anguish and ecstasy of a solitary soul seeking God. But this was the way to his advancement. The Queen chose him for her father confessor; and then this man, tall of stature, pale and thin, with deep-set, piercing eyes, an aquiline nose, and a forehead which even in his old age remained free from wrinkles, appeared now and again at court in his cowl, heard the Queen's confessions, and then returned again to his convent. On one occasion, in the year 1495, he had just finished conducting the spiritual exercises of the Queen during Lent, and had bidden his companion, Francisco Ruyz, to cook some vegetables, and saddle the asses to return,—for they intended to spend Good Friday in the monastery at Ocaña—when he was a second time summoned to the Queen's presence, and received from her hands a letter with the Papal seal and the superscription : " To our brother Francisco, Archbishop Elect of Toledo." Isabella, who sought for an archbishop who had no illustrious relations, who would not entail property, nor spend his revenues in any cause other than that for which they were originally intended, viz., in the defence of Granada and the coasts, and in every Moorish war, had chosen him. He exclaimed, " This is not intended for me," and rode away unperturbed to his convent. A second command of the Pope at length forced him to accept the dignity, while a third admonished him to comport himself accordingly. After that, he began to wear a silken outer dress, whilst his friar's frock remained underneath ; to wear valuable fur, but of ashen grey colour, in order that it should remind him of his observances ; to use soft and luxurious beds, and to keep a considerable staff of servants and a jester —a sort of clever dwarf. But he himself often slept as he formerly did ; and in the palace itself he maintained certain monks, to whom he spoke of nothing but of God and strict discipline, and for whose observance he drew up a table, teaching them how to abstain from worldly things.

In this union of spiritual and temporal affairs he lived

his life. He spoke very little, and scarcely ever laughed. His life was action and accomplishment : it forms a forcible contrast to the sufferings of the Queen. We read how, on one occasion, he came from the synod of his diocese, where he had said the daily mass and conducted ecclesiastical business, to the Aragonese Cortes, and induced them to take the oath, how he then proceeded without delay to lay the foundation of the University of Alcalá, which was all his doing, a work the King envied him ; how from here he hurried to Granada to convert the Moors, returned, and received (1502) the new Prince at Toledo ; how, then, instead of sitting at tournaments, he searched the manuscripts in his library, renewed the Mosarabic liturgy, discussed with seven scholars the plan of the Complutensian Polyglot, and also helped to found a society which every night searched the streets to see if any deserving poor were in need of shelter. To-day he would draw up a plan for a campaign in Africa, and on the morrow one for founding a convent, and would carry both into execution. His letters, dealing with the affairs of State, were sealed with the image of St. Francis.[1]

This man, who, it is generally believed, induced Isabella to order in her will a mitigation of the alcabala for the cities, and who was yet the first of all prelates and grandees, stood midway between the conflicting parties. He was not, as we have seen, successful in reconciling Philip and Ferdinand. But now, at least, he contrived to prevent an open civil war. He had also a guard, which was equipped in the Swiss style ;[2] his horsemen might be seen riding out daily to exercise. New weapons continually arrived from the Asturian forges ; and at last he brought it to pass that all other troops, save his own, quitted the court.

Now it was a matter of great import that Ximenes declared himself for Ferdinand. The Catholic King, probably, wished rather to reward him than gain him over by the dignity of Cardinal, which he had procured for him.[3] Maximilian's advent would beyond all doubt have resulted

---

[1] All from the Life of Ximenes by Alvar Gomez de Castro, of Toledo, in Schott's Hispania illustrata.

[2] Zurita, f. 119, 120.   [3] Brief, in Gomez.

in the complete disorganization of Castile, a war on all sides, and the most violent domestic strife. And when could or should Maximilian come, tied as he was by a Diet, weakened by revolt in the Netherlands, and his presence required in an Italian campaign? Ximenes decided for Ferdinand. The most powerful men in the land listened to his advice. Villena, who almost from the first had been on the side of Philip, came to him : " Is it right what the King demands? Swear to me that it is so." The Archbishop swore to him that it was right ; thereupon whilst still clasping his hand, he vowed to serve King Ferdinand in his government.[1] The rest of the opposition of the grandees Ferdinand contrived, in almost every case, to overcome by the grant of favours, so much so indeed, that his loyal supporters became quite jealous. Pimentel also gave in on receiving an encomienda and an annual stipend of 12,000 maravedi.[2] Accordingly, in August, 1507, after having been absent a year, Ferdinand entered Castile without encountering any resistance, with Alcaldes and Alguazils, his maces and heralds ; the grandees hastened to kiss his hand. In the North there were still left several, whom neither he nor Ximenes had been able to gain over. They fled or lost their castles ; Najara lost all save one. " And now," said Ferdinand, " we will open a new account together." In Andalusia, Priego and Giron were in open revolt. He deprived them also of their castles. The Inquisition abated its rigour somewhat, and Ximenes, whom the King had appointed Grand Inquisitor, set free all those whom Luzero had denounced.[3]

At Tortoles the King met his daughter. As soon as they set eyes on each other, the father took off his hat, and the daughter her mourning veil. When she prostrated herself to kiss his feet, and he sank on one knee in recognition of her royal dignity, they embraced and opened their hearts to each other. He shed tears. Tears she had none, but she granted his desire ; only she would not consent to bury the

[1] Letter of the King to Villena, in Zurita, 110. Also in the same, 142.
[2] Zurita, ii. 133.
[3] Zurita, 143, 148, 163. Also, Llorente, i. 352.

corpse. "Why so soon?" she inquired. Nor would she go
to Burgos where she had lost her husband. He took her to
Tordesillas. Here the Queen of such vast realms lived for
forty-seven years. She educated her youngest daughter,
gazed from the window upon the grave of her husband, and
prayed for his eternal happiness. From henceforth she was
dead to the world.[1]

These are the struggles engendered of the Neapolitan
war through the claims of the house of Austria. Maximilian, owing chiefly to the opposition of Louis, who
declared that he would consider every one who recognized
him his enemy, and, if he were a subject of his own, guilty
of high treason, could at first not even obtain the guardianship over his grandchildren in the Netherlands.[2] At last,
however, in 1507, he obtained it, when new dangers
threatened from Gelderland and from the French coast, and
made his assistance desirable. But in Spain and Italy
Ferdinand was triumphant. He at once turned his newly
consolidated power against the outer world and foreign
nations.

4. FERDINAND'S EXTERNAL ENTERPRISES

Prior to the commencement of the Neapolitan war of
1501, the Xeque of Gelves had offered allegiance to the
Spaniards, together with the whole coast line lying between Tripoli and Tunis. Isabella had often repented
that Naples had at that time been preferred. As soon as
the first period of quiet set in, between Ferdinand's reconciliation with France, in 1505, and the arrival of Philip,
Ximenes urged the renewal of the Moorish war, and himself subscribed the fourth part of the expense of fitting out a
fleet, which attacked and took the great port of Mers-el-
Kebir, an important station of the African trade. His
attention had first been drawn to this place by a Venetian;
Lopez el Zagal was the first to spring on land.[3] The
great domestic disturbances, at all events in Andalusia, had

---

[1] Petrus Martyr, 359. Zurita, 144.
[2] Letter of Louis in the Lettres de Louis XII, i. 106, 107.
[3] Zurita, i. ii. 26.

not been completely suppressed, when the Moorish pirates were driven away from Velez and the rock lying before it. But as soon as tranquillity had been restored at home, and Ferdinand was no longer occupied by his Italian enmities, he again commenced greater operations in the interest of universal Christendom. To these belong also the colonization of America. Hitherto the Spaniards had been content to explore the islands and bays of the West Indies, to look for gold, to fish for pearls, and to preach Christianity peacefully. All these operations had been conducted by an admiral from a colony in San Domingo. In the year 1509, Ferdinand having heard of the barbarous habits of the wild cannibals there, appointed two governors, Hoieda for the coast of Carthagena, and Niquesa for Veragua.[1] Their duties were: "to make the Indians his vassals and good Christians, but, should this be impossible, to reduce them to slavery or exterminate them." The governors themselves were not fortunate; but some of their companions founded a colony upon Darien, to which, in honour of the picture of Maria Antigua at Seville, they gave the name of Antigua. Nuñez Balboa, a man who was reserved for great discoveries,[2] became its head.

But at the time of which we speak, the operations in Africa appeared to be of greater moment both for Spain and Europe: yet the other was greater both in respect of the exertion expended upon it, and of its results. On the eve of Ascension-day, 1509, Ximenes and Pedro Navarra set sail with their fleet and landed on the day following at Oran, before which city they found 12,000 Moorish knights gathered ready to defend it. "Shall we attack to-day?" asked Navarra. "Immediately," returned Ximenes. Before him the Cross was borne, and his monks, with swords over their habits, also advanced in line. The Galicians first stormed the heights, and maintained themselves there; then, strengthened by the other troops, they drove the enemy back upon the water reservoirs of the city. Here

---

[1] Sommario dell' Indie Occidentali di Don Pietro Martire, in Ramusio, Viaggi, iii. 18. Benzoni, Novae novi orbis historiae, a Calvetone latinae factae, p. 72.

[2] Pietro Martire, f. 21.

they awaited their artillery. They fought with this at a distance, and with their swords at close quarters. The enemy at length turned and fled. Whilst they were being driven past their own city, other troops landed from the ships and took it. Thereupon the Spanish ensigns floated from the walls of Oran, and the troops shouted, "Africa! Africa for our lord, the King of Spain!" Ximenes, to whose prayers the victory was attributed ("owing to them the sun had stood still and had shone brightly over them, whilst gloom was spread over the Moors"), consecrated the Grand Mosque as a Church of Sta Maria de la Vitoria.[1]

Again, on the 1st January, 1510, in honour, as the Spaniards said, of the Saviour and His Mother, and of the Apostle St. James, and the blessed knight, St. George, Pedro Navarra set sail from Iviza. On this occasion he was very successful. Bugia, a great and wealthy city, full of mosques, schools, hospitals, inns, and every sign of prosperity, was taken by him at the first assault. Xeque, Almoxarife, Alcadi, Musti, and all the Alfaquirs of Algiers surrendered their city under the condition that Ferdinand should not demand a single farthing more in contributions than the Moorish king had received, and would leave them their laws. Tedelitz surrendered. Muley Yahya, King of Tenez, promised to come as Ferdinand's vassal, as often as he should be summoned to the Cortes, or to the wars. At last Navarra, with brigantines, sloops, and barks, succeeded one evening in forcing his way into the harbour of Tripoli, and on the following day, between nine and one, in taking this great city.[2]

But before all else it was now imperative to conquer Tlemcen, Tunis, and the island of Gelves; then the African coast would be assured to the Spaniards. The King of Tlemcen, a great potentate, swore with his Mezvar and Cadi to pay an annual tribute of 13,000 doblas in good gold. In Sicily, preparations were going on against Tunis. Garcia, Alva's eldest son, attacked Gelves. Garcia had to pay for his daring with his life on the burning sands.[3] But

---

[1] Zurita, ii. 180–182, whence Mariana, 275–287. Gomez, 1025.

[2] Zurita, ii. 211, 212, f.

[3] Zurita, 230. Fazellus, Historiae Siculae, 597.

Ferdinand was for setting out in person to take over the command of the army. Only when the interior of the country was his, could he be certain of securing the harbours and coasts. This accomplished, his intention was to continue his holy campaign as far as Alexandria, the next city to Tripoli, and thence to the holy temple of Jerusalem. For this object, the Cortes of Aragon, Valencia, and Catalonia voted an aid of 500,000 pounds, which, considering their liberties, was a very considerable sum. A thousand English musketeers also joined in the expedition. The rupture between the Moors and Arabs along the whole coast gave prospects of a great success, and they bethought themselves of an old prophecy, that ancient Carthage with its harbour would now fall into the hands of the Christians.[1]

With these hopes in his breast, Ferdinand set out for Malaga, in the year 1511, in order to begin the campaign. But on the way thither he was overtaken by ambassadors from Italy, who brought him such tidings from the Romagna that his plans were turned into other channels.

[1] Zurita, 227. Senarega, Annales Genuenses, 608.

CHAPTER III

VENICE AND JULIUS II

THE development of affairs in the Romagna resulted in a general war. Once more Venice showed herself in the fulness of her might: independent, vigorous, and with comprehensive and grand ideas and aspirations. A general consideration of her position is accordingly indispensable.[1]

1. VENETIAN COMMERCE, CONQUESTS, AND CONSTITUTION; ATTACK UPON THE ROMAGNA

The lagoons were originally covered with low mud hovels, having scarcely an aperture to admit of light and air, and full of poor fugitives.[2] About the year 1500, there were to be seen there about seventy-two churches, built of stone, and glittering with gold, whilst three broad canals were flanked by palace on palace, all faced with variegated and white marble.[3] Even humble people slept on beds of walnut wood, behind green silk curtains, ate from silver, and wore golden chains and rings.[4] The West and East paid tribute here on their wares, before they were bartered and exchanged. Many large islands and splendid cities received hence their governors.

This pitch of prosperity has been reached through conquest and commerce; but commerce was the original source

---

[1] I refrain from making any additions, acquired from recent research, to my original description. They will, I think, find a place in a later volume of my works. (Note to 2nd Ed.)

[2] Sansovino, Venetia, p. 140.

[3] Comines, Mémoires, 479.

[4] Sansovino. Hence Splendor Venetiarum clarissimus, in Graevii Thesaurus, v. 3, p. 282.

of its greatness. Just as those fishermen themselves originally belonged to the Greek, that is the Eastern Empire, whilst the first territory they acquired for their sustenance belonged to the Lombard, *i.e.* the Western Empire, and they were thus vassals to both, so now did the essence of their present trade lie in the connection of the distant East with the distant West. It was carried on in the following manner.

As soon as the public galleys were ready for sea, and delivered over to those of the Nobili, who, summoned by the cry of the heralds, had offered the best prices, some, according to primæval custom, sailed to Alexandria and the Black Sea, and others to Africa and the West.[1] The first were laden with copper and mercury from Hungary, with German steel, with alum from Italy, and velvet, camelot, cloth, mirrors, beads, and glass from their own city, each cargo worth about 100,000 ducats.[2] In Alexandria, the watchmen on the tower looked out for their arrival, and signalled it to the toll-gatherer. The chief business was done in Cairo, in the Khan el Halili, the Persian merchants'-hall.[3] Thither, the caravans from Mecca brought fine spices from the Moluccas, silk from Bengal, cinnamon from Ceylon, pepper from Malabar, precious stones and dyewood from the Deccan, and pearls from the Bahrein Islands. In case the Indians preferred consigning their goods to the caravans through Kabul and Persia, to Derbend, the gate of gates, and to Azov, rather than to the sea,[4] or if the dwellers on the coast of Asia Minor produced anything rare or useful, like the goat's hair of Angora, this they fetched from Ajas or Azov. They conveyed all to the halls on the Rialto.

The Western galleys were not laden with such wares ; these they left to the Western nations to fetch for themselves. Their cargoes were cloth and metal, gold chains

[1] Petrus Martyr, Legatio Babylonica (to Cairo) anno 1502. Basil. 1533, p. 7.

[2] Sommario de' Regni, Città, etc., in Ramusio, Viaggi, i. 324.

[3] Petrus Martyr, Legatio Babylonica, 80. Leo, Descriptio Africae, in Ramusio, 83.

[4] Pegoletti, Avvisamento del Viaggio and Aloigi di Giovanni, in Sprengel's Geschichte der Entdeckungen, 253, 257. Ritter, Erdkunde, ii. 859.

for France, wax candles for the Spanish churches, fiddle-strings from Pacasto, and glass from Murano. In Gelves they owned a great house close to the castle, in Tunis they shared with Genoese and Catalans a whole suburb of the town; in Oran and Tlemcen they did a great trade. Hence their goods found their way to the interior of the Sudan, to Timbuctoo, where the women wore veils of Venetian manufacture, and to Gago, where their most inferior cloth fetched one, and their scarlet forty ducats the yard, and hither came the gold in return, which they sent back to the East.[1] In Malaga they loaded silk and grain, and wool also, though this they principally fetched from England. They penetrated as far as Flanders and Denmark. It is computed that, besides these public vessels, nearly 3,000 private ships were engaged in trading on the same coasts, but chiefly with other ports. Their trading capital, some considerable time previously, had amounted to 28,800,000 ducats.[2]

All this commerce was controlled by the most rigorous laws. Save in the Fondaco, where the German cities had each their separate vaults, which they let to separate business houses,[3] no one was allowed to trade with Germans, and only here such as were, as they expressed it, internal and external citizens. No subject city was allowed to sell for export, or to buy goods from abroad except in Venice. No galley might stay away longer than a definitely specified time.[4] A law obtained that an emigrating manufacturer should at first be induced to return by persuasion; in case he did not obey, by the arrest of his relations; and, if he did not then return, he should be put to death.[5] By such measures their city was preserved as the source of trade and commerce.

It was necessity that prompted their first conquests. In these they were not always fortunate, and the war in 1379

[1] Paruta, Storia Venetiana, iv. 117, whence all in Lebret, History of Venice, ii. 1046. Also, Leo Africanus, Descriptio Africae, in Ramusio, f. 70, 66, 58, 78, 79.

[2] Daru, Histoire de Venise, iii. 189, p. 51 from Filiasi.

[3] Document in the Regensburg Chronicle, iv. ii. 141.

[4] Tentori, Saggio sopra l' historia Venetiana, i. 126; ii. 80, 85.

[5] Six-and-twentieth art. of the Inquisition Laws in Daru, iii. 90.

left them little more than Negropont, Coron, Modon, and Candia. But, after that time, fortune and shrewdness opened to them a new way.

After the death of Charles de la Pace, when one faction in Corfu did not desire to be reigned over by his son Ladislas, the people bethought themselves how frequently they had seen the victorious standard of Venice in their waters, and raised the ensign of the lion and founded a church to St. Michael, as an everlasting memorial. The same Ladislas, in the midst of the contention between the Horvaths and the Hungarian Queens, sold to them Zara, where he had been crowned.[1] For fear of the despot of Servia, Cattaro sent its Chancellor and begged for a Venetian magistrate who should judge according to the old laws. Filled with like apprehensions, Spalato and Trau were delivered over to them by the citizens; Argos, Napoli di Romania, Patras, and Lepanto, under certain conditions; and many other cities by their princes and for money. Athens received a garrison from Venice; and, in consequence of a quarrel with his father, a prince of Constantinople delivered Salonika into their keeping.[2]

And so it went on. Veglia refused to obey a Frangipani, whether Nicolò or Giovanni, and preferred their rule. During a feud between Queens Carlotta and Caterina, they gained Cyprus.[3]

Their policy was as follows: whenever their neighbours became involved in differences or were in peril, they appeared on the scene, and offered the one protection and the other money; thus effecting their subjugation.

The same process they followed in Italy. To begin with, when the quarrel between Cividale d'Austria and Udine had convulsed the whole of Friuli, and the neighbouring states became likewise involved, it happened one day that the citizens of Treviso, and all the peasants who had come into the city to defend it, shouted " San Marco ! " and delivered themselves into the hand of the Venetian captain.

[1] Sanuto, Chronica Venetiana, 843, 844.

[2] Navagero, Chronicon Venetum, 1075, 1080. Daru, from MSS. ii. 99.

[3] Navagero, in detail, 1137-1198, 1203.

This incident brought about the subjection of the whole of Friuli. This enterprise was not without sufficient motive, for they needed a market in the vicinity for their daily supplies of food. But should they then, when the Visconti, in feud with the Carrara, offered them their cities of Verona, Feltre, and Belluno, implicate themselves in the general Italian movements, so full of storm, insecurity, and danger as they were? All who stood in any relation to the Carrara, must first be excluded from the Pregadi, before the Doge and Francesco Foscari, the head of the Forty, could carry the day by the preponderating voice of a single ballot. Vicenza raised the standard of Venice. On the 12th July, 1405, there appeared in the square of St. Mark before the Doge and Signoria twenty-two envoys from Verona on horseback, all dressed in white, bearing the seal of the State, the three keys of the city for the three Estates, the white staff (the symbol of sovereignty), and two ensigns; and having delivered these insignia over, they took the oath of allegiance. The Doge answered them, "You are come from darkness into light," and gave them a gold embroidered standard of St. Mark. They shouted "San Marco!" and rode back home. The Paduans, in sore distress, being permitted by Francesco Carrara to do what they wished, stipulated for the maintenance of their liberties, and surrendered to Venice.[1]

In Venice there was not entire satisfaction at this policy. Upon the mosaic floor of the Church of St. Mark, two lions may be seen depicted; one in the sea, great, strong, and courageous, the other on land, thin and weak; a picture which corresponded with widespread opinions. The Doge Mocenigo especially was opposed to every new enterprise. "For whoever made conquests," as he expressed himself, "sought evil and found it too. He, for his part, would not maintain people with great billhooks in order to ravage this beautiful garden of Milan, which brought them in some millions every year. Did the conquests they had already made, recoup the expenditure? He prayed God, our Lady, and St. Mark for peace." So long as he lived, but no

[1] Navagero, 1070. Sanuto, 794–831. Bilue's Historia Patriae, 32.

longer, his opinion was considered wise.[1] A man of opposite views and ideas, a man of whom he had warned his countrymen, Foscari, was chosen to succeed him. He made use of the misunderstanding between Filippo Maria of Milan and Carmagnola, in order with the latter's help to acquire Brescia and Bergamo; he availed himself of the disturbances following on Filippo Maria's death to gain Crema, and utilized the tumults which had broken out between the nobles and the commons to gain possession of Ravenna, and subsequently of Cervia also. The revenue Venice derived from the mainland, as a result of this policy, rose to 800,000 ducats, and that accruing from the islands to 400,000 ducats.[2] Men said: "They have no rival on the seas, and are not minded to tolerate one on land."[3]

How the internal machinery of this marvellous power worked, can easily be told if we look at the peculiar traditional forms of its constitution, but can only be explained with the greatest difficulty, if we consider the real moving and living principle animating the whole. If we reflect that the Doge could not say "Yes" or "No" to anybody without first taking counsel with his Consiglieri,[4] but that, on the other side, the three Inquisitori without the interference of the Avogatori, and laying aside all formality, had the right to condemn to death clergy and laity, nobles and commons, to make use of the public treasury, and to command the governors and generals,[5] we shall perceive that the counterpoise of Doge, Consiglieri, Pregadi, and the Consiglio was not worth much, but that the supreme power, which in other cities reposed in the hands of a Balìa, here resided in the Inquisitori. It is certainly not at all clear from what families these were chosen, how the others tolerated it, and why there was here no trace of party feeling. Some remarks of Maximilian, that he was coming to liberate the old fathers from the

[1] Arrenghi, in Sanuto, 949, 958. Sansovino, Venetia.
[2] Epitome proventuum Italiae; also in Ludewig, Reliquiae, MSS. x. 445.
[3] Letter of Ferrante in Fabroni, Vita Laurentii Medici, ii. 237.
[4] In Sanuto, 785.
[5] Daru, Histoire de Venise from authentic documents, ii. 423.

violent oppression of the new aristocracy,[1] cast no real light but only a glimmer upon this matter. Within this hall, no personalities and no differences appear, only sometimes hatred against secret renegades manifests itself, otherwise there is always a common exertion and a common will. " They are very clever," says Comines, " they meet daily and hold council ; their neighbours will feel the effect."[2]

The disturbances which had taken place in Italy since Charles VIII's advent there, came very opportunely for their plans and policy. On every available occasion the Venetians extended their power round about them. In the struggle between Charles and Ferrantino they acquired five fine cities in Apulia, excellently situated for their requirements, which they peopled by the reception of fugitive Jews from Spain.[3] Moreover, in the kingdom of Naples, one party had declared for them ; we have seen, too, how Taranto raised their standard. During the Florentine disorders, they were within an ace of becoming masters of Pisa. In the Milanese feuds they acquired Cremona and the Ghiara d'Adda. Their power was all the more terrible, as they had never been known to lose again anything which they had once obtained. No one doubted that their aim was complete sovereignty over the whole of Italy. Their historians always talked as if Venice was the ancient Rome once more ; therefore it was that the bones of Titus Livius were honoured at Padua, like those of a saint : " they should learn of him to avoid the faults of Rome."[4]

Since the Turkish war, which had kept them a while employed, was now at an end, they next tried their fortune in the Romagna, and endeavoured, availing themselves of the quarrels between the returning princes and Caesar, to become, if not the sole, at all events the most powerful, vassals of the papal throne. Those princes who were often compelled to fly, and were accustomed to fly to them, were

[1] Maximilian's Manifestos of the Years 1510 and 1511, in Hormayr's Archiv für Historie, etc., 1810.

[2] Comines, Mémoires, 488.

[3] Leander Alberti, Descriptio Italiae, p. 369.

[4] Comines, 483.

all, even including Guidobaldo, their head, so much bound
to Venice, that "San Marco!" had even been shouted in
Guidobaldo's castles, with his approval and consent. The
Venetians prepared to espouse the cause of those whom
Caesar had overpowered. The cities reflected how genuine
and substantial was that peace which the lion of Venice
spread over all its dependencies. Having appeared in the
Romagna at the end of October, 1503, and having first
promised the Malatesta other possessions in their own
territory, they took Rimini, with the concurrence of the
prince and citizens. Without ado they attacked Faenza.[1]
That city had recalled a natural scion of the Manfredi,
and for a good omen had called him Astorre ; but the good
omen proved an ill-starred one, when the governor of the
castle surrendered. They were then also themselves obliged
to surrender.[2] Men said: "Faenza is for the Venetians
either a gate into Italy, or their ruin." They continued
their conquests, and, in the territories of Imola, Cesena,
and Forlì, took stronghold after stronghold. Cesena itself
had already previously announced through Guidobaldo its
subjection, and it was only the fear of Caesar's castles above
their head that kept the cities still loyal. Then it was that
the first minister of France stated his belief that, "had they
only the Romagna, they would forthwith attack Florence,
on account of a debt of 180,000 guilders owing them."[3] If
they were to make an inroad into Tuscany, Pisa would fall
immediately on their arrival. Their object in calling the
French into the Milanese territory was, that they considered
them more fitted to make a conquest than to keep it ; and,
in the year 1504, they were already negotiating how they
might wrest Milan again from them. Could they only
succeed in this, nothing in Italy would be able to withstand
them any longer. "They want to make the Pope their
chaplain,"[4] said Machiavelli.

[1] Bembus, Historia Veneta, 145–147. Baldi, Guidubaldo, ix. 127–
141.
[2] Sansovino, Origine, 79.
[3] Machiavelli, Legazione alla corte di Roma, p. 331.
[4] His phrase in the same Legazione, p. 301.

2. FIRST EXPLOITS AND DOUBLE INTENTIONS OF JULIUS II

But they met with the staunchest resistance in Julius, as in him they could discover no weak point to attack.[1] As pointedly as he could express himself, he declared to them, on the 9th November, 1503, that, " though hitherto their friend, he would now do his utmost against them, and would besides incite all the princes of Christendom against them ; "[2] and once more, on the 10th January, he declared that : "he was, and always had been, firm and constant in his intention to regain the temporalities of the Church ; and, further, that no terrorism, no treaty, nor conditions would prevent his carrying it out, for it was his duty."[3]   But as no warning availed aught, " for their right was clear and plain, and they would satisfy his claims with their newly-coined gold," in September, 1504, he entered into the league with Louis, Maximilian, and Philip, which was directed not only against Ferdinand, but against Venice as well.   We have seen how this league became dissolved. The Venetians then retreated a step.   They restored all parts of the territories of Imola, Cesena, and Forlì which they had occupied ; until they had done so, Julius would not accept their obedience.[4]   Yet he did not on this account abandon his project of conquering the rest also.

Julius was of a very impatient and violent character. When Michael Angelo painted the Sixtine chapel, and at last unveiled it, he could not wait until even the dust from the scaffolding had cleared away.[5]   Any thought that had once occurred to him possessed his mind unceasingly ; it was visible in his features, he murmured it ever between his teeth ; " he must die," he confessed, " did he not speak it out."[6]   But this did not make him stubborn and

[1] Machiavelli, Legazione alla corte di Roma, the forty-eighth letter, p. 391.

[2] *Ibid*. 304.

[3] Breve Julii Papae, in Rainaldus, Annales Ecclesiastici, xx. 9.

[4] Bembus, Historia Veneta, vii. 155.   Baldi, Guidubaldo, xi. 182.

[5] Vasari, Vita di Michel Angelo, p. 206.

[6] Zurita, ii. 28, which explains Paris de Grassis, Diarium, apud Hoffmannum, Collectio Nova, 450.

inconsiderate. He once threatened Michael Angelo, requiring him to make haste and finish some work, and then on the following day sent him 500 scudi to pacify him.[1] In the same way, as he had always abided by his opinion in opposition to his uncle Sixtus, to Innocent and Alexander, even when a fugitive and in peril, so when he became Pope, he unswervingly adhered to what he had once decided upon, mindful of Nicholas and Gregory [2] among his predecessors. His temperament can be gathered from his portrait by Raphael—the strongly-marked features, the closed mouth and long flowing beard, as he sits in an arm-chair in deep thought. All his actions gave evidence of his firmness. He aptly bore the oak on his coat-of-arms.

Now, as we have seen, Julius was resolved to tolerate princes in the Papal States, but only such as he could control. But it was not only the Venetians who were capable of offering him resistance, but others also. Giovanni Bentivoglio, of Bologna, in particular, was almost independent. He ruled his city by a council of twenty, of whom ten conducted the Imborsazioni, the elections, and all public business for the first half of the year ; and the other ten for the remaining half, yet both under his personal presidency. He was styled Prince, Governor, and permanent Gonfaloniere of justice; he could himself levy a tax.[3] He dwelt in a splendid palace, containing 370 rooms, among gardens, fountains, and fish ponds.[4] His sons, one of whom was designated to succeed him, built other palaces. He found a bell indispensable for calling his friends together; and a tower bears an inscription to the effect that, " he had built it, he, to whom virtue and fortune had granted all his wishes and abundance of wealth." [5] On his shield were emblazoned a lily and an eagle ; yet he trusted most in the lily and in French protection.

In the year 1506, when Louis XII and Ferdinand the

---

[1] Vasari, Vita di Michel Angelo, p. 225.

[2] Bull to Louis XII, in Hottingeri Historia Ecclesiastica, vii. 45.

[3] Hieronymus de Bursellis, Chronica Bononiensia in Muratori, xxiii. 881.

[4] Sansovino, Origine, 280, 289.

[5] Inscription in Bursellis, 909.

Catholic needed the papal sanction to their Neapolitan compact, Julius considered it practicable to compel the Bolognese to recognize their dependence. The latter appealed to tradition and to the old treaties made with the papal see. He, on his part, maintained the rights of a prince to alter a constitution even in the face of tradition; he announced that he would come and see their mode of life for himself; if it pleased him, he would confirm it, otherwise he would alter it: the old treaties, he averred, were obtained by coercion, and now an amelioration was possible.[1] The Venetians offered him their assistance in this enterprise, provided he would only ratify their possession of Faenza and Rimini. But he paid them no heed. With a guard of only twenty-five lances, a grey-haired man among grey-haired cardinals, on the 20th August, 1506, he took the field in order to conquer Bologna.[2] On the march thither he thought of reducing Perugia at the same time.

For Giampaolo Baglione, who after Alexander's death ruled Perugia again in the customary manner by a Balìa, the Dieci dell' Arbitrio, had always refused obedience.[3] He was now to be compelled to obey. What was there victorious in his mere advent? In Orvieto, Giampaolo, whom Duke Guidobaldo had persuaded to subject himself, met him and promised to deliver his fortresses and gates into the Pope's power, and his troops into his pay. Before the capitulation had even been signed, before his troops, who had begun to collect, were on the scene, and in order to show that he trusted the honour of his enemy, the Pope entered Perugia, reinstated in their possessions those who had fled the city, left to Giampaolo his legal rights, and restored peace.[4]

In the case of Bentivoglio, the pride of his wife, Ginevra Sforza, and his old confidential standing with Julius, with

[1] Machiavelli, Legazione al Papa, tom. v. p. 157.
[2] Machiavelli, *ibid*. lett. iii. Hadriani Cardinalis Iter Iulii in Roscoe i. appendix, p. 519, in hexameters.
[3] Machiavelli, Legaz. v. 160.
[4] *Ibid.* v. 136, and Discorsi sopra la prima Deca di Tito Livio, i. c. 27. Baldi, 192.

whom he had eaten and drunk, prevented a similar subjection. Were his four sons, to whom he had committed the
defence of the four quarters of the city, too weak to resist a
Pope? He replied to Julius' demand that he should furnish
quarters for him, his army, and 500 French lances, that
"only the Swiss guard could be admitted with the Pope's
person," and further asked to be informed how long he
intended to remain?[1] "So," exclaimed Julius indignantly,
"he prescribes laws for us, and will not receive us. Shall
he dictate to us?"[2] Hereupon the Pope declared Bentivoglio and his adherents rebels against the Church, gathered
to him his army and the troops Louis had promised him, and
winding through the ravines and passes of the highest part
of the Apennine range, carefully avoiding the positions
occupied by the Venetians, and passing frequently by kneeling peasants, marched to Imola.[3] At this juncture, the
French, whose arrival Bentivoglio had never expected,
actually advanced against him—for Julius and Louis were
still friends—and, at the same time, his old adversaries in
the city, who had so long kept silence, rose up in revolt,
and with them many new opponents, embittered by the
cruelties perpetrated on the Marescotti (of whom shortly
before nearly two hundred had been ruined on the accusa-
tion of Caesar Borgia), and detesting him, too, for the
arrogance of his sons.[4] Then he likewise perceived that
no one can be accounted happy before his death, and that
he had falsely boasted that no one would ever expel him;
accordingly, he entered into a compact with the French,
which secured to him his private possessions, and then,
after an uninterrupted prosperity of forty years' duration,
quitted his palace, the pillar of his fortune, and his city.
Julius, on the other hand, obeying the invitation of the now
free people, was borne in on the 11th of November, 1506,
through the gates of Bologna, on an ivory chair, clad in
his papal robes. He only deposed three members of the

---

[1] Machiavelli, Legazione, 121, 165.

[2] Paris de Grassis, Itinerarium Iulii in Rainaldus, xx. 10.

[3] Hadriani Iter, vs. 86. Baldi, Guidubaldo, 195.

[4] Georg. Florus, de bello Italico, p. 19. Arluni, de bello Veneto,
24. Monstrelet, Appendix, 239.

Twenty, whilst adding twenty-three to their body. To these Forty he committed a far more independent jurisdiction than that which they had enjoyed under the Bentivogli, and released the people from all burdens. He desired to establish a truly free city, and one devoted to him for his protection and favour.[1]

Now whilst entertaining other projects, as to which he was not reticent, and having delivered to the Marquis of Mantua the standard of the Church, bidding him under it wage just and victorious wars, and well pleasing to God,[2] it happened that affairs in Genoa were so far prejudicial to his objects as to divert his intentions into another channel.

In the years 1506 and 1507, Genoa passed through all the phases of a revolution. The first impetus was given by the leading plebeian families, who, for a long time past, had been wont to see one of them, Fregoso or Adorno, at the head of affairs, and the old aristocracy doing service to them. Since the French occupation, however, both these leading families were in exile, and the supreme power resided in the nobles, and especially in the family of Fiesco.[3] The Popolari, having for a long time vainly demanded that two-thirds of the public offices should be again entrusted to them, were at length aided in their demands by the indignation of the proletariat at the conduct of some aristocratic youths, who, instead of paying, drew swords, showing on the hilts the inscription : " Chastise the peasant."[4] Accordingly, one day some of them placed themselves at the head of the people, and, with the cry of " People and King," organized an insurrection, and succeeded in wresting to themselves two-thirds of the offices.[5] The effect of this was to show the lower orders that the public peace only depended upon their good will. Rapidly following up their success, these latter next opposed the magistrates of the upper classes by appointing eight tribunes from their own midst; they went

[1] Sansovino, Origine delle Case, 292. Nardi, History of Florence, iv. 114. Anton, Chronicques Annales, p. 40. Paris de Grassis, p. 13.
[2] Brief in Dumont, iv. 1, 20.
[3] Senarega, Rerum Genuensium Annales, in many passages, and 576.
[4] Anton, Chronicques Annales, p. 47.
[5] Ubertus Folieta, Historia Genuensis, 282.

further, and committed the supreme power to four men, and were still not content. At last, the Cappetti—people whose sole wealth consisted in an old cap and a pair of woollen stockings—obtained the upper hand, and gathering together daily in their societies of " Peace," " Concord," or whatever they were called, waxed more and more enthusiastic, chose a dyer for their chief, and made him an absolute Doge.[1]

The course of such revolutions often proceeds in the same way ; from an ascendency of the middle classes to the opposite extreme, next to the ascendency of the proletariat, and, finally, to a monarchy from the artisans. These Genoese paid no heed to the King of France, until, in April, 1507, he advanced against them with his hommes d'armes and Swiss Guards. They then fortified a hill lying immediately before their walls, and occupied it with two masses of troops, the one posted on the summit, and the other on a lower point of vantage. But they lacked courage and discipline; and when Bayard, with 126 hommes d'armes, stormed the hill from the one side, and the Obwalden arquebusiers and Bernese volunteers from the other, both divisions turned and fled, without even thinking of combining.[2] They had no other weapons left, but for all, aristocratic Anziani and plebeians, women and maidens, to cry " Misericordia." Louis gave to all, with the exception of seventy-nine, their lives and property; but he burnt before their eyes the book of their compacts with him, and the letters of their imperial liberties, took their arms away, and built with their money a castle to hold them in awe. And so they went about, with shrugged shoulders and bowed heads ; on their new coins they saw no longer the device of the griffin, but only that of the lily.[3]

But how could it be that the degradation of his country should not affect Julius II, who was proud to call himself, in his inscriptions, " Ligurian " ? It might be that he had

---

[1] Principally in Senarega, 577–587. Georg. Florus, 24.

[2] Bayard, 123. St. Gelais, 191. Letter of the Freiburgers in Fuchs' Mailändische Feldzüge, ii. 44, 45. Anshelm in Glutz. 202.

[3] Anton, 185. Louis' instruction for John de Cabellis, in Datt, de pace publica, 512. Senarega, 592 f.

found the French not so well disposed as he could have wished, even before Bologna, upon which, on Bentivoglio's flight, they had advanced, under an understanding with the nobles, and which they were only prevented by the people from occupying.[1] But Genoa was almost nearer to his heart. He was related to the house of Fregoso, and perceived in their exclusion by the French a slight offered to himself. It was generally believed that he had had a hand in the insurrection of the Popolari; and that it was with intention that Louis had brought three cardinals and thirty high prelates with him, planning, perhaps, to dispossess the Pope.[2]   As a matter of fact, Louis had been in negotiation with Ferdinand to make Amboise Pope;[3] and certain overtures made to England appear to point to the same thing.[4]   But Julius, instead of awaiting the King's arrival in Bologna, as he had originally intended, returned in haste to Rome.

The result of this was, that the Pope's original plan, that of uniting the States of the Church, was supplemented by another—to free Italy from the French.   With respect to the first, he quarrelled with Venice; in carrying out the second, he might have assured himself of its support.   Had both only been at one, and united with the greater part of the nation, which felt itself oppressed,[5] they might, perhaps, together have achieved some result.   But, just as in the whole nation itself, the feeling of faction entertained by certain communities against each other was doubtless far stronger than the feeling of the unity of the whole— the first hereditary and deeply rooted, and the latter only existing in theory and in writings—so also did Julius and Venice prefer to fight out their own particular quarrel, rather than to think of their common country.   Both wished to possess Rimini and Faenza, and otherwise would entertain

[1] Maximilian's reply (to French allegations) in Goldast, Reichs-handlung, 57.

[2] Folieta and Guicciardini, vii. 372.

[3] Mémoire, touchant les affaires de France in the Lettres de Louis, i. 62.

[4] Garnier, histoire de France, xxii. 84 ; sur la copie d'une négociation secrète.

[5] See, for instance, Galateus, de situ Iapygiae, ap. Graevium.

no alliance. So they stand opposed to one another, both having the same object in view, but their present attitude being one of mutual hostility.

3. DISCOVERIES OF THE PORTUGUESE. DECAY OF VENETIAN COMMERCE.

Now it had come about that Venice had incurred—and was still incurring—great danger on both sides of her existence; in her conquests and her commerce. To begin with, Venetian trade had suffered injury in the true basis of its prosperity, the East, at the hands of those who had quite other aims in view, and were really engaged on a mission of great importance in the world's history.

In the year 1497, the trade on the coasts of Arabia, East Africa, and the Indian peninsula was in the hands of the Moors; naturally on the Arabian coast, at Aden, where the favourable monsoons were eagerly awaited, and at Hormuz, "the house of safety."[1] But scarcely less theirs was the fertile expanse of plain upon the other two coasts, which lay opposite each other, up to where the tableland begins. On the African coast, the Moors penetrated as far as Zanzibar, whence they fetched gold and amber, and Cape S. Sebastian. The King of Quiloa, who was computed to receive annually 2,666,666 ducats of gold from Sofala, and the sheikhs at Malindi and Mozambique were Moors.[2] On the Indian coast, lay the three kingdoms of Guzerat, Deccan, and Malabar. Over the two first-named Moorish princes held sway, whilst in all their ports were Mongolian or Arabian governors. If a Banyan wished to engage here in trade, he did not venture to embark without an Arabian convoy. The third, Malabar, had still an Indian, the Zamorin of Calicut, for its chief; but he also was kept in no little dependence by 4,000 Mohammedans, who dwelt in his city and often supplied him with money. Whoever was not minded to obey him, went into the mosque. One

[1] Ritter, Erdkunde, ii. 287. Especially Barthema, Itinerario in Ramusio, i. 157.

[2] Barbosa in Ramusio, 289. Also Corsali Fiorent. *ibid.* 178.

of his vassals, the Prince of Cranganore, even wore a beard, and entrusted the government to an Arabian.[1]

Besides the three coasts, Malacca in further India was the most important emporium for the whole Eastern trade ; thither China sent its silk yarn, Bengal cotton fabrics, and the Thousand Isles real spices : [2] this place was the counterpart to Venice, sending to the latter the light, perfumed and shining wares of the East, to receive in return the thick, heavy, martial or more artificial products of the West. Malacca likewise belonged to a Moorish king.

It is worthy of remark, that like Aden, lying as it does upon a promontory and severed by high mountains from the rest of the world, or like Hormuz, itself an island, Malacca, and most of the other centres of this trade, have an insular position in common with Venice. Their wealth depended upon the Venetian traffic between West and East, which I have previously described, whilst the wealth of Venice depended upon the position of India and its connection with Europe.

It appeared quite impossible that this trade could ever be intercepted and ruined. The Indians were much too weak to rid themselves of the Moors, and no other nation had any access to these shores. But, even while it appeared so firmly established, it was in fact already seriously undermined. We must observe that many Europeans had by this time visited India, that a description by Edrisi of the African coast as far as Sofala already existed,[3] and that, since Bartolomeo Diaz had circumnavigated the Cape, there was only the small strip from its last promontory, near Santa Cruz, to Cape S. Sebastian which remained unexplored, unnavigated, and not drawn within the sphere of the world's intercourse. As soon as this small strip of coast was navigated, the Portuguese found themselves again face to face with their old enemies, the Moors, whom they had left in North Africa. Then, naturally, India became attached to Europe by a route other than that of the Moors and

---

[1] Barbosa, 296. Sommario de' regni et città in Ramusio, p. 326. Barros, Asia, i. vi. 5, after Soltau.

[2] Sommario de' regni et città, 336.

[3] Sprengel, Geschichte der geographischen Entdeckungen, 155.

Venetians, and a direct connection was set up. The Venetian trade then necessarily fell into decay.

We have already seen how Dom Manuel became King of Portugal, a prince, who, whilst still a youth, had taken an orb for a device, and one whom a bold and brave nobility were ready at any time to serve ; a nobility bold not against him—for Manuel's forefathers had clipped their wings, and it was now their ambition to serve the King in the palace, and accept a small remuneration from him[1]—but bold against the Moors, and fearless on the sea. With a view to explore that unknown coast, and to discover India, Manuel, in July, 1497, fitted out three baloniere, and a ravetta, with a crew of 180 men. He gave them pillars, on which were inscribed a cross and his arms, ten condemned prisoners who were to explore the countries of barbarous nations, and letters for Prester John and the Zamorin of Calicut; he then had his flag hoisted on the mast of the admiral's ship, and committed the whole expedition to the care of Vasco da Gama.[2]

Vasco, a man of a proud and great heart, as his poet describes him, and one who gladly offered his services in great enterprises, and was always favoured by fortune, prayed, the previous night, with the monks of a church of Our Lady, and, on the morning of the 9th July, embarked on his cruise. The friends of the sailors, on seeing their sails disappear, mourned for them, saying that they would never see any one of them again. The voyagers themselves lost heart in the violent currents off the Cape, and would certainly have mutinied had it not been for Vasco's brother. Even when they had already passed it, and were cruising along the east coast of Africa, they considered themselves lost men, and their sole solace and common comfort was to pray. For many days, they saw nothing on the coast but Kaffirs, and could not comfort themselves by obtaining any intelligence. At last, beyond Cape S. Sebastian, they descried coloured men, and five days later, on the 1st of March, 1498, they were received with shouts of joy and music by other coloured men, wearing turbans, shields, and

---

[1] Osorius, de rebus gestis Emanuelis, p. 364.
[2] Navigazione di Gama in Ramusio, i. 116. Osorius, i. 26.

swords, in whom they recognized Moors, and who on their part considered them also Moors. From these they learnt that the island before them was Mozambique, and belonged to the Saracens, that voyages thence were made to India and Arabia, and that Calicut was no great distance away. On hearing this, they raised their hands to heaven and thanked God; the greater part of their work seemed now to have been accomplished. The actual discovery of the really unknown had been effected. They were again amidst their well-known enemies; but it was now for them to escape from these Moors and reach their destination.[1]

Now their subsequent adventures, how they were threatened with death at Mozambique and Mombasa, how the good Prince of Malindi refreshed them with his sweet oranges and gave them a pilot, how they again caught sight of Orion, which had not shone upon them for a long period, are known to everyone from his early years. On the 29th of May, 1498, they, a remnant of about one hundred men, the first Christians of the Latino-Teutonic stock, lifted up their hands on the coast of Malabar, and poured out their thanks to the true God; they then liberated their prisoners, loaded their pilot with gifts, and cast anchor not far from Calicut.[2]

The Moors instantly perceived the danger that threatened them, and resisted the intruders to their utmost. With great difficulty, and more as a proof that they had really been there, than as a commercial transaction, the Portuguese took some spices and precious stones away with them: they themselves were now reduced to two ships and sixty men; Vasco lost his brother Paul just before the goal; but fortune must always be dearly bought, and, as a result, the unknown coast had been explored, India had been discovered, and, on their return, their fame was noised abroad in Lisbon, and thence through Portugal, Spain and the whole of Europe, and lives on even at this present day.[3]

[1] Barros, Asia, i. iv. 1 and 2. Navigazione. Osorius, 24. Lichtenstein, Entdeckung des Vorgebirges, from Castanheda in Hormayr's Archiv für Geographie, etc., 1810, p. 636.

[2] Osorius, i. 33.

[3] Barros, i. iv. 5, 10. Osorius, ii. 40.

After this exploit, Lisbon spoke of nothing else but of the wealth of Calicut; how a load of cinnamon, ginger, pepper, and cloves, which in Venice cost more than one hundred ducats, was to be had there for ten to twenty; how dyewood grew there in bushes, and lac cost almost nothing; how pearls were fished for on an island near, and how the Arabians, who were enjoying all this wealth, were only badly equipped, and their ships easy to take. Nation and King were thus fired to energy. On the spot where Da Gama prayed previous to his departure, Dom Manuel built a far finer church, dedicated to Our Lady, and called Belem, a monastery of the Hieronymites, and a mausoleum for the kings. He styled himself lord of the commerce, navigation, and future conquests in Ethiopia, Arabia, Persia, and India. He fitted out new ships without delay.[1]

These ships were not built only for trade, but for war. For since Pedro Alvarez Cabral, of whose crew forty-five men had been killed at Calicut, and Vasco da Gama, on his second voyage, had both been so much aggravated by the Moors and the Zamorin, that they were obliged to fire on the city,[2] it was evident that nothing would be able to be effected here without war to the knife. It depended upon the issue of these wars, whether the old international intercourse should or should not exist longer. Even Manuel's counsellors sometimes doubted whether Portugal would be able to continue them, and the Venetians never conceived it possible; but those who undertook them were quite the men for the task, their valour being guaranteed by their standing as knights, by their detestation of the Moors, and by their religion; and their achievements are truly marvellous.

The most wonderful is, perhaps, the first war undertaken by Pacheco Pereira, in the year 1503, in defence of the King of Cochin, against the whole power of the Zamorin; the former, although a vassal of the Zamorin, had allowed the Portuguese to land and take in cargo, and

---

[1] Navigazione di Gama in Ramusio, 120 f.

[2] Pilotto Porteghese in Ramusio, 121. Thome Lopez, Navigazione, in Ramusio, 143.

had, in consequence, already once been driven from his throne, and with difficulty restored to it again.[1] With four kings and the heir to the Crown, and with 75,000 infantry, and 160 ships, all furnished with good guns cast by Christian refugees, the Zamorin advanced to battle. He was opposed by three ships, bound together by ropes, which blocked the ford by which he had to cross, and seventy-one Portuguese. He lashed twenty prows together with chains, in order to board one of the vessels ; he made a simultaneous attack upon the ford and the city ; he planted artillery on the bank to bombard the enemy from a distance, and built towers on his ships to destroy them from above. He himself showed dauntless courage, even when some standing at his side were laid low by the enemy's bullets; he caused the laggards to be driven forward at the point of the sword; he made vows to his gods, and selected his days. But Pacheco broke his chains with his guns, and contrived to surprise his cannon at the right moment and to spike them, whilst he kept off his towers with bowsprits and booms. Sometimes he would remain quiet, until the enemy had come to close quarters ; he would then give the signal and fire his cannon ; the result was the defeat of the enemy, and the ford red with blood. He also planted sharp stakes in the mud, on which the enemy impaled themselves. The struggle lasted five months. The enemy is said to have lost 19,000 men, whilst Pacheco's warriors scarcely lost a single one. It appeared to them a miracle. " God had fought for them : they had escaped unscathed from bullets, which rebounding from them even broke stones in pieces; when Pacheco's ship was stranded in the morass, and the enemy had already seized his rudder, had not the flood risen at his prayer and floated the ship again? Nay more, when they were in peril of the enemy's floating towers, their guns were ineffectual, until Pacheco had prayed to God not to punish their sins on that one day, as the honour of the whole of Christendom was at stake." [2]

What was here conquered, however, was, although

---

[1] Giovanni da Empoli, Viaggio, in Ramusio.
[2] Osorius, iii. f. 101-116. Barros, i. vii. 8.

incited by the Moors, only an Indian power. From this time on both sides a greater war began. On the Soldan of Egypt declaring that, " If they did not cease warring, he would destroy the grave of Christ," the Indian Moors made preparations for a vigorous resistance. Dom Manuel, on the other hand, in whose name Duarte Meneses was waging a rapid and glorious war against the Moors in Morocco, and who was also himself, on one occasion, on the point of joining personally in the campaign (for this war was none other than that which the forefathers of the nation had begun many centuries previously upon the Asturian mountains), replied to the Soldan's threat thus : " If he had hitherto injured him, he intended to inflict even more injury upon him in the future." He hoped one day to seize Mahomet's house at Mecca.[1] Da Gama once said, " Moors and Christians have, since the foundation of the world, been in arms against each other." [2] Such were the feelings which animated King and nation ; their war appeared to them a veritable crusade.

On the 25th of May, 1505, Manuel despatched twenty-two sail under Don Francisco d'Almeida ; his object was to hold the Indian seas by a fleet permanently stationed there, and to secure the coasts by forts, such as had first been built in Cochin for the defence of the prince.

Beginning with the African coast, Francisco stormed and took Quiloa and Mombasa, both by nearly the same tactics. And when another, following in his footsteps, defying the hostility of the Sheikh and the unhealthy climate, had established himself at Sofala, at the source of the gold trade, and when at Mozambique a fort had been built without opposition, the coast throughout its whole length was in their hands. The Prince of Malindi was devoted to their cause.[3]

The arrival of Almeida brought joy and consternation in India ; joy to the enemies of the Moors, and not only to the Prince of Cochin, who received a golden crown from Almeida's hands, but also especially to the great King of

---

[1] Osorius, iv. 124. Manuel's letter to the Pope in Osorius.

[2] Thome Lopez, 138.

[3] Barros, i. viii. c. 4, 5, 6.

Narsinga, whose realm on the highlands of the Malabar peninsula extended as far as Coromandel, and from Comorin far northwards, who once had caused 10,000 Moors to be put to death on the same day, and who now offered one of his daughters as a wife to Manuel's son;[1] consternation to Calicut and the Moors themselves.

The first to bring the tidings were two Persian merchants. "Bad news," they said; "with our own eyes we have seen twelve ships, all full of Christians armed with glittering weapons." Hereupon the Moslems were summoned from their minarets to prayer; after having prayed, they fitted out eighty-four large vessels and 104 prows.[2] Lourenço, Francisco's son, was stationed with eleven sail not far from Cranganore, when they advanced to attack him; their masts were like a thick wood, their garments red, and they were armed with bows, swords, muskets, and cannon. Lourenço addressed his men saying, "Sirs, brothers, to-day is a day on which our Lord will receive some of us into His holy glory." He let them eat, until the Moors were on them. He then said, "Now, my brethren, let us prove ourselves good knights." Thereupon he attacked the enemy's leading ship, grappled it, and sprang on board. His example was followed by others. Simon Martin sprang single-handed amongst fifteen Moors, and shouted, "Now, Christ, defend Thy faith;" he slew seven, and drove the remainder overboard. As soon as their two leading ships were taken, the Moors fled as one man. Lourenço, seeing the great spoils that were his and his ships undamaged, exclaimed, "Praised be Jesus Christ;" and built a chapel on the shore in honour of Our Lady of Victories.

Thus did the Portuguese fight, and thus their enemies. The Moors now, full of shame, hatred, and dismay, went about in great bands; they shaved their heads and chins, and bound themselves together under terrible oaths. "They would now either conquer or die." They awaited their enemy in the harbour of Panian, under the cover of their

[1] Barbosa and Osorius.
[2] Lodovico Barthema, Itinerario, iii. c. 34, 35, 37, fol. 107 f. Osorius, v. f. 166.

batteries. One morning, two hours before daybreak, the Christians under Francisco and Lourenço were, before their very eyes, gathered, one and all, around the admiral's ship; a priest raised a great cross on high, and pronounced absolution and blessing upon all assembled. Many prayed to be permitted that day to enter into the glory of God. This scene lasted but a moment; the next, they separated and made for the shore. The first who reached it were thrust back. Then came Lourenço, a youth who would rather burn his booty than give it away under the price he demanded, but who, in spite of this obstinacy, was quite obedient to his father; tall, and splendid of stature, he was the first to spring on land. A Moor wounded him in the arm; but Lourenço replied by cleaving him asunder at one stroke, from the head to the breast. His father then, the royal ensign in his hand, came to his assistance. The victory was theirs. Francisco did not accede to the wishes of his soldiery to sack the city, for he knew that a strong enemy was in the vicinity, only waiting for them to begin the pillage. He himself threw the torches into the city to fire it.[1]

By this second battle of the Portuguese in India, the Moors also were vanquished. The forts in Cranganore, Cochin, and for the present, at all events, upon the Angedives, as well as a victorious fleet cruising off the shore, kept the greater part of the coast of the Indian Peninsula in subjection to them.

The Arabian coast northwards and Eastern India still remained; they next turned their attention to both of these. In 1507, they took the Arabian fortress of Sokotra, lying at the entrance of the Gulf of Aden; and Albuquerque succeeded in building a fort at Hormuz, and in compelling the prince to pay 15,000 ducats tribute. The King of Colombo in Ceylon was forced to pay them 15,000 pounds of cinnamon, as an annual tribute.[2] The terror spread by their deeds paralyzed the people. Before Cannanore the inhabitants saw a Portuguese slay sixteen to eighteen of the enemy each day. They said, " Is it a Frank? Is it a god

---

[1] Barthema, iii. 40. Barros, ii. i. c. 6.

[2] Barros, Dec. ii. i. cap. 3 ; ii. cap. 1-4.

of the Franks? It is *the* god of the Franks, and he is stronger than our gods." [1]

Now, although these events had quite another object than the advantage or detriment of Venice, yet it is certain that their effect upon the community of our nations was principally made important by the change in trade.

It was not until 1503 that Portuguese merchants came to Antwerp, and offered their wares to German houses. Nicholas Rechtergem is said to have been the first to enter into an arrangement with them, and, after him, the houses of Fugger, Welser, and Osterett. [2]   The South Germans were much surprised when the wares they were otherwise in the habit of sending to the Netherlands were now brought to them from there; for they were soon convinced that they were genuine. As a result, we find Augsburg now taking the lead among German cities; [3] and of German commercial houses, that of Fugger, which in the year 1506, owing to Maximilian's good offices, sent three ships of its own to India, [4] rose to pre-eminence, whilst in the Netherlands Bruges was displaced by Antwerp. The German trade with Venice decreased. In Italy itself, the Florentine houses, such as the Marchioni, participated directly in the new shipping trade. [5]   In Venice, the effect of this was at once felt.

Many other things also combined at this time. The Turkish war and the new ordinances of the Soldan of Egypt had already seriously damaged their commerce. In the year 1499, many houses on the Rialto went bankrupt at the same time, whilst others suffered in credit. A load of pepper, which in Calicut cost about ten ducats and was sold in Venice for forty, rose to one hundred and ten. How great was the panic then, when, in the year 1502, the news came that four barks had arrived at Lisbon bringing spices direct from Calicut. [6]   In a moment, the price of

---

[1] Barthema, iii. c. 39.

[2] Ludovicus Guicciardini, Descriptio Belgii, p. 164.

[3] Gasser, Augsburger Chronik, 259.

[4] Ehrenspiegel, 1269. Peutingeri, Sermones conviviales ap. Schardium, i. 202.

[5] Giovanni da Empoli, Viaggio, p. 145.

[6] Diarium Ferrarense, pp. 365, 380.

spices fell, to the great detriment of the Venetians. They had comforted themselves for a long time with the hope that King Manuel would not be able to bear the expenses of his campaigns, and would at last succumb to his numerous foes. Whenever a bark was lost, the news was announced to them from Cairo as though a victory had been won.[1]

In 1507, after Almeida's brilliant victories, the Zamorin, the Zabai of Goa, and the Prince of Cambay, all sent to the Soldan Khan Hassan of Egypt, imploring help ; and the latter, in order to save the intermediate trade between Asia and Europe, in which his whole wealth consisted, determined to assist them. Then there broke out immediately a great war of the Indians, and the Indian and Egyptian Moors against the Portuguese, and the Venetians hoped once more that the power of Portugal would be destroyed. Their own fortune, or misfortune, depended upon the issue of this undertaking, which would either destroy the Portuguese shipping trade, or prevent both Moors and Indians from ever again molesting them. The Venetians themselves engaged in it. They sent metal and gun-founders, as well as shipwrights, to the Soldan of Egypt, to whom in any case they paid tribute.[2] The fleet which the Soldan fitted out at Suez, and despatched under Mir Hossein, was manned in part by Venetians and Dalmatians.[3] His victory and his loss was their victory and loss also. Their maritime life and their command of the seas were alike dependent upon the issue that was to be fought out in India in the year 1508.[4]

[1] Machiavelli, Legazione al duca Valentino, lett. 25. Opp. iv. 202. Sandi, Storia Civile, vii. 91 (note to 2nd edition).

[2] Tentori, Saggio, ii. 135.

[3] Zurita, i. f. 342.

[4] Osorius, vi. 196

4. MAXIMILIAN'S ATTACK. FORMATION OF THE LEAGUE OF CAMBRAY AGAINST THE CONQUESTS OF THE VENETIANS.

In a description of Italy dating from these times,[1] the Venetian possessions are never referred to, save under the name of the prince from whom they had been taken: "the city acknowledges no superior; all her possessions she has robbed from her neighbours."

This was the sentiment animating Louis XII and Maximilian, on the occasion of their first league at Trent, and on that of their second with Julius at Blois, when they resolved to conquer what belonged to them of the Venetian territory. And just now, when the existence or destruction of the Venetian trade in India was at stake, a third league was concluded with the same object in view, a league which in truth imperilled all their acquisitions.

In the summer of 1507, Maximilian held a Diet at Constance. His object was to obtain aid against Louis, and resources sufficient to enable him to invade Italy. "Seeing that Louis had broken all compacts, his investiture of Milan was void; moreover, as he intended to depose the Pope and to endanger the imperial dignity of the German nation, the Empire was bound to attack him." [2] After the King of France had allowed his party to fall to pieces through sheer negligence, he was unable to form another immediately, and, besides this, his envoy at Constance had been made prisoner. Maximilian made these concessions: that the Cameral Tribunal should be paid by the Estates—the origin of the sole permanent imperial tax that has ever existed [3]—and that a deputation of the Empire should control the forces, money, and conquests of the

[1] Descriptio Italiae, in Ludewig, Reliquiae MSS., tom. x. p. 426; according to p. 437, written between Charles VIII's and Louis XII's operations against Italy; translated into Latin, 1540.

[2] Vindication of Maximilian in Goldast, Reichshandlung, 53. See also Spalatin, Leben Friedrichs des Weisen, in the Sammlungen zür sächsischen Geschichte, at end.

[3] Pütter, Entwickelung der Reichsverfassung, i. 313.

Empire; in return for these concessions, he obtained an aid of 12,000 men and 120,000 guilders for six months.[1]

Moreover, on this occasion he might expect from the Swiss not merely no resistance, but even support. Their envoys walked about at Constance in the mantles he had given them, were sometimes guests at his table, and received presents of silver goblets from him. The council of Zürich voted him 6,000 men, and at once arranged what contingent each canton should furnish.[2] Towards the beginning of the year 1508, Maximilian came to Trent. At the first report of his arrival, the Ghibellines in Italy became so active, that it was deemed wise to send many of them to France. The Florentines, who were at a distance, and were besides not weak in themselves, were under French protection; yet they sent in advance to conclude a compact with him.[3]

Fate willed it that Maximilian, whilst intending a Milanese war, embarked upon one with Venice.

The negotiations with the Venetian envoys at Constance led to no result. Was it likely that they would be willing to allow a man who had so often intended to rob them, and who had shortly before wrested Görz from them—the last count, their vassal, at whose decease it would have devolved upon them, had, in his old age, bartered it away to Maximilian—was it probable that they would be willing to permit him and his great army to march through their passes?[4] Accordingly, now that Venice was leagued with France against him, he resolved to attack that enemy which was less capable of resistance, and less dangerous to himself, in the event of his being attacked. On the 4th February, 1508,[5] at Trent, his heralds leading the way, and he himself following sword in hand, Maximilian held a great procession, and, with the concurrence of the Papal envoy, adopted the new title of Roman Emperor Elect, a title until then unknown.

---

[1] Müller's Reichstagsstaat, 643. Proceedings therein, 662.

[2] Report of the Diet of Constance in Ehrenspiegel, 1237; in Fuchs, Mailänd. Feldzüge, 71, 79.

[3] Florus de bello Italico, 53. Vettori's Report of the Embassy in Machiavelli's Legazioni.

[4] Müller, Reichstagsstaat, 649. Chronicon Venetum in Muratori, xxiv. 155.

[5] Cf. Deutsche Geschichte, vol. i. p. 348 (note to 2nd edition).

This he did, doubtless, in order to be able, as was actually done the same day, to arraign and condemn the Venetians, with all the greater show of right.[1] That very day, bread was baked for the army, and provisions were sent down the Adige. In the evening, the soldiers were ordered to hold themselves in readiness. The next morning early, at three o'clock, the trumpets sounded, and the march began. The Emperor advanced with 4,000 infantry, and 1,500 horses, up the mountains of Asiago, in the direction of Vicenza. He had with him a Vicentine emigrant, Leonardo Trissino. He took the intrenchments of the Sette Communi, and received the allegiance, at any rate to some extent and sufficiently to allow his passage, of half the mountain chain, where it sinks down to the Adriatic from the chalk hills between Monte Matajur and S. Pellegrino. On his right, Friedrich of Brandenburg marched down the Adige with 2,500 men, and besieged Roveredo. On his left, the army of Erich of Brunswick-Calenberg, with climbing-irons on their feet, descended from the hills, took Cadore, and advanced forty miles. All betokened a splendid result, and Loredano, Doge of Venice, no longer peremptorily prohibited the imperial envoys from passing through.[2] Yet, in the midst of his success, the Emperor suddenly stopped, before he had even reached Vicenza, and carefully closing the seven passes into his own country from the Isonzo to the Adige,[3] returned to Innsbruck and Ulm.

The reason was this : the French party in Switzerland had contrived, through the mediation of two envoys from Louis, after many contradictory resolutions, to gain entirely the upper hand.[4] As to the means which the French envoys adopted to attain their ends, we learn that one of them, Rocquebertin, once defrayed the expenses of all the strangers in Baden, and, besides this, kept open house

---

[1] Chief passage in Vettori's letter in the Legazioni of Machiavelli, v. 212. Proclamation to the Empire in Datt, de pace publica, 569.

[2] Vettori, up to 215. Second report to the Empire in Datt, 571 ; and letter of 4th March, 1508. Bembus, p. 160.

[3] Göbel, Chronica von den Kriegsthaten Kaiser Maximilians. From beginning.

[4] Passages from Anshelm, Bullinger, Tschudi MSS. in Fuchs, 98 f.

daily; the other, the Bishop of Roeux, once paid in
Lucerne the reckonings of all the peasants who had come
to market.[1] In the very midst of his operations against
Venice, Maximilian heard the resolution of the Swiss, of the
25th January, which ran as follows: "if he injured the
French king, he would force them to be mindful of their
obligations to him," these words being a direct threat
levelled at himself.[2] For how easily Louis could interpret
an attack directed against his allies as one against himself,
and how easily again kindle a war against the Emperor, as he
did in the year 1500! In March, the six months, for which
period the Empire had voted the supplies, expired. With
these thoughts he turned round and addressed himself first
to the Swabian League: "They had to fear an attack upon
the Tyrol, a member of their League, the perpetual estrangement of Allgau and Wallgau from the German nation, and
after that the revolt of Flanders and Gelderland, of Liège and
Utrecht; the assistance of the League, if it would support
the German confederates against the French with money
and arms, might save everything." [3]

If danger threatened here, his advent averted it. The
deputies of the Empire, at all events, voted him assistance
for six months longer,[4] and although the aid was but irregu-
larly paid—for the matricula, which in much later times
was still incorrectly made and contained the names of
mediate states as though they were immediate, must have
been inaccurate at that time also—it was still considerable.
With the Swiss he entered into fresh negotiations. Meanwhile another danger threatened. As he had intended a
French war, and undertaken one against Venice, so now
the danger threatening him did not come from France and
Switzerland, as he had feared, but from Venice, which he
did not fear.

The first move was made on Cadore by Bartolommeo
d'Alviano, Captain of the Signoria, against Sixt Trautson,
the commander there. The Emperor had bidden him pull
down the houses in the valley, and barricade himself.

---

[1] Various decrees in Fuchs, 93, 102, 104, 106, 111.
[2] Decree in Fuchs, Datt, Göbel, Dumont, iv. 1, 90.
[3] Letter in Datt, 572, f.   [4] Vettori, 230.

Trautson thought that mountains and snow were sufficient to protect him.[1] But Alviano sought him out through snow and defiles, surrounded him above with peasants, who pelted him with stones, and below with soldiers who attacked him with fire-arms, overcame his gallant band who preferred death to surrender, and captured Cadore.[2] Then Alviano looked further afield. All the passes, except that of Görz, were strongly defended. Then Hans Aursperg wrote to the Princes of Brandenburg and Brunswick, who were in the Pusterthal and at Trent, that, "with his Carniolans he was much too weak to hold this great broad road; but that they, on the other hand, were almost too well furnished with troopers and cannon for their narrow passes: they should come to his assistance."[3]

The Princes, though warned, paid no attention to the summons. Alviano knew how to take advantage of his opportunity. He had 10,000 Venetians, French, and Spaniards, took guns and scaling ladders with him, and on the 9th April, 1508, fell upon the Görz road, and first upon Kramaun, and stormed it. The country was unprotected, the inhabitants servile and discouraged, accustomed to look upon the Signoria of Venice as their suzerain. The danger was imminent. Letters were hurriedly sent to all their neighbours: "Help, speed, haste, only haste! How can the poor walls of Görz withstand their cannon? Trieste, the Karst, and the whole of Austria will soon be lost. Let us not be destroyed by these Italians."[4] Forthwith a summons was sent through Carinthia, Styria and Carniola: "every man must be ready with armour and weapons, as soon as he heard the bells ring and shots fired, otherwise not only the houses but the churches would be in danger" —the lonely churches which these people love.[5] But the Carinthians replied: "the 700 men in their passes, with the horses of the country, were their hope and defence, and

---

[1] Instruction of Maximilian in Göbel, f. 1, and letter to Trent, f. 5.
[2] Naugerii Oratio de Alviano, 3, 4; Vettori, 232.
[3] Aursperg to the princes in Göbel, f. 28 and 36.
[4] Three more letters of Aursperg, f. 38, 43, 45.
[5] Two summonses of Erich of Brunswick, 45, 46.

these could not be dispensed with." The Styrians replied: "they were threatened by the Hungarians." The Carniolans, whose nobles were equipped with 200 horses, said that, " they required the help of more experienced soldiers to save them; if the nobles meant to compel them, without bringing such troops into the field, they would rather strike them dead." Only Erich came with 1,400 men, but even he did not venture into the open field, " for he was much too weak for that." [1]

Thus it happened that, on Easter Eve, after Andreas Lichtenstein had held out in the crumbling walls of Görz a day longer than he had promised, and had repulsed an assault, he was obliged to surrender.

Immediately after, Wippach and Duino fell. When the people of Trieste saw for the third time a ship of the Venetian fleet approach before their eyes with a white flag, and their garrison again open fire, they murmured together, " that was a bad business; for 100 years past they had lived under the protection of Austria, and would still continue so to live; but they must have assistance." While they were being bombarded from the sea, they saw Bartolommeo approach from the land, and no help being visible they surrendered, and bought themselves free from pillage. Hans Thur still held out for a while upon the almost inaccessible rocks of Mitterburg, and Hans Räuber in S. Veit am Pflaum; but they also called in vain for men and weapons and they too surrendered. Portenau had long since fallen, and the garrison was seen flying to Laibach. In this general disaster, only Bernhardt Reiniger on the Adelsberg showed real German courage. He scattered the first horsemen who approached looking for plunder. He took Savorgnano prisoner, shortly before the end of his victories. His castle fired and in ruins, he accepted safe conduct, and marched away. [2]

What Aursperg had said, was fulfilled to the letter. The Germans had lost forty-seven good towns.

---

[1] Replies of the Carinthians, 65; of Reichenburg, 76; and of Aursperg, 65, to Erich, and his Letter, f. 79.

[2] Letter of the Kriegsräthe, 69; of the people of Trieste, 71; and of Thur and Räuber, 72, 75. Bembus, 164–166.

Maximilian, meanwhile, was journeying dejectedly up and down the Rhine.[1] Not only had the attack upon Venice proved so disastrous for him, but also on the Lower Rhine Charles of Gelderland, since the breach with France, was waging a successful campaign against him. At one time he was encamped in the strong Castle of Pouderoyen, at the confluence of the Waal and the Maas, whence he had levied toll upon seventy-two villages and upon all the ships in the rivers ; at another time he would ride through a rainy night upon bad roads, appear the next morning before a distant town, and fire it. In this way Weesp was burnt. The prophecy of their mermaid, "Muiden shall remain Muiden," availed the inhabitants of that city nought on this occasion, and it too was taken. In short, the Duke of Gelderland kept the whole of the Netherlands in terror.[2] And, in addition to all this, Maximilian was filled with the greatest fear of all—the fear of an insurrection in the Empire.[3]

For one moment he must take breath. Whilst then the Prince of Anhalt succeeded at this crisis in seizing Pouderoyen,[4] he directed his military operations against Gelderland alone, and ordered the Bishop of Trent to conclude a truce with Venice.

Some of the elders of the Venetian Senate had frequently, but vainly, warned their fellows that "it was sufficient to act on the defensive ; to attack would only arouse new enemies." Not therein alone did the difficulty of their position consist, but in the entanglement of their relations with the Great Powers. Louis XII, who regarded the war in the Alps and in the Netherlands as one single affair, both parts being connected through his influence in Switzerland, demanded that Venice should include Gelderland in the truce. Friends who were advantageously situated should protect him who was at a disadvantage. But to this the Venetians refused to agree. It is perhaps the grandest

---

[1] Diary of 1508, in Hormayr's Oesterreich. Plutarch, v.

[2] Hermannus, Bellum Gelricum in. Matthaei Analecta Medii Aevi, i. 503–523.

[3] Letter of Maximilian in Datt, 575.

[4] Letter of Maxim. in Beckmann's Anhaltische Chronik, v. ii. 128.

moment in their policy, that, after having overcome the Emperor, they refused to listen to the demands of France. They could not be prevailed upon to do more than restore Adelsberg to the Emperor : for the rest a truce was granted them for three years.[1] Maximilian, of course, felt himself terribly aggrieved, but Louis almost equally so, as the Venetians had refused him that consideration to which the services rendered them would appear to entitle him. And thus it came about, that Maximilian and Louis, between whom the struggle that had just burst forth principally lay, drew closer together. In July, 1508, Maximilian went to Hertogenbosch, and then to his daughter and grandchildren. Negotiations were entered into between Cardinal d'Amboise and Maximilian's daughter, Margaret ; they were, however, rendered difficult owing to Maximilian's refusal to desist from attacking Gelderland, while Louis, on the other hand, would not be restrained from an attack on Navarre. Margaret said her head ached from the business.[2] But at last an understanding was arrived at. Muiden and Weesp were restored to the Emperor, whilst the King was guaranteed the renewal of his Milanese investiture. Maximilian desisted from his schemes upon Gelderland, and Louis from his against Navarre. But the main outcome was this ; they resolved upon a joint attack upon Venice, by which they considered themselves aggrieved. Thus arose, the League of Cambray, concluded on the 10th December, 1508. It was an alliance of the two powerful princes against a city, which had the audacity to take up an independent position between them. All princes who had any claims upon Venice, or rather upon its lands and possessions, were to be invited to join in the operations. The frontiers of Milan and Naples were to be readjusted in favour of Louis and Ferdinand, those of the Empire and Austria in favour of Maximilian, and those of the States of the Church in favour of the Pope.[3] In this arrangement, the erroneous, but, as appears from

---

[1] Bembus, Histor. Venet., 167. Seissel, L'Excellence de la victoire d'Aignadel in Godefroy's collection for Louis XII, p. 268.

[2] Margaret to Maximilian, in the Lettres de Louis, i. 134, f.

[3] Treaty in Dumont, iv. 110-115.

the above-quoted description of Italy,[1] popular idea was followed, that Padua, Vicenza, and Verona primarily belonged to the Empire, to which they were consequently assigned.

True, Maximilian could not possibly change his loss into gain on the one side, and attain a victory on the other, more easily than by entering into this League. He was the first to swear the compact of Cambray. Then Louis affixed his seal to it in the palace of Bourges, after sermon and mass ; he showed himself very much delighted. An old plan had now ripened to accomplishment. Ferdinand delayed until March, 1509 ; he then laid his hand on the altar, and swore it by the Holy Eucharist.[2] The Pope unwillingly resorted to this extreme measure, often as he had threatened to do so, and although he had always incited Emperor and King to it. He went once more with the Venetian ambassador, Giorgio Pisani, to Città Vecchia. The sea was tranquil, only a light breeze filled the sails ; he was lively and kindly disposed. He thought if only vassals were placed in his cities, like the Malatesta, he could endure this, and spare Italy this war. He proposed this course to the ambassador. Pisani coldly and proudly replied : " It is not our habit to make kings," and did not even announce the proposal to Venice. Thereupon Julius also ratified the League, pronounced his ban upon Doge, senate, and subjects of Venice ; ordered his nephew, Francesco Maria, the young Duke of Urbino—for Guidobaldo was dead—into the field, and prepared for the struggle.[3]

5. FALL OF THE POWER AND TRADE OF THE VENETIANS IN 1509.

Thus the very existence of Venice was in extreme jeopardy. Her trade depended upon the relations between Asia and Europe, and now, in India, Portuguese and Moors

[1] Descriptio, 435.

[2] Gattinara's reports to the Austrian Court ; Lettres de Louis, i. 167, and Petri Martyris Epistolae, 410.

[3] Declaration to the League, p. 116. Bembus, 173. Rainaldus, Annales Eccl., xx. 65.

were engaged in a deadly struggle as to whether these should last longer or not. The acquisitions of Venice were due to the feuds of her neighbours, and now her neighbours had leagued together more powerfully than ever before to wrest her conquests from her. The first struggle was, for the most part, in foreign lands, the second in their own, and to this latter they devoted their whole strength, and were self-confident enough not to fear the issue.

As a matter of fact, the League was not as powerful as it appeared. Maximilian and Julius had both misgivings as to Louis, the first on account of Gelderland, and the latter on account of Amboise's old schemes. Louis and Ferdinand, on the other hand, were afraid of Maximilian; the former for Milan, the latter for Naples.[1] They were negotiating, and had concluded alliances against each other, even before their common League was carried into effect.

Should it not, then, have been possible for the Venetians to detach one or other from such an alliance? It must be confessed that, had they succeeded, they would have profited but little; besides which, Ferdinand never moved a finger until all was settled. At the beginning of April, Maximilian was at Xanten, instead of at Trent. The Venetians were not frightened by the Papal preparations: the only enemy they really feared was Louis—that Louis whom they themselves had invited to Italy. To gain him over, appeared to them perhaps unfeasible, and, it might be, not even to their advantage.

If we inquire what had really incited Louis against Venice, we shall at once perceive that it was not the election of Julius to the Papal chair in the stead of Amboise; for the share Amboise himself had in this election is much more certain than that of Venice. He must have had other reasons, which indeed had already been evident on several occasions. In the year 1501, he was impelled, as it appears, by nothing but his right, which he had from the Visconti; in 1504, by the open assistance the Venetians afforded the Spaniards; and, at present, the irritating factor was the truce they had concluded with Maximilian, without regard being paid to his demands. The hatred ever cherished by the prince and

[1] Lettres de Louis, i. 161. Zurita, ii. 178.

the nobles against the powerful communes was also a very powerful factor. " These fishermen," they said, " must be driven back again into their lagoons to catch fish." [1]   And thus Montjoye, the first French king-at-arms, appeared in his cotte, embroidered with golden lilies, on the threshold of the great hall in Venice, and there proclaimed war upon the Republic; war for life and death, with fire and sword, on land and sea, until the lands, which they had torn from others, were completely restored.[2]

"Sir herald," replied Loredano to Montjoye, " God, whom no one can deceive, will decide between us." Their envoy in France said: " the world will see whether brute force or intellect will be triumphant." [3] It was sure to come to a struggle between them one day, and it was probably in anticipation thereof, that they had summoned the French to Italy. Many entertained the hope that a glorious victory would be theirs, and Italy at last ridded of them.

With this thought they equipped and prepared for action. All the most tried knights of Italy—for the last glory of their country was at stake—entered into their service and formed their heavy cavalry.[4] From Apulia and the Romagna came their infantry, the best being that formed by Dionigi di Naldi, a party-leader in the Val di Lamone, from the inhabitants of this valley, and so well disciplined, that other companies also were organized after their pattern, dressed in red and green, and called Brisignels.[5] For the peasants and citizens, a kind of militia had been already organized. The coasts of Illyria, the Peloponnese, the Ægean sea, and the Hellespont sent light Greek horse. Half savage archers, the Sagdars, came from Crete.[6]

The supreme commander of this force was Pitigliano, a man who had never yet made a resolve, much less carried

[1] Chaumont's words in Machiavelli, Legazione alla corte di Francia, 1504.

[2] Garnier, Histoire de France, xxii. 163, and Daru, Hist. de Venise, iii.

[3] Fleuranges, Mémoires, 48.

[4] Senarega, de rebus Genuensibus, 596.

[5] Bayard, 133. Note to Machiavelli, Opp. iii. p. 6, from MSS.

[6] Bembus, 157.   Mocenicus, Historia belli Cameriacensis, in Graevius, v. 4, 9.

out any action, unless the stars were propitious, and whom years—he was already over sixty—had made still more circumspect.[1] His lieutenant, Alviano, commanded the infantry. Of constellations the latter knew this much, that Mars was in the highest heaven when he was cut from his mother's body. He was small of stature and weakly in appearance, but yet had slain bears; his troops sometimes mocked at his figure, but he held them so firmly in control, that not even a baggage boy would dare to desert the standard. His decisions sometimes looked like violence of temper, and his punishments seemed cruel; but afterwards, when he had cooled down, he was gentle and generous, and master of himself. By nature he was boldest of the bold.[2] Many ascribed to him Gonzalvo's victory on the Garigliano, and as he had conquered Istria and Görz, his renown was fresher, and his fame greater than that of Pitigliano. Only in one thing did both agree, that Pitigliano was justly proud of having never served a foreign prince, and that Alviano conceived that he would now be able to defend Italy from the barbarians. He of the two had the bolder hopes. "If he might give reins to his horse and outrun the train and transport of his army, he would have Milan within three days. Had he not driven the French out of Naples? Now the King was coming; but he would bring him back a prisoner to Venice." He had with him an ensign, upon which was emblazoned a winged lion tearing an eagle. His cry was "Italy, freedom."[3]

But we must remember that all were not as sanguine as he was. Many thought that they ought to be satisfied, if, perhaps, Cesena and Imola were captured from the Pope, and Genoa was roused by the Fregosi to revolt. The Signoria ordered that the attack be awaited behind intrenchments, and the campaign restricted to sending assistance to places attacked. Amongst the people there was a

---

[1] Alexander Benedictus, de rebus Caroli, p. 1617.

[2] Jovius, Elogium virorum bellica virtute illustrium, p. 219, from Alviano's Commentaries. Navagerus, Oratio de Alviano, pp. 5, 6, etc.

[3] Arluni, de bello Veneto, ii. 57. Seissel, L'Excellence, etc., 308. Senarega. Ehrenspiegel.

presentiment that some disaster was approaching. A great conflagration, which at that time burnt down the arsenal, was regarded as a heaven-sent sign. But more still was said to have happened. The Virgin Mary was said to have been seen in the sea sitting on a log and saying, "Weep, country, weep."[1]

In April, 1509, the war commenced. The French soon crossed the Adda crying "France," and then came the Venetians with their cry of "Libertà." Then the French attacked Treviglio, the Mantuans, who as well as the Ferrarese had joined the league, Casalmaggiore, and the Papal troops, Brisighella, and all three places fell. But, as they pushed on further, the first two were repulsed, and only the Papal troops succeeded in taking Russi. But the Venetians did not trouble themselves about the Papal army; they attacked the French with great fury. In Rivolta they drove out all who appeared to them to be suspicious, boys of fifteen and old men of seventy; they then marched upon Treviglio, eager for pillage, though it was in their own country.[2]

King Louis was at Milan, and intended remaining there two days, when, late in the night, Trivulzio came to him from the Adda with the tidings that "Treviglio was being bombarded, and torches were being incessantly waved from the walls, as a sign that it could barely hold out; but he felt himself too weak to save it." The King assembled his hommes d'armes in the morning, rode in full armour and with joyful looks through their lines, and set out.[3] On the way thither he learned that the White Knight, his commander in Treviglio, had been made prisoner, and that the city was lost; the citizens who, having been plundered and expelled by the Venetians, who spared neither nuns nor the Holy Sacrament, were seeking for shelter in Milan, came to meet him. He pressed on; on the 6th of May he transported his soldiers across the Adda, on two bridges

---

[1] Joh. P. Vallerianus, Carmen ad Sabellicum, in Roscoe, App. i. 586.
[2] Petrus Martyr, Epp., ep. 413. Especially Coelius Rhodiginus, Lectiones antiquae, v. 190.
[3] Rosmini, Vita di Trivulzio, i. 392. Arluni, 63. Seissel, 299.

of boats, the one for the infantry and the other for the horse, and confronted the enemy ;[1] he in the valley, they on the high ground. He could thus either attack the foe in their camp or force them to come down into the valley. The camp, however, was too strong to be taken by assault, and for four days he tried to induce them to come down by skirmishes ; on the fifth day, the King went to attack the towns in the rear of the enemy. He took Rivolta, and on Monday, the 14th of May, advanced upon Pandino. The roll of his army showed a strength of 28,232 men ; the first division was commanded by Chaumont, the second by the King in person, and the third by Longueville.[2] Thus had come about the situation which the Venetian Signoria had arranged beforehand, and Alviano's thirst for battle could no longer be restrained. "What use is a soldier to a country if he allows it to be pillaged?" Therefore, whilst the French slowly advanced along the valley of the Adda, the Venetians, 33,000 men strong, hurried along the shorter road over the high ground, in order to anticipate them by arriving first at Pandino. It cannot be denied that arms rule the world, and the result of centuries of wisdom depends upon the issue of a single battle. Just where their two roads met, Alviano and the first French division caught sight of each other, and the French began the attack.

Alviano, eager for the fray as soon as the first shots had been fired, being under the impression that the first division formed the King's whole army, and wishing to protect his rear and flank from the attacking enemy, planted his thirty-six guns in the brushwood, and summoning Pitigliano to his assistance, hurled himself with his infantry through the vineyards and over the ditches at the enemy. The French gave way. Chaumont sent to the King, saying : "Sire, you must fight." Louis immediately sent Bourbon and La Trémouille to his aid ; behind them, sword in hand, and surrounded by princes and pensioners, came the King himself; then the standards waved and the rest of the army came up. It was in the midst of a thunderstorm, and the

[1] Symphorian Champier, in Godefroy, 338. Bayard, 133.
[2] Bembus, 184-186. Champier's muster-roll, 344 354.

rain falling like hail appears to have concealed the arrival
of the King from the Venetians. But as soon as they saw
him—I can imagine that the lightning every now and then
burst through the gloom and shone on the steel armour,
illuminating the field of battle—when they realized that the
enemy was receiving assistance, their courage sank. Yet,
for a while, the Brisignels gallantly withstood the charge of
the King's Swiss and Gascons. With them lay the issue.
It was upon peasants and shepherds from the high valleys
of the Alps, the Apennines and the Pyrenees, that the fate
of Venice depended. What did it matter to them? They
were only bent on plunder. Now the Italians had their
booty with them from Treviglio, and their sole care was to
secure it, if not by victory, then by flight at the right time.
The French and Germans had gained no booty, and were,
therefore, all the more eager to obtain it; so it happened
that the Brisignels were driven back. Alviano, in the thick
of the fray, was wounded just as he was about to exchange
his tired steed for a fresh one, and was immediately taken
prisoner. All his troops fled, and communicating their
terror to Pitigliano's men, to whom they had not been able
to communicate their lust of battle, turned them also to
flight. The day was completely lost. The King gazed on
the great number of fallen and vowed a chapel to Our
Lady of Victories for the repose of their souls.[1]

According to most accounts, Alviano commanded the
last of four columns, and the others were too far ahead
to come to his assistance.[2] Others say that the first and
attacking column was under Alviano's command, but that
Pitigliano, who had quarrelled with him in Treviglio, looked
on at the battle from the hills, and would not stir to help
him.[3] That Pitigliano was in the rear, seems to be confirmed by the retreat, which took the road to Caravaggio;
had he been in front towards Crema, he would not have

---

[1] St. Gelais, Histoire de Louis XII, 213-215. Champier, 340.
Leferron, iv. 87. Fleuranges, Mémoires, 47. Bembus, 188.

[2] Bembus, Guicciardini, Petrus Martyr, 416. Many others.

[3] Nardi, iv. 23. Appendix to Monstrelet, 240. Arluni, 69.
Especially Coelius Rhodiginus, Lectiones antiquae, 190, and Carpesanus,
1264.

fled back, that is, upon the very swords of the victorious enemy.[1]

Pitigliano alone now endeavoured, though in vain, to rally his soldiers round the standard. They had lost their fame; but they would not lose their lives and booty as well. Some would not place their names again upon the rolls; some did so, received fresh pay, and then fled. The citizens of Brescia refused to be burdened with an army such as this; they would only receive such of their men as were amongst them. In Peschiera, the army despaired of holding together; it found the gates of Verona closed against it, and, having for a while bivouacked upon the plain, took its way to Mestre, on the coast.

Louis pursued the fugitives. The castle of Caravaggio held out three days; all other places surrendered at the first blast of the trumpet. In Brescia, the King rode up the steps into the upper court of the palace without meeting with resistance, and it was only Peschiera that needed to be stormed.[2] The inhabitants of Ferrara rang their bells, drove out the Visdomino, and retook the Polesina. The Pope proclaimed the victory in an Italian sermon, and occupied Rimini and Faenza. The Germans appeared on the Lago di Garda, in Friuli and beyond Vicenza. Many advised King Louis to press on to the coast, and crown his triumph by utterly destroying Venice.[3]

In Venice itself, when, after Alviano's many letters, all promising victory, the news of this great disaster arrived, the Senate speedily assembled, the merchants closed their shops, the monks, mindful of the Pope's ban, fled, and the people, crying aloud, surrounded the palace. The remnant of the army, 6,000 strong, had no inclination to fight more. Thereupon the Doge invited Pietro Barbo, an old, sick

---

[1] In the letters of Luigi da Porto (Lettere Storiche di Luigi da Porto Vicentino per cura di Bressan), which appeared in 1857, and which cannot properly be regarded as letters, but as a history, in the form of letters, of the years 1509-13, all is ascribed to fate: "che avea disposto il cielo, che uno esercito possente a vincere, e combattendo anche con gran valore, dall' inimico così tosto e compiutamente battuto" (p. 36).

[2] Mocenicus, 16. Petrus Justinianus, Rerum Venetarum libri, p. 375.

[3] Paris de Grassis ap. Rainaldum, 68, and the authorities cited.

man, to the council; he had not attended the sittings of the
Senate for a long time past, but he now put on his official
dress, and was carried in a litter into the hall; yet he
could give no other advice, but to trust in God's protection.
Matteo Priuli was the first to propose that they should give
up the subject towns.   This proposal was adopted : " Thus
does a skipper throw cargo overboard to save his ship."
Twelve men now examined the coast, to see where precautions against an attack were insufficient ; orders were
despatched to Cyprus to open all the reserve stores, and all
salt ships were commanded to load corn only ; the mills at
Treviso were grinding day and night, and preparations
were being made to utilize other islands and the sea ; and
strangers who had no business connections were expelled.
Meanwhile envoys were sent to Maximilian, assuring him
that " the Venetians would retire from Verona, Vicenza,
and Padua ; " others were on their way to Naples, saying
that " the harbours and cities of Apulia were open to the
King of Spain ; " others again repaired to the Pope, inviting
him to occupy Rimini and Cervia.[1]   These resolutions may
perhaps be called heroic.   The republic wished to get rid
of all its conquests on the mainland, in order to be able
to maintain itself, and perhaps compel its enemies to make
peace.   The surrendered towns were ordered to subject
themselves ; how, otherwise, could the Paduan nobles have
been enabled to boast that the Emperor, thanks to them,
was lord of Padua ?[2]   Their former surrender to Venice
had had the semblance of liberty, and so now, Venice being
unable to protect them, they received back from her, if not
their oath of allegiance, at all events the liberty to choose
their lord.   As the Venetians later speak of criminal faithlessness, they must have expected that these towns would
still hold out for them.[3]   But the towns too were dismayed,
and so surrendered themselves, each to one whose claims
the League had recognized.

[1] Bembus, 196 f.   Petrus Justinianus ; Ehrenspiegel, 1260.   Vettori,
Sandi, whence Daru, iii. 347.
[2] Machiavelli, Legazione of 1510.
[3] Coelius Rhodiginus, Lectiones ant. 191.   Arluni, i. 86.   Paul
Jovius, Epitome libri x., Histor. p. 89.

Thus perished the power of Venice, and the hope of the Italian patriots. Only one small consolation remained; all Italians engaged in the battle who were wounded had been wounded in the head and breast, and not in the back.[1]

During these months of preparation and decision, tidings reached Venice of the issue of the struggle in India. It was perhaps not less unexpected. For at first the operations of Mir Hossein and the Egyptian fleet were successful. Mir Hossein discovered Don Lourenço in the harbour of Schaul, where the shallow water never allowed the Portuguese to come to close quarters and board. As Lourenço was attempting to gain the open sea, his ship stuck fast between fishing poles, in which predicament Mir Hossein attacked him. The hero, covered with wounds, had himself carried to the foot of the mast, where he kept encouraging his men to the onslaught, until he was at last slain by a bullet in the breast.[2]

But the Mamelukes and Moors did not long rejoice over their triumph. Francisco, on hearing of the death of his only son, exclaimed, "Whoever loved him, let him not lament, but help me to avenge him;" and in December, 1508, four days after the League of Cambray had been concluded, he sailed out to find Hossein. He burnt Dabul, a city of the Zabai, who had summoned Hossein to his assistance, and spared not a soul therein. On the 3rd February, 1509, he sailed against his enemy into the harbour of Diu; each of his ships singled out one of the enemy's, attacked, and boarded it. Whilst the struggle was going on on the ships, the prows of Calicut, and the princes of Diu, anticipating what the issue would be, slipped away. Neither Dalmatians nor Venetians helped the Egyptians: they sank, or surrendered. Mir Hossein sprang on shore, mounted a horse, and escaped. Lourenço was at length avenged. The coast towns of the Soldan thereafter could not pay him any more tribute. The last hope of the Venetians was broken; and the Portuguese, without whose safe conduct no ship dared after this to enter the Indian Ocean, were completely masters of the situation. That was the

[1] Senarega, Res Genuens. 596.
[2] Barros, ii. ii. 8. Osorius, 170.

time, Queen Helena of Abyssinia wrote, which Christ fore-told to his blessed Mother: " In the land of the Franks a king shall arise, who shall destroy the whole race of the Moors and barbarians." [1]

From that time, Italy ceased to be the "inner court in the house of the world," as Ascanio Sforza expressed himself, and the centre of the European trade. The 3rd February, 1509, crushed the trade, and the 14th May, 1509, the power of Venice.

What is it that exalts nations, and brings them low? Is it their natural development, their growth and decline, as is the case with human beings? But external circum-stances often work together in a wonderful manner. Or is it a divinely pre-ordained destiny which drives them on either to destruction or prosperity? The growing and flourishing state is girt round by other living forces, which prevent its expanding beyond measure. Venice had sprung up when her neighbours were weak; she now came into collision with stronger powers, and whilst developing her-self widely and occupying an independent position in their midst, she was attacked by them and overcome. And simultaneously a new maritime power, which sought and found another centre, sapped those resources which had enabled her to rise so high. Venice could not become more than she now was; but she might still maintain her present position.

6. WAR OF THE VENETIANS TO SAVE THEIR CITY AND PART OF THEIR TERRITORY.

After these great blows had fallen upon her, and Venice was stripped of all save herself, and what she had once acquired in the oriental expeditions against the Turks, Julius and Ferdinand resolved to spare the remainder; the former, because the city was an eye of Italy; the latter, because he was involved at that moment in his Moorish campaigns, and was mindful of his Catalonian claims to

[1] Barros, ii. iii. 6.   Osorius, 196.   Literae Helenae, ap. Ramusium, i. 177.

Neopatri and Athens : " Had he only 3,000 landsknechts, in addition to 20,000 Spaniards, he would even take Constantinople itself." [1]   Louis and Maximilian, on the other hand, were for utterly annihilating Venice ; and to this intent they joined hands, through the intervention of Amboise.[2] It was not until after the battle, that Louis received the Duke of Savoy into his camp, who demanded Cyprus. It was not until the 29th of May, that Maximilian, through many princes, counts, knights, and servants of the realm, proclaimed hostilities against Venice. He was most urgent in the matter ; he declared to the princes of the realm that the territory of Venice had been already won, and that he was now minded to take to the sea, and annihilate also the rest of her power. His plan was, with Papal and Spanish fleets, to attack the city from the sea, whilst German and French armies, advancing down the Brenta, invested the city on the land side, and reduced it. It could be divided up into four districts, and each prince could have a castle there.[3]

With these schemes in view, he made his preparations. Shortly before this, the three ships which the Fuggers had despatched to Calicut returned, and the instant gain of 175 per cent. made this house wealthy enough to pay him the money which Julius, Ferdinand, and Louis, each for different reasons, had promised him; namely, 300,000 ducats,[4] so that the profits of the Eastern trade were not merely withdrawn from Venice, but were even employed against her. But before he had finished his preparations, the undertaking began to wear a different aspect.

On the return of Louis to Milan, he was received with a triumphal arch, upon which were represented his achievements, his councillors, his march and his battle, the nobili of Venice finding also a place thereon. In their flowing robes, with hand on breast and faces serious and thoughtful, they looked as though their sole purpose was not only to defend

---

[1] Paris de Grassis, in Rainaldus and Zurita, 185, 196.

[2] Zurita, 194, also Dumont, iv. 1, 117.

[3] Declaration of hostilities, in Goldast, Reichshandlung, 92. Handellunge auf dem Wormser Reichstage, 96. Zurita, 182, 195.

[4] Ehrenspiegel, 1295.

themselves, but also to repair the damage and to punish the faithless.[1] The facts are these. In the Venetian territories, both parties, rulers and subjects, appear at first to have believed that they could dispense each with the other. When the rulers saw that their enemies would not be satisfied with the possessions which they had renounced in their favour, but intended to subject even them themselves, and became aware that they needed a bulwark for their defence, and when at the same time their subjects were reminded, by the rigour of the new government, of the clemency of the old, they both perceived that communities of men are not so easily dissolved as formed, but grow into a natural cohesion, to rend which asunder is to endanger the life of the whole.

This truth was first realized at Treviso, which lay amidst the estates of the Venetian nobles, and at Padua, for whose daily traffic with Venice eighty boats were scarcely sufficient, and which yearly sold to Venice corn and the produce of its orchards and vineyards, to the value of 40,000 ducats.[2] When Leonardo Trissino appeared at Treviso, to occupy that city in the name of the Emperor, it only required a shoemaker to raise the standard and the cry of " San Marco ! " for the whole of the people to join him. Had it not, 175 years previously, in similar straits, of its own accord thrown its fate in with that of Venice ? It again received a Venetian garrison within its walls. The Imperialists were already in possession of Padua. Yet when, in the early morning of the 27th of July, 1509, Andrea Gritti had surprised one of the gates—masked sharpshooters behind hay waggons picked out each his man among the guard, and 2,000 were in reserve in a neighbouring thicket —and dashing through the streets raised the national cry, the people here also declared for Venice, and the landsknechts were forced to retire. The chiefs of the nobles were punished for having surrendered their city.[3]

But the war, hereupon, began to wear a changed aspect.

[1] Arluni, de bello Veneto, 81.

[2] Savonarola, Commentarius de laudibus Patavii, in Muratori, xxiv. 1176, 1180.

[3] Mocenicus, i. 21, 23. Coelius Rhodiginus, Lectiones ant. 191. Arluni, 86. Bembus, 203.

Towards the autumn, Maximilian arrived on the scene with twenty-six princes and 12,000 horse—La Palice, Bayard, and French and Spanish auxiliaries were with him—with more than one hundred cannon and so many landsknechts that his army was 50,000 men strong; he came like a true emperor, in the hope of a battle such as Louis had fought and won.[1] The peasants in the mountains surrendered, those living near the plain fled with wife and child, with cattle and chattels, to the lagoons, behind banks and dykes (they drove 10,000 head of cattle to Cavarzere, 20,000 to Montalban, and thus we can see how the lagoons may have been peopled in bygone days); but no army appeared.[2] Only Padua opposed its triangular fortifications, with walls sixty feet in height, and five-fold escarpments, to the enemy's advance. Loredano, now convinced that the fortune of Venice depended upon preservation of the towns on the mainland, set the Venetians a new example, and, though no noble had ever before served on land, now offered both his sons for the defence of Padua.[3] They were joined by 174 other young nobili, each accompanied by ten men, bound to them for life and death. Thus they came, in all 10,000 men, to Padua. One day they were all assembled on the Prato della Valle, before the church of Sta Giustina, Padua's patron saint. Here an altar was raised, on which was placed a copy of the Holy Gospels; after mass they one and all advanced to the table, and laying their hand on the Gospels swore to defend the city with true allegiance, and with their lives.[4]

Against this city Maximilian now advanced. His letters, which flew into the city attached to the points of arrows, were not heeded. The balls from his great mortars, the "Strauss," the "Scharfe Metze," and others, which were placed on special carriages, and could only be fired off four times a day, terrified them not. Unconcerned, Coelius

[1] Bayard, 144. Jovius, Vita Alfonsi ducis Ferrar. 156. Weiskunig, 290.

[2] Petrus Justinianus, 372. Mocenicus, 30.

[3] Naugerii Oratio in funere Leonardi Laureati, 1530, f. 31, 22, 36, 18. Savonarola, de laudibus, 1177. Carpesanus, 1269.

[4] Mocenicus, ii. 34. Petrus Justinianus, 384.

Rhodiginus worked on at his book " Lectiones antiquae."
Some Spanish companies, trained under the great Gonzalvo,
stormed a bastion, which they scaled; but the attack ended
in their own destruction, when the powder, concealed under
dry faggots, caught fire and exploded. The landsknechts
were ready to storm once more, if some heavy-armed troops
were associated with them; and Maximilian actually commanded the French hommes d'armes, who were with him,
to help them ; but this did not suit their temper. Bayard
was wrath and said : "Shall we rush into danger at the
side of mere tailors and cobblers ? Let him send his
German nobles with us." But these latter, on being
appealed to, replied, " They were come to fight on horseback, and not to storm."[1] Maximilian, in the vexation of
spirit which is aroused in every energetic man by the im-
pediments of prejudice, gave orders to break up the camp,
and throwing garrisons into the other fortresses, left Italy.

After this, the fortunes of the Venetians increased mainly
through the attachment of all the peasants to them. It
would often happen, when the Germans were marching
through the valleys between the vineyards, that, where the
defile was narrow, peasarts would come out from behind
the vines crying : "now they were going to avenge their
fathers, children, and wives," and attack them ; often they
would conceal themselves behind the bushes, until a
weak detachment came by, and then they would call the
Venetians, who were also concealed hard by, to the
slaughter. The Marquis of Mantua escaped from some
soldiers who suddenly attacked him ; but four peasants
found him crouching in some maize, and, in spite of
his great promises, they consigned him to the tower of
St. Mark's. The Bishop of Trent, whom the Emperor had
left behind in Verona, arrested a certain man who said he
was a Venetian. The bishop hanged him ; but he remained
firm to the last.[2] Every day the situation grew worse.
The Venetians then succeeded in placing even Verona in

[1] Arluni, iii. 108. Ehrenspiegel, 1265. Zurita, 204. Especially
Bayard, c. 37, p. 171.
[2] Especially Machiavelli, Legazione to Mantua, 1519, v. 319.
Mocenicus, 40, 46. Bembus, 214.

danger, and actually in taking Vicenza, Monselice, Montagnana, and many other towns. Immediately they took a place, they erected a statue of Saint Mark there, but no longer, as formerly, with a book, but with a sword.[1]

Maximilian once again, on the 7th April, 1510, commissioned his general, Rudolf of Anhalt, a man called by the neighbours at home "high crown of the lineage of Anhalt,"[2]—he was famed for his loyalty, and his army called him Anhalt the Loyal (Anhalt das treue Blut)—to make incursions and ravage the land with fire and sword, with pillage and murder.[3] The most horrible deeds were then done. In the Grotto of Masono, two thousand men, women, and children of good family had taken refuge; some of the French auxiliaries came to the grotto, and, as the wind was blowing into it, they made a fire at the entrance, so that all the unfortunates were suffocated by the smoke.[4] In Udine two angels with bloody swords were believed to have been seen above the church. In this war, in which sieges, stratagems, victories, counter-stratagems, defeats, and retreats interchanged in rapid succession, they appear to have fulfilled their omen throughout the whole of Friuli.[5] In Austria, some confessed that they had been hired by the Venetians to set fire to the country.

Venice no longer waged this war in order to conquer or to liberate Italy—these plans were past and gone; her aim now was to avail herself of the almost unexpected devotion of her people, and of the general state of affairs, to regain her territory, at all events in part. Therefore, now that her Indian trade was ruined, she busied herself with a new organization of commerce in the Mediterranean. Meanwhile fresh events took place.

---

[1] Machiavelli, *ibid.* 10th letter, p. 324.

[2] Letter of Hieronymus, Bishop of Brandenburg, in Beckmann's Anh. Chronik, v. ii. 127.

[3] Commissoriale Maximiliani, in Beckmann, 130.

[4] Maximilian's letter to the Count Palatine Louis, in Goldast, Reichshandlung, 93. Bayard, 199–201.

[5] Petrus Martyr and Mocenicus, 55, 59.

7. ENTERPRISES OF THE POPE TO EFFECT THE LIBERATION OF ITALY.

"Your Holiness knows," the Venetians wrote, after their first disaster, to the Pope, "how we are situated: your Holiness will pity us. Blessed Father and Lord, our gracious master! If we have obeyed your precepts, as we have done, may the hand that inflicted the wound deign to heal it."[1]

The Pope thought that the League of Cambray was now satisfied; "if the Emperor was not in possession of his cities, it was due to his own dilatoriness;" and, on the 20th February, 1510, in St. Peter's hall, he released Venice from the ban of excommunication, and, stretching out his hand, pronounced his blessing on the envoys of the republic.[2] His noble soul was full of grand plans, urgently needed for the whole of Italy.

Amboise had supported the Emperor's expedition against Venice with French forces, in order that he should make him Pope; and in the manuscripts of Bethune is contained a whole list of favours, which Amboise would confer upon the Emperor, as soon as he had attained his aim.[3] His own danger, accordingly, confirmed Julius in his old intention of liberating his native land, Genoa, whence his kinsmen, the Fregosi, had been exiled, so that he might thus drive the French from Italian soil. Formerly this had been the intention of the Venetians as well as his own; they had, however, first of all to fight out their quarrel together. This had now been done, and the power of Venice was broken. Julius now resolved to save the rest of the Venetian power, and to commence his work in league with the republic. The resolve was all the bolder, as it would certainly kindle the war against him, which his enemies at present hesitated to begin. Although his scheme was so dangerous that the galleys were kept at Ostia ready

[1] Epistolae Venetorum, in Senarega, Annales Genuenses, Muratori, xxiii.
[2] Paris de Grassis, ap. Rainaldum, Annales Eccles. xx. 75; Bembus, 200; Daru from MSS. iii. 381.
[3] Garnier, from the MSS. xxii. 219, and Zurita.

for sea, in order, if necessary, to enable him to escape, he yet adhered to it: "It suited Louis to make the other princes his vassals, and himself his chaplain; but he would not tolerate this tyranny any longer, he would drive the French from Italy, and if his sins were so grievous as to prevent his accomplishing his purpose, he would live no longer. He would shed his blood for the liberation of Italy." [1]

Without delay—hesitation was foreign to him—he proceeded to action, and first of all in Ferrara and Genoa.

Now in Ferrara, Alfonso d'Este held sway, as did his fathers, uncontrolled alike by his subjects, his relations, and his superiors. His subjects he ruled by tribunal and sword; he proclaimed his laws by sound of the trumpet, without asking any one, and punished the rebels with rack or sword.[2] He kept his brothers, Giulio and Ferrante, who had conspired against his life, in close confinement. As a result of the battle of Agnadello, he had ridded himself of the Venetian Visdomino, who with his processions and his drums and fifes had not even spared his court; instead of cleaving to his suzerain, the pope, he adhered to emperor and king.

The Pope now demanded of this Alfonso that he should make peace with Venice. To make an attempt upon Genoa, in July, 1510, he despatched Marc Antonio Colonna and the party of the Fregosi, who, in anticipation of his achievements, called him Julius Cæsar, and with the shout of "Libertà e Italia," came to the Riviera.[3]

But Alfonso, who, with cannon that he himself had cast, had shortly before, from his tower Pepos and the embankments on the river, annihilated a considerable Venetian fleet, which had advanced up the Po against him, would not assent to this peace.[4] Julius, wrath that he should still have vassals whom he could not control, demanded yet more: "Alfonso should not impose any fresh burdens upon his subjects, should moreover set free his brother

---

[1] Zurita, ii. 227, 235.
[2] Diarium Ferrarense, 229, 234, 290, *passim*.
[3] Lettres de Louis, i. 255.
[4] Bayard, 148. Coelius Rhodiginus, Lectiones ant. v. 194.

Ferrante, who was the Pope's godson, and should not, in defiance of his suzerain, manufacture salt at Comacchio—for Agostino Ghisi, who had rented the saltworks in the newly acquired Cervia, was already complaining of this [1]—which he had never dared to do as long as Cervia was Venetian." But the only answer Alfonso returned was either a flat refusal or a subterfuge : he would not obey him.[2]

The Fregosi in Genoa succeeded no better. They hoped that their partisans would rise, as soon as they appeared. But the French had, on this occasion, a well-disciplined body of men both inside and outside the city, and kept every one in terror. It is recorded that the peasants, when the heads of executed rebels were sent through their villages and stuck on stakes to strike terror into them, did not dare to touch them when they saw them blown down by the wind. Thus, while the Fregosi were expecting a movement on the part of their adherents, the latter, on their side, were waiting until the Fregosi achieved some success.[3]

This first misadventure aroused the Pope to fresh exertions. He put Alfonso under ban and fitted out a fleet against Genoa. But he conceived still greater schemes; with one stroke he would overcome Ferrara, rouse Genoa, drive the French from Milan, and help the Venetians to triumph over the Emperor. And in this he looked to the Swiss for assistance. The epoch arrived in which the Swiss attained the zenith of their renown, both in war and politics. Let us sketch in outline their position at this time.

In February, 1509, Louis had abandoned his alliance with them,[4] and it is patent for what reason. In spite of his annual subsidies, he had on two occasions, in 1501 and 1503, almost come to open war with them, had at last been obliged to confirm the rights of the people of Uri to Bellinzona, and had never been able to satisfy the claims

---

[1] Leonardo da Porto, letter in the Lettere di Principi, i. 3.

[2] Jovius, Vita Alfonsi, 160. Andrea del Burgo, in the Lettres de Louis, i. 250.

[3] Senarega, 600–603. Machiavelli, Legazione alla Corte di Francia. v. 347.

[4] Bullinger, in Fuchs, Mailänder Feldzüge, ii. 133. Garnier, 236.

of certain mercenaries to payments long due. And as often as a campaign was in prospect, the factions asserted themselves after his alliance, just as before. The negotiations of the year 1507 against Maximilian cost him the very considerable sum of 230,000 guilders.[1] He thought he was bargaining for obedient mercenaries, but found them very refractory allies. Now Louis, who never underestimated the value of money, no doubt thought that, even without annual subsidies, he would secure his true partisans by secret pensions, and an army by guaranteeing pay. Directly he had renounced the alliance, this supposition was confirmed. Without any annual subsidies, 6,000 Swiss joined him in his war with Venice and decided his victory on the very day that an alliance with Venice, which held out an even greater prospect of success, was proposed to them at home. After the battle, nothing of course came of this.[2]

Whilst then the Swiss were now released from all obligations to any prince, the patriots among them hoped that, in the future, every Swiss would be restrained from accepting foreign pay, and would hereafter live in true liberty, without serving in the field and accepting money for such service.

It must be confessed that this hope was not likely to be realized. To forego the money might not, perhaps, have been such a hardship either for the judges, who still sat in judgment beneath the fir-tree at Lastorf, or for the people of quality, who thought it too great an expense to warm a separate room for their servants, or for the respectable householders, who were content with windows of cloth or, if of glass, with roughly glazed panes, costing four pfennigs each, or even for the simple cowherds and peasants.[3] But they could not live without war. As soon as they were old enough, the boys dangled a sword over their left knee, stuck an ostrich feather in their caps, followed the drum,

---

[1] Stettler, under the year 1507.

[2] Anshelm, in Glutzblotzheim, 222 (iv. 122). Bembus, 177. Seyssel, 312.

[3] Glutzblotzheim, from MSS. 456. Anshelm, in Fuchs, ii. 224. Also the Life of Johann Orelli from his letters, though of somewhat later date, 478.

and practised musket shooting.[1] No fair, no church festival, not even the swearing-in of a new magistrate took place without a review and a musket-practice. Even the lame must have coats of mail, and the priest in the pulpit was girded with a sword.[2] A wedding party was honoured when many uninvited guests followed, so long as they had halberts and swords and marched three and three.[3] Whenever these martial fellows were gathered together, families and guilds in separate rooms—they all called each other "thou"—there would appear in their midst, perhaps, one who had just returned home from active service, and would clink the guilders that he had got as pay or booty, and fire the others with the wish that they also would be one day thought of in their homes in fine helmets and with halberts. Amman Reding rightly remarked: "Their youth must spend itself somewhere." [4]

In the conviction that this people would, of all allies, be the least dangerous for Italy, Julius, who was the first among the popes to surround his person with a Swiss guard, concluded with the Swiss, through the mediation of Matthäus Schinner, Bishop of the Valais, on the 26th February, 1510, an alliance for five years, in return for an annual subvention of 12,000 guilders ; in return, they were to furnish 6,000 men against every enemy that should cause trouble to the Church of Rome.[5] With this alliance, Julius thought that he would infallibly carry out his designs. In July, he sent 36,000 guilders to Martinach, and demanded the promised contingent.[6]

At the end of August, 1510, his comprehensive military scheme was developed. The Papal army occupied Modena and threatened Ferrara ; and the Venetians (the Germans having departed) rose up against Verona. The fleet, to which

<hr/>

[1] Wimphelingii Soliloquium, cap. 28 in Fuchs, 56.

[2] Instance in Glutzblotzheim, 488.

[3] Wimphelingii Soliloquium, cap. 31, *ibid.* Glutzblotzheim, from MSS. 492. Simler, Helvetia, ii. 50, in the Thesaurus Helveticus.

[4] Müller, Schweizergeschichte, vol. v. cap. 2, note 151.

[5] Article in Anshelm, iv. 100. Stettler, 444, and Fuchs, 158. Julius, Statement to the ambassadors, extract in Fuchs, 216.

[6] Maximilian's letter to Ernst of Magdeburg, in Beckmann, Anhalt. Chronik, 135.

the Pope had entrusted the ensign, the key and the triple
crown, had already put to sea for the purpose of attacking
Genoa, and the Swiss, 8,000 men strong, appeared simultaneously on the Tresa, with the intention of marching through
the Milanese, and falling upon the other side of Ferrara—as
Chaumont had done upon Bologna—and thus deciding
the day. "The papal party was already in great strength at
Ferrara, and Lucrezia wished to fly. The city would be forced
to surrender as Bologna did. And then—had not understandings with Brescia and Parma been arrived at, and was
not the Ghibelline party in the whole of Milan on their
side?"[1]   The Pope now himself left Rome and went to
Bologna.   The cardinals of French sympathies forsook
him; but he had no doubt of success.   In Loreto,
he dedicated a great silver cross to the Virgin, and the
superscription : "In hoc signo vinces."[2]

It often happened, in Switzerland, that the negotiations
which led to no result before the army took the field, were
immediately successful as soon as it had done so, and when
those who were most eager for the war had marched out
with it.   If we investigate, we find that this evil was often
the real cause of much mischief, and finally occasioned the
fall of the independent Confederation.[3]   On this occasion,
the army had scarcely crossed the St. Gotthard, when the
imperial and French partisans began to bestir themselves.
Maximilian's warning, that the Pope intended with their
soldiers to attack Milan and not Ferrara, and that, in the
event of the army not returning, he would invade their
territory with the collective might of the Empire, had some
effect upon them.[4]   Although the three old Forest cantons
which were always against Milan, opposed it, the majority
resolved to guarantee safe conduct to the French embassy ;
and, although Matthäus Schinner reminded them, that the

[1] Bembus, 256, 257.   Orelli, Life, p. 75.   Mocenicus, p. 60.

[2] Victorellus ad Ciacconii vitas paparum.   Vita Julii II, Paris de
Gr. 78.

[3] Mallet du Pan, Destruction of the Swiss Confederation, vol. ii.
cap. 8, p. 111.

[4] From the letter in Fuchs, 178, and Tschudi, Continuat. *ibid.*
Cf. Anshelm, iv. 125.

intention was to send troops to the Pope, and that, " if the King of France opposed the Pope, he became the Pope's enemy, and that they then by virtue of their compact with the Pope would be sworn foes of the King also," the majority nevertheless resolved to detain, until further orders, the army they had raised for the Pope.[1] Such an order would at any time have thrown into confusion troops who were already in the field, and who never attributed it to a single party, but believed it to be the outcome of an unanimous resolution. On this occasion, they had already left Varese and reached Chiasso on the lake of Como, but had become extremely discouraged through want of provisions—for they found nothing but chestnuts, grapes, and nuts, the mills having been stripped of their iron-work ; moreover, their road was blocked by rivers without bridges, and they were surrounded on all sides by French horse, who did not actually attack them—for they were afraid of rousing their vengeance—but kept harassing and threatening them.[2] In this plight, the order of the assembly found them ; in addition, some of their captains had been bribed ; thus their general distress, confusion, and ignorance of the state of affairs determined them to retreat. On the 12th September, the first ships conveying the returning troops came across the lake to Lucerne,[3] and, on the same day, the French ambassador appeared before the assembly. The deputies of Uri, Schwyz, and Unterwalden indignantly quitted the meeting ; the rest drew up a letter to the Pope, praying that " the father of peace would deal with the Christians peaceably and without guile." [4]

Instead of the promised aid, the Pope, on arriving at Bologna, received this letter. The Venetians had already besieged Verona ; but they were compelled to retreat by the French, who, now freed from all fear of the Swiss, hastened to the assistance of the city.[5] Moreover, the papal

---

[1] Fuchs, from the resolution, 184. Testimony of M. Walter, 231.

[2] Mocenicus, 63. Bayard, 205. Bullinger, in Fuchs, 192.

[3] Breve Julii, in Fuchs, 239. Anshelm, in Glutzblotzheim, 225.

[4] Glutz. from the resolution, 545. Walter, 231. Simleri Vallesia.

[5] Lettres de Louis, ii. 22. Maximilian, in Hormayr's Archiv. 1812, p. 588.

army had not been able to take Reggio, to say nothing of attacking Ferrara. The fleet despatched against Genoa showed itself in the harbour off Vado, and attempted to land, but it found itself confronted by another equally strong ; and nowhere a friend. It exchanged a few stone shot from its mortars with the enemy, and returned.[1] All had failed. Here, where everything depended upon the ascendency of the moment, and where the conviction of superiority must precede victory, the failure was without doubt due to the retreat of the Swiss.

And now, like the picador in a bull-fight, when he has missed the deadly stroke, or like the hunter in the mountains, when the chamois that he has missed threatens to drag him into the abyss, Julius perceived that instead of himself attacking and threatening, he had become the attacked and was in extreme danger.

Louis hesitated long before meeting him. "The Pope intended devilish things against his honour and his possessions, none of which he was minded to lose ; but, unfortunately, war with his Holiness would rouse the whole of Christendom against him."[2] In the year 1510, Amboise died ; and, as he left no one to inherit his position, as the King, in making his great plans, was in the habit of disregarding small ones, though these were the stepping-stones to his greater achievements, the government appeared less enterprising than formerly. "O my patron," cried Robertet, when a portrait of Amboise was brought to him, "wert thou alive, we should now be with our army in Rome."[3] At last, after Louis, through the intervention of the Florentines, had vainly attempted negotiations, and when blow was followed by blow, and attack by attack, he also, at last, decided on war. On the 16th of September, the clergy of the kingdom assembled at Tours, more for counsel than for action, and chiefly in order to obtain the opinion of the nation, and there decided thus : "A prince might certainly return an attack made upon him by the Pope, provided it

---

[1] Mocenicus. Senarega, 604. Folieta, Historia Genuens. 262.

[2] Lettres, i. 270. Machiavelli, Legazione a. c. di Francia, lett. 6, v. 349.

[3] Machiavelli, c. 383, 380.

were only to weaken the Pope, and were not to his total destruction."[1] But this is exactly what the King proposed to do. In the same month, the imperial ambassador, Matthäus Lang, Bishop of Gurk, came down the Loire. The heir to the throne invited him to a banquet. The Queen sent him wine from Beaune and victuals from her table. The King promised a small contingent for a winter campaign, but, for the summer, a force of 1,200 lances, 10,000 men, and his own person to boot.[2] He boasted that "he would create a new heaven and a new earth in Italy; the Pope should be deposed and the Emperor be as great as Charles the Great was." His looks showed how seriously he intended it. Day and night he pondered how to revenge himself.[3] In November, he sent his Milanese army into the field under Chaumont. The papal forces lay between Modena and Bologna, in order to protect both places. Chaumont marched up the Reno as if to threaten Modena. The papal troops at once retired thither, but thus cut themselves off from Bologna, and upon this city Chaumont threw himself without delay.[4] Julius himself was in the city.

Julius was cut off from his army, still without the assistance Ferdinand had promised him on account of the Neapolitan fiefs, without the stipulated help from Venice, and, withal, ill of a fever. And in Bologna, he himself was in peril. As the Bentivogli had sided with his enemy, the city was full of the mutterings of their friends and partisans, the Rinucceneti, the Fantuzzi, and the Caprara. Nothing but captivity seemed in store for him. In this sore distress, he found aid in his own resources. He first of all promised the leading Bolognese, whom he had summoned to his bedside, that he would give them a Cardinal from among them. This was repeated to the people assembled in the market-place; many other favours were also promised, so that they

[1] Burgo à Marguerite: Lettres de Louis, ii. 33. Article in Gilles, Chroniques, p. 122.

[2] Burgo à Marguerite and Responsa Ludovici, Lettres de Louis, ii. 53, 78.

[3] Machiavelli, Legaz. 365, 370.

[4] Mocenicus, 63. Maximilian, in Hormayr, 393.

were quite won over to the Pope. And what influence has not the holy and august presence of a living pope always exercised upon the people! They all came together before his palace, 5,000 on horseback and 15,000 on foot, led by two Cardinals. He rose from his bed, showed himself upon the balcony, and spread out his hands to bless them : then, as though he would show them that, in his sore need, he committed himself into their hands, he drew back his arms and laid them crossways on his breast.[1] This sign, which showed the people that their prince and the father of Christendom entrusted his person to their keeping and allegiance, moved their hearts more than any promises could do. They shouted for very joy. The Pope retired and said : "now we have triumphed." And in truth so it was. The parties in the city were at length silenced, and immediately afterwards the Spanish and Venetian horse rode into the city, and the English and Spanish envoys intervened with threats on the Pope's behalf. Thereupon the French retired; with joy Julius heard at an ever-increasing distance their din and firing. Whilst still lying in bed, he raised his arm and cried : "Away, ye French, away from Italy." Gladness of heart made him well in a short time. He collected his army, and, in the month of December, despatched three generals against Mirandola and Ferrara.

By these three he was not, as it would seem, very excellently served. The first, the Marquis of Mantua,[2] halted at a crossway, and said : "There is Mirandola and the enemy's country; here is Mantua and friendly country. Go ye thither, whilst I remain here; if ye need me, fire your arms until I hear." This man had been liberated from the tower of San Marco, principally owing to Julius' intervention.[3] The two others, the Cardinal of Pavìa and the young Duke of Urbino, near relatives of Julius, were every day at feud together, and the Cardinal, at all events, was a man of such a notorious character that one day, on seeing a man

---

[1] Paris de Grassis, Diarium in Rainaldus, 79. Sansovino, Origine, 299. Jovii Alfonsus, 166.
[2] Breve, in Dumont, iv. 1, 131. Also Machiavelli, Legazione, 352.
[3] Mocenicus, 67.

who had been hanged, some one exclaimed: "well for thee, that thou hast not to do with a Cardinal of Pavìa."[1]

Alfonso of Ferrara, whom they attacked, was a totally different man. He converted all his silver-plate into money, and pledged his wife's jewels to the usurers. The earthenware plates and dishes which were used at court, were, after this, remarkable as having been manufactured by the Prince's own hands. He always paid everybody at the appointed day. To this circumstance, he said, was due the obedience paid to him. The three hundred pieces of cannon, many of them cast from the metal which the citizens had delivered over to him, according to streets and guilds, ensured him the respect of friends and foes. The fortifications flanking his city were a model for many in the future.[2] The French whom Louis had sent to his assistance, were under ban, as he was, but were kept in allegiance and obedience by nature and the laws of chivalry.

In this situation, the operations of the Pope did not seem likely to be crowned with success. Mirandola would scarcely have been wrested from its lady defender, the widow of Galeotto Pico, were it not that Julius, though a pope and very old, had proceeded to besiege it in the coldest winter season.[3] It did not affect him at all, that, on one occasion, he only escaped from Bayard owing to a snow-storm, and that at the last minute he had to spring out of his litter, in order that a drawbridge should be pulled up behind him, or that a cannon-ball fell into his tent before the city. The ball, as large as a child's head, he sent to Loreto, to be treasured as a keepsake and thank-offering. At last he succeeded in reducing the town, marched into it over the frozen ditch and through the breach in its walls, and restored the rightful lord.[4] But he alone of all his party showed this determined courage. If Bastia del Genivolo was taken, Ferrara, according to Alfonso's own opinion, would be lost to

[1] Paris. Bembus. Leoni. Castiglione, Cortegiano, 205.

[2] Jovii Alfonsus, 170, f. 197. Fleuranges, 78.

[3] Paris de Gr. 100. Bayard, 216, to be compared with Benedictus Jovius, Hist. Novocom. p. 62.

[4] Fleuranges, 66, 72. Mariana, 301. Triulce au Roy, in Rosmini, Trivulzio, ii. 300. Alcyonius de Exil., ed. Menken, p. 62.

to him. But the papal generals neglected to occupy a ford that might have been held by twenty men; through this Alfonso came, and saved his castle. Julius sent him word that " if he would dismiss the French he should not be again attacked;" but the man who brought this news was not trustworthy. Alfonso replied, " Julius will soon be in his grave ; but a princely race rewards good services for ever." The man—his name was Agostino Gerlo—answered: "within six days he offered himself to kill the Pope, who received all his food from his hand." The Duke told it to Bayard as a fact. Bayard replied : " Sire, did I but know it for certain, I would communicate it to the Pope before nightfall." Alfonso shrugged his shoulders, and expectorated: "for Bayard's sake he would not do it;" thus the enemies of the Pope and those whom he had placed under ban did him better service than those he trusted.[1] When Julius, after the trifling war in the winter, in which the French and Papal troops only strove to keep open their connections, the former with Ferrara and the latter with the Venetians, as well as to cut their enemies' communications, at length found himself, in April, again in the field with 9,000 foot and 1,500 horse,[2] he no longer found Chaumont at the head of the enemy, but a man whom the disorganized state of the French army required. This man was none other than Gian Giacomo Trivulzio, a captain who often hanged or drowned his refractory soldiers ; a man who deducted from the pay of his Spaniards what they had stolen from a peasant; a man cursed by his soldiers—"this old man with the bald head had no strength nor life in him, and was yet so stern;" but he taught them again how to take fortresses.[3]

Thus did two septuagenarians, both grown grey in the turmoils of Italy, both brave and stern, oppose each other, and each desired battle. How could Julius be anxious to fight, he who was plainly so much weaker than his opponent? But he said : " Christ helps his warriors, and will find means

---

[1] Bayard, 223–231, 234–240.

[2] Leonardo da Porto, in the Lettere di Principi, 4. Paris de Grassis, 101.

[3] Rebucco, Andrea da Prato and Arluni, Historia Mediolanensis, in Rosmini, Trivulzio, i. 584. Arluni, Historia Veneta, iv. 55.

to destroy the house of Este and the schismatical king."
Trivulzio desired to make the way smooth for the King, for
Louis was already on his way to Grenoble, in order to cross
the hills, and fight out his cause himself. The crisis was at
hand, and the sword drawn.

At this moment, Matthäus Lang appeared between the
parties, and again an attempt was made to ratify a peace,
which should include both Venice and Ferrara. All the
ambassadors hurriedly met. The Scottish envoy, Murray,
was specially energetic in his endeavours to bring about an
understanding. The cardinals held frequent consultations.[1]
But how was any arrangement with Venice possible, when
Lang demanded Padua, Treviso, and 700,000 ducats
besides from Venice? He rejected all remonstrances and
all promises whatsoever. His boast was that he always
went straight like a candle.[2] As to Ferrara, Louis would
not even agree to a formal truce. "Such a truce would
break the heart of his people. He was now at an advantage,
and might expect victory. First victory, then peace. He
would recruit in the Grisons, would then take the field, and
not return until he had both victory and peace, otherwise he
would remain away altogether." He was all fire and flame,
when one of the Fregosi, who was taken in Ventimiglia,
confessed that he had been sent by the Pope to stir up a
revolution. Lang left the Pope.[3] Trivulzio crossed the
Panaro, and drove back the Papal army, which did not need
on this occasion to defend Modena—for Julius had shrewdly
delivered it into the hand of an imperial plenipotentiary—
under the walls of Bologna. Here, on the 22nd May, 1511,
Georg Frundsberg joined him with 2,500 Germans.[4]

The cause of the Pope, who had gone to Ravenna, lay in
the hands of the Cardinal of Pavia, who commanded in
Bologna, and of the Duke of Urbino, who had charge of
the army lying before that city.

[1] Coccinius, de bellis Italicis, ap. Freherum, Rerum Germanicarum,
ii. 268. Margaret to Henry, in the Lettres de Louis, ii. 96.
[2] Articles proposés, and Lang's letter in the Lettres, ii. 96, 139.
[3] Andrea del Burgo's letters, *ibid.* 150, 170, 183, 190. Paris de
Gr. 103.
[4] Andrea to Margaret. Reisner's Thaten der Frundsperge, f. 11.

Now the Cardinal, among his twenty constables, to whom he had entrusted the keeping of the city, had also committed one of the gates into the hands of the partisans of the Bentivogli, and, as often as he was warned of it, only replied: "It is all well, all precautions have been taken." But in the night of that 22nd of May, it came to pass, that the Bentivogli on the outside passed by the gates, whilst the Fantuzzi and Ariosti on the inside mounted the Torre degli Asinelli, and waved to them with a torch, and, thereupon, those on the outside and those within both hurried to the Porta San Felice, the latter to open it and the others to rush in. Some of the more loyal troops were already assembling to fall upon the Ariosti from behind, when the gate burst open, and with the shout of "Sega Popolo," the Bentivogli rushed into the city. The cry was taken up on all sides, and the Cardinal instantly fled with 100 horsemen. The city was in the power of the Bentivogli.[1]

The noise and tumult, the shouts and the waving of torches were also observed by the Duke, who was lying before the gates. "What are they shouting?" he asked of an attendant, and they believed at first that it was "Chiesa" that they heard. But in a short time they could distinguish quite clearly the cry "Sega," and immediately afterwards heard from the sentinels all that had taken place.[2] The Duke perceived that he could not possibly hold his ground. Forthwith then, in the depth of night, abandoning his tents and the baggage, but without further loss—he himself was with the rearguard—he withdrew with his army.[3] Only the Venetians who were with him were overtaken by the daylight and by the enemy in effecting their retreat. The French attacked them in the rear, and the peasants from the hills assailed their flank, whilst the Bentivogli threw themselves across their line of march. The last-named were cut through by some knights, to whom the urgency of their need gave courage. The peasants plundered the

---

[1] Report of Trivulzio in the Lettres, ii. 233. Nardi, 132. Especially Paris de Grassis.

[2] Leoni, Vita di Francesco Maria, duca d'Urbino, lib. i. p. 26.

[3] Leoni, Consideraz. sopra l' histor. di Guicciardini, from the mouth of Ricardo Alidosi, iii. 41.

baggage; the French took three prisoners—one of them with a wooden leg—and great booty. The same morning, the Bentivogli took the statue of the Pope, a work of Michael Angelo, from its niche, and after dragging it through the city, broke off its head, and resolved to melt down the rest to make a cannon.[1]

Julius was still at Ravenna. Contradictory news reached him every hour. Sometimes hoping, and sometimes lamenting that "he was betrayed by those whom he loved best," the tidings of the disaster at last reached him. The cup was not yet full. After a short time, the Cardinal of Pavia made his appearance with his horsemen. He threw all the blame upon the Duke, and effected that the command should be at once taken from him and entrusted to Altavilla of Capua. The Duke himself soon made his appearance, and found little attention given to his excuses. In bitter rage, defeated and calumniated, slandered to his uncle and before the whole of Italy, and, being an Italian, determined on revenge, the young man walked through the streets until his deadly enemy, seated on a mule, met him, and smiled a friendly greeting. In his wrath he threw himself upon him. Grasping the saddle with his left hand, and with the words, "Art thou guilty or I?" before he could even answer, with his right he plunged his sword into his side. The Cardinal's dying words were, "Punishment follows sin." The Duke rode away to Urbino.[2]

Now the Pope neither saw Ferrara conquered nor Italy liberated; what he did see was Bologna lost, his statue broken in pieces by a people whom he had loaded with favours, and a hostile army in his territory. Yet the heaviest stroke of all was the murder of his trusted friend by his nephew, whom he had brought up, and the consequent loss of them both. On the 28th May, he was brought in a litter from Ravenna to Rimini. He smote his breast, and wept bitterly, and, that no one might see him, he was brought to Rimini by night.[3]

[1] Leonardo da Porto, in the Lettere di Princ. 5. Coccinius, 271.
[2] Bembus, 274. Guicciardini, ix. 533. Ferry Carondele à Marguerite, Lettres, ii. 243. Leoni, Vita di Francesco Maria, 132.
[3] Paris de Gr. ap. Rainaldum, 89, 104.

After this disaster, the Venetians could make no further resistance. On the 1st of August, Maximilian declared to them that he would set free the good old fathers and the people from the thraldom of the new and tyrannical nobility now reigning; he would give the city the freedom of the cities of the empire.[1] On the 2nd of August, his troops marched out from Verona. The Venetians were driven out of all Lombardy and Friuli back upon a few strongholds; but even these, Laniago and Soave, Kofel and Beitelstein, with many others, were taken, some under the personal superintendence of the Emperor. Not till then did he turn his attention to Treviso and Padua, but Treviso was besieged with good prospects of success before the end of August.[2] Whilst the Germans scoured the country as far as Lido Maggiore and the lagoons, the Venetians, on their side, having no general worthy the name, were obliged again to avail themselves of the services of Luzio Malvezzi, with whom they were dissatisfied, and whom they had dismissed. They could not pay their troops, and these would have deserted in one body to the Emperor, could they have expected pay from him. But, worst of all, the good will of their subjects did not continue. We see with astonishment how the ruling body were ever and again obliged to order their nobili to pay the imposts that were due. They adjured them by all that was holy, by their country and their children; they did not merely threaten to eject the delinquents from the Pregadi, and to confiscate their estates, but they began carrying out their threats. Yet all their adjurations, threats, and penalties were of none effect.[3] It suffices to say that Venice was in no less peril than Julius was.

How could they ever have conceived the idea of liberating Italy from its enemies? No pulse at that time beat for the idea of the unity and freedom of Italy. Only those States which had become formed in the course of the

[1] A letter of Maximilian, from the Italian in Hormayr's Archiv. für Geographie, etc.

[2] La Palice au Roy; Burgo à Marguerite, in the Lettres, iii. 15, 21, 10.

[3] Principally Bembus, 275-288. Mocenicus, 79.

few preceding centuries, and the Papacy boasted of life. Their union only lay in a common understanding, by means of which the attacks of foreign nations might have been repelled. But whilst each asserted and endeavoured to advance its own cause, they became involved in feud with each other, appealed to foreign aid, and yet there was not one among all strong enough to place itself at their head and remove the invaders, who had also on their side justifiable claims and a strong body of adherents. Nothing remained for the determined Pope but to summon to his assistance, against the French and the King of France, the Spaniards and the Swiss. But the result of this was to be something other than the liberation of Italy.

MORAL REFLECTION

Such being the position of affairs, it cannot be said that it was impossible, but it must be confessed that it was exceedingly difficult, for Italy to become once more independent of foreign nations. Far be it from me to pass judgment upon the temperament of a great nation, which in those days was a source of intellectual stimulus to the whole of Europe. No one can say that it was incurably sick; but it is certain that it suffered from serious diseases. Pederasty, which extended even to the young soldiers in the army,[1] and was regarded as venial because practised by the Greeks and Romans, whom all delighted to imitate, sapped all vital energy. Native and classical writers ascribe the misfortune of the nation to this evil practice.[2] A terrible rival of pederasty was syphilis, which spread through all classes like the plague. How often did it not happen that generals were by it rendered incapable of service ! The sons of Ercole d'Este were once all suffering from it at the same time. Whole villages in the Venetian territory were affected by it and exterminated ; we read of ships, if not of a whole fleet, that required to be remanned in Corfu, because the whole crew had been rendered unserviceable by

[1] Ferronus, after the description of the battle of Pavia, 1525.
[2] Chronicon Venetum, in Muratori, xxiv. p. 12.

this disease.[1] Precautions such as we might perhaps take here in Germany appear to be nothing but child's play, in the face of so wide-spread an evil.

It is, however, difficult not to identify this depravation, everywhere and always existent, although ever afresh denounced by preachers of morality, with the peculiar character of an epoch or a nation. We shall not be able to maintain without fear of contradiction that aspiration to fine language rather than to noble deeds, the imitation of antiquity in what it has achieved in the shade, rather than in what it has performed in the sun, as Machiavelli says,[2] is mere luxury, and not healthy for a nation as such ; for instance, the training of boys not merely in drawing and in composing prose and verse, but also in " fine hypocrisy," as their teachers expressed it,[3] which consisted in making speeches in public, raising and lowering the voice by turns, now affecting the tone of complaint, now that of triumph, simulating an unreal passion on an unreal theme, a practice which they continued in a strange manner when grown up—in fact, this whole formal training, to which women, whom we find improvising Latin verses to the lyre, also aspired.[4] But no one can doubt that it is a weakness, when those who affect to be masters of life, recommend in the place of manliness, chastity, and strict self-control, nought but acuteness and the semblance of such virtues.[5] Besides this, there were youths who preferred to sit upon a mule rather than a horse, men who curled their hair, plucked out their eyebrows, and spoke to their superiors as softly as if they were at their last breath ; men who were afraid to move their heads lest they should disarrange their hair, men who carried a looking-glass in their hat and a comb in their sleeve. Many considered it the highest praise to be able to sing well in ladies' society, accompanying themselves on the viol.[6]

---

[1] Diarium Ferrarense. Chronicon Venetum, 73.
[2] Machiavelli, arte della guerra, i. beginning.
[3] Arluni, bellum Venetum, iv. 58.
[4] Gilles, Chroniques, 117. Sansovino, Venetia, 190.
[5] Machiavelli, Principe and Discorsi. Castiglione, Cortegiano.
[6] Cortegiano, p. 43, p. 111, p. 125.

The motive for imitation is always to be found in weakness; foreign manners and customs forced their adoption upon the nation. And the misfortune was, that two nations strove for the mastery, and that whoever loathed French customs fell a victim to Spanish. He who did not speak French, learnt Spanish: he who disliked the loose dress of the French, chose the tighter-fitting garb of the Spanish and Germans. There were many who, in order to imitate the French, did nothing but shake their heads, or made bows and plied their feet so vigorously in the street, that their servants could not overtake them.[1] There were others, who took for their pattern the short and witty replies of the Spaniards, and their discreet and unpretentious appearance in every company and in every court, where they became each day more indispensable; these excellent chess players, who never appeared to take any trouble in the matter.[2] In any case they were captivated by one or the other custom.

The literature is also to a certain extent influenced by these conditions. Shortly previous to and during this period, there appeared four important heroic poems, two at Florence, namely, Ciriffo and Morgante, and two at Ferrara, the Orlandos of Boiardo and Ariosto. Ciriffo deals with the crusade of St. Louis, the others with the paladins of Charlemagne. They mainly extol French heroes; they take for their subject rather the wars of the Spaniards against the Saracens than their own wars: if the matter of these poems had an effect upon the nation, it could only act in opposition to the national spirit.

[1] Cortegiano, 146, 147, 163.   [2] Ibid. 138, 169.

CHAPTER IV

RISE OF THE AUSTRO - SPANISH HOUSE TO ALMOST THE HIGHEST POWER IN EUROPE

I. JULIUS II IN LEAGUE WITH SPAIN

JULIUS was assailed not only in his temporal power, but also in his spiritual dignity. The five cardinals who had forsaken him and joined Louis, three French, Borgia, for the sake of Lucrezia Borgia of Ferrara, and Caravajal, on the 19th of May, 1511, called a General Council of the Church—arguing, that contrary to his duty and his time the Pope was neglecting it—and invited the Pope himself to take part in it.[1] In the same manner as Charles VIII, in league with Savonarola, opposed Pope Alexander, so now did Louis make use of these cardinals against Julius. The so-called ecclesiastical weapons were employed more by the Princes against the Pope, than by the Pope against the Princes. Julius knew how to meet the cardinals. "They ought to remember with what voice, what eye, and what countenance he had sworn to hold a council ; they would say that he had done so in genuine singleness of heart. Only the misfortunes and the restlessness of Italy had stood in his way. But now, whilst annulling their convention, he himself summoned a Council, but not at Pisa (which a siege of fourteen years had rendered unsuitable for the purpose), and fixed it not for the following September, which was much too short an interval, but for April, 1512, and at Rome."[2]

[1] Convocatio Concilii apud Pisam, in Goldast, Politica Imperial. 1194.
[2] Breve apud Rainaldum, Ann. Eccl. xx. 90–92. Paris de Gr. *ibid.* 115.

The real danger did not lie in the Council, but in the superior power of Louis, who intended to employ its resolutions to the destruction of the Pope. Like Alexander, who, when in dread of Charles, and in feud with Louis, on one occasion concluded an alliance with Ferdinand, and on another at all events intended doing so, Julius now, though hesitatingly and unwillingly, but under the compulsion of necessity, turned to an alliance with Spain.

Ferdinand was on the road to Malaga and the African war, when he received the Pope's missives complaining of Louis. He halted on his march. The Council of Castile considered that as there was already a domestic war, it was not necessary to seek an external one. Ximenes promised to contribute 400,000 ducats, and even to come in person.[1] Ferdinand, who, in the year 1510, owing to the Pope's investiture, which released him from all obligations to Louis,[2] had become complete master of Naples,[2] knew well that in league with the Church and by its sanction all could be attained; in feud with her, nothing. With new great schemes in his head, he relinquished all idea of conquering Alexandria, and, in return for 40,000 ducats, their monthly pay, he offered the Pope 1,000 lances and 10,000 infantry.[3]

In August, 1511, the Pope secretly accepted his proposals at Ostia. On the 1st of October, they proclaimed their alliance. Its object was stated to be : " To conquer Bologna with its territory, and all the immediate possessions of the Papal See, and to restore the unity of the Church." A further important stipulation was the following : " If any conquests should be made outside of Italy, the conqueror should be confirmed in their possession by the Pope." [4] Hereupon, after a grand procession through the city, the League was proclaimed from the "stone of decrees" in the grand square at Venice, which guaranteed half the stipulated pay. Ferdinand came from stag-hunting, from the woods between Aranda and Lerma, and swore it ; declaring that he moreover offered himself and his goods,

[1] Gomez, Vita Ximenis, ap. Schottum, 1057, 1058.
[2] Zurita, ii. 220. Passero, Giornale, 173.
[3] Zurita.
[4] Liga pro recussu Papae, in Rymer, Foedera, vi. 1, 23.

and all the goods and estates of his daughter, to the service of the Church.[1]

A fourth associate, with Pope, King, and Republic was the Swiss Confederation. The League was not published among the Swiss. Neither their pay nor their old treaty influenced them at all; but, of all the parties to the League, they were the soonest ready for war.

Through all the Swiss cantons there surged in this year a lively spirit of faction. Especially was this the case in the Valais and Freiburg. There Jürg uff der Flue and Matthäus Schinner of Mühlibach strove against each other. Jürg, a strong hardy man, almost a hundred years of age, proud of his twelve sons and eleven daughters, all of whom his house-wife had borne him, lived at Glis, on the Simplon, whither the people often went on a pilgrimage, and was distinguished by reason of his family, who mainly were instrumental in conquering the Lower Valais.[2] Matthäus Schinner, who at school at Como had worked his way up to be his teacher's deputy, afterwards, as priest, gained the affections of the common people through his ascetic life—he slept on the bare boards—and, after zealously studying the law, won over also the educated classes, until a Bishop of the Valais on a journey saw him, and promoted him to a higher dignity. Both were once friends: they had both together compassed the overthrow of the bishop, who had been Schinner's benefactor, and Matthäus, through Jürg's assistance, had himself now become a bishop.[3] As long as Louis and Julius remained friends, they both served together; but as soon as war had broken out between these potentates, they also quarrelled. It is said that the bishop offered his services to the King for too great a price, and had on that account been rejected; at any rate, it happened that Jürg became the King's adherent, whilst Matthäus favoured the Pope. Since that time, they persecuted each other even to exile and imprisonment. One after the other, they were obliged to avoid the Valais. In

[1] Bembus, 290. Petrus Martyr, Epp., 467, 468.

[2] Simleri Vallesia, ii. p. 13, 33, in Thesaur. Helveticus.

[3] Elogium Matthaei Schineri, in the Elogia Jovi, 249–251. Simler, *ibid,* Stettler, 444.

Freiburg, the bailiff, Franz Arsent, and Peter Falk, an adherent of the Pope, strove to the bitter death. Falk triumphed; thereupon the old friendship between Freiburg and Bern was at an end ; for, in the latter place, the Diesbachs and the French party were in the ascendant.[1]

During these struggles, the assemblies presented a curious spectacle. The covenant of succession with the Emperor, when an ally of Louis, had been assented to by the majority but not by the Forest cantons.[2] Many cantons had already once taken home the draft of a new French alliance, and were disposed to accept it ; but the three Forest cantons declared that, in the event of its being adopted, they would from that very moment, single-handed, march with their three standards against the King's land. Nothing was settled. Schinner, it is true, also visited the assemblies in the various cantons, and, wherever he was, there was a constant going and coming, writing, enlisting, and nego-tiating ; not a moment's repose. He showed himself so well informed, that it was believed that a private demon told him everything ;[3] but, in spite of all his exertions, he was not successful. A mere chance incident at length brought matters to a close.

A courier was despatched from Schwyz through the Milanese, in order to fetch the subsidy from the Pope, but in Lugano he was seized—for he was carrying letters from Schinner to the Pope—and drowned in the lake. The person of a courier, in his distinctive dress, was considered to be as inviolable as that of a herald. But his dress, a coat with the arms of Schwyz, was made jest of, and his symbol—the wooden box—was even sold by auction. The bailiff may have done this, in order to insult the Ghibellines in Lugano, who were of Swiss sympathies, rather than the Schwyzers themselves ; but, however this may be, the incident roused the Forest cantons, which were already ill-disposed, to a perfect transport of frenzy. They complained that " their honour had been wounded, and that they must devise a means of saving it ; "

---

[1] History of Arsent's imprisonment and death in Glutz. 233–240.
[2] Document in Dumont, iv. 1, 133. Recess in Fuchs, 251.
[3] Recess in Fuchs, 262, 264. Bullinger MS. in Fuchs, 254.

accordingly, in September, 1511, they resolved, on their own initiative, to take the field against the King, and to call upon their confederates to join them.[1]

As, in the year 1500, the affront given to the Grisons aroused all the Swiss against the Emperor, in spite of the imperial party in their midst, so now even the French party were obliged to obey this challenge, and prepare for war against France, no longer for pay or because of the league with the Pope, but on their own account, and without pay.

When, then, in October, Schwyz once more earnestly called upon all members of the Confederation, by virtue of the eternal alliance subsisting between them, to take the field, the deputies of the others hurriedly presented themselves before the assembly in that town, in the hope of being able to appease it. But they were not successful. Schinner was not there; the very moment he had been made Cardinal by the Pope, he had been obliged to fly from his countrymen to Italy, where in disguise, and after many risks, he arrived, and passed through the midst of his enemies to Venice. Here, he received 20,000 guilders from the Signoria[2] and found means to despatch a goodly portion of it to his friends in the Confederation. Instead of calming the excited feelings of the people, the deputies themselves were carried away. They promised to make the cause of the Schwyzers their cause, and to stake lives and property for their sake. But their masters at home who had sent them did not change their minds. The assembly was again reminded that the winter had arrived, the St. Gotthard was high and the passes narrow, and how was it possible to pay for provisions on the Italian side? The Emperor might meanwhile follow up his threat and attack. But all to no purpose. The assembled community declared for war: "they would find the King and punish him," and they despatched their letters of summons to the other cantons. They then provided themselves with provisions and arms; one after another they all took the field.[3]

---

[1] Fuchs from Schödeler, Silbereisen, 255.

[2] Ciacconius, Vitae Paparum et Cardinalium, 1383. Anshelm, in Glutz. 247. Bembus.

[3] Recess in Fuchs, 268 and 270.

Thus began a new war, the central figure in which was Julius. The despatch of money through Schinner appears to have been his work; and it was also his plan that the Spaniards at the same time, on the 2nd of November, set out for Naples. As the French had retired from Treviso from fear of the Swiss, and the Germans were too weak to undertake the siege alone, the ruin of the Venetians was stayed; they were even enabled themselves to advance through the country.[1] It would perhaps have been better had the Confederates awaited their advance and their arrival on the Po. But they could not be restrained.

On the 14th of November, 1,500 Schwyzers began the ascent of the St. Gotthard with the standard, under which they had vanquished Charles of Burgundy, and which they had never since unfolded. They were immediately followed by Peter Falk with 500 Freiburgers and some artillery. It was the first artillery that the St. Gotthard had yet seen. Gunners from Lucerne brought it over the lake, and oxen of Uri along the bridle-path from Flüelen; thence, with the assistance of the ammans of Urseren, they carried it in their arms across the heights! How the French on Lake Maggiore were terrified when they heard the first salvos![2]

Schwyzers and Freiburgers were the most zealous in the Papal cause, and now, without a moment's pause, they marched into the enemy's country. Four Freiburgers swam across the Tresa, in the face of a number of French arquebusiers, and threw a bridge across the river. It was not until Varese, where the plain begins, that they awaited the troops from Uri, Unterwalden, and Schaffhausen, and the rest only in Gallarate, where the French hommes d'armes were in force, and in advantage. They then pursued the enemy, "with all hands," as the chroniclers say, as far as the hazel-trees of Milan.[3] Now was the time for the Spaniards and Venetians to make their onslaught. But the former

---

[1] Caracciolus, Vita Spinelli, 95. Coccinius, 273. Burgo, Lettres, iii. 82.

[2] Bembus, 294. Letter of Peter Falk in Fuchs, 272.

[3] Letters of the Constable and Councillors of Freiburg in Glutz., Appendix 18, p. 535. Schwytzer, Schödeler, Bullinger in Fuchs, 285 *seq*. Bayard, 252.

were too far off, and the latter were occupied in retaking their castles from the Imperialists.[1] The Swiss, without horse and cannon in the face of a strongly fortified city, their first onslaught repulsed with severe loss, disheartened at the weather—for the winter was wet rather than cold and they had been rained upon for four whole days and nights—without provisions or money, and in a state of perplexity respecting Bern, were seized with what the Italians called the German mania, and which their chroniclers can only compare with a sudden rush of water from the hills—a cataract which forces a channel for itself, and breaks its force against a rock, then turns, perchance, and bursts away in an opposite direction, until by nature and circumstances it is restored to its right course. They now conceived the idea of turning back, and coming again later in greater strength. In their frenzy, they made their way home with fire and devastation; those from the Forest cantons leading the way. In the morning, they fired their bivouac ; before them, behind them, and for miles on either side the villages were in flames. Thus they made their way from the hazel-bushes of Milan back to the mill of Bellinzona ; even in Mesocco they burnt the castles of Trivulzio ; thence they rushed home across the mountains, still full of fury, saying that it was owing to them that the French had come to Italy, and through them they should retire again.[2] They returned to their cottages and awaited the coming of the spring.

Then, and not till then, came the Spaniards and Venetians.[3] They made their attacks simultaneously in different places. On the 25th of January, 1512, the Venetians, summoned by Luigi Avogaro, made their appearance before Brescia, and, in the dusk of the evening of the 26th, the Spanish arquebusiers, with the Gozadini and Pepuli, the old enemies of the Bentivogli, commenced the siege of

[1] Coccinius, 276. Reisner, Frundsperge, 113. Bembus, 205.
[2] Benedictus Jovius, Historia Novocom. 63. Bayard, Stettler. Schödeler and Anshelm in Glutz. 256, 257. Petrus Martyr, Epist. 474. Appendix to Monstrelet, 241.
[3] Paulus de Laude in the Lettres de Louis, iii. 109. Jovius, Vita Alfonsi, 172.

Bologna.[1] But, on this occasion, neither force was successful. They repeatedly renewed their attacks. On the 1st of
February, Pedro Navarra sprung the mines which he had
bored under the houses of Bologna, and his Spaniards
stormed. They were met by the counter-mines of Gabriel
von Sulz, and the overpowering fumes of kindled brushwood, so that Bologna was still safe. The Venetians, who
bombarded Brescia with their whole force, were more successful on the 2nd. Some with ropes, and others by tunnel-
ling, succeeded in effecting an entrance: the people then
rose and Brescia fell. Crema, Cremona, and Bergamo
declared for their old masters. In France, when this news
was first received, Milan was considered to be lost.[2] Yet
the army did not intend to give it up.

Gaston de Foix, the King's nephew, led the army. He
was a youth at the age when youthful bloom is passing into
riper manhood; the down of youth was still on his cheeks;
his eye fired whenever he laid hand on his sword; he drew
it, as he said, in love of his lady, whose colours, green
and white, he wore round his arm.[3] At Reggio, he heard of
the loss of Brescia and the peril of Bologna; he did not
long hesitate, but sought the strongest enemy, and, on the
4th of February, entered through the Porta San Felice.[4]
The Spaniards, as soon as they heard of his arrival, fell back
upon the Idice. After having strengthened the garrison, so
as to be certain of success, he turned about at once, forced by
surprise the approaches of Mantua, and drove the Venetians,
who opposed him, into the hands of the Germans, who
were advancing from Verona to meet him.[5] By the 17th
of February he was in the castle of Brescia—it is called the
Falcon of Lombardy, and is certainly high enough and
menacing enough to deserve this name[6]—determined with

---

[1] Coccinius, 280. Zurita, ii. 264. Bembus.

[2] Jean le Veau from Bologna, Lettres, iii. 132. Andrea del Burgo,
p. 147. Carpesanus, 1273. Coccinius. Zurita, 266. Arluni, iv. 175.

[3] Elogium Foxeji in Jovius, Elogia, 225. Brantôme, Capitaines,
142. Bayard.

[4] Jean le Veau, Lettres, iii. 153. Coccinius, 281. Zurita.

[5] Jean le Veau, Lettres, 173. Machiavelli, Discorsi sopra la prima
deca di Livio, 299. Mocenicus, 85.

[6] Octavii Rubei Monumenta Brixiensia in Graev. Thesaur. iv. 2, 91.

his French and Germans from this point of advantage to take the city lying beneath him.

On the morning of the 18th, two companies of soldiers formed in the castle yard; in the gate the vanguard of volunteers, consisting of Germans under Fabian and Spet, Gascons, and some hommes d'armes with short lances with long blades; further behind them the others, both Germans, who, at the word "to conquer the city or die," lifted up their hands as a sign of their good will, and cut notches in the pikes which long usage had worn smooth, and French. When, then, the citizens below, declining to listen to the repeated summons to surrender, gathered together for resistance at the sound of the bell, Gaston led the attack upon them with the cry of " Forward, in the name of God and St. Denis !" All the trumpets sounded.[1]

Whilst the Venetians, after their first ineffective fire, were again loading their muskets, the vanguard succeeded in descending the narrow path in single file; then, uniting their force, they made an onslaught upon the cathedral of S. Florian and the intrenchments of the Brisignels. Bayard, who had forced his way amongst the Venetians, made the greatest impression. Gritti cried: " Let us vanquish this Bayard and the victory is ours," and he was in fact severely wounded; but the assault was not thereby stayed. The cathedral and the cannon were taken. The advance guard pursued the Brisignels through the citadel to the very gate of the city: they alone had decided the day. When the rest of their force arrived on the spot, and the gate of the city was opened, the Venetians saw the cannon directed against their close ranks in the streets and they thereupon let down the drawbridge at the Porta S. Nazzaro—for flight, as they thought, whilst it was really for destruction, for 500 lances were concealed without and now rushed in. The ensuing struggle was more like a massacre than a fight. In the narrow streets, their light horses availed the Stradioti nothing, nor the heavy-armed their stout armour. They were all alike cut down. Only Avogaro, although

---

[1] Bayard, 261. Coccinius, 282. Epistola ad Episcopum Gurcensem in the Paralipomena ad Chronicon Urspergense, 467. Mythical, in Appendix to Monstrelet.

he threw himself into the midst of the enemy, was not slain ; his horse fell with him ; he was made prisoner and saved for a worse death. Gritti was also taken. In all the houses the hideous scenes of war and pillage were enacted ; the booty was carried off in 3,500 waggons.[1]

Thus were the attacks of the Swiss, Spaniards, and Venetians successively repulsed, and Gaston triumphant : he next resolved to go in search of the Spanish knights, whom he had been told it was a pleasure to behold, all in gold and azure, with their horses completely covered with mail armour. With them he now thought of contesting for the prize of valour.

The Council furnished him a special opportunity for advancing against them. It had only been opened on the 5th of November in Pisa by the Cardinals ; and on the 6th, Caravajal declared his readiness to remove it elsewhere.[2] After the first sittings, it was, in January, 1512, removed to Milan. Neither Maximilian nor Florence, nor even Flanders, although it was subject to Louis, sent any prelate. The Cardinals had been unwelcome in Pisa, and in Milan their presence was utterly ignored ; but after Gaston's victories they were more courageous. They sneered at the Pope, released Bologna and Ferrara from his ban, and sent two envoys, one to Avignon, and the other to Bologna : "for it was seemly that the whole temporal possessions of the Church should be in their hands." [3] Now Louis, who most particularly avoided the appearance of waging war in his own name with the Church, in March availed himself of this pretext, and, in the name of the Council rather than in his own, despatched his nephew accompanied by the legate, to the territory of the Church ; he had with him what was for those times a powerful army, consisting of 1,800 lances, 900 light cavalry and 15,000 infantry.[4]

---

[1] The foregoing and characteristically also Carpesanus, 1276–1280. Louis to Margaret, Lettres, iii. 178. Arluni, iv. 179. Fleuranges, 87, 88.

[2] Machiavelli's Legazione to the Council, v. 407.

[3] Petrus Martyr, Ep. 470, seq. Nardi, 130, seq. Guicciardini, x. 559, 580.

[4] Andrea del Burgo, Lettres, iii. 197. Reports to Louis, 211.

The Spaniards were not inclined to fight. Their King wrote to them : " Three things about which he was negotiating, must come about : the English invade France ; the Swiss again attack Milan ; and the Emperor conclude peace with Venice ; each of which events was by itself capable of annihilating the French. It would be better for the Pope to conquer late than to lose quickly." [1] Only they would not entirely abandon the country.

From the Apennines six important streams run down to the sea, the Silaro, the Santerno, the Senio, the Lamone, the Montone, and the Ronco, all reaching Ravenna in the plain. They all intersect the country in the same direction. The Spaniards resolved to make use of these for the purposes of resistance. They could either be defended below, and this course was advised by Fabrizio Colonna, general of the cavalry, but in that case the road across the Apennines to Tuscany, and possibly to Rome itself, would be open to the enemy, or above ; and the latter plan found favour with Pedro Navarra, captain of the foot, an enemy of Colonna, whose proud title angered him, but Ravenna would in the latter case be in danger. Navarra gained his point here, as he always did. Their first encampment was at Castel S. Pietro, on the first of those rivers. As soon as Navarra perceived that the French crossed lower down the stream, he broke up the camp ; at Imola he found that the French pursued similar tactics ; they crossed the second, third, and fourth rivers, and Navarra always entrenched himself ready to receive the enemy ; finally, the French swerved to the left from the Montone towards Ravenna, and on Good Friday, the 9th of April, 1512, they attacked the city. In Ravenna the Spaniards had their magazines, and they could not allow the city to be lost ; on the same Good Friday they advanced with their whole force between the Lamone and the Ronco down towards the city. The French attack was unsuccessful. On Easter Eve, the armies confronted each other.[2]

It was on Easter Day, at the hour when the rest of

[1] Zurita, ii. 279.
[2] Report to Louis, Lettres, iii. 215, 216. Zurita, ii. 281.

Christendom was waiting for the rising of the sun, before saluting each his fellow, when a herald of the Viceroy and Spanish commander-in-chief, Ramon de Cardona, had an interview with Gaston on the canal, which joined the Montone and the Ronco, and now separated both the armies. "Shall we fight to-day?" asked Cardona; Gaston replied: "If you will, we are ready." They both then broke asunder the white staves, which they held in their hands as a sign of peace, and rode back.[1] Gaston came to his captains; he said: "If fortune favours us, we will praise it, if not, God's will be done;" he shared with them the bread and the bottle of wine, which he still had; they vowed to live and die with him.

Gaston sat on horseback, arrayed in the arms of Foix and Navarre: his coat of mail only extended as far as the elbow of his right arm, and from there to the wrist he wore the colours of his lady.[2] The Bastard of Chimay warned him and said that an old seer at Carpi had prophesied the death of one of the commanders; the blood-red sunrise meant death for either Gaston or Cardona; but he answered: "I will go into the battle."

Whilst they were thus riding along the canal, they perceived Pedro de la Paz and some others of the enemy on the other side. "You appear to be amusing yourselves until this fine game begins," said Bayard. "Is it you?" asked Pedro, "then is your camp stronger by fully 2,000 men. If we could only amuse ourselves with you in peace! But who is the noble prince, whom I see among you?" "It is the Prince of Foix." Gaston de Foix was the brother of Queen Germaine. The Spaniards dismounted and saluted him. "My lord," said Pedro, "saving our master's service, we are at your disposal."[3]

Meanwhile, Jacob von Ems stood in the midst of the landsknechts, and addressed them thus: "Dear brothers, the French this day place their hopes upon you. You cannot, however, place your hopes upon any one except yourselves; for know this well, if you do not defeat the enemy,

---

[1] Coccinius, De bellis Italicis, apud Freherum, ii. 286.
[2] Senarega, Annales Genuenses, p. 613.
[3] L'histoire du bon chevalier Bayard, 310, 311.

you will never escape from the peasants. Be steadfast in the fight! Think of victory or death!" And then he led them, after each had vowed to God to fast the ensuing Saturday on bread and water, across the bridge over the canal. "I would rather lose an eye," said the captain of the French infantry, Molart, "than that they should go before us," and dashed with his soldiers through the water. They advanced against the enemy's centre, Alfonso of Ferrara with his cannon and La Palice with 800 lances supporting their flank. Behind them, at a short interval, came Gaston and the main body.

The Spanish camp was protected on the right, where the cavalry were posted, by the canal, and on the left, where the infantry was drawn up, by a ditch, and a little further away by a dyke. In front of his infantry, Navarra had, besides, two ditches; some little distance behind these, were posted his two-wheeled carts, upon which were mounted iron contrivances, long and pointed, and curved on the sides like sickles, and close by, a goodly number of mounted arquebuses and culverins.[1]

It was for Gaston's army to drive the enemy from this strong position.

On their left, on the dyke, Alfonso planted his artillery, while Ives d'Allègre mounted his on their right, on the other side of the canal. Navarra's infantry having thrown themselves flat on the ground, it happened that the balls thrown by both fell entirely among Fabrizio's knights. Their stout armour did not protect them; they fell in thirties and forties; the foremost and hindmost closed up and spoke among themselves; Fabrizio at last shouted, "Shall we all perish for the sake of a traitor?" The Spaniards cried, "God slays us, let us fight with men." With the shout, "España and St. Iago with the horse!" they advanced against the foe. On seeing this, Gaston said, "Now, Sirs, let us now see what ye will do for France and my lady," and closed up with La Palice. All cried, "France, France!"

[1] Fleuranges, Mémoires, 89–93. Coccinius and Novae e castris Gallorum in the Paralipomena ad Chronicon Urspergense, 467. Also Ulrich Zwingli, Relatio de iis, etc., ap. Freherum, ii. 122. Reisner, Kriegsthaten, i. 114.

and the cavalry battle, their fine art, commenced.[1] Meanwhile the infantry, in obedience to Gaston's orders to halt until he gave the signal, stood still; but Navarra's arquebuses and culverins wrought deadly havoc; two of the chief leaders, Molart and Freiberg, who were sitting together over a bottle, were both killed by one ball. Many distinguished captains, subaltern officers, and common soldiers fell; at last they would no longer stand still and endure this fire. As they surmounted the first ditch, which Navarra had dug in front of him, Jacob von Ems was hit. He exclaimed, "The King has been gracious to us, be firm," and died. When they came to the second ditch, the Spaniards held their pikes crossed to oppose them; whereupon Fabian von Schlaberndorf, a man of great size and strength, clutching his pike crosswise, beat down six or eight of the enemy's pikes, and opened a path. They forced their way to the open space between the ditches and the carts; here Fabian and Johann Spet placed green wreaths on their heads, and advancing, challenged the bravest of the Spaniards to mortal combat. Two came out to them. Spet was, before the fray, laid low by a bullet, but Fabian slew his opponent. At length, when they were close upon the arquebuses, the Spaniards sprang to their feet, and the real infantry battle began. Spears broke and swords snapped; some fought with fists, with clods of earth, and teeth; sometimes one or other, fearing a cavalry attack on the flank, would cry, "Back, ye Germans!" but the first line never moved; then fell the powerful Fabian, Linser, the boldest man in the world, and many others. The Spaniards frequently cried, "Victoria, Julius!" and it seemed probable that they would be victorious. But Navarra's hopes were always doomed to disappointment: the Germans remained unshaken.[2]

But at the same time Fabrizio and his horse, after a

---

[1] L'histoire du bon chevalier, 312. Bayard à Laurens Alemand in Expilly's Supplement à l'histoire, 451. Also Daru, iii. 441.
[2] Zurita, ii. 283. Guicciardini, x. 590. Petrus Martyr, Ep. 483. Especially Coccinius, 286, and Fleuranges, 94. *Vide* also Machiavelli, Principe, c. 26, p. 68. Hutteni Epitaphia in Empserum in the Epigrammata; Opera, t. i. 184, 185, ed. Münch.

cavalry engagement of three hours, felt that they were un-
equally matched with the French. Gaston himself ran an
enemy through the body; Bayard and La Palice com-
pleted what the cannon had begun; the King's Guard
used their iron firelocks with effect upon the helmets of
the enemy; the attack of the light cavalry was repulsed by
a short manœuvre. Ramon de Cardona fled. The young
Marquis of Pescara did not forget his shield and the words
"with or upon" emblazoned on his standard; but his
horse stumbled, and he was taken prisoner. The legate of
the Pope, Giovanni de' Medici, was led before the legates
of the Council. Fabrizio Colonna still defended himself,
unknown, as he thought. "Roman," said one to him,
"yield to fate, and surrender to me." "Dost thou know
me—who art thou?" "Alfonso d'Este!" "It is well, no
Frenchman;" he surrendered himself. The cavalry was
completely disorganized.[1]

At this juncture, Pondormy also with cavalry galloped
across Navarra's ditches, and attacked the infantry in the
flank. Ives d'Allègre broke into Ramazotto's company,
in order to avenge the death of his son, whom they had
killed in a riot. Others came to the assistance of the
Germans, who were with the artillery. Navarra looked
round, and saw that the battle was lost; he began to beat a
retreat, though in good order. Yet once again he made
a desperate onslaught upon the enemy, and was taken
prisoner. This decided the day. Don Diego Quiñones
lay wounded on the ground, and saw the horsemen dashing
past him. Half dead he raised himself, and inquired who
had won the victory. He heard, "The French," and parted
dissatisfied from the world.[2]

"Sir," said Bayard to Gaston, who was covered with
blood and brains, "are you wounded?" "No," replied
Gaston, "but I have wounded." Bayard answered, "Thank
God, now leave the pursuit to others." Whilst they spoke,
Gaston perceived the Bastard of Chimay: "Well, Master,

---

[1] The foregoing and Jovius, Vita Alfonsi Ferrariensis, 176. Vita
Leonis. Vita Davali Pescarae, 280. Ferry Carondelet à Marguerite,
Lettres, 228.

[2] The same and Passero, Giornale Napolitano, 180.

am I slain as you said?" "Sir, it is not yet over," was
the answer. At that moment a musketeer came: "Look,
Sir, two thousand Spaniards are on the height." These
Spaniards had fought with some Gascons at a distance from
the main battle, and, after having defeated and pursued
them, were now returning. Gaston again took up his helmet:
"Follow me, all who love me;" with twenty or thirty
men he rushed upon them; but there he found his death.
It is, doubtless, sweet for a young man, after glorious
achievements, and in the midst of great successes and
hopes, to die, while yet free from the blame which later
years bring only too easily. Memory immortalizes youth.
Gaston's horse fell, and he defended himself on foot.
Lautrec called to the Spaniards: "Spare him, he is the
brother of your Queen;" but no quarter was given. He
was slain, and thrown into the ditch: from chin to forehead
he had fourteen wounds.

When the French saw this, the joy of their victory was
damped.

This conflict is remarkable as having been the only one
in history, where Italians and Spanish, on the one side,
opposed an alliance between Italians, Germans, and French
on the other, since Italians and Germans were later always
united with the Spaniards; and it is especially remarkable
for the co-operation of guns with the pikes of the infantry
and the armour of the knights. The military discipline of
the French hommes d'armes, and the stubborn resistance of
the Germans bore off the victory.

The French came to the Germans, who were still drawn
up in line, and said: "That is our artillery that you took
from us in Naples, now give it back to us. Will you not
also go out for booty?" They answered: "We have stood
here, not for booty, but for glory and honour." They fell
on their knees and thanked God.[1]

A Spanish knight was the first to bring the news of the
battle to Rome. The Spanish ambassador at once shipped
all his household goods on the Tiber; the populace, summoned by some of the barons to liberty, closed their shops

[1] After Fleuranges, Bayard's Letter, 453, and Coccinius. Hutten,
183.

and rose in revolt. Julius shut himself up in the Castle of St. Angelo, and wished to leave Italy. Ferdinand, in anxiety for the peril of Naples, forgot his principles, and again appointed the Great Captain commander-in-chief of the forces in Italy.[1]

Thus the great war of the Pope, combined with the Venetians, Swiss, and Spaniards, against the French and Germans, had completely failed. Other forces must needs be summoned to take part in it.

2. FORMATION OF A NEW LEAGUE. THE SITUATION AND COALITION OF ENGLAND

At this time, with perhaps the exception of the French, there was no nation more subject to its King than the English. The numbers of the nobles had become thinned in the ruinous struggle between the rival houses of York and Lancaster, and, when one party triumphed, in the fresh rivalries which ensued between its members. Comines computes that eighty scions of the blood royal were, as far as he could ascertain, slain in these wars. King Edward IV in his battles cried: "Slay the lords; but spare the people!"[2] At length, Henry VII was conveyed in a covered carriage to London to be crowned, and had almost all the rest of the Yorkists imprisoned in the Tower, or put to death;[3] not even sparing the man, whose secession at the decisive hour had alone procured him victory and the Crown. Hereupon he limited the clergy's right of sanctuary, so far subjected the cities, that their liberties, without his Chancellor's confirmation, were a dead letter, and brought the peasants, after they had thrice risen in arms against him, to a more and more unquestioning obedience.[4] The organs of liberty—the tribunals and parliament—were subservient to him. His councillors in

---

[1] Infessura in Rainaldus, 112. Petrus Martyr, 484. Jovius, Vita Gonsalvi, 286.

[2] Comines, Mémoires, pp. 41, 155.

[3] Polydorus Virgilius, Historia Anglica, 728.

[4] Bacon, Historia Henrici VII. Opus vere politicum, pp. 18, 360.

the Star Chamber dealt with murder, robbery, and every apparent attempt at insurrection. His financial agents, Empson and Dudley, made use of the conflicting laws of the realm, given by conflicting powers, to hold, by means of fines payable for every transgression of the law, both the nation in obedience and the King in funds. But his Parliaments—following the precedent established in the civil wars, that each victor formed one of his own party, which was rather an organ of the supreme power, than an organ of the people—were from the first entirely sub-servient to him. The first consisted exclusively of men who had been condemned by former parliaments. Another parliament chose Dudley for its Speaker.[1]

This obedience was Henry VII's internal safeguard ; the external lay in his relationships. We have already seen that he married his daughter to the King of Scotland and his son Arthur to Katherine. Arthur having died before, as is believed, he was able to consummate the marriage, Katherine, much as she wished to escape from these hard hearts, her father and father-in-law, was compelled to remain, because through her each thought himself surer of the other. But Henry was not yet contented. By another alliance, the betrothal of Charles of Austria with his daughter Mary,[2] he united himself with the Austro-Spanish house.

This English prince, with his few hairs, few teeth, and a face that no painter would envy, parsimonious, and studying his advantage more than his reputation, whose servants were mere tools, left, in 1509, his realm to his son, who was in the first bloom of his youth, who could wield the two-handed sword and the battle-axe as deftly as he could play the flute and spinet, lavish by nature, in urgent need of a favourite, and eager for honour and glory.[3]

Yet being one flesh and blood they both went the same way. Although Henry VIII bore the red and white rose on his scutcheon, he put to death Suffolk and

[1] Bacon, 113, 236, 350. Polydor. Virgilius, 775. Cf. also Hume.
[2] Polydor. xxvii. 2. Zurita, ii. 155. Vettori in Machiavelli, Legazioni, v. 228.
[3] Bacon and Polydor. Especially Edward Herbert of Cherbury, The Life and Reign of Henry VIII, p. 4.

Buckingham, the old servants of the House of York, whose lives his father had spared. To put to death the financial agents was, at all events, as violent a deed on the part of the son as their employment had been on the part of the father. His first favourite, Wolsey, who used the whole lustre of his archbishopric and his dignity as Papal legate to bring the clergy into submission, and subordinated all the bureaucracy to the Chancellorship, which he also held, procured him all the essential advantages of supremacy, without the name. Parliament continued to vote what he wished, and, as he said to an opponent, " Man, to-morrow my bill or thy head passes." The whole manner and method of his father was his also ; only he brought them to bear still more inconsiderately and more rapidly.[1]

He also based his foreign policy upon his relationships. His object was not merely to secure his own position, but to procure for the great league, to which he belonged, the ascendency in Europe ; and herein he proceeded with more energy and passion than his father had done.

At the very outset, immediately after his marriage with the Spanish Katherine, he found himself, through her, allied to Ferdinand, and, through his sister Mary, to Charles and Maximilian. In the year 1511, he sent aid to both ; to the first against the Moors, and to the other against Gelderland ; and as long as they enjoyed it, he also had peace with France. In July, 1510, his envoys swore to the old treaties with Louis.[2] But when, in October, 1511, Ferdinand entered into a league with the Pope against France, matters wore a different complexion.

One important result of the League of 1495 was, as we have seen, the formation of the great Austro-Spanish alliance. At the present time, it was Ferdinand's plan to found in the same manner a new league, which, in name and pretext, should be in the interests of the Pope, but which, in fact, should work still more for the future greatness of his house.

But the foundation of all was the reconciliation between

---

[1] Herbert, 14. Goodwin, Annales Anglici, Henrico, Eduardo et Maria regnantibus, p. 17. Hume, Henry VIII, p. 117.
[2] Herbert, 15. Machiavelli, Legazioni, vi. 348. Zurita, ii. 249.

Ferdinand and Maximilian.   After the long feud respecting
Castile, Mercurino Gattinara was, of all Maximilian's councillors, the first to arrive at the conviction that this
reconciliation was the greatest need of his master.   How
was it that the campaign against Padua had failed?   Was it
not because Ferdinand had sent the Venetians supplies?[1]
In order to renew the old understanding, he betook himself
to Spain; and here, after at last abandoning Maximilian's
claim to a direct administration of Castile, which could
never be obtained, and, by contenting himself with an
arrangement, whereby Ferdinand assured the succession in
his realms to their common grandson Charles, he brought
about the reconciliation, and restored the old alliance and
the natural friendship between the two potentates.   Since
then, Ferdinand busies himself again with the affair of
Gelderland, and the Emperor in German state papers
devises war against the Moors.[2]

Ferdinand's next scheme was to draw the King of England
and the Emperor, his nearest relatives, into his war.

He first succeeded with King Henry.   When Louis
invited the latter to take part in the Council of Pisa, the
answer was given by the fact, that the King, whilst the
French ambassador was speaking, leant on the shoulder of
the Spanish envoy, Luis Carroz.[3]   The league between
Ferdinand and the Pope was concluded in the presupposition
that Henry would join it.   Henry hoped that the Pope
would give him the title of "the most Christian king," and
on the 4th of February, 1512, he despatched his plenipotentiaries to the Lateran Council.   He hoped, if not to
restore the greatness of the former English kings in France,
at all events to unite Guienne to his royal standard; and
for this purpose, his parliament, which assembled on the
same day, voted him a benevolence.   He granted privileges
for zealous captains,[4] and punishments for the dishonest.

---

[1] Gattinara à Marguerite, Lettres de Louis, 194.

[2] Zurita, ii. 203.   Letters of the Emperor of 1510 in Goldast,
Hormayr, Beckmann.

[3] Zurita, ii. 267.

[4] Herbert, 18, 19.   Jean le Veau in the Lettres, iii. p. 150, of
10th February.

One of his motives, perhaps, was that his house, owing to the betrothal of Mary to Charles, had a claim to Naples, which Ferdinand represented as being in danger; and the five and a half millions which his father had left him gave him support and confidence. Suffice it to say, he entered into the League, and promised to maintain the sea from the Thames to le Trade. In the winter, he sent two messages to Louis, one about Guienne, and one on behalf of the Pope. But as both were to no purpose, he declared war, and made common cause with Ferdinand; he agreed to supplement 8,000 Spanish infantry with 8,000 English arquebusiers, but to pay the cavalry jointly with him; whatever was conquered should belong to him whose forefathers had possessed it.[1]

Henry having now made his decision, both parties solicited the alliance of Maximilian. When, in August, 1511, Julius was lying sick unto death, Maximilian entertained a hope of becoming Pope himself. "He required 300,000 ducats to gain over the cardinals; and to raise this sum he would sacrifice his four chests full of jewels, and his feudal apparel. He had no higher ambition." Both parties entertained the same idea, even after Julius had recovered. The schismatic cardinals encouraged Maximilian, urging him only to come to Italy; there there were at his service 200 lances of Louis', the power of the Sanseverino of Mantua and Ferrara, as well as the prestige of the Council; the Pope would then be deposed, and he himself, if he desired it, be elected in his stead. Naples, they urged, was also open to him. On the other hand, Ferdinand reminded him that "friendship with the present Pope, and not enmity, was essential, if he wished to become his successor."[2]

We do not learn precisely when and why Maximilian abandoned this scheme, which was much too ambitious to be able to be realized; but, as he was allied with Ferdinand, nothing permanent could be done with regard to it so long as Julius was alive. Other matters were nearer his heart.

[1] Ratificatio Ligae ap. Rymer, vi. 1, 25, Articul. 2, 7. Polydorus, lib. xxvii. p. 7.

[2] Maximilian's Letter of 18th Sept., probably 1511, to Margaret in the Lettres and to Lichtenstein in Goldast. Zurita, ii. 260.

It had ever been his intention to conquer the Milanese and Venetian territory. But the one scheme really excluded the other, for he could not subdue the one without the assistance of the other. Ferdinand disclosed to him a way of attaining both objects successively : first of all, the conquest of Milan for Charles, their grandson (it would pass for the time being into the hands of Maximilian through the League) ; for this purpose, a truce to be made with Venice, who would then give her assistance ; finally, an attack upon Venice itself.[1] Julius was already so deeply entangled in the net of this family, that he agreed to whatever suited them. The Venetians declined to abandon Verona and Vicenza entirely, and in exchange for Treviso and Padua to acknowledge the Archduke Charles as suzerain, as the Emperor demanded ; but the Pope, having gathered from a secret letter of Louis, which, though the words were crossed out, was still legible, that an alliance between the King and the Republic was to be apprehended, lost no time in bringing about a truce between the Emperor and Venice, which left to both parties what they possessed, and procured for the Emperor, to begin with, a sum of 40,000 ducats.[2]

Thus, and owing also to the disturbances in Gelderland, which had recommenced, it came about that the Emperor joined the League. At the very moment that he forsook Louis, his Germans had gained a victory for the King. It is true that, shortly before the battle of Ravenna, a certain rumour as to this truce came to them from the enemy's camp; but this indefinite information was kept secret and had no influence upon their courage and their success. Venice also recognized the Lateran Council.

3. THE CONQUEST OF MILAN

Three things had been foretold to his army by Ferdinand, and two had already happened : England was involved in war with France, and the Emperor had made peace with

---

[1] Zurita, ii. 262. Another proof is afforded by the negotiations at Mantua in the summer of 1512.

[2] Bembus. Document in the Lettres de Louis, iii. 217.

Venice. In the days of the battle of Ravenna, the third was also realized: the invasion of Milan by the Swiss.

On that Good Friday on which Gaston stormed Ravenna and the Spaniards went forth to battle, the bitterest foes of the French, coming from all the cantons of the Confederation, assembled in Baden, and resolved, even singlehanded, to begin the war against the French. Each man of them was to announce the fact of their decision to his lords and superiors, and beg them for powder and muskets. The following Saturday week, they were to meet in Livinen, and, in God's name, advance against their enemies.[1] Neither the Diesbachs of Bern, who had mocked at Cardinal Schinner in a carnival play, nor yet those private individuals who had promised the French peace, in consideration of a sum of only 60,000 guilders, were able to cope with such a great rising of the people, and withstand the indignation of the Forest cantons;[2] and even Jürg uff der Flue negotiated at Milan in vain. The papal party had been encouraged by new promises of temporal and spiritual favours, and the imperial party also had come over to them, in consequence of Maximilian's new attitude. On that Saturday after Easter, the 19th of April—it was inevitable—the Swiss with the banners of their cities and lands, and fully accoutred with arms and armour, sallied forth to aid the Pope.[3] Their envoys were despatched to the various courts; some, instructed as it would seem, by the French party, repaired to Louis: "Why," they asked, "had he taken from them the subsidy which their poverty demanded, in return for which they had made France twice as great as it had been; but it often happened that God, through the instrumentality of despised creatures, broke the pride that was displeasing to him."[4] Others were sent to the Emperor. The Emperor said: "Both Italian and German Tyrol was open to them; the future prince of Milan should pay them 300,000 ducats immediately, and 30,000 ducats annually."[5] On the 6th of

---

[1] Letter in Fuchs, ii. 318.

[2] Anshelm and recess in Glutzblotzheim, 261. Lettres, iii.

[3] Report from embassy in Venice, in Stettler. Fuchs, 332.

[4] Petrus Martyr, and especially Garnier, from the Bethune MSS., p. 351. [5] Fuchs, 321.

May, the Swiss set out, in greater numbers and better
equipped than ordinarily. They were under the command
of a commander-in-chief, Jacob Stapfer, a chief master of
ordnance, and a provost-marshal, to whom the soldiers from
all the various cantons swore obedience. In all the taverns
in the Tyrol, they found bread and wine; at Trent their
captains, whilst seated at a meal in the bishop's garden,
heard the plans of the Emperor. At Verona, they received
a hat and sword, a consecrated banner, and, moreover, each
man, as first payment, a ducat, from the hand of their
Cardinal.[1]

They came just at the right moment for the Pope.
Encouraged by the victory of Ravenna, Louis' Council had,
at its eighth sitting, declared the Pope now and hereafter
suspended from all Papal authority; but, after the loss of
its commander-in-chief and so many brave men in the
battle, the French army was not by any means strong
enough to give effect to such a sentence.[2] La Palice, upon
whom the command had devolved, was obliged to content
himself with holding his strongholds in the Romagna. But,
on the 3rd of May, after passing the night in the Lateran
Church, Julius also opened his Council there, in order, as
he said, to weed out the thorns from the field of the Lord.[3]
On the 2nd, the Viceroy Cardona, who had fled without
halting from Ravenna to the Abruzzi, again started from
Naples, in order, with the troops that were left and with
fresh forces from Sicily, to make a new attack upon the
French.[4] On this occasion the plan was, to mass together
in one camp the four armies, to wit, the Papal army, which
had been organized under the Duke of Urbino, the Spanish,
the Venetian, and the Swiss. At Valeggio, the Swiss
actually joined forces with the Venetian cavalry and artillery; they were resolved, even if their way led through the
midst of the enemy, to find the two other armies.[5] How

---

[1] Letter of the Swiss, Peter Falk, in Fuchs, 335 *seq*. Glutz. 266.
Stettler.

[2] Acta Concilii Pisani, in Rainaldus, p. 113.

[3] Historia Concilii Lateranensis, in Roscoe, Life of Leo, i. App. 536.

[4] Caracciolus, Vita Spinelli, 59. Zurita, ii. 285.

[5] Mocenicus, 91. Lütener in Glutz. App. p. 538.

was La Palice to cope with such a hostile demonstration?
For, since the English in the same month of May had sailed
to Fuenterrabia and, not content with throwing an army upon
the Bidassoa, were harassing the coast of Brest, and since,
moreover, a great joint attack by English and Spanish upon
Guienne had also been announced, King Louis was more
inclined to recall his hommes d'armes from Milan, than to
send others thither.[1]   But it was still uncertain which of the
two Councils, that of the King of France, or that of the
Pope, would gain the upper hand.

Two events caused matters to come to a speedier issue
than could have been anticipated.   First, the Swiss intercepted a letter from La Palice, which was to the effect that
he would scarcely be able to hold the field against a strong
army.   As soon as this letter had been translated to his
comrades by the Freiburg captain, they were unanimous in
their decision, not to advance to the Po to join their friends,
as they had originally intended, but to march forthwith to
the Oglio and attack the enemy, and to rest not a night on
the way, save out of necessity; for in three or four days the
battle must be fought.[2]   The second event was really the
decisive one.   We remember that the King of France
vanquished Ludovico Sforza by withdrawing his landsknechts, and sending the Swiss upon him.   Curiously
enough, he was overcome by the same means with which
he had formerly conquered.   The Swiss were in the field
against him : on the 4th of June, strict orders were
received from Maximilian, addressed to the landsknechts
who had striven and conquered for him at Ravenna, that
their captains, lieutenants, corporals, and privates should
leave the French camp from that very moment.   Now they
were not in the Emperor's pay, but in the King's, but these
landsknechts were either Tyrolese, and thus the immediate
subjects of the Emperor, or related to the Swabian league,
and, as such, also, more or less in subjection to him.
Accordingly, when Burkhard von Ems, Jacob's nephew, and
Rudolf Häl, the captains of the landsknechts, came into the

---

[1] Andrea del Burgo, Lettres, iii. 256.
[2] Letter of Peter Falk, in Fuchs, 357.   The Solothurn captains, in
Glutzblotzheim, 541.

council of war, which La Palice had summoned to take counsel on the question of resistance, they declared in spite of all the fair promises of the general, that they must obey the Emperor's orders, and, on the 5th of June, begged the Confederation for safe conduct.[1] Some were for remaining six days longer, until the expiration of the term for which they had bound themselves ; and about eight hundred, probably North Germans and such as had nothing at home to lose, resolved to try their fortune with the French still longer.

Hereupon La Palice, seeing himself deprived of his faithful and victorious allies of Brescia and Ravenna, abandoned all idea of resistance, and retreated from place to place. For one moment, Trivulzio entertained the hope of being able to regain for Milan its old freedom, and he actually succeeded in winning over the leading Ghibellines. But what could be expected from these nobles, who only had a thought for their own immediate advantage. At the very first disturbance of the social order, they broke disguised into the houses of poor learned men and aged invalids, and forced them to give up their savings, the hope of their latter years. Trivulzio, like La Palice, abandoned all hope also, and left the city.[2] Whilst, then, the French were retiring from Ravenna before the Papal army, and had in Bologna burnt the episcopal palace which they had occupied, and retired from the city — the Bentivogli never afterwards returned thither—Cremona surrendered to the Swiss, with the cry of " Giulio, Chiesa ! " and placed itself in the hands of the League. The Swiss advanced to Pavìa.[3] Here they once more came upon a body of landsknechts. At first they met each other with their old jests of the Rhine and Garigliano, instead of with arms. But at last, when the French had retired, and the Swiss, invited by the citizens, entered the city, the landsknechts, who also wished to retreat, were prevented by the breaking of a bridge, and a desperate struggle ensued. The landsknechts saw that they were

[1] Missives and documents in Fuchs, 365. Roo. Especially Zurita, ii. 289.

[2] Arluni, de bello Veneto, ix. 195-201.

[3] Oath of Cremona in Daru, iii. 457. Falk's letter in Fuchs, 364.

doomed to die at the hands of their old enemies; they accordingly first went and threw the money, which they carried in their sleeves into the river, in order that their enemies should not profit by it; then they fought, and were all slain.[1] Four days later, the French crossed Mont Cenis; there was not a single city in the whole duchy that had not surrendered. Only the castles still held out.

Beyond all doubt it exceeded the expectations of the League, that Milan had so rapidly passed from the French hands, not into theirs, but into those of the Swiss.

When Julius received the tidings, he read them through silently; he then drew himself up and said to his master of the ceremonies, "Victorious, Paris, we have been victorious." "May it be of service to your Holiness," replied the latter, and knelt down. The Pope said, "May it profit you and all Italians, and all the faithful whom God hath deigned to deliver from the bondage of barbarians;" he then unfolded the letter and read it through from beginning to end.[2] Shortly after, the news arrived from Genoa that his country was at last free; upon Gian Fregoso's arrival in Chiavia and upon receiving a letter from Matthäus Lang, the French commander had fled to the Lanterna, his Swiss guard had disbanded, and Gian had thereupon entered the city.[3] Envoys from Bologna arrived, plainly clothed, and without their golden chains, to implore pardon of the Pope. Parma and Piacenza surrendered to him; he did not receive them as new, but as old subjects, whom an accident two hundred and fifty years previously had estranged from the Church.

Alfonso d'Este also came under the protection of the Colonna to be liberated from his ban and to appease his anger.[4] Rome was ablaze with torches and *feux de joie;* the Pope presented an altar cloth with the inscription, "Julius II after the liberation of Italy," to the Church of St. Peter.[5]

---

[1] Principally Zwinglii Relatio de rebus ad Paviam gestis, ap. Freherum, ii. 124. Falk's Letter, 368, 378. Bayard, 328. Fleuranges, 104. Jovii vitae virorum doctorum, p. 107. Leferron, iv. 102.

[2] Paris de Grassis, ap. Rainaldum, 121.

[3] Senarega, incomplete, 615; Folieta, 294. Also Zurita.

[4] Carpesanus, an Envoy of Parma, 1288. Jovii Alfonsus, 178 *seq.*

[5] Paris de Grassis, 122.

A great painting of Raphael has reference to these events.
In the Camera della Segnatura, he represents Heliodorus,
as the horse with the rider in gold mail prepares to kick
him at the moment when he is plundering the temple,
whilst two avenging angels hurl him down.[1]

These, beyond doubt, were the happiest days in the life
of Pope Julius; after so much exertion, danger, tribulation,
and tears, his object was, as it appeared, attained, his plan
had succeeded, and his name was immortalized in the glory
of his great deeds.

He owed the Swiss eternal gratitude, for it is evident
that it was they who rescued him at a single blow from his
great spiritual and temporal danger. The other members
of the League were not so happy; both Ferdinand and
Maximilian had expected quite a different issue. Ferdinand only made use of the victory, to stay Gonzalvo's
preparations. The army, which, in spite of this termination, and against the Pope's express desire, he sent across
the Tronto,[2] seemed to be intended for somewhat else than
to serve the Pope.

4. THE CONQUEST OF NAVARRE

At first, this same Ferdinand did not turn his eyes towards Italy as much as he did towards the French frontier,
where the Marquis of Dorset had make his appearance
with 8,000 English auxiliaries—that is towards Navarre.[3]

In those days, the kingdom of Navarre comprised the
valleys and hills, fruitful and barren, which extend on both
sides of the Pyrenees, on the one side from the Ebro, on the
other from the Nive, up to the snowy heights of the mountain chain. On both sides, the cattle were driven to the
Alduidos to pasture : herds might be seen all the way from
the Ebro valley as far as the church of S. Iago hard by
St. Jean-Pied-de-Port. Every loss caused by robbery was
made good by the district in which it had happened, even

---

[1] Speth, Kunst in Italien, ii. 294. Roscoe, Leo, iii. 393.
[2] Zurita, ii. 307.
[3] Herbert, Life of Henry VIII, p. 20.

across the hills.[1] Now this kingdom had for a long time been imperilled on both sides. In France, Louis defended the rights of Gaston de Foix, who was as much the grandson of old Gaston, King of Navarre, as the possessor of the throne, Catherine, was his granddaughter.[2] She had made her husband, Jean d'Albret, king of the country. On the Spanish side, Ferdinand, in opposition to this King and his adherents, the Grammonts, took the part of Count Lerin, the head of the Beaumonts; the Count had once been one of the most powerful vassals, a man, who had to be allowed to ignore the King's express invitations; but he had been driven out, and was now a fugitive in Andalusia. Moreover, King Louis was suzerain of one part of the territory of Navarre; in the remaining portion, all the alcaldes had sworn allegiance to Ferdinand; he held five strongholds in the land, and had even the King's daughter in his keeping. Many years before this, there lived and reigned in Navarre a King, Sancho the Wise; this monarch had emblazoned on his coat of arms two lions, both pulling at a golden band, which they held in their teeth; this device represented Castile and Aragon struggling for Navarre. The relation of Spain and France to this country was analogous. At the beginning of the year 1512, Ferdinand, in order to secure himself against attack on the part of Louis XII as a result of his concerted co-operation with the Pope against him in Italy, demanded of the alcaldes that they should renew their oath of allegiance, requiring besides the surrender of the prince into his keeping, and three additional fortresses.[3] It was just at the time that Gaston attained every day to greater renown in Italy, and had additional claims to the gratitude of Louis, to which he could only give effect by defending his rights to Navarre. Gaston's death was the good fortune of the sovereigns of Navarre. They immediately allied themselves with France, summoned the Estates of their realm from both sides of the mountains, obtained assistance, and

---

[1] Garibay, Compendio universal de las Chronicas, tom. iii.; historia de Navarra. Barcel, 1628, p. 11.

[2] Polydorus, in detail.

[3] Zurita, i. 12. Garibay, 500.

prepared to resist the claims of Ferdinand and his English allies.[1]

Now it was either an idle tale that was spread abroad, or it was an actual fact, that a secretary of the King of Navarre had been stabbed in the house of his paramour, and that the priest, who was called in to offer consolation, found on him the copy of a treaty, by which Louis pledged himself to restore the old frontier of Navarre against Castile, and sent it to Ferdinand. This enabled the latter to gain over Cardinal Ximenes and a part of the nation for his undertaking.[2] He declared that he had long had in his possession a bull putting under ban the King of Navarre, who was as much a schismatic as the French sovereign, to whom he was lending his support; he commanded the Duke of Alva, who had gathered a great army at Vitoria, under the pretence of joining the English, not to combine with these latter but to advance upon Pamplona.[3]

Jean was not yet ready, and no Frenchman was at hand, when the Duke of Alva appeared in the narrow gorge which divides the valleys of Biscay from those of Navarre. His muskets easily dispersed the 600 Roncalese who defended the pass. Don Luis, Count of Lerin, marched at the head of the Spaniards. The whole party of the Beaumonts rose in his favour, and the cities, which had once belonged to him, received him with jubilation. On the fifth day, the army was eight leguas from the city upon the heights which form the Cuenca, that is, the basin of Pamplona. Jean d'Albret was a king who went twice or three times daily to mass, and who would dance with a peasant woman and eat with a citizen; but he was not made for war and danger. He said, " Better be in the hills than a prisoner," and fled; two days later, his consort also fled away. She said, "Jean d'Albret you were born, and Jean d'Albret you will die. Had I been King and you Queen, we should not have lost this kingdom." On the 25th

[1] Zurita, i. 130; ii. 161; ii. 273–290. Garibay, 29, c. 25. Treaty in Dumont, iv. 1, 147. Zurita, 294.

[2] Petri Martyris Epistolae, ep. 491. Gomez, Vita Ximenis, 1060.

[3] Antonius Nebrissensis, de bello Navarrensi, in Hisp. illustr. ii. 911.

July, 1512, Pamplona surrendered to the Spaniards, and Alva guaranteed its general and special franchises and immunities; this done, with the exception of a few castles belonging to the Grammonts, and the valleys of Roncal, the whole of the kingdom lying on this side was reduced. On the 10th of September, Alva crossed the Pyrenees, and on the same day took St. Jean.[1]

The English saw with astonishment how the French war, which they had come out to fight, resolved itself into a conquest of Navarre for Spain. Bayonne lies more than twenty miles from St. Jean, and the former city they could, at all events, at once attack with combined forces. " But not to Bayonne," wrote Ferdinand, " where the battlements bristle with guns; before you there lies the open and unprotected country." The Marquis of Dorset, who was annoyed at this constant hesitation and delay, replied that, " his orders were to go against Bayonne, and not against the open country; he would not approach the Spaniards by a single inch." His King was sooner over-persuaded than he himself. But before any other arrangement could be come to, a mutiny among his troops compelled the Marquis to retreat.[2]

Yet, without their assistance, Ferdinand understood how to defend his conquest. Alva was still at St. Jean, when, in November, 1512, d'Albret succeeded, with French assistance, in penetrating into the kingdom through the defiles; closing them behind him, he began the siege of Pamplona with every prospect of success. But Alva, making his way by paths little known, arrived at Pamplona in the nick of time, and held out there, until fresh auxiliary forces from Spain showed themselves on the heights of Cuenca. Then d'Albret retired, and the peasants, who had come to buy and load their waggons with the plunder of the city, returned dissatisfied homewards. And now Ferdinand brought the whole of Navarre on this side of the Pyrenees, 800 pueblos, entirely into his power; the high chain of mountains formed an admirable frontier.

[1] Garibay, 506. Antonius, 911, 912. Fleuranges, 115. Zurita, 302. Petrus Martyr, ep. 499.
[2] Polydorus. Herbert, Life of Henry, 22.

Further, the territory on the other side, was never again united with it, and the whole memory of the old connexion entirely disappeared, leaving scarcely a trace. The conquered land desired the Aragonese and allodial law ; but it only received the laws of Castile and vassal rights. It retained its Cortes. The Procurators of the twenty-three cities held a sitting before the canopy of the throne, to settle the Servicio ; only under the canopy there sat, not their King, but a representative of the King of Spain. This also had become part of the great inheritance of Austria and Spain and of the great feud between this house and France.[1]

5. REVOLUTION IN FLORENCE.   OTHER SUCCESSES IN ITALY

In July, 1512, Navarre was conquered, and in November defended ; midway between both these events, in September, the Austro-Spanish house succeeded in an enterprise, which was perhaps of even greater influence upon international relations.

We have seen how the war, waged by Alexander's League some sixteen years previously, turned, after the French had been driven from Italy, against their principal supporters, the Popolari in Florence. While Louis was in Italy, these Popolari had enjoyed extended influence under the chief man in the city, Piero Soderini, who had been raised to the position of perpetual Gonfaloniere ;[2] and, after Louis had been expelled, they still adhered to their old allegiance to him. For a second time, a League, that of Pope Julius, now turned against them.

Pisa, which, after indefatigable exertions, they had at length again subjected, was their destruction. In four campaigns they laid siege to it, and put to death one of their leaders, Paolo Vitelli, because he did not take it. For three successive years, they came in May and ravaged

[1] Antonius, 912–924. Zurita, 318–328. Garibay.
[2] Filippo Nerli, 89. Jacopo Nardi, 83.

2 A

the crops of the Pisans right up to their walls; they even attempted to divert the course of the Arno, and employed 80,000 labourers on the work; they spared no money in order to obtain the sanction of the Kings of France and Spain to their undertaking. From podesteria to podesteria, and from valley to valley, with the assistance of their citizen Machiavelli,[1] they formed military stations of native soldiery. At length, in the year 1509, they succeeded in their object. They had invested the city with three camps, and had made the Arno impassable by a fortified bridge, and the Fiume Morto by piles bound together under the water by iron bands.[2] A famine broke out in the city, which resulted in a quarrel between the citizens, who were for holding out longer, and the country people, who violently demanded surrender. The latter obtained the upper hand. On the 8th June, 1509, the Florentines again entered Pisa.[3] But the reconquest of the place did not bring good fortune and prosperity to the Florentines. The name of Pisa, and the memory of an old Council in this city, incited both King and Cardinals to urge the summoning of a new Council there. The Florentines were under too deep an obligation to the King to be able to refuse; but the fact that they, although unwillingly, acceded to this demand, made the Pope their enemy.[4] This was, as far as could be seen, the principal reason for an attack upon them. In 1511, Julius appointed their great enemy, Cardinal de' Medici, legate with his army; and now that they had banished his Datario from their city, the Pope became all the more the supporter of this Cardinal, who intended to avail himself of the French reverse to make an attack upon Florence, and favoured his plans.[5]

Among Lorenzo de' Medici's shrewd schemes, one of the shrewdest was the employment of the prestige which

---

[1] Guicciardini, vi. 343; viii. 418.

[2] Istruttione of Machiavelli in the Legazioni, iv. 106. His letters, 262, 264. Vasari, Vita di San Gallo, p. 133.

[3] Reports of Machiavelli, 267–290. Treitschke, Geschichte der fünfzehnjährigen Freiheit von Pisa, p. 356.

[4] Jovius, Vita Leonis, ii. 35. Nerli, 104.

[5] Carondelet in the Lettres, iii. 78. Nardi, v. 144.

he possessed as mediator of Italy to utilize the ecclesiastical preferment of his son Giovanni in order to obtain the least invidious and most certain enhancement of his house.   When the Medici were driven from Florence, Giovanni's benefices, consisting of a preceptorate, a priory, a provostship, four canonries, six pastorates, fifteen abbeys, and an arch-bishopric, were one of their chief supports.[1]   We do not find that Giovanni either grossly neglected the original duties of these offices, or administered them with any special zeal ; it was his whole aim to live contentedly without incurring blame, to make friends and gain respect, and at some future time to restore his house to power.   His face, as shown in Raphael's portrait, if regarded hastily, displays but the pleasure and satiety seen in other ecclesiastics of high rank ; but if we regard it closer we are struck by an expression of deep thought, purpose, and firm will.   He had a comfortable and pleasant way of living.   It was also his wont to give way to other cardinals in the slightest matters of contention ; he jested or was serious, according to their mood ; he never dismissed their agents without their being able to tell their principals that Cardinal de' Medici was their obedient and humble servant.[2]   He proved to the Orsini in the chase that he was of their blood.   His palace was always full of music and song; here were gathered together the models, drawings, and works of the painters, sculptors, and goldsmiths of Rome.   Scholars found there a library ever open to them.   It contained the books of his father Lorenzo ; it gave him the greatest pleasure when he took up one and studied it page by page.   He then imagined he was earning the approbation of his deceased father. For the rest, his humblest visitor left him convinced only of his mildness and goodness.[3]

His life was not pretence ; but it availed him quite as much as if it had been most carefully studied.   He won the hearts of all Florentines of his acquaintance.   Men of

[1] Fabroni, Vita Leonis X.   Adnotationes, p. 245.

[2] Leonis X. Vita, autore anonymo conscripta, in Roscoe, Leo X, App. to 3rd vol. 581.

[3] Jovius, Vita Leonis, ii. 29, *seq*.   Especially Alcyonius, de exilio, edited by Mencken, 1707, i. 12.

quality did not fear from him Piero's arrogance. There were often assembled in Florence at that time, in the gardens of Cosimo Rucellai—a man more qualified for scientific conversation and poetic essays than for the service of his country—young men of the Vettori, Albizzi, Valori families, whom high birth, youth, wealth, and the consciousness of an excellent education had made, one cannot say otherwise, somewhat overbearing. They had read in Roman history of the glories of the Optimates, and thus they styled themselves ; they found out the weak points of the Gonfaloniere and the Consiglio, and mocked at them in masquerades. The good Soderini, meek and mild, did not interfere ; but they joined the party of Giovanni de' Medici, through whom they hoped to attain greater influence.[1]

The Cardinal intended to make use of them to the advantage of his house, when he summoned Ramon de Cardona to a campaign against Florence.

Cardona came in August to Mantua, and negotiated there with Matthäus Lang, with reference to the reorganization of Italy after the victory ; the Medici promised to pay his Spaniards, whilst Soderini refused Matthäus Lang the 100,000 ducats which he demanded.[2] Soderini was blamed for his action in this matter ; but how could Lang answer for the Spaniards ? How could the Emperor, who, in 1509, had guaranteed the position of Florence in return for a money payment, and who was even then negotiating about it, be depended upon to alter it ? Both Bishop and Viceroy resolved upon the undertaking, in favour of the Medici.

Soderini was a man who once demanded of the 300 priori, who had at various times been under him, that they should say, whether he had ever preferred a personal advantage to a public interest, and whether he had ever on any occasion recommended his friends for a judicial post.[3] He felt himself completely free from all the passions of the Italian party leaders, and trusted the people under him.

[1] Filippo Nerli, Commentarii, p. 106.

[2] Nardi, Historie, 147 ; cf. Mémoire concerning the meeting in Mantua, in the Lettres, iii. 289.

[3] From Ammirato and Cambi in Sismondi, Hist. d. républ. ital. xiv. 130.

When Cardona entered Tuscany, with the declaration that he was only coming against Soderini, the latter summoned the Grand Council and remonstrated with them, pointing out that he had gained his dignity by the will of the people, and not by force and deceit; and should all kings in the world, united, try to persuade him to lay down his office, he would not do so; he would only lay it down when the people who had conferred it demanded it of him; he was in their hands, and into their hands he surrendered himself. He urged them to go amongst their Gonfalonieri and decide the matter. They separated, and returned declaring their readiness to stake their lives and property for him.[1]

After this, Cardona found the Florentines more hostile than ever; their cities resisted him, especially Prato, which he besieged. On one occasion, being in straits, he declared his readiness to return, provided the affairs of the Medici were left to the arbitration of King Ferdinand, when all of a sudden everything was changed. Through a hole in the wall, which looked more like a window than a breach, the Spaniards succeeded in entering Prato.[2] They pillaged it, as Brescia had been pillaged, and by their doings filled all Florence with dismay. This first moment of dejection was turned to account by the followers of Rucellai. The youths, to the number of thirty, assembled under arms in the grand hall, and shouted at the door of the chamber where the Signori were assembled, that, "they would tolerate the Gonfaloniere no longer." As though they possessed the voice and the power of the people, they rushed forth, and bursting into Soderini's room, with the shout that "his life should be safe, but that he must follow them," they tore him away with them. They opened the prisons, wherein were some friends of the Medici, returned, forced from the Signoria the deposition of Soderini, and compelled him to flee; and before any terms had been agreed upon, they opened the gates to the Viceroy and Giuliano de' Medici, a brother of Giovanni.[3] A treaty was hereupon concluded, the basis of

---

[1] Speech from Nerli. Machiavelli, in the Lettere a una Signora, 7.
[2] Nardi, 147. Guicciardini, xi. ii. p. 13. Jovius, Leo, p. 53.
[3] The foregoing, and especially Nerli, 110, i.

which was the return of the Medici : between Ferdinand and
Florence—and this is the vital point—there should be, in
respect of Naples, an alliance for three and a half years,
similar to that which had existed with Louis in regard to
Milan, and by virtue of which the Florentines must, under
the Medici, be as Spanish as, under the Popolari, they had
been French.[1]

This arranged, Cardona left all internal matters to the
Medici. At first, Giuliano authorized a Gonfaloniere with
limited powers, and, following the advice of Rucellai's
friends, a council of the Optimates, and much liberty.
But this was not agreeable to Giovanni. Whilst yet outside
the walls, he had determined with his followers on a different
policy, and, after entering the city, arranged also with the
Condottieri there ; when morning broke, both parties rushed
to the palace to the cry of " Palle ! Palle ! " They first
forced the Signoria to summon the people to a parliament,
and then, by the weak and servile voices of this forcibly
collected assembly, to commit the supreme power to a Balìa
of fifty-five men. As soon as they were elected and assembled, a Medici carried the standard before the Signoria up
the steps of the Palazzo Pubblico. The fifty-five, with 200
others whom they had joined with them, formed the Grand
Council ; a council of seventy, and a council of a hundred
was formed after the model of the old Lorenzo. At the discretion of the Medici, new names were placed in the ballot
boxes at all elections. Suffice it to say, the supreme power
returned again to the Medici, Giovanni, Giuliano, and
Lorenzo, Piero's son. The sbirro would often come up to
two or three citizens and ask " about what they were con-
versing ; " among the first malcontents and suspects,
Machiavelli was arrested and imprisoned.[2]

Now the Popolari, though humbled, were so little
suppressed—as is shown by the fact that they afterwards
regained their strength and seized the supreme power—that
they were only awaiting the arrival of the French to rise
again ; and thus the Cardinal became bound to the Spanish

[1] Document of the treaty in Fabroni, Vita Leonis X, adnot. 266–69.
[2] Nardi, 156, *seq*. Nerli, 116. Machiavelli, Lettere famigl. p. 11.
Guicciardini, 17.

cause against the French, not only out of gratitude, not only owing to his alliance with Cardona, but owing to a constant and perpetual interest.   It must be confessed that this part of central Italy had now come, beyond all question, into the power of the Austro-Spanish house.   Lucca was forced to enter the League.   Siena received a garrison of 100 Spanish lances.[1]

At Mantua Cardona and Lang had resolved, after the Florentine undertaking, to settle Milanese and Venetian affairs.

In Milan they wished to appoint as prince, not the young Massimiliano Sforza, who had at length, after an exile of fourteen years in Regensburg[2] and the Netherlands, arrived at man's estate, but the Archduke Charles.   This proposal was repeatedly brought before the Swiss during August and September : there should be paid them for their expenses 300,000 ducats and 50,000 ducats yearly subsidy; for the present, Sforza was not allowed to return to Italy.[3]

The Venetian dispute was to be fought out as soon as the truce expired.[4]   Cardona would not be kept back with his troops, and replied to all objections, that he was captain-general of the League.   Brescia, before being taken by the French, had always belonged to Venice ; but this did not prevent Cardona from taking this city, in October, 1512.[5]

If these plans were successfully carried out, how would it then fare with the freedom of Italy, which the Pope thought he had achieved ?   The affairs of Ferrara compelled him to look to the interests at stake here.

For he had not come to an understanding with Alfonso d'Este, although the latter had come to Rome for that purpose.   One day, a page in the palace heard the Pope walking up and down his chamber, hissing between his teeth the words, "This Vulcan," and "Vengeance." Alfonso was called Vulcan, and he was immediately

---

[1] Zurita, ii. 314.
[2] Order of the Regensburg Council in the Regensburger Chronik, iv.
[3] Fuchs, 444.   Anshelm, iv. 289.
[4] Especially Zurita.
[5] Paul. Jovius, Vita Pescarae, 382 ; and Zurita, ii. 338.

informed of this incident.[1] It is possible that, at that moment, Julius was thinking of the Duke's plots against his life; however that may be, Alfonso, who had just been bidden to a banquet by the Pope, feared for his life if he accepted the invitation. With the aid of Fabrizio Colonna, who in this manner requited him for saving his life in the battle of Ravenna, he succeeded in effecting his escape. As a result of this, however, Cardona and Alfonso again became enemies. The Pope, who was determined to subject Ferrara, was again in need of the Spaniards, as the Swiss refused their assistance for this purpose. Yet he did not go so far as to allow them, in return, to carry out their intentions upon Milan; Massimiliano Sforza must, after all, be at last installed there; but he allowed them to have their will with regard to Venice. On the 25th November, he concluded an alliance with them, according to which the Venetians should leave Verona and Vicenza to the Emperor, retaining Padua and Treviso, for an immediate payment of 250,000 ducats and an annual tribute of 30,000.[2] This alliance promised him assistance against Ferrara.

This arrangement once carried out, and the greater part of Lombardy in the hands of the Emperor and the Spaniards, how could the remainder hold out for any length of time, seeing that the Swiss were venal and young Sforza very weak, and, moreover, in the hands of Andrea del Burgo and other imperial councillors? Italy, instead of enjoying liberty, would thus come into greater subjection than ever. Were not Julius' intentions themselves praiseworthy? Were not the means he adopted bold and heroic? But all his exertions, instead of tending to the emancipation of Italy, merely enhanced the Austro-Spanish power. For ideal aspirations directed towards attaining their highest aims can only be fulfilled under conditions which are subject to their own peculiar laws. Human actions are prompted by the first; their success, however, depends upon the second.

Before Julius saw the whole result of his schemes, yet

[1] Carpesanus, Historiae sui temporis ap. Martène, v. 286.
[2] Complaints of Bembus, 310. Paris de Grassis, 125. Paolo Paruta, historia Veneziana, p. 9.

while he dimly conceived it, it was vouchsafed to him, in February, 1513, to die. There is credible evidence that his anxiety as to the future of Italy was the cause of his death.[1] It was fated that even his decease should further the intentions of the Austro-Spanish house.

Upon whom should it desire to confer the Papal dignity, but upon that Cardinal, whom great favours had placed under an obligation, and whom, in consequence of the events in Florence, and the danger with which he was threatened by the French and the popular party, it was able to call its own? To this Cardinal the younger members of distinguished families in Florence were devoted heart and soul, as were also, in the Conclave, the junior cardinals, especially Petrucci of Siena and Sauli of Genoa, since, seeing how gentle and easy his nature was, they would share his power. It was, perhaps, his abdominal complaint, for which he was operated upon in the Conclave itself, and which, in spite of his comparative youth, held out little hope of old age, that contributed to his election; or perhaps it was due to his clever friend Bibbiena, who knew the weak points of all the cardinals and how to use them.[2] At last Cardinal Soderini, his natural enemy, also gave way, and was followed by all the other cardinals. He was elected. The people forthwith remembered his generosity; the poets prophesied that, as Numa followed Romulus, so would Leo X—thus he styled himself out of respect for a dream his mother had—follow the stormy Julius, to crown in times of peace every virtue, every toil, and every art. His marvellous fortune was the common theme, how he, but a year previously taken prisoner at Ravenna, was miraculously liberated from captivity, and had become lord of Florence and lord of the world. All the inscriptions to be seen on the day of his coronation, the anniversary of that battle—he was mounted on the Turkish horse upon which he had then ridden—extolled the "subduer of fortune." Of the treasure, which Julius had so carefully

[1] In Bembus. Also Zurita, ii. 336, 338, 341. Passero, 188.
[2] Pio of Carpi to Maximilian, Journal of the Conclave, in the Lettres de Louis, iv. p. 72, p. 65. Paris de Grassis in Rainaldus, 133. Vita anonymi, 583.

hoarded up, 100,000 ducats were thrown among the people. The cup of joy and hope was overflowing.[1]

First of all, it was certain that his policy would further the interests of the Spaniards, and that, among all their many successes, his election was not the least.

6. STRUGGLE OF THE FRENCH AND SWISS FOR MILAN

Between the two great powers of Europe, the French and the Austro-Spanish, both of which coveted Milan, stood the Swiss, withholding it from both. They had themselves not merely gained in glory and prestige, but had also acquired considerable tracts of land in the Milanese. The valleys and defiles through which the Tosa, Maggia, Onsernone, and Melazza, flowing from the Alpine chain, break their way through the rocky hills, not fruitful—they supply only stone and men who know how to carry loads and sweep chimneys — but the highways of the nations, had been occupied by them. Moreover, there had passed into their hands the pleasant shores of Lake Maggiore, so far as they belong to Locarno, and the slope of the mountain chain where it sinks down towards the Lake of Lugano, a land full of southern fruits and cornfields and vineyards: Locarno, Lugano, and Mendrisio, long since devoted to them, had come into their hands. The whole mountain chain from Monte Rosa to the Wormser Joch, with all the passes, for the possession of which nations had so often striven, had now, after passing from Italian into German hands, been brought to own obedience to the Confederation and the associated districts, through the instrumentality of the Grisons, which had not only appropriated the valleys of the Mera and Liro, but the Valtelline also, as belonging to the jurisdiction of Chur. Their cattle could now be driven in peace to the market at Varese, and the very first which was held, brought them extraordinary profits; wine and corn came up to them from Italy without trouble.

[1] Poems in Roscoe, ii. 387. Jovius, Fabroni Vita, p. 65.

It was now the Pope's care to instal Massimiliano Sforza as ruler of the rest of the Milanese, and this project was welcomed by the voice of the citizens of the capital, once more assembled on the green square before the Duomo;[1] but that it was carried out, was principally due to the staunch attitude of the Swiss. On the 30th December, 1512, Massimiliano received the key of the city from the hands of a citizen of Zürich, and made his entrance. The Swiss, whom he confirmed in the possession of their acquisitions, and to whom he promised a present payment of 200,000 ducats, and an annual subsidy of 40,000, entered into an alliance with him, promising " to defend him and his successors in the duchy by force of arms for all time." [2]

What a difference between the innocence of the early fraternities, designed only for defence, and this alliance, which amounted to an independent entrance into international disputes to defend a foreign land ! What a difference between that night on the Rütli and these days, when all the princes of our nations vied with each other for the favour of the peasants ! They felt it themselves. Marx Röust often narrated how, when he and the other deputies were sitting in the Diet at Baden to seal that alliance, three heavy blows were struck on the table by invisible hands.[3] There is a legend to the effect, that the three men who formed the Confederation on the Rütli now rest in the Seelisberg mountain, and keep watch over their people. To them the blows were attributed. Not only men, but nations also, have a zenith in their power and life; and never were the Confederates more powerful than at this moment. In spite of this weird fright, they affixed their seals.

War broke out immediately. Louis XII, who had always thought the conquest of Milan the glory of his reign, was determined to reconquer it. He had already, in September, 1512, offered the Swiss, through the intervention of Savoy, both peace and alliance. In February, 1513, he made a second attempt. In order to be able to send his envoys to the Confederates, he overcame his

---

[1] Fuchs, 439. Arluni, de bello Veneto, 204.
[2] Article from the Act in Fuchs, 478. See also *ibid*. 501.
[3] Bullinger in Fuchs, 481.

scruples, and made over to them the strongholds which he still held in the district they had occupied.[1] But when Trivulzio urgently warned them not to increase the power of their own friends, adding, "That he had been present when proposals had been made to his King, to make common cause with others, and to join in conquering their possessions,"[2] he did not quite hit the mark. It was in no wise in the interest of Austria, but in their own, that they kept Massimiliano Sforza at Milan, and this prince was quite as dependent upon them, through their soldiers and their cardinal, as he was upon the Emperor, through his councillors. Only a few in all, a son of Jürg uff der Flue, a son of Hetzel of Bern, and some captains from the Stein, gave the French envoys, Trivulzio and La Trémouille, an audience on their passage through.[3]

Louis was obliged to cast about for another alliance and other infantry for his undertaking.

This alliance he found in the Venetians. Both he and they had again the same enemy to face, viz. the Austro-Spanish house; on the 13th March, 1513, they allied themselves, the King promising to restore Cremona and the Ghiara d'Adda.[4] Foot soldiers, bidding the Emperor defiance, came through all parts of the empire, some from Bohemia,[5] some from Swabia, the greater number from North Germany, and joined the French. The black troop under Thomas of Mittelburg, consisting of landsknechts, with great broadswords and armour, almost like knights, were led by the young Fleuranges, who himself carried two standards, across the Meuse through Burgundy to Lyons;[6] other landsknechts were led by his brother, Jametz. Their father, Robert de la Mark, who had inherited from his uncle William the name of " The Boar of the Ardennes "—he

---

[1] Anshelm, iv. 311.

[2] Trivulzio to King Louis — Lucerne, 5th February, 1512—in Rosmini, Trivulzio, ii. 209. *Ibid*. Sforza's letters to Stampa. Anshelm, Berner Chronik, iv. 369.

[3] Gattinara to Margaret from the letter of La Trémouille; Lettres, iv. 99. Anshelm, iv. 409.

[4] Dumont, iv. 1, 182.

[5] Regensburger Chronik, iv. iii. 192, from the Emperor's letter.

[6] Fleuranges, Mémoires, 110.

had invented for the infantry a fence of iron chains, to rest the arquebuses upon—himself led 100 lances. In May, the French army, 1,200 lances and 8,000 foot, began their march across the mountains; on the 12th it was received at Alessandria, and the Guelphs were all astir in the whole country.[1]

Now it lay in the nature of the interested parties, as well as in the situation, that neither the Spaniards, though with a strong army in the vicinity, and bound by various promises and obligations, bestirred themselves to protect the Duke,[2] nor did the Emperor send the assistance he had promised. The 4,000 Swiss, who were in the country, retired from place to place. Meanwhile, when the whole country was in arms—the French from the Castle of Milan again marched through the city as masters—and the 4,000, with their Duke at their head, fled to Novara, the very city where Ludovico had been betrayed, all appeared to be at an end, and Trivulzio boasted that he had the Swiss like molten lead in a spoon.

But, on this occasion, he boasted prematurely. To his attempts to persuade them, the Swiss replied that he should prove them " with arms, not with words." They all followed in this matter the advice of Benedict von Weingarten, a man, according to Anshelm,[3] stout, upright, and wise, who, though he unwillingly took the command, led them bravely. The French attacks met with almost more contempt than resistance. The gates of Novara were left open, and the breach holes hung with sheets.[4] Whilst the Swiss, by this show of unanimous bravery, wiped out the shame which Novara had brought them fourteen years before, their confederates of the reserve crossed the mountains; the greater portion, from the Forest cantons and Bern, came over the St. Gotthard and down Lake Maggiore, whilst the smaller contingent, from Zürich and Chur, crossed the St. Bernardino,

[1] Bellay, Mémoires, 1 b. Petrus Martyr, Ep. 524. Morone in Rosmini, ii. 315.

[2] Contradictory correspondence in the Letters, iv. 118, *seq.*

[3] Anshelm, Berner Chronik, iv. 385.

[4] Stettler and Anselm in Glutz. 323. Jovius, Hist. sui temporis, i. 93.

and descended the Lake of Como.[1] A messenger soon arrived, asking, "Why they hurried? There was no danger;" a priest shortly afterwards made the announcement that, "The Duke and all the Swiss had been slain."[2] But they collected their forces, and resolved to find their comrades, dead or alive. Both contingents hastened; the nearest road from the St. Gotthard was chosen, and, on the 5th June, the greater part of the force had arrived close to Novara.[3]

On the same day, the French raised the siege. On the road to Trecate, Trivulzio selected a rising knoll, called Riotta, which, owing to ditches and marshes, was well suited for defence; they bivouacked here at night, mounted their guns, and intended the following morning to fix their iron palisade. Their good entrenchments emboldened them to await the coming of the 6,000 landsknechts, who, with 500 fresh lances, were already in the Susa valley.[4]

As soon as the Swiss appear in the field, their whole thought is battle. They have neither generals nor plans, nor yet any carefully considered strategy; the God of their fathers and St. Urs, their strong arm and the halberd are enough for them, and their bravery shows them the way. Those who had arrived at Novara on the 5th June, refreshed themselves with a draught, an hour's sleep and another draught, and then, without waiting long for the Zürichers, as the morning of the 6th June dawned, they all, both those who had been there and the fresh arrivals, rushed in disorder, like a swarm of bees flying from the hive into the summer sun, as Anshelm describes it,[5] through the gates and the breaches into the open. They were almost without guns, entirely without cavalry, and many were without armour; but, all the same, they rushed on the enemy, well entrenched as they were behind good artillery, and upon those knights, *sans peur et sans reproche*, in full armour.

They stood face to face with the enemy, on whose

---

[1] Stettler. Bullinger in Glutz. 315.

[2] Anshelm, iv. 383.

[3] Benedictus Jovius, Hist. Novocom. p. 66.

[4] Bouchet, Vie et gestes du cheval. de la Trémouille, 184, and Trivulzio's defence by Rosmini, i. 570.

[5] Anshelm, iv. 384.

coats of mail the first rays of the rising sun flashed; they seemed to them like a hill of gleaming steel.

They first attacked the lances and cannon of Robert de la Mark. Here was engaged the smaller body, in whose front ranks stood with their pikes the bravest heroes, two Diesbachs, Aerni Winkelried, and Niklaus Conrad, all distinguished for their ancestry or the nobility of virtue;[1] the greater body, almost more by instinct than intention, in the midst of the smoke and the first effect of the hostile artillery, made a detour round a copse;[2] they sought and found the landsknechts. When the cannon at once came to the assistance of the latter, the Swiss again separated. Some fought against the Black Flags;[3] the greater part, however, threw themselves upon the guns. Thus they fought in three distinct places; the first against the knights, who often broke up their own ranks and appeared behind their banners —but they always rallied again and held out; the next, 400 men, wielding their halberds in both hands, fought against a company of Fleuranges' Black Flags, dealing blow for blow, and thrust for thrust; whilst the third and greatest body was engaged with the landsknechts, who, besides cannon, had 800 arquebuses; but soon the rain of bullets ceased; only the clash of swords and the crash of pikes was audible. At length the standard of the landsknechts sank; their leaders were buried under a heap of slain; their cannon were lost and employed against them.[4] Meanwhile the Blacks also gave way. Robert de la Mark looked about him; he saw his foot soldiers and his sons lost; in order to save these, he also retreated. He found them among the dead, among the victors, bleeding still from wounds, and rescued them.[5] In vain did Trivulzio appeal to St. Catherine and St. Mark; he, too, as well as La Trémouille, who was wounded, was forced to retire.[6] The Swiss gave

---

[1] Nicolaus Konrad Hauptmann, Letter to his bailiff; Rosmini I, 549.

[2] Letters of Captains from Solothurn; *ibid.* 546.

[3] Fleuranges, Mémoires, 130, *seq.*

[4] The foregoing and Paulus Jovius, Historiae, s. t. i. 97. Carpesanus, 1291.

[5] Bellay, Mémoires, 4. Guicciardini, xi. 45.

[6] Rosmini, from Prato MS., and from "Un rozzo poema," i. 474.

no quarter to the fugitives whom they overtook; they then returned, ordered their ranks for prayer, and knelt down to give thanks to God and their saints. They next set about dividing the spoil and burying the dead.[1]

It was the second hour of the morning, when the news of the issue of the battle reached Milan. The French, who, in anticipation of victory, had left the castle, immediately fled; some back thither, others to the churches and the palaces of their friends; the Ghibelline faction at once rose, and city and country returned to their allegiance to Massimiliano Sforza. The Swiss undertook to chastise those who had revolted. They compelled the people of Asti who had left their houses to pay 100,000 ducats, Savoy, which had gone over to the enemy, 50,000, and Montferrat, which had insulted their ambassadors, 100,000. This event enabled the Spaniards to hold their heads high. In Genoa, they restored the Fregosi, who had been expelled for twenty-one days, and Ottaviano among them; they reconquered Bergamo, Brescia, and Peschiera, which also had revolted.[2]

After this victory, the Swiss enjoyed far greater power in Milan than ever before. " What you have restored by your blood and your strength," wrote Massimiliano Sforza, " shall belong for the future as much to you as to me," and these were not empty words. The Swiss perceived that they were strong enough to attempt other achievements. " If we could only reckon upon obedience in our men," they were heard to say, " we would march through the whole of France, long and broad as it is." [3]

7. GENERAL WAR MOVEMENT

Two great combinations confronted each other: the Emperor, the Pope, Spain, England, and Switzerland on the one side, and France, Venice, and Scotland on the other.

---

[1] Anshelm, iv. 385.

[2] Stettler. Jovii Historiae, 93. Vita Pescarae, 285. Passero, 197, in detail.

[3] Letter of Sforza, of 6th June, in Glutz. appendix, 545. May in Glutz. 329.

The first group seemed to have in view an immediate attack upon France. Affairs in France, under Louis XII, developed in a similar way as under Charles VIII. The commencement, in both cases, rapid conquest; the turning point, a quarrel with the Pope; then a League; the final result, a loss of the conquests, and jeopardising of the French position itself.

But as, on this occasion, all the factors were greater, the French exertions stronger, the Pope's enmity more violent, and the achievements of the League in Italy more brilliant, it followed that the attack upon France, which at present was more supported by Maximilian's guidance than by his actual forces, was proportionately important and dangerous.

Julius, who, on the 3rd of December, 1512, surrounded by 120 prelates, had pronounced an interdict against France, had prepared for the coming storm. Ferdinand advised that Burgundy, Normandy, and Guienne should be seized from the French;[1] Maximilian and Henry VIII also urged this course, as they had long-standing claims to these provinces; the Swiss also agreed, in the hope of rendering their Duke secure in Milan. The new Pope, Leo, was on account of the still prevailing schism obliged to follow the way of his predecessor. Thus, in April, 1513, a general attack upon France from all four sides, English, German, Italian, and Spanish, was determined upon in a formal treaty.[2]

But this scheme was not capable of being carried out on this scale, as the Venetians continued to side with the French, so that the arms of the League had also to be turned against them. Ferdinand, moreover, would never allow war on his frontiers. Pursuing his tactics of 1497 and 1503, he concluded an unexpected truce for his frontier territory.[3] It thus came about, that the Spanish and Italian attack, that is, the forces of Ferdinand and Leo, turned against Venice, whilst the attack upon France could only be left to the Swiss, who acted for the Germans, and to the English. Herein Maximilian showed himself once more

---

[1] Paris de Gr. in Rainald. 126. Zurita, ii. 333.
[2] Appunctuamentum of 5th April in Rymer, Foedera, vi. i. 92.
[3] Zurita, ii. 352. Jacob de Bannissis, Lettres, iv. 114.

very energetic and influential. He himself had, it is true, placed no large army in the field, but he had his hand in all the operations and was not slow to display his qualities of generalship.

On the 1st of August, 1513, the Spanish under Cardona, and 200 heavy and 2,000 light cavalry of the Pope, under Prospero Colonna, were arrayed before Padua against the Venetians. But the greatest strength of this force probably consisted in the Swabian and Tyrolese companies, which the Emperor had sent them, under the command of Count von Lupfen, and the captains, Frundsberg, Rogendorf, Landau, and Lichtenstein, who had been tried and proved in this war.[1]

On the same 1st of August, the Swiss promised him to make an attack upon Burgundy. In the Confederation, an extensive revolt of the peasants against the cities had just completely ruined the French party, and had even forced the Bernese to depose three new and two old magistrates, who were suspected of French leanings. This made the Emperor all the more certain of them; he promised them assistance, without which they could not undertake the expedition : artillery, horse, and some money.[2]

At the beginning of August, the King of England joined his army, which, since the 22nd of July, had been engaged in besieging Térouanne. This was, beyond doubt, the most important operation; it drew the attention of all eyes to it. The English were still just the same as ever, not celebrating St. Martin's day because he was the patron saint of their enemies, calling the painted man, used for a mark at their bow-practice, " the Frenchman," and saying to their children: " Hit the Frenchman in the heart;"[3] they had gladly offered themselves according to their counties, within and without their respective liberties, for selection and enrolment for military service; they were mainly armed with bows and crossbows, leaden clubs and

[1] Jean le Veau, Lettres, iv. 200. Ehrenspiegel, 1303. Reisner, Kriegsthaten, 16.

[2] Glutz. 332–340. From the Recess of 1st August, p. 343.

[3] Herbert, Life of Henry, 32. Hubert Thomas Leodius, Vita Friderici Palatini, 33.

halberds; they arranged their march so that they could always barricade themselves at once behind their waggons, for they only cared to fight behind a strong position. Their King came with them, true Lancastrian as he was. Before setting out, almost in imitation of Henry V, he caused the last Yorkist who was in his power, Edmund Earl of Suffolk, to be put to death. He then took with him Charles Brandon, son of that Brandon who had carried the standard of Henry VII in the battle of Bosworth Field, once the playmate and companion of his youth, a short time since created Viscount Lisle. In his suite were also Charles Somerset, all of whose ancestors had lived and died for the house of Lancaster, George Talbot, of the blood of the last hero in the struggle of the Lancastrians against France, and many others whose names are connected with the same events.[1] The fame of his generosity, the means for exercising which his father's wealth furnished him, allured the knights and soldiery of Brabant, Hainault, and Flanders, and even far into Germany, so much to him, that many sold all they possessed in order, well accoutred and equipped, to earn greater pay under him. He had splendid cannon, and amongst them probably those twelve large pieces of ordnance, called the Twelve Apostles, cast for him in the Netherlands.[2]

In order to inspire as much confidence as the Swiss and the Spanish forces did, his army needed nothing further than an experienced general. Henry VIII, on begging the Emperor to lend him, for this purpose, Duke Heinrich, the warrior of Brunswick, or Marshal Vergy, the Emperor himself offered to lead the army of his friend.[3] He hoped with it to gain in open battle the bank of the Somme and, with the assistance of the Swiss, Burgundy, whereupon the two princes would unite and visit the French with a campaign, which would be as disastrous for them as ever an English war had been. On the 9th of August, he met

---

[1] Martin du Bellay, Mémoires, 6. Goodwin, p. 16. Herbert, p. 33.

[2] Margaret to Henry, in December, 1513, in the Lettres, iv. 217. Hubert Leodius, iii. 1.

[3] Letters of Maximilian, first in June, iv. 157, and frequently.

the King near Aire. He himself wore Henry's red cross and the Tudor rose; he was not annoyed that his two hundred horse, whose whole adornment lay in their golden chains, appeared insignificant in comparison with the brilliant accoutrements of the King's troops, or that his servants stooped down to pick up the silver bells, which Henry's noble pages purposely let fall from their horses' trappings; he accepted from the King a tent, gorgeously fitted up inside with silk hangings, gilded trelliswork and golden vessels, and, if Bellay is to be trusted, 100 escus a day for his table, and came into his camp.[1]

Thirty-four years before, Maximilian had besieged the same town, and, on that occasion, gained his most brilliant victory over the French, who had come across the Lys to relieve it. Mindful of this former success—for on this occasion, also, Térouanne was only besieged from one side—after having reconnoitred the camp and the walls with his master of the ordnance, he threw five bridges across the river. His luck would have it, that on the very same day that they crossed (17th August), the enemy, about eight thousand strong, made their appearance before him on the heights of Guinegate, descended, halted at the foot of the hill, and sent out light troops with provisions for the town. A simultaneous attack was planned by the besieged and their friends outside upon both parts of the English camp. Thereupon Maximilian, sending his infantry to a brook in the rear of the enemy's camp, threw himself with 2,000 horse upon the troops who had been sent out in advance. These forthwith galloped back to their camp.[2] Here—for it was four o'clock in the afternoon, and the knights had been in the saddle since two in the morning—many had exchanged their chargers for lighter horses, had thrown off their helmets, and were refreshing themselves with a draught. All at once, a general confusion and stampede ensued; the fugitives, coming from the one side, shouted that " the enemy were at their heels," and dashed wildly on

---

[1] Paul Armestorf to Margaret in the Lettres, iv. 192. Ehrenspiegel, 1297 seq. Goodwin, 20. Herbert, 35.

[2] Baptiste de Taxis in the Lettres, iv. 195. Polydorus, 27, 24. Herbert. Weiskunig, 303.

without stopping, and from the other side, came the tidings that the enemy's infantry was falling upon their rear. In vain the shout was raised of " Turn about, Hommes d'Armes ! " Maximilian's flying artillery swept them before them ; and this day was known hereafter by the name of the Battle of the Spurs. And when at last the bravest of them rallied on the bridge over the brook we have referred to, it was only to their destruction ; the Burgundian cavalry found another way across the brook and cut them off. They were all obliged to surrender, one here and another there ; La Palice, the Duc de Longueville, and a hundred others, all the flower of the army. Bayard, perceiving one of the enemy's knights unconcerned and taking no care, since the victory was theirs, rushed upon him sword in hand and cried, " Surrender to me, or thou art a dead man." The knight was wounded and surrendered himself. " But who art thou ? " he asked. " I am Bayard, and surrender myself to thee again." Both the other attacks were likewise repulsed, and on the 22nd of August the town surrendered.[1]

About the same time—on the 27th of August — the Swiss, about 30,000 men strong, united with the horse of Württemberg and Burgundy under Duke Ulrich and Vergy ; they received the Emperor's siege guns from Landau, his mortars from Breisach, his field cannon from Ensisheim, and a hundred arquebuses. Their captains were em-powered to make peace, only if the King renounced all rights to Milan. On their march, they heard the news of the Emperor's victory. With all the greater courage they crossed the French frontier.[2]

This double attack could not but throw the French into great anxiety. Even before the English had arrived, Louis had found himself obliged to confess to the Parlement that

[1] Bellay, Mémoires, 6. Bayard, 345–350. Fleuranges, p. 145. Embellished in Jovius, 100. Heuterus, Birken. A letter of an eye-witness in Brewer shows us the characteristic trait of Maximilian, that, though entreated to do so, he did not unfurl his standard, but declared his intention of fighting under the standard of St. George and the King of England. Thus the English ascribed the victory to their King. Brewer, i. No. 4431 (note to 2nd edition).

[2] Captains from Solothurn and Zürich, in Glutz. 345. Stettler.

his pecuniary needs were so pressing, and his finances
so much in arrear, that he must sell his demesnes to raise
400,000 livres, in order, without overburdening his poor
people, to resist the old enemies of his realm.[1]   After
the battle of Guinegate, he despatched his marshal to Paris
in order to review the tradesmen and artizans.   Once more,
after so long a peace, the banners of the trade guilds were
seen flying in the streets of the capital, and the same was
probably the case in many other cities.   The arrival of the
Swiss terrified every one.   A murmur of despondency went
through the whole nation ; "the retribution for their misdeeds in Italy was now about to break over their heads." [2]
In this crisis, France looked with a certain confidence to
its old alliance with the Scots.

It was the lot of King James IV, who once had been
desirous of negotiating peace between the Pope and Louis,
with a view to an expedition to Jerusalem, to be drawn
into the whirlpool of this war.   After a long peace, differences again arose with England, which threatened to end
in a fresh breach.   One of the chief disputes affected
Andrew Barton.   Barton was a bold pirate, who had also
served King John of Denmark, James' nearest friend,
against the Hanseatic League.[3]   James had delivered to him
letters of marque against the Portuguese, who had killed
Barton's father ; but he—as the Portuguese, the English,
and the Hanseatic League appear to have been united in
a long-standing maritime alliance—employed them against
the English also ; for this he was sought for by the latter,
and, in spite of a resistance which has been immortalized
even by his enemies in a long ballad, was at length killed.[4]
James was still smarting from indignation at this, when he
was implored by Queen Anne of France, whom in knightly
manner he had ever declared to be his lady, to come to
her assistance : "for Henry's crossing to Calais threatened

---

[1] Garnier from the Parliamentary Records, MS. of Fontanicu,
p. 470.

[2] Monstrelet, App. 246.   Gilles, 124.

[3] Anonymi chronologia rerum Danicarum, in Ludewig, Reliq.
MSS. ix. 52.

[4] Goodwinus, Annales, p. 11.

both her and Brittany." The King assembled his barons, in whom their many tournaments had awakened thirst for a real fight, and who were not a little influenced by the entreaties of the French ambassador, who, moreover, offered them 50,000 livres for their equipment. Having arranged matters with his nobles, James sent Lyon King of Arms to Térouanne to summon his neighbour to return, and when this had no effect—Henry merely reminded him of the fate of Navarre—he equipped himself in Edinburgh with 50,000 men.[1]

The complicated situation became thus more complicated. From such a vigorous attack some degree of success was to be expected in England, which would oblige Henry to return to his realm. It would then be possible for the French, perhaps by an attack upon Italy, to compel the Swiss to retire, and at the same time to encourage the Venetians.

As soon as James crossed the Tweed, the shout of battle rang from village to village, and from town to town. Henry, who, in order to be more certain of the loyalty of his frontier provinces, had not compelled them to pay his benevolence, had entrusted them to the keeping of the Earl of Surrey, a scion of the famous house of Howard. Round him the nobles gathered at Alnwick; his son, an admiral of the kingdom, landed at Newcastle with 5,000 men; the northern and southern shires all sent their contingents. Meanwhile, James remained for six days at Norham, and dallied for a while with Lady Ford; he was delighted to see the enemy assembling; for it was for battle that he had come: "he would fight," he said, "even though 100,000 English were arrayed against him." Thus minded, he entrenched himself upon the hill of Flodden, situated between the river Till, where it flows at the foot of the Cheviots between high banks, and a morass.

No less enthusiastic for the fray were the English: on Sunday, the 4th of September, they sent their herald Rougecroix to the King, asking, "whether it was his intention to remain so long in England that they could fight on the ensuing Friday?" The King replied: "Were I in

[1] Buchananus, Rerum Scoticarum l. xiii. p. 172 seq. Herbert.

Edinburgh, I would haste to be there by that day." But
was it likely that the English would attack him behind his
entrenchments? In vain they begged of him to come
down upon the plain of Milfield, which lay between them.[1]
But when he saw that, following a report which had been
spread, they made a detour, as though to invade Scotland—
it was the 9th of September, and a Friday—he broke up
his camp, burnt his tents, and, under cover of the smoke,
marched, in order to anticipate them, along the heights, to
a hill called Piperdy. Here he halted. Towards the same
place, through the low ground, came the English, and here
the battle began.

Thomas Howard, who had killed Andrew Barton, stood,
in order to answer for his conduct, as he said, in the very
first line, and fought magnificently. Not less valiantly, in
another part, did James fight in the front ranks, and
repeatedly threw back the enemy's standards. Now one
side, and now again the other, retired. But at last, owing to
the English arrows hitting better up the hill than the Scottish
cannon did down, for they fired too high, the Scots abandoned
the offensive, and formed a square for defence; their king
was here also to be seen fighting heroically. Whilst they
were still fighting, and the flower of both armies falling, night
supervened. In this night the Scots sought their king,
and found him not. Had he fallen, had he fled, or was he
a prisoner? They retreated. The English, on visiting the
battlefield the following morning, saw the cannon abandoned,
and knew that they were victorious. They found a dead
body in royal dress, and brought it in triumph to Berwick.
The Scots maintained that, "it was Elphinstone, who on
that day had worn royal apparel, in order to deceive the
English; their king had been seen across the Tweed."
But they themselves could not show him anywhere. Some
said: "Alexander Hume, whose company alone remained
almost intact, and who thereafter insulted both churches
and monasteries, must have killed him;" others, again,
"that he had gone to Jerusalem to do penance for his
sins;" the English accounts merely mention that King

[1] Expostulations of the Earls, and Answer in the very words, in
Herbert, 39.

James IV died in defending his banner.[1] The issue of this conflict upon the British Isles was even more important than the events on the Continent. Henry VIII, whilst fighting against France, became master of Scotland.

Besides 8,000 others, twelve earls and seventeen barons fell in the battle. Margaret, Henry VIII's sister, had undertaken the government of the realm. The French, who could no longer avail themselves of Scottish aid, had to fear the worst from the English and Swiss. On that fatal 9th of September, 30,000 Swiss crossed the Tille, where it falls into the Saône, and formed three camps before the walls of Dijon. The fourth was formed by the Emperor's cavalry and artillery. On the same day, both Emperor and King were still at Térouanne, and were capable of making an inroad any day into French territory.

But on this occasion France was not doomed to fresh devastation, and was saved. If it be asked how it came about, we may answer, that the turning point was their temporary yielding to the Swiss. La Trémouille, on seeing his citadel at Dijon wrecked by bombardment, France undefended, and the Swiss ready for further operations, attempted to make arrangements with them, first through an agent, then by appearing in person, and finally through confidential persons, who went in and out of the camp at dusk.[2] To save France, he thought it to be the best policy to give up Milan. On the 13th of September, he had arranged terms of peace with them, according to which the King renounced his claims to Milan, Asti, and Cremona, paying the Swiss, moreover, 400,000 escus.[3] This was what they desired.[4] What did the conquest of Burgundy for the house of Austria interest them, especially since they had never bound themselves to assist in such an undertaking? Only it was a great

---

[1] Buchananus, Rerum Scoticarum l. xiii. p. 251-255. Goodwinus, p. 29. Especially Herbert. Polydorus, xxvii. p. 28. Jovius, Historiae sui temporis, i. 102-106. The English report of Ruthal to Wolsey : " The King fell near his banner," Brewer, i. 4461 (note to 2nd edition).

[2] Anshelm, iv. 470 (note to 2nd edition).

[3] Bouchet, la Trémouille, 191-199. Ehrenspiegel, 1301. Especially Stettler. Anshelm, iv. 471. In Glutz. p. 549, there is an extract from the document, which is preserved in the archives at Zürich.

[4] Jean le Veau, Lettres, iv. 192.

mistake on their part to return home, without obtaining any security for their peace, or the King's word. Meanwhile, the English also resolved to turn back within sight of the French frontier, which they were actually threatening, their object being to reduce a semi-free city, which lay at a distance from the sea. It is not very credible that this was done with the advice of Maximilian, who was especially interested in invading France, and we find, as a matter of fact, that immediately after this occurrence, he separated himself from Henry in a sort of quarrel.[1] Perhaps the latter was influenced by the example of Edward III, who had besieged this city at the beginning of his French campaigns; but the chief point, beyond all doubt, was, that he conceived this to be the easiest and most permanent conquest. For he had razed Térouanne to the ground, in answer to the entreaties of the Council of Flanders.

However this may be, on the 15th—and it is impossible to know how far this is connected with the Swiss retreat—he made his appearance before the walls of Tournay; on the 25th, he entered that city in his assumed quality of King of France.[2] This city of Tournay, which really belonged to the province of Flanders, had relations with the Crown of France similar to those subsisting between the German free cities and the Emperor. Henry likewise confirmed its liberties; but he did not suffer these liberties to prevent his building a castle there. And here his campaign ended. In his delight, that though he had not destroyed France, he had yet succeeded in his attack upon her, and in taking two strongholds, he amused himself now at Margaret's court at Lille, now in his royal camp at Tournay with tournaments,[3] when the tidings reached him of the result of the Venetian operations, to which we, too, must turn our eyes; for they are all part of the same chain of events, brought to pass in widely separated places.

In August, Cardona had left the walls of Padua behind him; he resolved to compel the Venetians to accept his

[1] Herbert, 36.

[2] In Brewer, p. 676 : de l'entrée du roi Henri comme roi de France et d'Angleterre (note to 2nd edition).

[3] Lodov. Guicciardini : Descriptio Belgii. Herbert.

proffered peace. The Germans, Italians, and Spanish with him, had penetrated into Venetian territory across the Bacchiglione and the Brenta as far as Mestre, in order, as they said, to see what the Venetians had reaped. The country people once more fled to the marshes by the sea; in Padua and Venice it could plainly be seen how the fine country houses on the shore burst one after the other into flames. Cardona rode up to the tower of Malghera, whence the streets and quarters of Venice were clearly discernible. From here Georg Frundsberg could not restrain himself from discharging a piece of ordnance against the city itself, although this had been forbidden.[1]

To this pitch matters were allowed to come, before Alviano received permission to march out. What the allies had formerly desired became a source of no little peril to them now that they had advanced so far, and were surrounded by rivers and difficult passes. The discovery of a ford enabled them to escape across the Brenta; but, on the Bacchiglione, when Alviano was posted in the pass of Olmo before them, Manfrone in their rear on the road by which they had come, and peasants with their muskets crowned the heights on both sides of the defile, whilst they had to shelter themselves through a whole night behind the trunks of trees, they appeared to be lost, spoils and all. Alviano said that: "he had the remainder of the barbarian brutes between his shears, and needed only now to close them." The next morning, the imperial troops having retired a short distance to an open plain near Creazzo, he sent his flying artillery on ahead, and made after them. An action took place. The Spaniards fought with desperate valour; Pescara cried to his men: "If I die, let me not be trampled upon by the enemy," and led them, all athirst for the fray, against the enemy's centre. The Germans were protected by the strength of their arms: Frundsberg, who was in the front line, plied his sword vigorously, and, taking breath like a woodman in a forest felling an oak, struck again and again. All fought in the certainty that they must either conquer, or die covered with disgrace; the Papal horse

---

[1] Especially Ehrenspiegel, 1304, and Carpesanus, 1293, Mocenicus, v. 110. Passero, 202. Reisner.

took Alviano's banner; the Venetian army was completely routed, and those who but just before thought themselves as good as lost, became at one blow masters of the land.[1]

Such was the result of the attack upon Venice. This took place on the 7th October, 1513. About the same time, the Emperor, with Frangipani's help—more by treason than force of arms—contrived to effect the conquest of Marano, a Venetian seaport with a splendid commercial situation. Everywhere the League was in triumph. Three battles had been won, the Scottish nobility in great measure annihilated, and Venice so far humbled as to be compelled to accept the Pope, only just before its deadly enemy, as arbiter of its fortune; besides this, Milan, by a fourth great battle, and by a peace, which only needed ratification, as well as by the actual occupation of the remaining strongholds, had been wrested from the French. Yet France as yet had only been attacked on her frontiers, and was by no means vanquished in the interior. To this end the next campaign was destined to lead. On the 17th October, 1513, it was agreed at Lille to begin the campaign of the ensuing year with three attacks upon France, not only from the German and English, but also from the Spanish side.[2] Henry promised to secure from his parliament the assurance that, in the event of his dying without

[1] Jovius, Historiae, III–114. Vita Pescarae, 287. Paruta, 47–56. Guicciardini, ii. p. 55. Zurita, ii. 372.

[2] Herbert, 41. In Brewer, i. 4511, is to be found another extract from this compact, which displays some deviations, but which is also still incomplete. According to it, Ferdinand pledged himself in express terms to surrender Guienne to Henry VIII. "He shall give up his conquests to England." Moreover, both fleets were to be at sea before April: "Each power to send a fleet to sea before the end of April." No mention is therein made of the agreement, which we hear of in Margaret's letter. The records prove that the arrangement with Maximilian had been already concluded on the 16th of October; on the 15th November it was confirmed by the Emperor. By it the Emperor also pledged himself to join in the attack upon France, for which purpose he promised to keep a certain number of troops in reserve in Artois and Hainault. The marriage of Charles and Mary is therein mentioned with the greatest certainty. (Brewer, i. No. 4560.) Some particulars have been modified thereby, but the main points remain the same (note to 2nd edition).

issue, the crown of England should pass to the Archduke Charles of Austria, who in the ensuing May was to wed his sister Mary.[1]

8. FURTHER SCHEMES FOR THE ADVANCEMENT OF THE AUSTRO-SPANISH HOUSE

In this perilous crisis, Louis XII also felt himself obliged to approach the victor. He would not forego his claims to Milan ; but he thereby caused another plan to be formed, which would be advantageous to the House of Austria.

One month after the treaty of Lille, on the 16th November, 1513, Louis XII declared before notaries that, " He did give and make over the Duchy of Milan to his younger daughter, Renée, without revocation, without any exception." [2] It was soon seen what his object was in doing so. On the 1st December, he concluded a treaty with Ferdinand : " the same Renée should be married to one of Ferdinand's two grandsons, who should then receive Milan, which should be taken from the Swiss." Ferdinand hoped by this marriage to unite the Guelphs and Ghibellines in Milan, as he had once, in Naples, succeeded in doing with the Angevins and Aragonese.[3] In deep secrecy he despatched an envoy to Milan, to represent to the Duke how badly he was situated under the power of the Swiss, and, if possible, to detach him from their alliance.[4]

Anne of Brittany, the old friend of the House of Austria, desiring to see her younger daughter well married, was the real negotiator of these terms of alliance. When, on the 2nd January, 1514, she died, one might have supposed that this incipient union would dissolve and disappear. But, on the contrary, this very occurrence gave it fresh life. For, as Louis still wished to have an heir of his body, he did not reject the proposal that he should take to

[1] Margaret to Henry VIII. Lettres, iv. 239.
[2] Donatio de ducatu Mediolani, etc., in Dumont, iv. 1, 177.
[3] Treaty of Blois, in Dumont, 178.
[4] Fragment d'une lettre, in the Lettres de Louis, iv. 250.

wife Eleanor, the eldest of Ferdinand's granddaughters, and should enter into a hereditary alliance with the Austro-Spanish house. Navarre would then still remain joined to Castile. Fray Bernaldo de Trinopoli, a Dominican, remained behind for the negotiations, which lasted a considerable time.[1] Quintana, the confidant of Almazan, journeyed in February, 1514, from Burgos to Blois, and from Blois to Innsbruck; on the 11th of March, he was for a long time closeted with King Louis; on the 12th, the King's council assembled once again, and finally, on the 13th, new treaties were signed. But the grand alliance had not as yet been arranged, but only a truce, to which, however, as Quintana declared, the Emperor, in Henry's name as well as his own, was a party, and during which, although Sforza was no party to it, Louis promised not to attack Milan.[2]

This truce was designed to lead to the grand alliance, and to universal peace.

It can readily be perceived that this was in no wise in harmony with the treaty of Lille, not merely in that the war, then resolved on, lost its whole *raison d'être*, but, also, in that the prospective marriage of Charles with the English princess became very doubtful; for it was to the interest of the House of Austria that the other of Maximilian's grandsons should be kept for the matrimonial alliance with Hungary, which, as the heir to the throne was a weakling, had every prospect of continuing the succession. But, on that account, no hostility was feared from Henry, who had moreover taken no steps, as yet, to obtain the sanction of his parliament: " he was Ferdinand's son-in-law; Maximilian, too, who had come into his camp, had shown him the greatest confidence that one man could show another. He would, accordingly, accept the truce, if he only did not hear of it too soon."

With the greatest secrecy then—the Spanish ambassador insisted that not even the Emperor's daughter should be informed of it—the grand alliance was at length to be

---

[1] Zurita, ii. 383.
[2] Treaty in Dumont, 179. Gattinara and Veau, Letters in the Lettres, iv. 289, 292, *seq.*

established.[1] In a contemporary French manuscript, the original draft of the compact has been found: "Eleanor to marry Louis; Renée, the second grandson of the Emperor; Milan and Genoa to be delivered over into Ferdinand's hands, in favour of the two above-named; Louis to lay claim neither to Naples nor yet to the money he was to receive thence, and not to support Navarre; the Swiss to be jointly driven back within their borders. In return for this Tournay to be restored to France."[2] It almost looks as though Ferdinand, among other things, was bent upon preventing a new Philip rising up in the person of Charles. In any case, all this was admirably calculated for the aggrandisement of his house: on the 12th of August, 1514, he sent to Bernaldo de Trinopoli the authorization to arrange these marriages and to conclude this treaty.

In these days, the prestige of the Austro-Spanish house in Italy, Germany, and the whole of Europe, was greater than it had ever been. In May, 1514, Ferdinand concluded a compact with Genoa, which was the basis of all the later relations, almost those of vassal and suzerain, between the Genoese and the Kings of Spain.[3] Already it was calculated how frightened Massimiliano Sforza would be, and how, under the pressure of his officials, who were quite devoted to the Emperor, he would surrender his citadels and his people in favour of the latter's grandson. The Swiss could be compensated with money.[4] Venice, which could not even retake Marano, was not a little weakened by a fresh disaster[5]—a conflagration, which, breaking out on the 14th January, in the linen warehouses on the Rialto, spread on both sides of the canal, and in one day and night destroyed property to the value of two millions. Leo was in alliance with this house; Naples was completely subservient. This much for Italy. In Switzerland, the people had again and again risen against the French party, so that it appeared as if a King of France

---

[1] Gattinara to Margaret, Lettres de Louis IV, 369, 371.
[2] Garnier, from the MSS. of Bethune, p. 509.
[3] Senarega, at end. Zurita, ii. 379.
[4] Francesco Vettori, in Machiavelli, lettere famigl. p. 16.
[5] Guicciardini, ii. 69. Jovius, Historiae, 115. Paruta, 45.

would never again be able to avail himself of their services. In Lucerne, six suspects were committed to prison, and two, who were found guilty, put to death. The country people of Baden seized old Caspar Hetel, whose son had gone over to the French, and, paying no heed to the fact that his son had acted against his wishes, tortured and beheaded him.[1] "Hans Rudolf," the mother wrote to her son, "thou hast not acted as an honourable man, thou hast put thy father to death : never shalt thou again address me as thy mother : I will never own thee more as my son."[2] This conflict penetrated into the inmost secrets of filial love and affection ; it redounded to the advantage of Spain and Austria over France ; in the next Swiss diets, there was no one to be found who spoke French. In Germany, the election of a bishop, even where the chapter was unfavourable to the candidate,[3] only cost the Emperor a word. For instance, a second Albrecht of the house of Brandenburg, which had always been devoted to the Austrian house, and from which, but shortly before this, another Albrecht had been appointed from the imperial camp in Padua to the office of Grandmaster in Prussia, received the Archbishoprics of Magdeburg and Mainz. A great tumult in Württemberg ended in the Estates advising their Duke to live at the court of the Emperor, only on no account to sever himself from Austria.[4] At Regensburg, which had long resisted an imperial administrator, there arrived at the beginning of the year 1514, Wolf von Wolfstall and the other imperial commissioners. Many of their opponents, "famous masters in their respective arts, old, honourable men with white hair," as the chronicle says, paid the penalty with their lives. Others were expelled and their wives sent after them. The imperial commissioners appointed a new council and made a new constitution at their discretion.[5] They boasted that the Emperor had, in the

---

[1] Letter of the father to the son, in Anshelm, iv. 410 (note to 2nd edition).

[2] Correspondence of the mother and son, in Stettler, 501.

[3] Hubert Thomas Leodius, Vita Frederici Palat. iii.

[4] Sattler, Württembergische Geschichte, etc., i. 180.

[5] Regensburger Chronik. vol. iv. part 3, pp. 234-245.

previous year, made a similar example of more than one city.[1] At the same time, in the interests of Austria, Georg of Saxony vanquished the Frisians in the west, whilst in the east, Heinrich of Brunswick, the warrior, overcame the Budjadings, and both united triumphed over Etzard Cirksena, Count of East Friesland, whom the Emperor had placed under his ban as his enemy, for having supported these peoples. The Budjadings were ruined by the winter of this year (which continued from October, 1513, to February, 1514, with such severity, that all the springs were frozen hard and the peasants for a long period counted their years from this great frost), and their privileges were abolished. Etzard, in April of this year, offered Georg fealty in respect of East Friesland, and tribute for Groningen and the Ommelande. But this did not content Georg. In July, he devastated Damm with great cruelty. Groningen was inclined for immediate submission. Etzard saw his enemy marauding as far as the gates of Emden.[2]

Among other motives, this great good fortune may have induced Christian II of Denmark to sue for the hand of Isabella, Maximilian's second granddaughter. His father John had, in the year 1511, pledged himself to aid the French. After his death he also was prepared to support the Scots.[3] But he now severed himself from the Franco-Scottish alliance. In April, 1514, the matter was settled, and Christian promised to side with the Teutonic Order on behalf of the Empire, and to oppose the claims of Sigismund of Poland.[4] In June, 1514, Maximilian's third granddaughter, Mary, journeyed through the Empire in order to wed Louis, the heir to the throne of Hungary.[5]

We see the position of affairs in Europe ; how the French had not merely lost Italy, but their party had almost everywhere perished or become Spanish, and how the two great combinations threatened to merge into one, and Louis XII was himself on the point of becoming a member of the

---

[1] Proclamation of the Commissioners, *ibid.* p. 238.
[2] Chytraei Chronicon Saxonicum, p. 207.
[3] Gebhardi, Geschichte von Dänemark und Norwegen, ii. 55.
[4] Marguerite à l'Empereur, Lettres, iv. 325.
[5] Regensburger Chronik, vol. iv. part 3, p. 243.

Austro-Spanish House. In July and August, it looked as though the Spanish monarchy would one day be able to embrace the whole of Europe. At the same time, the same house was further advantaged by the second chief discovery in America. In September, 1513, that Nuñez Balboa, who had founded Veragua, sailed from Darien to find the South Sea. After much toil and exertion, outstripping his comrades, he climbed the peak of a high mountain and saw, first of all our races, before him the great ocean that separates the two continents of the earth. He made a monument of stones and took possession of the mountain ; he proceeded down the coast, called his notaries to him, and took possession of the sea for Ferdinand the Catholic. The cacique, who had shown him the way, he baptized with the name of the heir to all this power in Europe and America, his prince, Charles.[1]

CONCLUSION TO THE SECOND EDITION

The narrative breaks off at the very moment of the crisis. A combination of dynasties and empires looms before us, which might seem destined to combine the nations of Latin and Teutonic origin in a unity such as has never existed, and which certainly would not have had a beneficial influence upon their development. We perceive, at the first glance, that the realization of such a scheme presented the greatest difficulties ; for both nations and countries were still engaged in their own peculiar impulses and were represented therein by their several dynasties. To combine all these into one political system would in itself have been an utter impossibility. The idea of such a possibility is nothing but an expression of that defeat, which the most powerful nation of all, the French, had just suffered.

'All had resulted from this, that the ever chivalrous France, superior in power to all other states, attempted, on the strength of old dynastic claims, to conquer Naples and

[1] Sommario dell' Indie occidentali del S. D. Pietro Martyre, in Ramusio, Viaggi, 29.

Milan. As a rule, it has only been said that by this Italy would have been utterly ruined; but it is indisputable that, at the same time, such a conquest would have imperilled the independent development of Europe. But it happened that, through the dynastic union of Burgundo-Austria and Spain, in the struggles and vicissitudes I have here depicted, an opposing force arose which maintained the balance of power.

The generation whose acts and struggles have led to this result belongs, from an historical point of view, to the most remarkable that have ever existed; its political work was the foundation of an European system of states; it brought the most heterogeneous elements of the north and south into a combination, wherein the unity of the Latin and Teutonic nations became more than ever conspicuous.

But such a state of things could not last, in the face of the ascendency which the House of Austria had attained to in the years 1513 and 1514. The life of Europe consists in the energy evolved by the great contrasts it presents. In the year 1515, the most chivalrous of the French kings again began the struggle with brilliant success. But that at the same time served to bring the Austro-Spanish combination to full reality. The antagonism which has since controlled the European world was becoming developed. In the years immediately following arose the generation which represented it most clearly and vigorously. The times henceforward completely changed their course.

It would, perhaps, be a task for a historian to describe successively the generations, as far as possible, in the order of their appearance on the stage of the world's history, showing how they belong together, and how they separate from each other. Full justice would have to be done to each one of them. It would be possible to portray a series of the most brilliant forms and figures, all of which have the closest connection with each other, and in whose contrasts the development of the world makes further progress. Events are in harmony with their nature.

INDEX

A

Abruzzi, the, to belong, with Lavaro, to Louis XII, 178, 191; Aragonese call Gonzalvo to, 191; influence of Gonzalvo in, 205; defeat of Angevin army in, 207

Abuayazid, known as Bajazet, 181. *See* Bajazet

Abyssinia, king of, a Christian, 68; Queen Helena of, 297

Adda, the, the French cross, 291; Louis XII transports troops across, 291

Adelsberg, courage shown by Bernhardt Reiniger on the, 284; restored by Venetians to Maximilian, 286

Aden, Moorish trade at, 268

Adolf of Nassau, struggle of, with Albert for German crown, 15; falls at Hasenbühel, 15

Adorno, family of, the leading plebeian family of Genoa, 265; flee from Genoa, 157; offer their services to Gonzalvo, 213

Adorno, Giovanni, reported on march from Naples to Genoa, 162

Adrian, Cardinal, of Corneto, his banquet to Alexander VI and Caesar Borgia, 210

Ægean Sea, coast of, sends light Greek horse for Venice, 289

Africa, expeditions against, give rise to scheme for conquest of India, 17; early colonization of, 18; Spanish operations in, 249–251; in 1497, trade on East coast of, in hands of Moors, 268; Almeida secures coast of, 274

Agnadello, battle of, 292–293

Aguilar, Alfonso de, opposed to Isabella, 64; slain in field against Moors, 183

Aguilar, Gonzalvo de. *See* Gonzalvo

Aguilar, Pedro de, Marquis of Priego, 232; in revolt against Ferdinand of Spain, 248

Aire, Maximilian meets Henry VIII near, 371–2

Ajas, Venetian trade with, 254

Albaycin, converts from the, baptised by Ximenes, 183

Albert, struggle of, with Adolf for German crown, 15

Albertinelli, painter, of Florence, becomes innkeeper, 126

Albizzi, the, at Florence, 356

Albrecht, Duke of Munich, and the Landshut succession, 221; Maximilian decides in his favour, 222

Albrecht of Saxony, with Archduke Philip of Austria, 111

Albret, Charlotte d', daughter of Alain d', marries Caesar Borgia, 172

Albret, Jean d', husband of Catherine of Navarre, made king of Navarre, 350; opposed by Ferdinand, 350; weakness of, 351; flies before Spaniards, 351; makes way back and besieges Pamplona, 351; retires before Alva, 352

Albuquerque, succeeds in building fort at Harmuz, 276

Albus, Brother, patriarch of Venice, 41

Alcalá, Archbishop Richard of Toledo leads Crusaders against, 8; Ximenes lays foundation of university of, 247

Alemanni, both Swabians and Swiss are, 14

Alessandria, Galeazzo Sanseverino at, 153; Galeazzo flies from, 153; fall of, 153; French army at, 365

Alexander VI, Pope, Rodrigo Borgia of Xativa, 41; bribes Brother Albus of Venice, 41; overcomes resistance of Ascanio Sforza, 42; opposed by Giuliano della Rovere, 42; elected Pope, 42; his family, 42; Alfonso II of Naples wins over, 44; connection of, with Alfonso alarms Cardinal Giuliano, 44-5; refuses food as Cardinal's guest, 45; Orsini reconciled with, 45; interviews Alfonso II at Vicovaro, 45; perplexed by claims of Charles VIII, 55; sends escort for Charles entering Rome, 56; Charles makes obeisance to, 57; promises conquest of Africa to Spain, 68; a friend of the Sforza, 72; under protection of Ferdinand and Isabella, 72; Ludovico hesitates to trust, 74; letters of Bajazet to, concerning Djem, 75; flies from Rome before Charles VIII, 77; resolves on opposition to Savonarola, 122; his quarrel with the Orsini, 122; summons Savonarola to Rome, 124; general sketch of position of, 169; sensuality, greed, and vices of, 170; washing of feet by, on Maundy Thursday, 170; cruelty of, 170; closely connected with Houses of Sforza and Aragon, 170; sudden death of Juan, favourite son of, 170; thinks of abdicating, 171; negotiates with France, 172; rewards messenger announcing Ludovico's captivity, 174; ill consequences for Italy of feud of, with Naples, 185; gives French legation to Cardinal Georges d'Amboise for life, 186; allied with kings of France, Denmark, and Scotland, 186; fights in the Romagna, 196; talks of resigning papacy to Cardinal Orsini, 199; death of Cardinal attributed to, 201; castles of Orsini, and cities of Perugia, and Città di Castello in hands of, 201; most powerful of popes in States of Church, 202; compels Sienese to expel Petruccio, 201-2; death of, 205; agitation for election of successor of, 205; complaints of French against, 208; had abandoned French cause to subdue Pisa, Siena, and Florence, 209; Francesco Trocces, chamberlain of, put to death, 209; had proposed to Ferdinand of Spain a league with Venice to expel French, 209; suspicions regarding death of, 210; prediction of astrologers concerning, 211; blood and cruelty stain acquisitions of, 211; alternately French and Spanish in sympathy, 216

Alexander the Black, of Veldenz, assails the Palatinate, 223

Alexandria, Ferdinand's designs on, 252; Venetian galleys carry trade to, 254

Alfonso of Calabria, Ludovico shrewdly uses, 140

Alfonso d'Este. See D'Este

Alfonso of Ferrara. See Ferrara

Alfonso I of Naples (Alfonso V of Aragon) founds power of House of Aragon, 30, 71; Ferrante, natural son of, 30

Alfonso II of Naples, son of Ferrante, 30; marries daughter of Francesco Sforza, 30; character of, 31; barons allied with Innocent VIII against, 32; defeats Pope, and besieges Aquila, 32; urges Ferrante to murder enemies, 33; Isabella, daughter of, betrothed to Gian Galeazzo, 39; Isabella appeals to, 40; calls upon Ludovico to retire from government, 41; comes to throne of Naples on death of Ferrante, 44; gains over Alexander VI, 44; crowned, 45; interview of, with Alexander VI, 45; resolves to attack Ludovico, 45; Piero de' Medici surrenders to France, in interest of, 50 n.; Charles VIII rejects overtures of, 57; proposes marriage of Ferrantino to daughter of King of Spain, 57; renounces realm, 58; flies to, Olivetan monastery, at Mazzara, 58

Alfonso V of Portugal betrothed to Juana of Castile, 63; defeated by

Ferdinand at Toro, 64; his dispensation to marry Juana, revoked by Sixtus IV, 64; renounces his claims, 65

Algau, men of, at Frastenz, 147

Alidosi, Francesco, Cardinal of Pavìa. *See* Pavìa

Allègre, Ives d'. *See* Ives

Almazan, "other self," of Ferdinand of Spain, 230, 234

Almeida, Jacobo, 129

Almeida, Don Francisco d', Dom Manuel of Portugal despatches fleet to India under, 274; takes Quiloa and Mombasa, 274; gives golden crown to Prince of Cochin, 274; tidings of successes reach Moors, 275; victorious in second battle, 276; sets out to avenge death of Lourenço, 296; burns Dabul, 296; avenges Lourenço at Diu, 296

Almeida, Don Lourenço d', son of Francisco, victorious over Moors in India, 275; wounded, 276; attacked by Mir Hossein at Schaul and killed, 296

Almeria, plunder of, by Alonso Ramon, 9; colonies established in, 18

Almirante of Castile, the, opposed to exclusion of Archduchess Juana from government, 243 *n.*

Almoravides, the, 8

Alonso the Noble, 8; gains battle of Navas de Tolosa, 8

Alonso the Sage, subjects Mercia, 8

Alonso Ramon, Spaniards under, take valley of Guadiana, 8

Altamura, factions, siding with France or Spain, fight for, 191

Altavilla, Juan de, fidelity of, 79

Alva, Duke of, 195; never wavers in loyalty to Ferdinand of Spain, 232; Garcia, eldest son of, attacks Gelves, 251; gathers large army at Vitoria, 351; ordered by Ferdinand to advance on Pamplona, 351; Pamplona surrenders to, 352; takes St. Jean, 352; holds Pamplona against Jean d'Albret, 352

Alviano, Bartolommeo d', with Venetian troops, opposes Paolo Vitelli, 139; assists Gonzalvo at

battle of the Garigliano, 207; captures Cadore, 283; storms Kramaun, 283; commands infantry for Pitigliano, 290; character and achievements of, 290; at battle of Agnadello, 292; defeated and wounded, 293; boasts that he has "barbarian brutes between shears" in pass of Olmo, 379; defeated by the Spaniards near Creazzo, 379, 380

Alzheimer Gau, ravaged by Wilhelm of Hesse, 223

Amalfi, given by King Ferrante to nephew of Pius II, 30

Amboise, Charles d'. *See* Chaumont

Amboise, Cardinal Georges d', Archbishop of Rouen, at Court of Louis XI, 136; takes side of Duke of Orleans, 136; visited by Mosen Gralla, ambassador of Ferdinand, 178; fears Spanish claims on Naples, 178; Alexander VI gives French legation for life to, 186; candidate for Papacy, 212; receives legation of Avignon, 213; receives investiture of Milan, Pavìa, and Anghiera for Louis XII, Charles, and Claude, 227; Louis XII negotiates to make Pope, 267; negotiations of, with Maximilian's daughter Margaret, 286; Louis XII and Maximilian join hands through intervention of, 298; supports Maximilian against Venice in hope of becoming Pope, 303; death of, in 1510, 310; Robertet's comment on seeing portrait of, 310

America, the gold of, promotes exploration, 18; colonization of, by Ferdinand, 250; second chief discovery in, 386

"Amman Reding," calf christened as, by Germans, at Bendre, 144

Anathema (accursed thing), burnt at Florence, 120

Andalusia, subdued by St. Ferdinand, 8; colonies move to, 18; cities of, visited by Queen Isabella, 64; 5000 houses in, emptied through Inquisition, 65; Priego and Giron in revolt against

Ferdinand in, 248 ; domestic disturbances in, 249

Andrada Caravajal. *See* Caravajal

Andrew of Hungary takes part in crusade, 7

Angevins, rights of the, in Naples, pass to crown of France, 71 ; summon French to Calabria, 191 ; Ferdinand recalls, to Naples, 239. *See also* Anjou

Anghiera, Louis XII receives investiture of, 227

Angles at enmity with Danes, 4 ; Egbert makes heptarchy of a monarchy, 5

Anglo-Germanic element in Ireland, 10

Anglo-Saxons, foes of Britons, 3 ; not finally able to resist Latin Christianity and culture, 3

Angora, Venetian trade in goats' hair with, 254

Angoulême, Francis of. *See* Francis

Anhalt, Rudolf of, in Rome, 55 ; Pope speaks to, on title of Maximilian, as Emperor, 55 ; seizes Pouderoyen, 285 ; known as " Anhalt, das treue Blut," 302 ; commissioned by Maximilian to ravage Italy, 302 ; horrible deeds consequent on commission of, 302

Anjou, claims of princes of, 14 ; Plantagenets of, 20 ; Duke of, dies without leaving son, 21 ; territory of, comes to French crown, 21 ; John of, 30, 71

Anne of Brittany (Queen of France) betrothed to Maximilian, 23 ; called Queen of the Romans, 23 ; married to Charles VIII, 23 ; disappointment of Maximilian at not obtaining, for wife, 96 ; Louis XII divorces Jeanne to marry, 137 ; favours betrothal of Claude to Charles, 228 ; afterwards consents to Claude's betrothal to Francis of Angoulême, 229 ; negotiates treaty with Ferdinand, 381 ; death of, in 1514, 381

Anne of Bourbon, sister of Charles VIII, 136 ; demands compensation for increment acquired by grandfather for crown, 136 ;

Suzanne, daughter of, is guaranteed succession, 136

Anne de Candale marries King Wladislav, 176

Antigua, colony on Darien, named in honour of picture of Maria Antigua, at Seville, 250

Antonello of Solerno, Prince, fugitive from Naples, at court of France, 26, 33

Antwerp, trade of, with Florence, 213–214 ; Portuguese merchants go to, 277 ; displaces Bruges in trade, 277

Anziani, the, of Genoa, 266

Apostles, the Twelve, twelve pieces of ordnance, for Henry VIII, called, 371

Aquila, Alfonso II of Naples besieges, 32 ; surrenders to Charles VIII, 57 ; goes over to Spaniards, 89

Arabia, trade on coast of, in hands of Moors, in 1497, 268 ; Dom Manuel of Portugal styles himself lord of future conquests, in, 272

Arabian governors at Indian ports, 268 ; convoys for Banyans, 268

Aragon, union of, with Catalonia, 8 ; lawful influence of Justicia established in, 16 ; House of, rules over great part of Italy, 29 ; power of House of, founded by Alfonso I, and maintained by Ferrante, 30 ; united with Castile 62 ; African kingdoms of Oran and Tlemcen claimed for crown of, 68 ; Barcelonese House of, 71 ; alliance of House of, with that of Hapsburg, 129 ; succession of, assured to Juana, wife of Archduke Philip, 188 ; Gonzalvo rules Naples in spirit of party of, 207 ; struggles of, with Castile, for Navarre, 350

Architecture, characteristic, 12

Aretins offer services to Gonzalvo, 213

Arevalo, Archduchess Juana conveyed to, 244 *n.*

Arezzo, Florentine commerce with, 113

Argos delivered to Venice, 256

Arias, feud between the, and the Lassos, at Madrid, 245

Ariosto, family of, help the Benti-vogli, 316

Ariosto, his Orlando, 321

Arno, Popolari attempt to divert course of, 354

Arrabbiati, party of,in Florence, 123; Franciscans join, 124; for Pope, against Savonarola, 124; struggle of, with Popolari, 125; attack Popolari in streets and convent, 127; devoted to League, 127; assert supremacy in Florence, 127; chose a leader, called "Duke," 157

Ars, Louis d', intercedes for Vog-heresi, 167

Arthur, King, cycle of tales of, 11, 25

Arthur, Prince of Wales, marriage of, arranged with Katherine of Aragon, 130

Asiago, Maximilian ascends mountains of, with troops, 281

Askemans, the, daring by land and sea, 5

Aspromonte, Spaniards retreat across the, 193

Asti, Ludovico Sforza and Charles VIII meet at, 47; Louis of Orleans at, 73; Charles VIII at, 85; Trivulzio fortifies, 109; Venetians will not give up, 112; hommes d'armes of Louis XII, collecting at, 150; pledged to Charles and Claude, if Louis dies without son, 226; Swiss compel people of, to pay 100,000 ducats after battle of Novara, 368; French king renounces claims to, 377

Astorga, Marquis of, with Arch-duke Philip, 232

Atella, Ferrantino defeats the French at, 92; Gonzalvo at, 192

Athaulf, King of Visigoths, dreams of gothicising Roman world, 1

Athens receives garrison from Venice, 256

Atlantic, from Canaries to Iceland, navigated by Columbus, 68

Aubigny, Robert d', brother of Matthew Stuart, joins Charles VIII, 28; Ferrantino incapable of resisting, 55; penetrates to Forlì, 73; at Tropea, 91; surrenders to Ferrantino, 92; sets forth from Naples to recover Tripalda, 192; advances to Cala-bria, 193; sacrifices silver plate to ransom Imbercourt, 193; defeated at Seminara and escapes to Gioia, 203; surrenders to Caravajal, 205

Augsburg, Diet of (1500), 168

Augsburg, festivities at, 111; takes commercial lead among German cities, 277

Aursperg Hans, asks for assistance against Alviano, 283

Austria, mark of, first founded round castles of Krems and Melk, 95; becomes an archduchy, 95; Maximilian lord of, 95; all the earth subject to (" Alles Erd-reich ist Oesterreich unterthan "), 96; Maximilian reconquers, 96; Switzerland hostile to, 102; quarrel of, with Spain, 218; House of, takes possession of Castile, 234; League of Cambray readjusts frontier of, in favour of Maximilian, 286

Austro-Spanish House, prestige of, in Italy, Germany, and all Europe, 383

Avignon, Cardinal Giuliano at, 45; Popes at, in power of French kings, 169; Amboise has lega-tion of, 213; Cardinals opposed to Julius II send envoy to, 331

Avogaro, Luigi, summons Vene-tians to Brescia, 328; defeated and made prisoner by Gaston de Foix, 330–331

Ayala, Pedro de, negotiates in Scotland, 130; uses persuasive powers on Perkin Warbeck, 130; persuades James IV not to invade England, 131

Ayalas, the, feud of, with the Silvas at Toledo, 245

Azov, Venetian trade with, 254

B

Bacchiglione, allied Germans, Italians, and Spanish penetrate into Venetian territory across the, 379

Baccio, Bartolommeo, takes figures

from workshop and gives up as "Anathema," 121

Baden, House of, friendly to the Emperor, 103; Swiss assemble at, and resolve on war with France, 344; blows by invisible hands said to be struck at Diet at, 363; Caspar Hetel tortured and beheaded at, 384

Baetica (Andalusia), Vandals take name from, 3

Baglione, family of, in pay of Caesar Borgia, 186, 198

Baglione, Giampaolo, under French protection, 211, 212; rules Perugia by a Balía, 263

Bagnolo, peace of, 35

Bahrein Islands, Venetian trade in pearls from the, 254

Bajazet, or Abuayazid, the Sultan, 56; fits out galleys in Constantinople, 57; letters of, to the Pope, regarding Djem, 75; Ludovico Sforza vainly relies on, 152; decides on war with Venice, 181; gives Andrea Zancani Italian letter of compact, 181; equips ships in Hellespont, 182; sends troops to pillage Zara, 182; Lepanto taken for, 182; takes Coron, Modon, and Navarino, 183; returns to Constantinople, 183

Balboa, Vasco Nuñez y, head of colony of Antigua, 250; founds Veragua, 386; sails from Darien to find South Sea, 386; takes possession of sea for Ferdinand, 386

Balzo, of Taranto, 30; family of, in open war with House of Aragon, 32; execution of three members of family of, 33

Barbo, Pietro, invited by Doge to Venetian Council, 294-295

Barcelona, claims of princes of, to Naples, 14, 71; market for Florence, 113

Bardonian Alp, separates Tuscany from Lombardy, 78

Bari, defended against French by Isabella of Aragon, 192

Barletta, attacked by French, 192; La Palice before, 193; Gonzalvo shut up in, 202

Barton, Andrew, James IV of Scotland gives letters of marque to, against Portuguese, 374; killed by Thomas Howard, 376

Basel, peace between Ludovico and the Swiss ratified at, 158

Basilicata, not included in treaty of partition between France and Spain, 191

Bavaria, Louis of, quarrels with Charles of Luxembourg for German crown, 15

Bavaria, Maximilian in, 224

Bavaria-Landshut. See Landshut

Bayard, Chevalier, character of, 194; at battle of the Garigliano, 207; attacks the Genoese, 266; with Maximilian in Italy, 300; refuses to fight at side of tailors and cobblers, 301; Julius II escapes from, owing to snowstorm, 313; hears indignantly of plan to poison the Pope, 314; wounded at siege of Brescia, 330; at battle of Ravenna, 333, 336-337; surrenders at battle of the Spurs, 373

Bayonne, Marquis of Dorset has orders to go against, 352

Beatrice of Hungary, daughter of King Ferrante of Naples and wife of King Wladislav, 176; divorced, 177; goes to Federigo in Ischia, 180

Beaumonts, Count Lerin head of the, 350

Bechadas, by Godfrey of Bouillon, the first novel, 11

Becket, Thomas à, quarrel of, with Henry II of England, 13

Beitelstein, taken from Venice, 318

Bejar, Duke of, with the Archduke Philip, 232

Bellincioni, Bernardo, pastoral plays and farces of, 36

Bellinzona, Swiss cross the St. Gotthard, to defend, 220; rights of people of Uri to, confirmed by Louis XII, 305; Swiss make their way back from Milan to, 328

Belluno, offered by the Visconti to Venice, 257

Bembo, Pietro, on Ludovico, and terms of peace with France, 87

Benavente, Pimentel, Count of, on the side of Philip, 232 ; opposes Ferdinand, 245 ; gives in to Ferdinand, 248

Benavides, Count, at battle of Seminara, 203

Benavides, the, feud of, with the Caravajals, 203, 245

Bendre, christening of calf as "Amman Reding," at, 144

Bengal, Venetian trade in silk from, 254 ; and in cotton fabrics from, 269

Benivieni, sent by the Signoria of Florence to Savonarola, 123

Bentivogli, the brothers, 29 ; Caesar Borgia attacks, 198 ; treaty between Caesar and, 199–200; family of, side against Julius II, 311 ; Bologna, in hands of the, 316 ; break statue' by Michael Angelo of the Pope, 317 ; Bologna not regained by, after French occupation, 347

Bentivoglio, Giovanni, opposes Caesar Borgia, 175 ; resists Julius II, 262 ; supported by Ginevra Sforza, 263 ; declared a rebel against the Church, 264

Bergamo, Doge Foscari takes, 258 ; reconquered by Swiss, 368

Bergstrasse, Wilhelm of Hesse ravages the, 223

Bern, Ludovico Sforza allied with, 141 ; joins League, 145 ; enlistment prohibited in, 163 ; common people of, implore bailiff to secure peace, 164 ; friendship of, with Freiburg at an end, 325 ; Diesbachs and French party in the ascendant in, 325

Berry, Duke of, dies without leaving a son, 21

Berthold, Count of Henneberg, Elector of Mainz, leads the Estates in opposition to the Emperor, 105 ; disapproves setting aside of Edict of Worms, 132 ; Maximilian complains of, 220 ; death of, in 1504, 225

Besigheim, people of, forced to acknowledge Ulrich of Württemberg, 223

Beutelstein, Maximilian's instructions how to shoot obliquely into kitchen with makeshift bullet at, 98

Bey, Mustapha, said to have killed Djem, with help of the Pope, 76

Bianchi, the, contrasted with Neri, 117

Bibbiena, Bernardo di, counsellor of Piero de' Medici, 49 ; influence of, at the election of Leo X, 361

Bidassoa, English army on the, 346

Bigi, the, in Florence, 123

Biragi, family of, have Guelph proclivities, 35

Bischofzell, men of, assemble at the Schwaderloch to assistance of Confederation, 146

Biseglia, taken by French, 192

Biseglia, Alfonso di, Lucrezia Borgia married to, 171 ; flies from Rome, 176 ; returns to Rome and is murdered, 176 ; tumult against the Pope after death of, 210–211

Bishops, influence of, in founding of France, 2 ; at first of Latin origin, 2–3 ; Frankish in Paris, 3 ; Metropolitan, instituted by Boniface, received pallium from Rome, 4–5 ; Spanish, not to be made without approval of Ferdinand, 66

Bisignano, Princess of, 33 ; on side of French, 192

Bitonto, unconquered, 93 ; Marquis of, on side of French, 192 ; Marquisate of, seized by Gonzalvo, 207

Black Prince, the, driven by avarice of Peter the Cruel to the hearthtax, 16

Blanche of Savoy, Charles VIII received by, at the gates of Turin, 47

Blois, treaty of (1504), 226, 261–279 ; points to general war on Venice, 227 ; broken, 229

Blumeneck, Lady of, carries her husband from castle taken by Swiss, 148

Boccaccio, works of, burned in Florence, 121

Boccalino cedes Osimo to Turks, 181

Bohemia, Austria extends to, 95 ; foot soldiers from, join French, 364

Bohemond of Tarentum, operations of, against Greeks, 7

Boiardo, heroic poem of Orlando by, 321

Bolgherelli, the, Faentines defend, against Frederick II, 175

Bologna, allies prepared to meet Charles VIII at, 79 ; Caesar Borgia threatens, 175 ; independence of, under Giovanni Bentivoglio, 262 ; Julius II takes field, to conquer, 263 ; Bentivoglio obliged to quit, 264 ; Julius enters, 264 ; reforms government of, 265 ; Julius, when forsaken by schismatic Cardinals, goes to, 308 ; Chaumont attacks, 311 ; Julius promises leading Bolognese a Cardinal from, 311 ; and rises from sick bed to give blessing to, 312 ; French retire from, 312 ; Trivulzio drives back papal army under walls of, 315 ; Cardinal of Pavia commands for the Pope in, 315 ; Bentivogli gain possession of, 316 ; object of Holy League to conquer, 323 ; failure of attack on, by Pedro Navarra, 328–329 ; Gaston de Foix enters, 329 ; released by Cardinals from ban, 331 ; Cardinals send envoy to, 331 ; French burn episcopal palace and retire from, 347 ; envoys from, implore pardon of the Pope, 348

Bona, Duchess, widow of Galeazzo Maria, Duke of Milan, takes possession of land and cities in name of her son, 34 ; Gian Galeazzo imprisons favourite of, and determines to rule, 35

Boniface, St., Apostle of Germans, goes forth from England, 4 ; made Archbishop of Mainz, 4 ; on Pipin's incentive brings clergy into subjection to Rome, 4

Borgia, Caesar, son of Pope Alexander VI, 42 ; Charles VIII assured of Pope if he has as hostage, 56 ; Swiss in pay of, 162–163 ; sensual and cruel character of, 171 ; death of brother, Don Juan, attributed to, 171 ; proposals for marriage of, to daughter of Federigo, 171 ; resigns his benefices, 172 ; his reception at French Court, 172 ;

made Duke of Valentinois, 172 ; marries Charlotte d'Albret, 172 ; plans to destroy vassals of the Church, 172 ; makes war on Caterina Sforza, 173 ; made a Gonfaloniere of Church, 174 ; successful campaign in the Romagna, 174 ; Faentines surrender to, 175 ; called Duke of Romagna, 175 ; hunts human beings with arrows like game, 176 ; outrages and murders Astorre Manfredi, 176 ; murder of Alfonso di Biseglia, by order of, 176 ; treaty of, with Giovanni Bentivoglio, 186 ; Baglione, Vitelli, and Orsini in pay of, 186 ; renews campaign in Romagna, 196 ; treachery of, to Guidobaldo of Urbino, 197 ; takes Urbino and Camerino, 197 ; murders Giulio Varano and his sons, 197 ; allies himself afresh with Louis XII, 197 ; attacks Bentivogli, 198 ; the Orsini conspire against, 198 ; makes a treaty with the Orsini, 199–200 ; treacherously captures and murders them, 201 ; twice dissuaded by Louis XII from attacking Florence, 208 ; Ferdinand proposes to make him King of Tuscany, 208 ; falls dangerously ill, 209 ; takes poisoned wine at banquet of Cardinal Adrian of Corneto, 210 ; position of, on death of Alexander, 211 ; Fabio Orsini slays attendant of, 211 ; adherents of, in the Romagna fly, 211 ; loses confidence after father's death, 214 ; vacillates in papal election, 214 ; offers to surrender castles to Julius, 214 ; goes to Ostia, 215 ; divergent accounts of his movements, 215 n. ; brought to Rome by papal guards, 216 ; his castles delivered to Pope, 216 ; Lescun and Marquis of Finale offer Spanish safe-conduct and French aid to, 216 ; surrenders to Runno de Ocampo and is imprisoned in Spain, 217 ; escapes and is killed in a skirmish, 217

Borgia, Francesco, Cardinal of Cosenza, one of the schismatic Cardinals, 322

Borgia, Gioffredo, son of Alexander VI, 42 ; Alfonso promises an estate and his daughter Sancia to, 44

Borgia, Juan, Duke of Gandia, son of Alexander VI, 42 ; marries Maria Enriquez, 44 ; murder of, 122, 170 ; Alexander's grief at loss of, 170–171

Borgia, Lucrezia, daughter of Alexander VI, 42 ; married to Giovanni Sforza, 43 ; married to Alfonso di Biseglia, 171 ; married to Alfonso d'Este, 187 ; wishes to fly before papal troops, 308 ; Cardinal Borgia forsakes Julius II for the sake of, 322

Borgia, Rodrigo. See Alexander VI

Borromei, family of, 34

Bourbon, Gilbert de, Duke of Montpensier, letter of Charles VIII to, 76 n.; appointed viceroy of Naples in absence of Charles, 77 ; hurries to San Severo to collect revenue, 90 ; at battle of Agnadello, 292

Bourges, Louis of Orleans released by Charles VIII from tower of, 22 ; Ascanio Sforza imprisoned at, 167–168 ; Louis XII in palace of, affixes seal to compact of Cambray, 287

Brabant, Maximilian and Archduke Philip meet in, 230 ; knights and soldiery of, with Henry VIII in France, 371

Brandenburg, Germans, real stock of inhabitants of, 9 ; peopled by Saxon colonists, 14–15 ; envoy of, holds Maximilian's sceptre at Diet of Worms, 99 ; House of, friendly to Imperial House, 103 ; against Landshut in war of Landshut succession, 222–223 ; Hans Aursperg tells princes of, that he is too weak to withstand Alviano, 283 ; two Albrechts of, 384

Brandon, Charles, Viscount Lisle, with Henry VIII at Térouanne, 371

Brazil, Portuguese in, 18

Bregenzerwald, Ludovico pays tribute levied on the, 158

Brescia, Doge Foscari takes, 258 ; citizens of, refuse to be burdened with Pitigliano's army, 294 ; Louis

XII enters, 294 ; Venetians before, 328; Venetians bombard and take, 329; Gaston de Foix captures castle of, 329 ; castle of, called the Falcon of Lombardy, 329 ; Gaston de Foix attacks and captures the city, 330–331 ; Ramon de Cardona takes, in 1512, 359 ; reconquered by Swiss, 368

Bresse, Philippe de. See Philippe

Brest, English harass coast of, 346

Bretten, defended against Ulrich of Württemberg by ordnance cast by Georg Schwarzerd, 223

Brisignels, companies organized to fight for Venice called, 289; at the capture of Brescia, 330

Brisighella, attacked and taken by papal troops, 291

Brittany, Duke of, Charles VII owes mastery over country to, 20 ; dies without leaving heirs, 21

Brittany, Louis purchases the rights of the Penthièvre in, 22 ; allied with England, the Netherlands, and Spain, 22 ; Germans make possession of, sure for France, 100 ; governor of, pledged to deliver to Charles and Claude if Louis XII dies without son, 226–227

Brittany, Anne of. See Anne

Bruges, displaced in trade by Antwerp, 277

Brunswick, estates of the realm at, 17 ; line of, attached to the Emperor, 103

Brunswick, Erich of. See Erich

Brunswick, Heinrich of. See Heinrich

Brusa, Florentine woollen factories send goods to the East by way of, 113

Budjadings, Heinrich of Brunswick overcomes the, 385; ruined by severe winter, 385

Bugia, Pedro Navarra takes, 251

Bulls, papal, no longer dated by years of reigns of Greek emperors, 5

Burgo, Andrea del, Massimiliano Sforza in hands of, 360

Burgos, architecture of, 12 ; Archduke Philip dies at, 237

C

Cabral, Pedro Alvarez, forty-five men of crew of, killed at Calicut, 272

Caçaça, and Melita, excepted when Portugal granted liberty to conquer Fez, 68

Cadiz, Ponce de Leon, Marquis of, against Isabella of Spain, 64 ; first order of Inquisitors threatens, 65

Cadiz, town of, recovered from family of Ponce de Leon, 70

Cadore taken by Erich of Brunswick, 281 ; attacked by Alviano, 282 ; and captured, 283

Cagli, Caesar Borgia advances on, 197

Cairo, business with Venetians in the Khan el Halili at, 254

Calabria, southern tableland of, conquered by Gonzalvo, 89 ; Ferrantino not quite safe in, 91 ; to belong, with Apulia, as dukedom, to Ferdinand, 178, 191 ; Angevins summon French to, 191 ; almost all taken from Spaniards by French, 193 ; Imbercourt in, 193

Calicut, Zamorin of, chief of Malabar, 268 ; talk in Lisbon of wealth of, 272 ; Cabral and Vasco da Gama fire on, 272 ; four barks bring spices to Lisbon from, 277

Calvo, a Genoese, brings to Charles VIII will of the younger Joanna, 25.

Cambay, Prince of, asks help of Soldan Khan Hassan of Egypt, 278

Cambray, League of, concluded, 286, 287 ; not so powerful as it appeared, 288

Cambuskenneth, battle of, 15

Cameral Tribunal (*Kammergericht*). *See* Tribunal

Candles, wax, Venetian trade in, for Spanish churches, 255

Cannanore, terror of Portuguese at, 276

Canosa, French force Pedro Navarra to retire from, 192 ; French stationed at, 204

Cantons, the Forest, League of the, hostile to Austria, 102 ; had not assented to covenant of succession with Maximilian, 325 ; frenzied by drowning of courier in lake of Lugano, 325 ; take field against Louis XII, 326 ; men from, come over St. Gotthard for battle of Novara, 365

Capets, the, twice conquer France, 20

Capitanata, not expressly named in partition between France and Spain, 191

Cappeler, Friedrich, of Pfirt, 85

Cappetti, the, gain upper hand in Genoa and appoint a dyer as chief, 266

Caprara, the, friends of the Bentivogli in Bologna, 311

Capri, beacons of, announce approach of Ferrantino, 79

Capua, Ferrantino sure of, 59 ; Ferrantino ventures to walls of, 60 ; Charles VIII in, 61 ; surrender of castle of, 88 ; captured by Gonzalvo, 179

Caracciolo, of Melfi, a leader of the revolt in Naples, 32 ; imprisoned and executed, 33

Caracciolo, Giacomo, opens gates of Naples to French, 60

Caravaggio, Pitigliano retreats towards, after battle of Agnadello, 293 ; castle of, surrenders to Louis XII, 294

Caravajal, Andrada, in command of Spaniards from Gerace and Reggio, 203 ; at battle of Seminara, 203 ; D'Aubigny surrenders to, 205

Caravajal, Cardinal, candidate for the Papacy, 212 ; forsakes Julius II, 322 ; ready to remove council from Pisa, 331

Caravajal, family of, feud of, with Benavides, 203, 245

Cardinals, the five schismatic, 322 ; call general council of Church, 322 ; release Bologna and Ferrara from ban of Pope, 331 ; encourage Maximilian to come to Italy, 343

Cardona, Ramon de, Viceroy and Spanish commander-in-chief in Naples, 333 ; interview of, with Gaston de Foix, 333 ; defeated at battle of Ravenna, and flies, 336 ;

reaches the Abruzzi, 345; starts from Naples to attack French, 345; sent for by Cardinal de' Medici, 356; undertakes campaign against Florence, 356; Florentine cities resist, 357; succeeds in entering Prato, 357; the gates of Florence opened to, 357; leaves Florentine internal affairs to Medici, 358; takes Brescia, 359; leads Spanish troops against Venetians, 370; penetrates into Venetian territory up to Malghera, 379

Cariati, Spinello becomes Count of, 240

Carinthia, summons sent throughout, for help against Italians, 283

Carlotta, Queen of Cyprus, feud of, with Queen Caterina, 256

Carmagnola, Francesco Bussone called, 258; feud of, with Filippo Maria, Duke of Milan, 258

"Carne Ammazza," war cry of, 197

Carniola, summons sent throughout, for help against Italians, 283; requires help of experienced soldiers, 284

Carpi, prophecy of seer of, 333

Carthagena, Ferdinand makes Hoieda governor of coast of, 250

Carrara, feud of the, with the Visconti, 257; all standing in relation to, excluded from Pregadi, 257

Carrara, Francesco, allows Paduans their choice, and they surrender to Venice, 257

Carroz, Luis, Spanish envoy, Henry VIII significantly leans on shoulder of, 341

Casale, Giovanni da, Ludovico's agent, 173

Casalonaggiere, Mantuans attack and take, 291

Casciano, Charles VIII receives youth of Pisa at, 55

Caspar, German captain, true to Ferrantino, 60

Castile, cities of, have seats in Cortes, 12; internal affairs of, affect history of Conradin, 13; Peter the Cruel and Henry of Trastamara contend for crown of, 15-16;

united with Aragon in kingdom of Spain, 62; Englishmen forbidden to visit, without permission of King of France, 62; succession of Isabella in, 63; contention of with Aragon, 63; traditional liberties in, 66; claims Mauritania and Tingitana, 68; quarrel of, with Portugal, 69; Isabella, the Infanta, receives at Toledo allegiance of, 188; succession of, devolves on Juana, wife of Archduke Philip, 188; Louis XII promises Philip 1,000 lances for conquest of, 219; Philip takes royal title and crown of, 227; House of Austria succeeds in taking possession of, 234; Philip's death throws affairs of, into confusion, 237, 244; Ferdinand realizes loss of, 237; proposal to exclude Philip's widow, Juana, from government of, 243 n.; factions in, 245; Ferdinand enters, without resistance, 248; Maximilian's claim to administration of, 341; struggle of, with Aragon, for Navarre, 350; Louis XII pledged to restore old frontier of Navarre against, 351; re-marriage of Louis would seal union of Navarre with, 382

Castrovillari, mountain chain sloping down to, subjected by Gonzalvo, 91

Catalans, enmity between Provençals and, 14, 71; take Sicily, 71; trade of, in Tunis, 255

Catalonia, union of, with Aragon, 8; Florentine factories import wool from, 113

Caterina, Queen of Cyprus, 256

Catherine of Navarre, wife of Jean d'Albret, 350–351

Cattanei, Vannozza de', 42 n.

Cattaro begs for Venetian magistrate, 256

Cavazere, peasants in flight from Maximilian bring 10,000 head of cattle to, 300

Cephalonia, Trevisano unable to capture, 183; Trevisano and Gonzalvo take castle of, 184

Cerignola, battle of, 204

Cervia, Doge Foscari takes, 258

Cesena, announces subjection to Venice, 260 ; Venice restores her part of territory of, 261

Ceylon, caravans from Mecca bring cinnamon from, for Venetian trade, 254

Châlons, Maximilian sends corps against, 134

Champagne, restored to French king by Maid of Orleans, 20

Chariteo, poet, and private secretary to Alonso Pescara, 85

Charlemagne, 1 ; frees Pope from Lombard enmity, 5 ; unites as Christians Latino-Germanic nations, 5 ; cycle of tales of, 11 ; legendary hero, 25

Charles of Anjou, 13

Charles the Bold, heritage of, brought to pitch of greatness by Maximilian, 95 ; defeated before Nancy, 101

Charles, Duke of Gelderland. *See* Gelderland

Charles of Maine, assigns the inheritance of Provence and Anjou to Louis XI, 21

Charles, Archduke of Austria, son of Archduke Philip and Juana of Spain, 188 ; born at Ghent, 188 ; great combination round life of, 188 ; to marry Claude, daughter of Louis XII, 189 ; Louis to pledge governors in Milan, Genoa, Asti, Brittany, Blois, and Burgundy to deliver provinces conditionally to, 226-227 ; betrothal of, revoked by Louis XII, 236 ; Najara anxious for Philip's death to appeal to Emperor regarding, 245 ; to marry Mary, daughter of Henry VII of England, 339 ; Ferdinand assures succession for, 341 ; and desires conquest of Milan for, 343 ; Venetians refuse to acknowledge, as suzerain, 343 ; Ramon de Cardona and Matthäus Lang desire to appoint, as prince of Milan, 359 ; crown of England for, if Henry VIII should die without issue, 380-381 ; prospective marriage of, to English princess becomes doubtful, 382

Charles IV, Emperor, grants "Golden Bull," 16

Charles VII of France, 20

Charles VIII of France, releases Louis, Duke of Orleans, from captivity at Bourges, 22 ; marries Anne of Brittany, 23 ; who assigns to him rights in Duchy, 23 ; journeys joyfully through France, 24 ; ambitious schemes of, 25 ; Ludovico Sforza stirs up, to attack on Naples and holy lands, 26 ; visions, prophecies, and poems regarding, 27 ; adopts title of King of Naples and Jerusalem, 28 ; comrades from many countries join army of, 28 ; rights of Paleologi to Constantinople and Trebizond ceded to, 28 ; character and appearance of, 28-29 ; Ludovico sends envoy to, 43 ; help from, in Italy, for Ludovico, 46 ; offers prayers for victory over Saracens, 46-47 ; attends mass at Grenoble, and starts for Italy, 47 ; received at Turin by Blanche of Savoy, 47 ; meets Ludovico at Asti, 47 ; sees Gian Galeazzo, who is sick at Pavia, 48 ; meets at Piacenza two of the Medici, 49 ; arrives at Pontremoli, 49 ; Florentines little inclined to support Piero de' Medici against, 49 ; Piero delivers fortresses to, 51 ; enthusiastically received in Pisa, 52 ; enters Florence, 53 ; comes to understanding with Florentines, 54; warned by Savonarola, 54 ; issues a manifesto, 54-55 ; his further progress, 55 ; enters Rome, 56 ; desires to have Caesar Borgia as hostage, 56 ; takes Djem with him, 56 ; receives the Pope's blessing, 57 ; rejects overtures of Alfonso II, 57 ; orders Monte San Giovanni to be stormed, 59 ; rapidity and fury of conquest of, terrifies Ferrantino, 59 ; Trivulzio goes over to, 60 ; welcomed in Naples, 61 ; Kings of Spain do not approve enterprises of, 71 ; and send envoys to, 72 ; formation of league against, 72-75 ; retreat of, 75-88 ; cautious reply of, concerning territory for Ferrantino, 76 ; his work in Naples, 76 ; hears of league, 77 ; realizes necessity of retreat, 77; appoints Montpensier viceroy of Naples, 77; Pope flies before, 77; his retreat, 78; allies invest Novara and intercept retreat of, 79; choses road across mountains, 80; difficulties of, with Swiss troops, 80; reaches Fornovo, 81; opposed by Lombards, accepts battle, 81; without gaining real victory is able to continue march, 84; dream of conquest by, ended, 85; must confine himself to rescue of Duke of Orleans shut in Novara, 85; despatches some Swiss to Provence to cross to Naples, 86; concludes truce with Ludovico, 87; comes to Lyons, 87; results of expedition to Italy, 93; thinks of returning to cities of which he is suzerain, 93-94; orders surrender of citadel of Pisa to Florentines, 108; governor of Pisa disregards order of, 108; fleet fitted out in Marseilles by, wrecked in storm, 119; ecclesiastical reforms of, 122; Savonarola invites to undertake reformation of Church, 122; death of, 127; at the last occupied with internal reforms, 127; succeeded by Louis, Duke of Orleans, as Louis XII, 135; interred at Blois, 136

Charles of Luxembourg, quarrel of, with Louis of Bavaria, 15

Charles de la Pace, faction in Corfu does not desire rule of Ladislas, son of, 256

Chaumont (Charles d'Amboise), commands division at battle of Agnadello, 292; attacks Bologna, 311; succeeded as head of French troops by Trivulzio, 314

Chiavenna opens its gates to Galeazzo, 160

China, trade of, in silk yarn, 269

Chinon, Caesar Borgia at, 172

Christian II of Denmark, sues for hand of Maximilian's granddaughter, Isabella, 385

Christianity, propagation of, animates colonization, 18

Chur, differences of, with the Tyrol, 143; Gossenbrod mocks people of bishopric of, 143; contingent from, at battle of Novara, 365

Church, State of the, dependent on idea of supreme hierarchy, 39; Alexander VI most powerful Pope in the, 202

Cibò, Franceschetto, son of Pope Innocent VIII, 37

Cid, the, Campeador of Spaniards, lives to see Crusades, 8

Cifuentes, Count of, makes Ximenes manager of estates, 245

Ciriffo, heroic poem of, 321

Cirksena, Etzard, Count of East Friesland, overcome by Georg of Saxony and Heinrich of Brunswick, 385

Città di Castello, falls into hands of Pope, 201; a golden calf, device of the Vitelli, carried through streets of, 211

Cividale d'Austria, quarrel between Udine and, 256

Città Vecchia, designs of Charles VIII on, 56

Claude of France, betrothed to Archduke Charles, 189; Juana gives large diamond to, 189; Ferdinand refuses to assign Naples to, with Charles, 227; Queen Anne favours betrothal of, to Charles, 228; but finally consents to betrothal of, to Francis of Angoulême, 229; Maximilian hears that betrothal of, to Charles is revoked, 236; betrothal of, to Francis ratified, 236

Clergy, Henry VII of England limits right of sanctuary of, 338; Wolsey strives to bring into subjection, 340

Cloth, factories of, in Florence, 113; galleys laden with, for Venetian trade, 254; Venetian inferior, fetches a ducat, and scarlet forty ducats, a yard at Gago, 255

Cochin, Pacheco Pereira defends King of, against Zamorin, 272; King of, driven from throne for allowing Portuguese to land, 272-273; King of, receives golden crown from Francesco d'Almeida, 274; forts in, keep greater part of Indian coast in Portuguese subjection, 276

Codito, a citizen of Como, bids farewell to Ludovico, 155

Cologne, architecture of, 12

Cologne, Diet of (1505), 225–226

Colombo, King of, pays tribute in cinnamon to Portugal, 276

Colonization of foreign countries, 2; crusading spirit gives birth to, 17

Colonna, the, in disfavour with Innocent VIII, 37–38; occupy Ostia and close Tiber, 45; have possession of the Abruzzi, 91; faithful to Federigo, 179; Ferdinand keeps in obedience, 240

Colonna, Fabrizio, general of cavalry at battle of Ravenna, 332, 334; an enemy of Pedro Navarra, 332; surrenders to Alfonso d'Este, 336; helps Alfonso to escape from Rome, 360

Colonna, Giovanni, Cardinal, comes from Sicily for Papal election, 212

Colonna, Marc Antonio, despatched by Julius II to Genoa, 304

Colonna, Prospero, commands light cavalry of the Pope against Venetians, 370

Columbus, Bartholomew, 68

Columbus, Christopher, 68; first voyage of, 69

Como, people of, welcome Ludovico in his flight, 155; French fly from, 160

Conrad, Nicholas, bailiff of Solothurn, 150; hears that castle of Dorneck is threatened by Count Fürstenberg, 150; falls upon enemy's camp, 151

Conradin, internal affairs of Castile affect history of, 13; Barcelonese House of Aragon, heirs of, 71

Constance, Diet of (1507), 279

Constance, jokes of the Germans at, 144; Swiss attack landsknechts on lake of, 144; strong army of Empire and League assembled at, 149

Constantinople, Latin Empire in, 7; Florentines export cloth to, 113; Ferdinand ambitious to take, 298

Coppola, Francesco, invaluable to Ferrante, 30; King enters into partnership with, as merchant,

31; made a Count, 31; leagues himself with Sanseverino of Salerno, 32; put to death, 33

Cordova subdued by St. Ferdinand, 81

Cordova, Gonzalvo de. See Gonzalvo

Cordova, Juan de, on side of Isabella of Spain at Seville, 64

Corfu, one faction in, against rule of Ladislas, son of Charles de la Pace, 256; whole fleet in, disabled by disease, 319–320

Corte, Bernardino da, Ludovico commits castle of Milan and jewels to, 154; treachery and death of, 156

Cortona, power exercised by Florentines over, 112

Cosentine villages, 89, 91

Cosenza, Gonzalvo subjects, 91; plan to relieve, 91

Council of Regency. See Regency

Courland, German rule over, 10

Cranganore, Prince of, entrusts government to an Arabian, 269

Crati, Gonzalvo subjects fortresses in valley of the, 91

Creazzo, Venetian army routed near, 379, 380

Creçy, battle of, 15

Crema, gained by Foscari, Doge of Venice, 258; declares for Venice, 329

Cremona, Venetians ask Louis XII to guarantee them a portion of territory of, 139; surrenders to Venice, 156; altar raised to San Marco in, 156; people of, wait occasion to revolt against Venice, 162; declares for Venice, 329; surrenders to Swiss, 347; Louis XII promises to restore to Venice, 364; French give up claim to, 377

Crete, half savage archers, the Sagdars, from, 289

Cronaca, Simone, honours Savonarola, 128

Cross, first adopted in war by Norwegian St. Olaf, 7; red, worn by citizens of Parma pledged to fight against Infidels, 17; of Jerusalem, worn by Charles VIII on coat of mail, 82; nobles decorated with Burgundian, of St. Andrew, accompany Maximilian, 110; marvellous apparition of, in France, Italy, Upper and Lower Germany, 189

Crown, Holy, Neapolitans welcome Charles VIII as, 61

Crucifixion, the, emblazoned on Swiss standards, 146

Crusades, the, 2; regarded as migration, 6; undertaken by Latin and Teutonic nations, 7; Low-Germans, English, and Flemish proceed on, 9; bull of Pope Eugenius III concerning, 9; stirring energy and intellectual impulse characterize, 11; share of, in foundation of modern poetry, 11; chivalrous spirit of, 88

Culture, Italy at zenith of, 39; perfection of, in Italy due to independence, 180

Cyprus, gained by Venetians during feud between Queens Carlotta and Caterina, 256; Venetians order all reserve stores to be opened at, 295; Duke of Savoy demands, 298

D

Dabul, city of the Zabai, burned by Francesco d'Almeida, 296

Dalmatians, taught by Venetians to speak Italian, 10

Damm, cruelly devastated by Georg of Saxony, 385

Danebrog, the, hung by Ditmarschers in a village church, 101

Danes at enmity with Angles, 4; unite with Saxons and Westphalians against Slavs, 9

Danube, mark of Austria first founded in valley of the, 95

Danzig, possessions of Knights of Sword and Teutonic Knights extend from Narva to, 10

Darien, colony founded on, 250; Balboa sails from, for the South Sea, 386

Davalos, Alfonso, at Monte San Giovanni, 59; holds castle of Naples, 60

Davalos, Inigo, gives keys of castle of Ischia to Gonzalvo, 205

Deccan, the, Venetian trade with, 254; Moorish princes hold sway over, 268

Denia, Marquis of, correspondence of, with Charles V, 243 n.

Denmark, Venetian trade penetrates to, 255. See Christian II of, and John of

Derbend, Indian caravans to, 254

Diaz, Bartolomeo, 269

Dieci dell' Arbitrio, at Perugia, 263

Diesbachs, party of the, 325; mock Cardinal Schinner in Carnival play, 344; two heroes of, in battle of Novara, 367

Diessenhofen, jokes of the Germans at, 144

Dijon, bailiff of, joins Charles VIII, 28; goes to Switzerland for troops, 86, 163

Dijon, Maximilian sends corps against, 134; Swiss form three camps before, 377; citadel of, wrecked by bombardment, 377

Ditmarschers, the, defeat the Danes, 101, 187

Diu, Francisco d'Almeida victorious at, 296

Djem, brother of Bajazet, 56; alleged letter of Bajazet to Alexander VI concerning, 75; sudden death of, 76; the Pope said to have had hand in death of, 76

Dominicans, convent of the, at Seville too small to hold those accused of heresy, 65; Tuscan separated from Lombard by Savonarola, 124; doctrines of, challenged by Franciscans, 126

Donato, treacherously surrenders castle of Valenza, 152

Dorneck, troops under Count Fürstenberg at, 149; Fürstenberg to make raid from, 150; battle of, 151

Dorset, Marquis of, with English auxiliaries in France, 349

Dresden, line of, attached to the Emperor, 103

Dudley, Edmund, financial agent Henry VII of England, 339; chosen Speaker, 339; put to death by Henry VIII, 340

Duero, castles on the, visited by Ferdinand of Spain, 64

Duino, fall of, 284

Dunois, negotiates with Anne of Brittany with regard to her marriage to Charles VIII, 22–23

Durazzo, Archbishop of, despatched by Charles VIII on expedition against Turks, 76

E

Ebro, valleys and hills extending from the, in kingdom of Navarre, 349

Edrisi, description by, of African coast as far as Sofala, 269

Edward III of England, Commons under, insist on responsibility of King's Council, 16

Edward IV of England, compunction of, for people, 338

Egbert, forms heptarchy of Angles into kingdom, 5

Egypt, might have been French colony but for ill-luck of St. Louis, 8.; Soldan of, threatens King Manuel of Portugal, 274; Zamorin, Zabai of Goa, and Prince of Cambay send for help to Soldan of, 278

Eighty, Council of the, in Florence, 118

Elba, Caesar Borgia gains, 175

Eleanor, eldest granddaughter of Ferdinand of Spain to marry Louis XII of France, 381-382, 383

Electors of the Empire, assemble at Gelnhausen and arrange yearly meetings, 219; afterwards resolve to meet every two years, 221; such meetings of, do not take place, 221; Maximilian gains Palatinate territory heedless of solicitations of, 224; Union of the, 225

Eletto, Neapolitans free to choose an, 76; fuller chosen as, 93; permitted to carry the Mappa on day of Corpus Christi, 93

Elphinstone, dead body in royal apparel at Flodden said to be that of, 376

Elsa, Florentines take castle on heights of the, 108

Emden, Georg of Saxony marauds as far as gates of, 385

Emperor, hallowed position of the, 103

Empire of Charlemagne, perishes through mistakes of successors, 5

Empire, Holy Roman, struggle of, with Papacy, 13; Maximilian and the, 95-107; constitution of, 101; blends all countries of Germany in legal bond of union, 102; only while a reality can rights of electors be maintained, 102; Ludovico Sforza called a vassal of the, 163; for six months neither Kammergericht nor Hofgericht held throughout the, 219

Empire, Roman, of West, conquered by Germanic nations, 3

Empson, Sir Richard, financial agent of Henry VII of England, 339; put to death by Henry VIII, 340

Ems, Burkhard von (nephew of Jacob von), at council of war, 346-347

Ems, Jacob von, taken prisoner by French, 166; addresses landsknechts at battle of Ravenna, 333; killed in battle, 335

Engadine, the, affected by differences between Chur and the Tyrol, 143; fighting in, 148

Engilbert of Cleves, loses Utrecht to Maximilian, 28; commands Germans and Swiss, 82

England, wars of, with France, 14; torn by War of the Roses, 14; exports wool to Florence, 113; in opposition to France, 230–231; Venetian trade in wool with, 255; no nation, France perhaps excepted, more subject to king than, 338; eighty scions of blood royal of, slain in War of Roses, 333; compunction of Edward IV for people of, 338; with Emperor, Pope, Spain, and Switzerland, confronts France, Venice, and Scotland, 368; attack on France left to Switzerland and, 369

English, the, Teutonic element in, 2;

alliance of, with Austrian House, 231; arquebusiers to supplement Spanish infantry, 342; sail for Fuenterrabia, throw army on Bidassoa, and harass coast of Brest, 346; discover that their French war means conquest of Navarre for Spain, 352

Enriquez, Enrique, pillages in France, 131; killed in riot at Perpignan, 137

Enriquez, Admiral Fadrique, 67

Enriquez, Maria, cousin of Alfonso II of Naples, marries Juan Borgia, 44

Era, castle on heights of the, taken by Florentines, 108

Eric, St., leads Swedes against Finns, 9; baptizes Finns in spring of Lupisala, 9

Erich of Brunswick-Calenberg, saves life of Maximilian, 224; takes Cadore, 281; too weak to venture into field against Alviano, 284

Este, family of, at Ferrara, 29

Este, Alfonso d', son of Ercole, makes terms with Caesar Borgia, 176; marries Lucrezia Borgia, 187; holds absolute sway in Ferrara, 304; keeps his brothers in prison, 304; the Pope orders him to make peace with Venice, 304; refuses to obey, 304-305; put under ban, 305; converts plate and jewels into money, 313; fortifies Ferrara, 313; saves the castle, 314; Julius promises not to attack if French are dismissed, 314; refuses offer to kill the Pope, 314; at battle of Ravenna, 334; Fabrizio Colonna surrenders to, 336; comes to Rome under protection of the Colonna, 348; anger of the Pope against, 359; fears to accept invitation from the Pope, and escapes, 360

Este, Beatrice d', daughter of Ercole, 39; Ludovico Sforza betrothed to, 39; honoured as bride in Milan, 40; her burial-place in Milan, 154; portrait of, by Leonardo da Vinci, 155

Este, Ercole d', 39; left by Venetians to settle affair of Pisa, 139; puts himself under protection of Louis XII, 157; freed from anxiety, 187; his son marries Lucrezia Borgia, 187; sons of, all suffering from syphilis at one time, 319

Este, Ferrante d', kept in prison by his brother Alfonso, 304; the Pope demands that he should be set free, 304-305

Este, Guilio d', kept in prison by his brother Alfonso, 304

Ethiopia, Dom Manuel of Portugal styles himself lord of commerce and future conquests in, 272

Eudons of Blois, Capets encounter the, 20

Eugenius III, bull of, 9

Eustachio, Ludovico Sforza shares sovereign power with, 35; Ludovico rids himself of, 35

F

Fabian (von Schlaberndorf), Germans under, at Brescia, 330; exploits of, at battle of Ravenna, 335; is killed, 335

Faenza, industrial cleverness of people of, 175; Caesar Borgia takes, 175; surrenders to Venetians, 216, 260; Venetians promise aid to Julius II, if he ratifies their possession of, 263; Julius occupies, 294

Falcon of Lombardy, castle of Brescia called, 329

Falk, Peter, strives with the bailiff, Franz Arsent, at Freiburg, 325; crosses St. Gotthard with Freiburgers and artillery, 327

Fantuzzi, the, side with the Bentivogli in Bologna, 311, 316

Federigo (Frederick II of Naples), begs Charles VIII for territory and title of King for Ferrantino, 76; takes Trani, 85; succeeds to kingdom, 93; reconciled to Ludovico Sforza, 93; Pope proposes marriage of Caesar Borgia to daughter of, 171; refuses proposal, 171-172; desperate position of, 176-177; asks Gonzalvo if he can depend on him, 177; asks for Ferdinand's daughter or niece for son, 177; proceedings against, by Ferdinand and Louis XII, 178; loses hope, 179; arranges to retire to France if he cannot collect army, 179; goes to Ischia, 180; Aragon dynasty and House of Sforza extinguished in, 180

Feltre, offered by Visconti to Venice, 257

Ferdinand, St., subdues Jaen, Cordova, and Seville, 8

Ferdinand the Catholic, of Spain, son of John I of Aragon, 63; marries Isabella of Castile, 63; takes castles on the Duero, 64; undertakes grandmastership of three orders of knighthood, 65–66; controls appointment of bishops, 66; refuses to make war on Ferrante, 71; consults the Pope on claims to Naples, 94; two children of, betrothed to children of Maximilian, 100; to invade France from Roussillon, 111; makes an alliance with Dom Manuel of Portugal, 129; negotiates with Henry VII of England, 129; plans advanced by marriage of Prince of Wales with Katherine of Aragon, 130; concludes truce with France, 131, 137; Federigo begs for matrimonial alliance with, 177; concludes treaty with Louis XII concerning Naples regardless of Federigo, 178; wishes to make Caesar Borgia King of Tuscany, 208–209; Alexander VI proposes league of, with Venice, to expel French from Italy, 209; quarrels with Archduke Philip, 218–219; Philip makes alliance with France against, 219; refuses to assign Naples to Charles and Claude, 226; on death of Isabella determined to remain real King of Castile, 227; despatches Enguera to French Court, 229; summons Cortes, 229; favoured by cities, 230; makes alliance with Louis XII, 230; promises to marry Germaine de Foix, 230;

forsaken by all except Duke of Alva on Philip's arrival in Spain, 232; has an interview with Philip, 233; renounces government of Castile to Philip, 233–234; dissimulation of, 234; secretly resolves to liberate Juana, 234; anxious about Naples, 237; Gonzalvo dissatisfied with, 237; thinks of imprisoning Gonzalvo, 238; changes mind and offers him grandmastership of Santiago, 238, 240; sets sail for Naples, 238; hears of Philip's death, 238; settles affairs in Naples, 239; possession of Naples assured to, 239; keeps Colonna in obedience and wins over Orsini, 240; his treatment of Gonzalvo, 240–241; hurries to Castile, 241; one party in Castile invites, on death of Philip, 245; Ximenes declares himself for, 247–248; grandees in Castile hasten to kiss hand of, 248; meets Juana, at Tortoles, 248; takes her to Tordesillas, 249; triumphant in Spain and Italy, 249; operations of, for colonization of America, 250; successes for, won by Pedro Navarra in Africa, 250–251; sets out for Malaga to begin holy campaign, 252; tidings from Romagna change plans of, 252; readjustment by League of Cambray of frontiers of Milan and Naples in favour of, 286; swears to League of Cambray, 287; Venetians surrender harbours and cities of Apulia to, 295; spares what is left to Venice, 297; mindful of Catalonian claims to Neopatri and Athens, 297–298; enters into a league with the Pope against France, 323, 340; schemes of, against France, 332; after defeat of Ravenna appoints Gonzalvo commander-in-chief in Italy, 338; allied to Henry VIII of England through marriage of Katherine, 340; reconciled with Maximilian, 340–341; arranges with Maximilian succession of Charles, 341; schemes to draw King of

England into his war, 341; discloses to Maximilian his schemes against Milan and Venice, 343; Swiss occupation of Milan a surprise to, 349; conquest of Navarre by, 349–353; treaty of, with Florence, 358; in alliance with Henry VIII, advises seizure of Burgundy, Normandy, and Guienne, 369; concludes unexpected truce for frontier territory, 369; forces of, with those of Leo X, turn against Venice, 369; makes a treaty with Louis XII (1513), 381; Louis XII contemplates marriage with Eleanor, granddaughter of, 381–382; grand alliance between Louis, Maximilian, and, 382–383; concludes compact with Genoa, 383; Nuñez Balboa takes possession of South Sea for, 386

Ferdinand and Isabella, marriage of, 63; defeat Alfonso of Portugal at Toro, 64; found convent of St. Francis at Toledo, 64; title of " Kings " given to, 64; granted right to appoint Inquisitors by Sixtus IV, 64; give the royal power a new basis, 66; aided by the Church, 66; invade and conquer Granada, 67; put caravels at disposal of Columbus, 69; turn attention to Naples, 70; never approved of enterprises of Charles VIII, 71; propose to Charles an expedition against Africa, 71; despatch an ambassador to Venice, 72; despatch envoys to Charles, 72; their treaty with Charles torn up, 72; take the Pope and Ferrantino under their protection, 72; form league against Charles, 72, 74; the Moors of Granada revolt against, 183; marriages of children of, 187, 189; ceremonial at court of, 187; birth of grandson Charles, 188 (*see also* Ferdinand *and* Isabella)'.

Fermo, Oliverotto murders seven leading citizens of, 198

Ferracut, herald of Robert d'Aubigny, sent to Spanish camp before battle of Seminara, 203

Ferrante (Ferdinand I of Naples), natural son of Alfonso I, 30; foreign alliances of, 30; marries son Alfonso to daughter of Francesco Sforza, 30; relations of, with Coppola and Petrucci, 30–31, 33; revolt of the barons against, 32; his vengeance on his enemies, 33; begins war with Florence, 34; helps the Sforza, 34; attacks Lorenzo de' Medici, 37; becomes Lorenzo's ally, 37; Pope Innocent VIII displeased by, 37; granddaughters of, Isabella and Beatrice, marry Gian Galeazzo and Ludovico Sforza, 39; Pope endeavours to divorce Wladislav of Hungary from daughter of, 43; weighed down by years and anxiety, 43; prophecy of destruction of race and dynasty of, 43; death of, 44

Ferrantino (Ferdinand II of Naples), son of Alfonso II, 46; leads army against the French, 46; driven back, 46; forsaken by Florentines and princes of Urbino and Pesaro advances towards Rome, 55; leaves Rome, 56; assumes realm on abdication of Alfonso, 58; friends of, terrified by conquests of Charles VIII, 59; appeals to the Neapolitans, 59; hears that enemy attacks Capua and rushes thither, 59; Trivulzio deserts and goes over with army to Charles VIII, 60; Germans alone faithful to, 60; returns to Naples and is in danger of being killed, 60; betrothed to Juana, niece of Ferdinand of Spain, 72; ally of Ferdinand, 74; Charles VIII would gladly have concluded treaty with, 76; pushes into Calabria, 78; driven back by French, 78–79; feeling for, in Otranto and Naples, 79; appears with sixty-nine sail in Gulf of Naples, 84; welcomed back to Naples, 85; hurries to Foggia to collect revenue, 90; attacked on road by French, 90; has advantage again, 90–91; aided by Ludovico and Venice, 91; defeats the French at Atella, 92; returns with young wife to Naples, 92–93 ; great love of people for, 93 ; death of, 93 ; owed much to Ferdinand, 134

Ferrara, family of Este at, 29 ; Savonarola, a native of, 114 ; frequent fasting and religious observance at, 12 ; French sympathy at, 121 ; shouting for Ludovico Sforza at, 162 ; inhabitants of, drive out the Visdomino and retake the Polesina, 294 ; papal army threatens, 307 ; Julius II despatches general against, 312 ; fortified by Alfonso d'Este, 313 ; Alfonso saves castle of, 314 ; French strive to keep open connection with, 314 ; schismatic Cardinals release from ban, 331 ; Julius II determined to subject, 360

Feudal system, decay of, in Germany, 104

Fez, Portugal to be allowed to conquer all, except Melita and Caçaça, 68 ; quarrel about, 70

Fiesco, Obietto, offers services to Alfonso II, 45 ; taken into service of Charles VIII at Naples, 72–73

Fiesco, family of, powerful in Genoa, 265

Figueroa, Lorenzo, despatched by Ferdinand to Venice, 72

Finale, Marquis of, offers French aid to Caesar Borgia, 216

Finland, becomes Christian and Swedish, 10

Finns, defeated by St. Eric, 9

Flanders, renewal of treaty between England and, 130 ; Venetian trade with, 255 ; Maximilian warns Swabian League of revolt of, 282 ; soldiers of, with Henry VIII in France, 371

Fleuranges, Robert III, Seigneur de la Mark, leads black troop, under Thomas of Mittelburg, 364 ; at battle of Novara, 367

Flodden, battle of, 375–377

Florence, at war with Ferrante, 34 ; dependent on artistic industry and manufactures, 39 ; Piero de' Medici's entrance into palace disputed in, 51 ; the Medici leave, 52 ; Medici treasures in, 52 ; Lion

of, thrown into Arno, 53 ; Charles VIII enters, 53 ; war of, against Pisa, 108 ; Ludovico Sforza and Venetians take part of Pisa against, 109 ; attack of Maximilian on, 112, 119–120 ; benefit of city of, 113 ; manufactures and trade of, 113–114 ; influence of Savonarola in, 114 et seq. ; formation of a Balìa in, 117 ; the Balìa dissolved, 117 ; Savonarola's constitution in, 118 ; "Anathema" given up under influence of Savonarola, in, 120–121 ; factious rising in, 123 ; dissensions between Franciscans and Dominicans in, 124, 126 ; Popolari and Arrabbiati in, 125 ; victory of the Arrabbiati in, 127–128 ; Popolari supreme in, 173 ; Caterina Sforza in, 173 ; Louis XII twice dissuades Caesar Borgia from attacking, 208 ; Pope opposes union of, with Siena, 209 ; literature in, 321 ; influence of Popolari under Piero Soderini in, 353 ; Cardinal de' Medici beloved in, 355 ; the Optimates in, 356 ; campaign of Cardona against, 356–357 ; return of the Medici to, 357–358 ; treaty with Ferdinand makes Spanish, as formerly French, 358 ; new constitution in, 358 ; supreme power in the hands of the Medici in, 358

Florentines, the, do not agree with French, 54 ; extent of power of, over subject towns and hamlets, 112–113 ; first Signori cloth and silk merchants, 114 ; daily life of a merchant, 114 ; Savonarola and, 114 et seq. ; reconquer Pisa, 354 ; enmity of the Pope to, 354

Foggia, revenue authorities at, 90 ; marvellous deed of Germans on road to, 91

Foix, Gaston de, nephew of Louis XII, leads French in Italy, 329 ; enters Bologna and strengthens garrison, 329 ; leads attack at Brescia, 330 ; success of, 331 ; resolves to contest with Spanish knights for prize of valour, 331 ; despatched with Legate to territory of Church, 331 ; interview of, with Cardona before battle of Ravenna, 333; at battle of Ravenna, 333–337; slain after fourteen wounds, 337; rights of, to Navarre, 350

Foix, Germaine de, Louis XII, uncle of, assigns Neapolitan rights to, 230; Ferdinand agrees to marry, 230; rides with Ferdinand through Naples, 238–239

Fontrailles, called the "Fearless," 193

Ford, Lady, James IV of Scotland with, at Norham, 375

Forlì, princes of, 29; Aubigny penetrates to, 73; Pope declares that Ludovico's great-nephews have forfeited, 172; Caterina Sforza defends citadel of, 173–174; Venetian conquests in territory of, 260; Venice restores occupied places in territory of, 261

Fornovo, Charles VIII at, 81; battle of, 82–84

Foscari, Francesco, Venetian envoy, 112 n.; head of the Forty, 257; chosen Doge, 258; successful policy of, 258

Fossombrone, taken by Caesar Borgia, 197

France, Latin element predominates in, 1–2; bishops exercise influence in founding, 2; free communes under magistrates in, 12; wars of, with England, 14, 15; decay of English power in, 16; twice during Middle Ages conquered by Capets, 20; king of, not completely sovereign, 20–21; second conquest of, by the Valois, 24; position of peasants in, 24; free chivalry develops into quasi-military service of second sons of lower nobility in, 24–25; name of *hommes d'armes* for such young men in, 25; new life given to nobility in, 25

Franche-Comté, assigned to French as dowry of Maximilian's daughter Margaret married to Dauphin, 21; recovered by Maximilian, 23; Guillaume de Vergy, marshal of, 134

Francis of Angoulême, heir presumptive to French throne, 228;

deputies of cities beg Louis XII to consent to betrothal of, with Claude, 236

Franciscans, join Arrabbiati and Pope against Dominicans and Savonarola, 124; conflict with Dominicans in Florence, 126–127

Franconia, split up into knightly and ecclesiastical domains, 14

Frangete, Ferrantino faces French at, 91

Frangipani, Veglia refuses to obey a, 256; Maximilian helped by, to take Marano, 380

Frankfurt, Maximilian delivers up the judge's staff to the justiciary at, 107

Frankish bishop, in Paris in 556 A.D., 3; independence of clergy, 4

Franks, enmities of, with Lombards and Saxons, 4

Frastenz, Swabians with men from Algau and Etschland collect at, 147

Frederick I (Emperor) invades Italy, 13

Frederick II (Emperor), ousted from Austria by Hungarians, 95–96; Swabian League under protection of, 102–103

Frederick II of Naples. See Federigo

Frederick the Wise (Frederick III), Elector of Saxony, 142

Fregoso, family of, 265; Julius II related to, 267; exiled from Genoa, 303; party of, to attack Genoa, 304; not successful, 305; Pope's revolutionary instigation to, 315; restored to Genoa, 368

Fregoso, Cardinal, places hopes in King of Naples, 45; in service of Charles VIII, 72–73; attacks Genoa, 80

Fregoso, Gian, arrives at Chiavia, 348; enters Genoa, 348

Fregoso, Ottaviano, 368

Fregoso, Tommaso, makes over Leghorn to Florentines, 113

Freiburg, cathedral of, 12

Freiburg, Diet of (1497), 133, 168

Freiburg (Switzerland), factions in, 324–325; men from, cross St. Gotthard, with artillery, 327; zealous in papal cause, 327

Friedrich, Arrogator of the Palatinate, 221

Friedrich of Brandenburg, besieges Roveredo, 281

Friesland, East, conquered by Georg of Saxony and Heinrich of Brunswick, 385

Friuli, Turkish incursion into, 181; pillage in, 182; quarrel of Cividale d'Austria and Udine convulses, 256; subject to Venice, 257; Germans at, 294; Venetians driven from, 318

Frundsberg, Georg, joins Trivulzio at Bologna, 315; sent by Maximilian to Padua against Venetians, 370; discharges ordnance against Venice, 379; fights desperately at Creazzo, 379

Fuenterrabia, English sail for, 346

Fugger, leading commercial German house of, 277; enormous profits of trade of, with the East, 298; supplies funds used against Venice, 298

Fürstenberg, Count Wolf von, at battle of Schwaderloch, 147; soldiers of Gelderland and Burgundy commanded by, 149; raid of, from Dorneck, 150

G

Gaeta taken by French after revolt, 78; French army flies to, from Spaniards, 205; Navarra at, 205

Gago, Venetian trade with, 255

Gallarate, French hommes d'armes in force at, 327

Gama, Vasco da, expedition of, to Mozambique and Malabar, 270–271

Gamboa, factions of, the, 14, 241

Gandia, Duke of. *See* Borgia, Juan

Garcia, eldest son of Duke of Alva, attacks Gelves and loses life, 251

Garda, Lago di, Germans appear on the, 294

Garigliano, Charles VIII on the, 59; French and Spaniards opposed on the, 205; battle of the, 206–207

Gascons, join Charles VIII to invade Italy, 28

Gattinara, Mercurino, favours Maximilian's reconciliation with Ferdinand, 341

Gaurus, ill-famed grottoes of the, 194

Gelderland, affairs in, 16; Archduke Philip gains, 227; Louis XII demands inclusion of, in truce with Venice, 285; Maximilian refuses to desist from attacking, 286; Henry VIII assists Maximilian against, 340; Ferdinand busied in affairs of, 341

Gelderland, Charles, Duke of, Maximilian's enmity to, 141; war in territory of, 142; gives up most of country to Philip and enters his suite, 227; renews war in the Netherlands, 236; successful campaign of, against Maximilian on Lower Rhine, 285; in castle of Pouderoyen, 285

Gelves, Xeque of, offers allegiance to Spaniards, 249; conquest of imperative for Spain, 251; Garcia, son of Duke of Alva, attacks, 251; Venetian trade in, 255

Genivolo, Bastia del, importance of holding, to Alfonso of Ferrara, 313

Genoa, consuls in, 11–12; attack on, by Alfonso of Naples, 45; Duke of Orleans, 46; Bartholomew and Christopher Columbus from, 68; Fregoso, Giuliano, and Philippe de Bresse attack, 80; recognizes suzerainty of Louis XII, 157; watch in, not given to any Italian, 162; pledged to Charles and Claude if Louis XII has no son, 226–227; trade of, in Tunis, 255; phases of revolution in, 1506 and 1507, 265; leading plebeian families of, in exile, 265; power of family of Fiesco in, 265; a dyer made absolute Doge in, 266; Louis XII advances against, 266; Bayard with French victorious at, 266; Julius II desires to liberate, 303; Pope sends Marc Antonio Colonna to, 304; ill-success of Fregosi at, 305; Pope sends fleet against, 305; failure of papal fleet against, 310; Gian Fregoso enters, 348; Swiss restore

Fregosi in, 368 ; treaty to deliver to Ferdinand, 383 ; Ferdinand concludes compact with, 383

Gerace, Spaniards hold their ground in, 193

Gerlo, Agostino, offers to poison Pope Julius II, 314

Germanic nations conquer Roman Empire of West, 3 ; possessions, 3 ; Normans carry Germanic life to Naples and Sicily, 6

Germano - Latin nations never united, 75

Germans, migration of nations proceeded from, 2 ; stock of the, in new inhabitants of Mecklenburg, Pomerania, Brandenburg, and Silesia, 9 ; rule of, extended over Esthonia, Livonia, and Courland, 10 ; as auxiliary troops, 100 ; Venetians not to trade with, except in the Fondaco, 255

Ghiara d'Adda, guaranteed to Venice by Louis XII, 139 ; Venetians acquire, 259 ; Louis XII to restore to Venice, 364

Ghibellines, feud between Guelphs and, 14 ; support Ludovico Sforza, 34 ; power of Visconti due to, 34 ; contrasted with Guelphs, 117 ; Ludovico commits government to, 154 ; people of Como in sympathy with, 155 ; of Milan will not obey Trivulzio, 160 ; open feud with Guelphs in Milan, 160-161 ; heads of leading, fixed on palace gates of Milan, 167 ; active in Italy, 280 ; many sent to France, 280 ; jests at Lugano insulting to, 325 ; Trivulzio wins over leading, 347 ; rise at Milan after battle of Novara, 368 ; Ferdinand hopes by marriage to unite with Guelphs, 381

Gié, Marshal, disgraced by Queen Anne of France, 228

Gioia, Aubigny escapes to, 203

Giron, Pedro, controls Henry IV of Castile, 62 ; accompanies Archduke Philip, 232 ; deprived of castle by Ferdinand, 248

Gisdar, Turkish commander at Cephalonia, defeated and killed, 184

Giustina, Sta, patron saint of Padua, 300

Glarus, wishes to join Swabian League, 145

Glis, on the Simplon, home of Jürg uff der Flue, 324

Goa, Portuguese in, 68 ; the Zabai of, asks help of Soldan Khan Hassan of Egypt, 278

Godfrey of Bouillon, " Bechadas," first novel by, 11

Golden Bull granted by Emperor Charles IV, 16

Gonzaga, family of, at Mantua, 2

Gonzaga, Francesco, Marquis of Mantua, leads the Venetians, 82 ; won over by Ludovico, 138 ; enters service of Louis XII, 157 ; opposes Gonzalvo on the Garigliano, 205 ; quits the army in disgust, 206 ; Julius II delivers standard of Church to, 265 ; captured by peasants, 301 ; strange conduct of, in campaign against Mirandola, 312

Gonzalvo d'Aguilar (known as Gonzalvo de Cordova) commands Spanish troops in Naples, 78 ; campaign of, in Calabria, 89 ; subjects Cosenza and fortresses of Crati valley, 91 ; seizes Laino, 91 ; blocks road against French, 92 ; Pope calls, to aid against Orsini, 122-123 ; takes Taranto, 123 ; subjects Sora to Federigo, 123 ; compels Orsini to make peace, 123 ; in Messina, 177 ; Federigo asks for assurance from, 177 ; master of fifteen towns, 179 ; younger brother of Alfonso d'Aguilar, 183 ; called the Great Captain, 183, 195 ; assists Venetians, 183 ; combines with Trevisano to capture Cephalonia, 183-184 ; turns towards Sicily and Naples, 184 ; in the Abruzzi, 191 ; meets Nemours in the chapel of St. Antony, 192 ; character and influence of, 194-195 ; combines Spaniards, Italians, and Germans in one corps, 195 ; shut up in Barletta, 196, 202 ; ventures out of Barletta, 202 ; reduces Ruvo and takes prisoner La Palice, 202 ; marches against French in force, 204; victorious at battle of Cerignola, 205; takes thirty castles in a day, 205; Marquis Gonzaga opposes, on Garigliano, 205; victorious in battle of the Garigliano, 207; rewards captains, including the Orsini, 207; Aretins, Pisans, French, and nobles of Tuscany offer services to, 213; tries to win over Caesar Borgia, 215 *n.*; fears Caesar's plots, 215 *n.*; promises ships to Maximilian, 237; very popular in Naples, 237; dissatisfied with Ferdinand, 237; inclined to side with Castilians and Archduke Philip regarding Naples, 238; Ferdinand promises grandmastership of Santiago to, 238; pledges himself to Ferdinand, 238; honours paid to, by Ferdinand, 240; Ferdinand's duplicity towards, 240

Görz, bartered to Maximilian, 280; Andreas Lichtenstein surrenders, 284

Gossenbrod, Georg, of Augsburg, royal councillor in Tyrol, 142–143; meets enemy, Count Jörg of Sargans, at Pfäffers, 143; Jörg tries to take prisoner, 143; encourages Tyrolese to invade Münsterthal, 143

Goths, the, in Italy, 4

Gotthard, St., Schwyzers and Freiburgers ascend, with artillery, 327

Gozadini, the, appear before Bologna, 328–329

Gralla, Mosen, Spanish ambassador, visits Cardinal d'Amboise, 178

Grammonts, the, adherents of Jean d'Albret of Navarre, 350; castles of, excepted in Alva's conquests, 352

Granada, conquest of, 67; joy of Ferdinand and Isabella at conquest of, 69; conquest of, celebrated in Christian lands, 70; Moors of, rise against Spain, 183; Ximenes advises Archduke Philip to leave to Ferdinand, 233

Gravina, Duke of (Francesco Orsini), prevails on Sinigaglia to surrender its castle, 200

Greek form of worship, Slavonic nations adopt, 5–6

Greeks, operations against, by Bohemond of Tarentum, 7

Grimani, Antonio, after being merchant leads Venetian forces, 182; retreats before Turks, 182; banished, 183

Grisons Confederation, the, 143

Grisons, men of, under Galeazzo's standard, 160

Gritti, Andrea, surprises one of gates of Padua, 299; attempt of, to vanquish Bayard, 330; taken prisoner, 331

Groningen, Etzard Cirksena offers tribute for, 385

Guadalquivir, Spaniards on the, 8

Guadiana, Alonso Ramon takes valley of the, 8

Gualterotti, family of, formerly Medicean, 51; member of family of, opposes Piero de' Medici, 51

Guelphs, faction of the, 14; opposed to Ghibellines, 14; Ludovico surrounds himself with Guelph families, 35; Trivulzio, head of, 46; contrasted with Ghibellines, 117; on side of Ludovico, 140; care more for Trivulzio than Ludovico, 152; open feud of, at Milan with Ghibellines, 160; astir at advance of French, 365; Ferdinand hopes to unite with Ghibellines, 381

Guidobaldo of Urbino. *See* Urbino

Guienne, restored to French king by Maid of Orleans, 20; Henry VIII hopes to unite to English royal standard, 341; joint English and Spanish attack planned upon, 346; Ferdinand advises seizure of, from French, 369

Guilds, rise in cities against families, 15; rights of, 101

Guinea, Portuguese right of navigating, 68

Guinegate, heights of, battle of the Spurs, 372

Gurk, Bishop of. *See* Matthäus Lang

Gutenberg, landsknechts and Swiss at, 144

Guzerat, Moorish rule in kingdom of, 268

H

Hagenau passes into hands of Maximilian, 224

Hainault, knights and soldiery of, with Henry VIII of England, 371

Häl, Rudolf, captain of landsknechts, 346–347

Hanseatic League, 102, 374

Hapsburg, House of, 95; alliance between House of Aragon and, 129

Hasenbühel, battle of, 15

Hassan, Khan, Soldan of Egypt, asked for help by Indian princes, 278; fits out fleet at Suez, 278

Hederlin, marvellous deed of Germans under, 90

Hegau, fighting in the, 151

Heinrich of Brunswick, Duke, Henry VIII of England asks Maximilian to lend, 371; overcomes Budjadings, 385; subdues East Friesland, 385

Helena, Queen of Abyssinia, 297

Henry of Trastamara, 15; law of, that no Englishman go to Castile without permission of King of France, 62

Henry II of ·England, quarrel of, with Thomas à Becket, 13

Henry III of England, English towns represented in parliament of, 12

Henry V of England, in possession of Paris and French crown, 20

Henry VII of England, appeased by money, returns to England, 23; Ferdinand negotiates with, 129; joins league and receives hat and sword from Pope, 129; dangers threatening, outside England, 130; entertains Archduke Philip at Windsor, 231; asks that the Earl of Suffolk should be given up, 231; imprisons and puts to death Yorkists, 338; limits clergy's right of sanctuary, 338; tribunals and parliament subservient to, 338; councillors of, in Star Chamber, 338–339; financial agents, Empson and Dudley, 339; daughter Mary betrothed to Charles of Austria, 339

Henry VIII of England, bears red and white rose on escutcheon, 339; puts to death Suffolk and Buckingham, 340; bases foreign policy on relationships, 340; allied to Ferdinand through Katherine, 340; and, through sister Mary, to Charles and Maximilian, 340; hopes for title of "most Christian king," 341; despatches plenipotentiaries to Lateran Council, 341; hopes to unite Guienne to royal standard, 341; claim of House of, to Naples, 342; enters into league with Ferdinand and Pope, 342; declares war on Louis, 342; together with Ferdinand and Maximilian seeks seizure of Burgundy, Normandy, and Guienne, 369; joins English army besieging Térouanne, 370ı; army and cannon of, 371; asks Maximilian for Duke Heinrich of Brunswick or Marshal Vergy, 371; Maximilian offers to come in person to, 371; meets Maximilian, 372; Maximilian under standard of, at battle of the Spurs, 373 n.; James IV of Scotland summons, from Térouanne, 375; becomes master of Scotland through battle of Flodden, 377; enters Tournay in assumed quality of King of France, 378

Henry III, Emperor, 101

Henry IV of Castile, controlled by Pacheco and Giron, 62

Hermandad, the, incompetent to deal with heresy, 64; Inquisition harmonized with, in form, 65; modelled on a coalition of citizens against nobles, 66; commits civic power to king, 66; Ferdinand, aided by, overcomes nobles, 230

Hertogenbosch, Maximilian meets daughter and grandchildren at, 286

Hesse, opposes Palatinate in war of Landshut succession, 222

Hesse, Wilhelm of, ravages Bergstrasse and Alzheimer Gau, 223

Hetel, Caspar, tortured and beheaded at Baden, 384

Hetel, Hans Rudolf, goes over to French, 384

Hetzel of Bern, has audience of French envoys Trivulzio and La Trémouille, 364

Hieronymites, Dom Manuel builds a monastery of the, 272

Hoeks, the, supply troops to Charles VIII, 28 ; Philip of Ravenstein, last of, surrenders Sluys, 96

Hofgericht, not held throughout Empire for six months, 219

Hohenstaufen, Papacy wrongly attributes gain in strength to fall of, 13 ; strife between Spain and France at death of the last, 71

Holland, affairs in, connected with those of other nations, 13

Holy League (1511), proclaimed, 323 ; objects of, 323

Holzinger, Doctor, Eberhard of Württemberg takes from prison, to be Chancellor, 132

Hormuz, " House of Safety," Moorish trade at, 268 ; Albuquerque succeeds in building a fort at, 276

Horvaths, contention of the, with Hungarian Queens, 256

Hospitallers, the, 11

Hovenden, Roger de, success of Crusades ascribed to Normans by, 7

Howard, Thomas, fights magnificently at Flodden, 376

Hume, Alexander, at Flodden, 376

Hungary, mark of Austria grows towards, 95 ; Maximilian's plans against, 96 ; German auxiliaries subduers of, 100 ; Maximilian turns eyes on, 227 ; Maximilian in, 234 ; Maximilian takes island of Schütt, called " heart of," 235 ; contention of Horvaths with Queens of, 256 ; Maximilian's granddaughter to marry Louis, heir to throne of, 385

Hungary, Wladislav, King of. See Wladislav

Huybert, the brothers, Philip of Castile embarks in ship of, 231

I

Iceland, Wilkinasaga and Niflungasaga, composed in, 11

Illyria, Goths in, 4 ; light Greek horse for Venice sent from, 289

Imbercourt, heroic qualities of, 193

Imola, Pope declares Ludovico's great-nephews to have forfeited, 172 ; taken, by Caesar Borgia, 173 ; Caesar defenceless at, 199–200 ; Venetians occupy country round, 213, 260 ; Julius II interferes against Venice on behalf of, 216 ; Venice restores part of territory of, 261

India, Portuguese desire to reach, as land of spices, 68 ; trade of, in year 1497, in hands of Moors, 268 ; Mongolian or Arabian governors in ports of, 268 ; too weak to rid itself of Moors, 269 ; many Europeans had visited, 269 ; direct connection set up between Europe and, 269–270 ; King Manuel fits out fleet to discover, 270 ; and calls himself lord of commerce, and future conquests in, 272 ; arrival of Francisco d'Almeida in, 274 ; Portuguese victorious over Moors in, 276 ; house of Fugger sends three ships to, 277 ; war of Moors of, and of Egypt, against Portuguese, 278 ; Venetian trade in, affected by struggle of Portuguese and Moors, 287

Inebecht (Lepanto), 181

Ingelheim, peasantry of, resist Wilhelm of Hesse, 223

Innocent VIII, Pope, desires possession of Naples, 32 ; defeated by Alfonso II, 32 ; anger of, with Ferrante, 37 ; Lorenzo de' Medici undertakes to pacify, 37 ; Lorenzo gives daughter to Franceschetto Cibò, son of, 37 ; Giovanni della Rovere and the Colonna in disfavour with, 37–38 ; death of, 41

Innsbruck, Maximilian's Court at, 111

Inquisition, dispensation granted by Sixtus IV for establishment of, in

Spain, 64 ; Torquemada has part in founding, 64–65; brought about by quarrel between converted and unconverted Jews, 65; harmonized with Hermandad, in form, 65; the Quemadero set up by Isabella before Seville, 65; rigour of, abated under Ximenes, 248

Intercursus Magnus, treaty between England and Flanders, 130

Ireland, Henry Plantagenet in, 10 ; Pope instigates attack on, 10

Isabella of Aragon, granddaughter of Ferrante and daughter of Alfonso II, 39; betrothed to Gian Galeazzo Sforza, 39; taken to Milan, 39; jealous of honours paid to Ludovico's wife Beatrice, 40; appeals to her father for assistance, 40 ; death of husband of, 48 ; hears that Ludovico is Duke of Milan, 48–49 ; goes to Federigo at Ischia, 180 ; Bari defended by, against French, 192

Isabella of Castile (see also Ferdinand and Isabella), sister of Henry IV of Castile, 62–63 ; succession in Castile for, 63 ; betrothed to Ferdinand, 63 ; married at Valladolid, 63 ; visits Andalusian cities, 64 ; presides at tribunals in Seville, 64 ; pardons all offences except heresy, 64 ; establishes Inquisition at Seville, 65 ; vigorous rule of, 67 ; aims at absolute power over orthodox kingdom, 67 ; death of, 227; regard of, for hand of, 246–247

Isabella the Infanta, daughter of Ferdinand and widow of Alonso of Portugal, marries Dom Manuel, 129 ; demands expulsion of Jews from Portugal, 129 ; becomes Queen of Portugal, 188 ; receives allegiance of Castilians, 188; death of, 188; death of Miguel, son of, 188

Isabella, granddaughter of Maximilian, Christian II of Denmark sues for hand of, 385

Ischia, Federigo, Beatrice of Hungary and Isabella of Milan at, 180 ; Inigo Davolos brings to Gonzalvo keys of castle of, 205

Isonzo, Maximilian closes passes from the Adige to the, 281

Istria, Alviano conquers, 290

Italiae, Descriptio, 279

Italy, feuds of Guelphs and Ghibellines in, 14 ; first independent, 39; at zenith of culture, 39; alliance of, with Spain, 71–75; Charles VIII in, 46–61 ; Louis XII most powerful potentate in, 157–158 ; God's judgment over, 176 ; kept free from foreign influence by Houses of Sforza and Aragon, 180; only three large States in, 181 ; ill-effects of feuds and papal authority in, 185 ; rivalry of knights of, 195–196 ; heir to, also heir to third of France, 227; Ferdinand triumphant in, 249 ; Julius II plans to free from French, 267, 303; Maximilian desires to invade, 279 ; no desire for unity and freedom of, 318; prevalence of vice and disease in, 319; training of boys in " fine hypocrisy " in, 320 ; Julius II presents to St. Peter's altar cloth commemorating liberation of, 348 ; anxiety about future of, causes death of Julius II, 361

Iviza, Pedro Navarra sets sail from, 251

Ivrea, Swiss march to, 86

Ivres d'Allègre, French general, message of, to Mendoza, 192; at battle of Cerignola, 204, 205 ; at battle of Ravenna, 334, 336

J

Jaen, subdued by St. Ferdinand, 8

James IV of Scotland, 28 ; supports Perkin Warbeck, 130 ; marries Margaret, daughter of Henry VII, 131 ; friendship of, with King John of Denmark, 131, 374 ; allied with Louis XII, 186–187 ; drawn into fresh war with England, 374 ; Queen Anne of France asks assistance of, 374 ; sends Lyon King of Arms demanding return of Henry VIII, 375 ; crosses Tweed, 375 ; remains six days at Norham, 375 ; English send herald Rougecroix to, 375; at Flodden, 376; question whether dead body at Flodden is that of, 376

Jametz, son of Robert de la Mark, leads landsknechts, 364

Jayme, Conquistador, exploits of, 8

Jeanne, wife of Louis XII, divorced, 137; retires to Bourges, where she is revered as saint, 137

Jerusalem, crusades to, 7; title and right of, belong to crown of 'Naples, 26; visions and prophecies of entrance of Charles VIII into, 27; Spanish expeditions to, 68; crosses of, on coat of mail of Charles VIII, 82

Jews, Marquis of Cadiz warned by Inquisition not to shelter, 65; quarrel between converted and unconverted brings about Inquisition, 65; influence of, in Spain, 65; to be expelled from Portugal, 129; fugitive, from Spain people cities in Apulia, 259

Joanna I, Queen of Naples, 25

Joanna II, Queen of Naples, will of, 25

Johannsen Erik, under ban of Empire, 228

John of Anjou, revolt of the Neapolitan barons in favour of, 30, 71

John of Aragon, attacked by Don Carlos and the Catalans, 63

John I of Castile, relies in battle on French, 62

John II of Castile, Alvaro de Luna favourite of, 62; defeats his son Henry at Olmedo, 63

John, King of Portugal, 129; receives Columbus and makes compact with Ferdinand with regard to discoveries, 69-70; death of (1495), 129

John, King of Denmark, related to James IV of Scotland, 131; unsuccessful expeditions of, against Ditmarschers and Sweden, 187

Jörg, Count, of Sargans, tries to take prisoner Georg Gossenbrod of Augsburg, 142-143; once schemed to bring Tyrol to crown of Bavaria, 143; outlawed, 143; forces Abbot of Pfäffers to leave monastery, 143

Jorge, Dom, natural son of John of Portugal, 129

Jovianus Pontanus, draws up document for resignation of Alfonso II, 58

Juan, son of Ferdinand of Spain, marries Margaret, daughter of Maximilian, 100; death of, and of infant child of, 188

Juan de Enguera, Inquisitor of Catalonia, 229

Juana Beltraneja, daughter of Henry IV of Castile, declared illegitimate, 62; succession of, disputed, 62-63; hand and realm of, offered to Alfonso of Portugal, 63; Sixtus IV revokes dispensation to Alfonso to marry, 64; report of Ferdinand's proposed marriage to, 229

Juana, daughter of Ferdinand and Isabella, marries Archduke Philip, 100; Castilian succession passes to, 188; birth of Charles, son of, 188; has great reception in Spain, 188; gives large diamond to Claude of France, 189; succession of Castile devised to, by Isabella, 229; kept prisoner by husband, 232; Ferdinand resolved to liberate, 234; state of health of, 241; discovers Philip's infidelity, 241; mind of, overshadowed, 242; disease develops after husband's death, 242; Bergenroth's opinion that her madness was a myth, discussed, 242 n.; takes husband's corpse with her from Burgos, 244; gives audiences at Furnillos round coffin, 244; strongholds seized in name of, 245; at Tortoles meets Ferdinand, 248; refuses to bury corpse of husband, 248-249; taken to Tordesillas, 249; where she lives forty-seven years dead to world, 249

Julius II, Pope (Giuliano della Rovere), had before election opposed three popes, 212; a man of his word, 213; election of, 213; remonstrates with Venetians, 214; Caesar Borgia ready to surrender towns and castles to, 214, 215 n.; refuses offer, 214; Caesar's castles delivered to, 216; interferes against Venice for Cesena, Imola, and Forli, 216 ; bent on regaining temporalities of Church, 261 ; joins league with Louis, Maximilian, and Philip against Venice (1504), 261, 279 ; violent and impatient, 261 ; treatment of Michael Angelo by, 261-262 ; firm character of, 262 ; portrait of, by Raphael, 262 ; takes field against Bologna, 263 ; enters Perugia, 263 ; declares Bentivoglio and adherents rebels against Church, 264 ; enters Bologna in state, 264 ; proud to call himself Ligurian, 266 ; related to House of Fregoso, 267 ; had hand in insurrection of Popolari, 267 ; returns to Rome, 267 ; plans to unite States of Church and free Italy from French, 267 ; quarrels with Venice, 267 ; ratifies League of Cambray, 287 ; pronounces ban on Venice, 287 ; has misgivings about Louis XII, 288 ; proclaims victory of Agnadello in Italian sermon, 294 ; occupies Rimini and Faenza, 294 ; invited to occupy Rimini and Cervia, 295 ; resolved to spare what is left to Venice after fall, 297, 303 ; releases Venice from ban of excommunication, 303 ; keeps galleys at Ostia ready for sea, 303-304 ; demands that Alfonso d'Este should make peace with Venice, 304 ; defied by Alfonso, 305 ; puts Alfonso under ban and fits out fleet against Genoa, 305 ; further schemes of, 305 ; first Pope to have Swiss guard, 307 ; concludes five years' alliance with Swiss through Matthäus Schinner, 307 ; army of, occupies Modena and threatens Ferrara, 307 ; dedicates in Loreto cross to Virgin, 308 ; retreat of Swiss troops of, 309 ; placed in danger by failure of his troops and fleet, 310 ; Louis XII decides on war against, 310-311 ; Chaumont attacks, at Bologna, 311 ; cut off from army and ill of fever, 311 ; promises the Bolognese a cardinal, 311 ; rises from sick bed to bless people of Bologna, 312 ; despatches three

generals against Mirandola and Ferrara, 312 ; besieges Mirandola, 313 ; escape of, from Bayard due to snowstorm, |313 ; sends cannon ball to Loreto as thankoffering, 313 ; sends message to Alfonso, 314 ; opposed by Trivulzio, 314-315 ; Bentivogli take Bologna and there break Michael Angelo's statue of, 316, 317 ; grief of, at murder of Cardinal of Pavia, 317 ; brought to Rimini, 317 ; summons Spaniards and Swiss to assistance, 319 ; five schismatic Cardinals invite to General Council, 322 ; himself summons Council at Rome, 322 ; sends to Ferdinand, 323 ; concludes Holy League (1511), 323, 340 ; central figure of a new war, 327 ; after defeat of Ravenna shuts himself up in castle of St. Angelo, 338 ; Henry VIII hopes for title, " Most Christian King," from, 341 ; Henry sends message to Louis XII on behalf of, 342 ; schismatic Cardinals talk of deposing, 342 ; question of Maximilian succeeding, 342 ; brings about truce between Maximilian and Venice, 343 ; schismatic Council deposes from papal authority, 345 ; opens Council in the Lateran, 345 ; army of, under Duke of Urbino massed with Spaniards, Venetians, and Swiss, 345 ; hears that Milan is in Swiss hands, 348 ; Bologna implores pardon from, 348 ; Parma and Piacenza surrender to, 348 ; gives to St. Peter's altar cloth commemorating liberation of Italy, 348 ; happiest days of, 349 ; eternal gratitude of, to Swiss, 349 ; League of, against Popolari of Florence, 353 ; reason for enmity of, against Florence, 354 ; appoints Cardinal de' Medici legate with his army, 354 ; heard to utter words of vengeance against Alfonso, 359 ; Alfonso fears to attend banquet of, 360 ; determined to subject Ferrara, 360 ; supports installation of Massimiliano Sforza in Milan, 360 ; death of, hastened by anxiety for

Italy, 361 ; pronounced interdict against France (1512), 369

Junge Pfalz, founded by Maximilian, 225

Jürg uff der Flue, feud of, with Matthäus Schinner, 324 ; account of, 324 ; negotiates at Milan in vain, 344 ; son of, gives audience to French envoys on passage through Switzerland, 364

K

Kabul, Indian trade through, 254

Kammergericht. *See* Tribunal, Cameral

Karst, the, in the Windish Mark, Maximilian goes to, 237

Katherine, daughter of Ferdinand, 187 ; goes to England to marry Arthur, Prince of Wales, 189 ; compelled to remain in England after Arthur's death, 339

Kaub, garrison of, resists Wilhelm of Hesse, 223

Kennemer, standard of the, with device of bread and cheese, 96

Knight, White, imprisoned in Treviglio, 291

Knights, of the Sword, 10 ; Teutonic, 10, 11 ; rise against cities, 15 ; Charles VIII dubs children as, 77 ; League of, in the Black Forest, 102 ; rivalry of Italian, French, and Spanish, 195, 331

Kofel taken from Venetians, 318

Krems, mark of Austria founded round castle of, 95

Kufstein taken by Maximilian, 224

L

Ladislas, king of Naples, sells Cortona to Florence, 113 ; faction in Corfu opposed to rule of, 256 ; sells Zara to Venice, 256

Laibach, garrison of Portenau flies to, 284

Laino, Gonzalvo takes, 91

Lancaster, rival houses of York and, 338

Landriani, the, will never obey Trivulzio, 160

Landriano, the treasurer, attacked in Milan, 154

Landschad Johann, opposes Alexander the Black of Veldenz, 223

Landshut, war of Succession in, 221–223

Landshut, Duke Georg of, desires succession for Ruprecht, 221 ; death of, 221

Landsknechts, army of, formed, 104 ; fear of irregular payment of, 106; boast of power, 133 ; performances of, at Gutenberg, 144 ; Swiss attack, on Lake Constance, 144 ; at battle of Schwaderloch, 147 ; ordered by Maximilian to leave French camp, 346; body of, all slain at Pavia, 347–348

Lang, Matthäus, Bishop of Gurk, Imperial ambassador in France, 311 ; attempts to negotiate peace, 315 ; writes to commander of Genoa, 348 ; Cardona negotiates with, at Mantua, 356, 359 ; Soderini refuses 100,000 ducats demanded by, 356

Langres, Maximilian send corps against, 134

Laniago, taken from Venetians, 318

Lanzengast, detachment of Swiss scale the, 147

Las Casas, Bartolomeo de, leads peasants to Cumana, 18

Lasla, the priest, compilation of chronicles by, 98

Lassos, feud of, with Arias at Madrid, 245

Lastorf, Swiss judges sit under fir-tree of, 306

Lateran Council, plenipotentiaries of Henry VIII at, 341 ; Julius II opens, 345

Latin element in French, Spanish, and Italian nations, 1–2 ; countries communicate religion and language, 2 ; Anglo-Saxons unable to resist Latin Christianity and culture, 3 ; Pope ecclesiastical head of Latin nations, 5 ; empire at Constantinople, 7 ; summary of position of Latin nations, 185 ; Maximilian desires to unite Latin nations with Teutonic, 228

Latino-Germanic nations, Charlemagne unites, 5

Lautrec tries to aid Gaston de Foix at battle of Ravenna, 337

Lavoro, with the Abruzzi, to belong to Louis XII, 178, 191

Leghorn, Piero de' Medici grants fortress of, to Charles VIII, 51; to remain in French hands till conclusion of expedition against Naples, 54; ceded to Florence, 108

Leo X (Giovanni de' Medici) elected Pope, 361 (see Giovanni de' Medici); operated on in Conclave for abdominal complaint, 361; coronation of, on anniversary of battle of Ravenna, 361; generosity and popularity of, 361–362; enmity of, against France, 369; follows policy of predecessor, 369; forces of, with those of Ferdinand, against Venice, 369

Leon, Ponce de. See Cadiz, Marquis of

Leonardo da Vinci, summoned by Ludovico Sforza to Milan, 36; painting by, of Beatrice d'Este, 154–155

Leonora of Aragon, daughter of Ferrante and wife of Ercole d'Este, 39

Lepanto (Inebecht), designs of Bajazet on, 181; taken by Turks, 182

Lerin, Don Luis, Count, Ferdinand supports claims of, on Navarre, 350; head of the Beaumonts, 350; marches at head of Spaniards against Jean d'Albret, 351

Lesbos, rule of Louis XII extends to, 157

Lescun, offers Caesar Borgia a safe-conduct, 216

Letts, land of the, made German, 10

Leventina, Val, inhabitants of, form eight Italian communes, 158; insults directed to people of Uri driving cattle through, 159; people of, forced to acknowledge protection of Uri, 159

Leyva, Antonio, famous Spanish leader, 195; at battle of Seminara, 203

Librafatta, Paolo Vitelli assists Ludovico Sforza to take, 138

Lichtenstein, Andreas, surrenders Görz to Alviano, 284; captain of Maximilian's forces before Padua, 370

Lido Maggiore, Germans scour Venetian territory as far as, 318

Liège, Maximilian represents possibility of revolt of, 282

Ligny, Louis, Comte de, inclined to allow escape of Ludovico Sforza, 165; treatment of Vogheresi by, 167

Lille, treaty of (1513), 380, 381, 382

Limburg, hereditary cupbearer of, 99; Eagle of Empire in hand of the cupbearer of, 150

Lindau, Maximilian orders soldiers to appear at, 110

Linser, "boldest man in the world," falls in battle of Ravenna, 335

Linz, Maximilian takes counsel with Philip at, 111

Liro, valley of the, belongs to jurisdiction of Chur, 362

Lisbon, Columbus at, 69; talk in, of wealth of Calicut, 272; four barks bring spices from Calicut to, 277

Lisle, Charles Brandon created Viscount, 371

Literature, affected by national conditions, 321

Livinen, Swiss to meet in, and then advance against French, 344

Livonia, German rule in, 10; Ivan Wasiljewitsch's attack on, repulsed by Walter von Plettenberg, 189

Locarno, Ludovico Sforza offers to cede, 164; becomes Swiss, 362

Loches, Ludovico imprisoned at, 168

Loja, Gonzalvo in, 241

Lombardy, French army in, 57; benefit to Italy of Francesco Sforza's lordship over, 180; Ascanio Sforza, with 600 nobles of, offer services to Gonzalvo, 213; Venetians driven from, 318

London, market for silk fabrics, brocade, and damask from Florence, 113

Longueville, Duke of, commands division at battle of Agnadello, 292; surrenders at battle of the Spurs, 373

Lope de Vega, poem of, commemorates Castilian services in Holy Land, 7

Loredano, Andrea, gallantry of, against Turks, 182; death of, 182

Loredano, Doge of Venice, permits passage of Imperial envoys, 281; replies to Montjoye, French herald, 289; offers sons for defence of Padua, 300

Loreto, Julius II dedicates silver cross to Virgin at, 308; Julius II sends cannon ball as thankoffering to, 313

Lorini, one of Florentine Signori, admits Piero de' Medici into assembly, 51

Lorraine, René of Anjou once hoped to join, to Anjou, 21

Louis of Bavaria, quarrels with Charles of Luxemburg for German crown, 15

Louis of Hungary, birth of, 235; marries Maximilian's granddaughter Mary, 385

Louis, Duke of Orleans, defeated at St. Aubin, 22; released from Tower of Bourges by Charles VIII, 22; comes to Genoa to assist Ludovico, 46; claims of, on Milan, 73; writes to France that troops are needed, 75; people of Milan and Pavia invite, 79; received in Novara and proclaimed Duke, 79; shut up in Novara, and in distress, 85; Charles VIII to rescue, 85; suffering from intermittent fever, 86; hardships of, 86; truce concluded and permission to leave Novara given to, 87; submits unwillingly to terms of peace, 87; Trivulzio spreads report of approach of, 109; suddenly changes mind about journey to Italy, 112; becomes King of France as Louis XII, 135 (see Louis XII)

Louis XI of France, aims at full possession of sovereign power, 21; Maximilian defeats schemes of, 95

Louis XII of France, comes to throne (1498), 135; draws Pope to his side and repulses Maximilian, 135; character of, 135-136; gives internal government to Georges d'Amboise, 136; shows mark of favour to La Trémouille, 136; divorces Jeanne and marries Anne of Brittany, 137; unites on coins arms of Brittany and France, 137; styled King of Naples and Milan, 137; enterprises of, with Venetians, Pope, and Ferdinand, 137-138; makes agreement with Venice against Ludovico, 139; reasons for enmity between Maximilian and, 141; Philip obliged to promise service to, 142; aids Duke of Gelderland, 142; resolves to stir up trouble in Germany, 142; opportunity for such trouble arises, 142-143; offers alliance to Swiss, 145; war in Swabia serves purpose of, 149; Swiss refuse to supply men against Milan for, 149-150; but some Swiss join, 150; acquires inheritance of Valentina, 156; greeted in Milan as deliverer, 156; lowers taxes in Milan, 157; most powerful potentate in Italy, 157-158; returns to France, 158; after successes of Ludovico gives supreme command to La Trémouille, 162; capture of Ludovico a victory over Maximilian for, 168; negotiates with Alexander VI, 172; promises Valentinois to Caesar Borgia, 172; receives Caesar at Chinon, 172; agrees to partition of Naples with Ferdinand (1500), 178; Maximilian promises investiture of Milan to, 180-181,189; power and policy of, 185-186; fond of hunting and hawking, 186; allies of, 186; German princes have understanding with, 187; proclaims crusade against Turks, 189; Pope gains power through, 202; destruction of Orsini advantageous to, 202; twice dissuades Caesar Borgia from attacking Florence, 208;

makes alliance with Philip, 218–
219; correspondence of, with Elector Palatine, 221; Count Palatine
sends son Ruprecht to, 223; enters
treaty of Blois with Maximilian
and Philip, 226; Maximilian proposes repeal of Salic law to, 228;
falls ill in spring of 1505, 228;
repents treaty of Blois, 228;
Claude, daughter of, to be betrothed to Francis of Angoulême instead of Charles, 229,
236; Ferdinand seeks reconciliation with, 230; assigns Neapolitan rights to Germaine de Foix,
whom Ferdinand promises to
marry, 230; subdues the revolution in Genoa (1507), 266; negotiates with Ferdinand to make
Amboise Pope, 267; Maximilian
seeks aid against, 279; envoy of,
made prisoner at Constance, 279;
demands of Venice to include
Guelderland in truce, 285; agrees
with Maximilian to attack Venice,
286; affixes seal to League of
Cambray, 287; Maximilian and
Julius II have misgivings about,
288; reason for enmity of, against
Venice, 288–289; proclaims war
against Venice, 289; hears at
Milan that Treviglio is bombarded, 291; victorious at battle
of Agnadello, 292–294; pursues
fugitives and takes castle of Caravaggio, 294; wishes to annihilate
Venice utterly, 298; receives
Duke of Savoy, who demands
Cyprus, 298; triumphant return
of, to Milan, 298; abandons
alliance with Swiss, 305; makes
war, after hesitation, on Pope,
310; on way to Grenoble, 315;
will not agree to truce for Ferrara, 315; makes use of five
Cardinals against Julius II, 322;
enters Holy League with the
Pope, 323; sends Gaston de
Foix to territory of Church, 331;
invites Henry VIII to Council of
Pisa, 341; Henry VIII declares
war on, 342; Swiss remonstrate
with, 344; harassed by English
on coast of Brest, 346; defends
rights of Gaston de Foix to

Navarre, 350; suzerain of one part
of territory of Navarre, 350; determined to reconquer Milan,
363; offers Swiss peace and
alliance, 363; sends envoys to
Confederates and makes over
strongholds, 363–364; makes alliance with Venetians, 364; pressing pecuniary needs of, 373–374;
gives Duchy of Milan to daughter
Renée, 381; makes treaty with
Ferdinand, 381; death of Anne
of Brittany, Queen of, 381; thinks
of marrying Eleanor, granddaughter of Ferdinand, 381–382;
treaty for royal marriages of, 383;
not to claim Naples or support
Navarre, 383
Louise of Savoy, mother of Francis
of Angoulême, 228
Lucca, forced to join Austro-
Spanish League, 359
Lucerne, bailiff of Dijon lives in
princely fashion at, 86; Ludovico allied with, 141; recess of
(1499), 144; flag of, appears at
battle of Dorneck, 151; people
of, not at one, 165; Bishop of
Roeux pays peasants' reckonings
at, 282; six suspects in, committed to prison, 384
Ludovico il Moro. See Ludovico
Sforza
Lugano, Ludovico offers to cede to
Swiss, 164; courier with letters
from Schinner to the Pope,
drowned in Lake of, 325; becomes Swiss, 362
Luna, Alvaro de, favourite of John
II of Castile, 62; Pacheco and
Giron overthrow, 62
Lupfen, Count von, 370
Lupisala, St. Eric baptizes Finns in
spring of, 9
Luxembourg, Charles of, quarrels
with Louis of Bavaria about
crown of Germany, 15
Luzero, an Inquisitor, uses false
witnesses, 232; Ximenes sets free
those denounced by, 248
Lyons, Charles VIII at, 87; Maximilian, Philip, and Ferdinand to
meet at, 111; alliance of Louis
XII and Philip proclaimed at,
219

M

Machiavelli, helps to form military stations in war against Pisa, 354

Magdeburg, gates of Novgorod Cathedral work of craftsmen of, 13; Albrecht of Brandenburg made Archbishop of, 384

Maggia, valley of the, Ludovico offers conditionally to Swiss, 164; Swiss acquire, 362

Maggiore, Lake, Swiss acquire shores of, 362; French on lake of, terrified to hear Swiss artillery, 327

Magione, war on Caesar Borgia decided upon at, 198

Magra, troops of Charles VIII at source of the, 81

Maino, Jasone de, lectures in Pavia, 36

Mainz, St. Boniface, Archbishop of, 4 (see Boniface); Berthold, Elector of (see Berthold); Doctor Stürzler, Chancellor of, 132; Albrecht of Brandenburg Archbishop of, 384

Malabar, caravans from Mecca bring pepper from, 254; Zamorin of Calicut, chief of, 268; Vasco da Gama on coast of, 271

Malacca, important emporium for Eastern trade, 269; belongs to Moorish king, 269

Malaga, Ferdinand to begin Holy Campaign from, 252; Venetians load silk, grain, and wool at, 255

Malatesta, Venetians purchase Rimini from the, 213, 260

Malghera, Ramon de Cardona sees Venice from tower of, 379

Malindi, sheikh at, a Moor, 268; Prince of, kindly entertains Vasco da Gama, 271

Malserheide, Tyrolese fly before men of the Grisons on the, 148

Malvezzi, Luzio, flight of, with Galeazzo, 153; employed as general by Venetians but soon dismissed, 318

Mamelukes, short-lived triumph of, 296

Manfredi, Astorre and Ottaviano at Faenza, 175; Astorre outraged by Caesar Borgia and both thrown into Tiber, 176

Manfredi, Astorre, natural scion of family recalled by Faentines and so named, 260

Manfredonia, factions fight for, 191; Hans von Ravenstein and Germans at, 203

Mantua, family of Gonzaga at, 29; people of, join League and take Casalmaggiore, 291; Gaston de Foix forces approaches of, 329; Cardona and Matthäus Lang confer at, 356, 359

Mantua, Marquis of. See Gonzaga

Manuel, King of Portugal, makes alliance with Ferdinand of Spain, 129; marries the Infanta Isabella, 129; death of wife and child of, 188; marries Mary of Spain, 189; will not give up to Ferdinand Juana Beltraneja, 229-230; fits out expedition under Vasco da Gama, 270; builds church on site of Da Gama's prayer before departure, 272; styles himself lord of commerce, etc., in the East, 272; Duarte Meneses wages war for, against Moors in Morocco, 274; threatened by Sultan of Egypt, 274; hopes to seize Mahomet's house at Mecca, 274; despatches fleet under Francisco d'Almeida, 274

Manuel, Juan, raises contingent of Germans for service in Naples, 203

Marano, taken by Maximilian, 380; Venetians unable to retake, 383

Marburg, Gothic architecture of, 12; House of, 103

Marchioni, house of the, in Florence participate in shipping trade, 277

Marescotti, cruelties of Caesar Borgia to the, 264

Margaret, daughter of Henry VII, marries James IV of Scotland, 131

Margaret, daughter of Maximilian, to marry Dauphin, 21; marries Juan of Spain, 100; widowed, 188; marries Philippe de Bresse, 189

Margaret of York, widow of Charles the Bold, 130; dangers of Henry VII from, 130

Margolina, country seat of Sannazzaro, 239

Marino, a city of the Colonna, Roman citizens resolve to destroy, 179

Marliani, the, will not obey Trivulzio, 160

Martin, St., English will not celebrate day of, 370

Martin, Simon, fights singlehanded against fifteen Moors, 275

Martinach, Swiss troops march from, 86

Martinswand, supposed rescue, by angel, of Maximilian from the, 97

Mary of Burgundy, Maximilian's marriage with, 21, 23; advantages to Maximilian of marriage with, 95; premature death of, 95

Mary, daughter of Henry VII of England, betrothed to Charles of Austria, 339, 340, 342

Mary, daughter of Ferdinand and Isabella, 187; marries Manuel of Portugal, 189

Mary, Maximilian's granddaughter, married to Louis of Hungary, 385

Mary the Virgin said to have been seen in the sea off Venice, 291

Masone, men, women, and children suffocated in Grotto of, 302

Massaria, field of, after battle, 90

Matienzo, Tomas de, Sub-prior of Santa Cruz, correspondence of, concerning Archduchess Juana, 242 n.

Matricula, payments computed by, in the Empire, 226; inaccurate, 282

Mauerstätten, taken by Maximilian, 224

Maulbronn, taken by Ulrich of Württemberg, 223

Mauritania, claimed by Castile, 68

Maximilian of Austria, Emperor, King of the Romans, marries Mary of Burgundy, 21; assigns to French Artois and Franche-Comté as daughter's dower, 21; fails to uphold wife's claim to Burgundy, 21; betrothed to Anne of Brittany, who marries Charles VIII, 23; recovers Artois and Franche-Comté, 23; Pope's message to, regarding title of Emperor, 55; confers investiture of Milan on Ludovico, 73; anxious for imperial dignity, 73; natural ally of Ludovico and Venice, 74; objects of, 95; effects of his marriage with Mary of Burgundy, 95; imprisoned at Bruges (1488), 96; set at liberty, becomes supreme in Netherlands, 96; reconquers Austria, 96; plans of, against Hungary and Burgundy, 96; disappointment at failure to marry Anne of Brittany, 96; summons Diet at Worms, 96; character and habits of, 97-99; at Diet of Worms, 99; makes arrangement with House of Württemberg, 99-100; children of, betrothed to children of Ferdinand and Isabella, 100; wants assistance of Empire against French, 100; accuses Charles VIII of assuming prerogatives of Church and Empire, 104; proposals of, to the Diet, 104; princes propose a Council of Regency to, 105; obtains promise of 100,000 guilders, which, however, are not paid, 106; again obtains promise of money, 106; adopts proposals of Diet, 106; Common Penny to be raised for, 107; delivers judge's staff at Frankfurt to Eitel Friedrich von Zollern, 107; plans thwarted, 107; visited by ambassadors of Italy, 108; Ludovico awaits, at Münster, 109; consents to wage war for Italians, 110; abandons decrees of Diet, 110; complains of his treatment at Worms, 110; takes counsel with Philip, 111; meets Ludovico and papal legate at Vigevano, 111-112 n.; invests Leghorn, 112, 119; sees wreck of French fleet, 119; hopeless of achievement, returns to Germany, 120; allied with Ferdinand and Henry VII, 131; Berthold of

Mainz complains of, 132; decides succession in Württemberg, 133; at Diet of Freiburg, 133; receives from Estates, 70,000 guilders, 133; sends army to Burgundy, 133; in year 1498 makes three-fold attack on France, 134; campaign unsuccessful, 135; interested in struggle for Milan, 141; reasons for enmity of, with Louis XII, 141; closely allied with Ludovico, 142; Swiss roused against, 144–145; involved in arduous war, 149; goes himself to Constance, 149; advances towards the Schwaderloch, 150; captains will not risk blood for, against peasants, 150; defeated at battle of Dorneck, 151; agrees to a conference at Schaffhausen, 151; fails to prevent Swiss from marching against Ludovico, 163; affected by disaster to Ludovico, 168; opens Diet at Augsburg, 168; four military enterprises of, have failed, 168; forced to acquiesce in Council of Regency, 168; Louis XII victorious over, 168; makes treaty of Trent with Louis, 181, 189, 219; in anticipation of crusade forms new order of knighthood, 190; sends contingent to Manfredonia, 203; induced by Philip to make alliance with France, 219; demands of, referred by Electors to yearly meetings, 220; bereft of judicial power, 220; complains of Berthold of Mainz, 220; three aims in view with regard to Landshut succession, 222; finally decides in favour of Albrecht of Munich, 222; ransacks archives for claims to Palatinate territory, 224; gains territory, with Hagenau and Ortenau, 224; defeats Bohemians at Regensburg, 224; commands truce and forms "Junge Pfalz," 225; holds Diet of Cologne, 225; opposition to Imperial authority dies, 225–226; makes treaty of Blois, 226; turns attention to Hungary, 227, 230; dreams of monarchy over Latin and Teutonic nations, 228; proposes to

Louis XII to repeal Salic law, 228; places Swedish leaders under ban of Empire, 228; asserts claims to Portugal and England, 228; concerned about Hungarian succession, 234; defied by Hungarian nobles, 235; reduces Pressburg and takes Schütt, 235; hears of birth of son to Wladislav, 235; leaves Hungary, 235; desires Imperial crown in Rome, 236; indignant with Louis XII, 236; resolves to invade Italy, 236; Venetians refuse passage to, 236; hurries to Carniolan ports, 237; goes to the Karst, 237; death of Philip puts end to schemes of, 237; sends message to Gonzalvo, 238; appealed to by party in Castile, 245; unable to go to Castile, 248; cannot obtain guardianship of grandchildren in Netherlands, 249; afterwards gains guardianship, 249; holds Diet of Constance, 279; makes concessions in return for aid against Louis and for invasion of Italy, 279; embarks on war with Venice, 280; adopts title of Roman Emperor Elect, 280; advances towards Vicenza, 281; takes entrenchments of the Sette Communi, 281; suddenly returns to the Tyrol, 281; reasons for his retreat, 281–282; Charles of Gelderland at war with, on the Lower Rhine, 285; fears an insurrection in Empire, 285; concludes peace with Venice and directs operations against Gelderland, 285; aggrieved by Venice, draws closer to France, 286; forms League of Cambray with Louis XII against Venice, 286; has misgivings about Louis, 288; Venetian envoys sent to, 295; on fall of Venice, is for her utter annihilation, 298; plans to attack Venice from sea, 298; house of Fugger supplies with money, 298; arrives in Italy with French and Spanish troops, 300; advances on Padua, 300; Bayard and French refuse to obey, 301; leaves Italy in disgust, 301;

orders Rudolf of Anhalt to ravage country, 302; warns Swiss against the Pope, 308; proposes to give Venice freedom of cities of the Empire, 318; troops of, march out of Verona, 318; allied to Henry VIII, 340; reconciled to Ferdinand, 340–341; has hope of becoming Pope, 342; requires 300,000 ducats to gain over Cardinals, 342; Ferdinand discloses plan of gaining Milanese and Venetian territory to, 343; makes truce with Venice, 343; Swiss envoys sent to, 344; orders landsknechts to leave French camp, 346; Venetians to leave Verona and Vicenza to, 360; desires seizure of Burgundy, Normandy and Guienne from French, 369; qualities of generalship of, 370; Henry VIII asks loan of Duke Heinrich of Brunswick or Marshal Vergy from, 371; offers Henry his own leadership, 371; meets Henry near Aire, 371–372; at battle of the Spurs, 372–373; fights under standard of King of England, 373 n.; separates himself from Henry VIII, 378; granddaughters Isabella and Maria marry Christian II of Denmark and Louis of Hungary, 385

Mazzara, Alfonso II flies to Olivetan monastery at, 58

Mecca, Portuguese intentions against, 17; trade carried on by caravans from, 254; Dom Manuel hopes to seize Mahomet's house at, 274

Mecklenburg, German inhabitants of, 9

Meda, Maximilian meets Ludovico and envoy of Pope at, 111

Medici, family of, friendly with that of Sforza, 37; two of the, meet Charles VIII at Piacenza, 49; Charles VIII enters palaces of, 53; Charles wishes to restore House of, 54; vigorous edicts against, withdrawn, 54; Savonarola foretells expulsion of, 117; again supreme in Florence, 358

Medici, Cosimo de', 37

Medici, Foligno de', complains of decrease of "State" of the Medici, 38

Medici, Giovanni de', made Abbot of Miramondo and Monte Casino, and Cardinal, 38; driven from Florence, 52; papal legate at battle of Ravenna, 336; appointed legate with papal army against Florence, 354; benefices of, chief support of family when driven from Florence, 355; character and habits of, 355; summons Cardona to campaign against Florence, 356; opposes policy of Giuliano, 358; becomes bound to Spanish cause, 358–359; elected Pope, 361 (see Leo X)

Medici, Giuliano de', offers services to Gonzalvo, 213; gates of Florence opened to, 357; his constitution not agreeable to Giovanni, 358

Medici, Lorenzo de', ruler of Florence, 37; makes cause with Bona, 37; pacifies Pope by marrying his daughter to Pope's son, 37; position of, as mediator of Italy, 38; death of (1492), 41; not spared by Savonarola, 115; employs his prestige to advance his house through preferments of his son Giovanni, 354–355

Medici, Lorenzo de', son of Piero, 358

Medici, Piero de', devoted to House of Aragon, 41; Florentines discontented with, 49; character and tastes of, 49; perceives that he is not supported by Florentines, 49; gives himself up to Charles VIII, 50; analysis of his motives and policy, 50 n.; returns to Florence, 51; revolution against, 52; flies from Florence and goes to Bologna, 52; the Arrabbiati endeavour to effect recall of, 123

Medina del Campo, Benavente's loss of market of, due to House of Aragon, 232

Medina Sidonia, Duke of, on side of Isabella of Spain, 64

Meinhard, Bishop, preaches in Esthonia, 9

Meissen, laid waste by wars, 14

Melfi, Caracciolo of, 32; description of Princess of, 77

Melita, excepted when Portugal allowed to conquer Fez, 68

Melk, mark of Austria founded round castle of, 95

Melzo, Count of, 153

Mendoza, Diego de, Ives d'Allègre sends message to, 192; Spaniards under, at Marino, 212

Mendoza, Pedro Gonzales de, Archbishop of Seville, makes Ximenes vicar of diocese, 245

Mendrisio, Ludovico Sforza offers to cede, 164; becomes Swiss, 362

Meneses, Duarte, wages glorious war against Moors, 274

Mera, valley of the, appropriated by Grisons, 362

Mers-el-Kebir, Spanish fleet takes, 249

Messina, Gonzalvo, in, 177

Mestre, alarm in, of Turks, 182; Pitigliano retreats to, 294; Germans, Italians, and Spaniards penetrate to, 379

Michael Angelo, and Julius II, 261–262

Michel, Jean, visions of, 27

Michelotto, executioner of Caesar Borgia, 176, 201

Migration of nations, a German movement, 2; ends in middle eleventh century, 6

Miguel of Portugal, death of, 188

Milan, ruled by Ludovico il Moro, 26; family of Sforza at, 29; Galeazzo Maria Sforza, Duke of, 34; Ludovico's court at, 36; Francesco Sforza, lord of, 37; duchy of, dependent on trade of war, 39; Ludovico and Beatrice honoured at, 40; Isabella, wife of Gian Galeazzo Sforza at, 40; Alfonso II to attack Ludovico, in territory of, 45; Ludovico, takes possession of, 48; claims of Louis of Orleans on, 73; League occupies territory of, 78; Duke of Orleans invited to, 79; Lombards protect territory of, 81; troops of, oppose Charles VIII, 82; Louis XII styled King of,

137; Venice offers to assist Louis against, 139; Ludovico commits government of, to Ghibellines, 154; Ludovico leaves, 155; Louis XII enters, 156; Louis lowers taxes and relieves burdens in, 157; reaction in favour of Ludovico in, 158; feud of Ghibellines and Guelphs in, 160, 161; Trivulzio driven out of, 161; Maximilian claims, as a crown land, 163; heads of leading Ghibellines fixed on palace gates in, 167; once devoted to Caterina Sforza, 173; feuds of, with Venice, 185; Maximilian promises Louis XII investiture of, 181, 189, 219; governor of, pledged to deliver castle to Charles and Claude if Louis XII has no son, 226–227; Amboise receives investiture of, for Louis, 227; Venice schemes to wrest, from French, 260; Maximilian declares Louis' investiture of, void, 279; renewal of Louis' investiture guaranteed, 286; League of Cambray to readjust frontier of, 286; great reception of Louis XII at, 298; Julius II seeks to drive French from, 305; schismatic Council removed from Pisa to, 331; Ferdinand desires conquest of, for grandson Charles, 343; conquest of, by the Swiss, 343–348; Cardona and Matthäus Lang propose Archduke Charles as prince of, 359; Massimiliano Sforza installed by the Pope as ruler of, 363; Louis XII determines to reconquer, 363; French again masters of, 365; French fly from, after battle of Novara, 368; French renounce claims on, 377; treaties between Louis XII and Ferdinand concerning, 381, 383

Mir Hossein commands fleet of Soldan of Egypt, 278; defeats Lourenço d'Almeida at Schaul, 296; defeat and escape of, 296

Miramondo, Giovanni de' Medici, Abbot of, 38

Mirandola, Julius II sends Marquis of Mantua against, 312; Julius II reduces, 313; cannon ball falls into tent of Julius II before, 313

Mittelburg, Thomas of, leads black troop under Fleuranges, 364

Mitylene, stormed by French eighteen times, 184

Mocenigo, Doge, opposed to conquests, 257

Modena, occupied by papal army, 307

Modon, Melchior Trevisano unable to relieve, 183; Bajazet takes, 183

Molart, captain of French infantry, killed at battle of Ravenna, 335

Molise, province of, 91

Moluccas, caravans from Mecca bring spices from the, 254

Mombasa, exploring party of Vasco da Gama threatened at, 271; Francisco d'Almeida storms, 274

Moncagliere, Swiss troops in, 86

Mongolian governors in Indian ports, 268

Monopoli, Venetians take, 85

Monselice, Venetians take, 302

Montagnana, Venetians take, 302

Montalban, peasants flying before Maximilian bring cattle to, 300

Montefiascone, peaceful reception of Charles VIII in, 55

Montferrat, Constantin de, 153

Montferrat, Marchioness of, death of, 87

Montjoye, French herald at Venice, 289

Montpensier, Duke of. See Bourbon, Gilbert de

Moors, campaigns against, 14; ineffectual rigour of Isabella of Spain against, 64; of Granada rise against Kings of Spain, 183; of mountains will not submit to baptism, 183; Alfonso d'Aguilar takes field against, 183; trade of, on coasts of Arabia, East Africa, and India, 268; penetrate to Zanzibar and Cape S. Sebastian, 268; sheikhs of, at Malindi and Mozambique, 268; oppose Portuguese explorers, 271; Duarte Meneses opposes, in Morocco, 274; 10,000 put to death in one day, 275; dismay of, after victory of d'Almeida, 275; again vanquished, in second battle of

Portuguese in India, 276; war of Indian and Egyptian, against Portuguese, 278; Francesco d'Almeida triumphs over, 296; Henry VIII of England sends troops against, 340

Morea, Despots of the, despatched by Charles VIII against Turks, 76

Morgante, poem of, 321; burned in Florence, 121

Morocco, Duarte Meneses wages war on Moors of, 274

Moscow, Russians of, marvel at a knight as a wonder, 13

Mozambique, sheikh at, a Moor, 268; Portuguese explorers reach, 271; voyages made from, to India and Arabia, 271; Portuguese threatened with death at, 271

Mühldorf, battle of, 14

Muiden, prophecy of mermaid of, 285; taken by Charles of Gelderland, 285; restored to Maximilian, 286

Muley Yahya, King of Tenez, promises to be Ferdinand's vassal, 251

Munich, Albrecht of. See Albrecht

Munich, line of, 103

Münster, Ludovico Sforza awaits Maximilian at, 109

Münsterthal, dispute as to administration of the minster in the, 143

Murano, Venetian trade in glass of, 255

Murcia, subdued by Alfonso the Sage, 8

Muscovites, led by Wasiljewitsch against Poles, 100

Music, first publicly taught at Milan, 36

N

Najara, Manrique of, opposed to Ferdinand, 229, 241; anxious that Maximilian should administer Castile in name of Charles, 245; loses castles, 248

Naldi, Dionigi di, the Brisignels organised by, 289

Nancy, Strassburgers meet Charles the Bold before, 101

Naples, Kings of. *See* Alfonso I, Alfonso II, Ferrante, Ferrantino, and Federigo

Naples, Germanic life in, 6 ; sundered from Sicily, 14 ; Ferdinand of Spain will not ally himself with, 23–24 ; Charles VIII believes in right to, 25 ; Ludovico urges Charles to come to, 26 ; title and right of Jerusalem belong to crown of, 26 ; Queen of, at convent of San Piero as beggar, 30 ; Pope Innocent VIII desires possession of, 32 ; Pope does not recognise Ferrante as King of, 37 ; kingdom of, depends on European balance of power, 39 ; Charles VIII resolved to take possession of, 54–55 ; Ferrantino rides through, on resignation of Alfonso II, 58 ; Ferrantino in despair rushes from, 59 ; Charles VIII welcomed in, as Holy Crown, King, and Lord, 61 ; Charles brings into harmony nobles, citizens, and people of, 76 ; League ridiculed in comedy at, 78 ; feeling for Ferrantino in, 79 ; Swiss tumultuous in, 80 ; Ferrantino received in, 85 ; war in, 88–94 ; procession in, for two days, 91 ; Ferrantino with young wife in, 92–93 ; Ferdinand consults Pope, on claims to, 94 ; German auxiliaries defenders and conquerors of, 100 ; Louis XII styles himself King of, 137 ; partition of, by Louis and Ferdinand, 178 ; ill consequence of feuds between Pope and, 185 ; effects of papal authority in, 185 ; war between Spaniards and French in, 191–196, 202–208 ; Gonzalvo enters, 205 ; plots of Caesar Borgia concerning, 215 *n*. ; to be governed in name of Charles and Claude, 218 ; Ferdinand refuses to consign, to Charles and Claude, 226 ; Louis XII assigns rights in, to Germaine de Foix, 230 ; Ferdinand anxious about, 237 ; popularity of Gonzalvo in, 237 ; Ferdinand with wife Germaine rides through five Saggi of, 238–239 ; exiled counts and barons reinstated in, 239 ; Ferdinand real King of, 241 ; frontier of, to be readjusted by League of Cambray, 286 ; Venetian envoys sent to Ferdinand at, 295 ; Louis XII consents not to claim, 383

Napoli di Romania, delivered to Venetians, 256

Narsinga, King of, rejoices at Almeida's arrival in India, 274 ; once caused 10,000 Moors to be put to death on one day, 275 ; offers daughter to son of Dom Manuel, 275

Navarra, Count Pedro, retires with honours from Canosa, 192 ; risen from ranks, 194 ; personal characteristics of, 194 ; at Gaeta, against French, 205 ; lands with Ximenes at Oran, 250 ; victory of, at Oran ascribed to prayers of Ximenes, 251 ; sails from Iviza and takes Bugia, 251 ; takes Tripoli, 251 ; springs mines under Bologna, 329 ; gains point, in dispute with Fabrizio Colonna, 332 ; at battle of Ravenna, 332–336 ; taken prisoner, 336

Navarre, Caesar Borgia slain in, 217 ; Louis XII to desist from schemes against, 286 ; Ferdinand turns eyes to, 349 ; Marquis of Dorset with English in, 349 ; extent of kingdom of, 349 ; French and Spanish claims in, 350 ; on death of Gaston de Foix sovereigns call in Louis XII to resist Ferdinand, 350–351 ; Spanish conquest of, 351–353 ; to remain joined to Castile if Louis XII married Eleanor, 382 ; Louis consents not to support, 383

Nemours, Louis d'Armagnac, Duke of, at Melfi, 192 ; defeated and killed at battle of Cerignola, 204–205

Neopatri, claims of Ferdinand to, 297–298

Nepi occupied by French force, 212

Neri, the, at Florence contrasted with the Bianchi, 117

Nerli, a, opposes Piero de' Medici, 51

Netherlands, the, Maximilian lord of, 95; ruled by Philip, 111

Nielsen, Schwente, under ban of Empire, 228

Niflungasaga, preface to the, 11

Niquesa, appointed governor of Veragua, 250

Nola, surrender of, 88

Normandy, Robert of, leads first Crusade, 6; restored to France, 20; Ferdinand, Maximilian, and Henry VIII desire seizure of, from France, 369

Normans, the, 5; established in France and England, 6; part of, in first Crusade, 6; Crusades originate with, 7

Novara, allies intercept retreat of Charles VIII at, 79; Duke of Orleans shut in, 85; Duke of Orleans allowed to leave, 87; peace of, 87–88; besieged, 106; Ludovico besieges castle of, 162; Ludovico retires to, 164; Ludovico betrayed in,165–166; bravery of Swiss at, 365–366; battle of, 366; French raise siege of, 366; Massimiliano Sforza acknowledges achievements of Swiss at, 368

Novgorod, gates of cathedral of, 13

Nuñez, faction of the, 14; Najara head of, 241

Nuremberg, city of, against Landshut in war of Landshut succession, 223

O

Obwalden, arquebusiers of, take part in conquest of Genoa, 266

Ocampo, Runno de, takes Caesar Borgia prisoner, 217

Odasio, tutor of Guidobaldo of Urbino, 197

Oedenburg, accepts terms of Maximilian, 235

Oesel, German colony of, 10

Oglio, the Swiss to attack French at, 346

Olaf, St., first to adopt cross in war, 7

Oliverotto of Fermo, Caesar Borgia makes use of, 198; murders seven leading citizens of Fermo, 198; strangled, 201

Olmedo, battle of, 63

Olmo, Alviano posted in pass of, 379

Ommelande, the, Etzard Cirksena offers Georg of Saxony tribute for, 385

Onsernone, valley of, becomes Swiss, 362

Optimates, title of, taken by young men in Florence, 356

Oran, colonies established in, 18; kingdom of, claimed for Aragon, 68; captured by Ximenes and Pedro Navarra, 250–251; Ximenes consecrates mosque at, 251; Venetian trade in, 255

Orange, Prince of, regains sovereignty, 136

Ordelaffi, Pino, fortifies Forlì, 173

Orlando, Simone, 52

Orlando, poems of Boiardo and Ariosto on, 321

Orleans, Duke Louis of. *See* Louis

Orleans, Maid of, obligations of Charles VII to, 20

Orsini, family of, Innocent VIII supports, 38; reconciled to Alexander VI, 45; castles of, surrendered to Charles VIII, 56; opposed to Alexander VI, 93; Duke of Gandia murdered by, 122; in pay of Caesar Borgia, 186; made use of by Caesar, 198; revolt against Caesar, 198; Caesar makes treaty with, 199, 200; leaders of, treacherously taken by Caesar and slain, 200–201; houses of, pulled down and castles in hands of Pope, 201; appear again after Alexander's death, 211; Ferdinand wins over, 240; Cardinal de' Medici and, 355

Orsini, Alfonsina, wife of Piero de' Medici, 41

Orsini, Fabio (son of Paolo), kills one of Caesar's attendants and washes mouth in blood, 211

Orsini, Francesco, Duke of Gravina, 200

Orsini, Giambattista, Cardinal,

Alexander VI speaks of resigning in favour of, 199 ; invited by Caesar Borgia and made captive, 201 ; mistress of, brings pearl to the Pope, 201 ; murdered, 201

Orsini, Niccolò, Count of Pitigliano. *See* Pitigliano

Orsini, Paolo, troops of Charles VIII at Florence under, 51–52 ; interviews Caesar Borgia, 199 ; persuades friends to sign treaty, 199 ; imprisoned and murdered, 201

Orvieto, Giampalo Baglione meets Duke Guidobaldo in, 263

Osimo, ceded to Turks, 181

Osterett, commercial house of, at Antwerp, 277

Ostia, Cardinal Giuliano della Rovere banded with discontents at, 45 ; Caesar Borgia goes to, 215 ; Julius II accepts proposals of Holy League at, 323

Ostrogothic empire, fall of, 4

Otranto, raises Aragonese cry of " Fierro," 79 ; once in hands of Turks, 181 ; Angevin army in, vanquished, 207

P

Pacasto, Venetian trade in fiddle strings from, 255

Pace, Charles de la, 256

Pacheco, Juan. *See* Marquis of Villena

Padua, bones of Livy honoured at, 259 ; Venetians promise to retire from, 295 ; Imperialists in possession of, 299 ; people of, declare for Venice, 299 ; Loredano offers both sons for defence of, 300 ; Maximilian advances against, 300 ; Matthäus Lang demands, from Venice, 315 ; Venetians decline, as exchange for acknowledging Archduke Charles as suzerain, 343 ; Venetians retain, 360 ; Spanish and papal troops before, 370

Palatinate, line of Veldenz, of House of, 103 ; House of, unfriendly to Imperial House, 103 ; Maximilian

finds opportunity to destroy opposition of, 221 ; Friedrich, Arrogator of, had successfully resisted Emperor, 221 ; Württemberg, Veldenz, and Hesse against, regarding Landshut succession, 222 ; assailed on three sides, 223 ; " Junge Pfalz " founded by Maximilian, 225

Palatine, the Elector (Philip), on good terms with Charles VIII, 132, 221 ; Eberhard of Württemberg flees to, 133 ; letters of Louis XII to, 142 ; marries his son to daughter of Georg of Landshut, 221 ; Louis XII refuses help to, against Maximilian, 223 ; maintains armies at Heidelberg and Landshut, 223 ; death of Ruprecht, son of, 225 ; despair of, 225 ; appeals to Maximilian, who commands truce, 225

Palenzia, Alonso de, manuscript of, 62

Paleologi, rights of the, to Constantinople and Trebizond ceded to Charles VIII, 28

Palice, La, title of Marshal ʃfirst given to, by the Spaniards, 193 ; taken prisoner at Ruvo, 202 ; with Maximilian in Italy, 300 ; at battle of Ravenna, 334 ; Swiss intercept letter from, 346 ; summons council of war, 347 ; deprived of allies, 347 ; retreats, 347 ; surrenders at battle of the Spurs, 373

Pamplona, surrenders to Spaniards, 352 ; d'Albret begins siege of, 352 ; Alva arrives at, and d'Albret retires, 352

Pandino, encounter between Louis XII and Alviano at, 292

Panian, Moors await Portuguese in harbour of, 275

Papacy, founding of, 4 ; establishment of real power of, 4 ; represents Latin principle of union of nations, 6 ; struggle of, with Empire, 13 ; supported by English gold, 13 ; did not gain, by fall of Hohenstaufen, 13 ; falls into captivity of French kings, 13

Paris, trade guilds at, 374

Parma, citizens of, pledged to fight

against Infidels, 17; Lombards protect, against Charles VIII, 81; surrenders to Julius II, 348

Patras delivered to Venice, 256

Pavia, Jasone de Maino lectures in, 36; Duke Louis of Orleans invited to, 79; investiture of, for Louis XII, Charles, and Claude, 227; Swiss advance to, 347

Pavia, Francesco Alidosi, Cardinal of, despatched by Julius II against French, 312; character of, 312-313; commands papal troops in Bologna, 315; flies from Bologna, 316; assassinated by Duke of Urbino, 317

Paz, Pedro de la, a squinting, deformed dwarf, 194; vanquishes Angevin army, 207; at battle of Ravenna, 333

Pederasty in Italy, 319

Peloponnese, the, sends light Greek horse to Venice, 289

Penny, Common, tax of, 107; object of, 107; annual diet to watch over application of, 107; paid by abbots and ecclesiastics, 110; Maximilian's support from, 111; administered by the government of twenty, 168

Penthièvre, the, rights of, in Brittany purchased by Louis XI, 22

Pepuli, enemies of Bentivogli, at Bologna, 328

Pereira, Pacheco, war of, in defence of King of Cochin, 272; victory of, over the Zamorin, 273

Perrault, Cardinal, persuades people of Montefiascone to receive Charles VIII peacefully, 55

Persia, Indian trade by caravans in, 254; Dom Manuel styled lord of future conquests in, 272

Perugia, Caesar Borgia uses the Baglioni of, 198; Paolo Orsini brings peace proposals to, 199; falls into hands of Pope, 201; ruled by Giampaolo Baglione, 263; reduced to obedience by Julius II, 263

Pesaro, princes of, 29; princes of, forsake Ferrantino, 55; Turkish agents well received at, 181

Pescara, Alonso, Marquis of, Ferrantino enters Naples with, 85; famous leader, 195

Pescara, Fernando, Marquis of, taken prisoner at battle of Ravenna, 336; valour of, at battle near Creazzo, 379

Peschiera, stormed by Louis XII, 294; reconquered by Swiss, 368

Peter, the Cruel, 15

Petrucci, Antonello, intimate counsellor of Ferrante, 30; enriched by Ferrante, 31; Alfonso considers wealth of, to belong to him, 32; put to death, 33

Petrucci, Pandolfo, chief of municipality of Siena, 187; allied with Alexander VI, 187; Caesar Borgia compels Sienese to expel, 202; offers services to Gonzalvo, 213

Petrucci, Cardinal (son of Pandolfo Petrucci), devoted to Cardinal de' Medici, 361

Pfäffers, Abbot of, 143

Pfirt, Friedrich Cappeler von, brings 10,000 Germans across Alps, 85-86

Philip, Archduke (son of Maximilian), marries Juana, daughter of Ferdinand, 100; rules Netherlands, 111; Maximilian discloses plans to, 111; never inclined for peace, 142; reception of, with Juana in Spain, 188; compact of, with Louis XII, for marriage of children, Charles and Claude, 189; journey of, through France; 189; treaty of, with Louis, 218; Ferdinand orders commander-in-chief to disregard orders from, 218; on bad terms with Ferdinand, 218; anxiety of, causes illness, 219; recovers, and concludes alliance with Louis XII, 219; induces father to join alliance, 219; gains Gelderland, 227; assumes royal title of Castile on death of Isabella, 227; meets Maximilian in Brabant, 230; on voyage to Spain driven by storm to Weymouth, 231; welcomed by Henry VII, 231; surrenders Suffolk to Henry, who swears to aid him, 231; embarks for

Corunna, 231; supported by nobles, 232; Ximenes arranges meeting between Ferdinand and, 233; Ferdinand renounces government of Castile to, 233–234; cities of Castile open gates to, 234; hears with indignation of renewal of war in Netherlands, 236; dies at Burgos, 237; jealousy of Juana concerning, 241; Juana takes corpse of, with her, 244, and gives audiences round coffin of, 244

Philip, Count Palatine. *See* Palatine

Philip the Fair, subjection of Pope to, 20

Philip of Ravenstein, brings troops for Charles VIII's expedition to Italy, 28; surrenders Sluys to Maximilian, 96; governor of Milan, 157

Philippe de Bresse, uncle of Duke of Savoy, 47; attacks Genoa, 80; becomes Duke of Savoy and marries Margaret, daughter of Maximilian, 189; demands Cyprus, 298

Piacenza, surrenders to Julius II, 348

Pianosa, Caesar Borgia takes, 175

Pico, Galeotto, Count of Mirandola, Countess Francesca, widow of, defends Mirandola against Julius II, 313

Piccolomini, Cardinal (Pope Pius III), election and death of, 212

Piedmont, French kings suzerains in, 47

Pietrasanta granted by Piero de' Medici to Charles VIII, 51

Pimentel. *See* Benevente

Piombino gained by Caesar Borgia, 175–176

Pisa, Politian lectures in, 36; surrendered by Piero de' Medici to Charles VIII, 50–51; Charles VIII enthusiastically received in, 52; no annals of, since day of enslavement, 53; youths of, bring offerings to Charles, 55; Charles greeted by inhabitants of, 100; Swiss offer to forego pay if liberty of, guaranteed, 80; attacked by Florence, 108; citadel given up to people of, 108; supported by Ludovico and Venetians, 109; Florentine influence over, 113; Florentines again attack, 138; Venice supports, 138; Florentines take castles round, 138; envoys from, offer city of, to Caesar Borgia, 209; Pope bent on subduing, 209; people of, offer services to Gonzalvo, 213; Venetians nearly masters of, 259; schismatic Cardinals open Council in, 331; Florentines lay siege to, 353; Paolo Vitelli put to death for failure to take, 353; Florentines conquer, 354; new Council summoned at, 354

Pisani, Giorgio, Venetian ambassador, Julius II goes with, to Cività Vecchia, 287

Pistoia, Florentine power over, 113

Pitigliano, Niccolò Orsini, Count of, escapes from French captivity, 83; at battle of Fornovo, 83; Venetians win over, 138; commander-in-chief of Venetian forces, 289–290; relations of, with Alviano, 290, 292; at battle of Agnadello, 292–294

Pius II, won over by Ferrante, 30; an enemy of the French, 212

Pius III, election and death of, 212

Plantagenets of Anjou, the, 20

Po, Lombards oppose Charles VIII on the, 81

Poland, Grandmaster of Prussia refuses allegiance to King of, 189

Pole, Edmund de la. *See* Earl of Suffolk

Poles, Muscovites led by Wasiljewitsch against, 100

Politian (Angelo Ambrogini), brilliant lectures of, 36

Polo, Marco, on "Sypango," 63

Pomerania, German stock of new inhabitants of, 9; claims of Brandenburg princes to, 15

Pondormy, cavalry of, at battle of Ravenna, 336

Pontremoli, Swiss pillage and murder at, 80

Pope, Anglo-Saxons recognise as Patriarch, 4; Boniface subject to, 4; Charlemagne frees, from Lombard enmity, 5; becomes ecclesiastical head of Latins and Teutons, 5; subjected to Philip the Fair, 20; office of, given to Cardinal who promises most, 41; provision of, for sons and nephews, 42; Savonarola teaches that the pious must not give way to a wicked and ignorant, 125; general sketch of position of, 169-170

Popolari, the, at Florence, attack Pisa, 108; struggle of, with Arrabbiati, 125; chose leader called King, 157; gain upper hand on fall of Ludovico, 157; make proposals to Caesar Borgia, 199; organize insurrection at Genoa, 265; enjoy extended influence in Florence, 353; Pisa subjected by, 353; humbled but not suppressed, 358; await arrival of French in order to rise, 358

Porcupine, selected for symbol by Louis XII, 136

Portenau, falls into hands of Venetians, 284

Portugal, kingdom of, founded, 8; originally fief of crown of Castile, 14; part taken by, in war for succession of Castile, 63-64; to be at liberty to conquer Fez, 68; navigation rights of, 68, 70; Isabella demands expulsion of Jews from, 129; Maximilian asserts claims to, 228; Venetians hope for fall of power of, in East, 278

Portuguese, expeditions of, to the East, 270-278; merchants at Antwerp; 277; masters of the Indian Ocean, 296

Posilippo, Charles VIII at Grotto of, 77

Pouderoyen, Charles of Gelderland encamped in castle of, 285; Prince of Anhalt seizes, 285

Prato, Spaniards pillage, 357

Préjean, French galleys under, 202

Pressburg, Maximilian reduces, 235

Prester John, King Manuel gives Vasco da Gama letters for, 270

Prie, Aymar de, twenty shields under standard of, attack Gonzaga, 83

Priego, Marquis of. See Aguilar, Pedro de

Priuli, Matteo, proposes giving up of towns subject to Venice, 295

Provençals, at enmity with Catalans, 14; take Naples, 71

Provence, St. Louis possesses himself of, 20; comes to French crown, 21

Pulgar, Fernando del, statement of, regarding Torquemada, 65

Purkhard, Georg, Maximilian defeats, as marksman, 97

Pusterli, the, disaffection of, against Duchess Bona of Milan, 34

Q

Quadrata, taken by French, 192

Quemadero, Isabella of Spain erects, on plain before Seville, 65

Quiloa, Moorish king of, 268

Quiñones, Don Diego, killed at battle of Ravenna, 336

Quintana, confidant of Almazan, confers with Louis XII, 382

R

Rabot, Jean, master of petitions to Charles VIII, 53; in Naples, 85

Ramazotto, at battle of Ravenna, 336

Randeck, Burkard von, falls at battle of Swaderloch, 147

Rapallo, Aragonese occupy, 46; sack of, by Swiss under Charles VIII, 80; assaulted by Genoese, 84

Raphael, portrait of Julius II by, 262; painting by, in the Camera della Segnatura, 349

Räuber, Hans, surrenders to Venetians in S. Veit am Pflaum, 284

Ravenna, Julius II at, 317; murder of Cardinal of Pavia at, 317; battle of, 332-337

Ravenstein, Hans von, commands contingent of Germans at Manfredonia, 203

Ravenstein, Philip of. See Philip

Recarred, becomes Catholic, 2

Rechtergem, Nicholas, the first to do business in Antwerp with Portuguese merchants, 277

Reding, Amman, calf christened as, at Bendre, 144

Regency, Council of (*Reichsregiment*), 105; Maximilian rejects, 106; intended composition of, 107; Maximilian agrees to establishment of, 168; passes resolutions which are not enforced, 219; origin of idea of, 225

Regensburg, Maximilian victorious at, 224; Wolf von Wolfstall and other Imperial commissioners at, 384

Reggio, Gonzalvo advances from, 89; Spaniards from, at battle of Seminara, 203; papal army unable to take, 309–310

Reiniger, Bernhardt, courage of, 284

René of Anjou, appoints nephew Charles as heir, 21

René of Lorraine, grandson of René of Anjou, 21; Maximilian acts in interests of, 111; tribunal decides against claims of, to Provence, 137

Renée, younger daughter of Louis XII, 381; Louis makes over Duchy of Milan to, 381; treaty for marriage of, to grandson of Ferdinand, 381

Reuchlin, Johann, favourite pupil of Demetrius Chalkondylas, 36

Rhine, Lower, Charles of Gelderland successfully opposes Maximilian on the, 285

Riario, Girolamo, marries Caterina Sforza, 35; fall of (assassinated 1488), 172–173

Rienzi, Cola di, Italian zealot, 16

Rimini, Venetians purchase, from the Malatesta, 213; Venetians to support Julius II if he ratifies possession of, 263; Julius occupies, 294; Venetians again invite Julius to occupy, 295; Julius brought to, in deep distress, 317

Rinucceneti, friends of the Bentivogli, at Bologna, 311

Rivolta, Venetians drive suspicious persons from, 291; Louis XII takes, 292

Robert of Normandy, leader in first Crusade, 6

Robert de la Mark, the "boar of the Ardennes," 364; at battle of Novara, 367

Robertet, Florimond, remark of, on seeing portrait of Amboise, 310

Rocca Guglielma, 93; falls from French hands to Spanish, 205

Rocquebertin, French envoy, defrays expenses of strangers in Baden, 281

Roeux, Bishop of, French envoy at Lucerne, 282

Rogendorf, Captain, serving under Maximilian, 370

Roger, King of Sicily, possessions of, 8

Romagna, the, Caesar's campaigns in, 172–176, 196–198; Louis XII wishes to make Caesar Borgia King of, 208–209; flight of Caesar's adherents from, 211; Venetians invade, 213, 259–260; infantry from, for Venice, 289

Rome, Rienzi establishes republican government in, 16; Ferrantino advances towards, 55; Charles VIII enters, 56; bad conduct of Swiss troops in, 80; Maximilian desires to receive Imperial crown in, 236; Spanish knight brings news of battle of Ravenna to, 337; revolt of populace in, 337–338; ablaze with torches for "liberation of Italy," 348

Roncal, valleys of, not included in Alva's conquests in Navarre, 352

Rosa, Monte, range from Wormser Joch to, becomes Swiss, 362

Rosendaal, Charles of Gelderland subjects himself to Archduke Philip at, 227

Roses, Wars of the, 14, 338

Rouen, Gothic architecture of cathedral of, 12; Georges d'Amboise, Archbishop of, 136

Roussillon, Ferdinand of Spain receives back, 23, 70, 71; restoration of, in vain, 77; Ferdinand to invade France from, 111; Ferdinand's apprehension for, 131; French and Spanish opposed on borders of, 207–208

Röust, Marx, tells of invisible hands

striking blows at Diet at Baden, 363

Rovere, Giuliano della, Cardinal, flies from Pope and Aragonese, 26; in disfavour with Innocent VIII, 37-38; opposes Borgia, 42; alarmed by alliance of Alexander VI and Alfonso II, 44-45; suspicions of Pope during visit to, 45; bands himself with discontents at Ostia, 45; sails to France, 45; obliged to come to terms with the Pope, 122; had opposed three popes, 212; elected Pope, 213 (see Julius II)

Rovere, Francesco Maria della, Duke of Urbino. See Urbino

Roveredo besieged by Friedrich of Brandenburg, 281

Rucellai, Cosimo, hears that Gian Galeazzo has been poisoned, 48; more qualified for scientific and poetic discourse than active service, 356; followers of, admit the Medici, 357.

Rudolf of Anhalt. See Anhalt

Runno de Ocampo makes Caesar Borgia prisoner, 217

Ruprecht, son of Philip, Elector Palatine, marries daughter of Duke Georg of Bavaria-Landshut, 221; succession of Landshut claimed for, 221; appears before Estates to urge claims, 221-222; Maximilian proposes arrangement for, 222; wife of, takes possession of Munich and part of Landshut territory, 222; dies during war, 225; Maximilian founds "Junge Pfalz " for children of, 225

Russi, papal troops take, from Venice, 291

Rütli, legend of men who formed Confederation on the, 363

Ruvo, taken by Gonzalvo, 202

S

Sabina, niece of Maximilian, wife of Duke Ulrich of Württemberg, 133

Sagdars, archers from Crete, 289

St. Aubin, Louis of Orleans defeated at, 22

St. Denis, standard of, 12; Charles VIII has body of, brought into church from vault, 47; Charles pays his vow in church of, 87

St. Jean-Pied-de-Port, 349; taken by Duke of Alva, 352

St. Malo, Archbishop of, letter from, to Queen Anne, 56 n.

St.Sebastian, Cape,Moors penetrate to, 268

S. Veit am Pflaum, Hans Räuber surrenders to Venetians in, 284

Salic law, Maximilian proposes repeal of, in France, 228

Salinas, Count of, 63

Salonika, delivered to Venetians, 256

Salsas, castle of, taken by the French, 131; Ferdinand orders cannon to be ready when Philip visits, 218

Sancia, daughter of Alfonso II, to marry Gioffredo Borgia, 44

Sancho the Wise, King of Navarre, 350

San Domingo, Spanish colony in, 250

San Germano, Ferrantino joins his army at pass of, 58; citizens of, unable to resist French longer, 59

San Giovanni held by Alfonso Davalos, 59; stormed and gained by Charles VIII, 59

San Leo, castle of, taken from Caesar Borgia, 198

Sannazzaro, reinstated by Ferdinand at Margolina, 239

Sanseverino, family of, in war against House of Aragon, 32; execution of members of family of, 33; on side of French, 192; Ferdinand and, 239

Sanseverino, Antonello, Prince of Salerno, 33

Sanseverino, Francesco, Ludovico Sforza summons, to help Galeazzo, 153; treachery of, 153

Sanseverino, Galeazzo, throws himself into Alessandria, 153; obtains permission to march out, and escapes across Po, 153; army of, annihilated, 153; presents himself to Ludovico Sforza at Novara, 165-166

Sanseverino, Count Marsico of,

Ferrante's brother-in-law, 30; Salerno made over to, 30; leagued with Francesco Coppola, 32

San Severo, cattle being driven to, taken by Stradioti from French, 91

Santa Cruz, Cardinal of, Caesar Borgia under care of, 215 *n.*; Gonzalvo sends message to, 215 *n.*

Santa Maura taken from the Turks but restored, 184

Santiago, order of, 66

Santo Spirito, French troops in plains of, 84

Sapienza, Turks defeat Christians at, 182

Saragossa, Queen Isabella dies at, 188; bishops, Ricoshombres, and deputies at, assure succession to Philip and Juana, 188; Jurado of, prepares to resist Ferdinand, 232

Sarno, Swiss repulsed at, 88

Sarzana and Sarzanella surrendered by Peiro de' Medici to Charles VIII, 51; Ludovico Sforza tries to obtain, 72

Sauli, house of, in Genoa, Charles VIII borrows money from, 47

Savonarola, Girolamo, prophesies coming of great king, 51, 117; interviews Charles VIII, 54; reassures, but warns, Charles, 78; account of, 114 *et seq.*; extracts from sermons of, 115-116; theory of government of, 117; Florentine constitution of, 118; popularity and influence of, 119; Florentines believe in prophetic mission of, 120; great number of children communicants due to, 120, influence of, in Ferrara, 121; head of enemies of the League and the Pope, 122; invites Charles VIII and Ferdinand to reform Church, 122; Mariano de Genazzano preaches against, 122; Signoria of Florence apply to, 123; allows his own law to be broken, against his opponents, 123-124; interdicted from preaching and summoned by Pope to Rome, 124; excommunicated, 124; his pulpit soiled, 124; publishes "Triumphus Crucis," 125; Franciscans challenge to ordeal by fire, 126;

result of the ordeal, 126-127; confessions by, on rack, afterwards denied, 127; visions of, 128; hanged and body burnt, 128

Savorgnano taken prisoner by Bernhardt Reiniger, 284

Savoy, Duke of. *See* Philippe de Bresse

Savoye, black charger of Charles VIII, 82

Saxons, at enmity with Franks, 4; unite with Danes and Westphalians against Slavs, 9; Western Pomeranians called Saxons by Eastern, 10

Saxony, Estates of the realm in, 17; Duke of, holds Maximilian's sword at Diet of Worms, 99; line of Dresden of House of, 103; in arms against Landshut, 223

Saxony, Duke Georg of, vanquishes Frisians, 385, devastates Damm, 385

Schaffhausen, Maximilian agrees to conference at, 151

"Scharfe Metze," great mortar, used by Maximilian, 300

Schaul, Mir Hossein defeats Lourenço d'Almeida in harbour of, 296

Schinner, Matthäus, Bishop of the Valais, Julius II concludes alliance with Swiss through, 307; feud of Jürg uff der Flue with, 324; ascetic life of, 324; shrewd and singularly well informed, 325; courier drowned carrying letter to Pope from, 325; made Cardinal, 326; forced to fly to Italy, 326; mocked at in carnival play by Diesbachs of Bern, 344

Schlaberndorf, Fabian von, at battle of Ravenna, 335

Schütt, Maximilian takes island of, 235

Schwaderloch, battle of, 146-147

Schwend, Rudolph, of Zurich, 28

Schwyz, earliest treaty of, with Uri, 102; allied with Ludovico Sforza, 141; joins League, 145; deputies of, help to draw up letter to Julius II, 309; calls on members of Confederation to take arms against France, 326

Schwyzers, 1500, begin ascent of St. Gotthard, 327 ; zealous in papal cause, 327

Scotland, Pedro de Ayala negotiates in, 130 ; with France and Venice confronts Emperor, Pope, Spain, England, and Switzerland, 368 ; Margaret (Regent of Netherlands) undertakes government of, 377

Scots, rebellion of, against English, 15 ; bodyguard of, for Aubigny, at battle of Seminara, 203

Seelisberg, legend of men who formed Confederation watching from the, 362

Seminara, battle of, 203

Senlis, peace of, 23

Sessa, Gonzalvo throws bridge across Garigliano at, 206

Seville subdued by St. Ferdinand, 8 ; Isabella presides at tribunals at, 64 ; Isabella has Quemadero, erected on plain before, 65 ; Dominican convent in, will not hold all accused of heresy, 65 ; market for Florence, 113 ; picture of Maria Antigua at, gives name to colony on Darien, 250

Sforza, family of, at Milan, 29 ; friendly with the Medici, 34 ; Pope nominates three Cardinals in interest of the, 43 ; claims of, to Milan, challenged by Duke Louis of Orleans, 73 ; French assist Pope against, in the Romagna, 157 ; privileges enjoyed by Grisons from the, 159 ; house of, extinguished, 180 ; achievements of, for Italy, 180

Sforza, Ascanio, 34; opposes Rodrigo Borgia, 42 ; is bribed and gives way, 42 ; keeps Ghibellines on side of Ludovico, 140 ; French fly from, at Como, 160 ; besieges castle of Milan, 162 ; announces capture of Ludovico, 167 ; imprisoned at Bourges, 168 ; released to vote at papal election, 212 ; calls Italy the " inner court in house of the world," 297

Sforza, Caterina, marries Girolamo Riario, 35 ; Caesar Borgia makes war on, 173 ; not supported by Florence or Milan, 173 ; commands citadel of Forlì against Caesar's

attack, 173 ; captured and brought before Caesar, 174 ; afterwards lives many years in Florence, 174

Sforza, Francesco, father of Ludovico, Lord of Milan, 37, 54, 180 ; had restored Val Leventina to Uri, 159 ; fate of five sons of, 167 ; star of, means disaster for descendants, 168

Sforza, Francesco, son of Ludovico, sent into Germany, 154

Sforza, Galeazzo Maria, Duke of Milan, murder of, 34

Sforza, Gian Galeazzo, mother of, governs in name of, 34 ; gives himself into power of Ludovico, 35 ; betrothed to Isabella of Aragon, 39 ; schemes of Ludovico against, 40 ; devotion of people of Milan to, 46 ; death of, attributed to Ludovico, 48

Sforza, Giovanni, lord of Pesaro, marries Lucrezia Borgia, 43 ; marriage annulled by the Pope, 171 ; flees to Venice on approach of Caesar Borgia, 174

Sforza, Ludovico, il Moro, urges Charles VIII to invade Italy, 26, 43 ; position of, after murder of his brother Galeazzo Maria, 34 ; agitates with Ascanio against action of Duchess Bona and is driven out, 34 ; returns and takes over conduct of affairs, 34 ; allies himself with Sixtus IV, 35 ; Venice well disposed to, 35 ; young Duke declares against his mother on initiative of, 35 ; shares sovereign power with Eustachio, 35 ; acquires sole authority, 35 ; kind and affable, 35 ; patronises the arts, 36 ; court of, 36 ; farm of, at Vigevene, 36 ; Lorenzo de' Medici ally of, 37 ; marries Beatrice d'Este, 39-40 ; marries Isabella of Aragon to nephew, Gian Galeazzo Sforza, 39 ; declares sovereignty belongs to him rather than to Gian Galeazzo, 40 ; Alfonso II calls upon to retire from government, 41 ; alliances and relations of, 43 ; Alexander VI leagued with, 43 ; attacked by Alfonso II, 45 ; meets Charles VIII at Asti, 47 ; takes complete possession of

Milan, 48 ; death of Gian Galeazzo ascribed to, 48 ; proclaimed Duke, 48 ; Ferdinand and Isabella offer alliance to, 72 ; differences arise between Charles VIII and, 72 ; Louis of Orleans claims Milan from, 73 ; addresses himself to Maximilian, 73 ; joins league against France, 74 ; new taxes of, excite people of Milan and Pavia, 79, who invite Louis of Orleans, 79 ; asks good services of Venetian envoy, 79 ; bids Genoa be ready, 80 ; opposed to battle at Fornovo, 82 ; reviews German troops, 85–86 ; concludes peace with Charles VIII, 87 ; has no intention of helping French in Naples, 88 ; helps Ferrantino to victory, 91 ; reconciled to Federigo, 93 ; takes part of Pisa against Florence, 109 ; transfers war to Emperor, 109 ; awaits Maximilian at Münster, 109 ; Venice in feud with, regarding ؛ isa, 135 ; when Florentines again attack Pisa, takes side of assailants, 138 ; indignation of Venice against, owing to failure of campaign, 139 ; not dismayed by failure of plans, 139 ; has faith in own cleverness, 139 ; accepts advice from astrologer, 140 ; allied with Swiss Cantons, 141 ; coins of, 141 ; close alliance of, with Maximilian, 142 ; desires to mediate between Swabians and Swiss, 145 ; deprived, as ally of Maximilian, of Swiss aid, 149 ; sends Galeazzo Visconti to Bern, 149 ; French throw themselves on, 151 ; sees fate approaching, 151 ; Trivulzio opposed to, 151 ; Guelph favourites of, go over to Trivulzio, 152 ; treachery of Francesco Sanseverino towards, 153 ; feelings of Milanese to, unreliable, 154 ; sends sons with treasure to Germany, 154 ; commits government to twelve Ghibellines, 154 ; visits his wife's grave, 154 ; goes to Como, 155 ; addresses people of Como, 155 ; crosses frontier into Germany, 156 ; believes himself sure of Milan, 158 ; makes peace with Swiss Cantons, 158 ; avails himself of state of affairs in Uri, 159 ; promises Bellinzona and Val Bregna to people of Uri, 159 ; at Innsbruck, hears of revulsion of feeling in Milan, 161 ; crosses Alps, 162 ; received in triumph at Como, 162 ; met by nobles before gates of Milan, 162 ; assisted by brother Tommaso, 162 ; besieges castle of Novara while Ascanio besieges Milan, 162 ; Maximilian represents him as vassal of Empire, 163 ; promises advantages to Swiss if they rid him of king, 164 ; opposes Swiss to Swiss who refuse to fight, 164 ; retires to Novara, 164 ; captains of, go over to enemy, 165 ; in embarrassment negotiates with French leaders, 165 ; endeavours to escape in disguise, 166 ; betrayed by a man of Uri, 166ᵗ; taken prisoner and imprisoned at Loches, 167–168 ; the Pope gives 100 ducats to messenger announcing captivity of, 174

Sforza, Massimiliano, sent into Germany, 154 ; fourteen years' exile of, 359 ; Julius II favours instalment of, at Milan, 360, 363 ; weak and in hands of Imperial councillors, 360 ; receives key of Milan from the Swiss and enters the city, 363 ; dependent on the Swiss, 364 ; flies to Novara on approach of French, 365 ; calculations on alarm of, 383

Sforza, Tommaso, brother of Ludovico, follows him into Italy, 162

Sicily, Goths in, 4 ; King Roger of, 8 ; sundered from Naples, 14 ; Tunis and eastern slope of Atlas claimed for, 68

Siena, Gothic architecture of cathedral of, 12 ; Charles VIII enters, 55 ; factions in, 78 ; Charles leaves garrison at, 78 ; bad discipline of Swiss at, 80 ; Pope opposes union of, with Florence, 209 ; receives garrison of 100 Spanish lances, 359

Sigismund of Poland, Christian II

of Denmark opposes claims of, 385

Sigurd of Norway earns name of "Jörsalafar," 7

Sila, La, conquered by Gonzalvo, 89

Silesia, Germans inhabit, 9

Silk yarn, sent by China to Malacca, 269; factories in Florence, 113

Simnel, Lambert, 130

Sinibaldo de' Sinibaldi, dies of grief at the election of Pope Alexander VI, 42

Sinigaglia, Caesar Borgia orders barons against, 200; surrenders castle to Caesar, 200; flies to arms, headed by Cardinal Giuliano della Rovere, 211

Sixtus IV, Pope, Ludovico Sforza allies himself with, 35; gives Ferdinand and Isabella right to appoint inquisitors, 64

Slavs, influence of, 3; irruption of, 4; practically exterminated west of Oder, 9

Slavonic nations, Christianized, 5; adopt Greek form of worship, 5-6; Danes, Saxons, and West-phalians leagued against, 9

Sluys, loss of, by Philip of Raven-stein, 28, 96

Smalandic heathen, coerced into Christianity, 9

Soave, taken from Venetians, 318

Soderini, Francesco, Cardinal, sent by Julius to Caesar Borgia, 216; gives way at election of Cardinal de' Medici as Pope, 361

Soderini, Piero, perpetual Gonfalo-niere, at Florence, 353; mocked at by Optimates, 356; refuses 100,000 ducats demanded by Matthäus Lang, 356; character of, 356; Cardona declares himself against, 357; summons Grand Council who declare in his favour, 357; compelled by followers of Rucellai to fly, 357

Sofala, large sums received by King of Quiloa from, 268

Solothurn, Nicholas Conrad, bailiff of, 150; castle of, threatened by landsknechts, 151

Somerset, Charles, in suite of Henry VIII, 371

Sonwald, Alexander the Black of Veldenz lies in wait at, 223

Sora, nephew of Sixtus IV invested with, by Ferrante, 30; uncon-quered, with Charles VIII as suzerain, 93-94; subjected by Gonzalvo, 123

South Sea, Balboa sails from Darien to find the, 386

Spagnuoli, visions of the monk, 27

Spain, intermarriages in, 2; factions of the Nuñez and Gamboa in, 14; wane of English power in, 16; consolidated into powerful king-dom, 62; Inquisition in, 64-65; alliance of, with Italy, 71-75; rivalry of monarchy of, with that of France, 88; strict ceremonial at court of, 187; quarrel of, with Austria, 218; monarchy of, seems likely to embrace Europe, 386

Spalato, in Dalmatia, delivered over to Venice, 256

Spet, Johann, Germans under, at Brescia, 330; at battle of Ra-venna, 335

Spices, Portuguese desire to reach land of, 68; Thousand Isles send to Malacca, 269; four barks bring, from Calicut to Lisbon, 277; fall in price of, detrimental to Vene-tians, 278

Spinello, Neapolitan envoy, 74-75; office of accountant of realm taken from and restored to, 240

Spurs, battle of the, 372-373

Stanga, Conradin, prepares to de-fend Genoa, 80; recalled, 157

Stapfer, Jacob, Swiss under com-mand of, 345

State of the Church, dependent on idea of supreme hierarchy, 39; League of Cambray to readjust frontier of, 286

"State," appellation of, 38

Stradioti, join Ferrantino, 91; lay waste country estates, 119

Strassburg, French form of oath pre-scribed at, 6; architecture at, 12

"Strauss," great mortar of Maxi-milian, 300

Stuart, Matthew, 28

Sture, Sten, Swedish General, 187

Stürzler, Doctor, Chancellor of Mainz, Maximilian tries to win over, 132 ; Maximilian takes into service, 225

Styria, call to arms sent throughout, 283 ; men of, plead preoccupation with Hungarians, 284

Sudan, Venetian trade in interior of, 255

Suez, Soldan of Egypt fits out fleet at, 278

Suffolk, Earl of (Edmund de la Pole), Archduke Philip obliged to give up, to Henry VII, 231 ; Henry VIII puts to death, 339

Sulz, Gabriel von, mines of, under Bologna, 329

Surrey, Earl of, border counties in charge of, 375 ; son of, lands with force at Newcastle, 375

Suzanne, daughter of Anne of Bourbon, 136

Swabia prayers for peace throughout, 148-149 ; against Landshut in war of Landshut succession, 223 ; troops of, join French against Maximilian, 364

Swabian League, the, 102 ; Tyrol calls to its assistance, 144 ; Maximilian appeals to, 282

Swabians, the, war of, with Swiss, 141 et seq. ; boasts of, 146 ; everywhere at disadvantage, 148 ; force of, sent by Maximilian to Padua, 370

Sweden, German auxiliary troops in, 100 ; John of Denmark claims, 131 ; Danish expedition against, foiled by Sten Sture, 187 ; leaders of, under ban of Empire, 228

Swedes, led by St. Eric against Finns, 9 ; in army of Frederick I invading Italy, 13

Swiss contend with Swabians, though both are Alemanni, 14 ; in field with Duke of Orleans, 79 ; with Charles VIII in retreat, 80 ; feeling roused against, 80 ; offer to forego pay if liberty of Pisa guaranteed, 80 ; harness themselves to cannon, 80-81 ; led by La Trémouille, 81 ; with Engilbert's Germans, 82 ; Charles VIII despatches to Provence, 86 ; in Charles's camp at Vercelli, 86 ; unwillingly submit to terms of peace, 87 ; repulsed at Sarno, 88 ;

war of, against Maximilian and the Swabian League, 144 et seq. ; united for war, 145 ; make treaty with Louis XII, 145 ; everywhere successful against Swabians, 148 ; Maximilian assembles army against, 149 ; peace made at Basel, 158 ; Cantons return to dissensions on conclusion of peace, 158 ; characteristics of, 163 ; enlisted on opposite sides, 163-164; Ludovico makes offer to, 164; those in Ludovico's pay go over to enemy, 165 ; called cattle-vultures, 206 ; cross St. Gotthard to defend Bellinzona, 220 ; support of, for Maximilian, 280 ; French party among, gain upper hand, 281 ; Julius looks to, 305 ; gain zenith of renown in war and politics, 305 ; position of, in 1509, 305 ; Louis XII abandons alliance with, 305 ; join Louis in war with Venice, 306 ; life without war impossible for, 306 ; Julius II first Pope to have, as papal guard, 307 ; Maximilian's warning to, regarding Pope, 308 ; majority of Cantons guarantee French embassy safe conduct, 308 ; resolve to detain army sent to aid of Pope, 309 ; retreat of troops, 309 ; join Holy League, 324 ; factions in Cantons, 324 ; aroused against Maximilian, 326; prepare for war against France, 326 ; cross St. Gotthard with artillery, 327 ; repulsed, 328 ; seized with "German mania," and retreat ravaging country, 328 ; resolve on war against France, 344 ; set out to aid Pope, 344-345 ; receive at Verona hat, sword, consecrated banner, and each man a ducat, 345 ; join Venetians at Valeggio, 345 ; determine to attack enemy on the Oglio, 346 ; enter Cremona and Pavìa, 347 ; obtain possession of Milan, 348 ; Julius II owes eternal gratitude to, 349 ; stand between French and Austrians, who covet Milan, 362 ; have considerable tracts of Milanese territory, 362 ; make alliance with Massimiliano

Sforza, 363; Louis XII offers peace and alliance to, 363; retire before the French, 365; Trivulzio boasts prematurely of power over, 365; bravery of, at Novara, 365; victorious in battle of Novara, 366–368; compel payment from Asti, Savoy, and Montferrat, 368; acquiesce in plan to take Burgundy, Normandy, and Guienne, 369; march into France, 373; alarm in France caused by arrival of, 374; form three camps before Dijon, 377; terms of peace and payment for, 377; compact between France and Spain to drive back, 383

Sword, Knights of the, 10

Sybang, Christopher Columbus speaks of land called, 70

Sypango, of Marco Polo, 68

Syphilis, scourge in Italy, 319

T

Talbot, George, in suite of Henry VIII in France, 371

Tancred, operations of Bohemond of Tarentum against, 7

Taranto, ancient prophecies of destruction of Ferrante's race said to be found in, 43; has permission to select syndic from middle class, 76; an unconquered city, 93; Gonzalvo takes, 123; flies Venetian colours in vain, 123

Taro, the, Charles VIII at springs of, 81; runs red with blood, 83

Tavoliera, royal meads of, 90

Tedelitz, surrenders to Spain, 251

Templars, the, 11

Ten Jurisdictions, the, 143

Térouanne, English siege of, 370; Maximilian joins Henry VIII before, 372; surrenders, 373; James IV of Scotland summons Henry VIII from, 375

Terracina, designs of Charles VIII on, 56

Terranova, Spaniards confront French near, 203

Terzagi, family of, have Guelph proclivities, 35

Teutonic element in Germans, English, and Scandinavians, 2

Teutonic nations, Athaulf hopes to combine with Romans of West, 1; union of, with Romans effected later, 1; adopt Roman law, 1; Pope ecclesiastical head of, 5; development in, 12; summary of position of, 185

Thiengen, landsknechts retire from, in shirts, 148

Thur, Hans, surrenders to Venetians, 284

Thuringian kingdom, destruction of, 4; wars of succession lay waste, 14

Timbuctoo, women of, wear Venetian veils, 255

Tingitana, Castile claims, 68; quarrel about, 70

Tlemcen claimed for crown of Aragon, 68; tribute paid by King of, 251; great Venetian trade in, 255

Toledo, Ferdinand and Isabella found convent at, 64; succession assured to Philip and Juana at, 188; feud between Ayalas and Silvas at, 245

Tordesillas, Archduchess Juana removed from, 244 n.

Toro, Ferdinand and Isabella victorious at, 64

Torquemada, Tomas de, representations of, bring about Inquisition, 64–65

Tortoles, Ferdinand meets Archduchess Juana at, 248

Tortona, fugitives from Milan come to, 34; Charles VIII crosses dyke of, 85; lost to Ludovico Sforza, 152

Tosa, valley of the, becomes Swiss, 362

Tournay, Henry VIII enters, in character of King of France, 378; Henry builds castle at, 378; to be restored by treaty to France, 383

Tours, request made in, for betrothal of Claude to Francis of Angoulême, 236; clergy assemble for consultation at, 310

Trade, Florentine, 113–114; Venetian, 253–255; danger to Venetian, 268; decay of Venetian, 270;

Florentine houses participate in shipping, 277

Trani, Federigo takes, 85

Trau, delivered to Venice, 256

Trautson, Sixt, commander at Cadore, 282; Alviano captures Cadore from, 283

Trémouille, Louis de la, leads and encourages Swiss, pulling cannon, 81; likened to Hannibal, 81; Louis XII shows mark of favour to, 136; in supreme command, 162; at battle of Agnadello, 292; envoy to Swiss, 364; wounded at battle of Novara, 367; arranges peace with Swiss, 377

Trent, Maximilian holds procession at, 280; Bishop of, arrests and executes Venetian, 301; Swiss captains in garden of Bishop of, hear Maximilian's plans, 345

Trent, treaty of, between Maximilian and Louis XII (Oct. 1501), 181, 189, 219

Tresa, Freiburgers throw bridge across the, 327

Treviglio, White Knight imprisoned in, 291; Venetians plunder, 291

Trevisano, Melchior, goes against Turks, 183; unable to take Cephalonia or relieve Modon, 183; proud of successes, 183; Gonzalvo combines with, to capture Cephalonia, 183-184

Treviso, inhabitants of, alarmed by Turks, 182; citizens of, deliver themselves to Venice, 256; mills of, grind day and night, 295; Leonardo Trissino received at, with cries of "San Marco," 299; Matthäus Lang demands, from Venice, 315; besieged by Maximilian, 318; French retire from, 327; Venetians will not accept, on condition of acknowledging Archduke Charles as suzerain, 343; Venetians to retain, 360

Tribunal, Cameral (Kammergericht), constitution of, 107; not held throughout Empire for six months, 219; subjects for deliberation of, 220; passes into hands of Maximilian, 226; Maximilian arranges payment of, by Estates, 279

Trieste, surrenders to Venetians, 284

Trinopoli, Fray Bernaldo de, negotiates Austro-Spanish marriages, 382; Ferdinand sends authorization to, 383

Tripalda, Spaniards forcibly enter, 192

Tripoli, taken by Navarra, 251

Trissino, Leonardo, with Maximilian in Italy, 281; opposed at Treviso, 299

"Triumphus Crucis," published by Savonarola, 125

Trivulzi, Guelph proclivities of family, 35

Trivulzio, Gian Giacomo, flight of, 35; taken into service of Charles VIII, 72-73; with his son at battle of Fornovo, 83-84; fortifies Asti, 109; marches against Ludovico Sforza, 151; castles surrender to, 152; opposed by Ghibellines in Milan, 160-161; with Guelphs, occupies square on approach of Sforza, 161; flies to Ticino, 161-162; brings to Louis XII news of bombardment of Treviglio, 291; at head of French troops against Julius II, 314; a hard captain, 314; drives back papal army under walls of Bologna, 315; joined by Georg Frundsberg, 315; Swiss burn castles of, 328; hopes to regain freedom for Milan, 347; wins over leading Ghibellines, 347; French envoy to Swiss, 364; prematurely boasts of power over Swiss, 365; compelled to retire at battle of Novara, 367

Trocces (Trocchio, or Troche), Francesco, favourite and privy chamberlain of Alexander VI, put to death, 209

Tropea, Aubigny at, 91

Tunis, claimed for Sicily, 68; imperative for Spain to conquer, 251; Venetian trade in, shared with Genoese and Catalans, 255

Turin, Charles VIII arrives in, 47

Turks, Charles VIII assures himself of success against, 56; scared by prestige of French, 61; Venice concludes alliance ostensibly against, 74; Otranto once in hands of, 181; lay claim to Naples, 181; war of, against Venice, 181-183; general campaign against, proclaimed by Louis XII, 189

Turmann (a man of Uri) betrays Ludovico Sforza, 166

Tuscany, scheme of Alexander VI for conquering, in league with Spaniards, 209; Aretins and Pisans offer services to Gonzalvo on part of, 213

Tyrol, the, secured to Maximilian, 96; Maximilian goes to, 107; Count Jörg of Sargans schemes to bring to crown of Bavaria, 143; calls Swabian League to aid, 144; three bands from, fly before men of the Grisons, 148; bread and wine for Swiss soldiers in all taverns of, 345

U

Udine, quarrels of, with Cividale d'Austria, 256; two angels with bloody swords said to be seen at, 302

Ulloa, Juan, fights against Rodrigo Ulloa, 63

Ulm, Count Eberhard escapes to, 132-133; landsknechts fly to, from Lake Constance, 145; Maximilian returns to, from Italy, 281

Unterwalden, Ludovico Sforza allied with, 141; joins League, 145

Urach, line of, 103

Urbino in the hands of Caesar Borgia, 198; revolt of, 198, 211; Caesar to receive back, 199

Urbino, Guidobaldo Montefeltre, Duke of, 29; forsakes Ferrantino, 55; does not encourage Giovanni Sforza against Caesar, 174; protects exiles and refugees, 186; lends artillery to Caesar Borgia, 196; deceived by Caesar, and flies, 197; leaves possessions in Caesar's hands, 197; returns, 198, 211; attached to Venice, 260

Urbino, Francesco Maria della

Rovere, Duke of (nephew of Julius II), takes field against Venice, 287; at feud with the Cardinal of Pavia, 312; leads papal troops against Ferrara, 312-313; in charge of army before Bologna, 315; retreats from Bologna, 316; blamed by Cardinal of Pavia, 317; murders the Cardinal, 317; organizes papal army, 345

Uri, earliest treaty of, with Schwyz, 102; summoned to aid of Chur, 143; people of, rule in valley of Urseren, 158-159; acquire Bellinzona and thus quarrel with Milan, 159; Ludovico Sforza promises Bellinzona and Val Bregna to people of, 159; Louis XII confirms rights of people of, to Bellinzona, 305

Urs, St., Swiss trust in, 366

Urseren, German settlement in valley of, 158-159; often in feud with Val Leventina, 159

Utrecht, lost to Maximilian by Engilbert of Cleves, 28; Maximilian gives warning of possible revolt of, 282

V

Vado, papal fleet confronted in harbour off, 310

Valais, factions in the, 324

Val Bregna promised by Ludovico Sforza to people of Uri, 159

Val di Lamone, Dionigi di Naldi party-leader in, 289

Valeggio, Swiss join forces with Venetians at, 345

Val Leventina, eight Italian communes in, 158; people of, insult people of Uri, 159

Val Maggia, Ludovico Sforza offers, conditionally to Swiss, 164; Swiss acquire, 362

Valentinois, Caesar Borgia receives from France as Dukedom, 172

Valenza, Donato, Governor of, lets in followers of Trivulzio, 152

Valladolid, marriage of Ferdinand and Isabella at, 63; Jurado of Saragossa enters, 232

Valois, the, 20; Charles VII of, 20

Valori, Francesco, comes to Florence with Piero de' Medici, 51

Valori, young men of family of, among the "Optimates," 356

Valtelline, the, Galeazzo Sforza collects troops for incursions into, 159; the Grisons had appropriated, 362

Vandals, the, 3

Vannozza de' Cattanei, mother of Caesar, Juan, Gioffredo, and Lucrezia Borgia, 42 n.; monument of, in Santa Maria del popolo, 42 n.

Varano, Giulio, murdered, with his sons, by Caesar Borgia, 197

Varese, Swiss cattle driven to, in peace, 362

Vaudrei, Claude de, Ludovico Sforza crosses Alps with Burgundian horse of, 161

Vega, Garcilasso de la, accompanies Archduke Philip, 232

Vega, Lope de, poem of, on Castilians in Holy Land, 7

Veglia, refuses to obey a Frangipani, 256

Veldenz, line of (House of Palatinate), 103; against Palatinate in war of Landshut succession, 222

Velez, Moorish pirates driven from, 250

Venice, teaches Dalmatians to speak Italian, 10; Doge and plebeians in league against nobles in, 16; Ludovico Sforza procures peace of Bagnolo for, 35; dependent on commerce, 39; Ferdinand and Isabella send an ambassador to, 72; Aubigny's advance alarms, 73; gathers forces against Charles VIII, 73; joins Maximilian and Ludovico in League against Charles, 74-75; Ludovico asks good services of, 79; Ferrantino pledges five places in Apulia to, 91; helps Ferrantino to victory, 91; takes part of Pisa against Florence, 109, 138; Doge, Consiglieri and Pregadi, above Grand Council of, 118; in feud with

Ludovico, 135, 138; sends coronation present to Louis XII, 137; failure of operations against Florence, 139; fits out two armies against Turks and Ludovico, 152; Ascanio Sforza in hands of, 167; Giovanni Sforza relies on, 174; declares for Pope, 174; requires salute from Turkish ships, 181; war with Turks, 181-183; ill-consequences, for Italy, of feuds between Milan and, 185; invasion of the Romagna by, 213, 259-260; operations of, against Caesar Borgia, 214, 260; treaty of Blois points to general war on, 227; refuse passage to Maximilian, 236; lagoons of, originally covered with mud hovels, 253; prosperity of, gained by commerce and conquests, 253; account of commerce of, 254-255; conquests of, 255-258; Doge Mocenigo opposed to conquests of, 257; Doge Foscari succeeds Mocenigo in, 258; constitution of, 258-259; Italian disturbances used for acquisition of territory by, 259; *bon mot* of Machiavelli on Pope as chaplain for, 260; Julius II stoutly withstands, 261; Imola, Cesena, and Forlì restored by, 261; offers to assist Julius II against Bologna, 263; danger to commerce of, 268; beginning of decay in trade of, 270; effect of Portuguese adventures on trade of, 277; many houses on Rialto bankrupt, 277; hopes for fall of Portuguese power, 278; sends metal and gun workers to Soldan of Egypt, 278; Maximilian embarks on war with, 280; success of, against Maximilian, 281-285; Maximilian orders Bishop of Trent to conclude peace with, 285; will not listen to demands of France, 286, or do more than restore Adelsberg to Emperor, 286; League of Cambray against, 286; Julius II excommunicates Doge, senate, and subjects of, 287; existence of, in jeopardy, 287; fears enmity of Louis XII, 288; France proclaims war on, 289; composition of army of, 289;

evil omens for, 291 ; commencement of war, 291 ; news of Alviano's defeat at Agnadello reaches, 294 ; monks mindful of Pope's ban fly from, 294 ; Matteo Priuli proposes giving up of subject towns by, 295 ; envoys of, to Maximilian, Ferdinand, and Pope promise surrender of cities, 295 ; Portuguese successes over Moors destroy last hope of, 296 ; ceases to be centre of European trade, 297 ; Julius and Ferdinand spare what is left to, 297 ; Louis and Maximilian for annihilation of, 298 ; attachment of peasants to, 301 ; organizes commerce in Mediterranean anew, 302; released from ban of excommunication, 303 ; Julius bids Alfonso d'Este make peace with, 304 ; demands of Matthäus Lang from, 315 ; obliged to accept services of Lucio Malvezzi as general, 318 ; loses good will of subjects, 318 ; Holy League proclaimed in grand square of, 323 ; Cardinal Schinner arrives in disguise at, 326 ; ruin of, stayed, 327 ; troops of, under Avogaro capture Brescia, 329 ; Gaston de Foix triumphant over, 331 ; truce of, with Emperor, 343 ; recognizes Lateran Council, 343 ; army of, to be massed with papal and Swiss troops, 345 ; Louis XII allied with, 364 ; forces of Ferdinand and Leo X against, 369 ; territory of, invaded by Germans, Italians, and Spanish, 379 ; Cardona at tower of Malghera commanding view of, 379 ; army of, routed, 380 ; compelled to accept Pope as arbiter of fortune, 380 ; great conflagration in, 383

Venosa, Gonzalvo blocks road from, 92

Ventimiglia, one of Fregosi taken in, confesses to revolutionary errand from Pope, 315

Veragua, Ferdinand appoints Niquesa Governor of, 250 ; founded by Balboa, 386

Vercelli, Swiss in camp of Charles VIII at, 86

Vergy, Marshal, Henry VIII asks Maximilian to lend, 371 ; unites with Swiss, who cross French frontier, 373

Verona offered by Visconti to Venice, 257 ; envoys from, in Venice, 257; by popular idea, belongs to Empire, 287 ; gates of, closed against Pitigliano's retreating army, 294 ; Venetians promise retirement from, 295 ; in danger from Venice, 301–302 ; Venetians rise against, 307 ; Venetians retreat from, 309 ; troops of Maximilian march out of, 318 ; Germans advance from, to meet Gaston de Foix, 329 ; Venetians refuse to abandon, 343 ; Swiss soldiers receive hat, sword, consecrated banner, and money at, 345 ; Maximilian to have, 360

Vettori, family of, young men of, among the "Optimates," 356

Vicenza raises standard of Venice, 257 ; Maximilian advances on, 281 ; by popular idea, belonged to Empire, 287 ; Germans appear beyond, 294 ; Venetians promise retirement from, 295 ; Venetians re-take, 302; Venetians decline to abandon, 343 ; Maximilian to have, 360

Vico, Ludovico Sforza takes, 138

Vigevano, Maximilian meets envoy of Pope and Ludovico at, 111

Vigevene, farm of Ludovico Sforza at, 36

Vigne, André de la, poem by, on Charles VIII, 27

Vikings, the, 5

Villena, Juan Pacheco, Marquis of, control of, over Henry IV of Castile, 62 ; loses estates, 239 ; opposes Ferdinand, 229 ; won over to Ferdinand by Ximenes, 248

Villenas, Grand Alcalde, Isabella orders his hand to be cut off, 67

Visconti, the, Ghibellines establish power of, 34 ; claim of Louis of Orleans to Milan through connection with, 73 ; offer Verona, Feltre, and Belluno to Venice, 257

Visconti, Filippo Maria, Duke of Milan, misunderstanding between Carmagnola and, 258

Visconti, Gabriele, sells Pisa to Florentines, 113

Visconti, Galeazzo, sent by Ludovico to negotiate with the Swiss, 149 ; negotiates peace with Germans, 158 ; collects troop for incursion into the Valtelline, 159 ; victorious, 160

Visconti, Gaspare, at the court of Ludovico, 36

Visconti, Valentina, grandmother of Louis XII, 141 ; Louis acquires inheritance of, 156

Visigoths, Athaulf, King of the, 1 ; question of intermarriage with, in Spain, 2

Vitelli, family of, in pay of Caesar Borgia, 186, 198 ; Swiss arms introduced into Italy by, 198

Vitelli, Paolo, commands Florentines, 138 ; Alviano opposes, 139 ; put to death for failure to take Pisa, 353

Vitelli, Vitellozzo, a head of the Orsini party, 200 ; murdered by Caesar Borgia, 201

Viterbo, Charles VIII at, 56

Voghera, lost to Ludovico Sforza, 152

Vogheresi, the, treatment of, by Ligny, 167

W

Walheim, people of, acknowledge Ulrich of Württemberg, 223

Wallgau, Confederates attack men of, 146 ; men of, ask mercy on battlefield, 148 ; Ludovico Sforza pays fine levied on, 158 ; Maximilian represents danger of estranging, 282

Warbeck, Perkin, 130

Warwick, Lambert Simnel declares himself Edward of, 130

Wasiljewitsch, Ivan, depends on German troops, 100 ; attack on Livonia by, repulsed by Walter von Plettenberg, 189

Weesp, burnt by Duke Charles of Gelderland, 285

Weingarten, Benedict von, brave advice to Swiss by, 365

Weinsberg, people of, acknowledge Ulrich of Württemberg, 223

Weiskunig, on wreck of French fleet, 119

Weissenhorn, claimed by Maximilian, 224

Welser, mercantile house of, trades with Portuguese, 277

Werdenberg, Hug von, refuses to be chamberlain for the younger Eberhard of Württemberg, 132

Weymouth, Archduke Philip lands at, 231

Wilkinasaga, the, 11

Winkelried, Aerni, at battle of Novara, 367

Wippach, fall of, 284

Wisby, Bishop Meinhard goes from, to preach at Esthonia, 9 ; in Gothland on Swedish soil, 12

Wisch, forsakes Duke of Gelderland, 227

Wladislav II, King of Hungary, question of divorce of, 43 ; Alexander VI pronounces divorce for, 176-177 ; marries Anne de Candale, 177 ; Maximilian to succeed if no heir for, 234 ; question of marriage of daughter of, to grandson, Maximilian, 235 ; birth of a weakly son to (afterwards Louis II of Hungary), 235

Wolfstall, Wolf von, imperial commissioner, comes to Regensburg, 384

Wolleb, Heini, leads Swiss, who scale the Lanzengast, 147 ; killed at battle of Schwaderloch, 148

Wolsey, Cardinal, tries to bring English clergy into submission, 340

Wool, Florentine factories import, from France, Catalonia, and England, 113

Worms, negotiations between Ferrantino's ambassadors and Maximilian at, 74

Worms, Diet of (1495), summoned, 96 ; ceremonial at, 99 ; important arrangements made by Maximillan at, 99 ; his real aims,

100; influence and position of Maximilian, 103; he asks for aid against Charles VIII, 104; proposal of the princes, 105–106; Maximilian is twice successful, 106; constitution of the Cameral Tribunal, 107; Maximilian complains of his treatment at, and abandons decrees, 110; decrees of, set aside, 132

Wormser Joch, mountain range from Monte Rosa to, becomes Swiss, 362

Württemberg, to be raised to dukedom, 100; weakly boy sole hope of family of, 100; line of Urach, House of, 103; Ulrich to be Duke of, 133; against Palatinate in war of Landshut succession, 222; Estates of, advise Duke not to sever himself from Austria, 384

Württemberg, Eberhard, the elder, Count (afterwards Duke) of, 99; character of, 99; Maximilian enters into compact with, 100; death of, 132

Württemberg, Eberhard, the younger, Count (afterwards Duke) of, 99; character of, 99; on death of his cousin dismisses old councillors, 132; the Estates seize his cities, 132; escapes to Ulm, 133; renounces the duchy and is imprisoned in Lindenfels until his death, 133

Württemberg, Ulrich, Duke of, 133; to marry Sabina, niece of Maximilian, 133; in war of Landshut succession, 223; unites with Swiss and crosses French frontier, 373

X

Xanten, Maximilian at, 288

Ximenes, Franciso, de Cisneros, Archbishop of Toledo, wins over Alfaquins and one Zegri, 183; arranges meeting between Ferdinand and Philip, 233; account of, 245–247; declares for Ferdinand, 247–248; Ferdinand procures dignity of Cardinal for, 247;

made Grand Inquisitor, 248; urges renewal of Moorish war and subscribes for fitting out fleet, 249; at siege of Oran, 250; consecrates mosque at Oran, as Church of Sta Maria de la Vitoria, 251; Ferdinand gains over, with regard to Navarre, 351

Y

York, House of, auxiliary German troops fight for, 100; Maximilian has pretensions of a fugitive member of, transferred to himself, 228; struggle of, with Lancaster, 338; members of, imprisoned or put to death by Henry VII, 338

Yxkull (Oesel), colony of, 10

Z

Zabai, the, of Goa, asks help of Soldan of Egypt, 278; Francesco d'Almeida burns Dabul, a city of the, 296

Zagal, Lopez el, first to spring on land at Mers-el-Kebir, 249

Zamorin of Calicut, the chief of Malabar, 268; Dom Manuel of Portugal gives Vasco da Gama letters to, 270; Pedro Alvarez Cabral and Vasco da Gama exasperated against, 272; Pacheco Pereira defends King of Cochin against, 272; asks help of Soldan of Egypt, 278

Zancani, Andrea, Abuayazid gives Italian letter of compact to, 181; sent against Turks, 182–183; dares not venture out of Gradisca, 183; banished, 183

Zanzibar, Moors penetrate to, 268

Zapolya, Count John of, aspires to crown of Hungary, 235

Zara, Grand Turk despatches troops to pillage, 182; sold by Ladislas, 256

Zegri, Ximenes baptizes a, 183

Zollern, Eitel Friedrich von, first

justiciary of Frankfurt, has judge's staff given by Maximilian, 107

Zug, troops from, attack landsknechts on Lake of Constance, 144 ; troops from, at battle of Dorneck, 151

Zuñiga, Pedro, fights against his father, 63

Zürich, Rudolph Schwend of, 28 ; troops from, attack landsknechts on Lake of Constance, 144 ; men of, chose captain, 163 ; Council at, votes 6,000 men for Maximilian, 280 ; Massimiliano Sforza receives key of city of, 363 ; contingent from, at battle of Novara, 365

THE END